Understanding
Business Strategy

Concepts and Cases

High Technology	Media/Entertainment/Communication	International Perspective	Social/Ethical Issues	Entrepreneurial	Industry Perspective	Chapters
	X			X	X	3, 5
		X				3, 8, 9
X	X					6, 7
X	X			X		3, 4, 5, 9
X				X		2, 9, 10
				X		6, 7
	X		X			2, 10
	X			X	X	2, 10
			X	X	X	2, 4, 10
		X				1, 9
		X	X		X	1, 2
		X				4, 10
				X	X	9, 10
		X			X	8, 9
		X				2, 8
	X				X	3, 4, 5
		X			X	3, 6, 8
	X		X	X		2, 10
		X			X	4, 5, 9
					X	1, 3

Understanding
Business Strategy

Concepts and Cases

R. Duane Ireland
Texas A&M University

Robert E. Hoskisson
Arizona State University

Michael A. Hitt
Texas A&M University

THOMSON
™
SOUTH-WESTERN

Australia · Brazil · Canada · Mexico · Singapore · Spain · United Kingdom · United States

THOMSON
SOUTH-WESTERN

Understanding Business Strategy: Concepts and Cases, 1st Edition
R. Duane Ireland, Robert E. Hoskisson, and Michael A. Hitt

VP/Editorial Director:
Jack W. Calhoun

VP/Editor-in-Chief:
Dave Shaut

Sr. Publisher:
Melissa S. Acuña

Executive Editor:
John Szilagyi

Sr. Developmental Editor:
Mardell Toomey

Marketing Manager:
Rob Bloom

**Marketing Communications
Manager:**
Jim Overly

Sr. Production Project Manager:
Emily Gross

**Manager of Technology,
Editorial:**
Vicky True

Technology Project Editor:
Kristen Meere

Web Coordinator:
Karen Schaffer

Manufacturing Coordinator:
Doug Wilke

Production House:
Lachina Publishing Services

Printer:
R.R. Donnelley & Sons Company
Willard Manufacturing Division

Sr. Art Director:
Tippy McIntosh

Internal Designer:
Christy Carr

Cover Designer:
Craig Ramsdell,
Ramsdell Design

Cover Images:
Terry Vine and Manfred Rutz,
Getty Images

Photography Manager:
John Hill

Photo Researcher:
Seidel Associates

Library of Congress
Control Number:
2005922997

For more information about
our products, contact us at:

Thomson Learning Academic
Resource Center

1-800-423-0563

Thomson Higher Education
5191 Natorp Boulevard
Mason, OH 45040
USA

To our son, Scott: Your courage and perseverance continue to inspire me. Following in your footsteps, I'll always try to be on that hill with everything I've got. I love you, Scott. Dad
R. Duane Ireland

To my wife, Kathy: Your lifetime of sacrifice for our family has made a major difference in my life and the lives our children. I love you so very much.
Robert E. Hoskisson

To my little granddaughter, Michelle (Michellebell): Your smiles light up my day. I love you. PaPa
Michael A. Hitt

Brief Contents

Contents

Part 2   Analyzing environments   50

chapter_3
Analyzing the External Environment   52

chapter_4
Analyzing the Firm   80

Part 3   strategy   106

chapter_5
Business-Level Strategy   108

chapter_6

Multiproduct Strategies   136

chapter_7
Acquiring and Integrating Businesses   164

chapter_10
Innovating through Strategic Entrepreneurship   238

Part 4 cases c-i

Preface

Firms are important to all of us. As customers, we buy products (goods and services) from them; as employees, we work for them; as suppliers, we sell raw materials to them; and, as perhaps many of us would agree, firms often are a vital part of the communities in which we live. Thus, for many reasons, all of us benefit when firms perform well. Think about it this way. When firms are successful, they are (1) producing, selling, and servicing products that customers want to buy, (2) providing employees with good-paying jobs, and (3) contributing in various ways to the communities in which they are located. But what influences a firm's performance? Why do some perform exceptionally well while others fail to perform adequately and end up in bankruptcy?

The strategic management process, the focus of this book, strongly influences firm performance. Stated simply, firms with executives who understand how to effectively use the strategic management process tend to succeed, while those with executives who do not, depend more on luck and often experience deteriorating performance that leads to failure. As you'll understand from reading this book, firms use the strategic management process to examine various alternatives in order to decide *what* objectives they should try to accomplish as well as *how* to pursue those objectives.

Our purpose in writing this text is to present to you, our readers, a succinct and action-oriented explanation of how to manage a firm strategically. As such, we cover a broad array of concepts in ten concisely written chapters. As you examine the following list of features, we think you will agree that this book is reader-friendly.

Let's examine some examples of how this book is accessible to you, our readers.

- The writing style is lively, engaging, and application-oriented. You'll find examples in each chapter of how firms that you likely know actually use strategic management concepts and tools. These examples bring the strategic management process to life and highlight its relevance to real firms around the globe.
- Each chapter is organized around **"Knowledge Objectives"** at the beginning of each chapter that clarify what you can expect to learn.
- Key terms are placed in the margins for easy mastery of terminology that is important to understanding strategy.
- We open each chapter with a feature called **"Focusing on Strategy."** Each "Focusing on Strategy" illustrates how a particular company uses the part of the strategic management process explained in the chapter. This feature quotes a strategic manager or observer of the strategic management process

and brings strategic management issues to life by showing their application in actual firms.

- In each chapter, we also include a feature (**"Understanding Strategy— Learning from Success"**) to explain how one or more actual firms have benefited by successfully using a particular part of the strategic management process. We include a related feature in each chapter (**"Understanding Strategy—Learning from Failure"**) to explain how one or more firms suffered poor performance because of their failure to effectively use one or more parts of the strategic management process.

- Each chapter closes with a feature called **"Your Career."** We use this feature to help you think about and understand how you can use the strategic management process concepts presented in the chapter to develop and enhance your career. This feature will help you understand the useful links between strategic management and your career success.

- The **"Strategy Toolbox"** end-of-chapter feature, expertly prepared by Paul N. Friga of Indiana University, presents you with a tool or technique firms actually use with the strategic management process. In addition to learning how firms use strategic management, you will be able to use these helpful tools to help analyze cases.

- An especially exciting feature located at the end of each chapter is **"Biz Flix,"** prepared by Joseph E. Champoux of the University of New Mexico. This feature consists of a carefully selected video segment taken from popular motion pictures that have appeared over the last 25 years and are familiar to you. These short video segments reinforce main text concepts in a fresh and compelling way and are highly interesting and appealing. The discussion questions integrate video and chapter content. You may view the videos on the student Xtra! product (described later).

- At the end of each chapter, we present a **"Mini-Case"** that deals with an actual firm and explains, in some detail, how that firm uses one or more parts of the strategic management process. Each "Mini-Case" is more comprehensive than the "Focusing on Strategy" and "Understanding Strategy" features. To help you learn more about the firm discussed in the case and to enhance your strategic management skills, each case closes with a set of discussion questions. These questions are designed to help you think about the issues in the case and enhance your learning of the chapter's concepts.

- Two **"Experiential Exercises"** are included in the end-of-chapter content. We are grateful to Tamela D. Ferguson of the University of Louisiana at Lafayette and William C. Bogner of Georgia State University for their fine work preparing these. Each cognitive or experiential exercise involves you, as an active learner, in a way that will help you develop a better understanding of the chapter's topics. Typically, you will be provided with some discussion questions that facilitate your efforts to apply the learning gained from each exercise.

- Cases! The second part of the text includes 20 highly current cases that include U.S. and international firms in many different industries. Extensive case notes are available for instructor support and the student Xtra! product includes tutorials that help you learn how to analyze cases.

- To increase the book's visual appeal, full color is used to enhance the presentation of the concepts presented in the book's ten chapters. The full-color format enables us to include interesting color photographs to further illustrate each chapter's content. Captions describing the strategic actions illustrated by each photograph provide an additional way to actively engage you with aspects of the strategic management process that are explained in the chapter.

Acknowledgments

We are especially grateful to those preparing end-of-chapter content: Paul N. Friga, Indiana University, who wrote the "Strategy Toolbox" materials; Joseph E. Champoux, University of New Mexico, who developed the "Biz Flix" items; and Tamela D. Ferguson, University of Louisiana at Lafayette, and William C. Bogner, Georgia State University, who developed the "Experiential Exercises."

The feedback and guidance provided by our reviewers for this text were especially helpful. We are grateful for their insights about how to present you with an interesting, accessible, and complete explanation of strategic management.

Todd Alessandri
Syracuse University

Kunal Banerji
Florida Atlantic University

Rocki-Lee DeWitt
University of Vermont

Bahman Paul Ebrahimi
University of Denver

Cameron M. Ford
University of Central Florida

Tamela D. Ferguson
University of Louisiana at Lafayette

Steven Hamilton
University of Alaska, S.E.

Reza Karim
California State University, Fullerton

Franz W. Kellermanns
Mississippi State University

Joseph T. Mahoney
University of Illinois at Urbana-Champaign

Brett P. Matherne
University of Dayton

Paul Mallette
Colorado State University

Donald Neubaum
University of Central Florida

Daewoo Park
Xavier University

Laura H. Poppo
Virginia Tech

Jude Rathburn
University of Wisconsin, River Falls

Mitrabarun Sarkar
University of Central Florida

Katsuhiko Shimizu
University of Texas, San Antonio

Thomas D. Sigerstad
Frostburg State University

f. l. Smith
Emporia State University

Laszlo Tihanyi
Texas A&M University

Klaus Uhlenbruck
University of Montana

Our focus group participants helped us a great deal in understanding instructors' and students' needs in teaching and learning about strategic management in an action-oriented manner. We are grateful for the excellent observations the following scholar-teachers provided.

Donald Baack
Pittsburg State University

Rick Crandall
University of North Carolina, Pembroke

Fred Doran
University of Mississippi

Chuck Englehart
Salem International University

Steven Hamilton
University of Alaska, S.E.

Ed Murphy
Embry Riddle University

Tyge Payne
University of Texas at Arlington

Bill Ritchie
Florida Gulf Coast University

Michelle Slagle
University of South Alabama

Eva Smith
Spartanburg Technical College

Supplements

We also want to express our sincere appreciation for the excellent support we've received from our editorial and production team at South-Western. In particular, we want to thank John Szilagyi, our editor; Mardell Toomey, our senior developmental editor; Emily Gross, our senior production project manager; and Rob Bloom, our marketing manager. We are truly grateful for their dedication, professionalism, and commitment to work closely with us to prepare a high-quality book and an excellent and comprehensive package of support materials. It has been a great team effort.

Instructor's Resource CD-ROM (0–324–29124–8)

The instructor's CD-ROM provides all key ancillaries for ease in preparing for classes and customizing lectures, presentations, and assessment. Included are instructor case notes, an instructor's resource manual, a test bank, ExamView® test creation software, PowerPoint slide presentations, a video guide, and support for the Business & Company Resource Center exercises that are offered to students on the Xtra! product.

Instructor's Case Notes (0–324–29126–4)

The case notes are team-prepared to ensure maximum usefulness and thorough coverage of all case content. Preparers are Joyce A. Claterbos, University of Kansas; Paul Mallette, Colorado State University; Mark P. Sharfman, University of Oklahoma; and Marta Szabo White, Georgia State University. An innovative feature, called "Case Consensus," precedes each case note entry for each case. This feature is new to case notes accompanying strategy texts. This summary feature, prepared by Eric Wiseman of the University of Colorado at Boulder, includes the following information for every case and is provided based on agreement among all case notes preparers:

- Leading questions for discussion
- Helpful ways to integrate case material into classroom presentations
- Identification of key success factors
- Identification of life cycle factors
- Brief industry context

This feature enables instructors to quickly assess case content, identify each case's relevance for classroom presentation, and reduce preparation time. Following this summary feature, case notes are provided in great detail, including questions and answers that are integrated throughout the discussion of each case. All case notes are prepared consistently, following the framework for case analysis developed by the authors of the text and explained in the second half of the text, "Preparing an Effective Case Analysis." Also included are complete financial analyses for 8 of the 20 cases. Spreadsheets for those financial analyses are available for instructors on our product support Web site. Wherever possible, we include resolutions and updates of the cases.

Test Bank (0–324–29125–6)

Prepared by Jude Rathburn, University of Wisconsin, River Falls. More than 1,000 test bank questions are linked to each chapter's knowledge objectives and are ranked by difficulty (easy, medium, difficult) and question type (definitional, conceptual, application). We have included many application questions throughout, as well as scenario-based questions that focus on helping students learn to think and act strategically. The test bank material is also available in computerized ExamView® format for creating custom tests in both Windows and Macintosh formats.

ExamView® (0–324–40766–1)

The ExamView test creation software, which is an easy-to-use Windows-based program, contains all of the questions in the printed test bank. Instructors can add or edit questions, instructions, and answers, and select questions by previewing them on the screen, selecting them randomly, or selecting them by number. Instructors can also create and administer quizzes online, whether over the Internet, a local area network (LAN), or a wide area network (WAN).

Instructor's Manual with Video Guide and Transparency Masters (0–324–20382–9)

Prepared by Janelle Dozier. The Instructor's Manual, organized around each chapter's knowledge objectives, includes ideas about how to approach each chapter and how to reinforce essential principles with extra examples. Included are lecture outlines, detailed answers to end-of-chapter discussion questions, instructions for using each chapter's "Experiential Exercises," and an integrative video guide that combines main text chapter content, case content, and video content so that instructors can create a dynamic classroom environment.

PowerPoint Slide Presentations

Prepared by Charlie Cook of the University of West Alabama, each chapter's slide presentation includes animated figures from the texts, reinforcement of all main concepts and terms, and discussion questions that help instructors guide classroom discussion and encourage students to engage in active learning while viewing the presentation in the classroom or on their own, using the Xtra! support product (described shortly).

Transparency Acetates (0–324–39538–8)

Key figures from the main text have been re-created as colorful and attractive overhead transparencies for classroom use. Instructors may wish to vary their means of content delivery and this provides a practical option.

Understanding Business Strategy Video Package (DVD: 0–324–32400–6; VHS: 0–324–29129–9)

These video segments include clips that accompany the "Biz Flix" feature found at the end of each chapter within the text as well as additional, very current clips that are linked to companies that will be familiar to students. Our instructor's manual supports these features through discussion questions and guidance for making your classroom presentation more dynamic through the use of video. This media package provides students with a fresh context for studying strategic management.

Xtra! (0–324-40795-5)

This student support product, available as an optional bundle, expands text content and helps students improve their ability to conceptualize and apply strategy. Included are quizzes for each chapter that enable students to quickly assess their own understanding. Corbis video clips (see the "Biz Flix" feature described in the discussion of end-of-chapter content) increase students' interest and reinforce concepts found within each chapter. There are also two exciting tutorials. The first is an **"Interactive Case Analysis,"** prepared by Paul N. Friga of Indiana University. Using the method of case analysis developed by the main text authors, this tutorial walks students through the process of analyzing a case step by step, helping to reduce anxiety and build confidence in students as they approach a case. Intended for students to use independently, outside class, this tutorial provides a clear and straightforward approach to case analysis that includes graphics, discussion questions, and examples. The tutorial will help free up time for instructors to focus on the cases themselves. The second tutorial, **"Creating an Oral Presentation,"** also prepared by Paul N. Friga of Indiana University, serves as additional support for students' approach to case analysis. Finally, the **Xtra!** product includes the PowerPoint presentation available to instructors that covers all main text concepts and terms and Business & Company Resource Center exercises that include a component, wherever possible, that requires students to perform a financial analysis. These exercises, drawing on additional information about the companies featured in the cases, blend qualitative and quantitative questions that require research and independent, critical thinking on the students' part.

Product Support Web Site (http://ireland.swlearning.com)

The product support Web site features "Instructor Resources" that include the instructor's manual, test bank, PowerPoint presentations, case notes, and test bank files (ExamView® testing creation software is located separately on the instructor's resource CD-ROM). For students, we include "The Strategy Suite," a compilation of Web-based materials including links to online academic journals and professional societies, business strategy–related sites, international business sites, and research and data sources. The "Case Analysis Method" explains the case approach to students. In most strategic management courses, cases are used extensively as a teaching tool. Cases provide active learners with opportunities to use the strategic management process to identify and solve organizational problems. Therefore, by analyzing situations that are described in cases and presenting the results, active learners become skilled at effectively using the tools, techniques, and concepts that combine to form the strategic management process. The "Your Career" feature appeals to students as a quick means of exploring their personal future in management. The Internet is increasingly becoming a mall for goods and services, including personnel recruiting, career advice, and resume help; this feature provides students with a little guidance in surfing the Net as they pursue their career goals.

The Business and Company Resource Center

Business & Company
RESOURCE CENTER
THOMSON GALE

Put a complete business library at your students' fingertips with *The Business & Company Resource Center (BCRC)*. The BCRC is a premier online business research tool that enables you to seamlessly search thousands of periodicals, journals, references, financial information sources, industry reports, company histories, and much more.

- **BCRC** is conveniently accessible from anywhere with an Internet connection, enabling students to access information at school, at home, or "on the go."
- **BCRC** is a powerful and time-saving research tool for students—whether they are completing a case analysis, preparing for a presentation or discussion, creating a business plan, or writing a reaction paper.
- Instructors can use the **BCRC** as an online course pack, assigning readings and research-based homework without the inconvenience of library reserves, permissions, and printed materials.
- **BCRC** filters out the "junk" information students often find when searching the Internet, providing only high-quality, safe, and reliable news and information sources.

Visit http://bcrc.swlearning.com or contact your local Thomson sales representative to learn more about this powerful tool and how the BCRC can save valuable time for both you and your students.

Resource Integration Guide

When you start with a new—or even familiar—text, the amount of supplemental material can seem overwhelming. Identifying each element of a supplement package and piecing together the parts that fit your particular needs can be time-consuming. After all, you may use only a small fraction of the resources available to help you plan, deliver, and evaluate your class. With *Understanding Business Strategy*, you don't have to figure out how everything fits together. We have created this resource guide to help you and your students extract the full value from the text and its wide range of exceptional supplements.

This resource guide, available on the product support Web site, organizes the book's resources and provides planning suggestions to help you plan and conduct your class, create assignments, and evaluate your students' mastery of the subject. Whatever your teaching style or circumstance, there are planning suggestions to meet your needs. The broad range of techniques provided in the guide helps you increase your repertoire as a teaching expert, and in so doing, enrich your students' learning and understanding. We hope this map and its suggestions enable you to discover new and exciting ways to teach your course.

About the Authors

R. Duane Ireland

R. Duane Ireland holds the Foreman R. and Ruby S. Bennett Chair in Business in the Mays Business School, Texas A&M University. He teaches courses at all levels (undergraduate, master's, doctoral, and executive). He has won multiple awards for his teaching during his career. His research, which focuses on diversification, innovation, corporate entrepreneurship, and strategic entrepreneurship, has been published in a number of journals including *Academy of Management Journal, Academy of Management Review, Academy of Management Executive, Administrative Science Quarterly, Strategic Management Journal, Journal of Management, Human Relations,* and *Journal of Management Studies.* His published books include *Competing for Advantage* (2004), *Strategic Management: Competitiveness and Globalization,* sixth edition (2005), and *Mergers and Acquisitions: A Guide to Creating Value for Stakeholders* (2001). He is coeditor of *The Blackwell Entrepreneurship Encyclopedia* (2005) and *Strategic Entrepreneurship: Creating a New Mindset* (2001). He is serving or has served as a member of the editorial review boards for a number of journals such as *Academy of Management Journal, Academy of Management Review, Academy of Management Executive, Journal of Management, Journal of Business Venturing, Entrepreneurship Theory and Practice, Journal of Business Strategy,* and *European Management Journal.* He has coedited special issues of *Academy of Management Review, Academy of Management Executive, Journal of Business Venturing, Strategic Management Journal,* and *Journal of High Technology and Engineering Management.* He received awards for the best article published in *Academy of Management Executive* (1999) and *Academy of Management Journal* (2000). In 2001, his article published in *Academy of Management Executive* won the Best Journal Article in Corporate Entrepreneurship Award from the U.S. Association for Small Business & Entrepreneurship (USASBE). He is a Research Fellow in the National Entrepreneurship Consortium. He received the 1999 Award for Outstanding Intellectual Contributions to Competitiveness Research from the American Society for Competitiveness and the USASBE Scholar in Corporate Entrepreneurship Award (2004) from USASBE. Currently, he is an Associate Editor for *Academy Management Journal.* Previously, he served as a representative-at-large on the Board of Governors of the Academy of Management.

Robert E. Hoskisson

Robert E. Hoskisson is a Professor of Strategic Management and he holds the W. P. Carey Chair in the Department of Management at the W. P. Carey School of Business at Arizona State University. He was formerly on the faculty at the University of Oklahoma as well as Texas A&M University. He also has a special appointment at the University of Nottingham in the United Kingdom. He received his Ph.D. from the University of California–Irvine. His interest in strategic management topics has allowed him to teach overview as well topical courses in strategic management at the undergraduate, master's, and doctoral levels. He has taught topical courses in international strategy and strategic alliances and has made a number of specialized presentations on corporate governance, mergers and acquisitions, divestitures, strategy in emerging economies and corporate entrepreneurship, privatization, and cooperative strategy. These presentations were derived from his active research agenda in these topical areas. His teaching and research expertise in these areas has been recognized. For example, in 1998, he received an award for Outstanding Academic Contributions to Competitiveness, American Society for Competitiveness. He also received the William G. Dyer Distinguished Alumni Award given at the Marriott School of Management, Brigham Young University. He is a Fellow of the Academy of Management and a charter member of the Academy of Management Journals Hall of Fame. These recognitions come from his academic oriented publications in top peer-reviewed journals including the *Academy of Management Journal, Academy of Management Review, Strategic Management Journal, Organization Science, Journal of Management,* and *Journal of Management Studies.* Because of his interest in managerial practice and application, his advice has been published in journals that specialize in translating academic research into prescriptions for managerial practice, such as the *California Management Review, Academy of Management Executive, Long Range Planning,* and *Journal of World Business.* His research has been reviewed in the *MIT Sloan Management Review.* He has also coauthored a number of textbooks to foster instruction in Strategic Management including the 6th edition of *Strategic Management: Competitiveness and Globalization* and *Competing for Advantage* (1st edition). He has also coauthored *Downscoping: How to Tame the Diversified Firm* (Oxford University Press), a masters level text on restructuring large businesses. In serving the academic community, Hoskisson has served on several editorial boards for publications such as the *Academy of Management Journal* (including Consulting Editor and Guest Editor of a special issue), *Strategic Management Journal, Journal of Management* (including Associate Editor), *Journal of International Business Studies* (Consulting Editor), *Organization Science,* and *Journal of Management Studies* (Guest Editor). He completed three years of service as a representative-at-large on the Board of Governors of the Academy of Management and currently is on the Board of Directors of the Strategic Management Society.

Michael A. Hitt

Michael A. Hitt is a Distinguished Professor and holds the Joseph Foster Chair in Business Leadership and the C. W. and Dorothy Conn Chair in New Ventures at Texas A&M University. He received his Ph.D. from the University of Colorado. He has authored or coauthored over 120 journal articles and coauthored or coedited 25 separate books. Those books include: *Downscoping: How to Tame the Diversified Firm* (1994); *Mergers and Acquisitions: A Guide to Creating Value for Stakeholders* (2001); *Handbook of Strategic Management* (2001); *Strategic Entrepreneurship: Creating a New Integrated Mindset* (2002); *Managing Knowledge for Sustained Competitive Advantage* (2003); *Competing for Advantage* (2004); *The Blackwell Entrepreneurship Encyclopedia* (2005); *Strategic Management: Competitiveness and Globalization* (2005); and *Great Minds in Management: The Process of Theory Development* (2005). He has served on the editorial review boards of multiple journals and served as Consulting Editor (1988–1990) and Editor (1991–1993) of the *Academy of Management Journal*. He serves as President Elect of the Strategic Management Society and is a past president of the Academy of Management. He received the 1996 Award for Outstanding Academic Contributions to Competitiveness and the 1999 Award for Outstanding Intellectual Contributions to Competitiveness Research from the American Society for Competitiveness. He is a Fellow in the Academy of Management and a Research Fellow in the National Entrepreneurship Consortium, and received an honorary doctorate from the Universidad Carlos III de Madrid for his contributions to the field. He received the Irwin Outstanding Educator Award and the Distinguished Service Award from the Academy of Management.

Understanding
Business Strategy
Concepts and Cases

part 1

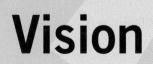

Vision

The Foundations of Strategic Management

Reading and studying this chapter should enable you to:

*Knowledge Objectives

1_
Define strategic management.

2_
Discuss why firms use the industrial organization model to analyze their external environment.

3_
Discuss why firms use the resource-based view of the firm model to analyze their internal environment.

4_
Define stakeholders and understand their importance.

5_
Explain the work of strategic leaders.

Focusing on Strategy

Solidly Focusing on Customers: The Foundation for Best Buy's Success?

"We are in the midst of a strategic transformation to put the customer at the center of all that we do." (Brad Anderson, vice chairman and chief executive officer [CEO], Best Buy)

Consumer electronics is a highly competitive business. Just think of the options you have as a consumer when buying a LCD television, which is only one of many electronic products you could buy. First, you could use the Internet to learn more about LCD televisions made by Sony, Samsung, Hitachi, Panasonic, and a host of other firms. With some information about LCD televisions, you could then shop at retailers such as Circuit City and Best Buy, smaller retailers located in your city or region, or even specialized stores focusing on tailoring home theater systems that include a LCD television. You can even purchase a used LCD television through an eBay auction.

As a "big box retailer," Best Buy competes with all of these sellers (Circuit City, local retailers, specialized stores, and eBay) to serve customers shopping for a LCD television as well as many other electronic products. While Best Buy is fully aware of the competitors mentioned so far, the firm's leaders are increasingly concerned about new competitors from different sources. Dell and Gateway, for example, now sell their own LCD televisions (as well as other consumer electronic products) via the Internet. While Gateway's future remains cloudy, Dell's ability to produce high-quality products at a low cost and to use the Internet to sell directly to consumers presents a clear competitive threat to electronics retailers such as Best Buy. Perhaps even more daunting is the threat Wal-Mart poses as it moves further into electronics retailing. Given this threat, if you were the CEO of Best Buy, what actions would you think of taking to compete against Wal-Mart?

A transformation to what the firm calls *customer centricity* is Best Buy's answer to these competitive threats. According to the firm's CEO, Best Buy is "in the midst of a strategic transformation to put the customer at the center of all that it does." The firm is launching customer centricity as a preemptive strike to its new competitive threats and to continue competing successfully against current competitors.

In the initial stage of its efforts to put the customer at the center of all that it does, Best Buy developed five prototypical customers, each of whom was given a name. Over the next several years, Best Buy stores will be converted to concentrate on serving the needs of one, but no more than two of the firm's five customer segments. *Jill* is a busy suburban mom who wants to enrich her children's lives with technology and entertainment. *Buzz* is a focused, active, younger male seeking the latest technology in his entertainment purchases. *Ray* is a family man wanting to purchase electronics that improve his and his family's life. *BB4B* (short for Best Buy for Business) is a small-business customer who can use Best Buy's product solutions and services to increase productivity and profitability. Finally, *Barry* is an affluent professional who wants to buy the best technology and entertainment experience and demands superior customer service.

Is customer centricity a success at Best Buy? It's too early to tell. The firm may change aspects of the program as it is introduced across all stores. But Best Buy's same-store sales for the ending of the first quarter in 2004 increased 8.3 percent. *Same-store sales* compares the sales revenue for a store that has been open for one or more years on a similar basis (such as a full year to a full year or a specific quarter of the current year to a specific quarter of the previous year). *Same-store sales* is an important performance measure because it allows investors to understand the part of a firm's growth in sales revenue accounted for by stores that were opened in a given year as well as the part of growth in sales revenue accounted for by existing stores within a year.

In addition to sales revenue growth, profitability was also improving in 2004 at Best Buy. In fact, the firm estimated that its earnings from continuing operations during the fourth quarter of 2004 would jump by 55 percent. Best Buy's leaders will study the increases in the firm's sales revenue and profits to determine the degree to which the strong focus on the consumer contributed to them.

SOURCES: 2004, Best Buy accelerates customer centricity transformation, Best Buy Home Page, http://www.bestbuy.com, June 3; J. Freed, 2004, Marketing to "Jill," "Ray," and "Barry," *Richmond Times-Dispatch*, May 23: D1, D2; M. Higgins, 2004, New retail offering: Geeks on call, *Wall Street Journal Online*, http://www.wsj.com, May 20; J. Seward, 2004, Best Buy same-store sales rise, sees earnings in-line, *Wall Street Journal Online*, http://www.wsj.com, June 3.

*
strategic management
the ongoing process companies use to form a *vision, analyze* their external environment and their internal environment, and select one or more *strategies* to use to create value for customers and other stakeholders, especially shareholders

*
vision
contains at least two components—a mission that describes the firm's DNA and the "picture" of the firm as it hopes to exist in a future time period

Do you sometimes wonder why some firms are more successful than others? Why, for example, is Best Buy's sales revenue more than twice that of Circuit City, its closest competitor?[1] Why is Toyota, traditionally a marginal player in Europe, now becoming a significant force in European markets? (Hint: Some believe that Toyota's new design studio in southern France and its new highly efficient manufacturing facility in Valenciennes in northern France account for its recent European success.)[2]

Although the reasons for Best Buy's and Toyota's success as well as the successes of many other firms sometimes seem mysterious, they really aren't. As with Best Buy and Toyota, firms use strategic management to achieve success. The purpose of this book is to carefully explain each of the three parts of strategic management—*vision, analysis,* and *strategy.* We think you will enjoy learning about strategic management and know that you will benefit from doing so.

What Is Strategic Management?

Strategic management is the ongoing process companies use to form a *vision,* *analyze* their external environment and their internal environment, and select one or more *strategies* to use to create value for customers and other stakeholders, especially shareholders. Let's define the parts of the strategic management process so we can see the differences among them. We merely introduce you to the parts of strategic management in this chapter. You'll learn more about each part in the book's remaining chapters.

The **vision** contains at least two components—a mission that describes the firm's DNA and the "picture" of the firm as it hopes to exist in a future time period. DNA includes the core information and characteristics necessary for the firm to function. The vision is intended to inspire the firm's employees to realize or "picture" the future aspirations of what the firm can become. A **strategy** is an action plan designed to move an organization toward achievement of its vision. The mission of the firm is focused on the markets it serves and the products (either goods or services) it provides. Basically, the **mission** defines the firm's core intent and the business or businesses in which it intends to operate. The **external environment** is a set of conditions outside the firm that affect the firm's performance. Changes in population trends and income levels, competition between firms, and economic changes are examples of the many conditions in a firm's external environment that can affect its performance. For example, think of the effect of increases in mortgage rates (which are part of the *economic* external environment) on home builders. The **internal environment** is the set of conditions (such as strengths, resources, capabilities, and so forth) inside the firm affecting the choice and use of strategies.

Strengths are resources and capabilities that allow the firm to complete important tasks. Being able to effectively manage the flow of its inventory is one of Best Buy's strengths that help it complete the important task of having the right merchandise on its shelves for customers to buy. **Resources** are the tangible and intangible assets held by the firm. A strong balance sheet is one of Coca-Cola's tangible assets, while the knowledge held by its employees is one of Microsoft's intangible assets. **Capabilities** result when the firm integrates several

capabilities the firm
emphasizes and performs
especially well while
pursuing its vision

core competencies that
differ from those held by
competitors

different resources to complete a task or a series of related tasks.[3] 3M integrates the knowledge of its scientists (an intangible asset) with other resources, including its sophisticated scientific equipment (a tangible asset), to create its innovation capability. **Core competencies** are capabilities the firm emphasizes and performs especially well while pursuing its vision. The distribution and inventory competencies Dell uses to sell computers directly to customers are considered core competencies. Core competencies that differ from those held by competitors are called **distinctive competencies.** Dell's distribution and inventory competencies differ from those of its competitors (for example, HP and IBM) and thus are also distinctive competencies. When core competencies allow the firm to create value for customers by performing a key activity (such as Dell's distribution competencies) *better* than competitors, it has a **competitive advantage.** A firm can also have a competitive advantage when a distinctive competence allows it to perform an activity that creates value for customers that competitors can't perform.

Figure 1.1 is a diagram of strategic management, while Table 1.1 presents a set of strategic management's key characteristics. We continue our introduction of strategic management's parts in the next few sections.

FIGURE 1.1   The Strategic Management Process

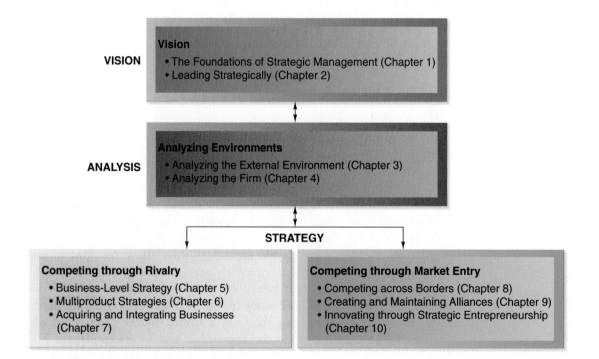

VISION

Vision
- The Foundations of Strategic Management (Chapter 1)
- Leading Strategically (Chapter 2)

ANALYSIS

Analyzing Environments
- Analyzing the External Environment (Chapter 3)
- Analyzing the Firm (Chapter 4)

STRATEGY

Competing through Rivalry
- Business-Level Strategy (Chapter 5)
- Multiproduct Strategies (Chapter 6)
- Acquiring and Integrating Businesses (Chapter 7)

Competing through Market Entry
- Competing across Borders (Chapter 8)
- Creating and Maintaining Alliances (Chapter 9)
- Innovating through Strategic Entrepreneurship (Chapter 10)

TABLE 1.1 Key Characteristics of Strategic Management

Strategic management is:
- Performance oriented
- Ongoing in nature
- Dynamic rather than static
- Oriented to the present and the future
- Concerned with conditions both outside and inside the firm
- Concerned with performing well and satisfying stakeholders

*
competitive advantage

when the firm's core competencies allow it to create value for customers by performing a key activity *better* than competitors or when a distinctive competence allows it to perform an activity that creates value for customers that competitors can't perform

Rivals Coca-Cola and PepsiCo use various strategies to compete with each other. In what ways are their strategies unique?

© Daniel Acker/Bloomberg News/Landov

The Three Parts of the Strategic Management Process

As suggested in Figure 1.1, strategic leaders are responsible for forming a firm's vision and mission (we talk about this further in Chapter 2). As noted earlier, an effective mission provides direction to the firm while an effective vision "inspires people to subsequent efforts."[4] We present additional vision statements and mission statements from different types of organizations in Table 1.2. Which of the vision statements shown in Table 1.2 inspire you? Which of the mission statements does the best job of telling you about the direction a firm is taking? Would you make changes to any of the vision or mission statements shown in Table 1.2? If so, why, and what would those changes be?

Figure 1.1 also suggests that firms must *analyze* their external environment and their internal environment before strategies can be chosen and *implemented*. Here's how this worked at Best Buy. Following careful study, Best Buy spotted an opportunity in its external environment to group customers based on their different needs. After analyzing its internal environment, Best Buy decided to use its capabilities in supply chain management and customer relationship management systems to serve the unique needs of each customer group.

As mentioned earlier, a strategy is an action plan designed to move an organization toward achievement of its vision. Strategy is about finding ways for the firm to be different from its competitors. The most effective companies avoid using "me-too" strategies—strategies that are the same as those of their competitors. A firm's strategy should allow it to deliver a unique mix of value to customers.[5]

As shown in Figure 1.1, firms use business-level strategies, multi-product strategies, and international strategies to directly compete with rivals. With product names such as

TABLE 1.2   Vision and Mission Statements

Vision Statements

McDonald's

To give each customer, every time, an experience that sets new standards in value, service, friendliness, and quality.

NASDAQ

To build the world's first truly global securities market . . . A worldwide market of markets built on a worldwide network of networks . . . linking pools of liquidity and connecting investors from all over the world . . . assuring the best possible price for securities at the lowest possible cost.

Petsmart

To be the premier organization in nurturing and enriching the bond between people and animals.

Wachovia

Wachovia's vision is to be the best, most trusted and admired financial services company.

Mission Statements

Bristol-Myers Squibb

Our mission is to extend and enhance human life by providing the highest-quality pharmaceuticals and health care products.

GlaxoSmithKline

GSK's mission is to improve the quality of human life by enabling people to do more, feel better and live longer.

Merck

The mission of Merck is to provide society with superior products and services by developing innovations and solutions that improve the quality of life and satisfy customer needs, and to provide employees with meaningful work and advancement opportunities, and investors with a superior rate of return.

Wipro

The mission is to be a full-service, global outsourcing company.

Mastiff and Pitbull, Big Dog Motorcycles' strategy is to build premium, heavyweight motorcycles that are targeted for customers with needs for this unique product. Big Dog competes directly against Harley-Davidson with its business-level strategy, as do Coca-Cola and PepsiCo with their business-level, multiproduct, and international strategies. Companies also use certain strategies (such as mergers and acquisitions, alliances, and new ventures) to enter new markets. To expand into additional markets, for example, Aqua America, a water utility company, acquired more than 90 firms in the last several years. Beginning with locations in Pennsylvania, the firm now serves more than 800,000 customers in 13 states.[6] As the term implies, the firm uses market-entry strategies to begin competing in new markets.

Once chosen, strategies must be put into use. **Strategy implementation** is the set of actions firms take to use a strategy after it has been selected. PetMed Express is a pet pharmacy with a strategy of providing the largest selection of prescription and nonprescription pet medications to consumers at competitive prices. Part of how PetMed Express implements this strategy is by using the Internet and telemarketing to sell its products to customers.[7]

*

strategy implementation

the set of actions firms take to use a strategy after it has been selected

In "Understanding Strategy," we describe the initial success of Netflix. As you'll see, the firm has a vision and a strategy that it is successfully implementing. Thus, the strategic management process is being used effectively at Netflix. Indeed, the firm has experienced much success in its early years. Shareholders and employees hope that Netflix will continue to grow and will become a consistently profitable corporation. However, organizational success can be transitory, even for very famous companies. Levi Strauss, for example, was quite successful for many years. However, between 1996 and 2001, the firm's sales dropped from $7.1 billion to $4.3 billion.[8] When a firm such as Levi Strauss experiences trouble, some top-level managers become paranoid about their own company's future success. Patricia Sueltz, executive vice president of Salesforce.com, feels that she has to keep looking over her shoulder to see what competitors are doing to determine whether those actions are a threat to her firm's performance.[9] There are no guarantees that what currently works for any firm will work for it in the future. When used properly, though, the strategic management process contributes to a company's desire to reach its vision by competing successfully across time. Let's see how Netflix has used the strategic management process and learn about the challenges the firm faces to remain successful.

After reading about Netflix, what do you think? Will this firm continue to grow? On a long-term basis, will Netflix be able to compete against the likes of Wal-Mart and Blockbuster?[10] Given what you know, would you be willing to invest in Netflix? Why or why not?

We've now introduced you to the parts of strategic management, provided you with examples of vision statements and mission statements, and described how one firm—Netflix—is using the strategic management process. We'll use the remainder of this chapter to tell you a bit more about how firms analyze their external environment and their internal environment. Decision makers use the information gathered from the analyses of their firm's external environment and internal environment to select one or more strategies (see Figure 1.1). Before closing the chapter with a brief discussion of the contents of the book's remaining chapters, we'll introduce you to stakeholders and strategic leaders. In essence, stakeholders are the individuals and groups that firms try to satisfy when using the strategic management process, while strategic leaders are responsible for making certain their firm effectively uses the process.

*

opportunities

conditions in the firm's external environment that may help the firm reach its vision

The Industrial Organization Model

Firms use what is called the industrial organization (I/O) model to analyze their external environment. We introduce you to this model here and provide you with a fuller discussion of it and its use in Chapter 3. Using this model helps firms identify opportunities and threats. **Opportunities** are conditions in the firm's external environment that may help the firm reach its vision. **Threats** are conditions in the firm's external environment that may prevent the firm from reaching its vision. Performance often declines in firms that do not carefully study the threats and opportunities in their external environment. Firms use their resources to pursue environmental opportunities and to overcome environmental

*

threats

conditions in the firm's external environment that may prevent the firm from reaching its vision

understanding strategy:

ONLINE RENTALS: USING STRATEGIC MANAGEMENT TO PIONEER A MARKET

Frustrated by recurring late fees, Reed Hastings developed the concept of an all-you-can-rent online movie business in 1997. Hastings established his firm, Netflix, after studying the external environment and concluding that "People love to rent movies, they hate late fees, and they like the Net." Netflix works like this: For a flat monthly fee beginning at $11.99 per month in January 2005, customers rent all the DVDs they want, three at a time, without incurring late fees. Viewed rentals are returned in prepaid mailing envelopes. Netflix then sends customers the next items on their own personalized list (called a "rental queue") that is retained for them on Netflix's Web site.

Netflix serves a niche in the movie rental market, and a growing number of analysts consider it "a brilliant idea (that) is well executed." In terms of strategic management, this comment suggests that as a strategic leader, Hastings worked with others to establish a vision for his company and then chose a strategy to reach it after analyzing the firm's external environment and its internal environment. Essentially, the vision is for Netflix to "provide superior service to movie buffs." "Well executed" means that the strategy is being effectively implemented. Carefully placed distribution centers and continuous efforts to understand and respond to customers' needs are examples of what Netflix does to implement its strategy.

What does the future hold for Netflix? Strong competition from Wal-Mart and Blockbuster is a significant challenge. Analysts warn that "Wal-Mart's brand name, in-store marketing and world-famous distribution system could eventually loom large" as a competitive threat similar to Blockbuster's Online rental service which was priced at $14.99 per month in January 2005. In addition, Blockbuster was still trying to acquire Hollywood Entertainment Corporation in the first part of 2005. If this effort succeeds, Blockbuster would become an even larger competitor for Netflix and Wal-Mart. In spite of the challenges from Blockbuster and Wal-Mart, Hastings is undeterred, believing that his firm has only "scratched the surface" of the value it can bring to customers. To continue delivering that value, Netflix should remain committed to using its strategic management process.

SOURCES: S. H. Meitner, 2004, Netflix flexes video rental muscle, *Richmond Times-Dispatch*, March 14: D9; D. Oestricher, 2004, Netflix won't match Blockbuster's price cut, CEO says, *Wall Street Journal Online*, http://www.wsj.com, December 22; E. J. Savitz, 2004, Netflix may be overvalued, *Wall Street Journal Online*, http://www.wsj.com, February 29; 2004, Netflix issues profit warning, citing subscriber growth costs, *Wall Street Journal Online*, http://www.wsj.com, February 24; 2004, Wrangling for rentals, *Barron's Online*, http://www.barrons.com, February 23.

threats. We demonstrate this point in "Understanding Strategy," which discusses Levi Strauss & Co.

The case of Levi Strauss shows how important it is for firms to understand the meaning of conditions in their external environment. As explained in "Understanding Strategy," Levi Strauss failed to detect changes in its external environment such as those in customers' preferences. Changing preferences among the firm's customers, which were threats to Levi Strauss, mandated that the firm begin to produce more fashionable jeans and related clothing items. Thus, firms must carefully analyze their external environment to anticipate its effects on their current strategy.

understanding strategy:

THE "501" JEAN: A CLOTHING ICON LOSES SOME OF ITS PANACHE

"One of America's most durable apparel brands is fighting for its life in the midst of a tough environment for apparel retailing." This comment by a business analyst suggests that difficult times are on hand for vulnerable jeans manufacturer Levi Strauss. Indeed, losses in market share and profit declines from the late 1990s into the early 2000s appear to demonstrate Levi's problems.

© GAMBARINI MAURIZIO/DPA/Landov

Established in 1873, Levi Strauss was the clear leader in the global jeans market as late as the 1970s. The famous 501 jean was the firm's flagship product and the foundation of its success. However, this product remained essentially unchanged through the 1970s, even though customers began to view jeans differently. Historically, jeans were generally thought to be a utilitarian, durable clothing item—something people could comfortably wear when working, especially for manual labor. By the end of the 1970s, though, jeans became fashionable as a result of the efforts of a number of firms such as Calvin Klein, Gloria Vanderbilt, Ralph Lauren, and Jordache. Indeed, these companies' stylish jeans revolutionized this product, damaging Levi Strauss's market share as a result. Soon, fickle customers were frequently changing their choice of jeans, moving from the current fashion trend to the next "hot" one on a regular basis. Jeans also were distributed more broadly, including through the channels of discounters such as Wal-Mart and Target. However, Levi Strauss chose not to sell through discounters' stores, preferring to remain focused on its traditional distribution channels (such as JCPenney and Sears, Roebuck). Thus, Levi Strauss's inability to handle threats in its external environment found the firm in a situation in which it was trying to sell items that customers didn't perceive as fashionable through distribution channels that were losing market share. Successful use of the strategic management process likely would have helped Levi Strauss deal more effectively with changes in its external environment (such as the changes in customers' preferences for jeans). In other words, if Levi had made a full-scale commitment to strategic management, it would have carefully studied its external environment in order to identify trends that might affect its operations.

Although it was slow to respond, Levi Strauss is now launching major product initiatives. "In late 2002," for example, "Levi Strauss overhauled its market strategy and, for the first time since the introduction of Dockers in 1986, rolled out a series of new brands," including the unusually cut Engineered Jeans, the Superlow for women, and the Type 1. Levi Strauss viewed the Type 1 as a product with truly innovative styling, as reflected by its exaggerated pocket details and superdark denim finishes. Levi promised that the Type 1 would be "the boldest, most provocative Levi's jeans in decades." However, early reaction was that the Type 1 was too cutting-edge for Levi's mainstream customer while it failed to appeal to other potential customers. Thus, only time will tell if Levi Strauss will return to its glory days as a top performer in its industry on the basis of the actions it is now taking.

SOURCES: S. Beatty, 2004, Levi Strauss plans to continue its sales strategy on jean styles, *Wall Street Journal Online*, http://www.wsj.com, March 3; D. K. Berman & S. Beatty, 2004, Levi to sell its Docker brand to Vestar for $800 million, *Wall Street Journal*, September 27: B6; D. Gross, 2004, Seams to be, *USAirways Attache*, March: 13–14; 2004, Levi Strauss & Co., *Hoover's*, http://www.hoovers.com, March 14; 2004, Levi Strauss & Co. Home Page, http://www.levistrauss.com, March 15.

Similar to Levi Strauss, the global airline industry illustrates the influence of the external environment on a firm's choice of strategy. Let's describe this influence.

Economic conditions, which as we said before are part of the firm's external environment, influence travel decisions. During poor economic times, for example, people might choose not to travel at all or to reduce the number of times they travel by air. Unrest in the global environment created by war and international tensions affect the demand for airline services. The cost of fuel can have a dramatic effect on each airline company's profitability; in mid-2004, for example, industry observers suggested that fuel costs could contribute to the bankruptcy of several airlines including Delta Airlines. Increasing fuel costs have also prevented United Airlines from emerging from bankruptcy. To deal with this matter and to avoid bankruptcy, United is aggressively trying to reduce its costs where it can. In mid-2004, United was studying the possibility of abandoning its employee pension plan in order to lower its costs.[11]

A lack of control over the conditions in the external environment reduces a firm's strategic options. A lack of options results in firms within an industry using similar strategies, such as is the case with airline companies. As a customer, think of your travel on airlines. The firms use the same planes to offer you essentially the same service at virtually the same price. While variances do exist, of course, do you think that customers can differentiate greatly among airline companies? If not, this could indicate that the external environment is influencing these companies to follow similar strategies.

In Figure 1.2, we diagram how firms use the I/O model to analyze their external environment. The information gained from this analysis is used to help decision makers choose one or more strategies. We'll explain the I/O model and its use in greater detail in Chapter 3.

The Resource-Based View of the Firm Model

While the I/O model focuses on the firm's external environment, the resource-based view (RBV) model describes what firms do to analyze their internal environment. The purpose of analyzing the internal environment is to identify the firm's strengths, resources, capabilities, core competencies, distinctive competencies, and competitive advantages. Thus, the I/O and RBV models complement each other; one (the I/O model) deals with conditions outside the firm and the other (the RBV model) deals with conditions inside the firm. We introduce you to the RBV model here and offer a fuller description of it in Chapter 4.

The RBV model suggests that effective management of the firm's operations creates resources and capabilities that are unique to that firm. This means that the bundle of productive resources across firms can vary quite substantially.[12] Louis Vuitton's resources and capabilities, for example, differ from those of competitors Prada, Gucci, Hermes, and Coach. With unique resources and capabilities, ones that are different from competitors', each of these firms has a chance to create competitive advantages that it can use to produce a product that creates value for a group of customers. Let's describe how Louis Vuitton uses its unique resources and capabilities to develop competitive advantages that in turn allow the firm to create value for a group of customers.

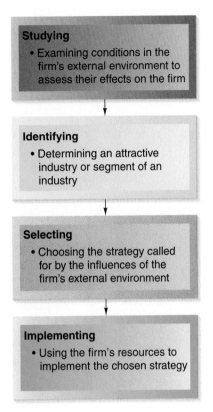

Studying
- Examining conditions in the firm's external environment to assess their effects on the firm

↓

Identifying
- Determining an attractive industry or segment of an industry

↓

Selecting
- Choosing the strategy called for by the influences of the firm's external environment

↓

Implementing
- Using the firm's resources to implement the chosen strategy

Customers of Louis Vuitton buy into the dream of owning luxury brand products.

© Doug Kanter/Bloomberg News/Landov

The world's most profitable luxury brand, Vuitton has design skills and manufacturing efficiencies that are considered superior to those of its competitors. These capabilities allow Louis Vuitton to generate higher operating margins. In the words of an executive at competitor Coach, Vuitton's "operating metrics are second to none."[13] Because of Vuitton's superiority relative to its competitors, these capabilities are the foundation for the company's competitive advantages in product design and manufacturing.

Although expensive, the firm's products do create value for a group of customers. One customer sees this value as "buying into a dream." In this particular customer's words, "You buy into the dream of Louis Vuitton. We're part of a sect, and the more they put their prices up, the more we come back. They pull the wool over our eyes, but we love it."[14]

Unlike the external environment, firms have direct control over conditions in their internal environment. Each firm's decision makers make choices about the resources

FIGURE 1.3 Using the RBV Model to Analyze the Internal Environment

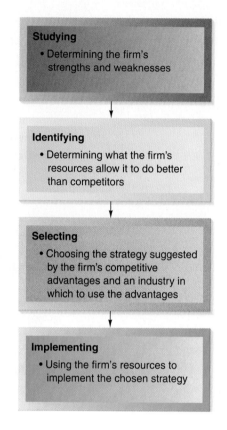

Studying
- Determining the firm's strengths and weaknesses

Identifying
- Determining what the firm's resources allow it to do better than competitors

Selecting
- Choosing the strategy suggested by the firm's competitive advantages and an industry in which to use the advantages

Implementing
- Using the firm's resources to implement the chosen strategy

and capabilities the firm wants to control and about how they'll be nurtured and used. The ability to control the firm's resources and capabilities and to develop them in ways that differ from those of the competitors' increases the number of strategic options. Thus, from the RBV perspective, the uniqueness of the firm's resources and capabilities influences the choice of one or more strategies.

Figure 1.3 diagrams how firms use the RBV to analyze their internal environment. Notice how the firm's resources and capabilities influence the choice of a strategy.

Next, we discuss stakeholders—the individuals and groups the firm seeks to satisfy by using the strategy or strategies it has selected.

Stakeholders

Stakeholders are individuals and groups who have an interest in a firm's performance and an ability to influence its actions.[15] In essence, stakeholders influence firms by deciding the degree to which they will support the firm's strategy.

*

stakeholders

individuals and groups who have an interest in a firm's performance and an ability to influence its actions

Shareholders, customers, and suppliers are stakeholders, as are a firm's employees and the communities in which the firm conducts business. Shareholders, for example, exercise their influence by deciding whether they will keep their shares in the firm or sell them. Employees decide whether they will remain with their employer or work for another firm, perhaps even a competitor. Not surprisingly, firms use strategic management to select and implement strategies that create value for stakeholders.[16]

As shown in Figure 1.4, firms have three major stakeholder groups—owners (shareholders), external stakeholders, and internal stakeholders. Each stakeholder wants the firm in which it has an interest to satisfy its needs. Generally speaking, stakeholders continue to support firms that satisfy their needs. However, stakeholders withdraw their support from firms failing to meet their needs.

Stakeholders' interest in performance, coupled with their ability to influence the firm through their decisions to support the firm or not, suggests that companies have important *relationships* with their stakeholders. These relationships must be managed in a way that keeps the stakeholders committed to the firm. Firms that can manage relationships with their stakeholders better than their competitors may gain a competitive advantage.[17] Firms that see stakeholders as their partners and keep them well informed about the company's actions provide an example.[18] Notice how the firm discussed in this chapter's Mini-Case openly communicates with its stakeholders. This communication may be a competitive advantage for that particular firm.

Firms and stakeholders have relationships because they need each other. To launch a company and operate it on a continuing basis, firms need capital (that is, money) provided by investors (such as stockholders) and financial institutions (such as banks), materials from suppliers that are used to produce a good or provide a service, and employees to complete necessary tasks. In addition and importantly, firms need customers to buy their good or service. Similarly, investors (individual stockholders and institutional stockholders such as pension funds) need to find viable businesses in which they can invest and earn a return on their capital. Employees need to work for organizations for income and at least some personal satisfaction. Customers want to buy goods and services from companies that will satisfy their various needs. Thus, firms need stakeholders, but stakeholders also need firms.

FIGURE 1.4 | Stakeholder Groups

Owners
Shareholders
• Individual
• Institutional

External Stakeholders
• Customers
• Suppliers
• Local communities
• Governmental agencies
• General society

Internal Stakeholders
• Employees
• Managers

Managing relationships between the firm and its stakeholders is difficult because satisfying one stakeholder's needs may come at the expense of another stakeholder. Consider, for example, employees' desire to be paid more for their work. If wages are increased without an identical increase in productivity to offset the higher costs, the firm's cost of goods sold will increase, reducing the return on investment for shareholders. Alternatively, think of customers wanting to buy higher-quality products from a firm at ever-decreasing prices. The net result of the firm's lowering the price of its good or service without reducing the cost to produce it is fewer resources for wages and salaries and for returns to shareholders.

While other examples could be offered, the main point here is that firms must manage their relationships with stakeholders in ways that will keep all stakeholders at least minimally satisfied. In other words, the firm wants to retain quality suppliers, loyal customers, and satisfied employees while providing returns to shareholders that cause them to retain their investment in the firm. As these comments show, managing relationships among various stakeholders is a challenging, yet important task for the firm's strategic leaders.

Strategic Leaders

*

strategic leaders

the individuals practicing leadership

Strategic leaders are the individuals practicing strategic leadership. (We define and fully discuss strategic leadership in the next chapter.) Strategic leaders make certain that actions are being taken that will lead to their firm's success.[19] As CEO of Apple Computer, for example, Steve Jobs must make certain that his firm uses strategic management to continue benefiting from its highly successful iPod digital music player.[20] A firm's board of directors holds the CEO and her top management team responsible for ensuring that an effective strategic management process is developed and properly used throughout the organization. When doing their work, top-level managers concentrate on the "big picture" to envision their firm's future and the strategies necessary to achieve that vision.[21]

In small firms, the CEO may be the sole owner and may not report to a board of directors. In this instance, of course, she is responsible for both designing and using strategic management. Decisions that strategic leaders make when using the strategic management process include determining the resources acquired, the prices paid for those resources, and how to manage those resources.[22] Through the firm's vision statement, strategic leaders try to stimulate their employees' creativity to develop new products, new processes to produce the firm's products, and the administrative routines necessary to successfully implement the firm's strategies.[23]

*

organizational culture

the set of values and beliefs that are shared throughout the firm

The CEO and his top management team are also responsible for shaping and nurturing the firm's culture. **Organizational culture** is the set of values and beliefs that are shared throughout the firm. *Values* reflect what is important, while *beliefs* speak to how things should be done. In 3M's organizational culture, respecting the contribution of each employee and continuous innovation are important values.[24] The most effective organizational cultures let people know that they are appreciated. When this happens, culture can be a strong motivator of excellent performance by employees.[25]

Intangible in nature, culture can't be touched or seen but its presence is felt throughout every organization. Think of companies where you've worked, university classes you've attended, or other groups to which you've belonged. Consider the values and beliefs held by each of those groups. How did it feel to be a member of those groups? The groups you are thinking about are different in terms of their values and beliefs, aren't they? The same can be said of business organizations.

Increasingly, strategic management is becoming more decentralized in companies. The reason for this is to have the people who are "closest to the action" making decisions and taking actions.[26] Thus, the strategic management process is often shared among many people in an organization.[27] As a result, we need to be prepared to take on leadership roles regardless of our position in an organization. Additionally, frequent communication among all involved with the strategic management process helps ensure that changes are made when and where they are needed. Because of changing conditions, adjustments are often necessary when implementing strategies.

We should understand, though, that while many different people may be involved, the final responsibility for effective strategic management rests with the firm's strategic leaders. In addition, it is important to note that the best strategic leaders also act ethically in all that they do. *Ethics* are concerned with the standards for deciding what is good or bad, right or wrong[28] as defined by most members of a particular society.[29] In an organizational context, ethics reveal a value system that has been widely adopted by the firm's employees[30] and that other stakeholders recognize as an important driver of decisions and actions. Firms can record their ethics in documents such as a code of conduct. On a daily basis, however, ethics can be inferred by observing the actions of the firm's stakeholders, especially its employees.[31] Even a brief review of events in the business world shows that an organization's ethics are of interest to the general society as well as to other stakeholders whose interests can be negatively affected when a firm acts unethically. Thus, as explored further in Chapter 2, ethical practices are a vital part of effective strategic leadership and strategic management.[32]

How the Book Is Organized

The book has three major parts, corresponding to the three parts of the strategic management process. Part One of this book comprises two chapters. This first chapter introduces you to strategic management. In Chapter 2, we describe leadership from a strategic perspective. Strategic leadership is being effectively practiced when everyone in a firm is aware of the vision being pursued and the important role each person plays in pursuing that vision. We also describe the most important actions strategic leaders take to guide their organizations.

In Part Two, which also has two chapters, we focus on two analyses that firms use to obtain and evaluate the information needed to choose strategies for pursuing the firm's vision. Chapter 3 focuses on the external environment. A firm analyzes the external environment to identify factors outside the company that can affect the strategic actions the firm is taking to achieve its vision. Firms can influence but not control conditions in their external environment. The focus of Chapter 4 is inside the firm. Here, the purpose is to understand how the firm's unique resources and capabilities can be shaped to form competitive advantages (that is, create superior value for customers) and satisfy stakeholders' needs.

Part Three examines different types of strategies. The strategies the firm selects are a product of the vision and the conditions in its external environment and its internal environment. This means that the insights gained from the topics presented in the book's first four chapters strongly guide the selection of strategies. In Chapters 5, 6, and 7, our concern is with different strategies (business-level, multiproduct, and international) that firms use to successfully compete in different markets. Each chapter also provides guidelines for implementing different strategies. We follow these discussions with explanations in Chapters 8–10 of strategies (mergers and acquisitions, cooperative alliances, and new ventures) that firms use to enter new markets.

Summary

The primary purpose of this chapter is to introduce you to strategic management and to discuss how firms use this important organizational tool to continuously improve their performance for stakeholders. In doing so, we examined the following topics:

- **Strategic management** is the ongoing process that firms use to form a vision, analyze their external and internal environments, and select one or more strategies to create value for customers and satisfy other stakeholders. The external and internal environments are analyzed to determine which strategies should be used (and how to use them) to achieve the vision. Firms use the strategic management process to select one or more strategies to implement to reach their vision. Strategic management is concerned with both formulation (selection of one or more strategies) and implementation (actions taken to ensure that the chosen strategies are used as intended).
- Firms use the industrial organization model (the I/O model) to examine their **external environment** in order to identify opportunities and threats in that environment. Firms use the resource-based view of the firm model (the RBV model) to analyze their **internal environment** in order to identify their resources and competitive advantages. A firm must use both models to have all of the knowledge needed to select strategies that will enable it to achieve its vision.
- **Stakeholders** are individuals and groups who have an interest in how the firm performs and who can influence the firm's actions. Firms and their stakeholders are dependent on each other. Firms must operate in ways that satisfy the needs of each stakeholder (such as shareholders, customers, suppliers, and employees). Firms failing to do this lose a stakeholder's support. Owners, external stakeholders, and internal stakeholders are the three primary stakeholder groups with which firms are involved. But stakeholders need firms as well. Consider, for example, that owners want to invest in profitable firms, employees want to work for acceptable wages, and customers want to buy products that create value for them.
- **Strategic leaders** practice strategic leadership. When doing this, strategic leaders make certain that their firm is effectively using the strategic

management process. Increasingly, effective strategic management results when many people are involved with the strategic management process and when strategic leaders demand that everyone in the firm act responsibly and ethically in all that they do.

Key Terms

capabilities 7
competitive advantage 8
core competencies 8
distinctive competencies 8
external environment 7
internal environment 7

mission 7
opportunities 11
organizational culture 18
resources 7
stakeholders 16
strategic leaders 18

strategic management 7
strategy 7
strategy implementation 10
strengths 7
threats 11
vision 7

Discussion Questions

1. What is strategic management? Describe strategic management's importance to today's organizations.
2. What is the industrial organization (I/O) model? Why do firms use it to analyze their external environment?
3. What is the resource-based view of the firm model? Why do firms use this model to examine their internal environment?

4. Who are stakeholders? Why are stakeholders important to firms? What does it mean to say that the firm has relationships with its stakeholders?
5. What is the nature of the strategic leader's work?

Endnotes

1. J. Freed, 2004, Marketing to "Jill," "Ray" and "Barry," *Richmond Times-Dispatch*, May 23: D1, D2.
2. G. Edmondson & A. Bonnet, 2004, Toyota's new traction in Europe, *Business Week*, June 7, 64.
3. M. Byler & R. W. Coff, 2003, Dynamic capabilities, social capital and rent appropriation: Ties that split ties, *Strategic Management Journal*, 24: 677–686.
4. H. Mintzberg, 1990, The manager's job—folklore and fact: Retrospective commentary, *Harvard Business on Leadership*, Boston: Harvard Business School Press, 29–32.
5. M. E. Porter, 1996, What is strategy? *Harvard Business Review*, 74(6): 61–78.
6. P. Loftus, 2004, Aqua America CEO sees flood of water co. consolidation. *Wall Street Journal Online*, http://www.wsj.com, June 8.
7. 2004, Pets—PetMed Express Inc., *Fidelity Investments*, http://www.fidelity.com, June 9.
8. A. Kandybin & M. Kihn, 2004, Raising your return on innovation investment, *Strategy & Business Online*, http://www.strategyandbusiness.com, May 10.
9. J. Kerstetter, 2004, A long climb to Salesforce.com, *Business Week Online*, http://www.businessweek.com, May 12.

10. D. Oestricher, 2004, Netflix won't match Blockbuster's price cut, CEO says, *Wall Street Journal Online*, http://www.wsj.com, December 22.
11. A. Borrus, L. Woellert, & Nanette Byrnes, 2004, Pensions on a precipice, *Business Week*, September 6: 52.
12. E. T. Penrose, 1959, *The Theory of the Growth of the Firm*, New York: Wiley.
13. C. Matlack, R. Tiplady, D. Brady, R. Berner, & H. Tashiro, 2004, The Vuitton machine, *Business Week*, March 22: 98–102.
14. Ibid., 99.
15. S. L. Hart & S. Sharma, 2004, Engaging fringe stakeholders for competitive imagination, *Academy of Management Executive*, 18(1): 7–18.
16. M. Beer & R. A. Eisenstat, 2004, How to have an honest conversation about your business strategy, *Harvard Business Review*, 82(2): 82–89.
17. A. J. Hillman & G. D. Keim, 2001, Shareholder value, stakeholder management, and social issues: What's the bottom line? *Strategic Management Journal*, 22: 125–139.
18. R. E. Freeman, A. C. Wicks, & B. Parmar, 2004, Stakeholder Theory and "The Corporate Objective Revisited,"

Organization Science, 15: 364–370; R. E. Freeman & J. S. Harrison, 2001, A stakeholder approach to strategic management, in M. A. Hitt, R. E. Freeman, & J. S. Harrison (eds.), *Handbook of Strategic Management,* Oxford, U.K.: Blackwell, 564–582.

19. P. F. Drucker, 2004, What makes an effective executive, *Harvard Business Review,* 82(6): 58–63.

20. P. Burrows, 2004, Rock on, iPod, *Business Week,* June 7, 130–131.

21. R. E. Kaplan & R. B. Kaiser, 2003, Developing versatile leadership, *MIT Sloan Management Review,* 44(4): 19–26.

22. D. G. Sirmon, M. A. Hitt, & R. D. Ireland, 2005, Managing resources in dynamic environments to create value: Looking inside the black box, *Academy of Management Review,* in press.

23. S. J. Shin & J. Zhou, 2003, Transformational leadership, conservation, and creativity: Evidence from Korea, *Academy of Management Journal,* 46: 703–714.

24. 2004, About 3M, 3M Home Page, http://www.3m.com, June 11.

25. R. Myers, 2004, The human capital vision, *NYSE Magazine,* January/February, 18–22.

26. C. L. Pearce, 2004, The future of leadership: Combining vertical and shared leadership to transform knowledge work, *Academy of Management Executive,* 18(1): 47–57.

27. H. M. Guttman & R. S. Hawkes, 2004, New rules for strategic management, *Journal of Business Strategy,* 25(1): 34–38.

28. E. Aronson, 2001, Integrating leadership styles and ethical perspectives, *Canadian Journal of Administrative Sciences,* 18: 244–256.

29. J. S. Harrison, 2004, Ethics in entrepreneurship, in M. A. Hitt & R. D. Ireland (eds.), *Entrepreneurship Encyclopedia,* Oxford, U.K.: Blackwell, 122–125.

30. J. S. Harrison & C. H. St. John, 2002, *Foundations in Strategic Management* (2nd ed.), Cincinnati, Ohio: South-Western College Publishing.

31. M. A. Hitt, R. D. Ireland, & G. W. Rowe, 2005, Strategic leadership: Strategy, resources, ethics and succession, in J. Doh & S. Stumpf (eds.), *Handbook on Responsible Leadership and Governance in Global Business,* New York: Edward Elgar Publishers.

32. S. Worden, 2003, The role of religious and nationalist ethics in strategic leadership: The case of J. N. Tata, *Journal of Business Ethics,* 47: 147–164.

Your Career

This first chapter introduces you to strategic management. We hope this introduction encourages you to carefully study the book's remaining chapters as a means of learning more about strategic management.

The strategic management process described in this chapter should be used by organizations of all types—large and small, whether producing goods or providing services; new ventures as well as established, ongoing corporations; and public-sector agencies in addition to for-profit organizations. You can also use the essence of strategic management to guide your career. Remember that we defined strategic management as the ongoing process companies use to form a vision, analyze their external and internal environments, and select one or more strategies to implement to create value for customers and other stakeholders, especially shareholders.

Just as companies require a vision, so do we to both launch and sustain our careers. What is your vision? What shape do you want your career to take and what do you want to achieve in the next few years as well as over the course of your career? What are your goals as you begin or continue with your career? To answer these questions, you can analyze the external environment to recognize different opportunities you may want to pursue. In addition, you can assess your strengths to select opportunities for which you are most qualified. This activity is similar to what firms do to analyze their internal environment. After you know what you want to achieve, given the opportunities and your strengths, you can choose the paths (or strategies) to follow. Of course, making these decisions and taking the actions flowing from them allows you to satisfy those with whom you have relationships (your stakeholders) in addition to satisfying yourself. Family members, mentors and friends, the firm for which you work, and society in general are examples of stakeholders you may wish to satisfy through your career-related decisions and actions.

The possibility of using the strategic management process to help develop your career may seem a bit overwhelming. After all, you have read only the first chapter of this text. For now, just give some preliminary thought to how strategic management could influence your career. We'll return to this topic and issues related to it in the "Your Career" segments in the book's remaining chapters.

Strategic management is the study of how business leaders take their organizations to new heights. A key player in this process is the chief executive officer (CEO). Chapter 1 provides the foundation for the strategic analysis the CEO must perform. With that in mind, the first tool in the strategy toolbox is the "CEO Strategy Checklist" for successfully completing this significant responsibility.

The CEO Strategy Checklist

1. Have I, along with the rest of the top managers in my company, established a clear vision for our firm? Yes/No

2. Do my employees understand the vision and use it to guide their day-to-day decision making? Yes/No

3. Have I adequately considered the dominant external forces beyond my company and industry that may affect our progress toward our vision? Yes/No

4. Have I adequately considered our internal strengths and weaknesses, honestly, to determine whether we are capable of achieving our vision? Yes/No

5. Do we have a clear strategic plan related to improving our resources and capabilities to take the company to the next level? Yes/No

6. Are the incentive programs in our company aligned with our strategic vision? Yes/No

7. Do I involve my entire organization in the strategy formulation process by means of formal and informal channels? Yes/No

8. Have we considered all of our stakeholder perspectives (shareholders, customers, suppliers, and employees) in setting our strategy? Yes/No

9. Does our organization have a clear ethical lens that permeates throughout all employee activities? Yes/No

10. Do I spend the majority of my time considering true strategic management issues rather than urgent but less important daily operational issues? Yes/No

✳ BIZ FLIX — *U-571:* SETTING STRATEGY

Watch the scene from *U-571*. It shows several aspects of strategic management and strategic planning described earlier in this chapter.

This action-packed World War II thriller shows a U.S. submarine crew's efforts to retrieve an Enigma encryption device from a disabled German submarine. After the crew gets the device, a German vessel torpedoes and sinks their submarine. The survivors must now use the disabled German submarine to escape from the enemy with their prize. The film's almost nonstop action and extraordinary special effects look and sound best with a home theater system.

The scene comes from the "160 meters" segment toward the film's end. Lt. Andrew Tyler (Matthew McConaughey) is now the submarine's commander following the drowning death of Lt. Commander Mike Dahlgren (Bill Paxton), the original commander. Lt. Tyler says, "Chief." Chief Petty Officer (CPO) Henry Klough (Harvey Keitel) approaches the map table. The film continues to its dramatic end with the execution of the strategy Tyler described.

What to Watch for and Ask Yourself

1. Does Lt. Tyler analyze the submarine's external environment?
2. What is Lt. Tyler's assessment of the submarine's resources and competitive advantage?
3. Does Lt. Tyler consider threats and opportunities in forming his strategic plan?

Mini-Case

Telkom SA Ltd.: Socially Responsible, Growing, and Profitable

With roots deeply embedded in South Africa, Telkom SA Ltd. (TKG) has an interesting history. According to company documents, the firm has "evolved from state control to public ownership, from monopoly outlook to competitive mindset, from providing plain old telephone services to delivering integrated communications solutions." TKG is now Africa's leading communications company. The firm's 225 global corporate customers, 550,000 smaller business and government accounts, and more than 2.6 million residential customers indicate the breadth and depth of its subscriber base.

How did this happen? What caused a state-controlled firm to morph into a globally competitive technology company? What factors or conditions have significantly influenced the firm's evolution and continuing growth?

The origins of TKG's current success can be traced to the 1998 hiring of Sizwe Nxasana as the firm's CEO, an individual with impressive credentials. Using his training, Nxasana became one of only a few (perhaps no more than ten) black chartered accountants in apartheid South

Africa. Later, he launched his own venture, which was the first black accounting firm in what today is known as the Nkonki Sizwe Ntsaluba province of South Africa. Wanting to make a significant contribution to his nation and its people, Nxasana immediately accepted the opportunity to be TKG's CEO when the position was offered to him.

Working with employees, government officials, suppliers, customers, and others, Nxasana is committed to creating a common vision of TKG as a world-class company. He also has changed the firm's management structure. In 1994, not a single woman or black person held a managerial position in TKG. Currently, 15 of the firm's top 18 executives are black and 4 are female. In total, black employees now comprise 35 percent and women comprise 18 percent of the management structure. This increased diversity legitimizes TKG as a South African company and generates high levels of commitment among the firm's employees. A high commitment level makes it more feasible to successfully implement a firm's strategy. Nxasana also has guided TKG through an initial public offering (IPO) of stock. TKG is now listed on both the JSE Securities Exchange in Johannesburg and on the New York Stock Exchange; the IPO is part of a broader government strategy to "achieve black economic empowerment and bring in foreign investment" to TKG. Because employees are now shareholders, the company officials believe the IPO has created an organizational culture of shared ownership.

Nxasana is a strong proponent of effective corporate governance and of business ethics. He expects to be held accountable for his performance by an independent board of directors and demands that employees act with integrity in everything they do. Believing in the value of open dialogue, Nxasana communicates regularly with employees to help them learn how to think like owners.

TKG sees general society as one of its important stakeholders: "As a responsible corporate citizen, Telkom complies with all legal, commercial and governance requirements, but for us, model corporate citizenship goes beyond compliance. It's a question of trust and accountability, of creating a company culture in which every person does what is right because it is right, and of contributing to South Africa's long-term economic development." Flowing from this commitment are decisions to establish the Telkom Foundation as the firm's social investment unit and the Safety, Health and Environmental Management (SHE) program. SHE studies occupational job-related risks and environmental effects of the firm's operations, trying to reduce the seriousness and frequency of both.

As TKG's CEO, Nxasana has also made difficult, yet important decisions in his efforts to be a successful strategic leader. Product lines and some staff positions have been eliminated. Employees have been asked to learn new skills so TKG can increase the technological sophistication of its products, especially its new offerings. These actions have been taken to improve TKG's operating efficiencies and reduce its capital expenditures.

SOURCES: M. Bidoli, 2004, Making the right call, *NYSE Magazine*, January/February: 28–32; 2004, Telkom SA Ltd. Home Page, http://www.telkom.co.za.

Questions

1. Use the materials in this chapter to describe Sizwe Nxasana's actions as a strategic leader. Would you want to work for Nxasana? Why or why not?
2. Under Nxasana's leadership, TKG seems to be committed to serving its stakeholders. Using materials in the Mini-Case as well as additional secondary materials found through an Internet search, can you determine what stakeholder groups TKG is serving? How well do you believe each of the stakeholders' interests are being served?
3. Using the information in the Mini-Case as well as other materials you may find, use the I/O (external analysis) and RBV (internal analysis) models to examine this firm. On the basis of your brief analysis, what conditions do you believe are the most important for Nxasana and TKG to carefully study while using the firm's strategy?

EXPERIENTIAL EXERCISES

EXERCISE ONE: THE CULTURE, VISION, AND STRATEGY LINKAGE

Vision and mission statements of firms need to be aligned with organizational culture. Together they give employees direction in any situation by providing them with values and purpose that set key priorities and orient action.

In Small Groups

In a small group, determine what your group thinks is the culture for each of the following companies. Then link that culture to your view of the firm's vision or mission, as you understand it. How does your concept of the firm's culture and vision fit with what you understand about its strategy, which is the basis for its success?

Whole Class

Groups should then compare their answers to the question that was answered in small groups. The purpose of this activity is to highlight differences as well as similarities in the small groups' answers. Finally, go to each firm's Web site and find its mission or vision statement. How well does the statement align with the culture and strategy you identified?

- Target
- Mary Kay Cosmetics
- UPS
- Starbucks

EXERCISE TWO: GATHERING ORGANIZATION-SPECIFIC INFORMATION

As an informed member of the business community, you will often need to gather information about specific organizations from a variety of sources. Your professor may assign an organization to you for research purposes. Using your research skills, find, print out, and read at least three popular business press articles (*Fortune, Business Week, Forbes, Wall Street Journal,* etc.) published in the last year focusing on your assigned organization. Discuss in class the various sources of information, their reputation for quality, their relevance to business research, and so on.

Leading Strategically

*Reading and studying
this chapter should
enable you to:*

*Knowledge Objectives

1_
Define and explain
strategic leadership.

2_
Explain how vision
and mission create
value.

3_
Define the meaning
of a top manage-
ment team and the
value of having a
heterogeneous top
management team.

4_
Explain the impor-
tance of managerial
succession.

5_
Define human capital
and social capital and
describe their value to
the firm.

6_
Describe an entrepre-
neurial culture and its
contribution to a firm.

7_
Explain the impor-
tance of managerial
integrity and ethical
behavior.

8_
Discuss why firms
should have a control
system that balances
the use of strategic
controls and financial
controls.

Focusing on Strategy

Evolution and Revolution in Strategic Leadership

"Humility, service and lifting the human spirit work as well in the board-room as they do in the classroom." (Ed Breen, CEO of Tyco)

Dell Inc. is known as one of the world's best-managed technology companies. Yet its CEO and founder, Michael Dell, recently decided to give up the CEO position and serve only as chairman of his company. Dell's then chief operating officer (COO), Kevin Rollins, was elevated to the CEO position. So while the leadership team was evolving, the primary leadership of Dell and Rollins remained intact. Why are they regarded as an excellent leadership team? There are several reasons. In 2001, for example, Dell and Rollins surveyed employees shortly after the firm's first large layoff. The survey showed that employees were unhappy and distrustful of Michael Dell and Kevin Rollins. Dell and Rollins took actions to turn the employees' attitudes around. Based on the survey's results, Dell met with his top 20 managers and presented a self-critique; he vowed to develop a stronger relationship with his management team, despite his shyness. He taped that session and showed it to every manager in the firm. Rollins placed a Curious George doll on his desk to remind him to obtain ideas from his management team before making important decisions.

Tyco has been one of the worst-managed firms in the United States. Former CEO Dennis Kozlowski made hundreds of acquisitions, building up huge debts and poorly managing the companies acquired. His successor, Ed Breen, is trying to create a revolutionary change in the company. Breen's leadership style is almost the opposite of Kozlowski's extravagant approach.

Breen stated in a recent talk at his alma mater that business leaders should display humility and provide service to the community. The quote from Breen at the beginning of this "Focusing on Strategy" illustrates his philosophy. Breen's comment suggests that strategic leaders should try to build the human spirit in the workforce and in society. He is applying these values in his attempt to reform Tyco after it was left in disarray by its former leadership team. His efforts appear to be working; Tyco announced that in the first quarter of 2004 it earned more than seven times the profit of the same quarter a year earlier.

Jack Stahl at Revlon and Daniel Carp at Kodak are trying to do the same as Breen. They are new CEOs and have to install almost revolutionary changes to ensure the survival of their firms. Both have to find a way to increase market share and return their firms to profitability to build market value for shareholders. Stahl has to develop a way to pay down a mountain of debt, and Carp must make his firm more innovative. Kodak is faced with significant changes as it moves from a chemical base to a digital base for its imaging products. Both new CEOs have only a little time to accomplish their revolutionary turnarounds, as their shareholders are becoming anxious for positive results.

Lastly, Cisco was once a Wall Street darling with a very high market value. Then the Internet boom busted and Cisco's fortunes tumbled. For a while its CEO, John Chambers, continued with the same practices, but he abruptly stopped when he realized that the markets were not going to return to the heady days of the 1990s. He analyzed the company and rebuilt its foundation. He began making fewer and more carefully planned acquisitions. Now, instead of having substantial individual autonomy, Cisco's managers work as a team to decide what markets to enter and how to enter them. Cisco also has become more efficient in its operations and more productive as well.

So continuing leaders (Dell, Chambers, and Rollins) have tried to create evolutionary changes, and new leaders (Breen, Stahl, and Carp) are working to implement revolutionary changes. Strategic leaders creating revolutionary change are likely to enjoy varying degrees of success because of the significant challenges involved in implementing such change. However, dealing with major strategic challenges underscores the importance of strategic leadership to a firm's success.

SOURCES: J. Thottam, 2004, Can this man save Tyco? *Time,* February 9: 48–50; Tyco basks in burst of profit, 2004, *Houston Chronicle,* May 5: B3; D. Brady, J. Carey, & A. Tsao, 2003, Putting a pretty face on Revlon, *Business Week,* November 3: 92–95; P. Burrows, 2003, Cisco's comeback, *Business Week,* November 24: 116–124; A. Park & P. Burrows, 2003, What you don't know about Dell, *Business Week,* November 3: 74–84; W. Symonds, 2003, The Kodak revolt is short-sighted, *Business Week,* November 3: 38.

*
strategic
leadership

developing a vision for the firm, designing strategic actions to achieve this vision, and empowering others to carry out those strategic actions

Strategic leadership involves developing a vision for the firm, designing strategic actions to achieve this vision, and empowering others to carry out those strategic actions. As defined in Chapter 1, *strategic leaders* are the individuals practicing strategic leadership. Strategic leaders hold upper-level organizational positions. Remember from your reading of Chapter 1 that today's strategic leaders are involving people throughout the firm in strategic management. Thus, any person in the firm responsible for designing strategic actions and ensuring that they are carried out in ways that move the firm toward achievement of the vision is essentially playing the role of a strategic leader.

Is strategic leadership important? You bet it is![1] "Focusing on Strategy" shows major differences in the performance of companies due largely to the leaders. Michael Dell and Kevin Rollins have provided the leadership needed to build Dell into a major technology corporation. However, Tyco is suffering because of Dennis Kozlowski's prior leadership. Ed Breen is trying to build new values and return Tyco to profitability.

In this chapter, we examine important strategic leadership actions: establishing the firm's vision and mission, developing a management team and planning for succession, managing the resource portfolio, building and supporting an entrepreneurial culture, promoting integrity and ethical behavior, and using effective organizational controls. These strategic leadership actions are displayed in Figure 2.1. We begin with a discussion of how vision and mission are used to direct the firm's future.

FIGURE 2.1 Strategic Leadership Actions

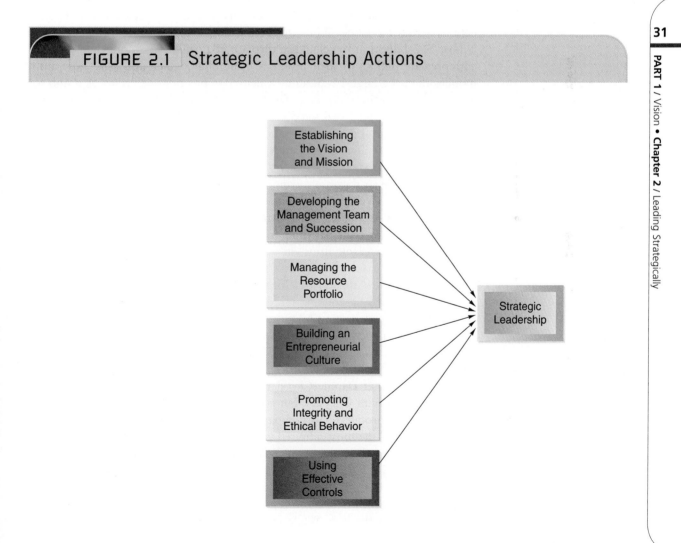

Establishing the Vision and Mission

While most strategic plans are designed for a 3-to-5-year time period, a vision is usually targeted for a longer time, say 10 to 20 years. As explained in Chapter 1, the *vision* contains at least two components—a statement describing the firm's DNA and the "picture" of the firm as it is hoped to exist in a future time period. The second part of the vision is *mission,* which defines the firm's core intent and the business or businesses in which it intends to operate. The mission flows from the vision and, compared to the vision, is more concrete in nature.

Visions can differ greatly across firms depending on the strategic leaders' intentions. For example, Steven Jobs, CEO of Apple, develops visions of new products and markets. He developed not only Apple but also Pixar, a hugely successful animation company that teamed with Disney to make *Finding Nemo.* He created the Mac revolution with the Apple Macintosh computer and more recently reshaped the music industry with Apple's iPod, which can store as many as 10,000 songs. Complementary to the iPod is Apple's iTunes online music venture, also a part of Jobs's vision to dramatically change this industry.[2]

In contrast, Meg Whitman, CEO of eBay, envisions her firm as a "dynamic self-regulating economy" using the eBay network to conduct all forms of transactions across the globe. While this seems almost crazy, 30 million people sold almost $22 billion in merchandise through eBay in 2003. More than 150,000 entrepreneurs sell all of their products using eBay, which also sells more automobiles than the largest U.S. auto dealer. eBay has been described as a hub for global commerce in a *Business Week* article.[3] Indeed, the fact that eBay had 125 million confirmed registered users as of September 2004 reflects the firm's standing as a central point in global commerce. Whitman's vision entails replacing the current retail stores. Can you imagine this happening over the next 10–20 years or do you think this vision is impossible to achieve because people want to touch what they are buying?

Other firms have simpler visions even though they still may be very difficult to achieve. For example, some firms may envision being among the most respected firms for their performance and effective management. A number of organizations now rank firms on a regular basis. For example, the *Financial Times* publishes a list of the world's most respected companies based on the *Times*/PWC survey; the top ten firms in 2003 are shown in Table 2.1. The rankings are based on creating the most shareholder value, but also exhibiting the strongest social responsibility and integrity and having the most effective corporate governance (such as the board of directors and executive compensation). The presence of some firms on the list is surprising. However, while Wal-Mart does not fare as well on social responsibility, it has strong financial performance. Likewise, DaimlerChrysler has had many publicized problems in the Daimler merger with Chrysler, but seems to rank highly because of the quality of many of its products. To compare, the top ten companies from *Fortune*'s annual survey of the most-admired companies for 2003 are also listed in Table 2.1. As you'll see, there is some overlap but the rankings differ and some firms appear on one list, but not the other. For example, Wal-Mart is ranked first on *Fortune*'s list but is fifth on the *Financial Times* list. *Financial Times* and *Fortune* use some different criteria for ranking the firms, thereby leading to the variance between the lists. While most of the firms on the *Financial Times* list

TABLE 2.1

Rankings of the Most Respected and Admired Firms

Financial Times Rankings	*Fortune* Rankings
1. General Electric	1. Wal-Mart
2. Microsoft	2. Berkshire Hathaway
3. Toyota	3. Southwest Airlines
4. IBM	4. General Electric
5. Wal-Mart	5. Dell
6. Coca-Cola	6. Microsoft
7. Dell	7. Johnson & Johnson
8. Berkshire Hathaway	8. Starbucks
9. DaimlerChrysler	9. Federal Express
10. Sony	10. IBM

Sources: M. Skapinker, 2004, Brand strength proves its worth, *Financial Times*, http://www.ft.com, January 19; A. Harrington, 2004, America's most admired companies, *Fortune*, March 8: 80–82.

are based in the United States, it is a world ranking, whereas *Fortune*'s ranking includes only U.S. firms.

An effective strategic leader not only can develop a vision of the future but also can inspire stakeholders' to commit to achieving it. It is especially important for the leader to gain the support of the company's shareholders and employees. If the shareholders do not support the vision, they may pressure the board of directors to change it or to find new strategic leaders. Similarly, employee commitment to the vision is needed because they must help implement the strategy designed to achieve the vision. Consider the case of Porsche. Company officials believe that they have a clear strategy in place to develop a group of new models through 2012. The firm's vision entails growth and maintaining its strong brand image by introducing these new products. One of the new models Porsche launched recently is a new, sporty SUV. In 2003, versions of this product were priced between $56,000 and $110,000. It is interesting to note that in 2004, Porsche was the most profitable automaker in the world; its shareholders probably support the firm's vision, while employees seem to be committed to helping achieve that vision through their work.[4]

As we mentioned earlier, strategic leaders often use their team of managers as well as others in the firm to help make major decisions, especially to define a vision for the firm. This team also helps formulate the firm's strategy. Next, we examine the teams of managers that strategic leaders use.

Porsche's shareholders and employees seem committed to the firm's vision of launching new models, such as this Cayenne Turbo model in Germany.

© Wolfgang von Brauchitsch/
Bloomberg News/Landov

Developing the Top Management Team and Succession

top management team

the group of managers charged with the responsibility to develop and implement the firm's strategies

Top Management Team

Because of the complexity of their roles, most strategic leaders form teams to help them complete their work. A **top management team** is the group of managers charged with the responsibility to develop and implement the firm's strategies. Generally, the top management team is composed of officers of the company with the title of vice president and higher.[5]

Typically, when people select individuals for a team to work with them, they prefer to choose people who think like them and are more likely to agree with them. While such a team can facilitate making fast decisions (because members of the team more easily agree), these teams are more prone to making mistakes. A team of people with similar backgrounds (a *homogeneous team*) may achieve a quick consensus about issues, but may lack all of the knowledge and information needed to make an effective decision. Additionally, because they "think alike," they may overlook important issues and make errors in judgment. Therefore, to be most effective, strategic leaders need a management team composed of members who see and think differently. This may mean that they have different types of education (such as engineering versus business) or varying amounts and types of experience (working in different functional areas, companies, or industries). We refer to this as a *heterogeneous team*. A heterogeneous team is likely to take more time to make decisions but also likely to make better decisions.[6]

Historically, Toyota included only Japanese employees in its management teams. However, as Toyota has begun to compete in more international markets, its managers have discovered the value of including other people in management teams to bring new perspectives to strategic management decisions. For example, Toyota's operations in the United States have many Americans on management teams. In fact, one author in *Fortune* described Toyota as "becoming more American." The CEO, Fujio Cho, has been making major changes in management teams to improve the design of Toyota vehicles as a complement to the firm's highly efficient manufacturing skills.[7] Someday, these changes may lead to succession of an American or a person from a country other than Japan to be Toyota's CEO, similar to the appointment of Sir Howard Stringer as CEO of Sony in 2005.

Management Succession

In addition to forming the management team, strategic leaders must develop people who can succeed them. In fact, having people with skills to take over a job when needed is very important to a firm's success. Some companies use sophisticated leadership screening systems to select people with the skills needed to perform well as a strategic leader.[8] The people selected then normally participate in an intensive management development program to further hone their leadership skills. The "ten-step talent" management development program at General Electric (GE) is considered one of the most effective programs for developing strategic leaders.[9]

Obviously, a change in CEO is a critical succession event in firms. The effects of CEO succession can be different based on whether the new CEO is from inside or outside the firm. The majority of CEO successions are from the inside, with a person groomed for the position by the former CEO or the board of directors. "Hiring from the inside" motivates employees because they believe that they have opportunities to receive promotions and better jobs if they perform well. Recent inside CEO successions were announced at Dell and Continental Airlines. In both cases, the COO was chosen to become the new CEO. As noted in "Focusing on Strategy," Kevin Rollins, COO of Dell, was selected to succeed Michael Dell as CEO. Likewise, the COO of Continental Airlines, Larry Kellner, was selected to succeed Gordon Bethune as CEO.[10] Both Michael Dell and Gordon Bethune had done a good job and the boards of the companies wanted to continue with the strategies they had put into place at each firm. Most new CEOs selected for the job in an inside succession are unlikely to change in any drastic way the strategies designed under the leadership of the former CEO.[11] However, when the firm is performing poorly, it is more common to select an outside successor.

When new CEOs are chosen from outside the organization, the board often does so with the desire to change the firm's strategies. A change in strategies may be desired because the firm is performing poorly or because opportunities and threats in the competitive landscape require adjustments to avoid performing poorly in the future.[12] For example, Motorola's board of directors chose Ed Zander as its new CEO in order to change the firm's strategy and turn around Motorola's poor performance in recent years. Zander was formerly president of Sun Microsystems, where he was highly regarded for his strategic leadership. Zander stated that he hoped to provide the value for Motorola that Lou Gerstner had for IBM when Gerstner was chosen to move from a consumer goods firm to become CEO of IBM. Gerstner transformed IBM into a successful performer again with a major change in its strategy.[13] Under Gerstner, IBM moved from a strategy based on selling separate pieces of hardware to a strategy calling for the firm to emphasize its service solutions and consulting services.

At times, it is more difficult to determine whether a succession is from the inside or outside. For example, in the 2004 CEO succession at Coca-Cola, the two major candidates were Steven Heyer, Coca-Cola's president and COO, and Neville Isdell, a former executive retired from Coca-Cola. Heyer was recruited to Coca-Cola in 2001 and many people felt he was the likely successor to Douglas Daft, the CEO at the time. However, Coca-Cola was not performing to the level desired by the board and they selected Isdell, who had the deep knowledge of the business and industry that was necessary to improve the firm's performance.[14]

Interestingly, industry analysts suggested that J. P. Morgan's acquisition of Bank One may have been partially motivated to find a good successor to William Harrison, CEO of J. P. Morgan. Harrison was scheduled to retire approximately two years after the merger was completed. Jamie Dimon, CEO of Bank One, is considered an excellent candidate to succeed Harrison. We can label this as an inside/outside succession.[15]

As discussed next, managing the firm's resource portfolio is another critical component of strategic leadership.

Managing the Resource Portfolio

Resources are the basis for a firm's competitive advantages and strategies (see Chapter 4). While we often think of physical resources such as buildings, manufacturing plants, offices, machinery, and computers as being important, intangible resources may be more important. Indeed, recent estimates suggest that as much as 75 percent of a firm's value may be contained in its intangible resources.[16] Intangible resources include human capital, social capital, and organizational capital (such as the organizational culture). Additionally, financial capital is a critically important resource.

Intellectual property can be an especially valuable intangible resource in high-technology companies. For example, Daniel Carp, Kodak's new CEO, discovered that the firm owned almost 600 patents on ink-jet technologies. However, for these patents to be of value, the technology had to be developed and introduced to the marketplace in the form of a product. As such, Kodak's patents (intellectual property) had not been properly managed. As an effective strategic leader, Carp set out to resolve this problem by commercializing the valuable technologies on which Kodak owned patents.[17]

A firm's intellectual property is developed by its human capital. **Human capital** includes the knowledge and skills of those working for the firm. Employees' knowledge and skills are critical for all organizations. According to Ed Breen, "Companies compete with their brains as well as their brawn. Organizations today must not only outgun and outhustle competitors, they must also outthink them. Companies win with ideas."[18] To outthink competitors, a firm must depend on the knowledge of its workforce (managers and nonmanagerial employees) and continuously invest in developing their knowledge and skills. Such organizations are focused on learning. Knowledge can be acquired in training programs or through experience on the job. Most experience is positive, but learning also usually occurs with failure. Unfortunately, learning through failure is difficult and can be costly. For example, Mark Mitchell, CEO of Mitchell & Company, an advertising agency, learned a valuable lesson. The company had 42 employees and approximately $4.5 million in annual revenue. But the revenue was highly dependent on one major customer, Owens Corning. Owens Corning had asbestos liability problems and filed for bankruptcy. To reduce its costs, Owens Corning decided to consolidate all of its advertising business with one agency and stopped doing business with Mitchell's firm. While Mitchell obtained some new business, it was not enough to pay his debts; he had to file for bankruptcy and close the firm. He said that he had been naïve to assume that his company was invaluable to Owens Corning. Mitchell is now the CEO of another advertising firm in Toledo, Ohio, and claims that he won't allow his new firm to become overly dependent on one customer again.[19] Not only must the CEO learn, however. It is the strategic leader's responsibility to help her firm learn faster than others. For example, if Mitchell & Company had been in a learning mode, it might have learned faster and spread its risk by obtaining more customers.

Effective strategic leaders base their strategies on the organization's human capital.[20] They do this because the human capital in the organization must have the skills and motivation needed to implement chosen strategies. As such, leaders must help develop skills throughout the firm's workforce, motivate employees to use their skills when working to implement strategies, and reward them for doing so.[21] Anne Mulcahy, the CEO who saved Xerox, credits much of her success to a talented and committed workforce. She suggests, "People always are the difference. That is why attracting them, motivating them, keeping them—making Xerox an employer of choice—is critical to our drive back to greatness."[22]

Anne Mulcahy, CEO of Xerox, believes human capital is the key to the success of an organization.

---

*

social capital

includes all internal and external relationships that help the firm provide value to customers and ultimately to its other stakeholders

Another important resource is social capital. **Social capital** includes all internal and external relationships that help the firm provide value to customers and ultimately to its other stakeholders. *Internal social capital* refers to the relationships among people working inside the firm. These relationships help each organizational unit effectively complete its work while contributing to the overall value of the firm's human capital.

External social capital refers to relationships between those working within a firm and others (individuals and organizations) outside the firm. Such relationships are essential because they provide access to needed resources. Few firms have all of the resources they need. Furthermore, most firms cannot do everything well. It may be better to outsource some activities to partner companies who can perform those activities exceptionally well, thereby increasing the quality of the focal firm's ability to produce products. External social capital can also help firms enter new markets. New companies may seek the financial support and expertise of venture capitalists, whereas more established companies often develop alliances with reliable suppliers or joint ventures with highly competent partners. In a sense, strategic leaders serve as key points of effective linkages for their firm in a network of relationships with other organizations. Some relationships involve strong ties, where trust exists between the parties and reciprocity is expected, whereas other relationships represent weaker ties that serve more informational roles and allow strategic leaders to stay on top of the latest developments—even outside their industry—that may affect their firm (such as technology developments). So both strong and weak ties are important in strategic leaders' networks.[23]

The most effective social capital occurs when partners trust each other (strong ties). Effective strategic leaders have well-developed relational skills that help them establish trusting relationships with others inside and outside the organization. Andrea Jung, CEO of Avon Products, suggests that compassion is one of the key characteristics of effective leaders. As such, she believes that leaders should treat people fairly, with dignity and respect. In so doing, leaders are leading with their heart as well as their head.[24]

Other resources such as financial capital are also important. In fact, firms with strong human capital and social capital will more likely be able to build a good base of financial capital.[25] Some also believe that an organization's culture can be a valuable resource. We discuss this topic next.

Building an Entrepreneurial Culture

*

entrepreneurial culture

encourages employees to identify and exploit new opportunities

Strategic leaders are concerned about the organization's culture because it can have major effects on employees' actions. An organizational culture is based on the core values of an organization, largely espoused by its leaders. When these values support opportunities to innovate, an entrepreneurial culture may develop. An **entrepreneurial culture** encourages employees to identify and exploit new opportunities. It encourages creativity and risk taking but also tolerates failures.

Championing innovation is rewarded in this type of culture.[26] Building an entrepreneurial culture is of particular importance to strategic leaders, as explained in "Understanding Strategy."

Innovation is important in high-technology industries such as computers and in creative industries such as music and film animation, as shown in "Understanding Strategy." Thus, Steve Jobs is an appropriate strategic leader for Apple with his emphasis on creativity and innovation. However, 3M operates in several different industries with lower technology, such as adhesives (for example, Scotch tape, traffic signs, and sandpaper). Yet the firm has been a pioneer, being the first to introduce new products in its markets, such as the Post-it note. Therefore, an entrepreneurial culture is important in both firms.

Being innovative in high-technology industries is challenging and the payoff is often low. For example, innovations in the biotechnology industry require an average of 15–18 years to develop and introduce to the market (partly because of the time necessary for testing the product). A gene-therapy vaccine called Vical, for example, has been under development for 16 years with approximately $100 million invested, but the product is not ready for the market. Most venture capitalists are unwilling to wait even ten years to earn a return on their investments, much less 15–18 years. Therefore, some entrepreneurs seek to acquire firms that have products in which the development is 50 percent or more completed.[27]

Because of the pressure to be innovative yet profitable, many leaders try to focus their firm's innovation to increase the chances of success. For example, Scott Cook, founder and CEO of Intuit, tries to focus his firm's innovation activities on the customer. He strongly believes that profitable innovation is based on having an intimate understanding of the customer.[28] Similarly, Jim McNerney at 3M targets innovation by integrating the research scientists with marketing and manufacturing people. As a result, development is targeting new products requested by customers.[29]

The preceding discussions suggest the importance of innovation and strategic leadership. While the type and focus of innovation may vary, it is important in nearly all industries. As a result, building an entrepreneurial culture is a vital task for strategic leaders. Strategic leaders also must demonstrate ethical behavior. Next, we discuss the importance of integrity and ethical behavior for strategic leaders.

Promoting Integrity and Ethical Behavior

Strategic leaders not only develop standards for behavior among employees, but also serve as role models in meeting and exceeding those standards. While quality of performance is an important criterion, showing integrity and behaving ethically are also essential. So strategic leaders should determine the boundaries of acceptable behavior, establish the tone for organizational actions, and ensure that ethical behaviors are expected, praised, and rewarded. Lack of integrity and unethical behavior can be serious and highly costly for a firm and for the person lacking integrity and behaving unethically. In fact, extraordinary unethical behavior can even lead to a firm's demise; Enron is a well-known example.

Recently, cases in which strategic leaders acted opportunistically in managing their firms have been a major concern. Acting opportunistically means that managers are making decisions that are in their own best interests rather than

understanding strategy:

RESTORING INNOVATION THROUGH LEADERSHIP

Jim McNerney became 3M's CEO in 2001, the first CEO selected from outside the firm. The reason for selecting an outsider as CEO was the perceived need by 3M's board to restore the firm's orientation to innovation. At one time, 3M was considered one of the most entrepreneurial firms in the United States. However, its innovative capability and innovations have decreased over time. 3M devotes considerable resources to produce innovation. The company invests $1.1 billion annually in research and development (R&D) and has almost 1,000 scientists and engineers doing research to develop innovative products.

Rebuilding an entrepreneurial culture has been a challenge for McNerney. First, he acquired some firms with strong R&D operations. He is

also trying to increase innovation by building a culture that expects and rewards entrepreneurial actions. He is investing in 3M's human capital. He also operates as a team leader. He has high expectations of those working with him but also rewards high performance. He emphasizes his people rather than himself, exemplifying a strategic leader who values teamwork.

Similarly, Steve Jobs is credited with restoring the entrepreneurial culture at Apple. He did it largely through leadership and exhibiting creativity himself. There is little doubt that he expects people working for Apple to create innovative products. Apple first restored innovation by developing creative new designs for the PC. However, Jobs has gone beyond computers and has developed new product lines that he sees as the future of Apple. Before returning to Apple, Jobs started Pixar, now the leader in animated films. He is now leading Apple into a new segment in the music industry with iTunes online music access and the iPod, which can store and play a large number of songs.

SOURCES: M. Arndt & J. Brady, 2004, 3M's rising star, *Business Week Online*, http://www.businessweek.com, April 12; R. Grover, 2004, Pixar twists the mouse's tail, *Business Week Online*, http://www.businessweek.com, January 30; C. Hawn, 2004, If he's so smart . . . : Steve Jobs, Apple, and the limits of innovation, *Fast Company*, http://www.fastcompany.com, January; P. T. Larsen, 2004, Pixar head Jobs slams Disney over split, *Financial Times*, http://www.ft.com, February 5.

in the firm's best interests. Enron and Tyco are examples of firms in which opportunistic behavior likely occurred.

Because of opportunistic behavior in a number of companies, significant emphasis has been placed on how firms govern themselves (*corporate governance*). Corporate governance begins with the board of directors, whose members are responsible for overseeing managerial activities and approving (or disapproving) managerial decisions and actions. The outcry from shareholders and the public in general has placed pressure on board members to be more diligent in examining managerial behavior. Legislation (such as the Sarbanes-Oxley Act of 2002) has even been passed in the United States requiring more managerial responsibility for the firm's activities and outcomes. Institutional owners in particular have pressured boards to enact better governance practices. For example, they generally want to have more independent outsiders than inside officers on the board. They believe that independent outside board members will be more objective and are less likely to agree with the CEO if he is taking actions that appear not to be in the firm's best interests. In this way, managers' opportunistic actions can be curtailed.[30]

One form of potential opportunism, **related-party transactions,** involves paying a person who has a relationship with the firm extra money for reasons other than his or her normal activities on the firm's behalf. For example, Apple CEO Steve Jobs was reimbursed $1.2 million for costs he incurred while using his personal jet on company business. Two directors for Ford Motor Company, William Clay Ford and Edsel Ford, receive hundreds of thousands of dollars in consulting fees in addition to their compensation for serving as directors. Many of these transactions are legitimate, but some can be for questionable purposes as well. The Securities and Exchange Commission has begun carefully scrutinizing related-party deals because of the opportunity for unethical behavior. Related-party deals were curtailed in the United States by the Sarbanes-Oxley Act.[31]

As explained in "Understanding Strategy," Michael Eisner was once a highly successful CEO at Disney. However, his strategies in recent years have been ineffective and Disney's performance has suffered. Worse, Eisner seems to have deliberately avoided developing a successor for his job. He appointed a number of friends and associates to Disney's board, which has approved extraordinarily high compensation for Eisner at a time when the company's performance was poor. Thus, Eisner has been criticized for managerial opportunism and ineffective strategic leadership, and, at the same time, the firm has been criticized for weak corporate governance.

Often worse than opportunistic actions by managers are fraudulent and other unlawful activities in which managers and companies' representatives engage. The costs of white-collar fraud are substantial, with estimates as high as $600 billion in losses by U.S. firms annually. White-collar crime is the reason for at least 30 percent of new-venture failures as well.[32] In 2002, the board of Peregrine Systems requested the resignation of the CEO and chief financial officer (CFO) because of an alleged falsification of $100 million in revenues. Eventually, three former Peregrine executives were convicted of criminal fraud. The investigations showed that as much as $500 million was nonexistent, more than half of which was because of fraud. These actions caused the firm to file for Chapter 11 bankruptcy protection. While Peregrine has partially recovered from these terrible actions, it still has significant problems and more work to do before it can achieve a level of stability.[33]

Only leaders who demonstrate integrity and values respected by all constituents of the company will be able to sustain effective outcomes over time. Those who engage in unethical or unlawful activities may go unrecognized or undetected for a time, but eventually they will fail. People working under the leader often demonstrate the same values in their actions that are evident in the leader's behavior. Thus, if the leader engages in unethical activities, the followers are likely to do the same. Therefore, the leader will suffer from the poor performance that results from their own and others' unethical behaviors. However, when the leader displays integrity and strong positive ethical values, the firm's performance will be enhanced over time because the followers will do the same. Opportunism and unethical activities evident in several companies in recent times clearly show the importance of having effective control systems, which are discussed next.

understanding strategy:

BREAKDOWNS IN GOVERNANCE AND MANAGERIAL OPPORTUNISM

Michael Eisner saved the Walt Disney Company when he became the CEO in 1984. He implemented many creative and insightful strategic actions that turned around Disney's fortunes. However, Eisner's leadership has been criticized in recent years because of a multitude of problems culminating in the firm's weak financial performance. Eisner has been criticized for exceptionally high levels of compensation, especially at times of weak firm performance, and for not developing a person to succeed him as CEO. His last five or more years as CEO have been controversial.

Disney (and Eisner) has been criticized for having a weak board with many members having ties to Eisner. In fact, the board has awarded Eisner compensation at levels highly criticized in the media and has also taken no action against Eisner for his ineffective decisions, strategies, and actions.

© REUTERS/Tim Shaffer/Landov

However, the situation at Disney changed in 2004. Powerful shareholders such as Roy Disney and the California Public Employees Retirement System (CalPERS), a large institutional investor, stated they would vote against reappointing Eisner as CEO. CalPERS representatives said, "We have lost complete confidence in Mr. Eisner's strategic vision and leadership in creating shareholder value in the company."

The vote of no confidence for Eisner as CEO was supported by 43 percent of the shareholders. Such a vote is almost unprecedented. While the board did not oust Eisner as CEO, they withdrew his position as chairman of the board and gave it to George Mitchell, a former U.S. senator. While some feel that Eisner has "nine lives," he may have used all of them. The board reported that it is developing a detailed succession plan and is working to increase its independence from the CEO. Of course, a critical issue is the need for improvement in Disney's performance. All of these actions may have influenced Eisner to state in late 2004 that he would step down as CEO in September 2006. However, critics were not quieted until the board announced that it would hire a search firm no later than June 2005 to move forward with the succession plan.

SOURCES: H. Yeager, 2004, Disney board taking the right steps, *Financial Times*, http://www.ft.com, May 21; L. M. Wilson, 2004, Eisner vote forces Disney to catch up, *New York Times*, http://www.nytimes.com, March 10; B. Orwall & J. S. Lublin, 2004, Disney shareholders' revolt widens, *Wall Street Journal Online*, http://www.wsj.com, February 27; P. T. Larsen, 2004, CalPERS turns against Disney's Eisner, *Financial Times*, http://www.ft.com, February 26; B. Orwall & J. S. Lublin, 2004, Eisner's critics now like the script: Roy Disney, Stanley Gold suspend bid to oust CEO after board pledges action, *Wall Street Journal*, September 29: B3.

Using Effective Controls

Controls are necessary to ensure that standards are met and that employees do not misuse the firm's resources. Control failures are evident in such dismal outcomes as exemplified by Enron and Tyco. Unfortunately, in both of these cases, the strategic leaders with responsibility for implementing the controls violated them, and the governance in both firms was weak and unable to identify and correct the problems until they became excessive and external entities expressed concern about them. However, the potential value of controls goes beyond preventing fraud and managerial opportunism. Properly formed and used controls guide managerial decisions, including strategic decisions. Effective strategic leaders ensure that their firms create and use both financial controls and strategic controls to guide the use of the strategic management process.

Financial controls focus on shorter-term financial outcomes. These controls help the firm stay on the right path in terms of generating sales revenue, maintaining expenses within reason, and remaining financially solvent. Of course, a prime reason for financial controls is to generate an adequate profit. However, if financial controls are overly emphasized to increase current profits, managers are likely to limit their expenditures more than is necessary. Too many expense reductions in certain categories (such as R&D) can damage the firm's ability to perform successfully in the future. Money spent on R&D helps the firm develop products that customers will want to buy.

Alternatively, **strategic controls** focus on the content of strategic actions rather than on their outcomes. Strategic controls are best employed under conditions of uncertainty. For example, a firm may employ the correct strategy but the financial results may be poor because of a recession or unexpected natural disasters or political actions (such as the 9/11 terrorist attacks). To use strategic controls, the strategic leader or board must have a good understanding of the industry and markets in which the firm or its units operate in order to evaluate the accuracy of the strategy. Using strategic controls encourages managers to adopt longer-term strategies and to take acceptable risks while maintaining the firm's profitability in the current time period.

The most effective system of controls is balanced using strategic *and* financial controls. Controlling financial outcomes is important while simultaneously looking to the longer term and evaluating the content of the strategies used. To obtain the desired balance in control systems, many firms use a **balanced scorecard**,[34] which provides a framework for evaluating the simultaneous use of financial controls and strategic controls.

Four foci are used in the balanced scorecard—*financial* (profit, growth, and shareholder risk), *customers* (value received from the firm's products), *internal business processes* (asset utilization, inventory turnover) and *learning and growth* (a culture that supports innovation and change). In addition to helping implement a balanced control system, the balanced scorecard allows leaders to view the firm from the eyes of stakeholders such as shareholders, customers, and employees.

*
financial controls
focus on shorter-term financial outcomes

*
strategic controls
focus on the content of strategic actions rather than on their outcomes

*
balanced scorecard
provides a framework for evaluating the simultaneous use of financial controls and strategic controls

Summary

The primary purpose of this chapter is to explain strategic leadership and emphasize its value to an organization. In doing so, we examined the following topics:

- **Strategic leadership** involves developing a vision for the firm, designing strategic actions to achieve this vision, and empowering others to carry out those strategic actions. Establishing the firm's vision (and mission), developing a management team and planning for succession, managing the resource portfolio, building and supporting an entrepreneurial culture, promoting integrity and ethical behavior, and using effective organizational controls are the actions of strategic leadership.

- Strategic leaders, those practicing strategic leadership, develop a firm's vision and mission. The vision contains at least two components—a statement describing the firm's DNA and the "picture" of the firm as it is hoped to exist in the future. The mission of the firm focuses on the markets it serves and the goods and services it provides, and defines the firm's core intent and the business or businesses in which it intends to operate.

- A **top management team** is the group of managers responsible for developing and implementing the firm's strategies. A heterogeneous team usually develops more-effective strategies than a homogeneous team because it holds a greater diversity of knowledge, considers more issues, and evaluates more alternatives.

- Managerial succession is important for the maintenance of the firm's health. Individuals should be developed and prepared to undertake managerial roles all up and down the firm's hierarchy.

- **Human capital** includes the knowledge and skills of those working for the firm. Employees' knowledge and skills are an important resource to all organizations. Another important resource is social capital. **Social capital** includes all internal and external relationships that help the organization provide value to customers and ultimately to its other stakeholders. Strategic leaders must help develop the skills within the firm's workforce, motivate employees to use those skills to implement strategies, and reward them when they successfully use their skills.

- Strategic leaders shape an organization's culture. In the current competitive environment, all firms need to be innovative to remain competitive. Therefore, building an entrepreneurial culture is of particular importance to strategic leaders. An **entrepreneurial culture** encourages employees to identify and exploit new opportunities. It encourages creativity and risk taking and tolerates failures as a result.

- Strategic leaders develop standards for behavior among employees and also serve as role models for meeting these standards. Integrity and ethical behavior are essential in today's business environment. Lack of integrity and unethical behavior can be serious and highly costly—to the firm and to individuals lacking integrity and behaving unethically. Ethical strategic leaders guard against managerial opportunism and fraudulent actions.

- Effective controls guide managerial decisions, including strategic decisions. **Financial controls** focus on shorter-term financial outcomes, whereas **strategic controls** focus on the content of the strategic actions rather than their outcomes. An effective control system balances the use of financial controls and strategic controls. The balanced-scorecard approach is a useful technique that can help balance these two types of control.

Key Terms

balanced scorecard 42	human capital 36	strategic controls 42
entrepreneurial culture 37	related-party transactions 40	strategic leadership 30
financial controls 42	social capital 37	top management team 34

Discussion Questions

1. What is strategic leadership? Describe the major actions involved in strategic leadership.
2. How do a vision and a mission create value for a company?
3. What is a top management team? Why does a heterogeneous top management team usually formulate more effective strategies?
4. Why is it important to develop managers for succession to other managerial jobs?
5. What do the terms human capital and social capital mean? What is the importance of human capital and social capital to a firm?

6. How can a strategic leader foster an entrepreneurial culture and why is such a culture valuable to a firm?

7. Why are managerial integrity and ethical behavior important to a firm?

8. Why should strategic leaders develop a control system that balances strategic controls and financial controls?

Endnotes

1. J. E. Post, L. E. Preston, & S. Sachs, 2002, Managing the extended enterprise: The new stakeholder view, *California Management Review*, 45(1): 6–28; D. Sirmon & M. A. Hitt, 2003, Managing resources: Linking unique resources, management and wealth creation in family firms, *Entrepreneurship Theory and Practice*, 27: 339–358.

2. P. Burrows, R. Grover, & T. Lowry, 2004, Showtime, *Business Week*, February 2: 56–64.

3. R. D. Hof, 2003, The eBay economy, *Business Week*, August 25: 125–128.

4. G. Edmondson, 2004, Porsche's CEO talks shop, *Business Week Online*, http://www.businessweek.com, January 19.

5. I. Goll, R. Sambharya, & C. L. Tucci, 2001, Top management team composition, corporate ideology and firm performance, *Management International Review*, 41(2): 109–129.

6. M. Jensen & E. Zajac, 2004, Corporate elites and corporate strategy: How demographic preferences and structural position shape the scope of the firm, *Strategic Management Journal*, 25: 507–524; L. Markoczy, 2001, Consensus formation during strategic change, *Strategic Management Journal*, 22: 1013–1031.

7. A. Taylor III, 2004, The Americanization of Toyota, *Fortune*, http://www.fortune.com, February 29.

8. W. Shen & A. Cannella, 2002, Revisiting the performance consequences of CEO succession: The impacts of successor type, post succession, senior executive turnover and departing CEO tenure, *Academy of Management Journal*, 45: 717–734.

9. R. Charan, 2000, GE's ten-step talent plan, *Fortune*, April 17: 232.

10. E. Souder, 2004, Continental's Bethune leaves Co in good hands, *Wall Street Journal Online*, http://www.wsj.com, January 19.

11. W. Shen & A. Cannella, 2003, Will succession planning increase shareholder wealth? Evidence from investor reactions to relay CEO successions, *Strategic Management Journal*, 24: 191–198.

12. L. Greiner, T. Cummings, & A. Bhambri, 2002, When new CEOs succeed and fail: 4-D theory of strategic transformation, *Organizational Dynamics*, 32: 1–16.

13. T. Foremski, 2004, Motorola's new boss aims for Zander-du, *Financial Times*, http://www.ft.com, May 9.

14. B. Liu & N. Buckley, 2004, Coca-Cola veteran named new chief, *Financial Times*, http://www.ft.com, May 5.

15. S. Tully, 2004, The dealmaker and the dynamo, *Fortune*, February 9: 77–82; E. Thornton & J. Weber, 2004, A made-to-order megamerger, *Business Week Online*, http://www.businessweek.com, January 15.

16. M. Reitzig, 2004, Strategic management of intellectual property, *MIT Sloan Management Review*, 45(3): 35–40.

17. A. Perez, 2003, What it boils down to for Kodak, *Business Week Online*, http://www.businessweek.com, November 24.

18. B. Breen, 2004, Hidden asset, *Fast Company*, March: 93.

19. L. Randall, 2004, Lessons learned the hardest way, by going belly-up, *New York Times*, http://www.nytimes.com, February 29.

20. B. C. Skaggs & M. Youndt, 2004, Strategic positioning, human capital and performance in service organizations: A customer interactionist approach, *Strategic Management Journal*, 25: 85–99.

21. J. Champ, 2003, The hidden qualities of great leaders, *Fast Company*, November: 139.

22. A. M. Mulcahy, 2003, From survival to success: Leading in turbulent times, speech in the U.S. Chamber of Commerce Leadership Series, Washington, D.C., http://www.uschamber.com, April 2.

23. J. Nahapiet & S. Ghoshal, 1998, Social capital, intellectual capital and the organizational advantage, *Academy of Management Review*, 23: 242–266; R. D. Ireland, M. A. Hitt, & D. Vaidyanath, 2002, Alliance management as a source of competitive advantage, *Journal of Management*, 28: 413–446.

24. A. Jung, 2004, You will stand on our shoulders, keynote address at the WWIB Conference, Knowledge @ Wharton, http://knowledge.wharton.upenn.edu, November 5.

25. R. A. Baron & G. D. Markman, 2003, Beyond social capital: The role of entrepreneurs' social competence in their financial success, *Journal of Business Venturing*, 18: 41–60.

26. R. D. Ireland, M. A. Hitt, & D. Sirmon, 2003, A model of strategic entrepreneurship: The construct and its dimensions, *Journal of Management*, 29: 963–989.

27. A. Pollack, 2004, Is biotechnology losing its nerve? *New York Times*, http://www.nytimes.com, February 29.

28. D. Lidsky & D. Whitford, 2004, Cook's recipe, *Fortune*, http://www.fortune.com, February 15.

29. M. Arndt & D. Brady, 2004, 3M's rising star, *Business Week Online*, http://www.businessweek.com, April 12.

30. R. E. Hoskisson, M. A. Hitt, R. A. Johnson, & W. Grossman, 2002, Conflicting voices: The effects of ownership heterogeneity and internal governance on corporate strategy, *Academy of Management Journal*, 45: 697–716.

31. J. R. Emshwiller, 2003, Many companies report transactions with top officers, *Wall Street Journal Online*, http://www.wsj.com, December 29.

32. K. Schnatterly, 2003, Increasing firm value through detection and prevention of white-collar crime, *Strategic Management Journal*, 24: 587–614.

33. C. Hawn, 2004, Surviving a corporate death, *Fast Company*, http://www.fastcompany.com, February.

34. R. S. Kaplan & D. P. Norton, 2001, Transforming the balanced scorecard from performance measurement to strategic management: Part I, *Accounting Horizons*, 15(1): 87–104.

Your Career

We examined strategic leadership in this chapter. At the beginning of your career, you are likely to be a follower. As your career begins, you should observe leaders in your firm to learn as much as you can about leadership. During your career, you will likely have many opportunities to take on leadership roles. Some will be formal leadership roles such as managerial positions with people reporting to you while others may be more informal or temporary such as a project leader. Your performance in these leadership roles will affect the success of your career. Therefore, you should learn as much as possible, at all points in your career, about the requirements of being a successful strategic leader.

You can begin this development process by learning well this chapter's contents. Given the definition of strategic leadership and the activities of strategic leaders, what specific skills are needed to be successful in these roles? Which of these leadership skills do you now possess? Which ones do you lack? We encourage you to prepare a long-term plan to develop the skills you need and to hone and improve the ones you now hold. The plan may include gaining experience in leadership roles. For example, if you join student organizations, we encourage you to volunteer for leadership roles. You can also practice the skills you have and apply the knowledge you have learned for courses such as the one for which you are reading this book. Keep in mind that recruiters will often ask questions about leadership positions in which you have served. Being able to describe your work as a leader and what you have learned from it can be a huge plus when interviewing with recruiters.

Think about the following questions as you prepare to assume a leadership role in an organization. What actions will be necessary to build an entrepreneurial culture? How can I develop a management team that is heterogeneous enough, yet willing to cooperate to achieve common goals? What can I do to explicitly encourage colleagues, peers, and employees to display ethical behavior and strong integrity in all of their actions? How can I develop a control system that balances strategic and financial controls?

Chapter 2 focuses on key issues associated with strategic leadership. One of the major problems business leaders face is maintaining strategic focus, given the dynamic and overwhelming nature of today's competitive environment. We would like to offer you a tool that can help sort through the ambiguity. It is intended to be simple to use, but comprehensive in its application.

The 4 Ps of Strategic Management

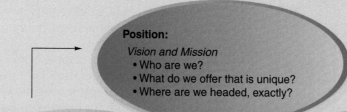

Position:

Vision and Mission
- Who are we?
- What do we offer that is unique?
- Where are we headed, exactly?

Performance:

Success Metrics
- How do we measure success?
- What controls should we implement?
- How is our return vs. competitors?

Strategic Leader

Priorities:

Values and Actions
- What is critical for success?
- What activities must we do?
- What should we not do?

Payments:

Budget
- How much do we have to spend?
- How should we allocate resources?
- What budgeting process should we use?

BIZ FLIX *BACKDRAFT:* STRATEGIC LEADERSHIP

Watch the scene from the film *Backdraft* to see dramatic examples of the strategic leadership discussions in this chapter. Use the discussion questions that follow as guides to your viewing of the scene.

Two brothers follow their late father, a legendary Chicago firefighter, and join the department. Stephen "Bull" McCaffrey (Kurt Russell) joins first and rises to the rank of lieutenant. Younger brother Brian (William Baldwin) joins later and becomes a member of Bull's Company 17. Sibling rivalry tarnishes their work relationships, but they continue to fight Chicago fires successfully. Add a plot element about a mysterious arsonist, and you have the basis for an extraordinary film. The intense, unprecedented special effects give the viewer an unparalleled experience of what it is like to fight a fire. Chicago firefighters applauded the realism of the fire scenes.

The scene comes from the "Time to Move On" sequence that appears about 50 minutes into the film. A woman has told the firefighters that her baby is in the burning building. The film continues after this scene with many more dramatic moments in a Chicago firefighter's life.

What to Watch for and Ask Yourself

1. Does Stephen have a vision for how to fight the fire in the burning building? Does he design strategic actions to reach that vision?
2. Does Stephen empower Brian to help reach his vision for fighting the fire? Why or why not?
3. Risk is often part of strategic leadership. What risks does Stephen take? Does he appear to take excessive risks in trying to rescue the child from the fire?

Mini-Case

Was There Strategic Leadership Failure at Boeing?

One analyst described Boeing's problems as a flawed strategy, lax controls, a weak board, and shortcomings in leadership. Philip Condit served as chairman and CEO of Boeing for seven years, but resigned because of Boeing's performance problems. Condit was described as a brilliant engineer with excellent problem-solving skills and a capability to envision elegant designs. This suggests that he has good decision-making skills and is creative, both of which can be valuable in a formal leadership role. However, as CEO, Condit did not seem to display these skills.

Some described Condit as indecisive and isolated from Boeing's operations. Condit and his management team failed to understand the determination of the firm's major competitor, Airbus, and thus were surprised by its announced intention to build a new extralarge (555-seat) passenger jet. They were even more surprised by Airbus's ability to obtain orders for this new aircraft. In fact, Airbus began to outcompete Boeing. In 2003, Airbus had more orders for aircraft than Boeing for the first time. Condit and his team also had lapses in judgment, and their actions raised questions of unethical actions. For example, controversial allegations were made about inappropriate contact with Pentagon officials to obtain knowledge about a lower Airbus bid on a contract. In turn, the official providing the information was allegedly offered a job at Boeing. Additionally, the Pentagon placed an indefinite ban on bids by Boeing on military satellite launches because the company possessed documents about rival Lockheed's activities, helping Boeing win contracts.

Additionally, Boeing had to fight a class-action lawsuit alleging sex discrimination by top company officials. Condit's personal life was also questioned, with four failed marriages and a suite at Seattle's Four Seasons hotel that had been remodeled to add a bedroom at Boeing's expense.

Condit's decision to diversify Boeing from its core business caused a loss of focus on competition, and the new business markets did not develop as envisioned. Of course, the ethical lapses in the defense contract business were especially harmful. The new top management team moved quickly to overcome the ethical problems and restore stakeholder confidence. But the firm still must undergo thorough examination by external parties, such as congressional subcommittee investigations of potential wrongdoing in obtaining government contracts.

Boeing now has an Ethics and Business Conduct section on its Web site. Included in this section is an Ethics Challenge that employees are encouraged to take.

The new top management team also decided to develop the 7E7 Dreamliner. This new plane is smaller (217–289 passengers) and designed to fly faster and farther (up to 8,500 nautical miles) than many competitive aircraft. So Boeing needs to balance financial controls (to improve its performance today) with strategic controls (to develop products, such as the 7E7 Dreamliner, with the potential to be successful tomorrow).

SOURCES: 2004, Boeing Home Page, http://www.boeing.com; M. Duffy, 2003, How Boeing got lost, *Time*, December 15: 49; S. Holmes, 2003, Boeing: What really happened, *Business Week*, December 15: 33–38.

Questions

1. What are the strategic leadership failures in Boeing that you can identify?
2. Will the actions of Boeing's new top management team resolve the firm's problems? Why or why not?
3. If you were Boeing's CEO, what actions would you take to correct the firm's problems?

EXPERIENTIAL EXERCISES

EXERCISE ONE: MANAGERIAL SUCCESSION

In "Understanding Strategy" in this chapter, you read about how 3M brought in Jim McNerney to be its CEO and to inject the firm with a fresh culture. For this exercise, use the Internet to search for these people:

- Jeff Immelt
- Gary Wendt
- Larry Johnston
- Bob Nardelli

Based on what you find, consider these questions:

1. What do they all have in common with Jim McNerney?
2. How is Jeff Immelt different from the rest?
3. What does this research tell you about the success of U.S. firms in finding top candidates for the CEO position?

EXERCISE TWO: CODES OF ETHICS

Many types of organizations try to define expectations and deal with the behavior of their leaders, employees, agents, and perhaps even business partners by establishing codes of ethics. The content of codes can vary greatly and is often linked to the mission of the organization. Explore http://www.e-businessethics.com, especially the "Ethics Links." Be prepared to discuss the prevalence and importance of ethics dialogues across various business, government, and professional organizations.

part 2

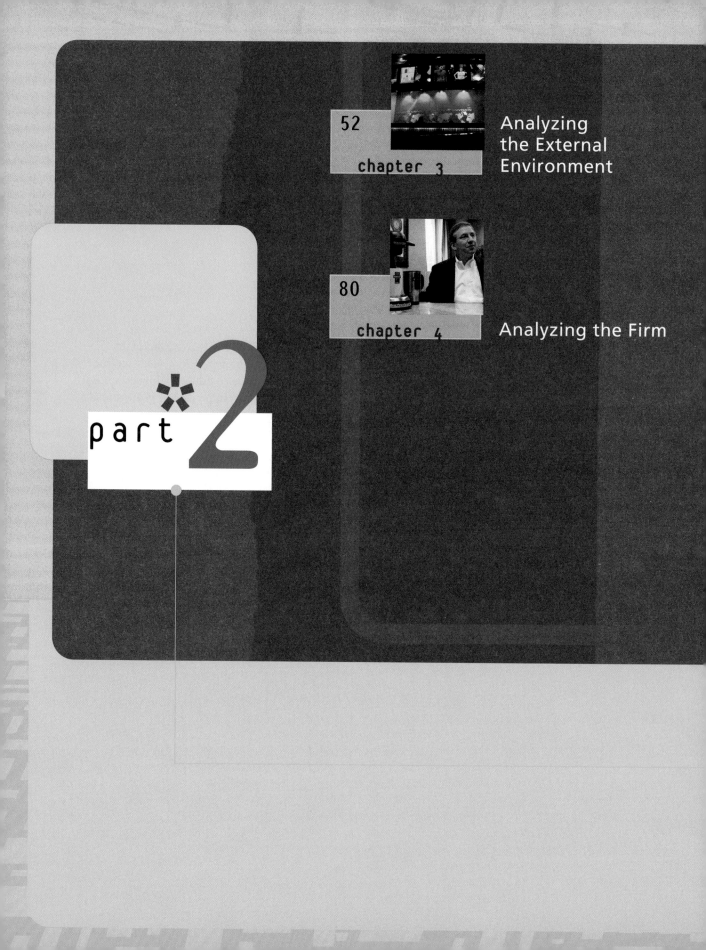

Analyzing Environments

Analyzing the External Environment

*Knowledge Objectives

1_
Explain the importance of analyzing the firm's external environment.

2_
Identify the categories of trends in the general environment that create opportunities or threats for the firm.

3_
Describe the five forces of an industry analysis.

4_
Understand how to complete a competitor analysis.

5_
Identify potential reactions to significant strategic moves by competitors.

6_
Understand how complementors support value creation for the firm in a competitive situation.

Focusing on Strategy

Changing Population Bases in the United States Lead Businesses to Change Their Focus

"$700 billion a year is spent by U.S. Hispanic consumers, a figure that is growing by eight percent per year (three times as fast as the overall U.S. rate)." (Joel Millman, *Wall Street Journal*)

Hispanic demographics are influencing the strategies firms are using to serve the needs of the growing Hispanic population in the United States. Almost half of all new workers to the workforce in the 1990s were Hispanic, and Hispanics are expected to account for nearly 25 percent of the workforce by 2010, up from 12 percent in 2004. This growth is likely to significantly increase the buying power of Hispanics in the United States. Furthermore, Spanish-speaking members of society are experiencing increasing political power. It is expected that both Texas and California will become Hispanic-majority states over the next decade. This growth in the Hispanic population suggests that Spanish could become a second accepted language in the United States, similar to French in Canada. Interestingly, Hispanics often retain more of their cultural and language heritage than other U.S. immigrants from Europe.

Given its increasing size, firms will likely see the Hispanic segment as one that is changing from a niche market to a major independent market in the United States. For instance, ad revenues for Spanish-language TV climbed 16 percent in 2004. Revenues of Univision, the number one Spanish-language media firm in the United States, soared 44 percent between 2001 and 2003, with a 146 percent increase in the 18–34 age segment. Clear Channel Communications, a vast network of radio stations based in San Antonio, Texas, has formed a partnership with Group Televisa, Mexico's leading broadcaster and media company. Clear Channel is interested in making a bigger push in to Spanish programs and advertising. Most Hispanics (63 percent) speak both Spanish and English, and this is expected to increase to 67 percent by 2010. In comparison, Hispanics are four times as likely to keep their native language relative to immigrants from the Philippines, Vietnam, and China.

With this significant growth, new businesses will likely be launched to cater to Hispanics' needs. As such, the number of firms using Spanish as their language to communicate with customers will probably increase. For instance, Procter & Gamble spent $90 million on advertising directed at Latinos for 12 products, including Crest and Tide. This was ten percent of its ad budget for the 12 brands and represented a 28 percent hike over the previous year (2002).

Citigroup is also seeking to serve the needs of a larger Hispanic population. Because more than half of the Hispanic community in the United States is Mexican, Citigroup is introducing a binational credit card that can be used by Mexican citizens living the United States and by members of their family living in Mexico. As we'll explain in this chapter, one of the outcomes the firm seeks when analyzing its external environment is to understand demographic trends such as those we are describing about the growing Hispanic population in the United States.

SOURCES: R. O. Crockett, 2004, Why are Latinos leading Blacks in the job market?, *Business Week,* March 15: 70; Dow Jones Newswire, 2004, Citigroup eyes Hispanic market, *Wall Street Journal,* June 16: D12; B. Grow, R. Grover, A. Weintraub, C. Palmeri, M. Der Hovanesian, and M. Eidam, 2004, Hispanic nation, *Business Week,* March 15: 59–70; M. Jordan, 2004, The economy: Latinos take the lead in job gains, *Wall Street Journal,* February 24: A2; J. Millman, 2004, "El gringo malo" wins fans airing Spanish baseball, *Wall Street Journal,* September 14: B1; G. Smith, 2004, Can Televisa conquer the U.S.? *Business Week,* October 4: 79.

Recall from Chapter 1 that the external environment is the set of conditions outside the firm that affect the firm's performance. As "Focusing on Strategy" suggests, the external environment can indeed affect the firm's choice and use of strategy. External events, such as the war in Iraq and changes in demographics (such as the growing number of Hispanics), illustrate how changes can create opportunities as well as threats for firms. To pursue an opportunity or to protect itself against a threat, the firm might choose to change how it is implementing a current strategy or may even change to a different strategy.

In this chapter, we examine the three parts of a firm's external environment—the general environment, the industry environment, and the competitor environment (see Figure 3.1). Firms analyze their external environment to collect information that will help them select a strategy. The conditions in the external environment influence what the firm might choose to do. In other words, the firm might choose to pursue a certain opportunity or it might choose to take action to avoid an impending threat. The firm's decisions about these choices are affected by conditions inside the firm itself. We will discuss the conditions inside the firm in the next chapter. The actual choice of a strategy is a function of conditions in the firm's external environment and the conditions in its internal environment.

As mentioned in Chapter 1, being able to identify opportunities and threats is an important reason why firms study their external environment. *Opportunities* are conditions in the firm's general, industry, and competitor environments

FIGURE 3.1 | External Environment Analysis

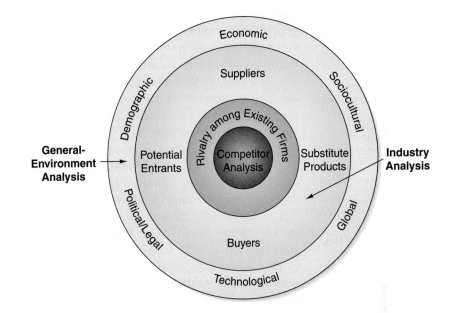

that enable the firm to use its core competencies to achieve its vision. *Threats,* on the other hand, are conditions in the firm's general, industry, and competitor environments with the potential to prevent the firm from successfully using its core competencies. Evaluating trends in the firm's general environment, evaluating the effects of competitive forces in the industry in which the firm intends to compete, and studying competitors are actions the firm takes to recognize the opportunities and threats it faces.

Firms should not rely on personal opinions and casual observations to study their external environment. In-depth study is required, and it is important to ask the right questions. There is no substitute for continually studying all parts of the firm's external environment—the general, industry, and competitor environments. In addition, complements to industry competition should be examined. Beginning with the general environment, we discuss each analysis the firm performs to fully understand the conditions in its external environment.

Analyzing the General Environment

*

general environment

the trends in the broader society that influence an industry and the firms in it

The **general environment** is composed of trends in the broader society that influence an industry and the firms in it. Firms must pay attention to six trends in the general environment: demographic, economic, political/legal, sociocultural, technological, and global. Each category has conditions that affect the firm's choice of strategy. Conditions in the general environment are outside the firm's direct control; no firm can control demographic trends, for example.

Keep this in mind while reading about each category and while thinking about how conditions that are part of each trend could influence different types of firms.

Demographic Trends

Demographic trends are changes in population size, age structure, geographic distribution, ethnic mix, and income distribution. Analysis of these trends is important to determine whether the firm might be able to serve additional customer groups with its products. For example, increasing population rates in international markets might represent opportunities for a firm to sell its products to a new set of consumers. As the largest economies in the world, China and India may offer enticing opportunities for a number of firms to use their products to satisfy new customer groups' needs.

Change in the average age of a population is another important demographic trend. Consider the prediction that the number of Americans over age 65 will increase to 55 million by 2020, up 56 percent from 2000. This prediction could signal an opportunity for pharmaceuticals companies to increase their revenues through product innovations.[1] "As baby boomers get older, they're increasingly going to be less 'do-it-myself' and more 'do-it-for-me,'" and so The Home Depot's and Lowe's customer installation service business is growing more rapidly than their other business segments.[2] Other demographic trends such as changes in a population's ethnic mix can affect patterns of consumer demand. As discussed in "Focusing on Strategy," the increasing Hispanic population in the United States and the simultaneous increase in these customers' purchasing power will influence firms' decisions about the customers they seek to serve and the types of products they sell to serve those needs.

Shifts in the geographic distribution of a population can also affect firms. For example, the U.S. population continues to migrate from north and east to west and south. This trend may reduce the number of customers for some firms in the north and east while increasing the number of customers for firms offering similar products in the west and south.

As the average age of the American population increases, how will home improvement stores such as Lowe's stay competitive?

© WENN/Landov

Economic Trends

Economic trends concern the direction of the economy in which a firm competes or may choose to compete. Gross national product, interest and inflation rates, income growth or decline, savings rates, and currency exchange rates in companies across the globe are examples of economic factors that firms examine to understand current economic trends and to predict future economic trends. Of course, economic trends also affect customers' purchasing decisions. Isn't that true for you? Doesn't your current and expected income influence what you decide to buy and from whom? In addition, economic trends affect the broader society, such as when there is a recession. A recession in 2001 that extended into 2002 in the

United States began to turn to expansion toward the end of 2003 and through 2004. The Federal Reserve reduced interest rates to record lows during this time period to help bring the economy out of recession.[3] The recessionary conditions have significant effects on firms in most industries. When facing less-than-favorable economic trends, firms must decide how to allocate their resources so they will be positioned to grow when domestic and/or global economies improve.

Political/Legal Trends

Political/legal trends pertain to changes in organizations and interest groups that compete for a voice in developing and overseeing the body of laws and regulations that guide interactions among firms and nations. Because political conditions affect how business is conducted, firms try to influence legislation in ways that benefit them through political strategy.[4] The means used to influence political and legal trends must be ethical, moral, and consistent with the laws of the land.

Increasingly, privatization of government-owned and government-regulated businesses has transformed many state-owned enterprises to private firms (as in eastern Europe) and has deregulated formerly regulated businesses (such as U.S. utility firms); consequently, the global competitive landscape is increasingly dynamic (open to competition) and deregulated. This trend is being fostered by countries such as China's admittance to the World Trade Organization (WTO). The Geneva-based WTO helps establish trade rules in the global environment. China's recent entry into the WTO signaled a significant trend in emerging countries regarding the reduction in trade barriers across multiple industries such as telecommunications, banking, airlines, automobiles, movies, and professional services.

Managers must carefully examine political trends in antitrust, taxation, and industry regulations as well as labor laws because of their potential importance to the implementation of strategies. Often, firms develop political strategies before establishing competitive positions within an industry.

Specific regulatory bodies frequently oversee industry activities. The airline industry is greatly affected by the Federal Aviation Administration (FAA) and the food and drug industries are strongly influenced by the Food and Drug Administration (FDA). The influence of regulations and antitrust laws on a firm's strategy is shown in the example of Microsoft.

Microsoft is a highly successful company with a market capitalization of $279 billion, second only to General Electric, and approximately $1 billion per month in cash flow. Accordingly, it is the most profitable company in the technology sector. On March 25, 2004, the European Commission announced a judgment that Microsoft was abusing its power in technology markets. In particular, Microsoft's linking of computers and players of music and video clips concerned European regulators. Accordingly, the company was ordered to reveal code from its "dominant Windows desktop operating system to help rivals' competing in similar software." The commission fined Microsoft $612.7 million, a single-company record in Europe. Because Microsoft at the time of the fine had $50 billion in cash and short-term liquidity investments, the fine was less important than the order to modify its business model.[5] Similar fines were also levied against Microsoft in the United States. After these judgments, Microsoft also settled a longtime dispute with Sun Microsystems subsequent to the European fine and injunction against Microsoft. These descriptions of Microsoft's experiences show how political trends in the general environment can affect a firm and how it will implement its chosen strategy or strategies.[6]

Sociocultural Trends

*
sociocultural trends
changes in a society's attitudes and cultural values

Sociocultural trends deal with changes in a society's attitudes and cultural values. These trends often differ across countries. For example, the emphasis on saving the environment is relatively strong in Europe and throughout the developed world; however, these issues are less important in emerging economies such as Russia, India, China, and Latin America. Health consciousness is also a trend that has increasingly been important in many countries around the world. Especially in the United States, women have been increasingly entering the workforce rather than remaining in traditional family roles. Additional talented workers, such as women, represent human capital that a firm might hire to pursue an opportunity. Do you see any sociocultural trends on the horizon that you believe are important for U.S. businesses to understand? What are they? What should firms do to be prepared to successfully deal with these trends?

Technological Trends

*
technological trends

changes in the activities involved with creating new knowledge and translating that knowledge into new products, processes, and materials

Technological trends concern changes in the activities involved with creating new knowledge and translating that knowledge into new products, processes, and materials. Some firms require a thorough examination of technological trends because of swift technological changes and shortened product life cycles in their industries. In particular, Internet technology has played an increasingly important role in domestic and global technological change. Furthermore, the Internet is an excellent source of data to help understand the three parts of the external environment. Significant changes in communications technology, especially wireless communications technology, have provided opportunities for many firms. For example, new industries have been created by combining handheld devices and wireless communications equipment in a variety of network-based services. This technology enables individuals to use their handheld computers for scheduling, as mobile phones, and to send e-mail or conduct Web-based transactions (such as online purchases of stock and other investments).

As our discussion is suggesting, firms must study technological trends to identify opportunities and threats. In "Understanding Strategy," we describe how Nokia lost market share to competitors because it failed to effectively deal with changes in the cell phone industry regarding flip-top or "clamshell" phones.

Global Trends

*
global trends

changes in relevant emerging and developed country global markets, important international political events, and critical changes in cultural and institutional characteristics of global markets

Global trends concern changes in relevant emerging and developed country global markets, important international political events, and critical changes in cultural and institutional characteristics of global markets. Table 3.1 lists five important global trends that some expect to significantly influence global markets in future years. Examining trends such as the ones shown in Table 3.1 helps the firm identify opportunities and threats outside its domestic market. Being able to do this is important, because firms are sometimes able to grow by pursuing opportunities in other countries. Furthermore, moving production overseas through global outsourcing enables some firms to increase productivity.

understanding strategy:

NOKIA MISSES A SIGNIFICANT TREND IN CELL PHONES

Nokia was the leader in cell phones with 35 percent of the market in 2003. However, by the end of the first quarter of 2004, Nokia had lost three percentage points of market share since the last quarter of 2003. At the same time, Samsung, which ranks third by sales volume after Nokia and Motorola, gained significant ground. Samsung has a goal of obtaining 40 percent of worldwide mobile phone sales, from its current approximate ten percent. Nokia's first-quarter 2004 profits dropped two percent, while first-quarter 2004 profits for Samsung rose 178 percent with sales up more than 50 percent for the quarter. How did this change in market share and profits occur? Nokia indicated that it was "not satisfied with our sales development during the first quarter," which seems to be an understatement. What happened to Nokia?

While Samsung focused on high-end products such as "clamshell" cell phones, Nokia has

SOURCES: K. Belson, 2004, As Nokia falters, Motorola rides strong sales to higher profits, *New York Times,* http://www.nytimes.com, April 21; A. Cowell, 2004, Slow to adapt, Nokia loses market share in latest cell phones, *New York Times,* http://www.nytimes.com, April 14; N. Fildes, 2004, Nokia forecasts growth in handsets; maker of mobile phones launches five new models to halt market-share loss, *Wall Street Journal,* June 15, B6; T. Hanrahan and J. Fry, 2004, Catch me if you webcam; Nokia flips its phone strategy, *Wall Street Journal Online,* http://www.wsj.com, April 19; M. Hansson, 2004, Sony Ericsson swings to profit on strong camera-phone sales, *Wall Street Journal Online,* http://www.wsj.com, April 20.

yet to launch a set of clamshell products. Also, Nokia has emphasized sales in emerging economies that require low-end phones rather than in richer markets such as the United States and Europe. Although Nokia introduced five new models in mid-2004, including the clamshell-type products, Samsung and Motorola have been quick to offer innovative products with improved features such as color screens and digital camera capabilities.

As Nokia has grown in size, it has encountered difficulties in responding quickly to changing trends such as the clamshell-type phone. As a result, Nokia's stock price has fallen while other companies such as Ericsson and Siemens in Europe have experienced positive changes in market value. While sales of cell phones increased 25 percent on an annual basis in the first quarter of 2004, Nokia's shipments rose only by 19 percent. As a result, its mobile phone division profits fell considerably relative to competitors' financial performances. This illustrates the importance of keeping abreast of important technological trends and consumer fashions in the marketplace. Making adjustments to successfully respond to trends in the general environment can greatly affect firm performance.

Consider the variety of purposes for which you use the Internet. The many ways most of us, likely including you as well, use the Internet demonstrate its power. From a global trends perspective, it is interesting to understand that to date, the Internet has had the greatest impact on firms competing in the United States. However, this is predicted to change. China, for example, has the potential to become the second major business power on the Internet. In fact, by 2006, it is expected that more people from China will use the Internet than any other nation on earth. For this reason, Nortel Networks decided to invest $200 million in a research-and-development facility in Beijing that will manufacture networking and wireless equipment. One reason why Nortel made this decision is the prediction that China will have more broadband users than the United

1. **The advent of nanotechnology.** Advances in manipulating organic and inorganic material at the atomic and molecular levels will lead to the ability to create smaller, stronger products. Michael D. Mehta, a sociology professor at the University of Saskatchewan, says, "Nanotechnology will usher in a new industrial revolution, have impacts on global trade and intellectual property, and will ultimately shape how we view the world and our place in it." Recently, the U.S. government earmarked $3.7 billion over four years for nanotech research.

2. **Globalization.** One of the consequences of globalization is an increasing gulf between rich and poor countries. Steven M. Kates, an associate professor of marketing at Simon Fraser University in Burnaby, British Columbia, predicts that many corporations may play an increasingly paternalistic role in third-world countries, developing infrastructure and stepping in where governments have failed.

3. **Global warming.** Earth's average surface temperature has risen by about 1°F in the past century, with accelerated warming during the past two decades, largely due to the buildup of greenhouse gases. Climate change will affect everything from human health and agriculture to forests and water supplies.

4. **Water shortages.** Population growth will increase pressure on water supplies. "Blue gold" is in short supply throughout much of the world. The management and conservation of potable water will become increasingly important.

5. **The employment power shift.** By 2006, two North Americans will be leaving jobs for every one available to refill those positions. Two years after that, projections show a worker deficit of 10 million people. This will shift the balance of power between employees and companies, and firms will have to compete to acquire talent.

SOURCE: "The 5 Most Important Global Trends" by Laura Pratt as appeared in *Profit,* December 2003, p. 24. Reprinted by permission of Laura Pratt.

States by 2006. The opportunities suggested by this expectation are contributing to the launch of many startup firms in Internet retailing, mobile services, and gaming services in China.[7]

Although the Chinese Internet market represents a significant opportunity, global trends can also present significant threats both from foreign competitors and in regard to the complexity in competing in different countries. Companies must understand the sociocultural and institutional differences in global markets in order to be successful. Significant changes in currency and political risks because of war and nationalization of assets also need to be considered.

As you have seen, firms focus on the future when studying the general environment. However, that future must take place within a particular context. An **industry**, which is a group of firms producing similar products, is the context within which a firm's future is experienced. Firms analyze the industry environment to understand the profitability potential of a particular industry or of a segment within an industry. We discuss how firms study an industry in the next section.

*
industry

a group of firms producing similar products

Analyzing the Industry Environment

Michael Porter developed a framework for classifying and analyzing the characteristics of an industry's environment.[8] His five-forces model of competition examines competitive forces that influence the profitability potential in an

FIGURE 3.2 The Five-Forces Model

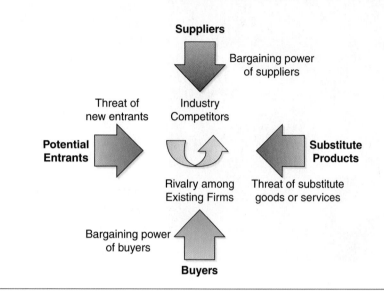

SOURCE: Adapted with the permission of The Free Press, an imprint of Simon & Schuster Adult Publishing Group, from *Competitive Advantage: Creating and Sustaining Superior Performance* by Michael E. Porter, p. 5. Copyright © 1985, 1988 by Michael E. Porter. All rights reserved.

industry or of a segment within an industry. Each force can reduce the probability that a firm can earn profits while competing in an industry. You'll see how this is the case while reading the following descriptions of each force. As shown in Figure 3.2, potential entrants, substitute products, suppliers, buyers, and rivalry among existing firms are the five forces that affect the profitability potential of an industry. Firms competing in an industry want to understand these forces so they can position themselves in the industry to maximize their ability to earn profits. Firms thinking of entering an industry want to understand these forces to decide whether the industry profitability potential is sufficient to support a decision to enter that industry.

Potential Entrants

Potential entrants can be a threat to firms already competing in an industry; by entering that industry, new firms may take market share away from current competitors. Potential entrants also pose a threat to existing competitors because they bring additional production capacity, which can lead to overcapacity in the industry. Overcapacity reduces prices for consumers, but results in lower returns for industry firms. On the positive side, new entrants may force incumbent firms to learn new ways to compete. For example, initiating a new Internet-based distribution channel has been important for established pharmacy competitors such as Walgreen's, given new Internet drug distributors in the United States and Canada.

In the highly competitive airline industry, American Airlines has been weakened by new entrants such as JetBlue. As smaller, more nimble, and more focused competitors such as Southwest Airlines and JetBlue have increased market share,

old-guard airlines with traditionally high cost structures have had to dramatically change their strategies and their implementation or fail. American, unlike United, barely managed to avoid bankruptcy by bargaining for concessions from labor unions and by cutting costs significantly. Though bankruptcy is no longer an immediate threat, American continues to face numerous challenges (such as rising fuel costs). American has trimmed its maintenance costs by finding new suppliers and by reducing the number of different aircraft in its fleet.[9] In spite of the airline industry's significant barriers to entry by new firms, new market entrants have changed the nature of competition in the airline industry.

Entry barriers make it difficult for new firms to enter an industry and often place them at a competitive disadvantage even when they are able to enter. Therefore, existing competitors try to develop barriers that new firms must face when deciding whether to enter an industry. The barriers we will discuss next are briefly described in Table 3.2.

The entrance of lower-cost airlines such as Southwest into the industry has forced veteran competitors to rethink their strategies.

Economies of Scale

Economies of scale are the improvements in efficiency a firm experiences as it incrementally increases its size. Economies of scale can be realized through increased efficiencies in almost all business functions such as marketing, manufacturing, research and development, and purchasing. The important point about economies of scale is that they reduce the costs the firm incurs to produce additional units of its products. Without economies of scale, new entrants are at a cost disadvantage trying to compete against established competitors.

*

economies of scale

the improvements in efficiency a firm experiences as it incrementally increases its size

Capital Requirements

A significant amount of financial capital is often needed for a firm to establish operations in an industry. Financial capital enables the entering firm to build or lease physical facilities, purchase supplies, support marketing activities, and hire talented workers (human capital) who know how to compete in a particular industry. If the amount of financial capital needed isn't available, a firm may not be able to enter an industry at all, or it may do so at a competitive disadvantage (because it lacked the capital to build or acquire what is needed to successfully compete against established competitors).

*

switching costs

the one-time costs customers incur when they decide to buy a product from a different supplier

Switching Costs

Switching costs are the one-time costs customers incur when they decide to buy a product from a different supplier. Switching costs can be low, high, or anywhere in between. Think of the costs you would incur to fly with one airline instead of a competing airline. Assuming the ticket costs are about the same, it costs you essentially nothing to check in at a different ticket counter after arriving at the airport and to land at a different terminal or a different part of a terminal at your destination city. On the other hand, deciding to transfer as a last-

TABLE 3.2

Barriers to Entry into an Industry

Barrier	Description
Economies of scale	Without economies of scale, potential new entrants are likely to be at a cost disadvantage relative to established competitors with economies of scale.
Capital requirements	If the amount of financial capital needed isn't available, a firm may not be able to enter an industry at all or may lack the resources to compete against an established competitor.
Switching costs	A firm thinking of entering an industry would want to determine how costly it would be for an industry's customers to buy from a new firm compared to continue buying from an established competitor.
Differentiation	If customers decide that an established firm's product uniquely meets their needs, then it may be difficult for a new firm to enter that segment of the market.
Access to distribution channels	If established firms have developed relationships with the majority of distribution channels, potential entrants may find it difficult to gain access because a change may create switching costs for a distributor.
Government policy	Some industries are more regulated than others and require a government license or permit before business can be conducted; entry then becomes more difficult.

semester senior in college to another university or college could be quite costly because most educational institutions require students to complete the last 60 or so hours of course work on site. So the cost to switch to another university or college as a last-semester senior is quite substantial. Existing competitors try to create switching costs for customers. Airline frequent-flyer plans are an example of this. A firm thinking of entering an industry would want to determine how costly it would be for an industry's customers to buy from a new firm compared to continue buying from an established competitor.

Differentiation

Over time, customers may decide that an established firm's product uniquely meets their needs. Such perceptions of uniqueness are defined as *differentiation* (see Chapter 5 for a more formal definition). Even in a commodity-type business such as soft drinks, firms such as Coca-Cola and PepsiCo have been effective at establishing customer loyalty through strong marketing programs. In these circumstances, a potential entrant must invest significant resources to overcome existing customer loyalties. Often this means entering with low-end products that compete on price rather than brand image. However, low-end products often require lower prices because of incumbent firms' economies of scale. New entrants may have difficulty in matching the low prices because realizing similar economies of scale without experiencing losses is difficult.

Access to Distribution Channels

Over time, established firms learn how to build and use effective distribution channels. Often relationships develop between firms and their distributors, creating switching costs for the distributors. Thus, potential entrants frequently find it difficult to gain access to distribution channels. Price breaks and cooperative-advertising allowances might be proposed by a potential entrant. But, if taken, these actions can be expected to reduce the new entrant's profit. Beyond this, there is no reason to believe that firms already competing in the industry wouldn't be able to match these actions.

Government Policy

Entry can also be limited by government policy through licensing and permit requirements. Some industries are more regulated than others. Liquor retailing, banking, and trucking, for example, are highly regulated. Substantial regulations limit entry by new firms. The Federal Communications Commission (FCC) grants licenses to radio and television stations. In 1997, the FCC took bids on licenses for satellite radio and only two licenses were granted to bidders. From these licenses only two competing companies were formed: XM Radio and Sirius Radio. XM has an agreement with General Motors, while Sirius has agreements with Ford and DaimlerChrysler.[10] In early 2005, rumors began circulating that XM Radio and Sirius Radio might try to merge. Government regulations, in terms of antitrust policies, would have a significant bearing on this possible transaction. So while regulations may protect established competitors from the challenges of new entrants, excessive regulations generate costs that reduce the industry's profitability potential.

Substitute Products

Substitute products also have the potential to influence an industry's profitability potential. **Substitute products** are goods or services that perform similar functions to an existing product. Consider the music industry as an example of an industry that has experienced a number of substitute products over the years. Cassette tapes became substitutes for phonograph records, and compact discs (CDs) became substitutes for tapes. Currently, MP3 and other digital formats are being substituted for CDs. In general, product substitutes present a strong threat to an incumbent firm when the substitutes are more effective and sold at a lower price. Thus, the product performance relative to the price is the relevant concern, especially if the incumbent firms' products lack switching costs. However, if the incumbent firms can differentiate the existing product in ways that customers value (such as after-sales service), a substitute product's attractiveness will be lower.

Bargaining Power of Suppliers

Suppliers' actions can also reduce the ability of firms to earn profits while competing in an industry. Think of it this way: If a supplier can either increase the price of its product or reduce the quality while selling it at the same price, the effect on established firms' profitability is negative. A supplier that can do one of these things is said to be a powerful supplier. Suppliers tend to be powerful when:

- There are a few large suppliers and the buying firms' industry is not concentrated.
- Substitute products are not available to the buying firms.
- The buying firms are not a significant customer for the suppliers.

- The suppliers' goods are essential to the buyers' marketplace success.
- The suppliers' products have high switching costs for the buyers.
- The suppliers pose a credible threat to integrate forward into the buyers' industry.

As illustrated in "Understanding Strategy" focused on Nokia, there are many cell phone suppliers such as Nokia and its competitors who are competing against one another to supply wireless phone service companies such as Sprint. Thus, in this industry, suppliers do not have much power and therefore do not negatively affect the profitability potential of cell phone service companies.[11] However, Electronic Arts (EA) has power as a supplier. Because EA has done an excellent job of developing high-quality, innovative games, electronic game box manufacturers such as Sony (Playstation), Nintendo (GameCube), and Microsoft (Xbox) are willing to pay a premium to contract for EA's products. EA's best-selling titles—MVP Baseball, Madden NFL, FIFA Soccer, Harry Potter, Lord of the Rings, and James Bond—have all been hits on these game platforms.[12] As a powerful supplier, EA's actions have the potential to reduce the profits that Sony, Nintendo, and Microsoft can earn while competing in the electronic game box industry.

Bargaining Power of Buyers

Firms selling a product want to increase their profitability, while their customers (buyers) want to buy high-quality products at a low price. These goals mean that buyers try to reduce their costs by bargaining with selling firms for lower prices, higher quality, and greater levels of service. In contrast, firms try to offer value to customers at prices that clearly exceed the costs of providing that value. Of course, powerful customers have the potential to reduce the profitability potential of an industry. Buyers or customers tend to be powerful when:

- They buy a large portion of the selling firm's total output.
- The selling firm is dependent on the buyers for a significant portion of its sales revenue.
- They can switch to another seller's product with few switching costs.
- The selling industry's products are undifferentiated or similar to a commodity.
- They present a credible threat to integrate backward into the sellers' industry.

As buyers, cell phone carriers such as Verizon and Sprint in the United States and DoCoMo in Japan have been gaining power over cell phone manufacturers such as Nokia, Motorola, Sony, and Samsung. The buyers' power is increasing in this case because the average consumer does not have a strong preference to buy, for example, a Nokia phone instead of a Motorola phone. Phone service companies often lure customers with cell phone giveaway programs; customers' indifference to cell phone brand makes this possible. Unless cell phone manufacturers have sufficient market share to maintain the scale of their operation and keep costs low, their ability to earn profits likely will be reduced because of the power of their main customers.[13]

Rivalry among Existing Firms

Competitive rivalry is the set of actions and reactions between competitors as they compete for an advantageous market position. For example, competitive

*

competitive
rivalry

the set of actions and reactions between competitors as they compete for an advantageous market position rivalry is highly visible and intense in the airline industry. When one airline lowers its prices in a market, that action is likely to affect a competitor's business in that market; so the tactical action of reducing prices by one airline invites a competitive response by one or more of its competitors. Competitive rivalry is likely to be based on dimensions such as price, quality, and innovation. Next, we discuss conditions that influence competitive rivalry in an industry.

Degree of Differentiation

Industries with many companies that have successfully differentiated their products have less rivalry, resulting in lower competition for individual firms and less of a negative effect on the industry's profitability potential. This usually results because competing companies have established brand loyalty by offering differentiated products to their customers. Differentiated products to which customers are loyal cannot be easily imitated and often earn higher profits.[14] However, when buyers view products as undifferentiated or as commodities, rivalry intensifies. Intense rivalry finds buyers making their purchasing decisions mainly on the basis of price. In turn, intense price competition negatively affects an industry's profitability potential.

Switching Costs

The lower the buyers' switching costs, the easier it is for competitors to attract them. High switching costs partially protect firms from rivals' efforts to attract customers. Interestingly, the government has lowered the switching costs of cell phone carriers by reducing regulation of phone numbers. Consumers can now transport their old cell phone number to a new cell phone service provider, which reduces the switching cost for the customer. However, lower switching costs for customers are likely to increase rivalry among cell phone service providers.[15]

Numerous or Equally Balanced Competitors

Intense rivalries are common in industries in which competing firms are of similar size and have similar competitive capabilities. An intense rivalry is evolving between SABMiller and Anheuser-Busch (AB).[16] These large competitors are battling to gain a dominant position in the global beer market. In China, one of the hotly contested markets, AB recently outbid SABMiller to acquire Harbin Brewery Group. This acquisition gives AB ownership of the fourth-largest Chinese brewer and serves as a platform for selling AB's own products in China.[17] Because of their intense rivalry, though, AB can anticipate that SABMiller will react to its acquisition of Harbin.

Slow Industry Growth

Growing markets reduce the pressure to attract competitors' customers. However, when sales growth declines, the only way to increase sales for current products is to take market share from competitors. Therefore, rivalry usually increases in no-growth or slow-growth markets. The battle often intensifies as firms react to actions by competitors to protect their market shares. One of the worst downturns in the information and communication technology industry occurred between 2000 and 2003. In 2004, the industry began to recover, but firms vary in their financial conditions. Lucent Technologies, for instance, cut R&D very deeply, while network giant Cisco invested considerable amounts in

R&D to retool its product line. As John Chambers, CEO of Cisco noted in 2004, "We have never invested more, looking out three years plus, than we are at the present, and that is at a time when almost all of our global peers did the exact opposite."[18] As the recovery continues, firms with abundant resources are able to take advantage of the weaker firms.

High Strategic Stakes

Competitive rivalry tends to be high when it is important for competitors to perform well in their chosen market(s). For example, the competition for global market share between SABMiller and Anheuser-Busch represents high strategic stakes for both firms. Similarly, as airlines compete with lower demand for their services and with the growth of low-cost airlines, many larger carriers are not as competitive as they once were. Alitalia, the flagship Italian airline, has been struggling and seeking to restructure even though Italy is a leading tourist destination.[19] Besides mismanagement and political problems due to government involvement, Alitalia is facing a number of low-cost carriers such as Ryanair. Ryanair handles about 9,000 passengers per employee, while the ratio at Alitalia is about 1,100 passengers per employee; the cost structure differences are significant.[20] Because of the importance of the Italian market to Alitalia and its competitors, increased competitive rivalry can be expected.

High Fixed Costs or High Storage Costs

When fixed or storage costs are a large part of total costs, companies try to spread costs across a larger volume of output. However, when many firms attempt to better utilize their capacity, excess capacity often results in the industry. Therefore, firms try to reduce their inventory by cutting the price of their product. Alternatively, they may offer rebates and other special discounts. This practice is quite common in the automobile industry and leads to more-intense competition. This pattern is also often found in perishable-goods industries; as perishable-goods inventory grows, intense competition follows, with price cutting used to sell products and avoid spoilage. When this happens, rivalry increases.

High Exit Barriers

Firms facing high exit barriers often continue competing in industries even when their performance is less than desired. In such industries, there is intense competition because firms often make desperate choices to survive. Barriers to exiting from an industry include the following:

- Specialized assets (assets with values linked to a particular business or location)
- Fixed costs of exit (such as labor agreements)
- Strategic interrelationships (relationships of mutual dependence, such as those between one business and other parts of the company's operations, including shared facilities and access to financial markets)
- Emotional barriers (aversion to economically justified business decisions because of fear for one's own career, loyalty to employees, and so forth)
- Government and social restrictions (more common outside the United States; often based on government concerns for job losses and regional economic effects)

© BLOOMBERG NEWS/Landov

For what reasons might satellite radio companies such as Sirius have high exit barriers?

The airline industry has high exit barriers because of the specialized assets associated with air travel, agreements with airports and other partners, government restrictions, and unions. Satellite radio rivals XM and Sirius, who are in a battle to gain customers, have high exit barriers as well. Sirius recently signed Howard Stern, a talk-show host who often uses colorful language. XM, the industry subscriber leader, is trying to sign other celebrities to counter this move.[21]

With an understanding of the potential of each of the five competitive forces to influence an industry's profitability, the firm can determine the attractiveness of competing in that industry. In general, the stronger the competitive forces, the less attractive the industry. An industry characterized by low barriers to entry, strong suppliers, strong buyers, the potential of product substitutes, and intense rivalry among competitors suggests little potential for firms to generate significant profits while competing in that industry. On the other hand, an industry characterized by high entry barriers, suppliers and buyers with little bargaining power, few potential substitutes, and moderate rivalry suggests that the profitability potential of that industry is strong.[22]

A competitor analysis is the final part of the external environment that firms must evaluate to fully recognize their opportunities and threats. The purpose of the competitor analysis is to fully understand the firm's competitors.

Competitor Analysis

Studying competitors is often the most important part of the external environment analysis (see Figure 3.1). Answering the questions in Table 3.3 can help a firm recognize its most important current and future competitors.

Armed with a list of critical competitors, the firm is prepared to conduct a thorough analysis of each, focusing on the competitor's strategic intent, current strategy, and major strengths and weaknesses.

Recently, Airbus seems to be winning in its continuing competitive battles with Boeing, its main rival.[23] We describe the intense competition between these competitors in "Understanding Strategy." After reading about these two firms, decide which of them you believe will be more successful over the next ten years or so.

Competitor Strategic Intent

Strategic intent is the firm's motivation to leverage its resources and capabilities to reach its vision. Understanding a competitor's strategic intent increases

*
_____
strategic intent

the firm's motivation to leverage its resources and capabilities to reach its vision

learning from success

understanding strategy:

AIRBUS SURPASSES BOEING AS THE LEADING MAKER OF COMMERCIAL JETS

Historically, Boeing has been the global leader in manufacturing commercial airplanes. Today, though, Airbus is outperforming Boeing—for several reasons. First, Airbus's intermediate-sized A330, which carries approximately the same number of passengers as the Boeing 767, is more fuel-efficient and has a greater flying range than the 767. Additionally, because Airbus cockpits share a similar design across planes, buyers experience lower costs to train their pilots. Although Boeing is trying to undercut the success of the A330 with its new fuel efficient 7E7 Dreamliner, it is concerned about Airbus underpricing this aircraft. If Airbus moves substantially ahead in the current economic cycle, Boeing will face significant hurdles in its effort to regain the largest share of the global market for commercial airplanes.

Airbus's CEO, Noel Forgeard, suggests that Airbus's planned superjumbo jetliner, the A380, has the potential to widen the gap between the two firms. The A380 has about 35 percent more seats than Boeing's largest jetliner, the 747–400. The size of the A380 could also work in Airbus's favor because of the chronic shortage of departure slots in airports such as London Heathrow. Moreover, Airbus believes that the fuel efficiency of the A380 will result in a fuel-consumption reduction of about 20 percent per passenger on most routes. However, reaching this goal means that the plane's weight must be reduced—a technological challenge. Increasing the percentage of the A380 that is made of composite materials is one action Airbus is taking to reduce the plane's weight.

As we expect, Boeing is trying to become more competitive in its battles with Airbus. Currently, Boeing is seeking support from the U.S. government to develop a "blended-wing design." Boeing believes that this technology has the potential to dramatically increase the efficiency of airplanes such as the military tanker plane Boeing wants to build for the U.S. government. If successful in an application to military aircraft, Boeing intends to use the blended-wing design technology to produce commercial planes as well.

SOURCES: S. Holmes, 2004, A silver lining for Boeing: The loss of a big contract could help its blended-wing tanker get off the ground, *Business Week*, May 24: 44; D. Michaels, 2004, Jumbo bet: For Airbus, making huge jet requires new juggling acts, *Wall Street Journal*, May 27: A1; C. Matlack & S. Holmes, 2003, Mega Plane: Airbus' A380 is the biggest superjumbo ever, and airlines have ordered more than 120 already, *Business Week*, November 10: 88.

a firm's ability to predict how that competitor will react to a competitive action.

The strength of strategic intent can be gauged by examining important competitor characteristics such as the competitor's market dependence. *Market dependence* is the extent to which a firm's revenues or profits are derived from a particular market. Competitors with high market dependence are likely to respond strongly to attacks threatening their market position.[24] Boeing is not as dependent on the commercial aircraft business as it once was;

TABLE 3.3

Basic Questions for Conducting an Industry Analysis to Screen Key Competitors

Threat of new entrants:
- Which firms have developed economies of scale and how strong are they?
- How differentiated are the industry's products and services?
- Would buyers encounter switching costs to purchase from a new entrant?
- Which firms pose the most significant threat of potential new entry?

Substitute products:
- What product functionalities can be duplicated in some other fashion?
- Are there lower-cost alternatives to current products?

Bargaining power of suppliers:
- Is the supply chain dominated by only a few companies?
- How important is the industry to its suppliers?
- How differentiated are suppliers' products?
- Do suppliers pose a threat of forward integration into the industry?

Bargaining power of buyers:
- Are there large concentrations of buyers in the industry?
- Are products a high percentage of buyers' costs?
- Do buyers pose a threat of backward integration into the industry?

Rivalry among existing competitors:
- How many competitors are there?
- How differentiated are they?
- What are the exit barriers?
- Which competitors are most likely to respond to a specific competitive move?

the firm has diversified into military aircraft and other defense-related equipment, as well as a space and satellite-launching business, to reduce its dependence on commercial aircraft production. Understanding Boeing's strategic intent in the commercial aircraft business can help Airbus in formulating its strategy to compete with Boeing. Understanding the strategic intent and actions of competitors clearly contributes to the firm's ability to compete successfully.[25]

Current Competitor Strategy

Gathering data and information to understand a competitor's current strategy is critical to conducting an effective competitor analysis. Meaningful information about a competitor's current strategy helps the firm predict that competitor's behavior. Despite the importance of studying competitors, evidence suggests that only a relatively small percentage of firms use formal processes to collect and disseminate such information. Some firms forget to analyze competitors' future objectives as they try to understand their current strategies, thereby yielding incomplete insights about those competitors.[26] Even if research is inadequate, appropriate interpretation of that information is important. "Research found that how accurate senior executives are about their competitive environments is indeed less important for strategy and corresponding organizational changes than the way in which they interpret information about their environments."[27] Thus, although competitor scanning is important, investing money to appropriately interpret that information may be just as important as gathering and organizing it. Therefore, assessing whether a competitor represents an opportunity or a threat and what that competitor's strengths and weaknesses are is extremely important.

Strengths and Weaknesses of the Competitor

Assessing a competitor's strengths and weaknesses is the final component of a competitor analysis. Firms with few or competitively unimportant strengths may not be able to successfully respond to a competitor's actions. Boeing has a number of strengths and resources that have enabled it to respond to Airbus's introduction of the A380 jumbo jet. But smaller jet producers such as Bombardier may be unable to respond to this action. Basic areas that firms study to understand where a competitor is strong and where it is weak are financial resources, marketing capability, human resource management, and innovation capability. A firm will want to avoid attacking a competitor where it is strong, and instead attack where it is weak.

Complements to Competitive Interaction

*

complementors

the network of companies that sell goods or services that are complementary to another firm's good or service

When a product is sold, complementary products may be necessary to facilitate the sale or to increase the functionality of the product as it is used.[28] **Complementors** are the network of companies that sell goods or services that are complementary to another firm's good or service. If a complementor's good or service adds value to the sale of a firm's good or service, it is likely to create value for that firm. For example, a range of complements are necessary to sell automobiles, such as financial services to arrange credit and luxury options (stereo equipment, extended warranties, and so on). Personal computers are complemented by peripheral devices and services such as printers, scanners, personal digital assistants, operating systems, software and games, and Internet service providers. Digital cameras are complemented by digital storage disks, software that creates usable and storable digital images, and printers and services for printing digital photographs.

As illustrated in Figure 3.3, complementors are a part of understanding the nature of value creation in an industry. A firm can increase its chances of achieving value creation by paying attention to customers, suppliers, competitors, and complementors.

FIGURE 3.3 Value Creation in an Industry

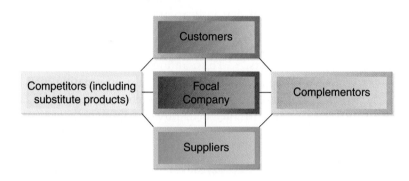

Summary

The primary purpose of this chapter is to describe what firms do to analyze the three parts of their external environment—the general, industry, and competitor environments. In doing so, we examined the following topics:

- Although the firm's external environment is challenging and complex, examining it is important. Careful analysis of the external environment enables a firm to identify opportunities and threats. The firm cannot directly control its external environment; however, the firm can use information about the external environment when choosing strategies to implement.
- The external environment has three major parts: (1) the **general environment** (trends in the broader society that affect industries and their firms), (2) the industry environment (forces that influence a firm in relationship to its buyers and suppliers and current and potential competitors), and (3) the competitor environment (in which the firm analyzes each major competitor's current and potential strategic actions).

- The general environment has six categories of trends that need to be analyzed: demographic, economic, political/legal, sociocultural, technological, and global.
- The five-forces model of competition examines the threat of entry, the power of suppliers, the power of buyers, product substitutes, and the intensity of rivalry among competitors. By studying these forces, the firm tries to find an attractive position in an industry. Compared to the general environment, the industry environment has a more direct effect on the firm's strategic actions.
- Competitor analysis informs the firm about the strategic intent, current strategies, and strengths and weaknesses of its major competitors. Competitor analysis helps the firm understand how its competitors likely will compete in its chosen industry.
- Understanding how complementors' products or services add value to the sale of the focal firm's product or service will help the focal firm improve its competitive position.

Key Terms

competitive rivalry 65
complementors 71
demographic trends 56
economic trends 56
economies of scale 62

general environment 55
global trends 58
industry 60
political/legal trends 57
sociocultural trends 58

strategic intent 68
substitute products 64
switching costs 62
technological trends 58

Discussion Questions

1. Why is it important for a firm to study and understand the external environment?
2. What are the six segments of the general environment that are important to study? Explain the relationships and differences among them.
3. How do the five forces of competition in an industry affect its attractiveness?
4. What three components are necessary to conduct a competitor analysis?
5. When would a competitor likely respond to a strategic competitive move?
6. How can complementors add value to a firm's competitive situation?

Endnotes

1. D. Armstrong, 2004, Sale of Eckerd to CVS, Coutu appears close, *Wall Street Journal*, April 1: B1.
2. D. J. Hanford, 2004, Installation help is growing market for home retailers, *Wall Street Journal*, December 28: B6.
3. G. Ip, 2003, Federal Reserve maintains interest-rate target at 1%, *Wall Street Journal Online*, http://www.wsj.com, August 13.
4. A. J. Hillman, G. D. Keim, & D. Schuler, 2004, Corporate political activity: A review and research agenda, *Journal of Management*, 30: 837–857.
5. J. Kanter, D. Clark, & J. R. Wilke, 2004, EU imposes sanctions on Microsoft, *Wall Street Journal*, March 25: A2.
6. J. Greene, J. Kerstetter, P. Burrows, S. Hamm, & S. E. Ante, 2004, Microsoft's midlife crisis, *Business Week Online*, http://www.businessweek.com, April 19.
7. B. Einhorn, 2004, The Net's second superpower, *Business Week*, March 15: 54–56.
8. M. E. Porter, 1980, *Competitive Strategy*, New York: Free Press.
9. M. Maynard, 2004, No longer on the brink, American Air is still in peril, *New York Times*, http://www.nytimes.com, March 18.
10. C. DeLeon, 2004, Daimler-Chrysler to bundle 1-yr Sirius subscription, *Wall Street Journal Online*, http://www.wsj.com, April 6.
11. T. Hanrahan & J. Fry, 2004, Catch me if you webcam: Nokia flips its phone strategy, *Wall Street Journal Online*, http://www.wsj.com, April 19.
12. C. Edward, 2004, Keeping you glued to the couch: In video games, top developer Electronic Arts zaps the competition, *Business Week*, May 27: 58–59.
13. R. O. Crockett, A. Reinhardt, & M. Ihlwan, 2004, Cell phones: Who's calling the shots? *Business Week*, April 26: 48–49.
14. D. M. De Carolis, 2003, Competencies and imitability in the pharmaceutical industry: An analysis of their relationship with firm performance, *Journal of Management*, 29: 27–50.
15. B. Stone, 2003, Cutting the (phone) cord, *Newsweek*, December 8: 103.
16. J. Ewing & J. Weber, 2004, The beer wars come to a head, *Business Week*, May 24: 68.
17. C. Lawton, 2004, Anheuser, with Harbin in tow, sorts through China options, *Wall Street Journal Online*, http://www.wsj.com, October 12.
18. D. Pringle, 2004, Top tech firms to boost R&D spending, *Wall Street Journal*, January 29: B6.
19. K. Johnson & L. DiLeo, 2004, Alitalia can't stanch red ink, *Wall Street Journal*, April 21: A16.
20. J. Spencer, 2004, The discount jet-set: Europe's budget airlines, *Wall Street Journal*, April 27: D1.

21. J. Helyar, 2004, Radio's Stern Challenge, *Fortune,* November 1: 123–127.
22. Porter, *Competitive Strategy.*
23. J. L. Lunsford, 2004, Dog Fight—Behind Slide in Boeing Orders: Weak Sales Team or Firm Prices? *Wall Street Journal,* December 23: A1.
24. K. G. Smith, W. J. Ferrier, & C. M. Grimm, 2001, King of the hill: Dethroning the industry leader, *Academy of Management Executive,* 15(2): 59–70.
25. G. McNamara, R. A. Luce, & G. H. Thompson, 2002, Examining the effect of complexity in strategic group knowledge structures on firm performance, *Strategic Management Journal,* 23: 153–170.
26. L. Fahey, 1999, Competitor scenarios: Projecting a rival's marketplace strategy, *Competitive Intelligence Review,* 10(2): 65–85.
27. K. M. Sutcliffe & K. Weber, 2003, The high cost of accurate knowledge, *Harvard Business Review,* 81(5): 74–82.
28. A. Brandenburger & B. Nalebuff, 1996, *Co-opetition,* New York: Currency Doubleday.

Your Career

© Getty Images

Most of us prefer to work for a company with multiple opportunities and few threats. Thus, when you are seeking employment, analyzing a potential employer's external environment can help you understand a firm's situation relative to opportunities and threats. In addition to informing your decision about whether you would want to work for a particular company, being aware of a firm's opportunities and threats is useful information during an employment interview. In fact, interviewers are often impressed when an interviewee demonstrates knowledge of the industry and the firm. Such knowledge shows that you have taken the time to obtain information to understand the firm's situation relative to its external environment. Gathering information about a potential employer's external environment will help you positively differentiate yourself from other job candidates; it shows the interviewer that you have personal initiative as well as an interest in the company. Doing this also helps develop your analytical skills, which are often desired by today's companies.

Also, when you consider a job offer or choose an industry or firm where you would like to work, having an in-depth understanding of threats and opportunities may help you decide which opportunity presents less risk and/or is the best fit for your career interests. Firms and industries with significant threats might be too risky; those with significant opportunities might provide better initial jobs and have greater potential for you to develop a successful career path.

STRATEGY TOOLBOX

Successful strategic management is based on the ability to navigate turbulent macro environmental and competitor conditions. There is no shortage of data to assist in the strategic management process. In fact, with the advent of the Internet and electronic databases, a plethora of data can be used in ways never imaginable 20 years ago. This chapter's tool is designed to provide special guidance in searching for critical data to be used in analyzing external environments in a focused and efficient manner.

State-of-the-Art Research

Electronic Resource	Description/Comments	Focus: Industry	Focus: Companies/Competitors
Factiva	Specializes in general news and business information, providing access to nearly 8,000 sources in 22 languages from 118 countries; detailed company reports. Read daily editions of the *Wall Street Journal, New York Times,* and other newspapers—for free!	Medium	High
Datamonitor	Quick hits on an industry and/or a company. Access industry and succinct company reports. Company reports include an effective SWOT analysis.	Medium	Medium
Market Research Monitor	Reports on consumer markets around the globe, with in-depth industry reports for hundreds of industries in France, Germany, the United Kingdom, and the United States.	High	Low
S&P Industry Reports	Outstanding industry data. Previously available only in hard copy; now available online through S&P NetAdvantage.	High	Medium
Mergent Online	Best for deep data on firms; downloadable financials for the past 15 years. Provides full-text SEC filings of U.S. and international company annual reports submitted to U.S. and foreign exchanges. Basic company information, annual and quarterly financials, earnings information, fundamental ratios, officers and directors, institutional and insider ownership, and a complete list of company subsidiaries.	Low	High

This chapter emphasized the importance of accurately assessing a firm's external environment to identify opportunities and threats. The scene from *The Bourne Supremacy* shows Jason Bourne (Matt Damon) making such assessments but at a much faster pace than faced by typical firms.

Jason Bourne and Marie (Franka Potente) have taken assumed names and now live in a Goa, India, seaside village. They hope to live normal lives, although Jason has repeated nightmares about his former CIA agent life.

Kirill (Karl Urban) arrives to kill them. Bourne quickly discovers that he must return to the life he left, that of a skilled CIA assassin. This exciting sequel to *The Bourne Identity* closes with a hint of its scheduled sequel, *The Bourne Ultimatum*.

This scene is an edited sequence from the "Blown" and "No Choice" segments that appear in the first 15 minutes of the film. The scene starts with Bourne calling to Marie from a jeeplike vehicle. He says, "Get in. We're blown." This sequence ends just before Marie is shot. The film continues with Bourne trying to avenge Marie's murder and clear his name.

What to Watch for and Ask Yourself
1. What threats does Jason Bourne assess before and during the chase?
2. What opportunities does Bourne assess during the chase?
3. Think of Kirill, who is pursuing Jason and Marie, as the competitor in a firm's environment. What is his strategic intent? Does Jason accurately assess Kirill's strategic threat?

Mini-Case

Verizon and Other Baby Bells Face Significant Competitive Challenges

Verizon and other local "baby bell" phone companies were formed in 1984 when the government required the breakup of AT&T. The original seven baby bells have merged into four giants: Verizon, SBC, BellSouth, and Qwest. Originally, each baby bell had a local monopoly, which meant that they didn't have to worry about customer defections to competitors; they kept customers locked in through the copper wires that ran through all homes and busi-

nesses in their region. Because of the monopoly positions, the baby bells were long regarded as the winners of the AT&T breakup. Verizon dominates the northeast and is the largest baby bell, with 35 million local phone customers and $68 billion in annual revenue.

However, the government has now deregulated different parts of the telecommunications industry. This deregulation allows all long-distance, local baby bell, and cell phone companies to compete in each different business. Because of this competition, Verizon has reduced its workforce by 30 percent since 2000 while adding new businesses such as wireless telecommunications. The newer businesses now account for more than half of Verizon's sales. On the other hand, Verizon lost nearly two million line subscribers in 2003 to telephone services provided via cable TV wires.

Verizon sales agents are trying to overcome the "monopoly mentality" by seeking to upgrade customers to newer services such as high-speed DSL Internet lines. Furthermore, Verizon now sells satellite TV service through a collaborative venture with DirecTV Group.

In densely populated areas, Verizon is laying high-speed fiber-optic lines to millions of customers' homes. For example, it has laid 300 miles of fiber-optic lines in suburban areas of Los Angeles, Seattle, and Dallas. These lines are the conduit through which Verizon can sell television programming in direct competition with cable companies such as Comcast. But cable companies are responding to Verizon's actions. Comcast, for example, recently suggested that it is going to enter the telecommunications industry. This is a significant competitive challenge because it would find Comcast entering some of the baby bells' markets.

In addition, Verizon and the other baby bells are competing directly with long-distance carriers such as AT&T and Sprint. Because the long-distance ban has been eliminated for local phone companies, most baby bells offer a range of services including long distance, DSL Internet service, cable TV service, and wireless service. These large combined packages are often discounted significantly to be competitive. Furthermore, each company, including Verizon, is going after both consumer and corporate business.

To remain competitive in this industry in the years to come, Verizon and its competitors will need to carefully monitor all parts of their external environment—the general, industry, and competitor environments. Clearly, the external environment will continue to have a strong influence on these firms' performance.

SOURCES: A. Atour, 2004, Defensive linemen: After 20 years, baby bells face some grown-up competition, *Wall Street Journal,* May 28: A1, A5; J. Creswell, 2004, Verizon bets big on cable, *Fortune,* May 31: 120–128; P. Grant, 2004, Comcast pushes into phone service, *Wall Street Journal,* May 26: A3; S. Rosenbush, T. Lowery, R. O. Crockett, & B. Grow, 2004, Verizon: Take that, cable: It seeks to reclaim lost ground with a gutsy plunge into pay-TV services, *Business Week,* May 24: 81.

Questions

1. What trends in the general environment have influenced Verizon's decisions as well as those of other baby bell companies?
2. Which of the five competitive forces seems to be having the most influence on Verizon's decisions? Justify your answer.
3. What competitive reactions do you expect Verizon to experience as a result of its entry into cable TV, long-distance, and Internet services?
4. What other actions would you recommend that Verizon take to remain competitive in the telecommunications industry?

EXPERIENTIAL EXERCISES

EXERCISE ONE: APPLE'S INDUSTRY

In December 2004, Steve Jobs, CEO of Apple Computer, announced the expansion of the company's hottest product line, the iPod, to include the new $99 iPod Shuffle. Many analysts saw the Shuffle, priced well below other iPods, as an effort to pre-empt the entry of Sony and several Korean and Chinese firms into the low end of the MP3 player market. With this move, Apple positioned itself to compete against firms such as Sony and Samsung, as well as handheld phone manufacturers such as Motorola and Nokia, all of which were potential providers of small MP3 players. Using the MP3 format, Apple's iTunes is in competition with others to supply digital music onto the iPod. Not only was the rejuvenated Napster selling songs, but firms such as Microsoft and Yahoo! were considering getting into the digital music business more heavily.

Part One
Just what is Apple's industry? Can you say that iPods and Macintosh computers compete in different industries when they are sold by the same sales force in the same stores? Are there two different industries in which Apple competes with respect to iPods and iTunes—one for hardware and one for music?

Part Two
In light of your conclusions in Part One, consider Apple's rivals and potential rivals mentioned in the brief story. Do they all fit in the same industry or industries that you defined for Apple? If not, do you have to rethink your definitions?

Part Three
Regardless of your answers in Part Two, how do you explain the wide range of industries from which Apple's competitors and potential competitors are coming?

EXERCISE TWO: FIVE FORCES AND PHARMACEUTICALS

The pharmaceuticals industry in the United States is one of the most publicly discussed and least understood. The pharmaceuticals market has several unique traits. Products must be ordered by physicians, not by consumers. The party paying for the prescription may be the patient, but more often today it is a pharmaceutical benefits management (PBM) firm. PBMs work with managed-care organizations to acquire drugs at lower cost by using formularies, which list preferred drugs for any given malady. Many drugs are very similar to other drugs in both effectiveness and likelihood to cause side effects, so these products should compete against each other largely on price. But, patients cannot choose one drug over another based on price; they have to take what the doctor prescribed. PBMs try to create this missing price competition by telling pharmaceuticals firms that if they offer the PBM's managed-care partners a lower price, the PBM will pressure doctors to write prescriptions for the firm's product. The PBMs also encourage patients to use formulary drugs by charging a lower copayment for using these "preferred" products.

Developing new drugs is a major undertaking, particularly for truly unique drugs. Although the Food and Drug Administration tries to "fast track" the approval of important new drugs, the time between identifying a molecule that may be a valid "drug target" and approving a new drug may be 7–10 years or more. By that time, a firm may have invested more than $400 million in development. Most approved drugs will not earn that much back in gross revenues. In addition, most drug targets never get to market, leaving the few successful drugs to cover their costs as well. Research expenses are a drug's main cost, as the product is often mass-produced in bulk with basic chemical inputs.

One reason people are so interested in the pharmaceuticals industry is that it directly affects their health. Most illnesses that pharmaceuticals treat effectively today were not treated effectively just a century ago by any medical product or procedure. As a result, drugs have an almost mystic quality for consumers who look to their pills and potions as the key to good health.

Using the information provided about the pharmaceuticals industry, systematically examine the industry, using the five-forces model, as well as industry complementors such as physicians and PBMs.

CHAPTER 4

Analyzing the Firm

Reading and studying this chapter should enable you to:

*Knowledge Objectives

1_
Explain how to identify the firm's strengths and weaknesses through an internal analysis.

2_
Define resources, capabilities, and core competencies and explain their relationships.

3_
Describe the four characteristics that core competencies must have to be competitive advantages.

4_
Explain the value chain and describe the differences between primary and support activities.

5_
Describe the advantages and disadvantages of outsourcing.

6_
Explain the relationship between a firm's resources and its performance.

© AP Photo/David Kohl

Focusing on Strategy

Building Resources for Innovation

"The consumer is boss; Reframe the Brands [defining P&G's brands more broadly]; Connect and develop; 360 degree innovation [differentiating products not just by formulating but also by design]. There is a lot of jargon. But we have to find things that are simple for 100,000 people to understand. And more than half my organization doesn't have English as a first language. So it's intentional." (A. G. Lafley, CEO of Procter & Gamble, speaking about what he is doing to make P&G more innovative)

Innovation's importance is no longer limited to high-technology industries. Indeed, innovation has become highly important for firms striving to be competitive in almost all types of industries. For example, Procter & Gamble (P&G), once considered a staid and bureaucratic company, has introduced many new innovative products since 2000. With new CEO A. G. Lafley emphasizing innovation, P&G has regained an image as a growth company. According to Lafley, P&G lost its market-leading positions in toothpaste and diapers because of competitors' superior innovation capabilities. Lafley is taking many actions to enhance innovation at P&G, including partnering with and acquiring other firms with innovation skills. Focusing on creating synergy by combining the skills of acquired firms with those already inside P&G has resulted in several innovative products such as Iams Dental Defense (a tartar-fighting pet food), developed after P&G acquired Iams. The same objective of combining synergy as a source of product innovations was the reason for P&G's intention to acquire Gillette for $57 billion (this intended transaction became public in January 2005). Other actions Lafley has taken to build his firm's innovation capabilities include expanding P&G's one-on-one consumer research, encouraging expansions of each brand, reaching outside the firm for new product ideas, and delegating more authority to product designers. These efforts seem successful, in that some believe that under Lafley's leadership, P&G now "takes mundane products and make[s] them so glamorous and distinctive that the world's largest retailer [Wal-Mart] won't be able to resist them."

Jeffrey Immelt, GE's CEO, is intent on building a culture of innovation at GE. One of the actions Immelt took was to appoint an outsider to head a new business, which was created by merging GE's health-care business unit with Amersham PLC, a U.K.-based firm that GE had acquired. Rather than appoint one of GE's homegrown managers to head the new unit, Immelt named Sir William Castell, CEO of Amersham, to be in charge of the new business. Castell is charged with fostering a new concept called *personalized medicine* that refocuses the level of research and diagnosis. Immelt believes that the personalized-medicine concept will create many innovations in this new business unit as well as provide a testing ground for applying versions of the concept in other GE units in the future. Immelt's interest in this new unit and its use of the personalized-medicine concept is high because of his conviction that innovation is the only way to truly jump-start GE growth. Immelt also strongly believes that innovation is the entry price that firms must pay to be able to effectively compete in the global economy.

Evidence shows that innovation also characterizes most "hot growth companies," firms that are growing rapidly. Currently, though, hot growth company Amgen is changing the way it operates. It is moving from being a pure biotechnology firm focused on basic and creative innovation to integrate its innovation skills with the more traditional R&D activities of large, established pharmaceutical firms. Large pharmaceutical firms are interested in gaining access to the innovation skills of firms such as Amgen primarily because during the last decade, R&D spending by large pharmaceutical firms doubled, but the number of new products decreased. Firms such as Sony have gone to external parties and even to consumers to foster development of new computer games. The retailer Sharper Image has its own R&D staff developing new product ideas. Both of these approaches are quite different from those of competitors in their industry. Regardless of whether the ideas come from inside or outside the firm, the capability to be innovative and create superior value for consumers is critical for a company to be competitive.

SOURCES: S. Ellison, A. Zimmerman, C. Forelle, 2005, P&G's Gillette edge: The playbook it honed at Wal-Mart, *Wall Street Journal,* January 31, A1, A12; M. Boyle, 2004, Growing against the grain, *Fortune,* May 3: 148–156; D. Brady & K. Capell, 2004, GE breaks the mold to spur innovation, *Business Week,* April 26: 88–89; P. O'Connell, 2004, Sharper Image's broader, richer focus, *Business Week Online,* http://www.businessweek.com, May 23; A. Overholt, 2004, Smart strategies: Putting ideas to work, *Fast Company,* April: 63–70; P. Sellers, 2004, P&G: Teaching an old dog new tricks, *Fortune,* May 31: 167–174.

As we discussed in Chapter 3, firms must be concerned with their competitors' actions as well as with other conditions in the external environment. At the same time, though, there must be concerns about the *internal environment,* which we defined in Chapter 1 as the set of conditions inside the firm affecting the choice and use of strategies. The reason managers must devote attention to understanding their firm's internal environment is that any strategy a firm chooses must be based on its resources. This means, for example, that Procter & Gamble's objective of becoming more innovative won't be reached if it lacks the resources needed. In "Focusing on Strategy," we explained some of the actions being taken at P&G to increase the firm's ability to innovate. GE's CEO, Jeffrey Immelt, is trying to do the same in his company. Sharper Image and Sony each have different approaches to increase innovation. Both focus on the use of human capital. However, Sharper Image uses internal human capital (people already working for the company) for new product ideas, while Sony additionally relies on external human capital (people outside the firm such as customers and suppliers) to identify and sometimes develop ideas for new products such as computer games.

In Chapter 1, we defined *resources* as the tangible and intangible assets held by a firm. To implement a strategy, managers integrate or combine different resources so the firm will be able to complete different work-related tasks. We also defined capabilities in Chapter 1. As we noted, *capabilities* result when the firm integrates several different resources so it will be able to complete a task or a series of related tasks. As we described in "Focusing on Strategy," P&G is combining resources between its former health-care business unit and a firm it acquired to form capabilities as the foundation for improving its ability to innovate.

We described how to conduct an external analysis (analysis of the firm's external environment) in Chapter 3. In this chapter, we discuss how to complete an internal analysis of the firm. To discuss this topic, we first describe how resources are integrated to create capabilities and how some capabilities are then developed into core competencies. Core competencies that satisfy certain conditions help the firm achieve a competitive advantage. We describe these important conditions in this chapter as well. Finally, we end the chapter with discussions of managing the firm's value chain and outsourcing. All of these terms, such as *core competencies, competitive advantages, value chain,* and *outsourcing,* are defined in this chapter.

Conducting an Internal Analysis

To develop and implement the best strategy, managers need to understand what the firm's resources and capabilities make possible. Indeed, as we noted earlier, a firm cannot successfully implement any strategy without being able to use the appropriate set of resources and capabilities. Think of it this way: A U.S.-based firm that wants to begin selling its products in Mexico won't be able to do so unless it has the resources and capabilities needed to properly distribute its products in Mexico, the financial capital to support the new distribution channel, the manufacturing capacity to produce additional quantities of its products, the capability to sell its products in a market outside the United States, and so on.

Therefore, because of the importance of resources and capabilities to the effectiveness of all strategies, managers conduct an internal analysis to identify and understand them as a precursor to selecting a strategy.[1] Through an internal analysis, the firm discovers many things, including its strengths and weaknesses.

As defined in Chapter 1, *strengths* are resources and capabilities that allow the firm to complete important tasks. **Weaknesses** are the firm's resource and capability deficiencies that make it difficult for the firm to complete important tasks. In general terms, *strengths* suggest possibilities while *weaknesses* suggest constraints. Think of a firm in your local community. What do you think are its strengths and weaknesses? Do you think the owners are aware of their firm's strengths and weaknesses?

The analysis of a firm's internal environment focuses on resources, capabilities, core competencies, and competitive advantages. We discuss these important concepts next.

Resources, Capabilities, and Core Competencies

Resources

There are two kinds of resources—tangible and intangible. **Tangible resources** are valuable assets that can be seen or quantified, such as manufacturing equipment and financial capital. **Intangible resources** are assets that contribute to creating value for customers but are not physically identifiable. They often accumulate and become more useful over time. Reputation, brand name, know-how, and organizational culture are examples of intangible resources. Both tangible and intangible resources play an important role in creating value for customers. **Value** is judged in terms of the satisfaction a firm's product creates for customers and can be measured by the price customers are willing to pay for the firm's product.[2]

Tangible resources such as financial capital are important for acquiring other physical assets (such as technology). Financial capital is also necessary for obtaining human capital. Tangible resources alone, however, will not create value for customers. Intangible resources play a critical role in the value creation process. For example, manufacturing equipment must be operated by employees (human capital) or by computers programmed by and using software developed by human capital. In fact, human capital is likely the most valuable intangible resource for most firms,[3] because of the importance of human knowledge in gaining and maintaining a competitive advantage.[4]

Human capital at upper managerial levels can have a strong influence on a firm's performance, as demonstrated by Coca-Cola. Although Coca-Cola is a well-known global brand name with much potential value for customers, the firm's stock has performed poorly in the market in recent years. This poor performance has been attributed largely to the firm's human capital in the form of its CEO and top management team. Analysts have been highly critical of the two successive CEOs and management teams that governed the firm after the unfortunate death of former CEO Roberto Goizueta. Articles detailing the poor strategies, indecisiveness, and political infighting among Coca-Cola's top executives and board of directors leave little doubt that the firm suffered from a weakness of strategic leadership for a number of years.[5]

Managers constantly take action to acquire resources, including human capital. The full set of resources a firm holds is called a *resource portfolio*. The need for managers to acquire resources and to develop an effective resource portfolio applies to organizations of all types, including professional sports teams. For example, the owners of the Boston Red Sox acquired the rights to two new pitchers, Curt Schilling and Keith Foulke (see "Understanding Strategy"). These pitchers represent specific human capital in the Red Sox resource portfolio, just as Magic Johnson and Larry Bird were human capital in the Los Angeles Lakers and Boston Celtics resource portfolios in the 1980s. Because they are pitchers, Schilling and Foulke do not play in every game. Their ultimate value to the team is affected by the decisions of the team's manager (another source of human capital) regarding against which teams each pitcher should pitch. Likewise, Johnson & Johnson acquired firms with resources the firm needed to compete. The managers making these acquisitions were filling out the firm's resource portfolio. The Home Depot acquired White Cap to gain access to an important share of a new market. In order to capitalize on White Cap's positive reputation in the commercial builders and tradesmen industry, a valuable resource, The Home Depot did not change the name of the firm.

The firms described in "Understanding Strategy" hope that their actions have shaped an effective resource portfolio—an important move, because failing to do so can limit a firm's strategy or its ability to implement a particular strategy. For example, Danone's expansion plans into China were constrained by its lack of qualified managers. Peng Qin, chairman of Danone's Chinese operations, stated that his company did not have the necessary caliber of human capital to expand at the pace desired by Danone, especially in the wealthy Guangdong province.[6]

Intangible assets require constant attention to retain and extend their value. For example, employees' skills should be continuously updated so that the firm's human capital can perform at peak levels. Intangible resources such as brand names also must be reinforced with customers or their value will diminish. That is why Coca-Cola continuously advertises the Coca-Cola brand, even though it is well known globally.[7] Additionally, negative events can harm a firm's reputation. For example, investigations by the Securities and Exchange Commission and the Department of Justice into Computer Associates' accounting practices have harmed the firm's reputation. As a result of these concerns, the CEO resigned and the company restated its financial results for 2000 and 2001. The new interim CEO had to address these problems at the firm's annual customer conference in 2004, but emphasized positive actions that were being taken to minimize harm to the firm's reputation.[8]

While it may seem easy to identify a firm's strengths and weaknesses, this generally isn't the case for several reasons. First, managers need full information about the firm's resources and capabilities to accurately evaluate them. Tangible resources (such as plants and equipment) aren't hard to identify, but intangible resources (such as organizational culture and brand name) are more challenging for managers to identify and evaluate. Tangible resources—financial resources, for example—are usually identified in the firm's accounting system and audited and certified by an external accounting firm (however, given recent problems identified in some firms' financial reports, we recognize that they are not always accurate). Physical resources can be visually identified and values placed on them by standard (accepted) practices. Yet a firm's intangible

understanding strategy:

ACQUIRING AND MAINTAINING VALUABLE RESOURCES

The value of human capital is clearly evident in professional service firms and in professional sports teams. For example, major accounting firms, management consulting firms, and law firms base how they operate on two major resources: human capital and the firm's reputation. The reputation is based on the quality of the services that clients have received over time. These services are

© (MLB)(Kyodo)/Landov

provided mainly by the firm's human capital. Likewise, professional sports teams also provide value to customers primarily with the human capital held by the organization. The Boston Red Sox, for example, satisfy their fans (customers) by winning baseball games, especially when they beat their traditional rival, the New York Yankees. While highly successful in 2003, the Red Sox lost the American League championship to the New York Yankees in the seventh game of the series. Because of this, the owners decided to change some key personnel. For example, they fired the team's manager and hired a new one. They also acquired new players, such as Curt Schilling and Keith Foulke, two all-star pitchers, and made other strategic moves as well. Their intent is to win future championship games and to become world champions. They know that they can do so only with the best human capital. The New York Yankees have been world champions 26 times since 1920, the most of any professional baseball team. The Yankees are also widely regarded to have the strongest human capital in the major leagues. However, the Red Sox's decisions about human capital brought dividends in the 2004 American League championship series. Schilling pitched an excellent game to win Game Six for the Red Sox, who then beat the Yankees 10–3 in the seventh and deciding game of the series. This was the first time since 1986 that the Red Sox had advanced to the World Series, and they went on to win it. So it seems that the changes in human capital paid off handsomely for the team and for the Red Sox organization.

Johnson & Johnson (J&J) has been a highly successful firm operating in health-care products industries. However, due to increasing competition, J&J decided to acquire other businesses to gain access to resources needed to compete effectively. It also invested more money into its drug development activities because drugs generate 60 percent of the firm's profits. Likewise, Nissan has developed value-creating resources in its manufacturing activities. In fact, its manufacturing flexibility gives it a competitive advantage over its competitors—not because of high-quality output but because of its ability to manufacture a variety of vehicles at lower costs. Nissan has also integrated external suppliers into its manufacturing process more effectively than its competitors have.

Use of a more intangible resource is exemplified by an acquisition made by The Home

Depot. The firm has been trying to use its reputation to move into related markets such as
sales to commercial builders, but has had limited success. The Home Depot then chose a different approach and acquired White Cap, a firm
with $500 million in annual sales to commercial
builders and tradesmen. Because of the strength
of White Cap's reputation with its customers,
The Home Depot decided to continue using that
name for its newly acquired stores.

SOURCES: F. Arner & A. Weintraub, 2004, J&J: Toughing out the drought, *Business Week*, January 26: 84–85; D. Fonda, 2004, Revenge of the bean counters, *Time*, March 29: 38–39; D. Morse, 2004, Home Depot looks to lure builders, buys supply firm, *Wall Street Journal Online*, http://www.wsj.com, May 7; W. C. Symonds, 2004, Breaking the curse, *Business Week*, April 26: 75–82; D. Welch, 2003, How Nissan laps Detroit, *Business Week*, December 22: 58–59.

resources, such as human capital, brand names, and reputation, are harder to
evaluate. Ultimately, the judgment of either a tangible or intangible resource is
made in terms of its ability to help create value for customers.

Resources as Options

Resources may be acquired or developed to use at a future time. When this
happens, resources are thought of as *options*. For example, a firm may purchase a piece of land and hold it for future expansion. The land can be used as
a location for a future plant or store. Thus, in this instance, the firm holds the
purchased land as an *option* to expand. Some refer to these as *real options*
because without the land, for example, the firm could not expand in that particular location if it decided to do so. By buying the land now and holding it,
managers can always decide to use the land later to expand. The thought is that
the land will be more expensive later, which is why the firm took out an option
on the land by buying it at a lower price today. Real options create strategic
flexibility for firms. Effectively executed options normally hold their value or
may even increase in value. Therefore, if the firm decides not to use the
resource being held as an option, it can be sold to recoup the original investment and possibly additional returns. In this way, real options represent investments having value and also provide options to support future strategies.[9]

Resources acquired as real options can be especially useful for firms competing in highly uncertain environments. This is the case for pharmaceutical
companies. These firms (such as Pfizer, Merck, and Johnson & Johnson) invest
large sums of money in R&D and develop a number of new drug compounds,
some of which are used as real options. In other words, they invest to develop a
variety of drugs that are intended to treat different illnesses, even though the
firms know that many of the drugs they develop won't succeed. Also, although
some of the new drugs will succeed, this will be true only in the long run. These
firms do not focus on only one or a few drugs because of the uncertain success
of new products (drugs) and the highly competitive nature of their industry.
Each firm's competitors are also investing heavily to discover the next "blockbuster" drug. Investing to develop a variety of drugs provides the firm with a
portfolio of potential drugs that can be developed and marketed.[10]

Many firms in high-technology industries also use their resources to create
options. They invest in the development of a variety of technologies to provide

flexibility to use if needed, given conditions in their highly competitive environments.[11] Some firms that compete in highly uncertain industries even invest in resources that provide options to move into totally new industries. Firms take these actions to maintain flexibility in case the industry changes dramatically and they find themselves lacking the resources needed to adapt to those changes.[12] This was the case with U.S. Steel. Once only a steel manufacturer, the firm now uses its resource portfolio to compete in a range of other businesses such as coal mining, transportation, real estate development, and mineral resource management. U.S. Steel initially took options in these different fields because of the intense competition facing it as a steel manufacturer.

However, regardless of whether resources are held as options or are designed for current use only, simply having them is not enough to build a competitive advantage.[13] The true value of a firm's resources emerges when they are integrated to form capabilities.[14] Another way of saying this is that Boston Red Sox pitcher Curt Schilling can't win a ball game alone, even if he pitches a strong game. Fielders must catch balls that are hit to them, and Schilling's teammates must get hits and score runs. This is how it is in companies as well. Individual resources must be integrated into capabilities to complete work-related tasks. The capabilities then must be leveraged with a strategy to satisfy customer needs. Some capabilities are developed into core competencies. We show how resources are managed to develop capabilities and competencies in Figure 4.1.

Capabilities

Many of the companies mentioned in "Focusing on Strategy" have developed capabilities that help them produce innovation, which means that they have successfully integrated some of their resources to form capabilities. For example, the capabilities of P&G and GE that we described are in each firm's research and development (R&D) unit. Each firm's R&D unit is composed of human capital (such as research scientists and engineers, a resource) and scientific research equipment (another resource). These resources have been combined to form R&D capabilities at P&G and GE. Apple is known as a highly innovative company. In fact, according to an article in *Fast Company*, "since its earliest days, Apple has been hands down the most innovative company in its industry—and easily one of the most innovative in all of corporate America."[15] In 2003, Apple introduced the new iTunes digital music store and the iPod digital music player. These products resulted from Apple's innovation capabilities.

FIGURE 4.1 Managing Resources to Develop Capabilities and Core Competencies

© Royalty-Free/CORBIS

One of the "hot growth companies" identified by *Business Week* in 2004, Shuffle Master, invests 12 percent of its annual revenues in R&D to support its capability in this area. The percentage that Shuffle Master allocates to R&D exceeds the percentages allocated to R&D by the firm's competitors. But the money is well spent; Shuffle Master continues to be the leader in its industry in product innovations. One of its newest machines can rapidly shuffle through a deck of cards and determine whether the deck is complete. This new machine saves casinos money by allowing them to open fewer new decks of cards. Shuffle Master's R&D capability also has produced new proprietary card games such as Let It Ride and Crazy 4 Poker.[16]

Other firms try to build their capabilities to successfully manage their operations in international markets. In recent times, superior customer service has become a capability many firms want to develop. For example, Rackspace, a Web-hosting company based in San Antonio, recognizes an employee each month with the "Straightjacket Award" for providing fanatical customer support. In fact, Rackspace has trademarked the term "Fanatical Support" to highlight what it believes is the unique service it provides to customers throughout the world.[17] So Rackspace has integrated some of its tangible (such as financial) and intangible (such as people) resources to develop a capability in customer and product service.

According to some sources, as many as 20 million Americans own iPods—clearly a successful product innovation for Apple.

Capabilities are normally based on the knowledge held by the firm's employees (its human capital).[18] For example, Apple's new products are developed based on ideas from the software engineers and designers in its R&D function. The same is true for Shuffle Master, a firm in a significantly different industry. Employees of Rackspace are trained to provide superior customer service. They then apply this knowledge and develop relationships with the customers that eventually result in social capital (explained in Chapter 2). Capabilities are often formed in functional areas such as marketing, R&D, and manufacturing. As noted earlier, some capabilities may be developed into core competencies.

Core Competencies

As defined in Chapter 1, *core competencies* are capabilities that the firm emphasizes and performs especially well while pursuing its vision. When the firm's core competencies are different from those held by competitors, they may be referred to as *distinctive competencies*,[19] another term we defined in Chapter 1. When core competencies enable a firm to complete activities effectively and thereby provide products to customers that are superior to those provided by competitors, the core competencies help the firm achieve a *competitive advantage*.

So what causes core competencies to produce competitive advantages? As you will see in the following materials, core competencies must have four characteristics to help a firm achieve a competitive advantage for the firm. These characteristics are summarized in Table 4.1.

TABLE 4.1

Characteristics of Core Competencies That Lead to a Competitive Advantage

Valuable	Contribute to value creation for customers by exploiting new opportunities or neutralizing threats
Rare	Held by few if any competitors
Difficult to imitate	Difficult to recreate because intangible resources or their specific contribution to the capability cannot be easily identified
Nonsubstitutable	No resources/capabilities exist that can complete the tasks and provide the same value to customers

1. Competencies must be *valuable.* Valuable competencies help the firm create value for the customer, exploit market opportunities, or neutralize threats from competitors. For example, firms with core competencies in R&D develop new products that exploit opportunities in the external environment. These opportunities represent customer needs that haven't been satisfied. Apple's iTunes digital music store provides a substantial selection of music at reasonable prices with easy access for customers, satisfying their need to listen to the music they prefer at a time that is convenient for them. Likewise, Shuffle Master's new machine that rapidly shuffles decks and counts the cards satisfies casinos' need to keep games moving along quickly. Rackspace's competence in customer service neutralizes threats from competitors by keeping customers satisfied while building social capital with them and, ultimately, customer loyalty.

2. Competencies must be *rare.* Rarity means that few if any competitors can perform an activity with the same quality. If many firms hold a valuable capability that isn't also rare, it can only contribute to competitive parity.[20] Earlier, we noted that Nissan is highly efficient and productive with its manufacturing activities, much more so than many of its global competitors. However, most major Japanese car manufacturers have developed a capability to build a common vehicle architecture or platform that can be used for several different cars. For example, Honda builds four different vehicles on the Civic platform. Because the major Japanese firms have this manufacturing capability, it leads to competitive parity among them. However, because some of their global competitors lack this capability, it gives them an advantage over non-Japanese rivals.[21] General Motors (GM) is trying to develop the capability of a common platform. If developed, GM hopes to quickly use its common platform to produce its products.[22] If GM is able to develop and successfully use a common platform, its Japanese competitors would no longer have a capability that is rare compared to GM.

3. Competencies must be *difficult to imitate.* Competitors want to imitate another firm's valuable and rare capabilities. However, some of a competitor's capabilities, such as an R&D capability, are not simple to identify or to imitate. An R&D capability results from combining some of the firm's

resources, such as integrating its engineers and scientists with laboratories and providing appropriate financial support to R&D activities. When these resources are effectively integrated, a positive and productive culture evolves. Because it is a tangible, visible resource, a firm's laboratory is the easiest resource for competitors to imitate. However, as intangible resources, the skills and knowledge of the engineers and scientists along with a supportive, productive culture are much more difficult for competitors to understand and certainly to imitate.

4. Competencies must be *nonsubstitutable*. This means that for a core competence to be a competitive advantage there cannot be equivalent competencies possessed by a competitor that can perform the same function. Customer service may be performed in a variety of ways, but the most valuable usually varies with the type of product sold. With some products, before-sales service is most important. Usually service before or with the sale is more important with simpler products. However, with complex products such as computers or automobiles, after-sales service is often the most important. When customers have problems with their computers or automobiles, they expect to receive fast and courteous service. Dell is known to provide quality service after the sale of its computers for its corporate accounts. This characteristic is often acknowledged by analysts as one of the factors contributing to Dell's competitive advantages of speed and an unrelenting sense of urgency to constantly do better.[23] No competitor has been able to duplicate or substitute Dell's service competence applied to its corporate customers or direct-sales ability. These two competencies have contributed significantly to a competitive advantage for the firm.[24] Yet, some have criticized Dell's service quality for individual customers; Dell outsources much of this service to IT operations in India.

Competitive Advantages

Firms with valuable and rare core competencies are able to achieve competitive advantages over their rivals. Competencies that are difficult to imitate and non-substitutable as well as being valuable and rare often produce competitive advantages that last for a relatively long time. But no competitive advantage can be sustained forever; competitors eventually learn how to imitate another firm's core competencies or how to use their own capabilities to produce products that create more value for customers.

Competitive advantages are important because they enable firms to capture larger shares of the market and to increase their returns. When they do so, they also create value for their owners and other stakeholders. As a result, managers are continuously searching for ways to develop competencies that are valuable, rare, difficult to imitate, and nonsubstitutable. Alternatively, if a competitor holds a competitive advantage, firms try to imitate it or substitute for it. Firms can try to imitate a core competence in many ways. For example, while a productive R&D capability is difficult to imitate, firms might acquire a company with an identified capability in R&D. Similarly, a firm could develop an alliance with companies having complementary capabilities that, when integrated with their own, form a unique and valuable core competence. As described in "Focusing on Strategy," Procter & Gamble acquired firms with strong R&D capabilities. Integrating P&G's own capabilities with the acquired firms' capabilities helps it create core competencies that it can use to develop innovative products. As we noted earlier, Johnson & Johnson is also acquiring firms so it can integrate their capabilities with its own to build new and valuable core competencies.

Next, we examine how firms use value-chain activities to develop a competitive advantage.

The Value Chain

*

value chain

consists of the structure of activities that firms use to implement their business-level strategy

*

benchmarking

the process of identifying the best practices of competitors and other high-performing firms, analyzing them, and comparing them with the organization's own practices

*

primary activities

inbound logistics (such as sources of parts), operations (such as manufacturing, if dealing with a physical product), sales and distribution of products, and after-sales service

*

support activities

provide support to the primary activities so that they can be completed effectively

The **value chain** consists of the structure of activities that firms use to implement their business-level strategy. Firms analyze their value chain to better understand the activities that contribute the most strongly to creating value for customers and the cost incurred to complete each activity. Of course, to succeed, the firm must create value that exceeds the costs incurred to produce, distribute, and service products for customers.[25] Based on the firm's analysis of its value-chain activities, it can compare them to those of its competitors. One common means of making these comparisons is through benchmarking. **Benchmarking** is the process of identifying the best practices of competitors and other high-performing firms, analyzing them, and comparing them with the organization's own practices.[26] Through these comparisons, firms sometimes identify better ways to complete activities that create greater value for customers. FedEx studied the activities and best practices of transportation companies to invent the overnight-delivery business. Other firms may develop means of handling the value-chain activities differently from competitors because they could not complete the activity in a comparable way. For example, Dell decided to handle distribution activities differently from its competitors. As we know, Dell decided to sell its computers directly to customers rather than through retail outlets. It would have been highly difficult for Dell to obtain the needed retail agreements to market its computers and outsell its competitors. The growth and popularity of the Internet greatly enhanced Dell's ability to reach customers and sell its products using the direct-sales approach.

The focus of value-chain analysis is on primary and secondary activities. **Primary activities** include inbound logistics (such as sources of parts), operations (such as manufacturing, if dealing with a physical product), sales and distribution of products, and after-sales service. Therefore, primary activities are directly involved in creating value for the customer. **Support activities** provide support to the primary activities so that they can be completed effectively. Support activities, then, are only indirectly involved in creating value for the customer as they support the primary activities. Below we examine primary and support activities to more fully explain the value chain.

Focusing on the primary activities, the product moves from raw-material suppliers to operations, to finished-goods inventory, to marketing and distribution, and finally to after-sales service. These activities are shown in Figure 4.2. Each stage of the value chain's primary activities adds costs, but hopefully cre-

FIGURE 4.2 The Value Chain

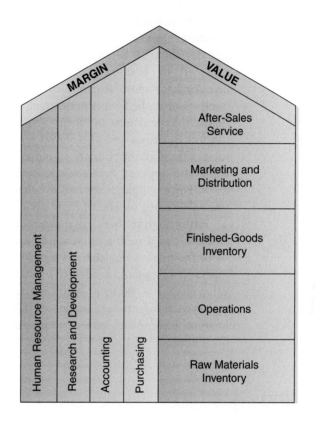

ates value as well. Some firms are especially effective in managing the *supply chain* and relationships with suppliers. In this way, they know where and when to buy specific supplies and usually have developed good working relationships with suppliers. In so doing, they can obtain high-quality goods when needed and at an appropriate price.[27]

A critical component of the value chain is knowledge of the customer.[28] This knowledge must be injected into each stage of activities to ensure that all activities are intended to create value for the customer. For example, using knowledge about customers, the firm ensures that its raw materials are of appropriate quality to build a product that meets or exceeds customer needs. These materials should be delivered in a timely matter so that the firm can provide the finished product on the dates required by the customer. Of course, the firm must be able to transform the raw materials into a high-quality finished product. These products are then sent to inventory so that marketing can distribute them to the customer when needed and at the lowest possible distribution cost. Marketing develops sales and promotion campaigns to attract customers and to ensure that they understand the value provided by the product. Finally, after-sales service helps customers use the product and makes certain that the product meets the customers' standards. The value provided is reflected in the size of the margin shown in Figure 4.2.

Support activities are important even though their effect on creating customer value is indirect. As shown in Figure 4.2, purchasing, accounting, research and development, and human resource management are support activities. The human resource management function is responsible for recruiting the human capital needed to complete all primary and support activities. Research and development helps to create the new products that then are produced and provided to customers through the primary activities. Shareholders and investors pay close attention to the reports provided by accounting to determine whether the firm is performing well and whether they want to invest more financial capital into the firm. This discussion emphasizes the necessity of the support functions and also shows how they affect the creation of value for customers through the primary activities. With today's new technologies, some primary and support activities are being performed in new and more efficient ways. For example, firms can use the Internet to communicate with customers, track deliveries, and learn more about customers' needs.[29]

Firms analyze their value chain continuously to find ways to operate more efficiently as a means of creating more value for customers. Continuous analysis of the firm's value chain is a prerequisite to developing a competitive advantage and sustaining it against substantial competition. In fact, analysis of the value chain has led to a significant amount of outsourcing of support activities and even some primary activities. When a firm identifies serious inefficiencies in how it completes one or more activities, they then become candidates for outsourcing.

Outsourcing

*

outsourcing

acquiring a capability from an external supplier that contributes to creating value for the customer

Outsourcing has become a popular and yet controversial activity among U.S. firms. **Outsourcing** involves acquiring a capability from an external supplier that contributes to creating value for the customer. Outsourcing is being used more frequently because of the increased capabilities in global markets by firms specializing in specific activities. An external supplier can often provide output of the same quality or better at a lower cost.[30] It can provide the higher quality because of supplier specialization that cannot be achieved by the acquiring firm and the economies of scale that the specialization produces. Therefore, by outsourcing, a firm benefits from the value created by another company's use of its core competence in a primary or support activity. Outsourcing of a support activity is depicted in Figure 4.3.

In spite of these benefits, outsourcing is controversial because of the job losses that some critics suggest result from decisions to outsource work to firms in other nations.[31] This controversy may exist for a while, in that companies in countries to which a great deal of low level work is being outsourced, such as China and India, are developing core competencies in higher value activities (such as an aspect of R&D, a support activity) of the value chain.[32]

In addition to the value provided by the external supplier, firms that outsource increase their flexibility, reduce their risks, and decrease their capital

FIGURE 4.3 Outsourcing the HRM Function

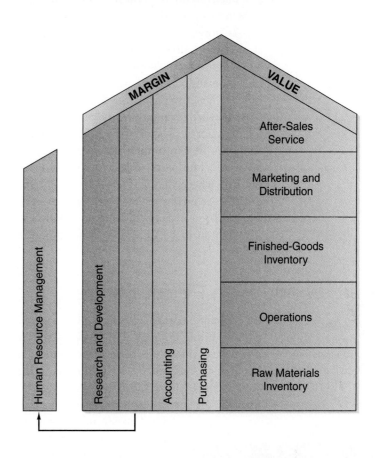

investments. Firms that outsource one or more primary or support activities have more flexibility because they can change suppliers, reduce the number of activities performed (if those activities become less important to producing value for customers), and more easily change their strategies and make other capital investments when needed. Outsourcing also allows the firm to focus on properly nurturing the core competencies it possesses.

Outsourcing, however, is not a panacea. In fact, firms must carefully evaluate outsourcing decisions because they are difficult to reverse.[33] The firm doesn't want to outsource an activity in which it has a capability that could become a core competence. Developing a capability that has been outsourced requires the firm to obtain the necessary human capital and to organize a new structure and internal mechanisms to insert it into the value-chain activities of the firm. This process is often time-consuming and costly. Some firms respond to this threat by outsourcing only part of an activity. For example, a firm such as Merck would likely never outsource its complete R&D function, given R&D's critical contribution to creating value for customers and its importance for competitive advantage in the pharmaceutical industry. However, Merck has begun to undertake alliances with small high-potential research-intensive firms that have promising drugs under development. In 2003, Merck paid $5 million for an exclusive license and a multiyear collaboration with Amrad Corporation, a small Australian biotech firm with a promising drug under development to treat respiratory diseases.[34]

As noted in "Understanding Strategy," IBM's CEO is delighted with outsourcing because of the new business it is generating for his company. The $750 million deal with the Indian telecommunications company is only the tip of the outsourcing iceberg for IBM. However, not all companies will receive significant benefits and some firms can be harmed by outsourcing if they are not careful when evaluating potential outsourcing activities. The example of AM Communications shows the potential harm that can accrue. Additionally, while some people can obtain lucrative jobs because of outsourcing, such as with Relativity Technologies, others are likely to lose jobs and enter the contract labor market, where they will earn less and have fewer or no fringe benefits such as health-care coverage. So there are perils along with benefits from outsourcing. The decision about whether to outsource should be made in terms of what the firm can do to create the greatest amount of value for customers.

Resources and Firm Performance

Ford tries to excite European customers with vehicles such as the Astin Martin DB9, but are Ford's efforts enough to improve its performance?

© Andrew Fox/Alamy

As explained earlier, resources play a critical role in developing and implementing the firm's strategy. However, as implied by this statement, resources may not have a direct effect on performance; rather, they may affect the quality of the activities or processes that in turn affect performance.[35] An example can be seen in Ford Motor Company's attempt to turn its performance around. Ford's financial performance has suffered in the 2000s. To deal with this problem, Ford needs to improve its capabilities in several areas, especially product design and manufacturing efficiency. Unfortunately, analysts believe that Ford's efforts have not been successful. For example, some analysts argue that the firm continues to design vehicles that are boring to European customers. Analysts also suggest that because the company hasn't produced competitively designed and manufactured vehicles for several years, the Ford brand image has been tarnished. Therefore, its weak capabilities in design and manufacturing are having a negative effect on its brand image,[36] an important intangible resource. A tarnished brand image is likely to hurt the sales of Ford vehicles; in turn, weak sales lead to poor financial performance.

It is important for Ford and all other companies to have strong resources, because strong resources support the use of value-chain activities and are the foundation for a strategy that can produce positive performance. For example, firms desiring to enter China need a partner for access to local markets. Many firms are interested in China because of the current large and growing markets (see Chapter 8). However, to

understanding strategy:

THE PROS AND CONS OF OUTSOURCING

Very few primary and support activities are not subject to outsourcing. Staffing customer service help lines, installing expensive and sophisticated medical equipment, interpreting medical X rays, servicing computers, and providing software and design services are examples of activities firms can outsource to other companies.

There are positive stories about the use of outsourcing. One of these stories concerns Relativity Technologies. Currently, this firm employs approximately 50 Russian programmers. If the firm were unable to outsource the programming function, the CEO, Vivek Wadhwa, claims that the firm and its 100 jobs in the United States, paying an average of about $100,000 annually, would not exist. Additionally, CEOs such as IBM's Samuel Palmisano argue that outsourcing provides major benefits to firms. Besides allowing the firm doing the outsourcing to focus on what it does best, the firm receiving the outsourcing business benefits by offering the outsourcing service. In recent years, IBM has generated significant revenues by completing activities (such as data-processing tasks) that firms have outsourced to it.

However, outsourcing also has negative aspects. For example, outsourcing has produced an explosion in temporary employment (often referred to as casual labor), even for highly professional jobs. Unfortunately, this "contract labor" is largely unregulated by U.S. labor laws. Additionally, some firms have learned that outsourcing can produce a form of brain drain. By outsourcing, firms can lose their capabilities to create value for the customers. For example, AM Communications outsourced a number of activities and then experienced some difficult times due to an economy in recession. When the original owners sought investors to revive the firm, they experienced problems because the investors felt that the firm's manufacturing, development services, and software and engineering know-how existed primarily in its external suppliers (firms to which AM had outsourced activities). The investors did not want to invest in the firm, which eventually filed for bankruptcy.

Some argue that outsourcing is being used primarily because of efficiencies that involve transfers to low-wage contexts. This scenario certainly exists in many services provided by Indian companies and contract manufacturing provided by Chinese companies. However, a critical component is whether they are also providing the quality of service needed. It should also be noted that outsourcing activities are not only in one direction. For example, IBM's CEO is excited about outsourcing because he expects his company to be a major supplier. In 2004, IBM obtained a new ten-year contract with Bharti Tele-Ventures to provide computing and information technology services. The contract is worth approximately $750 million over its life. Thus, while outsourcing has a rough edge, some firms can benefit but should realize that they are living on "the razor's edge"; the service they provide must be cost-efficient for the customer or they may be replaced by other firms that specialize in producing the outsourced service.

SOURCES: W. M. Bulkeley, 2004, IBM's Palmisano sees huge gains in outsourcing, *Wall Street Journal Online*, http://www.wsj.com, May 20; D. Gumpert, 2004, An unseen peril of outsourcing, *Business Week Online*, http://www.businessweek.com, March 3; C. Salter, 2004, Surprise package, *Fast Company*, February: 62–66; P. Taylor & R. Marcelo, 2004, IBM wins Indian telecoms outsourcing deal, *Financial Times*, http://www.ft.com, March 26; V. Wadhwa, 2004, My son, it's time to talk of outsourcing . . . , *Business Week Online*, http://www.businessweek.com, March 12; B. Grow, 2003, A day's pay for a day's work—maybe, *Business Week*, December 8: 100–103.

find a good local partner, they may need to provide something that partner needs in exchange, as General Electric (GE) discovered in its quest to sell power equipment in China. GE had to agree to transfer technology for building the equipment to its new partners; therefore, its resources allowed it to have access to a huge new international market. Similarly, Motorola invested more than $300 million in 19 different technology research centers in China to gain better access to markets there. Microsoft and Siemens AG have also made significant investments in China as one step to gaining access to Chinese markets.[37]

Firms should understand, though, that resources can constrain their strategy as well. For example, Volkswagen has a "middle-class" brand image. Because of this brand image, VW's recent attempt to develop and market high-priced luxury autos has been largely unsuccessful. However, its brand image is facilitating VW's efforts to reach the growing middle class in China, a potentially huge market. Chinese firms are simultaneously trying to develop the capabilities to compete in international markets. One resource needed is an international brand image. A few Chinese firms have already developed an international brand. For example, Haier manufactures small refrigerators in South Carolina and has about 50 percent of the U.S. mini-refrigerator market. As a way to develop their image, many other Chinese firms are venturing into other Asian countries to develop their competitive capabilities before they enter Western markets.[38]

Summary

The primary purpose of this chapter is to explain how a firm's resources can be managed to develop one or more competitive advantages. In doing so, we examined the following topics:

- To develop and implement the best strategy, managers need to understand the firm's resources and capabilities. Therefore, managers need to conduct an internal analysis to identify the firm's strengths and weaknesses. Strengths are resources and capabilities that allow the firm to complete important tasks. **Weaknesses** are the firm's resource and capability deficiencies that make it difficult for the firm to complete important tasks.
- Resources are either tangible or intangible. **Tangible resources** are valuable assets that can be seen or quantified, such as manufacturing equipment and financial capital. **Intangible resources**

are assets that contribute to creating value for customers but are not physically identifiable.
- Resources may be acquired or developed to use in the future. These resources are considered *options*. Resource options provide firms with strategic flexibility. These options normally hold their value and may even increase in value.
- Capabilities are formed by integrating several resources with the intent of accomplishing a major task or series of related tasks. Capabilities are normally based on the knowledge held by the firm's employees (its human capital).
- Core competencies are capabilities that are performed especially well and are emphasized by the organization in its quest for a competitive advantage. If these core competencies are different from those held by competitors, they may be referred to as distinctive competencies. To be a competitive advantage for the firm, a core

competence must be valuable, rare, difficult to imitate, and nonsubstitutable.

- The **value chain** is the structure of activities the firm uses to implement its business-level strategy. Firms analyze their value chain to better understand the activities that contribute the most strongly to creating value for customers and the costs of each of them in order to understand how to ensure efficient operations. A firm examines its primary and support activities when studying the value chain.

- **Outsourcing** involves acquiring a capability from an external supplier that contributes to creating value for the customer. Outsourcing has become common because of increased capabilities in global markets by firms specializing in specific activities.

- Without adequate resources, a firm will be unable to compete effectively. In fact, competitive advantages are based on valuable and rare resources. Therefore, managers must seek to obtain and manage superior resources effectively to achieve firm success.

Key Terms

benchmarking 92	primary activities 92	value 84
intangible resources 84	support activities 92	value chain 92
outsourcing 94	tangible resources 84	weaknesses 84

Discussion Questions

1. What are strengths and weaknesses and how does the firm identify them?
2. What are resources, capabilities, and core competencies? How are these concepts related?
3. What four characteristics of core competencies are necessary for them to become a competitive advantage?
4. How would you explain the value chain to a classmate? What are primary and support activities?
5. What is outsourcing? How does outsourcing create value for the firm? What are the potential problems with outsourcing?
6. How do resources contribute to a firm's performance?

Endnotes

1. C. M. Christiansen, 2001, The past and future of competitive advantage, *Sloan Management Review*, 42(2): 105–109; C. M. Christiansen & M. E. Raynor, 2003, Why hard-nosed executives should care about management theory, *Harvard Business Review*, 81(9): 66–74.
2. D. G. Sirmon, M. A. Hitt, & R. D. Ireland, 2005, Managing firm resources in dynamic environments to create value: Looking inside the black box, *Academy of Management Review* (in press).
3. M. A. Hitt, L. Bierman, K. Shimizu, & R. Kochhar, 2001, Direct and moderating effects of human capital on strategy and firm performance in professional service firms, *Academy of Management Journal*, 44: 13–28.
4. S. K. McEviley & B. Chakravarthy, 2002, The persistence of a knowledge-based advantage: An empirical test for product performance and technological knowledge, *Strategic Management Journal*, 23: 285–305.
5. B. Morris, 2004, The real story: How did Coca-Cola's management go from first-rate to farcical in six short years? *Fortune*, May 31: 84–98.
6. L. Chang, 2004, Groupe Danone builds a major market in China, *Wall Street Journal Online*, http://www.wsj.com, March 4.
7. D. G. Sirmon & M.A. Hitt, 2003, Managing resources: Linking unique resources, management and wealth creation in family firms, *Entrepreneurship Theory & Practice*, 27:

339–358; M. Maynard, 2004, Wrapping a familiar name around a new product, *New York Times,* http://www.nytimes.com, May 22.

8. M. LaMonica, 2004, CA shifts focus to product strategy, *New York Times,* http://www.nytimes.com, May 23.

9. R. G. McGrath & A. Nerkar, 2004, Real options reasoning and a new look at R&D investment strategies of pharmaceutical firms, *Strategic Management Journal,* 25: 1–21.

10. Ibid.

11. K. D. Miller & A. T. Arikan, 2004, Technology search investments: Evolutionary, option reasoning, and option pricing approaches, *Strategic Management Journal,* 25: 473–485.

12. T. B. Folta & J. P. O'Brien, 2004, Entry in the presence of dueling options, *Strategic Management Journal,* 25: 121–138; D. Harding & S. Rovit, 2004, Building deals on bedrock, *Harvard Business Review,* 82(9): 121–128.

13. Sirmon, Hitt, & Ireland, Managing firm resources; D. L. Deeds, D. De Carolis, & J. Coombs, 2000, Dynamic capabilities and new product development in high-technology ventures: An empirical analysis of new biotechnology firms, *Journal of Business Venturing,* 15: 211–229.

14. M. Blyler & R. W. Coff, 2003, Dynamic capabilities, social capital and rent appropriation: Ties that split pies, *Strategic Management Journal,* 24: 677–686.

15. C. Hawn, 2004, If he's so smart . . . : Steve Jobs, Apple, and the limits of innovation, *Fast Company,* January: 68–74.

16. A. Barrett, C. Palmeri, & S. A. Forest, 2004, Hot growth companies: The 100 best small companies, *Business Week Online,* http//:www.businessweek.com, June 7.

17. A. Overholt, 2004, Cuckoo for customers, *Fast Company,* January: 86–93.

18. S. E. Jackson, M. A. Hitt, & A. DeNisi, 2003, *Managing Knowledge for Sustained Competitive Advantage,* San Francisco: Jossey-Bass.

19. M. A. Hitt & R. D. Ireland, 1985, Corporate distinctive competence, strategy, industry and performance, *Strategic Management Journal,* 6: 273–293.

20. J. Barney, 2001, Is the resource-based view a useful perspective for strategic management research? Yes, *Academy of Management Review,* 26: 41–56.

21. D. Welch & K. Kerwin, 2004, Detroit tries it the Japanese way, *Business Week Online,* http://www.businessweek.com, January 20.

22. Ibid.

23. B. Breen, 2004, Dell time, *Fast Company,* November: 86–95.

24. A. Serwer, 2002, Dell does domination, *Fortune,* January 21: 70–75.

25. M. A. Hitt, R. D. Ireland, & R. E. Hoskisson, 2005, *Strategic Management: Competitiveness and Globalization,* Cincinnati, Ohio: South-Western; M. Porter, 1985, *Competitive Advantage,* New York: Free Press.

26. M. A. Hitt, J. S. Black, & L. W. Porter, 2005, *Management,* Upper Saddle River, N.J.: Pearson Prentice Hall.

27. L.-Y. Li & G. O. Ogunmokun, 2001, Effect of export financing, resources and supply-chain skills on export competitive advantages: Implications for superior export performance, *Journal of World Business,* 36(3): 260–279.

28. J. W. Boudreau, 2003, Strategic knowledge measurement and management, in S. E. Jackson, M. A. Hitt, and A. DeNisi (eds.), *Managing Knowledge for Sustained Competitive Advantage,* San Francisco: Jossey-Bass, 330–359.

29. R. Amit & C. Zott, 2001, Creating value in e-business, *Strategic Management Journal,* 22(Special Issue): 493–520.

30. F. T. Rothaermel, M. A. Hitt, & L. Jobe, 2004, Organizing for innovation: Product portfolios, new product success, and firm performance, paper presented at the Strategic Management Society, November: San Juan, Puerto Rico.

31. M. Forney, 2003, Tug-of-war over trade, *Time,* December 22: 42–43; K. Madigan & M. J. Mandel, 2003, Outsourcing jobs: Is it bad? *Business Week,* August 25: 36–38.

32. B. Einhorn & M. Kripalani, 2003, Move over India: China is rising fast as a services outsourcing hub, *Business Week,* August 11: 42–43.

33. M. J. Leiblein, J. J. Reuer, & F. Dalsace, 2002, Do make or buy decisions matter? The influence of organizational governance and technological performance. *Strategic Management Journal,* 23: 817–833.

34. J. Greene, J. Carey, M. Arndt, & O. Port, 2003, Reinventing corporate R&D, *Business Week,* September 22: 74–76.

35. G. Ray, J. B. Barney, & W. A. Muhanna, 2004, Capabilities, business processes, and competitive advantage: Choosing the dependent variable in empirical tests of the resource-based view, *Strategic Management Journal,* 25: 23–37.

36. G. Edmondson & K. Kerwin, 2003, Can Ford fix this flat? *Business Week,* December 1: 51–52.

37. K. Kranhold, 2004, China's price for market entry: Give us your technology, too, *Wall Street Journal Online,* http://www.wsj.com, February 26.

38. C. Prystay, 2004, VW makes bet on a new class of Asian buyers, *Wall Street Journal Online,* http://www.wsj.com, March 3; B. Dolven, 2004, China grooms global players, *Wall Street Journal Online,* http://www.wsj.com, February 24.

Your Career

Understanding how resources contribute to performance is important to you personally. This importance will be particularly true when you have managerial responsibilities. For example, you are reading this book and taking the course for which the book has been assigned to increase your knowledge and skills so you can manage a unit of a firm in the near term and an entire organization later in your career. Studying strategic management increases your personal resources (your human capital). As your personal resources grow, your career opportunities are greater because you have the knowledge and skills to perform a variety of tasks and to accept jobs with greater levels of responsibility and complexity.

As a leader or manager of a work group or unit in an organization, you will be assigned tasks that you must facilitate until they are accomplished. To accomplish the tasks, you will analyze the resources you have and integrate them (for example, by assigning teams of people) to create the needed capabilities. You will then oversee the work to ensure that the tasks are completed effectively. This process begins with an understanding of resources and how they can be used to develop capabilities.

We encourage you to think about the resources you have as an individual as you prepare to either start or continue your career. In particular, what intangible assets do you possess, such as knowledge and unique work experiences? How can you combine your resources to create capabilities that will enable you to complete important organizational tasks? Which of your capabilities are likely to give you competitive advantages relative to others in the job market?

As you can see, we are proposing that you conduct an internal analysis of yourself. Doing this on a regular basis will enable you to understand what you are capable of doing to create value for customers. As a manager, you will want to complete an internal analysis of your unit to identify how you can fulfill your managerial responsibilities in ways that create value for customers. An effective knowledge of resources, capabilities, core competencies, and competitive advantages and of how to apply this knowledge could be invaluable throughout your career.

After examining the external environment for opportunities to move a company forward, business leaders must carefully examine their firm's internal organization to identify capabilities. A vision that is disconnected with the reality of internal capabilities is doomed for failure. One of the most common elements of this analysis is a review of the industry value chain and an honest assessment of how the company compares to the competition. This chapter's tool summarizes how to systematically complete this review.

The Value Chain Assessor

Activity	Importance (Low, Med, or High)	Comparison of Company's Competency to Key Competitors				
		Significantly Lower	Somewhat Lower	Neither Higher nor Lower	Somewhat Higher	Significantly Higher
After-Sales Service						
Marketing and Distribution						
Finished-Goods Inventory						
Operations						
Raw Materials Inventory						
Human Resource Management						
Research and Development						
Accounting						
Purchasing						

Watch the scene from the film *Ray*. Think of Ray Charles as a recently bought resource of Atlantic Records. While watching this scene, recall this chapter's discussion about analyzing the firm.

Jamie Foxx gives an engaging 2004 Academy Award–winning portrayal of legendary American musician Ray Charles. This engaging film tells the story of how far Ray Charles rose in music despite almost impossible odds against his success. Great performances, music, cinematography, and film editing give unbeatable cinematic entertainment. If you do not already own Ray Charles's music before watching this film, you will after you see it.

The selected scene is an edited version of the "Messing Around" sequence that appears early in the film. This scene starts after Ahmet Ertugen (Curtis Armstrong) met Ray Charles in his Harlem apartment in 1952. He tells Charles that his company, Atlantic Records, bought Charles's contract from Swingtime. Charles has gone to an Atlantic Records studio to try some recordings. Ahmet and others in the control room have noted that Ray sounds like Nat King Cole or Charles Brown and does not have a unique sound.

The scene begins with Ahmet coming into the studio. Charles says, "Ahmet, What you think of that?" This scene ends with Charles starting his version of "The Mess Around." The film continues with its engaging chronicle of Ray Charles and his musical career.

What to Watch for and Ask Yourself

1. Is Ray Charles a tangible or intangible resource of Atlantic Records?
2. What are Ray Charles's strengths and weaknesses?
3. What capabilities and core competencies does Ray Charles bring to Atlantic Records?

Mini-Case

Wal-Mart versus the World: Can a Firm Have Too Many Resources?

Wal-Mart is the largest retailer in the world, with total annual sales revenue that is 50 percent higher than the combined annual sales of Target, Costco, and Sears Holding Corp. (the merger of Sears and Kmart). Wal-Mart is also the world's largest private employer, with 1.5 million employees. As of spring 2004, it had 3,500 stores around the globe. For 2004, Wal-Mart's sales volume was $287 billion.

The size of Wal-Mart's operations provides a number of benefits, especially economies of scale and market power. Both help the firm hold down costs and offer customers the lowest possible prices. As its size implies, Wal-Mart also has a reservoir of resources that enable it to enter markets in a big way. For example, in 2004, Wal-Mart acquired the Bompreco supermarket chain in Brazil. With this acquisition, Wal-Mart became the third-largest grocery chain in Brazil, with a total of 143 stores (13 supercenters, 10 Sam's Club stores, and two Todo Dia stores). Because of its global size and market power, Wal-Mart's foothold in Brazil places significant pressure on the two largest grocery chains in that country—Comapanhia Brasileira de Distribuico (based in Brazil) and Carrefour SA (based in France).

Bringing products to customers at lower prices is positive, but critics complain that Wal-Mart may not always use its resources in the correct manner. For example, some critics claim that Wal-Mart slashes prices with the intention of driving out competitors. This may be the case in the toy market. Wal-Mart has become the largest toy retailer in the United States, ahead of competitors Toys "R" Us, Target, KB Toys, and Kmart. In 2003, some argued that Wal-Mart intentionally lowered its prices on toys to capture Christmas sales and damage its competitors. The competitors are searching for other ways to compete because they cannot match Wal-Mart's economies of scale.

Although Wal-Mart's efficient use of its resources allows it to contribute to low inflation and growing productivity in the United States (and globally), some criticize Wal-Mart's practices with its employees and suppliers. For example, the firm is being investigated for knowingly using contractors who employ undocumented workers. Others have accused Wal-Mart of not promoting women relative to men in key positions, denying overtime pay to employees who have earned it, and prohibiting many of its employees from being covered by health-care benefits.

Others believe that Wal-Mart uses its substantial purchasing power when dealing with its suppliers. However, although Wal-Mart agrees that it pressures suppliers to provide low costs, it argues that doing so makes those suppliers more efficient and productive. This has been the case for Procter and Gamble (P&G). As noted in the "Focusing on Strategy" in this chapter, P&G "takes mundane products and make them so glamorous and distinctive that the world's largest retailer won't be able to resist them." But others suggest that Wal-Mart often goes too far. For example, it is alleged that Wal-Mart pressured Vlasic to sell pickles to it at cut-rate prices. Wal-Mart then sold the pickles for the very low price of $2.97 for a gallon jar. Vlasic had developed its brand image based on premium pickles and priced them accordingly in much smaller containers. Yet when Wal-Mart started selling Vlasic pickles, it sold 240,000 gallons of them per week. Although this meant large sales for Vlasic, it harmed the sales of Vlasic pickles elsewhere. Eventually, the company had to file for bankruptcy. Although many factors contributed to Vlasic's bankruptcy, Wal-Mart's approach of being able to use its massive resources to its advantage seemingly added to Vlasic difficulties.

SOURCES: S. Ellison, A. Zimmerman, C. Forelle, 2005, P&G's Gillette edge: The playbook it honed at Wal-Mart, *Wall Street Journal,* January 31, A1, A12; J. E. Garten, 2004, Wal-Mart gives globalism a bad name, *Business Week,* March 8: 24; A. Welsh & A. Zimmerman, 2004, Wal-Mart snaps up Brazilian chain, *Wall Street Journal Online,* http://www.wsj.com, March 2; C. Fishman, 2003, The Wal-Mart you don't know, *Fast Company,* December: 68–80; D. Fonda, 2003, Will Wal-Mart steal Christmas? *Time,* December 8: 54–55.

Questions

1. What are Wal-Mart's major resources and capabilities? In addition to facts included in the Mini-Case, go to Wal-Mart's Web site (http://www.walmart.com) to obtain additional information.
2. Is it bad for Wal-Mart to use its resources to significantly outperform its competitors? Why or why not?
3. Are Wal-Mart's actions regarding Vlasic an example of inappropriate behavior with suppliers? Please explain your answer.

EXPERIENTIAL EXERCISES

EXERCISE ONE: VALUE CHAINS AND COMPETENCIES

Organize into at least five groups (if you need more groups, have different groups do the same company), making sure that there are members in each group from different functional discipline majors (accounting, marketing, finance, management, information systems, etc.).

Each group should draw the value chain of the following five companies:

- Disney
- General Motors
- Nike
- McDonalds
- Starbucks

Highlight any elements of each value chain that you think represent areas in which the firm has a core competence. Be able to defend your selection by showing that the capability satisfies all four requirements of a core competence. Also, indicate any outsourced functions and explain why these have been taken out of the value chain.

When the class reassembles, compare value chains and defend your choices.

EXERCISE TWO: SWOT ANALYSIS

Read a case assigned for the class period or the Mini-Case in the chapter that presents the opportunity to create a simple strengths-weaknesses-opportunities-threats (SWOT) analysis as the basis for recommending some change in strategy. Half the class, in small groups of three to five, will prepare a list of strengths and opportunities, while the other half of the class will prepare a list of weaknesses and threats. Have the groups share their SWOT analyses with the class to build a shared understanding of their meanings. Next, groups must develop opposing arguments for their positions—for example, why is the specific strength they identified also a weakness? Students will learn to recognize that most attributes of the firm and its environment are double-edged; that is, they have a strength side and a weakness side or an opportunity side and a threat side.

Strategy

Business-Level Strategy

Reading and studying this chapter should enable you to:

1_
Define business-level strategy.

2_
Define and explain the differences among five business-level strategies.

3_
Describe how to successfully use each business-level strategy.

4_
Identify the risks of each business-level strategy.

5_
Describe the structures to use to implement each business-level strategy.

Focusing on Strategy

Brown: "How Can We Help You Today?"

"We'd lost track of whole trainloads of cars. It was crazy." (Jerry Reynolds, president, Prestige Ford, Garland, Texas)

This comment from a person running a car dealership highlights what was once a serious problem. The problem was that Ford Motor Company typically wasn't able to tell dealers exactly which cars and trucks were being shipped to them or when they would arrive. Put yourself into Reynolds' shoes: Can you imagine trying to run a business without knowing what you were going to have available to sell to customers and when?

To correct its distribution problem, Ford turned to United Parcel Service (UPS) for help. Based on information and data provided by Jerry Reynolds and other U.S. dealers, UPS engineers redesigned Ford's entire North American delivery network. The redesign involved UPS streamlining the routes taken by cars and trucks from Ford's factories as well as the processing procedures at regional sorting hubs before the vehicles are sent to their final destinations.

Have these changes helped Ford? To date, the answer to this question is a resounding "Yes!" The delivery network UPS designed for Ford has reduced the time it takes for cars and trucks to arrive at dealer locations by 40 percent. This time reduction enables dealers to receive vehicles much more quickly while saving Ford money. Thus, cars and trucks spend less time being transported and more time in front of prospective customers. What UPS accomplished for Ford was no small feat, given that the UPS-designed network is delivering more than four million cars annually from Ford's 19 North American manufacturing facilities. In describing the results of UPS's work, Jerry Reynolds said, "It was the most amazing transformation I had ever seen."

UPS's Supply Chain Solutions group is responsible for the redesign of Ford's distribution network. This fast-growing UPS business unit provides logistics and distribution services, international trade management, and transportation and freight services using multimodal transportation. Analysts believe that this business unit could be the fastest growing of UPS's business operations for some time to come. UPS wants to use this business unit to "serve as the traffic manager for Corporate America's sprawling distribution networks," which would enable UPS to provide a variety of new services to customers, including the scheduling of planes, ships, and trains on which goods are shipped. This has opened a new area of business for UPS—services—in addition to its standard delivery business. UPS is using its decades-long experience in managing its own global delivery network as the foundation for understanding how to help other companies solve their distribution woes. Its proprietary distribution-related skills enable UPS to provide services to customers that its competitors are not able to imitate. UPS is spending large sums of money to upgrade its capabilities so it can continue to provide superior logistics services to its clients.

SOURCES: D. Foust, 2004, Big Brown's new bag, *Business Week,* July 19, 54–56; 2004, United Parcel Service, *Argus Research,* https://argusresearch.com, July 15; United Parcel Service, Inc., *Callard Research,* https://www.callardresearch.com, July 9.

*
business-level strategy

an action plan the firm develops to describe how it will compete in its chosen industry or market segment

In Chapter 1, we defined *strategy* as an action plan designed to move an organization toward achievement of its vision. The different types of strategies firms use to do this are shown in Figure 1.1 in Chapter 1.

Business-level strategy, the topic of this chapter, is one of the types of strategies firms develop to achieve their vision. A **business-level strategy** is an action plan the firm develops to describe how it will compete in its chosen industry or market segment. A business-level strategy describes how the firm will compete in the marketplace on a day-by-day basis and how it intends to "do things right."[1] UPS's Supply Chain Solutions group has a business-level strategy as does each of UPS's other business units (such as UPS Consulting, UPS Air Cargo, and Mail Boxes Etc.).[2] Additional information about UPS's business units is presented in the next chapter's "Focusing on Strategy."

A firm's main objective in using a business-level strategy is to consistently provide a good or service to customers that they will buy because it creates more value (in the form of performance characteristics or price) for them than does a competitor's good or service. This is illustrated in "Focusing on Strategy" in this chapter which describes Ford's satisfaction with the new delivery system designed by UPS's Supply Chain Solutions group. A business-level strategy is most successful when everybody in the firm fully understands the chosen strategy[3] and when it is used with relentless zeal and efficiency.[4] In other words, firms must be precise in describing what they seek to accomplish with their strategy. The strategy must "connect" with the target customers as well. For example, the goal of BMW North America's business-level strategy is clear: "to be the leader in every premium segment of the international automotive industry."[5] Of course, as is the case with all of the firm's strategies, ethical practices should guide how the business-level strategy is used.[6] Often, a firm's intended ethical practices are made public by recording them in written documents such as a code of ethics, a code of conduct, and a corporate creed. The statements in these documents signal to stakeholders how the firm intends to interact with them. This means that a firm's employees are expected to adhere to the behaviors specified in these documents.

A business-level strategy is intended to help the firm focus its efforts so it can satisfy a group of customers.[7] In the case of BMW North America, the group of customers to be satisfied is the one wanting to purchase a high-quality vehicle that is different from "average" automobiles. Customers are satisfied when a firm's product creates value for them.[8] An effective business-level strategy has a clear statement of the value to be created for customers. This point is illustrated by the founding of Wal-Mart. Through the strategic leadership of Sam Walton, its founder, Wal-Mart initially formed a business-level strategy that was intended to offer a large assortment of many different products, at very low prices, to consumers living in towns with a population no greater than 25,000.[9] Thus, for early Wal-Mart customers, the value this firm provided to them was the opportunity to buy goods at prices that were always lower than the prices of those goods from locally owned stores. Everyone working at Wal-Mart understood the value the firm was creating for its customers, which helped the firm effectively implement its chosen business-level strategy. In addition, by comparison shopping and then buying from Wal-Mart, customers quickly understood the value the firm was providing to them in the form of lower prices on a wide assortment of items.

We fully discuss five business-level strategies in this chapter. These five strategies are sometimes referred to as *generic* because they are used in all industries and by all types of firms. A properly chosen business-level strategy favorably positions the firm relative to the competitive forces we talked about in Chapter 3. Being effectively positioned enables the firm to simultaneously create value for customers and returns for shareholders. We also use the value chain (see Chapter 4) to show the primary and support activities that are required to successfully use each business-level strategy. Not surprisingly, the firm accepts some risks when it decides to use a particular business-level strategy. We also discuss the risks of each type of strategy. Strategic leaders ensure that these risks are carefully monitored so the firm will recognize when it is time to make changes to its business-level strategy. As we discuss in "Understanding Strategy," JCPenney has changed its business-level strategy to improve its performance. In this chapter, we also describe the particular organizational structure (defined later in the chapter) that should be used to effectively implement each generic strategy. Because it affects the behavior of individual employees, the responsibilities assigned to them, and the leadership style they experience, organizational structure is an important aspect of how business-level strategies are implemented.

As the JCPenney example shows, a firm's business-level strategy is never set in stone. As an action plan, a business-level strategy is a living document that is

understanding strategy:

CHANGING FOR THE BETTER AT JCPENNEY

"The turnaround story is in the sixth inning and continues to be fueled by technology, merchandising and marketing initiatives that will drive and sustain margin improvements going forward." This comment from an industry analyst is great news for those interested in JCPenney's success.

© Neal Hamberg/Bloomberg News/Landov

ute a wide assortment of items at lower prices and with a level of service that was at least comparable to some firms, including JCPenney. In essence, JCPenney's poor financial performance during the 1990s resulted from the firm's inability to compete against competitors who had used their re-

But this analyst paints a picture that is strikingly different from what was said about the firm's fortunes beginning in roughly the 1990s. Let's see how this firm has emerged from less-than-desirable performances to again become an impressive retailer.

According to company documents, JCPenney has always aspired to be the customers' first choice when buying the goods and services it offers. Moreover, the firm claims that it always had a single goal—"to serve the public as nearly as we can to its complete satisfaction." The breadth of this goal, though, contributed to JCPenney's loss of customers in the 1990s. Think of it this way. The "general" public is certainly a broad target market with multiple needs. This is why mass merchandisers, which is what JCPenney was from the time of its founding until about five years ago, carry a wide assortment of merchandise. Clothing for all members of a family, tools for the person wanting to handle repairs around the household, lawn mowers, refrigerators, perfumes, lawn equipment, and sporting goods are just some of the items a mass merchandiser stocks to satisfy the "general" public's needs. However, discount retailers such as Wal-Mart and Target had developed core competencies that enabled them to distrib-

sources and capabilities to form core competencies that enabled them to better serve the needs of the "general" public.

What was JCPenney to do to improve its situation? A first step, newly appointed top-level managers concluded, was for JCPenney to identify a specific target market and thus shed its image as a mass merchandiser. Today, JCPenney is a moderately-priced department store chain serving the needs of middle-class consumers (households with income ranging from $30,000 to $80,000). In particular, the firm is concentrating on serving middle-class women between the ages of 35 and 54. Focusing on middle-class consumers' needs, JCPenney now provides competitive, fashionable assortments of merchandise. For 35–54 year-old women, JCPenney is offering what it calls "dressy causal" clothing items. Thus, JCPenney has changed its target customer from the "general public" to middle-class consumers. This means that JCPenney's market scope is now narrower than it was previously.

To present the firm's new assortments of merchandise to middle-class consumers in the most positive manner, JCPenney stores have been refurbished; the firm's marketing program is also thought to be more vibrant and certainly more oriented to telling its target customers exactly how its products can satisfy their needs. To support this change from being a mass merchandiser to a moderately priced department store chain, JCPenney is emphasizing its human capital. The firm has hired experienced personnel and continuously trains its workforce—a

SOURCES: E. Byron, 2005, New Penney: Chain goes for "missing middle," *Wall Street Journal Online,* http://www.wjs.com, February 14; M. Halkias, 2004, So far, so good. *Dallas Morning News,* October 19: D1, D12; 2004, JCPenney Home Page, Short history of JCPenney, http://www.jcpenney.com, October 23; 2004, JCPenney Company, Inc., *Standard & Poor's Stock Report,* http://www.standardandpoors.com, October 16.

workforce the firm's executives see as the key to providing maximum satisfaction for its customers. The firm has developed a new distribution channel network to make certain that its products are delivered to its stores in a timely manner. Today, JCPenney is able to create value in the distribution part of the value chain while only a few short years ago, its distribution channel was a source of competitive disadvantage. For 2005, JCPenney was expected to reach profit margins of six to eight percent, something that was unthinkable at the end of the 1990s.

constantly subject to changes based on opportunities and threats emerging in the firm's external environment as well as changes in the competitive advantages that are a product of the resources, capabilities, and core competencies in the firm's internal environment.

Types of Business-Level Strategies

Firms choose from five business-level strategies: *cost leadership, differentiation, focused cost leadership, focused differentiation,* and *integrated cost leadership/differentiation* (see Figure 5.1). As shown in this figure, the firm's business-level strategy has two key dimensions—competitive advantage and competitive scope. This means that the business-level strategy the firm chooses is a function of its competitive advantage (either cost or uniqueness) and the breadth (either broad or narrow) of the target market it wishes to serve. When using the cost leadership or differentiation strategy, the firm seeks to apply its competitive advantage in many customer segments. When using either focused cost leadership or focused differentiation, the firm uses its cost advantage or its uniqueness advantage in narrower market segments. Specifically, with focus strategies, the firm "selects a segment or group of segments in the industry and tailors its strategy to serving them to the exclusion of others."[10]

Procter & Gamble's Tide soap is an example of a product that has a broad target market, while Porsche's 911 Carrera is designed to serve the needs of a narrow group of customers.[11] Each firm's decision about competitive scope (broad or narrow) is influenced by opportunities and threats in its external environment. Interestingly, though, the fact that markets today are increasingly being segmented into smaller and smaller groups with clearly identifiable needs[12] is affecting firms' decisions about competitive scope. A *market segment*

FIGURE 5.1 Five Business-Level Strategies

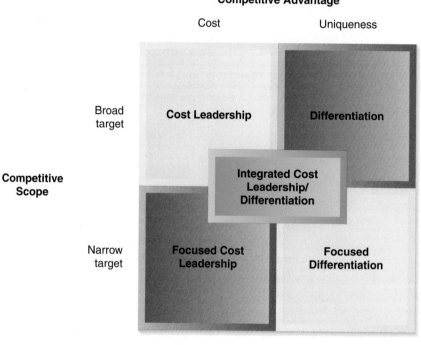

is a group of people with similar needs with respect to certain variables such as price, quality, and product features. Segmenting markets into smaller and smaller groups with similar needs can be a threat to firms with a relatively standardized product serving the needs of multiple customer segments. Tide, for example, in terms of competitive scope, is designed to fit a broad target market. Simultaneously, though, being able to identify people with a specific need that isn't being satisfied by the product aimed at a broad target market creates opportunities for other firms. For instance, a company named SoapWorks produces a laundry detergent as well as other hypoallergenic cleansing products for people who want to avoid the types of chemicals in products such as Tide that are targeted to broader customer segments.[13]

In general, a firm's competitive advantages enable it either to produce standardized products at lower costs than those of their competitors or to produce unique products that differ from competitors' products in ways that create value for customers. In the first instance, the firm has a *cost competitive advantage* while in the second it has a *uniqueness competitive advantage* (see Figure 5.1).

By *standardized* products, we mean products that are widely available and have a large customer demand. Think of automobile tires as an example. We all need tires for our vehicles, such as cars, trucks, and motorcycles. Cooper Tire & Rubber is known for producing relatively inexpensive (yet reliable) tires for cars and trucks. Cooper can do this because its production, distribution, and service costs are lower than those of its rivals (such as Michelin, Goodyear, and Pirelli). Cooper remains committed to being lean in all of its operations as a way of continuously holding its costs down relative to competitors' costs.[14]

Unique products have features different from or in addition to the standardized product's features. SoapWorks' products, for example, are made without certain chemicals that some customers believe may harm users' health. As another example, although more expensive than beers designed for the broad target market, Guinness believes that its beers "awaken the taste buds in the consumer's mouth."[15] Guinness beers are more expensive because Guinness targets customers who may be willing to pay more for what some perceive to be a distinctive taste—a taste that is more expensive to produce. Let's turn our attention to learning about each of the five generic business-level strategies.

Cost Leadership Strategy

cost leadership strategy

an action plan the firm develops to produce goods or services at the lowest cost

A **cost leadership strategy** is an action plan the firm develops to produce goods or services at the lowest cost.[16] Producing at the lowest cost enables the firm to price its product lower than competitors can, and therefore gain a larger share of its target market. Firms using the cost leadership strategy sell standardized products to the industry's typical or "average" customer because this is usually the largest target segment. Thus, Cooper Tire & Rubber intends to sell its tires to the customer with "average" or "typical" needs. Successful use of the cost leadership strategy across time results when the firm continuously finds ways to lower its costs relative to competitors' costs by constantly thinking about how the costs of its primary activities and support activities could be lowered without damaging the functionality of its products. Firms implementing the cost leadership strategy have strong process engineering skills, emphasize manufacturing processes permitting efficient production of products, have performance evaluation systems that reward employees on the quantity of their output, and know how to buy raw materials needed to produce their products at low costs.

In Chapter 4, we described how firms use value-chain analysis to identify the primary activities and support activities in which they are able to create value. In Figure 5.2, we show how the cost leader could create value in each primary activity and in each support activity. A firm does not need to outperform competitors in every one of these activities to successfully use the cost leadership strategy; however, the more primary and support activities in which the firm can outperform its competitors, the more likely that its costs will be lower than its competitors' costs.

Effective use of the cost leadership strategy positions the firm in the marketplace in a way that enables it to create value for customers, especially through lower prices. Also, as we describe in the next five subsections, effectively implementing the cost leadership strategy enables a firm to establish a strong market position relative to the five competitive forces we introduced in Chapter 3.

FIGURE 5.2 Examples of Value-Creating Activities Associated with the Cost Leadership Strategy

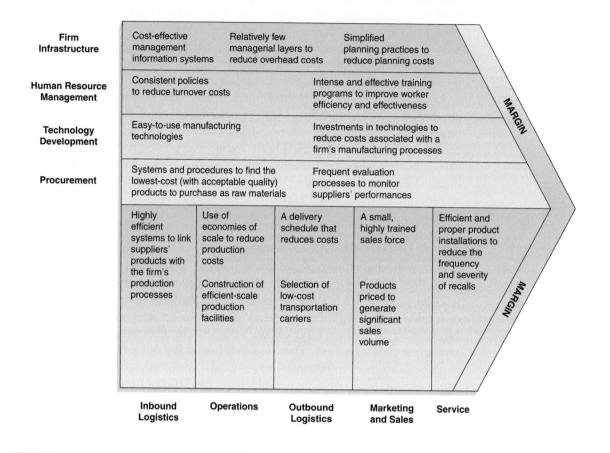

Rivalry with Existing Competitors

Competitors find it extremely difficult to compete on the basis of price against the cost leader. To meet the cost leader's sales price, a competing firm must reduce its profit margins when selling its products. In turn, lower margins leave that firm with less capital to invest to improve its operational efficiency. Therefore, competing on the basis of price against the cost leader places a competitor in a cycle of falling farther and farther behind in terms of efficiency and cost reductions. Kmart encountered this competitive circumstance when trying to compete against cost leader Wal-Mart on the basis of price. Kmart's cost structure, compared to Wal-Mart's, was higher. The higher cost structure prevented

Kmart from being able to offer products at prices as low as Wal-Mart's. Having emerged from bankruptcy, Kmart no longer attempts to compete against Wal-Mart on the basis of costs and product prices. Instead, the firm is changing its product mix to reduce the degree to which it competes directly with cost leader Wal-Mart.[17] Moreover, the proposed merger between Kmart and Sears (announced in late 2004) makes it even less likely that Kmart will directly compete against Wal-Mart.

Bargaining Power of Buyers (Customers)

As buyers, customers can exercise power against the cost leader under several conditions, but especially if they purchase a large quantity of the cost leader's output. The cost leader successfully positions itself against buyers' potential power by selling to a large number of buyers to avoid becoming dependent on any one customer for a significant portion of its sales.

Bargaining Power of Suppliers

A supplier can exercise power over the cost leader if it provides a significant amount of a key input to the cost leader's production process. Firms dependent on key natural resources to produce their products when sources of supply are limited may have to pay higher prices. Airline companies, for example, are highly dependent on aviation fuel, a product that is sold by a relatively small number of firms. Successfully positioned cost leaders try to develop long-term contracts with a number of suppliers at favorable rates to reduce the potential of suppliers raising their prices, which would affect the cost leader's position in terms of costs. Cost leader Southwest Airlines is quite savvy about forming long-term contracts with fuel suppliers. These contracts often keep Southwest's fuel costs lower than those of its competitors.

Potential Entrants

The favorably positioned cost leader operates at a level of efficiency that can't be matched by firms thinking of entering the industry in which the cost leader is well established. The cost leader's ability to continuously drive its costs lower and lower while still satisfying customers' needs makes it very difficult for potential entrants to the market to compete against the cost leader.

Product Substitutes

A *product substitute* is a product that can replace the focal product because it has essentially the same functionality. For example, NutraSweet is a replacement or substitute for sugar. To compete against a cost leader, though, a substitute must offer something in addition to the same functionality. This "something different" could be a lower purchase price (which is unlikely when competing against the cost leader) or a feature that customers value that isn't a part of the cost leader's product. (As you know, NutraSweet's "something different" is a taste similar to that of sugar but without sugar's calories.) The successfully positioned cost leader thwarts product substitutes by lowering the purchase price of its product, which makes it difficult for a substitute to attract the attention of the cost leader's customers.

Competitive Risks of the Cost Leadership Strategy

The cost leadership strategy has two major risks. First, competitors' innovations may enable them to produce their good or service at a cost that is lower than that of the cost leader. For the price-conscious, "typical" consumer, the lower cost is attractive. Second, concentrating too much on reducing costs may eventually find the cost leader offering a product at very low prices to customers who are less inclined to purchase it. While the cost leader must keep its costs down, it can't lose contact with its customers to the point that it fails to fully understand changes in customers' expectations relative to the product in terms of price and features. At some point, for example, customers wanting to buy low-cost products may become willing to pay more for additional features such as increased product safety and extended product warranties. The cost leader must stay in close touch with its customers so it will be able to detect changes in their needs.

Differentiation Strategy

*

differentiation strategy

an action plan the firm develops to produce goods or services that customers perceive as being unique in ways that are important to them

A **differentiation strategy** is an action plan the firm develops to produce goods or services that customers perceive as being unique in ways that are important to them. UPS's Supply Chain Solutions business unit, discussed in this chapter's "Focusing on Strategy," uses a differentiation strategy.

The "uniqueness" a firm provides when using the differentiation strategy may be physical or psychological. It can be created by the way in which the firm uses one or more of either the primary activities or the support activities. Product durability, ease of repair, and superior installation services are examples of physical sources of differentiation. Perceptions of the quality of service after the sale and of the courtesy of salespeople are examples of sources of psychological differentiation. Think of differentiated products you buy. Are the sources of these products' differentiation physical or psychological? Does the source of differentiation make a difference to you as long as the product you buy creates the unique value you want?

The cost leader serves an industry's typical or average customer. In contrast, the firm using the differentiation strategy serves customers who want to buy a good or service that is different from the good or service purchased by an industry's typical or average customer. Think of goods offered by Ralph Lauren as an example of differentiated items. The logo appearing on many of the firm's clothing products is one way these goods differ from those made for the clothing industry's typical customer. In addition to the logo, the firm's dress shirts for men, for example, are made of high-quality raw materials and lack a pocket. The logo, the materials, and the absence of a pocket are differentiated features that create value for customers desiring to wear something other than a "typical" dress shirt.

Think about goods and services (cars and clothes, for example) that you believe are different from those serving the typical customers in an industry. In all likelihood, you'll conclude that the ways goods and services can differ from one another are virtually endless. Different tastes, responsive customer service, product design, alternative distribution methods, and customer loyalty programs are but a few examples of how goods or services can offer unique value to customers.

© TANNEN MAURY/Bloomberg News/Landov

Pottery Barn started in 1949 as a single store in lower Manhattan and now has stores in more than 40 states. Are its loyal customers buying more than furniture?

Pottery Barn is another example of a firm using the differentiation strategy. The firm is known for the eclectic mix of its products, clever merchandising, and first-rate customer service as ways that its goods and services differ from those offered to the furniture industry's typical customer. The combination of these differentiated features has created a loyal group of customers who want to be a part of the Pottery Barn lifestyle, as suggested by an analyst who believes that Pottery Barn "has built a furniture brand into a lifestyle brand in a way that nobody else has done."[18]

The value chain can be used to highlight the primary and support activities where value should be created to use the differentiation strategy. The focus here is for the firm to emphasize the primary and support activities shown in Figure 5.3 to create more value than competitors can create for customers. This means, of course, that the firm using the differentiation strategy wants to develop core competencies in one or more of the primary and support activities. The more unique value the firm can create for customers, the more likely that the firm will be able to successfully use the differentiation strategy.

Next, we explain how the firm effectively using the differentiation strategy is able to position itself in the marketplace. In the next five subsections, we explain how an effective differentiation strategy results in a strong market position for the firm by countering each of the five competitive forces discussed in Chapter 3.

Rivalry with Existing Competitors

Customers tend to be loyal buyers of products that create unique value for them. Because of this, firms using the differentiation strategy do everything they can to increase the loyalty of their customers. With increasing loyalty, customer sensitivity to the price of the product they are buying is reduced. This is important, because the firm using the differentiation strategy needs to establish large profit margins on its products to earn the resources required to continuously reinvest in its products so that the valued sources of difference can be maintained. Think of it this way: providing differentiated goods and services can be expensive. The firm needs to earn high returns on what it sells to be able to pay for the costs of creating differentiated features while producing its products.

Bargaining Power of Buyers (Customers)

The uniqueness of a differentiated good or service reduces customers' sensitivity to the product's price. Firms using the differentiation strategy continuously stress the uniqueness of their products to customers (often through advertising campaigns) to reduce their sensitivity to price. Think of the Lexus slogan of "The Relentless Pursuit of Perfection" as an example. Toyota, the manufacturer of Lexus products,[19] is signaling to the customer that while the product's price is higher than that of cars aimed at the typical customer, the Lexus is a superior product because it is made by people seeking perfection in their work. When a

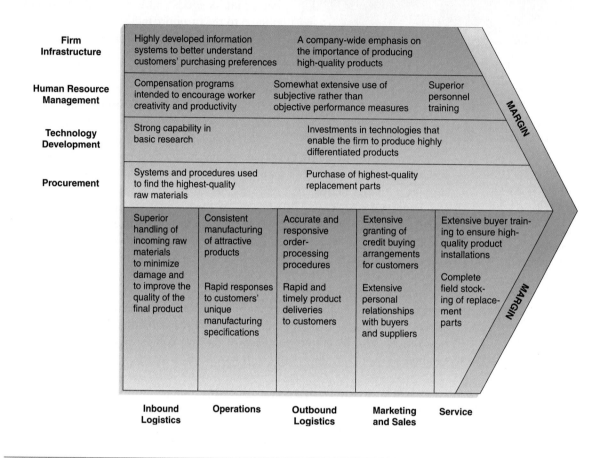

firm's effort to emphasize product uniqueness is successful, customers' sensitivity to price will be reduced, thus enabling the firm to continue selling its products at a price that permits constant reinvestment in the products' differentiated features.

Bargaining Power of Suppliers

The firm using the differentiation strategy typically pays a premium price for the raw materials used to make its product. For a good, this means that some of the raw materials will be expensive (think of high-quality cotton used to make expensive, yet differentiated clothing items). Alternatively, for a service, the firm may pay a premium price to hire highly talented employees (think of the consultants McKinsey & Company must hire to provide differentiated service to its clients). However, the returns earned from a premium sales price of a differentiated good or service yields the funds the firm would need to pay its suppliers' higher prices. In addition to this, a firm providing goods or services that create differentiated value to customers may be able to pass supplier price increases on to its satisfied and loyal customers in the form of higher prices.

Potential Entrants

Customer loyalty and the need to provide customers with more value than an existing firm's product provides to them are strong challenges for those thinking about competing against a firm successfully using the differentiation strategy. Customer loyalty is hard to earn (doesn't a firm have to consistently meet your needs for quite a while before you'll become loyal to it?), meaning that a new entrant typically faces a long battle. In addition, the established firm has the margins necessary to reinvest in ways that will further enhance the differentiated value it creates for customers, making it even more difficult for a new competitor to compete against it.

Product Substitutes

It is difficult for competitors to create substitute products that will satisfy loyal customers of a firm that provides them differentiated value in the form of a good or service. Perceived unique value is hard to replace, even when a product substitute has a better performance-to-price ratio that favors substitution. Think of a good or service to which you have a great loyalty. What would it take for you to switch to a product substitute? For most of us, it would take a lot to get us to switch to a substitute when we are satisfied with the product we've been buying for perhaps a long time. Thus, firms with loyal customers tend to be insulated from competitors' substitute products that are intended to provide different value to the focal firm's customers.

Competitive Risks of the Differentiation Strategy

The differentiation strategy is not risk free. The first risk is that customers may decide that the price they are paying for a product's differentiated features is too high. This can happen especially when a cost leader learns how to add some differentiated features to its product without significantly raising the product's price. When this occurs, the customers buying the differentiated product may decide that the value being received is simply too expensive relative to the combination of some differentiation and low cost of the cost leader's good or service. A second risk is that the source of differentiation being provided by the firm may cease to create value for the target customers. For example, men buying Ralph Lauren dress shirts might conclude that the logo, lack of a pocket, and high-quality cotton no longer provide value for which they are willing to pay. Customer experiences are the third risk; by using a differentiated product and comparing its performance with lower-cost alternatives, the customer may conclude that the cost of the differentiation isn't acceptable. When first introduced, the IBM brand name enabled the firm to charge premium prices for its personal computers (PCs). However, through experience, many customers learned that the performance of competitors' lower-priced products was virtually equivalent to that of the IBM PC. Finally, differentiated products run the risk of being somewhat effectively counterfeited. Haven't many of us seen counterfeit purses, wallets, watches, and jewelry offered by street vendors?

Some of us may have even purchased one of these products! Although of much lower quality, the counterfeit product that looks like "the real thing" can be appealing, even for the customer capable of buying the true differentiated product. Here, the customer thinks about why he or she should pay the higher price for "the real thing" when the counterfeit product looks about as good.

Focus Strategies

A **focus strategy** is an action plan the firm develops to produce goods or services to serve the needs of a specific market segment. Therefore, focus strategies serve a narrower segment within a broader market. Firms using the focus strategy intend to serve the needs of a narrow customer segment better than their needs can be met by the firm targeting its products to the broad market (see Figure 5.1). A particular buyer group (such as teenagers, senior citizens, or working women), a specific segment of a product line (such as professional painters rather than "do-it-yourself" painters), and particular geographic markets (such as the West Coast or the East Coast of the United States) are examples of different target market segments on which a firm might focus. Recall that SoapWorks serves the segment of the household cleaning products' market that wants to buy hypoallergenic products. The firm uses either the focused cost leadership strategy or the focused differentiation strategy to successfully serve the needs of a narrow market segment.

Focused Cost Leadership Strategy

The **focused cost leadership strategy** is an action plan the firm develops to produce goods or services for a narrow market segment at the lowest cost. Based in Sweden, Ikea uses the focused cost leadership strategy.

Ikea is a global furniture retailer with locations in more than 30 countries. Some of you reading this book may be customers Ikea is targeting, in that the firm focuses on young buyers desiring style at a low cost.[20] Ikea offers home furnishings with good design and function and acceptable quality at low prices to young buyers who, according to Ikea's research, aren't wealthy, work for a living, and want to shop at hours beyond those typically available from firms serving the broad furniture market.

To successfully use its focused cost leadership strategy, Ikea concentrates on lowering its costs and understanding its customers' needs. According to the firm, "low cost is always in focus. This applies to every phase of our activities."[21] To keep the firm's costs low, Ikea's engineers design low-cost modular furniture that customers can easily assemble. To appeal to young buyers, who often are short of time and are inexperienced when it comes to buying furniture, Ikea arranges its products by rooms instead of by products. These configurations enable customers to see different living combinations (complete with sofas, chairs, tables, and so forth) in a single setting.

Focused Differentiation Strategy

The **focused differentiation strategy** is an action plan the firm develops to produce goods or services that a narrow group of customers perceive as being unique in ways that are important to them. Thomas Pink is a business unit of LVMH Moet Hennessy Louis Vuitton, which produces clothing and apparel.

All of LVMH's business units, including Thomas Pink, use the focused differentiation strategy. Recently, Thomas Pink introduced men's shirts made of 170-count cotton. This count of cotton is quite high and is the main way the product is differentiated in the marketplace (in comparison, a T-shirt from Old Navy is made of 18-count cotton). When introduced, these shirts were priced at $195 each. What unique value does a 170-count cotton shirt provide to a customer? According to a company official, one of these shirts helps a man "feel comfortable and confident in himself. This could be the one shirt he wears to board meetings."[22] Thus, this shirt is targeted to a very narrow target market—men who have achieved a great deal of success in corporate settings and who want to feel comfortable about the shirt they are wearing.

To successfully use either focus strategy, the firm must perform many of the value chain's primary and support activities in ways that enable it to create more value than competitors can create for a narrow group of target customers. The specific activities required to successfully use the focused cost leadership strategy are identical to those shown in Figure 5.2, while the activities needed to be successful with the focused differentiation strategy parallel those shown in Figure 5.3. The difference in the value chains shown in these two figures is that each activity is performed with a narrow market instead of a broad market segment in mind. Therefore, Figures 5.2 and 5.3 and the text regarding the five competitive forces describe how a firm successfully using one of the focus strategies is favorably positioned against the five competitive forces. However, to maintain its favorable position, the firm must continually drive its costs lower compared to competitors when using the focused cost leadership strategy and continue to find ways to differentiate its product in ways that are meaningful to the target customers when using the focused differentiation strategy.

Designers reevaluate their focus strategies each season in order to compete. These models are showing the Polo Ralph Lauren fall collection.

© AP Photo/Richard Drew

Competitive Risks of Focus Strategies

Using a focus strategy carries several risks. First, a competitor may learn how to "outfocus" the focusing firm. For example, Charles Tyrwhitt Shirts is using its skills to try to outfocus Thomas Pink in men's high-quality dress shirts. Tyrwhitt introduced a 180-count cotton shirt priced at $160, creating significant competition for Thomas Pink.[23] Second, a company serving the broad target market may decide that the target market being served by the focusing firm is attractive. Ralph Lauren, for instance, could introduce a dress shirt with a cotton count lower than that used by Thomas Pink and Charles Tyrwhitt and a slightly lower price. Ralph Lauren could rely on its brand image to entice its competitors' customers to try its dress shirt. Finally, the needs of the narrow target customer may change and become very similar to those of the broad market. Increases in their disposable income and experience with buying furniture might change some of Ikea's young buyers' needs to those that can be satisfied by a firm serving the broad market.

Integrated Cost Leadership/Differentiation Strategy

The **integrated cost leadership/differentiation strategy** is an action plan the firm develops to produce goods or services with strong emphasis on both differentiation and low cost. With this strategy, firms produce products that have some differentiated features (but not as many as offered by firms using the differentiation strategy) and that are produced at a low cost (but not at a cost as low as those of the firm using the cost leadership strategy). This strategy can be used to serve the needs of a broad target market or a narrow target market. McDonald's uses this strategy to serve the needs of a broad market, while Anon uses it to focus on the needs of a narrow target market. (Anon makes semicustomized rooftop air-conditioning systems for large customers such as The Home Depot, Wal-Mart, and Target.) Because the integrated cost leadership/differentiation strategy requires firms to be somewhat differentiated while producing at relatively low costs, firms must develop the flexibility needed to serve both of these objectives.

The possibility of being "neither fish nor fowl" is the main risk of using the integrated cost leadership/differentiation strategy. This means that when a firm fails to produce somewhat differentiated products at relatively low costs, it becomes "stuck in the middle."[24] The risk of this strategy and the problem of being stuck in the middle is highlighted in the following quote from the CEO of BMW North America: "The car market seems to be bifurcating between more expensive, prestige products and very inexpensive, high-volume products. The middle ground is the killing fields—the worst business to be in."[25]

Implementing Business-Level Strategies

To be successful, business-level strategies must not only match the needs of the marketplace, they also need to be implemented effectively. Organizational structure is an important dimension of implementing strategies. An **organizational structure** specifies the firm's formal reporting relationships, procedures, controls, and authority and decision-making processes.[26] Matching the right structure with the chosen strategy enhances firm performance.

Three major types of organizational structure are used to implement strategies: a simple structure, a functional structure, and a multidivisional structure.[27] Only the simple structure and the functional structure can be used to implement business-level strategies. A **simple structure** is an organizational structure in which the owner/manager makes all of the major decisions and oversees all of the staff's activities. This structure calls for very few rules, a dependence on informal relationships, and limited task specialization. The work is coordinated through frequent informal communications between the owner/manager and staff. This type of structure is best suited for use in a small business. The **functional structure** is an organizational structure consisting of a CEO and a small corporate staff. Here, the managers of major functional areas usually report to the CEO or a member of the corporate staff. This structure emphasizes functional specialization and facilitates active information sharing within each function. However, the functional orientation sometimes makes it difficult to communicate and coordinate across functions.

Implementing the Cost Leadership Strategy

Firms implementing the cost leadership strategy use a functional structure with highly centralized authority in the corporate staff (see Figure 5.4). Recall that the cost leadership strategy finds the firm producing a relatively standardized product that is sold to the industry's average customer. To ensure that the product is produced at low costs and with standard features, the firm's structure calls for a high degree of centralized authority. To create efficiency, jobs are highly specialized and organized into homogenous subgroups, and highly formalized rules and procedures are established. The substantial efficiency resulting from this structure helps firms keep their costs low. The operations function is emphasized in this structure to ensure that the firm's product is being produced at low costs.

Implementing the Differentiation Strategy

The functional structure used by firms implementing the differentiation strategy differs from the one used by firms implementing the cost leadership strategy. In this version of the functional organizational structure, the R&D and marketing functions are more important; R&D is emphasized so the firm can continuously differentiate its products in ways that create value for customers, and marketing is emphasized so customers will be aware of the unique value being created by

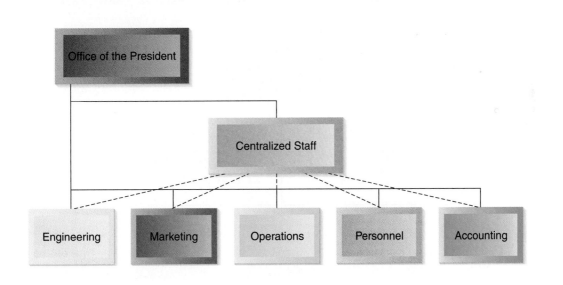

FIGURE 5.4 Functional Structure for Implementing the Cost Leadership Strategy

NOTES:
- Operations is the main function
- Process engineering is emphasized rather than new product R&D
- Relatively large centralized staff coordinates functions
- Formalized procedures allow for emergence of a low-cost culture
- Overall structure is somewhat rigid, causing job roles to be relatively structured

the firm's products (see Figure 5.5). Authority is decentralized in this structure so people "closest to the customer" can decide how to appropriately differentiate the firm's products. Jobs in this structure aren't very specialized and employees work without a large number of formal rules and processes. The characteristics of this form of the functional structure enable employees to frequently communicate and to coordinate their work. Communication and coordination are vital parts of being able to understand customers' unique needs in order to produce unique products to satisfy those needs.

Implementing the Focus Strategies

When firms following a focus strategy have only a single product line and operate in a single geographic market, a simple structure is effective for implementing the strategy. These firms are often small and the focus is direct. However, in firms that are larger and more complex (such as those that have several product lines or operate in multiple geographic markets), a functional structure usually is more effective. The type of functional structure used is matched to the type of strategy. Firms using a focused cost leadership strategy should use a centralized functional structure that emphasizes efficiency. However, firms using a focused differentiation strategy should use a functional structure that is decentralized and encourages interaction across functions to create innovation that the firm relies on to continuously differentiate its products.

FIGURE 5.5 Functional Structure for Implementing the Differentiation Strategy

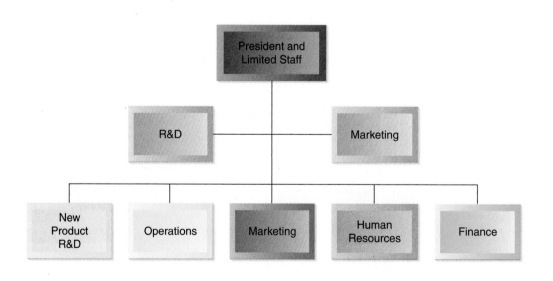

NOTES: • Marketing is the main function (to track new product ideas)
   • New product R&D is emphasized
   • Most functions are decentralized, but R&D and marketing may have centralized staffs that work closely with each other
   • Formalization is limited so that new product ideas can easily emerge and change is more readily accomplished
   • Overall structure is relatively flexible, causing job roles to be less structured

Implementing the Integrated Cost Leadership/Differentiation Strategy

Because of the competing demands of the cost leadership strategy's concern with efficiency and the differentiation strategy's concern with innovation, an integrated cost leadership/differentiation strategy is difficult to implement. To satisfy these competing demands, a firm using this strategy needs a structure in which decisions are partly centralized and partly decentralized. Jobs are semispecialized and some formal rules and procedures are needed, as well as some informal behavior. In short, flexibility is required. This strategy requires efficient processes to maintain lower costs. Yet the ability to change is also important in order to develop and maintain differentiated goods or services. Flexible manufacturing systems, quality-control systems, and sophisticated information systems can all contribute to simultaneous efficiency and flexibility. For example, ABB Ltd., a Swiss company manufacturing power and automated technologies that other firms buy to help them improve their performance, was well known for decentralizing decision-making authority to individual profit centers (the company once had 5,000 profit centers). But it also had effective information systems that gave top managers real-time information about each profit center's revenues and costs.[28]

Business-Level Strategy Success across Time

As we've described in this chapter, a business-level strategy is based on the firm's competitive advantages and is used to position the firm favorably in the marketplace relative to its rivals. Once formed, though, the firm must continuously evaluate its business-level strategy and change it as needed to create more value for customers or bring the firm back on course. Being "on course" means that the strategy is helping the firm reach its vision as well as the mission that is a core part of the vision, as explained in Chapters 1 and 2. Recently, brokerage house Charles Schwab concluded that the business-level strategy it was using to broaden its target market and product offerings wasn't working well. An important reason for this was the fact that the new strategy was taking Schwab too far from its original mission. According to a business writer, "Schwab executives [are saying] that salvation lies in returning to the firm's original mission of serving mom-and-pop, buy-and-hold investors who generate recurring advisory fees."[29] Schwab is changing its business-level strategy so the firm will again be "on course."

One way the firm can learn how to create more value for customers by using its business-level strategy is to ask them how it can do so. Sam Walton was known for recommending that firms trust their customers and frequently talk to them to find out what they want. In "Understanding Strategy," we describe how two firms talk to their customers to learn how to create more value for them.

Diversified firms, ones with multiple businesses competing in many industries and market segments, develop business-level strategies for each of their business units. For example, GE has more than a dozen business units, each of which develops a business-level strategy to describe how it intends to compete in its industry or market segments. In addition, UPS, the company described in this chapter's "Focusing on Strategy," has seven business units, each of which has a separate business-level strategy. We describe the multiproduct strategies that firms like UPS and GE use in the next chapter.

understanding strategy:

MINING GOLD BY TALKING TO CUSTOMERS

"Companies very often employ bright people but only use them to do the task at hand," says Mark Turrell, CEO of Imaginatik, a firm that helps companies interpret information from customers in ways that will enable them to create new, innovative products. The CEO's comments reflect his belief that companies too often fail to use all of their employees' skills. One of their unused skills, he believes, is identifying customers' unmet needs.

In a recent assignment, Imaginatik worked with Grace Performance Chemicals, a division of W. R. Grace, to make sense of customers' innovative applications of the division's products. Grace sales representatives observed customers using the products they had sold to them in unexpected, creative ways. The uses from these observations are being integrated and catalogued to see if the chemicals unit can find ways to sell its current products to different customers or to tap latent demand (suggested by how current customers are using the unit's current products) as the foundation for developing new products.

Dow Chemical recently launched a new stretch fiber, XLA. This product was created after asking customers to describe the functionality they wanted in fibers. Dow gathered insights from firms competing in 26 industries to understand the characteristics of fiber that these firms thought would best serve their needs. What Dow learned is that apparel makers (one of the 26 industry groups Dow surveyed) wanted a "soft stretch" fiber with a natural feel and an ability to resist heat and chemicals. Armed with this insight, Dow's scientists developed XLA. To date, three apparel makers have introduced shirts using XLA as the core fiber. This was important customer input for Dow. Prior to learning about customers' preferences, Dow believed that it should concentrate its efforts to develop a spandex-type fiber that could be sold at a price lower than competitors' prices for this type of fiber. According to business writers, "That critical insight—that the market wanted an alternative to spandex, not a low-cost imitator—helped Dow avoid a huge error."

Customers may not always know what they want. Grace Performance Chemicals is trying to develop new products based on latent customer needs as inferred by observing their innovative uses of current products. Dow, on the other hand, directly asked customers what functionality they wanted in a product and then used its scientific skills to develop a product that could deliver what customers wanted. Both of these companies are working with customers to learn how to better serve those customers' needs.

SOURCES: 2004, About Imaginatik, Imaginatik Home Page, http://www.imaginatik.com, September 22; J. Esty, 2004, Those wacky customers! *Fast Company*, January: 40; L. Lavelle, 2004, Inventing to order, *Business Week*, July 5: 84–85.

Unlike UPS and GE, nondiversified firms that compete in a single product market develop only one business-level strategy. Your neighborhood dry-cleaning store and favorite locally owned restaurant are examples of firms with a single business-level strategy. Every firm needs a business-level strategy, and diversified firms need multiple business-level strategies plus a multiproduct strategy (see Chapter 6) as well as an international strategy (see Chapter 7) if they compete in more than a single country's markets.

Summary

The primary purpose of this chapter is to discuss the different business-level strategies firms can use to compete in the marketplace. In doing so, we examined the following topics:

- **Business-level strategy** is an action plan the firm develops to describe how it will compete in its chosen industry or market segment. A business-level strategy details how the firm intends to compete in the marketplace on a day-to-day basis to satisfy customers' needs.

- There are five generic business-level strategies. These strategies are called generic because they can be used by any firm regardless of the industry. Opportunities and threats in the external environment and the firm's core competencies and competitive advantages suggest the business-level strategy the firm should choose to implement.

- Each business-level strategy has two dimensions— competitive advantage (either a cost advantage or a uniqueness advantage) and competitive scope (either broad or narrow). The cost leadership and differentiation strategies are used to serve a broad market, while the focused cost leadership and focused differentiation strategies serve the specialized needs of a narrow market. The integrated cost leadership/differentiation strategy strikes a balance between the competitive advantage and competitive scope dimensions.

- When using the **cost leadership strategy**, a firm produces standardized products that are intended to satisfy the needs of the typical or "average" customer, which is usually the largest market segment. These products are produced at costs lower than those of competitors. To use this strategy successfully across time, the firm must continuously drive its costs lower than competitors' costs so it can sell its products at lower prices.

- Firms use the **differentiation strategy** to produce products that customers consider unique in ways that are important to them. Target customers for this strategy are willing to pay for product uniqueness. Uniqueness can be physical (such as superior reliability) or psychological (such as perceived status). Earning margins that are sufficient to support continuous reinvestment in sources of differentiation that customers value is the key to long-term success with this strategy.

- **Focus strategies** (cost leadership and differentiation) rely on either the cost or uniqueness advantage to better serve the specialized needs of a narrow target market, as compared to serving a broad target market.

- Firms use the **integrated cost leadership/differentiation strategy** to produce products that have some differentiation at a relatively low price. With this strategy, a firm's products have some differentiated features (but not as many as products coming from the firm using the differentiation strategy) and are produced at a low cost (but not as low as are the cost leader's costs). Because both low cost and differentiation are sought simultaneously, the firm must be very flexible to successfully use this strategy so it won't become "stuck in the middle." The main risk of the integrated cost leadership/differentiation strategy is being outperformed by firms successfully using the cost leadership or differentiation strategy.

- Two versions of the **functional structure** are best suited to implement the cost leadership strategy and the differentiation strategy. These two versions differ in their degree of centralization, specialization, and formalization. To promote efficiency, the functional structure for the cost leadership strategy holds decision-making authority in centralized staff functions, is highly specialized, and uses formal rules and procedures. In contrast, the functional structure used to implement the differentiation strategy is decentralized to different organizational functions. The emphasis here is on R&D and marketing to promote innovation. There is less specialization, with the use of cross-functional teams and fewer formal rules and procedures. Structures for the focus strategies largely match the emphasis of structures used to implement the cost leadership or differentiation strategy. However, if a firm using a focus strategy is small, a **simple structure** is used. The structure for the integrated cost leadership/differentiation strategy is more complex. It must be flexible with some centralization and some decentralization. The structure must be flexible in order to promote efficiency and innovation. Use of flexible manufacturing systems, quality-control systems and sophisticated information systems aid the flexibility.

Key Terms

business-level strategy 110
cost leadership strategy 115
differentiation strategy 118
focus strategy 122

focused cost leadership strategy 122
focused differentiation strategy 122
functional structure 124

integrated cost leadership/
  differentiation strategy 124
organizational structure 124
simple structure 124

Discussion Questions

1. What is a business-level strategy? Why is a business-level strategy important to a firm's success?
2. What are the definitions of the five business-level strategies discussed in this chapter? What are the differences among the five business-level strategies?
3. What specific and unique set of actions should a firm take to effectively use each business-level strategy?
4. What risks are associated with using each business-level strategy?
5. What organizational structures should be used to implement the business-level strategies?

Endnotes

1. M. E. Porter & E. Olmstead-Teisberg, 2004, Redefining competition in health care, *Harvard Business Review*, 82(6): 64–76.
2. 2004, UPS Home Page, About UPS, http://www.ups.com, September 21.
3. M. Beer & R. A. Eisenstat, 2004, How to have an honest conversation about your business strategy, *Harvard Business Review*, 82(2): 82–89.
4. G. Stalk Jr. & R. Lachenauer, 2004, Hardball: Five killer strategies for trouncing the competition, *Harvard Business Review*, 82(4): 62–71.
5. B. Breen, 2002, BMW: Driven by design, *Fast Company*, September: 123–127.
6. L. K. Trevino & M. E. Brown, 2004, Managing to be ethical: Debunking five business ethics myths, *Academy of Management Executive*, 18(2): 69–81.
7. B. C. Skaggs & M. Youndt, 2004, Strategic positioning, human capital, and performance in service organizations: A customer interaction approach, *Strategic Management Journal*, 25: 85–99.
8. E. Waaser, M. Dahneke, M. Pekkarinen, & M. Weissel, 2004, How you slice it: Smarter segmentation for your sales team, *Harvard Business Review*, 82(3): 105–111.
9. 2004, Becoming the best: What you can learn from the 25 most influential leaders of our times, Knowledge @ Wharton, http://www.knowledge.wharton.upenn.edu, February 11.
10. M. E. Porter, 1985, *Competitive Advantage*, New York: Free Press, 15.
11. G. Edmondson, 2004, Porsche's latest entry hits a crowded track, *Business Week*, July 5: 55.
12. A. Bianco, 2004, The vanishing mass market, *Business Week*, July 12: 61–67.
13. D. M. Osborne, 2000, Bootstrap marketing: Taking on Procter & Gamble, *Inc.*, http://www.inc.com, October.
14. 2004, About Cooper, Cooper Tire & Rubber Home Page, http://www.coopertire.com, September 18.
15. D. Sacks, 2004, Guinness: Brew a connection, *Fast Company*, August: 39–44.
16. M. E. Porter, 1980, *Competitive Strategy*, New York: Free Press, 35–40.
17. A. Bary, 2004, Barron's insight: Attention, Kmart holders: Game plan has pitfalls, *Wall Street Journal*, July 25: 2.
18. J. Samuelson, 2003, How Pottery Barn wins with style, *Fast Company*, June: 106–110.
19. S. J. Spear, 2004, Learning to lead at Toyota, *Harvard Business Review*, 82(5): 78–86.
20. K. Kling & I. Goteman, 2003, Ikea CEO Andres Dahlvig on international growth and Ikea's unique corporate culture and brand identity, *Academy of Management Executive*, 17(1): 31–37.
21. 2004, About Ikea, Ikea Home Page, http://www.ikea.com, September 22.
22. K. H. Hammonds, 2004, Thread-count wars, *Fast Company*, January: 31.
23. Ibid.
24. Porter, *Competitive Advantage*, 16.
25. Breen, BMW: Driven by Design.
26. B. Keats & H. O'Neill, 2001, Organizational structure: Looking through a strategy lens, in M. A. Hitt, R. E. Freeman & J. S. Harrison (Eds.), *Handbook of Strategic Management*, Oxford, UK: Blackwell, 520–542.
27. R. E. Hoskisson, M. A. Hitt, & R. D. Ireland, 2004, *Competing for Advantage*, Mason, Ohio: South-Western, 44.
28. Ibid.
29. 2004, Schwab is renovating to be more competitive, *Dallas Morning News*, September 14: D3.

Your Career

As employees, we want to continuously develop unique skills that enable us to be valued members of a workforce. Although it may sound a bit harsh, each of us should try to differentiate ourselves from other workers in ways that will matter to employers. We should remember that just as customers have choices to make when deciding what goods or services to buy, employers have choices when deciding which workers to hire. Indeed, each employee should have skills that enable him or her to perform a work task better than others can, or to perform a work task that other potential employees can't perform. Remember from Chapter 4 that firms develop a competitive advantage when they have the core competencies that enable them to perform tasks more efficiently than competitors or when they can perform value-creating tasks competitors can't perform. In a similar manner, as employees, each of us should try to develop a competitive advantage that we can sell to a prospective employer.

Sell to a prospective employer is the key phrase for this application of the strategic management process to your career. When seeking an individual job or when contemplating the path you want your career to take, think of both your current and future employers as your customers. You can develop your career by determining whom you want to work for today as well as in the future. You may wish to work for a large financial institution today to hone your analytical skills in ways that will help you gain employment as a controller in a software manufacturer later in your career. You should also identify goals the firm has that you believe your competitive advantage enables you to address. Perhaps, for example, a firm wishes to increase its sales in a certain region of the country with which you are quite familiar. You could make your familiarity with that region known to people in the firm in hopes of gaining an opportunity to use that knowledge to your benefit as well as to the firm's benefit. Finally, when seeking a job, be prepared to clearly explain to your customer (the prospective employer) how you will be able to create value for the firm by describing how using your competitive advantages will create value for the firm as you complete various tasks.

Thinking of your employer as a customer who wants to buy your skills helps you create a mindset that will enable you to understand how you can create value for a firm. Having such an understanding may be vital to demonstrating to a prospective employer that you are the one to be hired!

STRATEGY TOOLBOX

The Pareto Principle, or the "80/20 rule," can be applied to the analysis of customers targeted and served by a company. At a given point in time, many companies find that 80 percent of the profit is derived from 20 percent of the customers. This chapter's tool builds off this possibility and provides a lens by which strategists can examine their customer base, with a particular focus on the identification of the profit per customer or customer segment.

Customer Value Analysis

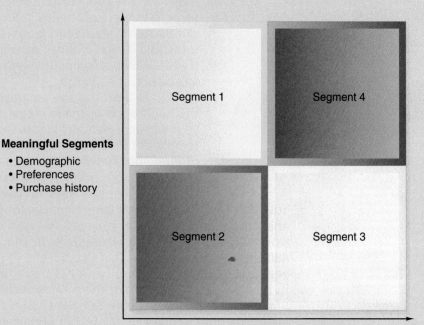

Meaningful Segments
- Demographic
- Preferences
- Purchase history

Profitability
Annual profit per customer

✳ BIZ FLIX

ABOUT A BOY: FOCUSED DIFFERENTIATION OF THE WILL LIGHTMAN PRODUCT

This chapter discussed differentiation strategies that firms can use to their competitive advantage. Watch this scene from *About a Boy* and assess Will Lightman's (Hugh Grant) strategy to attract eligible women to him.

Will Lightman lives on the royalties of his father's hit song, "Santa's Super Sleigh." A self-absorbed bachelor, Will has mastered getting through a day with no responsibilities. In his constant search for guilt-free short-term relationships, he stumbles on the idea of dating single mothers. He successfully presents himself as a single father at a Single Parents Alone Together (SPAT) meeting that leads to him meeting a boy named Marcus (Nicholas Hoult). Marcus is an outcast at school, so Will teaches him how to be cool. Marcus, in turn, teaches Will about the value of long-term relationships.

The scene comes from the SPAT sequence about 15 minutes after the film starts. Will attends his first meeting after seeing a SPAT advertisement while looking at magazines. The scene starts with Will describing his (fictional) son Ned. It ends as Will compliments himself for his performance. The film continues with Will's enthusiastic involvement in the meeting and the group's activities.

What to Watch for and Ask Yourself

1. Does Will use a focused differentiation strategy to distinguish himself from other men for this target group? What does he emphasize that appears important to SPAT members?
2. Does he emphasize physiological or psychological differences? What are they?
3. Does he create "perceived unique value" as discussed earlier in this chapter? Could a competitor easily replace what Will offers to SPAT members? Why or why not?

Mini-Case

Krispy Kreme—Will Dough Continue to Flow to Shareholders?

Launched in 1937, Krispy Kreme Doughnuts is a branded specialty retailer of premium doughnuts. It sells more than three billion doughnuts annually. Its Original Glazed doughnut is the firm's most recognizable product. However, Krispy Kreme's commitment to innovation results in frequent tests of potential new doughnuts. From February 7 to March 27, 2005, for example, Krispy Kreme test marketed its Chocolate Kreme doughnut. New products that are well received by customers are then added to the stores' inventory of doughnuts. As we can imagine, the variety of flavors Krispy Kreme can incorporate into its doughnuts is virtually endless.

As this brief discussion shows, Krispy Kreme uses a differentiation strategy. It seeks to sell its premium doughnuts to customers who value their uniqueness. The firm's Doughnut Theatre is a source of differentiation between Krispy Kreme and its competitors. The Doughnut Theatre is the in-store manufacturing process we as customers can watch to see employees actually make doughnuts.

Are Krispy Kreme doughnuts really significantly different from competitors' offerings? As we noted earlier in this chapter, some differentiation is tangible while other differentiation may be more psychological in nature. Some believe that Krispy Kreme's uniqueness is more psychological than tangible. One analyst even suggested, "It isn't what's inside a Krispy Kreme doughnut that creates the demand. It's what's inside the customer's head that makes a Krispy Kreme Krispy Kreme." Regardless of the nature of the differentiation, Krispy Kreme has achieved great success with its differentiation strategy for many decades.

However, things seem to be changing for Krispy Kreme. One indicator of the seriousness of the change is the firm's stock price. After hitting a high of $39.74 in March 2004, it fell to roughly $7.50 per share in February 2005. In addition, at the end of 2004 and continuing into 2005, Krispy Kreme was conducting internal investigations of alleged accounting irregularities. Let's describe more fully some factors that appear to be influencing Krispy Kreme's fortunes.

We noted in Chapter 3 that firms can't control events in the external environment, but those events can significantly affect a firm's performance. One phrase—*low-carb diet*—describes a trend in the general environment that is having a major effect on Krispy Kreme. Stated simply, the firm's doughnuts are high fat, high carbohydrates, and high sugar items. No matter how much customers may want this not to be the case, Krispy Kreme's doughnuts aren't friendly to those wanting to restrict their intake of carbohydrates and sugar.

But other events affecting performance were under the firm's control. How the firm accounted for the price it was paying to reacquire some of its franchisees concerned some analysts. In an unusual decision, the firm decided to book the price it paid for each franchise as an intangible asset called *reacquired franchise rights*. The issue is that this asset doesn't amortize over time, a situation that some critics

claim artificially inflates the firm's profits. In addition, the Securities and Exchange Commission (SEC) launched a formal inquiry into the firm's repurchase of six stores that were owned by its former chairman. The charge was that the price paid for these stores was more than three times the typical price paid to reacquire a store.

In spite of Krispy Kreme's difficulties, some of which are under the firm's control while others are not, some analysts remain positive about the firm's long-term potential. Improving the focus on operations, becoming more transparent in its repurchasing program, and being less aggressive in its accounting practices are actions analysts think may help Krispy Kreme use its differentiation strategy as the source of profitable operations.

SOURCES: 2004, Krispy Kreme to close Ravenna plant, blames low-carb fad, *Wall Street Journal Online,* http://www.wsj.com, October 5; M. E. Lloyd, 2004, Legg Mason cuts Krispy Kreme to hold from buy, *Wall Street Journal Online,* http://www.wsj.com, September 24; M. Maremont, 2004, Krispy Kreme suit raises questions on repurchases, *Wall Street Journal Online,* http://www.wsj.com, October 14; D. Stires, 2004, Krispy Kreme is in the hole—again, *Fortune,* November 1: 42–44.

Questions

1. Go to the Krispy Kreme Web site (http://www.krispykreme.com) and read about how the firm operates. Based on what you read, prepare a list of each source of differentiation the firm is using to differentiate its doughnuts and their presentation from what the firm's competitors are doing.
2. Using the information collected in responding to the first question, determine the sustainability of Krispy Kreme's differentiation strategy. Are the firm's sources of differentiation sustainable over the next ten years? Why or why not?
3. If you were appointed CEO of Krispy Kreme, what actions would you take and why?

EXPERIENTIAL EXERCISES

EXERCISE ONE: MOTOROLA SHIFTS STRATEGY

Motorola has long been one of the world's leading manufacturers of handheld cell phones. *Forbes* magazine reported that cell phones accounted for 40 percent of the firm's revenue and 60 percent of its operating profit in 2003. However, the Chicago-based firm was also being squeezed in 2003. Korean and Chinese firms had entered the market for basic handsets and had bid down prices to the point that Motorola's profit margins were approaching one percent.

Motorola's response to the situation it faced was two-pronged. First, the firm slashed costs by reducing the model variations of its phones and outsourced a large segment of the remaining models' production. By doing so, the firm was able to stay ahead of price drops, but only barely.

Second, Motorola hired Geoffrey Frost away from Nike to become the firm's "chief brand officer," and Tim Parsey away from Apple to be a corporate vice-president. Motorola, proud of its engineering orientation, was shocked when Frost ripped out walls and instilled a culture more reminiscent of a California start-up than an established midwestern manufacturer. Frost then opened a design studio in Milan and doubled the number of designers on the payroll. Soon new Motorola phones that were also MP3 players, FM radios, and cameras commanded $200–$300 and were available only from service providers that promoted the firm. Parsey ensured that the engineers did not undo the stylish contributions made by Frost's staff. Motorola's new goal was to turn out a stream of cutting-edge products to compete against Nokia, which in 2003 was selling more than twice as many handheld devices as Motorola, and other manufacturers of high-end products.

First, decide whether Motorola is really changing strategies. Is Motorola exhibiting the traits of a firm that has successfully executed a low-cost leadership strategy? Is Motorola establishing an effective differentiation strategy? What is the firm doing, if anything, that is consistent with an effective differentiation strategy?

Second, reproduce Figure 5.3 for Motorola. Identify the elements in the value-chain arrow that Motorola is focusing on as its source of competitive advantage in differentiation. Distinguish between areas where the firm has an existing advantage and where it is seeking one. If Motorola succeeds in establishing differentiation skills in the segments of the value chain that you have identified, will the firm have established itself as an effective differentiator in the cell phone manufacturing industry?

Source: M. Tatge, 2003, Recharged, *Forbes,* September 15, 62.

EXERCISE TWO: IDENTIFYING BUSINESS-LEVEL STRATEGIES

Using the Internet, the library, and other resources available to you, identify the business-level strategy from among the five discussed in this chapter that is being predominately used by firms competing in (1) the personal computer (PC) industry and in (2) the pharmaceutical industry. Please list the reasons why these strategies are being used in each of the two industries.

CHAPTER 6

Multiproduct Strategies

Reading and studying this chapter should enable you to:

*Knowledge Objectives

1_
Define a multiproduct strategy.

2_
Understand the differences between the levels of diversification.

3_
Discuss the related-diversification multiproduct strategy.

4_
Explain the unrelated-diversification multiproduct strategy.

5_
Understand two motives that top-level managers have to diversify the firms they lead.

6_
Describe the organizational structures used to implement the different multiproduct strategies.

Focusing on Strategy

Brown: How Many Services Does It Offer?

"We see every aspect of our business working cohesively to synchronize commerce—helping companies simultaneously manage goods, information, and funds with speed, precision, security, and efficiency." (Michael L. Eskew, chairman and CEO of UPS)

In Chapter 5's "Focusing on Strategy," we described how UPS's Supply Chain Solutions group worked with Ford Motor Company to solve Ford's distribution problem. Do you recall that the president of a Ford dealership said that UPS's work brought about the most amazing transformation he had seen over his career as a dealer? Not surprisingly, being able to solve customers' logistics or supply-chain management problems is the goal of people working in UPS's Supply Chain Solutions group.

But logistics or supply-chain management isn't the main product (we use the word *product* to refer to either a good or a service) that comes to mind for most of us when we think about UPS and what it does. In fact, many of us likely picture a large brown truck delivering packages to individuals or businesses when we think of UPS. And such an image is quite understandable, in that UPS is the world's largest express and package delivery company. However, UPS has diversified its product lines, meaning that it sells multiple products. For example, the firm has formed what it calls its "non-package businesses" group as well as its "international package delivery service." The Supply Chain Solutions group is at the core of UPS's non-package businesses, although UPS Capital (which provides asset-based lending to businesses) and UPS Consulting (which provides supply-chain design and re-engineering advice to clients) are also part of the group. In essence, the Supply Chain Solutions group helps firms increase the efficiency of their supply chains, viewed as a network of actors or companies that convert raw materials into products for distribution. Currently, UPS's international package delivery service is growing faster than its domestic service.

The decisions to move into non-package businesses and to deliver packages in more than 200 countries means that UPS is using a multiproduct strategy along with an international strategy. Collectively, this means that UPS is diversified in terms of the services it offers and is diversified in terms of the countries it serves.

Why would UPS choose to diversify? For example, why would the firm decide to make a major commitment to delivering packages in China? The president of UPS International answers this question by noting, "The most exciting and fastest growing market is China." The growth in package delivery in China and other countries outside the United States exceeds the growth in UPS's domestic package delivery business. Therefore, building its operations in China and other emerging economies outside the United States is understandable. UPS diversified into non-package services as a result of building a sophisticated technological infrastructure to support its international transportation network, as follows: The decision to expand internationally resulted in the firm's developing technological and information processing capabilities that could be used to complete tasks in addition to servicing the firm's sprawling international delivery service. With its technological and information processing capabilities, UPS decided to diversify its service offerings by adding logistics or supply-chain management services as well as other related services to its portfolio of services. Given all of UPS's actions to diversify, we can understand CEO Eskew's comment indicating that UPS is working to "synchronize commerce."

SOURCES: 2004, Today's UPS, UPS Home Page, http://www.ups.com, December 2; D. Foust, 2004, Big Brown's New Bag, *Business Week,* July 19: 54; N. Harris, 2004, UPS expands direct control of China business, *Wall Street Journal Online,* http://www.wsj.com, December 3; B. Stanley, 2004, Delivery services expand role, *Wall Street Journal Online,* http://www.wsj.com, November 26.

*
multiproduct strategy

an action plan that the firm develops to compete in different product markets

As described in "Focusing on Strategy," UPS has diversified its service offerings and is using a multiproduct strategy. A **multiproduct strategy** is an action plan the firm develops to compete in different product markets. The focus of this chapter is on diversification in the form of multiproduct strategies, while the next chapter focuses on diversification in the form of international strategies. Think about Figure 1.1 and consider that UPS is using a multiproduct strategy and an international strategy to compete against its rivals such as FedEx and DHL. Of course, UPS is using business-level strategies in each of its three product groups (U.S. domestic package, international package, and non-package).

As with business-level strategies, a firm's multiproduct strategy is used to improve its performance.[1] A firm improves its performance by using a multiproduct strategy when it learns how to use its core competencies to pursue opportunities in the external environment in more than one product market.[2] Successful multiproduct strategies enable a firm to smooth out its revenue and earnings flows and earn additional profits by using its core competencies in additional ways.[3] We present additional reasons why firms use multiproduct strategies to diversify their operations in Table 6.1.

Firms such as UPS deal with two issues when developing a multiproduct strategy: What products will be offered and how will those products be man-

TABLE 6.1

Reasons Why Firms Use Multiproduct Strategies to Diversify

- Achieve profitable growth
- Reduce the risk of being involved with a single product line
- Learn how to apply core competencies in other value creating ways
- Gain exposure to different technologies
- Develop economies of scope
- Extend the firm's brand into additional product areas

aged?[4] As noted earlier, the groups of services that UPS offers are U.S. domestic package (74 percent), international package (17 percent), and non-package (nine percent). The percentages shown indicate the percentage of total sales revenue generated by each group during UPS's 2003 fiscal year.[5] The manner in which UPS generates sales revenue across its product divisions means that the firm is using a dominant-business multiproduct strategy. We define this and the other multiproduct strategies in the next section. Later in the chapter, we discuss the type of organizational structure UPS uses to implement its multiproduct strategy.

To explain multiproduct strategies, we first describe how diversified a firm becomes (from low to high) when it selects a particular multiproduct strategy. We then examine two levels of diversification (related and unrelated) in some detail. We do this because of how frequently firms use these multiproduct strategies. Following these discussions, we describe two motives that top-level managers have to diversify the firm in ways that may or may not create value for stakeholders. The chapter closes with presentations of the different organizational structures firms use to implement the different multiproduct strategies.

Levels of Diversification

We show five levels of diversification (from low to high) in Figure 6.1. Firms using the single-business multiproduct strategy are the least diversified, while companies using the unrelated-diversification multiproduct strategy are the most diversified. A firm with low levels of diversification has a smaller total number of different products and generates a larger percentage of its sales from its major product group; a firm with high levels of diversification has a larger number of different products and generates a smaller percentage of its sales revenue from one product group.

Low Levels of Diversification

As shown in Figure 6.1, the sources of a firm's sales revenue are used to determine its level of product diversification. This technique of determining a firm's degree of diversification is based on a classic work completed by Richard Rumelt.[6]

FIGURE 6.1 | Levels of Diversification

Low Levels of Diversification

Single business: More than 95 percent of revenue comes from a single business.   **A**

Dominant business: Between 70 and 95 percent of revenue comes from a single business.   **A** **B**

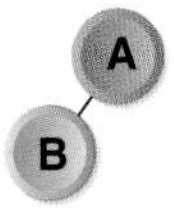

Moderate to High Levels of Diversification

Related constrained: Less than 70 percent of revenue comes from the dominant business, and all businesses share product, technological, and distribution linkages.   **A** **B**—**C**

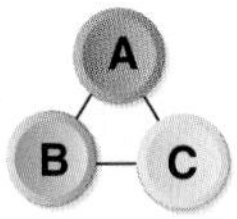

Related linked (mixed related and unrelated):   Less than 70 percent of revenue comes from the dominant business, and only limited links exist between businesses.   **A** **B**—**C**

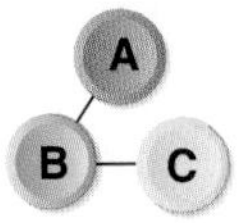

Very High Levels of Diversification

Unrelated: Less than 70 percent of revenue comes from the dominant business, and no common links exist between businesses.   **A** **B** **C**

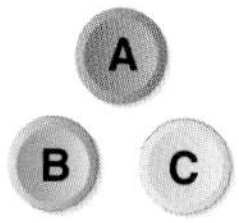

SOURCE: Adapted from R. P. Rumelt, 1974, *Strategy, Structure, and Economic Performance,* Boston: Harvard Business School.

Single-Business Diversification Multiproduct Strategy

A firm pursuing low levels of diversification uses either the single- or dominant-business multiproduct strategy. With the single-business multiproduct strategy, the firm generates at least 95 percent of its sales revenue from a single business. A *single business* is one in which the firm makes and sells a single product or a variety of a single product. Let's consider a famous chewing-gum manufacturer to understand the single-business diversification multiproduct strategy.

Historically, Wrigley has used the single-business multiproduct strategy. Chewing and bubble gums, of course, are the firm's core product. Wrigley produces and sells multiple types of gums, including Juicy Fruit, Spearmint, Doublemint, and Hubba Bubba. The few other products Wrigley produced for many years (which accounted for less than five percent of total sales revenue) were all related to derivatives of chewing gum. Therefore, for many decades, Wrigley produced and sold a number of versions of a single type of product—chewing gum and bubble gum.

Recently, though, Wrigley decided to diversify its product offerings so it could become a global confectionery business. Chewy and hard candies are a primary new product area for Wrigley. In this chapter's Mini-Case, we discuss

Wrigley has traditionally produced one product, gum, in a variety of flavors, such as Big Red, advertised here by Carmen Electra.

Wrigley's increasing level of product diversification where you will learn more about how and why Wrigley is diversifying its product offerings.

Dominant-Business Diversification Multiproduct Strategy

A firm using the dominant-business multiproduct strategy generates between 70 and 95 percent of its sales revenue from a single business. As mentioned earlier, UPS, the focal firm in "Focusing on Strategy," recently earned 74 percent of its revenue from its U.S. package delivery business, 17 percent of revenue from its international package business, and nine percent of revenue from its non-package business. This means that UPS has three businesses, with each business delivering some unique services. Therefore, compared to firms using a single-business multiproduct strategy, companies similar to UPS produce and sell a larger number of products and so are more diversified.

Given current trends, the nature of UPS's diversification is likely to change. There are two reasons for this. First, its international package delivery business is growing faster than its domestic package delivery business. Second, UPS's non-package business is also growing rapidly and is the product area that company leaders believe holds the most promise for UPS's future growth. Indeed, if the "world of synchronized commerce" evolves as UPS's leaders anticipate, the percentage of the firm's total revenue generated by its non-package products and its international package delivery businesses may continue to increase and eventually eclipse the amount of revenue generated by its U.S. package delivery business. If this trend continues, UPS is likely to pursue either a moderate or a high level of diversification.

Moderate to High Levels of Diversification

Related-Diversification Multiproduct Strategy

A firm generating less than 70 percent of its sales revenue from its dominant business is using either the related-diversification or the unrelated-diversification multiproduct strategy (see Figure 6.1). Let's see what the differences are between these strategies.

Firms using a related-diversification multiproduct strategy try to create economies of scope. **Economies of scope** are cost savings the firm accrues when it successfully shares some of its resources and activities or some of its core competencies between its businesses.

The related-diversification strategy actually has two forms, with a subtle but important difference between the two. With the *related constrained*

*

economies of scope

cost savings that the firm accrues when it successfully shares some of its resources and activities or some of its core competencies between its businesses multiproduct strategy, most (but not necessarily all) of the firms' businesses are related to each other.[7] The relatedness between the businesses occurs as they share some products, markets, and/or technologies.[8] As shown in Figure 6.1, the hypothetical firm using the related constrained multiproduct strategy has three businesses (A, B, and C). The lines connecting all three businesses show hypothetically that the three businesses are somewhat constrained in the activities used to produce their goods or services because they share some products (such as raw materials as inputs to the manufacturing processes used to make the business's final product), markets (that is, they serve the same customers), and/or technologies (that is, the same or very similar technologies are used to produce the three business's products). Consumer product giant Procter & Gamble (P&G) uses the related constrained strategy. A few paragraphs below, we describe an example of how P&G's businesses are related to one another.

In the *related linked* diversification strategy, only limited links or relationships exist between the firm's businesses. As shown in Figure 6.1, the hypothetical firm using the related linked strategy has three businesses (A, B, and C). The line connecting business A and business B reflects a hypothetical relationship, as does the line between business B and business C. Notice however, that business A and business C do not share products, markets, and technologies. In addition to some sharing of resources and activities between businesses, a firm using the related linked strategy concentrates on transferring core competencies between businesses. Firms using this strategy organize strategic business units (SBU). A **strategic business unit (SBU)** is a semiautonomous unit of a diversified firm with a collection of related businesses. An important point about strategic business units is that resources and activities are shared and core competencies are transferred among the product divisions within each SBU. However, resources, activities, and core competencies are not shared or transferred respectively between product divisions *across* SBUs. We'll talk more about this at the end of the chapter when we describe relationships between multiproduct strategies and organizational structures. Also, firms using the related linked strategy share fewer resources and activities between divisions within individual SBUs, concentrating on transferring core competencies (such as knowledge) between the businesses instead.

Unrelated-Diversification Multiproduct Strategy

A firm that does *not* try to transfer resources, activities, and/or core competencies between its businesses or divisions is using an unrelated-diversification multiproduct strategy. Commonly, firms using this strategy are called *conglomerates*. The unrelated-diversification multiproduct strategy is frequently used in both developed markets (for example, the United Kingdom and the United States) and emerging markets. In fact, firms using this strategy dominate the private sector in Latin American countries and in China, Korea, and India.[9] Conglomerates account for the greatest percentage of private firms in India.[10] Similarly, the largest business firms in Brazil, Mexico, Argentina, and Colombia are family-owned, highly diversified enterprises.[11]

We now turn our attention to discussing the related- and unrelated-diversification multiproduct strategies in detail and how firms use them to gen-

operational relatedness

achieved when the firm's businesses successfully share resources and activities to produce and sell their products

corporate relatedness

achieved when core competencies are successfully transferred between some of the firm's businesses

erate economies of scope by achieving either operational relatedness or corporate relatedness. **Operational relatedness** is achieved when the firm's businesses successfully share resources and activities to produce and sell their products. **Corporate relatedness** is achieved when core competencies are successfully transferred between some of the firm's businesses. Most commonly, these transfers involve intangible core competencies such as marketing knowledge, design skills, and brand name.

Notice by looking at Figure 6.2 that firms using the related constrained multiproduct strategy create economies of scope by achieving operational relatedness (see cell 1 in Figure 6.2), while firms using the related linked multiproduct strategy create economies of scope by achieving corporate relatedness (see cell 2 in Figure 6.2). As noted earlier, we concentrate on the related- and unrelated-diversification multiproduct strategies instead of on the single-business and dominant-business multiproduct strategies because they are more frequently used by larger firms.

FIGURE 6.2 Value-Creating Strategies of Diversification: Operational and Corporate Relatedness

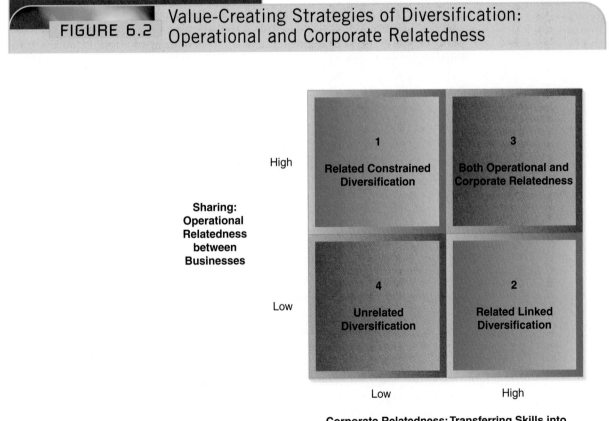

Corporate Relatedness: Transferring Skills into Businesses through Corporate Headquarters

Operational Relatedness and the Related Constrained Multiproduct Strategy

Economies of scope are created through operational relatedness when the firm successfully shares primarily tangible resources (such as plant and equipment) and/or when a primary activity (such as inventory delivery systems) or a support activity (such as purchasing procedures) is successfully used in more than one of the firm's businesses. We'll use Procter & Gamble (P&G) to describe how economies of scope are created in firms using the related constrained multiproduct strategy.

Currently, P&G has five businesses (Personal and Beauty, House and Home, Health and Wellness, Pet Nutrition and Care, and Baby and Family) that share some resources and activities. (P&G calls its businesses product divisions.) The total number of P&G's businesses may change as it integrates its recent acquisition, Gillette, into its operations. All five businesses produce one or more products that use materials based on paper. P&G operates a paper production facility that provides raw materials to all five businesses. Of course, there are some differences in what the paper production facility makes for each business. However, the paper-based raw material inputs needed by the five businesses are similar enough that one facility can produce many if not most of those items. Because many of the businesses' products are sold in some of the same outlets (grocery stores, for example), these products also share distribution channels and networks of sales representatives.[12] The sharing of these resources (raw materials) and activities (distribution) enables P&G to generate economies of scope. Specifically, P&G reduces its overall costs by combining assets to produce similar raw materials in a single facility and then using similar channels to distribute the products produced with those materials. To show these relationships at P&G in Figure 6.1, we would use five circles (A–E) to represent P&G's different businesses. We would draw lines between the businesses to demonstrate the links among all the businesses and P&G's use of the related constrained multiproduct strategy. However, it is important to emphasize that P&G's businesses share many, but not *all* of their resources and activities.

Firms must ensure that efforts to share resources and activities are effectively implemented. For example, the people responsible for P&G's paper production facility must communicate successfully with all businesses its products serve. Through these communications, those in the production facility learn about the quantity of raw materials they need to supply to P&G's five businesses.

A risk with resource and activity sharing is that the demand for the output of a unit servicing the needs of several of the firm's businesses may fall below the unit's production capacity. Reduced demand could lead to a situation in which the unit producing shared products doesn't generate enough sales revenue to cover its fixed costs. This outcome complicates efforts to share resources and activities among a diversified firm's businesses.[13] However, research evidence suggests that efforts to achieve economies of scope through operational relatedness are worthwhile in that they help create value for stakeholders.[14] Creating value through operational relatedness is what Hyatt intends to do as a result of acquiring the AmeriSuites chain. We discuss how Hyatt will attempt to do this in "Understanding Strategy."

understanding strategy:

HYATT CORPORATION: CREATING VALUE BY SHARING ACTIVITIES

The privately held Hyatt Corporation uses the related constrained multiproduct strategy. Hyatt Regency hotels are the core brand of accommodations offered by this firm.

As with other multiunit hoteliers such as Hilton Hotels, Hyatt offers a number of different hotel concepts as parts of its core brand. For example, Hyatt introduced the Grand Hyatt and Park Hyatt concepts in 1980 "to further identify and market the diverse types of Hyatt properties worldwide." Grand Hyatt units serve leisure and business travelers as well as conventioneers wanting a "grand scale" of refinement during their stays. Park Hyatt is the firm's smaller, luxury hotel that caters to "the discriminating individual traveler seeking the privacy, personalized service, and elegance of a small European hotel." But Hyatt has diversified beyond hotel accommodations, offering other products and services. The firm owns and operates time-share properties, freestanding golf courses, and gaming operations. Hyatt opened its first freestanding golf course in 1995 in Tierra del Sol on the island of Aruba. Hyatt also provides management services to golf

© EMILE WAMSTEKER/
Bloomberg News/Landov

© TANNEN MAURY/
Bloomberg News/Landov

courses owned by other companies. Hyatt entered the riverboat gaming industry in 1994 when it opened the Grand Victoria Casino in Elgin, Illinois. As you see, Hyatt is much more than a collection of hotels.

Hyatt continues to diversify its hotel accommodation concepts or products, as shown by its recent purchase of AmeriSuites for more than $600 million. When it was purchased, AmeriSuites was an upscale limited-service hotel chain with 143 hotels in 32 states. Hyatt acquired AmeriSuites partly to diversify away from its core high-end lodging accommodations. By buying AmeriSuites, Hyatt entered the fastest-growing segment of the lodging industry—limited service, all-suites hotels targeting frequent travelers.

Hyatt intends to generate economies of scope through its acquisition of AmeriSuites by sharing resources and activities. In particular, Hyatt uses its purchasing power (a support activity) to buy upgraded furnishings for AmeriSuites rooms at a lower cost than AmeriSuites could have obtained as an independent company. Additionally, AmeriSuites facilities will use Hyatt's reservations systems and will participate in Hyatt's frequent-stayer program. Thus, by sharing activities (such as its reservations systems) and resources (such as its frequent-stayer program) with its new AmeriSuites unit, Hyatt intends to gain economies of scope based on operational relatedness while using its related constrained multiproduct strategy.

SOURCES: 2004, Company overview, Hyatt Corporation Home Page, http://www.hyatt.com, December 15; 2004, Hyatt to buy AmeriSuites hotel chain, *Reuters*, http://www.reuters.com, December 9; C. Binkley, 2004, Hotels are lifting rates, profits a deals disappear, study finds, *Wall Street Journal Online*, http://www.wsj.com, December 9; J. Kimelman, 2004, Real estate pro likes hotels, retail, *Barron's Online*, http://www.barrons.com, December 7; M. Maremont, 2004, Hyatt to buy AmeriSuites hotel chain, *Wall Street Journal Online*, http://www.wsj.com, December 9.

Corporate Relatedness and the Related Linked Multiproduct Strategy

Economies of scope are generated through corporate relatedness when the firm successfully transfers core competencies between one or more of the businesses within individual SBUs. Remember that with the related linked multiproduct strategy, only limited relationships exist between the firm's businesses in each SBU and that core competencies are transferred only between the businesses *within* each SBU. A firm using the related linked multiproduct strategy does not seek to transfer core competencies between businesses housed in its different SBUs. Next, we examine how GE (a firm using the related linked strategy) transfers core competencies between the businesses within individual SBUs.

GE has 11 "primary business units, each with its own number of divisions."[15] As an SBU, GE Commercial Finance has eight divisions (such as Aviation Services, Fleet Services, and Healthcare Financial Services). Fleet Services is another division in this SBU. This division received the 2004 CRM (Customer Relationship Management) award from Gartner,[16] a firm that provides research and analysis on the global information technology industry. CRM is a technique firms use to establish and maintain long-term, positive relationships with their customers. Because the division's CRM system received an award for its excellence, this system may be a core competence that could be transferred from Fleet Services to one or more of the remaining seven divisions in the GE Commercial Finance SBU.

One way that intangible core competencies can be transferred from one business to another within a particular SBU is to reassign personnel. In these cases, the people in charge of an activity in a core competence within one business are assigned to another business to teach those employees how to develop the value-creating core competence. Personnel can sometimes be reluctant to transfer from one business to another; in these instances, the firm may have to pay them a premium to gain their cooperation.

Another way that core competencies are transferred is through knowledge acquired by participating in managerial and leadership training programs. One of the objectives of GE's executive education programs, for example, is for participating managers to develop knowledge (an important source of core competencies) that can be shared between some of the firm's businesses within one of its strategic business units. Here's an example of how this works in one of GE's SBUs. GE's NBC Universal SBU was formed in May 2004 "through the merger of NBC and Vivendi Universal Entertainment."[17] Managers from Universal are participating in executive education programs to work on the "integration" of its businesses with other parts of the SBU that GE has created, while "GE is shipping company-trained CFOs west to scope out the Hollywood units."[18]

Simultaneously Seeking Operational Relatedness and Corporate Relatedness

As shown in cell 3 in Figure 6.2, firms can develop economies of scope by simultaneously seeking high levels of operational relatedness and corporate relatedness.[19] Essentially, this means that the firm's multiproduct strategy is a hybrid with characteristics of both the related constrained and related linked multiproduct strategies.

Experience shows that it is very difficult for firms to simultaneously achieve operational and corporate relatedness.[20] Although sharing is difficult with tangible resources, in which primary and support activities are combined to achieve operational relatedness, transferring intangible resources can be even more challenging. Transferring intangible resources (such as knowledge about how to interpret market trends) between businesses within a SBU to generate economies of scope by achieving corporate relatedness is more difficult because the potential outcome is less visible (that is, it is difficult to know that an intangible resource is being transferred unless that resource is an individual manager). So you can imagine how difficult it is for a firm to simultaneously focus on *sharing* tangible resources and activities among businesses within each SBU while simultaneously concentrating on *transferring* intangible core competencies among those businesses. Although it is challenging to simultaneously attain operational relatedness and corporate relatedness, evidence suggests that firms able to do so have developed a competitive advantage that is difficult for competitors to imitate.[21] Walt Disney Studios, one of Disney's divisions, can share resources and activities as it creates, produces, and promotes movies in its different studios (such as Walt Disney Pictures and Miramax). However, within the same division, knowledge about how to promote movies as a source of entertainment could be transferred to other parts of the division such as television programs and live theater productions, which are also attempting to promote activities as a source of entertainment.[22]

Unrelated-Diversification Multiproduct Strategy

As indicated by cell 4 in Figure 6.2, firms using the unrelated-diversification multiproduct strategy do not attempt to develop economies of scope by achieving either operational relatedness or corporate relatedness. When using the unrelated-diversification multiproduct strategy, firms try to generate financial economies instead of trying to develop economies of scope through operational relatedness and/or corporate relatedness.

Financial economies are cost savings or higher returns generated when the firm effectively allocates its financial resources based on investments either inside or outside the firm.[23] With respect to internal investments, the firm creates financial economies when it allocates its resources efficiently through the efforts of corporate headquarters personnel who represent a capital market for the entire organization. In terms of investments outside the firm, the company using the unrelated-diversification strategy creates financial economies when it is able to buy another firm, restructure that firm's assets in value-creating ways, and then sell that company at a price exceeding its investment (price paid plus amount invested to increase the quality of the purchased company's assets). We consider each type of financial economy in greater detail in the next two sections.

Efficient Internal Capital Market Allocation

As you'll recall from your study of economics and finance in particular, capital markets are assumed to be efficient in the allocation of capital. Efficiency

*
financial economies

cost savings or higher returns generated when the firm effectively allocates its financial resources based on investments either inside or outside the firm results as investors take an equity position in firms by purchasing shares of stock in companies they believe have high future cash flow value. Efficient markets also allocate capital in the form of debt as shareholders and debtholders seek to improve the value of their investments by taking stakes in firms that they believe have high growth and profitability prospects.

In companies using the unrelated-diversification multiproduct strategy, corporate headquarters personnel allocate the firm's capital across its portfolio of product divisions. At Textron, which uses the unrelated-diversification strategy, corporate headquarters personnel allocate capital across the firm's five strategic business units—Bell, Cessna, Fastening Systems, Industrial, and Finance (Bell accounts for the largest amount of Textron's revenues—24 percent).[24]

At Textron and other firms using the unrelated-diversification strategy, capital is allocated on the basis of what headquarters personnel believe will generate the greatest amount of financial economies for the organization as a whole. At Japan Tobacco, for example, additional capital is currently being allocated to the firm's cigarette manufacturing SBU so it can acquire other firms. The purpose of the acquisitions is for Japan Tobacco's cigarette manufacturing SBU to increase the breadth and depth of its cigarette product lines. Financial capital is allocated to the firm's cigarette SBU because headquarters personnel believe that its growth and profitability prospects are greater than those of the firm's other SBUs (foods, pharmaceuticals, agribusiness, engineering, and real estate).[25] In Japan Tobacco and Textron, as well as in other firms using the unrelated-diversification multiproduct strategy, financial capital is allocated only after extensive, in-depth analyses of each SBU's prospects for revenue and profitability growth.

Internal capital market allocations in firms using the unrelated-diversification strategy may be the basis for superior returns to shareholders compared to returns shareholders would receive as a result of allocations by the external capital market.[26] Access to information is the main reason for this possibility. Indeed, while managing the firm's portfolio of SBUs, headquarters personnel may gain access to detailed information that isn't available to the external capital market about the ability of one or more of the firm's SBUs to create value by growing its revenue and profitability streams. In addition, those evaluating the performance of all of a firm's SBUs can internally discipline poorly performing units by allocating fewer or different types of resources to them.[27] Disciplined SBUs' managers are likely to respond favorably by working hard to improve their units' performance as the first step to receiving a larger percentage of the entire firm's financial capital.

The external capital market relies on information produced by the firm to estimate the organization's ability to generate attractive future revenue and earnings streams. Annual reports, press conferences, and filings mandated by various regulatory bodies are the most common sources of information available to the external capital market. In these communication media, firms may overemphasize positive news while either ignoring or de-emphasizing negative news about one or more of their SBUs. Beyond this, firms may not want to divulge information when using these media because it might help competitors better understand and imitate the competitive advantages of product divisions within SBUs. Therefore, in-depth knowledge about the positive and negative performance prospects and competitive advantages for all of the firm's SBUs creates a potential informational advantage for the firm relative to the external capital market.

As we've described, the firm's internal capital market can create value in the form of financial economies when it efficiently allocates the organization's total set of financial capital. However, firms sometimes fail in their efforts to do this effectively. When this happens, the conglomerate must either improve its internal capital market allocation skills or divest either SBUs or product divisions within SBUs until it reaches the point where once again, the SBUs the firm owns are creating more value through financial economies than they would generate while operating as independent entities.

We describe a failed unrelated-diversification multiproduct strategy in "Understanding Strategy." As noted earlier, firms may decide to become less diversified (often referred to as refocusing or downscoping[28]) when they are unable to achieve financial economies through allocations of their financial capital. This is what happened at Campbell Soup.

Restructuring

A firm using the unrelated-diversification multiproduct strategy can also produce financial economies by learning how to create value by buying and selling other companies' assets in the external market.[29] As in the real estate business, buying assets at low prices, restructuring them in value-creating ways, and then selling them at a price exceeding their purchase cost plus the restructuring cost generates a positive return on the firm's invested capital.

United Technologies Corporation (UTC) uses the unrelated-diversification strategy and restructures purchased firms' assets to create financial economies. In May 1999, for example, UTC sold its long-held automotive division (a composite of several previous acquisitions) to Lear for $2.3 billion because UTC's top-level managers concluded that the firm could not create additional value by further restructuring the unit's assets. UTC takes a deliberate approach in buying and selling restructured assets, often requiring several years to realize full value from restructuring its assets.[30]

In general, it is easier to create financial economies by restructuring the assets of firms competing in relatively low-technology businesses because of the uncertain future demand for high-technology products. All businesses that UTC purchases, for example, are involved in manufacturing industrial and commercial products, many of which are relatively low-technology (such as elevators and air conditioners). Of course, firms seeking financial economies by buying and selling restructured assets must be able to restructure those assets at a cost below their expected future market value when they are sold to another company.

Managerial Motives to Diversify

In addition to the reasons for diversification that are shown in Table 6.1, top-level managers may have two additional motives to diversify their organization. These motives may or may not be in the best interests of the firm's stakeholders.

Reducing the risk of losing their job is the first motive for top-level executives.[31] If a firm has multiple businesses and one business fails, the firm is unlikely to experience total failure if the other businesses are doing well. Therefore, additional diversification reduces the chance that top-level executives of a diversified firm will lose their jobs.

understanding strategy:

CAMPBELL SOUP RETURNS TO LOWER LEVELS OF DIVERSIFICATION TO IMPROVE ITS PERFORMANCE

Founded in 1869, Campbell Soup is a global manufacturer of high-quality convenience foods. Today, Campbell operates with four product divisions: North American Soup and Away from Home (39 percent), North America Sauces and Beverages (19 percent), Biscuits and Confectionery (26 percent), and International Soups and Sauces (16 percent). The percentages indicate the total of the firm's sales revenues earned by each product division during Campbell's 2003 fiscal

© David Young-Wolff/ Photo Edit

year. Obviously, Campbell is using a related diversificaton multiproduct strategy. Because some resources and activities are shared among the firm's divisions, we know that Campbell is using the related constrained multiproduct strategy. Only a few years ago, though, the firm was using the unrelated diversification multiproduct strategy. Let's talk about why the firm first became more diversified and then why it decided to reduce its level of diversification to again use the related constrained strategy.

R. Gordon McGovern was CEO of Campbell Soup from 1980 to 1989. McGovern decided early in his tenure to rapidly expand Campbell's product lines to increase its revenues and profits. McGovern felt that it was difficult to rapidly expand a packaged-goods company's product lines by developing new products internally. Therefore, McGovern concluded that Campbell should acquire other firms to quickly gain access to new products and new product markets. Instead of acquiring only food products, though, Campbell began to use the unrelated diversification strategy to acquire firms that it felt were positioned to capital-

ize on consumer trends, whatever they might happen to be. So McGovern and his top-level managers intended to create financial economies through their efficient allocation of financial capital across Campbell's increasingly diverse product divisions. During the course of McGovern's tenure, Campbell bought firms involved in all types of businesses. Triangle Manufacturing Company, a fitness products maker, is an example of a firm Campbell acquired that is clearly unrelated to what were historically the firm's core products. At one time during McGovern's tenure as Campbell's CEO, the firm had 50 product divisions.

A major reason for Campbell's failure to generate financial economies while using the unrelated diversification strategy is that the firm's approach to managing its core product divisions never changed. This means that instead of managing the core product divisions to control costs and use financial capital as efficiently as possible (which is necessary to achieve financial economies), managers in the firm's historical core product divisions continued to focus on creating economies of scope by sharing resources and activities. At the same time, corporate headquarters personnel didn't implement the strong financial controls necessary to efficiently manage an internal capital market.

David Johnson succeeded McGovern as CEO in 1990. He quickly decided that Campbell should no longer use the unrelated diversification strategy and that it should divest businesses that weren't related to its historical core products and product markets. As a result of divestitures that continued throughout much of the 1990s, Campbell is again using the related constrained multiproduct strategy to create value through operational relatedness.

SOURCES: 2004, Campbell Soup Co., *Reuters*, http://www.reuters.com, December 1; 2004, Campbell Soup, *Standard and Poor's Stock Report*, http://www.standardandpoors.com, November 27; 2004, Campbell Soup Company, About us, Campbell Soup Company Home Page, http://www.campbellsoup.com, December 2.

However, the managerial/leadership challenge increases greatly when a firm diversifies beyond the level of the single-business multiproduct strategy. The risk here is that managers who believe that keeping their top-level positions depends on greater levels of diversification may overdiversify the firm. Similar to business-level strategies, the multiproduct strategy used by the firm should be a function of opportunities in the firm's external environment and the degree to which the firm has core competencies that can create value in product markets beyond its core product market. A firm's board of directors must ensure that the level of diversification top-level managers pursue is based on a match between opportunities in the external environment and the company's core competencies.

The relationship between firm size and executive compensation is the second managerial diversification motive. Research shows that as a firm's size increases, so does the compensation for top-level managers.[32] Of course, increasing a firm's level of diversification increases the firm's overall size. The relationship between firm size and managerial compensation is perhaps not surprising, in that larger, more diversified organizations are more difficult to manage than smaller, less diversified firms.[33] Common sense suggests that more complex and difficult work should be more highly compensated. However, the board of directors desires to use compensation incentives that encourage managers to diversify the firm in value-creating ways rather than compensating them simply on the basis of the firm's size.

In Chapter 5, we noted that after choosing a business-level strategy, the firm must effectively implement it to fully benefit from its use. Organizational structure plays a major role in implementing a strategy. Because of their importance, we next discuss the appropriate organizational structures for implementing the different multiproduct strategies.

Implementing Multiproduct Strategies

We mentioned the multidivisional structure in Chapter 5 and indicated that it is not used to implement business-level strategies. Indeed, the multidivisional structure is used only to implement multiproduct strategies with moderate and high levels of diversification. Firms using the single-business and dominant-business multiproduct strategies still rely on the different forms of the functional structure used to implement the cost leadership strategy or product differentiation strategy. UPS uses a functional structure to implement its business-level strategies in its three product groups. Because UPS is rapidly becoming more diversified, a new structure will be required to implement the related constrained multiproduct strategy. When this happens, UPS will likely discard its functional structure in favor of a form of the multidivisional structure. Indeed, firms often change their multiproduct strategy from dominant-business to a related-diversification strategy (typically related constrained first) as they grow. With the change in strategy, the firm must also change its structure from the functional form to the appropriate form of the multidivisional structure.

The **multidivisional (M-form) structure** is an organizational structure in which the firm is organized to generate either economies of scope or financial economies. The M-form has three versions (see Figure 6.3). As we describe next, the different versions of the M-form are designed to implement multiproduct strategies in firms with moderate to high levels of diversification.

*
multidivisional (M-form) structure

an organizational structure in which the firm is organized to generate either economies of scope or financial economies

FIGURE 6.3 Three Variations of the Multidivisional Structure

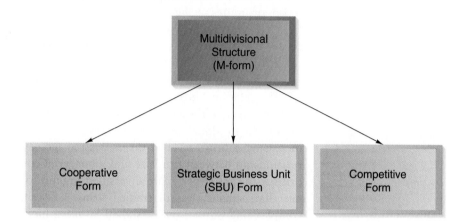

The Cooperative M-Form and the Related Constrained Multiproduct Strategy

*

cooperative M-form

an organizational structure in which horizontal integration is used so that resources and activities can be shared between product divisions

The **cooperative M-form** is an organizational structure in which horizontal integration is used so that resources and activities can be shared between product divisions. As you can see in Figure 6.4, firms using the related constrained multiproduct strategy (such as P&G) adopt the cooperative M-form. The product divisions in a firm's M-form structure must cooperate with one another to share resources and activities and generate economies of scope by achieving operational relatedness.[34] Thus, as we noted earlier, P&G's five product divisions share some resources and some activities.

Success with the cooperative M-form is significantly affected by how well product divisions process information about the resources and activities they intend to share and how they intend to share them. *Horizontal linkages* are the mechanisms used to facilitate information sharing between product divisions. One obvious horizontal linkage is holding frequent meetings among product division managers in which they discuss each division's products. In addition, each division head describes his or her division's available resources (especially new ones) and how they are used to complete different activities in the value chain. A key objective of division heads during these meetings is to determine whether two or more divisions' resources could be combined to create an intangible capability that could become a core competence.

Temporary teams or task forces are a second horizontal integrating mechanism. These groups are typically formed for a project that requires sharing the resources and activities of two or more divisions. Developing a new product or finding a way to create more value by completing one or more activities in the value chain are the objectives sought by temporary teams and task forces.

As shown in Figure 6.4, division managers in the cooperative M-form are held accountable for their divisions' performance. Because of this, headquarters personnel should also use compensation systems that reward sharing. As a

FIGURE 6.4

Cooperative Form of the Multidivisional Structure for Implementing the Related Constrained Strategy

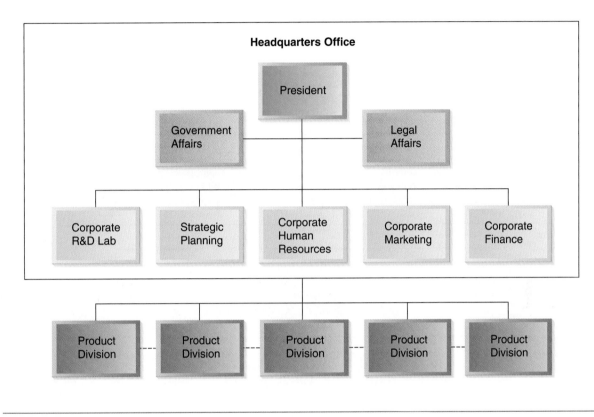

NOTES: • Structural integration devices create tight links among all divisions
• Corporate office emphasizes centralized strategic planning, human resources, and marketing to foster cooperation between divisions
• R&D is likely to be centralized
• Rewards are subjective and tend to emphasize overall corporate performance in additon to divisional performance
• Culture emphasizes cooperative sharing

result, for example, each division head's compensation might be based on a composite of her division's performance as well as that of the firm's other divisions, especially those that are cooperating on joint product development and management. This type of compensation signals to division heads that each person's success is at least partly a function of the success of cooperation.

The SBU M-Form and the Related Linked Multiproduct Strategy

The **strategic business unit (SBU) M-form** is an organizational structure in which the divisions within each SBU concentrate on transferring core competencies rather than on sharing resources and activities. As you can see in Figure 6.5, firms using the related linked multiproduct strategy (such as GE) adopt the SBU M-form.

In the SBU M-form, each SBU is a profit center that is evaluated and controlled by corporate headquarters. Although both strategic controls and financial controls are used (recall our discussion of these two types of controls in

*
strategic
business unit
(SBU) M-form

an organizational structure
in which the divisions
within each SBU concentrate
on transferring core
competencies rather than
on sharing resources and
activities

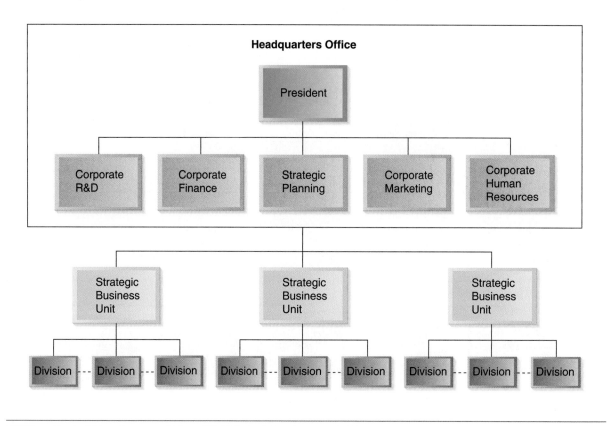

NOTES: • Structural integration among divisions within SBUs, but independence across SBUs
- Strategic planning may be the most prominent function in headquarters for managing the strategic planning approval process of SBUs for the president
- Each SBU may have its own budget for staff to foster integration
- Corporate headquarters staff serve as consultants to SBUs and divisions, rather than having direct input to product strategy, as in the cooperative form

Chapter 2), financial controls are vital to headquarters' evaluation of each SBU. Strategic controls, on the other hand, are critical when those leading each SBU evaluate the performance of the divisions in their SBU. Strategic controls are also valuable to headquarters personnel as they try to determine whether the businesses the organization has chosen to enter (as shown by its collection of SBUs) are the right ones. As you can imagine, the SBU M-form can be a complex structure. Think of GE's size (11 SBUs with multiple divisions in each SBU). It doesn't take much imagination to conclude that GE's organizational structure is immensely complicated.

*
competitive
M-form

an organizational structure
in which there is complete
independence between the
firm's divisions

The Competitive M-Form and the Unrelated-Diversification Multiproduct Strategy

The **competitive M-form** is an organizational structure in which there is complete independence between the firm's divisions. As shown in Figure 6.6, firms using the unrelated-diversification multiproduct strategy adopt the competitive M-form structure. Recall that with the unrelated-diversification strategy, the

FIGURE 6.6 Competitive Form of the Multidivisional Structure for Implementing the Unrelated-Diversification Strategy

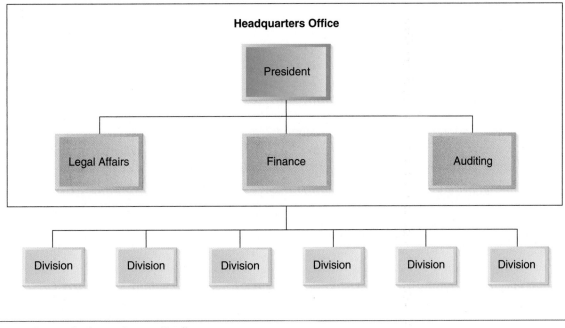

NOTES: • Corporate headquarters has a small staff
- Finance and auditing are the most prominent functions in the headquarters office to manage cash flow and ensure the accuracy of performance data
- The legal affairs function becomes important when the firm acquires or divests assets
- Divisions are independent and separate for financial evaluation purposes
- Divisions retain strategic control, but cash is managed by the corporate office
- Divisions compete for corporate resources

firm seeks to generate financial economies rather than develop economies of scope through either operational relatedness or corporate relatedness.

Divisions operating in a competitive M-form structure actually compete against one another for the firm's resources. Indeed, an efficient internal capital market allocates resources to the divisions with the greatest probability of generating excess returns on the firm's financial capital. Because of this focus, corporate headquarters personnel make no effort to find ways for sharing to occur between the firm's divisions. Instead, the focus of the headquarters office is on specifying performance criteria that will be used to evaluate the performance of all divisions. At Textron, for example, return on invested capital is the primary criterion used by corporate headquarters to judge the performance of the firm's divisions. According to Textron, "return on invested capital serves as both a compass to guide every investment decision and a measurement of Textron's success."[35]

With the competitive M-form, headquarters personnel rely on strategic controls to establish financial performance criteria; financial controls are then used to monitor divisional performance relative to those criteria. So the focus of headquarters is on performance appraisal, resource allocations, and long-range planning to ensure that the firm's financial capital is being used to maximize financial success.[36]

Summary

The primary purpose of this chapter is to discuss the different multiproduct strategies firms can use to enter new product markets. In doing so, we examined the following topics:

- A **multiproduct strategy** is an action plan that the firm develops to describe how it will compete in different product markets. When using multiproduct strategies, firms become more diversified in terms of the number and types of products they produce and sell to customers. Firms that use multiproduct strategies effectively use their core competencies to pursue opportunities in different product markets.

- There are five multiproduct strategies, ranging from low levels of diversification (the single-business and dominant-business strategies) to moderate to high levels of diversification (the related constrained, related unlinked, and unrelated-diversification strategies). As a firm becomes more diversified, the number of products it offers and the number of product markets in which it competes increase.

- A firm using the single-business multiproduct strategy makes and sells a single product or a variety of a single product and generates at least 95 percent of its sales revenue from its dominant business or product line. As firms continue to develop the ways in which their core competencies can be used to create additional products or to compete in different product markets, they may begin to pursue the dominant-business strategy—a multiproduct strategy through which the firm generates between 70 and 95 percent of its sales revenue from a single business.

- Firms using a related-diversification multiproduct strategy try to create **economies of scope**, which are cost savings that result from successfully sharing some of their resources and activities or core competencies between their different businesses. There are two types of related-diversification multiproduct strategies, both of which suggest that the firm is experiencing a moderate level of diversification. With both strategies, the firm earns less than 70 percent of its sales revenue from its dominant business.

- In the related constrained strategy, most or all of the firm's businesses share some resources and activities in order to generate economies of scope. Markets, products, and technologies are examples of what firms can share between their businesses. Firms that can share resources and activities between their businesses achieve **operational relatedness**.

- With the related linked strategy, few relationships exist between the firm's businesses. Firms share some resources and activities when using this strategy. However, the focus is on transferring core competencies between businesses to generate economies of scope instead of on sharing resources and activities. Firms that can do this achieve **corporate relatedness**.

- In the unrelated-diversification multiproduct strategy, resources, activities, and core competencies are not shared between the firm's businesses. Firms using this strategy are often called conglomerates. With this strategy, the firm tries to create financial economies instead of economies of scope. **Financial economies** are cost savings or higher returns generated when the firm effectively allocates its financial resources based on investments inside or outside the firm. The firm's divisions compete against one another to gain access to a larger share of the entire organization's financial capital. Firms generate financial economies when they successfully allocate their own financial capital across their businesses or by buying other companies, restructuring those firms' assets, and then selling the acquisitions in the marketplace at a profit.

- Managers often have personal motives for increasing the diversification of their firm. For example, increasing the number of product markets in which the firm competes reduces the managers' risk of losing their job (balances firm performance across markets). Additionally, compensation of executives is often related to the size of the firm. Thus, growing the size of the firm through diversification may increase executives' pay. Engaging in a multiproduct strategy for these reasons may or may not create value for the firm's shareholders.

- It is important to match each multiproduct strategy with the proper organizational structure. Firms using the single-business and dominant-business strategies continue to use the functional structure that we discussed in Chapter 5. However, the related- and unrelated-diversification strategies are effectively used only when supported by a version of the **multidivisional structure** (in which the firm is organized to generate either economies of scope or financial economies). The **cooperative M-form** supports the related constrained strategy, the **SBU M-form** supports the related linked strategy and the **competitive M-form** supports the unrelated-diversification multiproduct strategy.

Key Terms

competitive M-form 154
cooperative M-form 152
corporate relatedness 143
economies of scope 141

financial economies 147
multidivisional (M-form)
    structure 151
multiproduct strategy 138

operational relatedness 143
strategic business unit (SBU) 142
strategic business unit (SBU)
    M-form 153

Discussion Questions

1. What is a multiproduct strategy? Why do some firms use this strategy?
2. What are the different levels of diversification (from low to high) that firms experience when using a multiproduct strategy?
3. What are the related-diversification multiproduct strategies? How can the firm create value by using these strategies?
4. What is the unrelated-diversification multiproduct strategy? What are the ways that a firm can create value by using this strategy?
5. What are the two additional motives that top-level managers have to diversify their firms?
6. What organizational structure is used to implement each of the different multiproduct strategies?

Endnotes

1. H. Kim, R. E. Hoskisson, & W. P. Wan, 2004, Power dependence, diversification strategy, and performance in Keiretsu member firms, *Strategic Management Journal*, 25: 613–636.
2. W. P. Wan & R. E. Hoskisson, 2003, Home country environments, corporate diversification strategies and firm performance, *Academy of Management Journal*, 46: 27–45.
3. G. T. M. Hult, D. J. Ketchen Jr., & S. F. Slater, 2004, Information processing, knowledge development, and strategic supply chain performance, *Academy of Management Journal*, 47: 241–253.
4. M. E. Porter, 1987, From competitive advantage to corporate strategy, *Harvard Business Review*, 65(3): 43–59.
5. 2003 UPS Annual Report, UPS Home Page, http://www.ups.com, 8.
6. R. Rumelt, 1974, *Strategy, Structure, and Economic Performance*, Boston: Harvard Business School.
7. R. A. Bettis, 1986, The dominant logic: A new linkage between diversity and performance, *Strategic Management Journal*, 7: 485–501.
8. Rumelt, *Strategy, Structure, and Economic Performance*.
9. L. Fauver, J. Houston, & A. Naranjo, 2003, Capital market development, international integration, legal systems, and the value of corporate diversification: A cross-country analysis, *Journal of Financial and Quantitative Analysis*, 38: 135–157.
10. S. Manikutty, 2000, Family business groups in India: A resource-based view of the emerging trends, *Family Business Review*, 3: 279–292.
11. 1997, Inside story, *The Economist*, December 6: 7–9.
12. 2004, P&G products, Procter & Gamble Home Page, http://www.procterandgamble.com, December 15.
13. M. A. Hitt, J. S. Harrison, & R. D. Ireland, 2001, *Mergers and Acquisitions: A Guide to Creating Value for Stakeholders*, New York: Oxford University Press.

14. A. Van Oijen, 2001, Product diversification, corporate management instruments, resource sharing, and performance, *Academy of Management Best Paper Proceedings* (on CD-ROM, Business Policy and Strategy Division).

15. 2005, Our company, GE Home Page, http://www.ge.com, January 11.

16. 2004, GE Commercial Finance and Pitt Ohio Express win Gartner CRM excellence awards, Yahoo Finance, http://www.yahoo.com, October 28.

17. 2005, NBC Universal, GE Home Page, http://www.ge.com, January 11.

18. R. Grover, D. Brady, & T. Lowry, 2004, Lights! Camera! Bean Counters! NBC is set to get its Hollywood studio. Can the GE unit handle the culture clash? *Business Week,* May 17: 82.

19. K. M. Eisenhardt & D. C. Galunic, 2000, Coevolving: At last, a way to make synergies work, *Harvard Business Review,* 78(1): 91–111.

20. R. Schoenberg, 2001, Knowledge transfer and resource sharing as value creation mechanisms in inbound continental European acquisitions, *Journal of Euro-Marketing,* 10: 99–114.

21. Eisenhardt & Galunic, Coevolving, 94.

22. 2005, The Walt Disney Studios, Walt Disney Home Page, http://www.waltdisney.com, January 11.

23. D. D. Bergh, 1997, Predicting divestiture of unrelated acquisitions: An integrative model of ex ante conditions, *Strategic Management Journal,* 18: 715–731.

24. 2004, Textron Inc., *Standard and Poor's Stock Report,* http://www.standardandpoors.com, December 27; M. Maremont, 2004, More can be more, *Wall Street Journal,* October 25: R4.

25. J. Singer & R. G. Matthews, 2004, Investors bid up tobacco, *Wall Street Journal Online,* http://www.wsj.com, October 28.

26. O. E. Williamson, 1975, *Markets and Hierarchies: Analysis and Antitrust Implications,* New York: Macmillan.

27. D. Miller, R. Eisenstat, & N. Foote, 2002, Strategy from the inside out: Building capability-creating organizations, *California Management Review,* 44(3): 37–54.

28. R. E. Hoskisson & M. A. Hitt, 1994, *Downscoping: How to tame the diversified firm.* New York: Oxford University Press.

29. R. E. Hoskisson, R. A. Johnson, D. Yiu, & W. P. Wan, 2001, Restructuring strategies and diversified business groups: Differences associated with country institutional environments, in M. A. Hitt, R. E. Freeman, & J. S. Harrison (eds.), *Handbook of Strategic Management,* Oxford, U.K.: Blackwell, 433–463.

30. D. Brady, 2004, The unsung CEO, *Business Week,* October 25: 76–84.

31. W. Shen & A. A. Cannella Jr., 2002, Power dynamics within top management and their impacts on CEO dismissal followed by inside succession, *Academy of Management Journal,* 45: 717–733.

32. J. J. Cordeiro & R. Veliyath, 2003, Beyond pay for performance: A panel study of the determinants of CEO compensation, *American Business Review,* 21(1): 56–66.

33. J. G. Combs & M. S. Skill, 2003, Managerialist and human capital explanation for key executive pay premiums: A contingency perspective, *Academy of Management Journal,* 46: 63–73.

34. C. C. Markides & P. J. Williamson, 1996, Corporate diversification and organizational structure: A resource-based view, *Academy of Management Journal,* 39: 340–367.

35. 2002, Textron profile, Textron Home Page, http://www.textron.com, February 4.

36. T. R. Eisenmann & J. L. Bower, 2000, The entrepreneurial M-form: Strategic integration in global media firms, *Organization Science,* 11: 348–355.

Your Career

© Michael Newmann/Photo Edit

There are at least two reasons for you to understand the materials in this chapter. First, as an employee, you may be involved with your firm's efforts to use a multi-product strategy and further diversify its operations by offering new products to markets. If you worked for Wrigley, for example, as discussed in the Mini-Case, understanding how each multiproduct strategy works and what it is intended to achieve would serve you well. In fact, your understanding of multiproduct strategies could position you well to contribute to a firm's efforts to diversify its product offerings.

The second reason for you to master the chapter's content is that you may wish to diversify your career options. Let's think about this possibility and how it might come about.

As we know, people at the beginning of their career will likely change jobs at least five or six times before they retire. Even in retirement, the number of people starting a second career continues to grow. Often what was once an avocation (such as gardening) becomes a vocation (such as starting one's own land-scaping business). You can prepare today for these possibilities. Recall that while studying the "Your Career" in the last chapter you were asked to identify your competitive advantages. Think about those advantages again. On what core competencies are your advantages based? If one of your core competencies is an ability to learn quickly, for example, how might you use that competence to diversify your skills so you could work for different firms in different industries? Having diverse skills that can be used to work for different employers increases your probability of being continuously employed.

To maximize your value, list your core competencies on which your competitive advantages are based. How can you use your core competencies to diversify your skills? With more diverse skills, in what multiple businesses or industries would you be qualified to work? Responding to these questions will make you think about how your core competencies can be used in different job settings to create value. Also, think about how your core competencies could be combined with those held by other individuals to create synergy. Having this knowledge is as important for us as individuals as it is for firms trying to maximize their performance.

Competitive analysis is a critical step in the strategic management process. A competitor analysis should include identifying, studying, and comparing the focal firm with all competitors. All too often, CEOs and others involved with the firm's strategic management process focus only on *direct* or *immediate* competitors, as they have been announced and are already under study. This chapter's tool takes this analysis two steps further and considers *impending* and *invisible* competitors as well.

3 I's Competitor Radar Screen

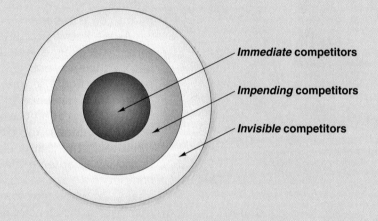

Immediate competitors	Already major players in your particular industrial segment(s); publicly admit competitive position and market share; high knowledge base
Impending competitors	Small players making a move to grow and gain market share; major players from other (related) industrial segments announcing entry into your market; medium knowledge base
Invisible competitors	Large players considering an unanticipated move from other (unrelated) industrial segments into your market—in secret; low knowledge base

✳ BIZ FLIX

JOSIE AND THE PUSSYCATS: RELATED OR UNRELATED MULTIPRODUCT STRATEGY?

Recall this chapter's discussion of multiproduct strategies and especially the Campbell Soup case. Assume while watching this scene that a single firm produces and markets all products and services shown in the scene.

Riverdale's little-known rock-and-roll trio The Pussycats gets an unexpected career boost following the mysterious disappearance of renowned rock group Dujour. Wyatt Frame (Alan Cumming), a MegaRecords executive, discovers the group on a city street. His scheming mind combines with the maniacal scheming mind of Fiona (Parker Posey), MegaRecords chief executive officer, to propel the newly named Josie and the Pussycats to national success. Unknown to this talented group, Fiona plans to use subliminal advertising embedded in their recordings to control the minds and spending habits of the nation's teenagers.

This scene is an edited composite from different parts of the film. The scene does not appear exactly as shown in the film. If you have seen *Josie and the Pussycats*, you may recall some of these moments.

What to Watch for and Ask Yourself

1. How many products and services does this hypothetical company produce and market? You may need to view the scene more than once to get a good count. You can also pause the scene to closely study any part of it.
2. What level of diversification does the scene imply for the firm—low or high?
3. Assess the multiproduct strategy implied by the scene. Could any firm successfully carry out this strategy?

Mini-Case

Wrigley: Diversifying beyond Chewing Gum
Most of us are quite familiar with Wrigley's core products. Selling trademarked chewing-gum and bubble-gum brands such as Spearmint, Doublemint, Juicy Fruit, Big Red, and Hubba Bubba across the globe for more than 100 years, Wrigley is the world's dominant chewing-gum and bubble-gum manufacturer. As we noted earlier in the chapter, this firm historically has used a single-business multiproduct strategy. This means that no more than five percent of its sales revenues were generated by products other than its core gum products.

However, Wrigley is now committed to transforming itself into a global confectionery business. Clearly, the firm is becoming more diversified. In fact, Wrigley is now using the dominant-business multiproduct strategy. Why did Wrigley's leaders decide that the firm's future growth in sales revenue and profitability would be through additional diversification of its products? The answer to this question is interesting, yet perhaps not surprising.

As with other firms, Wrigley wants to increase its revenues and profits. The firm's leaders believe that growth with its chewing gums can occur organically; Wrigley is confident that it already has the core competencies necessary to continue developing innovative chewing gums and bubble gums that will satisfy the needs of customers in many countries. But the firm also believes that the same core competencies (such as its research and development and sales and marketing capabilities) are the foundation for pursuing what Wrigley calls "strategic diversification" into related confectionery businesses (such as chewy and hard candies) and to increase its profitability by doing so. So Wrigley executives believe that the firm can create synergy by sharing some of its current resources and primary and support activities with processes used to manufacture and sell chewy and hard candies. Because of these beliefs, the firm is discarding its single-business multiproduct strategy in favor of a dominant-business multiproduct strategy.

Wrigley is aggressively pursuing its goal of strategic diversification to become a global confectionery business. In January 2004, Wrigley reached an agreement with Agrolimen, a privately held Spanish food conglomerate, to buy certain confectionery businesses from Agrolimen's Joyco Group. Pim Pom lollipops, Boomer bubble gum, and Solano candy are three of the products Wrigley acquired from Joyco. Bill Wrigley, president, CEO, and chairman of Wrigley, described the reason for acquiring these products: "The addition of strong brands, people and confectionery expertise from Joyco will increase the long-term success of our business and enhance our ability to weave our brands into the fabric of everyday life around the world." As this comment suggests, Wrigley wants his firm to expand the number of confectionery products it produces for people to use on virtually a daily basis.

In late 2004, Wrigley continued its expansion into new confectionery products when it spent $1.48 billion to acquire certain brands from Kraft Foods. Life Savers and Altoids were the most appealing of the brands Wrigley acquired through this transaction. Analysts viewed this strategic diversification favorably, suggesting that Kraft's sweets were a strong fit with Wrigley's growing presence as a global confectionery business.

SOURCES: 2004, Wrigley to buy Kraft candies, *Dallas Morning News,* November 16: D3; 2004, Wrigley to add Life Savers and Altoids to its confectionery unit, Wrigley Home Page, http://www.wrigley.com, December 1; 2004, Wrigley announces acquisition of confectionery businesses, *Consumer M&A Weekly,* http://www.piperjaffray.com/476, January 8.

Questions

1. Go to Wrigley's Web site (http://www.wrigley.com) and find out what other acquisitions the company has made since the Mini-Case was written to continue its progress toward becoming a global confectionery business. Do you think the firm is making good progress with its dominant-business multiproduct strategy? Why or why not?
2. Can you imagine a time in which Wrigley would change its multiproduct strategy from dominant-business to related constrained diversification? If so, why might it do so, and into what product categories can you imagine Wrigley attempting to use its core competencies to become more diversified?
3. Discuss the ultimate structural choices that Wrigley will need to contemplate in order to manage its increasing level of diversification.

EXPERIENTIAL EXERCISES

EXERCISE ONE: UNRELATED DIVERSIFICATION DEBATE

The corporate strategies of both Illinois Tool Works and Newell-Rubbermaid suggest that the age of unrelated diversification lives on. Illinois Tool Works (ITW), for example, had 650 operations in 445 countries in 2005. CEO W. James Farrell told *Forbes* in 2001 that the firm buys any company serving the auto, welding, construction, and food industries. As long as the business is number one in its niche and somewhat poorly run, ITW feels it can make money by acquiring the firm. After a purchase, ITW refocuses an acquired firm on the top 20 percent of the business's customers and reduces the product line to serve those clients. Farrell told *Forbes* that ITW could add another 600 businesses before 2010 and still make money! Since early 2000, ITW's stock price has risen from about $60 a share to around $90 in early 2005 with analysts expecting a price well over $100 in the near future.

Newell-Rubbermaid produces and distributes a wide range of consumer products to mass merchandisers such as Wal-Mart and Target. In fact, Newell-Rubbermaid is Wal-Mart's top supplier and has been its key partner in developing Wal-Mart's efficient supply logistics systems. Newell owns fewer businesses than ITW, but they represent a wide range of products including cookware, marker pens, and window blinds. Like ITW, Newell-Rubbermaid acquires poorly run but well-positioned businesses, sharpens their competitive focus, and keeps each business after fixing it up rather than spinning it off. Unlike ITW, however, Newell-Rubbermaid's multibusiness portfolio has done poorly due to difficulties in executing its clean-up-and-refocus strategy with the acquisition of Rubbermaid. After climbing to around $35 a share in mid-2002, NWL stock was trading around $21 a share in early 2005.

Group Analysis

Form small groups and decide which type of diversification ITW and Newell-Rubbermaid are following: related-linked, related-constrained, or unrelated. Be able to defend your group's conclusion to the whole class.

Role Play

Two students will take roles as the CEOs of the firms and the remaining students will be stock analysts. Each CEO must appear before the analysts to defend the firm's strategic choices and stock performance. The CEOs should prepare to describe and defend the diversification approach described earlier using the logic and rationale for that strategy in Chapter 6. The analysts will ask follow-up questions challenging the CEOs' diversification rationales based on their potential disadvantages described in the chapter.

Source: "Conquer and Divide," *Forbes*, April 16, 2001.

EXERCISE TWO: DIVERSIFICATION ALTERNATIVES

Use the Internet or a business library to find information on the firms in the following chart. Use each firm's Web site or other sources to review its products and services. Study the percentage of their sales and profits that come from various product categories to help you with your classification. Fill in the columns using the descriptions provided in Chapter 6 and be prepared to defend your choices.

Firm	Your Diversification Classification	Supporting Rationale
Dover Company (DOV)		
Emerson Electric Co. (EMR)		
Fortune Brands, Inc. (FO)		
Jacuzzi Brands, Inc. (JJZ)		
LVMH (Moet Hennessy Louis Vuitton) (LVMUY.PK)		
3M Company (MMM)		

Acquiring and Integrating Businesses

*Knowledge Objectives

1_
Define acquisitions, takeovers, mergers, and acquisition strategy.

2_
Discuss the five basic reasons why firms complete acquisitions.

3_
Describe target screening, target selection, target negotiating, and due diligence.

4_
Understand the importance and process of successful postacquisition business integration.

5_
Discuss the four major pitfalls of acquisitions and remedies for their prevention.

6_
Describe the major restructuring strategies for failed acquisitions.

Focusing on Strategy

What Makes an Acquisition Successful?

"European banks have been quaking in their boots since last October, when Bank of America swallowed FleetBoston Financial for $47 billion. J. P. Morgan Chase offered even more for Bank One three months later. The Europeans have been slow to merge among themselves—across national borders, at any rate—and fear that big American banks might look across the Atlantic for their next purchases. Some Americans have indeed taken a close look at European targets." (*The Economist*)

Acquisitions are a popular growth strategy for firms competing in many industries. In the banking industry, for example, less restrictive regulations and the sanctioning of branch banking, which permits consumer banking across state lines in the United States as well as across country borders, are contributing to the greater use of the acquisition strategy. As noted in the quote above, two large acquisitions—Bank of America's acquisition of FleetBoston in late 2003 and J. P. Morgan Chase's acquisition of Bank One in 2004—illustrate the use of an acquisition strategy. Transactions such as these between large banks may create economies of scale that often are achieved by combining firms' technology and information systems. After integrating different systems, the larger combined banks can employ powerful systemwide software applications that significantly reduce costs. For example, at the time of its announcement, Wachovia's acquisition of SouthTrust was projected to save $250 million after taxes by cutting 4,300 overlapping jobs (four percent of the combined labor force) and closing 130 to 150 redundant branches.

Firms use an acquisition strategy to compete successfully against their competitors. In the spirits industry, for example, Bacardi, a U.S. producer famous for its rum brands, recently tried to acquire Grey Goose, a dominant vodka producer, to expand its product line. Grey Goose has been growing at a rate of 80 percent annually and has about 50 percent of the market in high-end vodka. If completed, this acquisition would increase Bacardi's strength with distributors relative to Diageo. In 2000, Diageo, a large food and spirits company in the United Kingdom, bought Seagram's liquor business. After this acquisition, Diageo had 25 percent of the U.S. spirits market, compared to Bacardi's eight percent. With larger efficiencies in distribution and power with distributors, Diageo has an advantage relative to Bacardi. Therefore, Bacardi is trying to use an acquisition strategy to gain the product lines, resources, and market power it needs to successfully compete against Diageo.

Acquisitions are also resulting in consolidation in parts of the global retail clothing industry. For example, Philip Green, a billionaire retail entrepreneur, has shaken up the British retail landscape by acquiring nine store chains. As a result of these acquisitions, Green controls about 13 percent of the women's clothing market in the United Kingdom. Green is now targeting Marks & Spencer, a venerable U.K. retailer selling clothing and food. Marks & Spencer also owns King Supermarkets in the United States. If he is able to acquire Marks & Spencer, Green intends to cut costs by using more direct sourcing from overseas factories and more direct purchasing from manufacturers rather than using multiple distributors as Marks & Spencer has traditionally done. Although the Marks & Spencer board has rejected Green's offer, he is determined to buy the admired chain.

SOURCES: 2004, Finance and Economics: Westward, ho!; Retail banking, *The Economist,* May 8, 90; R. D. Atlas, 2004, Wachovia hopes SouthTrust deal repeats success of 2001 merger, *New York Times,* http://www.nytimes.com, June 22; D. K. Berman & C. Mollenkamp, 2004, Wachovia, SouthTrust in talks as hunt for consumers intensifies, *Wall Street Journal,* June 21: A3, A11; A. Dolbeck, 2004, M & A in the U.S., making mergers work, *Weekly Corporate Growth Report,* April 19, 1–3; C. Lawton, 2004, Bacardi aims for vodka shot, *Wall Street Journal,* June 18: B5; C. Mollenkamp, Wachovia to acquire SouthTrust for $13.7 billion, *Wall Street Journal,* June 22: A2; E. White, 2004, Wooing a dowdy retailer, *Wall Street Journal,* June 18: B1, B5.

*
_____

acquisition

a transaction in which a firm buys a controlling interest in another firm with the intention of either making it a subsidiary business or combining it with its current business or businesses

An **acquisition** is a transaction in which a firm buys a controlling interest in another firm with the intention of either making it a subsidiary business or combining it with its current business or businesses. It is important to understand that for some firms, an acquisition is a "one-time only" event. For example, a firm using a differentiation business-level strategy might decide to acquire only one other company because it has truly specialized skills that the focal

*
acquisition strategy

an action plan that the firm develops to successfully acquire other companies

*
takeover

a specialized type of acquisition in which the target firm does not solicit the acquiring firm's offer

*
merger

a transaction in which firms agree to combine their operations on a relatively equal basis

firm requires to create unique value for its customers. It is rare, though, for a firm to complete only a single acquisition. Most firms involved with acquisitions form an acquisition strategy. An **acquisition strategy** is an action plan that the firm develops to successfully acquire other companies. An effective acquisition strategy enables significant firm growth.[1] Philip Green (see "Focusing on Strategy") is using an acquisition strategy to establish a prominent competitive position in the United Kingdom's retail clothing industry. Through its acquisition strategy, Green's company has grown to a point where it controls about 13 percent of the women's retail clothing market in the United Kingdom. A **takeover** is a specialized type of acquisition in which the target firm does not solicit the acquiring firm's offer. For instance, in 2004, Comcast made an unsolicited offer to buy (take over) Walt Disney. Disney's board of directors and top-level managers reacted very negatively to the Comcast bid. When a target firm reacts negatively to a proposal, the proposed transaction is called a *hostile takeover*. A **merger** is a transaction in which firms agree to combine their operations on a relatively equal basis. For example, DaimlerChrysler was created by the merger between Daimler-Benz and Chrysler. Mergers are more common than takeovers, while acquisitions are more common than mergers. Because of their frequency of use, our focus in this chapter is on acquisitions and the acquisition strategy. However, we also describe some mergers.

You may not be surprised to learn that the number of acquisitions being completed with firms from different countries (called *cross-border acquisitions*) continues to increase (see Chapter 8). Relaxed regulations and improved trade relations among various countries are contributing to the growth of cross-border acquisitions such as the one between Daimler-Benz and Chrysler. In the European Union, as more countries have been added, the number of regulations and restrictions between firms in these countries has been reduced. As home markets mature, it is expected that governments would facilitate the efforts of firms in their country to seek growth in other countries' markets.

Although the number of opportunities to complete cross-border acquisitions is increasing, it is important to understand that these transactions are challenging. Among the challenges are the difficulties of screening firms, selecting a target firm, and then negotiating with target firm managers. Differences in languages and cultures require understanding and sensitivity from both sides of the transaction.

We think the trend of cross-border acquisitions will continue for years to come. What do you think? Do you think working for a company completing a cross-border acquisition would be exciting as well as challenging?

We use Figure 7.1 as the framework for this chapter's discussion of acquisitions and the acquisition strategy. First, we describe the five major reasons firms complete acquisitions. We then examine target screening and selection, target negotiating, and due diligence. We discuss four questions firms should answer when engaging in due diligence. Our attention then turns to what should be done to successfully integrate the target firm into the acquiring firm. We discuss four major pitfalls to successful integration and what firms can do to avoid them. In spite of good intentions, acquisitions sometimes fail. We close the chapter with a discussion of what firms do when this happens.

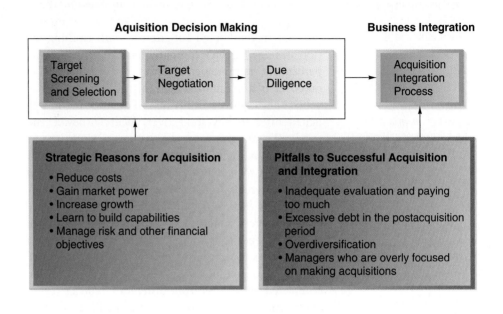

FIGURE 7.1 Acquisition Decision-Making and Business Integration Processes

Reasons for Acquisitions

Firms complete acquisitions and use an acquisition strategy for many reasons. We discuss five major reasons in the following sections.

*
horizontal
acquisition

the purchase of a competitor competing in the same market or markets as the acquiring firm

Reduce Costs

Firms often use horizontal acquisitions to reduce costs. A **horizontal acquisition** is the purchase of a competitor competing in the same market or markets as the acquiring firm. A manufacturer of women's shoes buying a competitor that also makes women's shoes is an example of a horizontal acquisition.

Firms gain scale economies through horizontal acquisitions. This is one reason why so many horizontal acquisitions take place in the pharmaceuticals industry. As you might imagine, the ability to combine two firms' R&D skills often drives horizontal acquisitions between pharmaceuticals firms. Let's consider the experiences of Aventis with horizontal acquisitions to demonstrate this point.

Aventis, a large French drug manufacturer, is the largest producer of vaccines in its home country. Swiss drug maker Novartis AG wanted to acquire Aventis, primarily to gain access to its competitor's R&D skills. Stalling this transaction was the French government's hesitancy to allow a Swiss company to buy Aventis and thereby gain control over the production of many vaccines used in France. Ultimately, Sanofi, another French drug maker, agreed to purchase Aventis for more than $65 billion, a price greater than what Novartis offered. At the time, the newly formed firm, Sanofi-Aventis, was the third-largest drug producer in the world, behind Pfizer and GlaxoSmithKline PLC (both of which increased their size through acquisitions as well).[2] Sanofi-Aventis believes that combining its complementary skills through this horizontal acquisition makes it a formidable competitor to the industry's other two giants.

A **vertical acquisition** is the purchase of a supplier or distributor of one or more of a firm's goods or services.[3] Vertical acquisitions can also be used to increase scale and to gain market power, which is discussed in the next section. Rupert Murdoch built News Corporation and continues to manage it today. He began acquiring British newspapers in the 1970s, and then began an acquisition program in the United States in 1976 when he acquired the *New York Post*. Books (HarperCollins), magazines (*TV Guide*), television networks (Fox), and movie studios (Twentieth Century Fox) have been added to create News Corporation. Murdoch acquired a controlling interest in DirecTV by offering $6.6 billion to buy General Motors' 20 percent stake in Hughes Electronics. The acquisition of DirecTV by News Corporation is a vertical acquisition, as DirecTV is a satellite TV company through which News Corporation can distribute more of its media content: news, movies, and television shows.[4]

Gain Market Power

Market power exists when the firm sells its products above competitive prices or when its costs are below those of its primary competitors. Firms commonly use horizontal and vertical acquisitions to gain market power. Horizontal acquisitions have been used in the business software industry. Declines in corporate spending because of the global economic malaise in the early part of the twenty-first century influenced the use of horizontal acquisitions in this industry. Because of declining demand for its products, the business software industry continues to suffer from overcapacity. Acquisitions enable the acquiring firm to reduce overcapacity by eliminating duplicate operations during the integration process.

An opportunity to reduce overcapacity may have influenced Oracle's hostile takeover bid and ultimate acquisition of rival PeopleSoft. After Oracle announced its bid for PeopleSoft, Microsoft and SAP, two other large players in the technology infrastructure and application software area, discussed a possible merger. Antitrust concerns prevented serious pursuit of this proposed merger, however. Nonetheless, the highly visible nature of the announced acquisition (involving Oracle and PeopleSoft) and possible merger (involving Microsoft and SAP) signaled the need for smaller firms in this industry to do something to be able to compete against the market power these transactions would create for the two newly formed firms (if the proposed transactions were completed). Some feel that these proposed transactions sent a message to smaller competitors that they needed to "eat or be eaten."[5]

BMC Software seems to understand this message. Acquiring firms with software applications to run on mainframe computers created

*
vertical acquisition

the purchase of a supplier or distributor of one or more of a firm's goods or services

*
market power

power that exists when the firm sells its products above competitive prices or when its costs are below those of its primary competitors

Craig Conway, former Peoplesoft CEO, was opposed to the takeover of the company by Oracle and its CEO, Larry Ellison, which occurred in January 2005. The combined companies will now represent more applications and database customers than any other company in the world.

© Noah Berger/Bloomberg News/Landov

some market power for BMC in its competitive battles with IBM and Computer Associates. BMC's sales grew to $1.7 billion in 2000. However, the firm then began to lose ground, as shown by a decline in its sales revenue to $1.42 billion in 2003. This sales decline suggests that BMC no longer has adequate market power. To address this competitive disadvantage, the firm acquired five additional companies beginning in 2002. Each horizontal acquisition was completed so that BMC could couple its current software with "tools to predict failures and automate fixes so computers one day might remotely patch errant systems without the need for costly technicians."[6] BMC hopes these acquisitions will help it regain lost market power.

However, pursuing market power can be problematic as well. As "Understanding Strategy" suggests, firms can pay too much for an acquisition as they compete to gain market power and the larger share of a market.

Increase Growth

Some industries have significant fragmentation, with many small competitors of equal size. In these instances, some firms use an acquisition strategy to increase their growth rate relative to competitors.[7] Sports Authority's merger with Gart Sports in 2003 demonstrates how this is happening in the sporting-goods retail market. Similarly, Russell and Reebok have acquired equipment companies to expand their apparel businesses. K2, a sports equipment maker, is responding to this consolidation in segments that surround its sporting goods market. Richard Heckman, CEO of K2, is seeking to grow in the sporting-goods equipment industry as Nike and Germany's Adidas-Salomon AG and Reebok International have grown and come to dominate the athletic footwear and apparel businesses. Since 2002, K2 has completed five acquisitions. Furthermore, K2 has agreements to purchase ski maker Volkl Sports Holding AG and Marker Group (a ski bindings manufacturer) as well as Marrot Mountain (an outdoor apparel company). Although K2 started out as a winter sports gear company, it now has 35 brands, which has resulted in the firm's becoming a year-round sports equipment manufacturer and distributor. As Heckman notes, "you don't drive growth from cutting costs, you do it from revenue synergy."[8]

In another example, MGM Mirage has an agreement to acquire Mandalay Resort Group. The acquisition would create the largest casino company in the industry. This acquisition would enable MGM Mirage to grow by expanding its operations and the opportunity to expand along the Las Vegas strip. Mandalay owns a large percentage of the land still available for development in the strip area and had been planning to use some of its land to build a huge beach-theme resort complex. Potential opposition from antitrust regulators is the major hurdle with this proposed acquisition. If the proposed acquisition is allowed, the combined company could control half of the 72,000-room capacity of the Las Vegas strip hotels. If regulators define competition more broadly than the Las Vegas market, then the acquisition is likely to be approved.[9]

Learn to Build Capabilities

Learning from a target firm and building new capabilities are more reasons firms acquire other companies. Target companies often have unique employee skills, organizational technologies, or superior knowledge that are available to

understanding strategy:

THE LACK OF SUCCESS IN LARGE FOOD COMPANY MERGERS HAS PRODUCED CAUTION AMONG INVESTORS REGARDING FURTHER ACQUISITIONS

Several acquisitions of larger food companies were completed during 2000 and 2001. Kellogg acquired Keebler Foods, Philip Morris (now Altria Group) purchased Nabisco, and Diageo acquired Pillsbury, a part of General Foods. There is speculation that General Mills, Campbell Soup, and Heinz may be acquired next. These midsize firms lack the market power of their larger competitors in dealing with strong distributors and retailers (such as Wal-Mart). To reduce their distributors' and retailers' power, some of these firms may merge or agree to be acquired.

However, complications surround these potential transactions. Nestle, which already has a joint venture with General Mills outside the United States focused on cereals, could make an acquisition a long-term goal by buying a piece of General Mills through Diageo. Nestle's goal of growing in health products does not necessarily fit with the bulk of General Mills' products. Additionally, an acquisition of General Mills would likely increase Nestle's debt by six times and thereby threaten its triple-A credit rating. Kraft may have difficulty acquiring General Mills as well because General Mills' recent purchase of another food company, Keebler, may disturb antitrust authorities. Furthermore, Kraft desires smaller acquisitions in its healthy food categories and in areas where it needs additional scale, such as beverages, snacks, and conven-

ience meals. Similarly, Unilever, the largest food company in Europe, is still paying down its $24 billion in debt due to an acquisition of Best Foods in 2000.

In addition, because the market has been disappointed by previous deals, potential shareholders may be unimpressed by the low returns they are likely to receive from the "value-destroying deals" made earlier by these companies. So firms announcing an acquisition might experience a significant decrease in their stock price.

Although General Mills' stock is priced low, its stock has not gained relative to gains in general stock market averages; this lack of performance may suggest to investors that it is unlikely to provide the growth necessary to increase stock prices in the potential acquiring firms. Accordingly, these deals will probably not be made any time soon even though pressure continues for additional transactions. Usually a premium is required to acquire another firm. Currently, though, those investing in firms in the food industry may not support the idea of their firm paying a premium to buy another firm in this low-margin industry. In slightly different words, shareholders of firms in the food industry may feel that acquisition targets are not worth the price that their firm might have to pay to acquire another firm in this industry. In summary, although there are reasons for continued acquisitions, there are also a number of reasons why such acquisitions are not likely to occur among large food companies.

SOURCES: D. Ball & J. Adamy, 2004, Don't ring up a sale of General Mills Inc. just yet, *Wall Street Journal*, June 7: C1, C2; A. Bary, 2004, Cereal appeal: General Mills and Nestle? *Barron's*, June 7: 14.

the acquiring firm only through acquisitions. Additionally, pooling the companies' combined resources and capabilities may enable development of new "centers of excellence" for specialized products in new markets. Cisco Systems, Microsoft, and Intel are examples of firms completing technology-driven acquisitions to build their capabilities.[10]

"Building capabilities" through acquisitions is a future-oriented reason to complete acquisitions compared to the reasons of reducing costs, gaining market power, and increasing growth. The first three reasons for acquisitions are about exploiting current advantages, while learning how to build the firm's capabilities is about exploring to create tomorrow's advantages. In general, exploitation was the base for many acquisitions in the 1980s and 1990s, while financial reasons (discussed next) influenced acquisitions in the 1970s. It appears that capability-building acquisitions are a dominant reason for many acquisitions in the first decade of the twenty-first century.[11]

A leader in networking for the Internet, Cisco Systems, founded by a small group of computer scientists in 1984, now has more than 34,000 employees worldwide. Headquarters are in San Jose, California.

Manage Risk and Other Financial Objectives

Facing stiff competition, some firms choose to use acquisitions to diversify their operations, thereby reducing their dependence on performance in an intensely competitive market. Many years ago, GE diversified away from the consumer electronics market into financial services to reduce its dependence on the consumer electronics area. Furthermore, GE has diversified into other service areas rather than basing its revenue solely on industrial products.[12] At times, firms also make acquisitions to gain access to tax advantages or to reduce business or financial risk. Of course, such acquisitions need to be done in a way that cannot be replicated by shareholders through portfolio diversification.

Screening, Selecting, and Negotiating with Target Firms

Research suggests that financial acquirers (such as Kohlberg Kravis Roberts [KKR]) experience higher valuations in their acquisitions than do corporate acquisitions.[13] Financial acquirers such as leverage buyout (defined later in the chapter) firms often complete two or three acquisitions per year. However, these firms may explore as many as 400 or 500 possibilities and examine closely perhaps 25 targets before selecting the four or five transactions they'll actually complete. Acquisition opportunities can come without warning and usually need to be quickly evaluated. Accordingly, it is important for firms to balance the need to think strategically with the need to react to an acquisition opportunity in a timely way. Cisco Systems, a network gear manufacturer that has completed a large number of acquisitions, may examine three potential markets and decide to enter only one of them, and may evaluate five to ten candidates for each deal that it closes. This extra amount of screening enables the acquiring party to identify the acquisition opportunities that exist while at the same time determining the right price. Although this process takes time, it helps managers develop experience in screening, and over time they can increase the speed *and* effectiveness of the screening process.

To focus too strongly on an "exciting" opportunity and set aside the firm's basic strategy can be a major mistake. It is often problematic when one of the senior executives "falls in love" with a target firm and everyone else falls in line, knowing that "we are going to do this deal." After the screening process is completed in a rational and strategic way, negotiations are initiated.

Key issues requiring careful analysis should be identified early in the negotiating process. For instance, it is important to clarify what role the top executives will play in the newly combined organization. Determining the executive positions needed in the newly created firm and who will fill those positions is an important topic for negotiating.

Because most proposed transactions are greeted with skepticism by those in the target firm, acquirers with experience often try to develop a spirit of cooperation to negotiate a mutually beneficial transaction. A cooperative relationship between personnel in the acquiring and acquired firms is the foundation on which the most serious issues can be successfully negotiated. Table 7.1 provides a list of suggestions that are helpful in the negotiation process. In particular, government officials may also need to be included in order to successfully negotiate a deal, especially in cross-border transactions.

TABLE 7.1	Considerations in Successful Acquisition (Including Cross-Border) Negotiation Processes

1. Be very clear about the strategic logic behind the proposed acquisitions.
2. Be patient, acting decisively when needed but in a way that does not create emotion. Take a long term view, which often runs counter to the strategic objective among participants in the negotiation process.
3. Seek to develop government, industry, and company contacts well before the transaction takes place.
4. Identify the potential players in the proposed deal-making process, including government administrators. Understand who will be for the deal and differentiate between those who will be unconditionally opposed and those whose objectives can be met in the negotiation process.
5. Understand who will defer to which group and sequence the negotiation process in a way that will maximize the chance of success.
6. Think about how you will negotiate with potential deal blockers and how you can give them a vision that meets your needs while enabling them to persuade others among their constituents of the transaction's value for their particular group's interests.
7. Act to ensure the sustainability of the deal. Remember that once the transaction is completed, negotiations are not finished. Integration between deal participants can be facilitated by taking a long-term view of the participants involved.

SOURCES: Adapted from J. K. Sebenius, 2002, The hidden challenge of cross-border negotiations, *Harvard Business Review,* 80(3): 76–85; J. K. Sebenius, 1998, Negotiating cross-border acquisitions, *Sloan Management Review,* 39(2): 27–41.

Due Diligence

Due diligence is the rational process by which acquiring firms evaluate target firms. Due diligence is concerned with verifying that the reason for the proposed transaction is sound strategically and financially. To understand how to improve due diligence, Bane and Company, a strategy consulting firm, studied 20 companies, both private and public, known for the quality of their due diligence processes. We summarize the results of their research into four basic questions around which an acquiring firm's due diligence efforts should be framed.[14]

What Is the Acquiring Firm Really Buying?

Acquiring firms frequently form a team to pursue due diligence. Rather than relying on what might be biased secondary sources for information, the due diligence team should build its own "bottom-up view" of the target firm and its industry. To do this, the team collects information from multiple parties, including customers, suppliers, and competitors. This information helps the team carefully examine each assumption the acquiring firm has made about the target and its value.

Studying customers and suppliers enables the due diligence team to answer important questions about the target firm, such as the following: is the target customer group growing? Has the target firm fully explored the needs of its target customers? What distribution channels is the target firm using to serve customers? Are superior channels available? Has the target firm negotiated favorable deals with its suppliers? If not, why hasn't it done so?

Analyzing competitors is another important source of information when it comes to understanding what the acquiring firm may buy. Important questions to pose in terms of the target firm's competitors include the following: is the target firm more profitable than its competitors? In what part of the value chain are most of the profits made? Is the target underperforming its competitors in the key parts of the value chain? How will the target firm's competitors react to an acquisition, and how might this influence competition between the target and its competitors?

Finally, the due diligence team should assess the target firm's capabilities. This is done by considering a host of questions: Does the target have cost advantages relative to its competitors? How could the target's cost position help the acquiring firm's cost position? Could the target's capabilities be used to create sources of differentiation? If so, how valuable would those be and how long would it take to develop those capabilities?

The due diligence team's answers about what the firm is really buying are studied to ensure that no "deal breakers" exist and to verify that the proposed transaction is logical strategically. On a positive note, answering this question sometimes uncovers more expected value for the proposed acquisition than originally anticipated.

What Is the Target Firm's Value?

Acquisitions can be glamorous, a fact that sometimes biases decision makers to quickly conclude that a proposed acquisition is virtually without potential flaws. To thwart this bias, the due diligence team must assess the target's true financial value. True financial value is determined through an objective, unemotional process.

An objective analysis verifies the absence of accounting anomalies at the target firm. Accounting anomalies may signal problems and possibly unethical decisions as well. The team should consider rapid and significant increases in sales revenue a possible accounting anomaly. As we know, rapid and significant increases in sales revenue may be a function of dramatically lower sales prices rather than true growth. While dramatically reducing prices to sell more products makes revenue look good in the current time period, such sales can't be sustained. Of course, the acquiring firm is very interested in future sales when evaluating a target firm. Another accounting anomaly occurs when the firm treats recurring items as extraordinary costs, thus keeping them off the profit-and-loss statement. These and other accounting anomalies must be stripped away to reveal the historical and projected cash flows. The only way to accomplish this is for the due diligence team to extensively interact with target firm personnel about entries to the target's financial statements. Given your knowledge of accounting and finance, what other anomalies do you think might surface when an acquiring firm works to determine a target firm's true financial value? What should be done to deal with the anomalies you have identified?

Where Are the Synergies between the Combined Firms?

Although evaluating the target firm to determine its actual value is wise, caution must be exercised when doing so. The due diligence team should also evaluate the target in light of the synergies that might be created by integrating the target with the acquiring firm. This evaluation should identify specific synergies that might be created, the probability of developing the synergies, and the time and investment required to do so. Acquisitions often fail because of an inability to obtain expected synergies, an outcome that highlights the importance of carefully studying proposed synergies and their costs.

What Is the Acquiring Firm's Walk-Away Offer Price?

The emotional pressure to make an acquisition can be significant. Think of the pressure executives in the acquiring firm might encounter once a proposed transaction is announced to the press. Extensive coverage highlights a transaction's visibility and can make it harder for the acquiring firm to walk away from the possible deal. However, as we would expect, successful acquisitions result from logical, not emotional decisions. To increase the probability that a rational decision will be made, the acquiring firm should develop a purchase price it will not exceed. To do this, the acquiring firm must determine who makes the top-price decision and the decision criteria he or she will use. These determinations should be made before final negotiations begin. Additionally, creating incentive systems for those negotiating transactions can be fruitful. For example, Clear Channel Communications, an international radio, billboard, and live entertainment company, has an incentive system that is focused on an acquisition's results. Thus, Clear Channel's integration teams' compensation is partly based on the profitability of the completed acquisitions.

Based on the results of its due diligence process, the acquiring firm decides whether it will acquire the target firm. If the acquisition is completed, the focus shifts to what must be done to integrate the acquired firm into the acquiring firm's operations. We discuss this topic next.

Integrating the Newly Acquired Business

The activities leading to an acquisition decision (target screening, target selection, target negotiating, and due diligence) influence the success of individual acquisitions as well as acquisition strategies. However, in the final analysis, a particular acquisition will succeed or fail on the basis of how well the target firm and acquiring firm integrate their operations.[15] Integration success is more likely when an integration team, including employees from the acquiring firm and the acquired firm, is formed and charged with full responsibility to integrate the two companies to create value. In "Understanding Strategy," we describe Hilton Hotels' purchase of Promus Hotel Corporation. As you'll see, these firms successfully integrated their operations.

Although there are many difficulties in implementing acquisitions, as acquiring and target firms begin to integrate their operations, unanticipated opportunities for creating new value may be discovered. This is especially true for firms bent on learning from each other or where complementary assets are brought together in ways that enable such value creation.[16] Other research suggests that creating a culture of a merger of "equals" is likely to reinforce existing organizational identities and create expectations for strict equality.[17] Instead, it is suggested that the organization develop a new identity by asking the question, "Who are we?" instead of framing an acquisition or merger as a combination of equals.[18] If the integration process is carried out thoroughly and appropriately, opportunities are likely for increased growth as learning occurs.[19] In a merger such as that between Sears and Kmart, firms with different retail cultures, it will be important not only to perform integration activities well, but also to establish a joint brand that will enable better differentiation than both firms have currently. They will be in a difficult battle with the likes of Wal-Mart, Target, and Best Buy, who have better-recognized brands for value creation in the consumer's mind.[20]

After filing bankruptcy in January 2002, Kmart closed more than 300 stores. Will its recent merger with Sears be beneficial for both companies?

© Getty Images

Pitfalls in Pursuing Acquisitions and Their Prevention

The importance of successful integration in the postacquisition period cannot be overestimated.[21] Because combined firms often lose target firm managers through turnover, it is important to retain key executives and other valuable human capital, especially if the acquiring firm wants to gain new skills from the acquired firm.[22] In addition, because much of an organization's knowledge is contained in its human capital,[23] turnover of key personnel from the acquired firm should be avoided.[24] Involving these employees in the

understanding strategy:

HILTON HOTELS' SUCCESSFUL ACQUISITION OF PROMUS HOTEL CORPORATION

In 1999, Hilton Hotels' CEO and co-chairman, Stephen F. Bollenbach, spearheaded the acquisition of Promus Hotel Corporation, owner of several midpriced hotel chains. At the time, the transaction seemed risky, because the cash and stock acquisition valued at $3.7 billion pushed Hilton's debt significantly higher to a total of $5.5 billion. Concerned about the transaction and its potential effects on earnings, investors pushed Hilton's stock price down seven percent. At the time, a number of analysts were concerned about the "fit" of Promus's midpriced hotel chains (such as Hampton Inn, Doubletree, Homewood Suites, and Embassy Suites) with Hilton's luxury brands (such as Hilton's Waldorf-Astoria in New York and Palmer House in Chicago).

However, six-plus years later, this acquisition is yielding impressive dividends for Hilton shareholders. Hilton now generates one-third of its sales and profits from the brands it purchased from Promus. Hilton now owns 2,185 franchise hotels versus the 269 it owned before the Promus acquisition. On sales of $4.1 billion, Hilton's 2004 earnings were expected to be $214 million, up 30 percent from 2003's earnings.

SOURCES: 2004, Hilton Hotels Home Page, http://www.hilton.com, October 24; C. Palmeri & C. Yang, 2004, The light is on at Hilton, *Business Week*, June 28: 66–68; J. Barsky & L. Nash, 2003, Improved loyalty programs target a dwindling number of travelers, *Hotel and Motel Management*, July 7: 16; M. Frankel, 1999, Hilton's buy brings only yawns, *Business Week*, September 20: 43.

What is contributing to this successful acquisition? As you have imagined, there are several keys to this acquisition's success. One key is the complex reservation system the newly formed firm was able to create by integrating the capabilities of the formerly independent hotel chains. This system enables the seven Hilton hotel brands to operate in a unified way. A reservation operator who receives a request for a Hilton property that is full can secure a reservation for the customer at another Hilton facility that is close to the location of the customer's first choice. This cross-selling of Hilton brands is generating more than $300 million in revenue each year.

Other actions were taken to integrate the acquired and acquiring firm. The HHonors loyalty program was expanded to include customers using the former Promus brands. Also, franchisees can offer rooms on the central Hilton Web site at the same price as third-party Web sites such as Expedia and Travelocity. The technology improvement program has created kiosks in major locations where guests can do self check-in and get a room key in the lobby. The kiosks also enable guests to book rooms online they'll use in the future. This acquisition is the source of Hilton's ability to grow at an average annual return of 12.5 percent from 2001 to 2003. This growth rate is superior to those of rivals Marriott International and Starwood Hotels and Resorts Worldwide.

integration process reduces the likelihood that they will leave the newly combined firm.

History tells us that acquisitions are risky. However, learning how to deal positively with prominent pitfalls increases the chance of acquisition success. Next, we discuss four major pitfalls.

Inadequate Evaluation and Paying Too Much

As we've discussed, effective due diligence is important in ensuring that once negotiations start, a rational approach is used. We also highlighted the importance of the acquiring firm's establishing a price above which it will not go. Notwithstanding due diligence and the use of investment bankers to help with this process, many firms still become too romantic about acquiring the target, with the result being that they pay too much for it. Research suggests that "a combination of cognitive biases and organizational pressures leads managers to make overly optimistic forecasts in analyzing proposals for major investments" such as acquisitions.[25] *Anchoring* (quickly becoming committed to a position and being highly resistant to changing it) and overconfidence in one's opinion are two examples of cognitive biases that may surface during an acquisition process. Regardless of the causes, those evaluating a target firm as an acquisition candidate must ensure that the acquiring firm's evaluation of that target is complete and that the acquiring firm doesn't overpay to acquire the target.

Excessive Debt in the Postacquisition Period

As illustrated in "Understanding Strategy," many companies in the food industry have significantly increased their debt levels. As we discussed, it is unlikely that Nestle will acquire General Mills or another large target anytime soon because additional debt would probably threaten Nestle's credit rating. When credit rating agencies such as Moody's and Standard and Poor's reduce a firm's credit rating, the firm will likely incur higher costs to obtain additional financial capital. This makes sense, because firms with lower credit ratings are thought to be riskier investments. And, as we know, investors expect higher returns from risky investments. An acquiring firm should also remember that if its debt load becomes too high, it will have less cash to invest in R&D, human resources, and marketing.[26] Investments in these organizational functions are important parts of what the firm does to be successful in the long term.

Overdiversification

Frequent acquisitions help meet capital markets' expectations for the firm to grow and have the potential to increase top-level managers' salaries. Top-level managers' salaries tend to increase with increases in the firm's overall size. Therefore, capital markets and the relationship between organizational size and salaries for top-level managers may influence top-level managers to make frequent acquisitions. This can be problematic, though, in that firms can become too diversified. When this happens, a firm is said to be overdiversified. In the late 1990s and early 2000s, a number of media companies such as AOL Time Warner, Vivendi, and Bertelsmann completed several acquisitions that did not turn out well. A number of analysts concluded that these firms had become overdiversified, a condition that makes it very difficult for the firm to effectively manage each successive acquisition. The response to overdiversification is for the firm to divest acquisitions that it can't successfully manage. Vivendi has indeed divested a number of the firms it acquired during the late 1990s and early 2000s.[27]

Managers Who Are Overly Focused on Making Acquisitions

Acquisitions require significant managerial time and energy. Managers have opportunity costs for the time and energy spent searching for viable acquisitions, completing due diligence, preparing for and participating in negotiations, and managing the integration process after an acquisition is completed. Time and energy spent to deal with potential acquisitions obviously can't be spent on managing other aspects of the firm's operations. Furthermore, when acquisition negotiations are initiated, target firm managers often operate in suspended animation until the acquisition and integration processes are completed.[28] Therefore, it is important for managers to encourage dissent when evaluating an acquisition target. If failure occurs, leaders are tempted to blame it on others or on unforeseen circumstances. Rather, it is important that managers recognize when they are overly involved in the acquisition process. "The urge to merge is still like an addiction in many companies: doing deals is much more fun and interesting than fixing fundamental problems. So, as in dealing with any other addictions or temptations maybe it is best to just say no."[29]

In Table 7.2, we summarize the four major pitfalls of acquisitions and present possible preventive actions firms can take to avoid a pitfall or to reduce the negative consequences experienced because of a pitfall. As suggested in the table and as we've discussed, it is important for the firm to establish a rational due diligence process and to make certain that the walk-away offer price is fixed when there is temptation to surpass the rational price to pay for a target firm. Paying too much often happens when there are many bidders; this is called the "winner's curse" in the research literature.[30] Similarly, in regard to the problem of taking on too much debt, it is important to ensure that the firm has enough cash on hand and debt capacity to complete the transaction at or

TABLE 7.2 Major Pitfalls of Acquisitions and Their Prevention

Pitfall	Prevention
Paying too much	Establish rational due diligence processes with a walk-away offer price and make certain that when this price is reached, managers involved do walk away.
Taking on too much debt	Ensure that the firm has adequate cash as well as debt capacity to complete the transaction at or below the walk-away offer price.
Becoming overdiversified	Understand fully the nature of synergy in the acquisition and the integration processes necessary to achieve it. Also, ensure that any unrelated transactions are justified based on strong financial rationales. However, even when such justification is in place, the deal may not be positive for strategic-fit reasons because it may lead to overdiversification. Therefore, make certain that strategic fit does not lead to overdiversification.
Managers who are overly focused on acquisitions	Establish checks and balances so that top managers are challenged by the board and other stakeholders regarding proposed acquisitions. These actions are especially important in firms making frequent acquisitions.

below the established walk-away offer price. Regarding the possibility of becoming overdiversified, it is necessary for managers to fully understand the nature of synergy and the actions necessary to create it in the business integration stage. Even if there are potential synergies and the transaction is justified based on its expected financial outcomes, a deal may not be good to execute due to lack of strategic fit with the acquiring firm's core strengths. Finally, it is important to establish a "checks and balances" system in which managers are challenged to support the acquisition decision. This is especially true when a firm regularly uses an acquisition strategy. If these checks and balances can be established with integrity, they will likely protect managers from becoming overly focused on completing acquisitions to the detriment of other issues warranting managerial attention.[31]

Acquisition Failure and Restructuring

divestiture

a transaction in which businesses are sold to other firms or spun off as independent enterprises

Regardless of the effort invested, acquisitions sometimes fail. When this happens, divestiture may be the best course of action. A **divestiture** is a transaction in which businesses are sold to other firms or spun off as independent enterprises. Some divestitures occur because the firm wants to restructure its set of businesses to take advantage of new opportunities.[32] Commonly, though, divestitures are made to deal with failed acquisitions. Sears, Roebuck is a famous example of a firm that failed with its acquisitions. In 1981, Sears acquired Dean Witter Reynolds to diversify into financial services and Coldwell Banker to diversify into real estate. At first, the results of these acquisitions seemed positive. Quickly, though, it became obvious that the synergies Sears expected among its retail, financial services, and real estate businesses would not materialize. The inability to rapidly create synergies caused Sears executives to focus too much time on trying to develop those synergies. The net result of these efforts was that Sears' core retail business received little managerial attention, causing it to lose market share and perform poorly. Pressured by institutional investors to correct the problems, Sears announced the divestiture of its financial services and real estate businesses so that it could concentrate on its retail business. Research suggests that despite initial gains over the period when Sears was diversified, the firm's shareholders suffered significant opportunity losses when compared to a portfolio of firms that maintained a focus on their core retailing sector.[33]

leveraged buyout (LBO)

a restructuring strategy in which a party buys all or part of a firm's assets in order to take the firm or a part of the firm private

Leveraged buyouts are commonly used as a restructuring strategy to correct for managerial mistakes. A **leveraged buyout (LBO)** is a restructuring strategy in which a party buys all or part of a firm's assets in order to take the firm or a part of the firm private. Once the transaction is completed, the company's stock is no longer traded publicly. Usually, significant amounts of debt are incurred to finance a buyout; hence the term "leveraged" buyout. To support debt payments, the new owners may immediately sell a number of assets in order to focus on the firm's core businesses.[34] Because leverage buyout associations (such as KKR, mentioned earlier) often control these firms, the intent is to restructure the firm to the point that it can be sold at a profit within five to eight years. However, besides improving efficiencies, such buyouts can also represent a form of firm rebirth to facilitate entrepreneurial efforts and stimulate strategic growth.[35]

Summary

The primary purpose of this chapter is to describe acquisitions as the foundation for an effective acquisition strategy. In doing so, we examined the following topics:

- An **acquisition** occurs when one firm buys controlling interest in another firm with the intention of either making the acquired firm a subsidiary business or combining it with a current business. An **acquisition strategy** is an action plan that the firm develops to successfully complete acquisitions. A **takeover** is a specialized acquisition strategy in which a target firm does not solicit the acquiring firm's offer. Takeovers are often hostile transactions. A **merger** is a transaction in which firms agree to combine their operations on a relatively equal basis.
- There are five basic reasons to complete acquisitions: (1) to reduce costs; (2) to gain market power; (3) to increase growth; (4) to learn and to build new capabilities; and (5) for other managerial, financial, and risk-reduction motives.
- Target screening, target selection, and target negotiating are activities firms complete to make an acquisition. Effective screening enables the acquiring firm to gain an overall sense of the acquisition opportunities that exist and helps establish the right price. Once the screening and selection are completed, negotiating with target firm leaders begins. When negotiating, it is important to clarify what roles top executives of the acquiring and target firms will play in the new firm. Also, government officials may need to be consulted to conclude negotiations, especially in cross-border deals.

- Effective **due diligence** is critical to making the right decision about a possible acquisition. Four basic questions are answered when engaging in due diligence: (1) What is the acquiring firm really buying? (2) What is the target firm's true financial value? (3) Where are the synergies between the acquiring and acquired firms? (4) What is the acquiring firm's walk-away offer price?
- Efforts to integrate the acquired firm with the acquiring firm after the transaction is completed may be the strongest predictor of acquisition success or failure. After a transaction is completed, it is critical to assess and improve, as required, the morale of all employees, but especially target firm employees. Building bridges between personnel in the target firm and personnel in the acquiring firm increases the likelihood that the firms will be effectively integrated.
- Besides integration difficulties, there are other pitfalls for acquisitions: (1) inadequate evaluation of the target firm and paying too much for the target; (2) excessive debt in the postacquisition period; (3) overdiversification; and (4) managers who are overly focused on making acquisitions.
- Acquisitions sometimes fail. When this happens, firms divest businesses that are causing performance problems so that they might again focus on their core operations. **Leveraged buyouts** are also used to restructure firms when particular acquisitions have failed or when a firm's whole acquisition strategy has failed.

Key Terms

acquisition 166	horizontal acquisition 168	takeover 167
acquisition strategy 167	leveraged buyout (LBO) 180	vertical acquisition 169
divestiture 180	market power 169	
due diligence 174	merger 167	

Discussion Questions

1. What are the definitions of an acquisition, takeover, merger, and acquisition strategy? Why are acquisitions this chapter's focus?
2. What are the five basic reasons why firms complete acquisitions? Over the next ten years or

so, do you think any of these reasons will become more important than the other four? If so, why?

3. What are target screening, target selection, target negotiating, and due diligence? In your

opinion, why do some firms fail to successfully complete these activities?

4. What process should be used to successfully integrate acquisitions and why is the process important?

5. What are the four major pitfalls of acquisitions? How can these pitfalls be prevented?

6. What major restructuring strategies do firms use to deal with a failed acquisition? What are the tradeoffs among the restructuring strategies?

Endnotes

1. J. E. Ashton, F. X. Cook Jr., & P. Schmitz, 2003, Uncovering hidden value in a midsize manufacturing company, *Harvard Business Review*, 81(6): 4–12.

2. A. Raghavan, J. Carreyrou, & G. Naik, 2004, Sanofi to swallow Aventis in a deal set at $65 billion, *Wall Street Journal*, April 26: A1, A8.

3. T. S. Gabrielsen, 2003, Conglomerate mergers: Vertical mergers in disguise? *International Journal of the Economics of Business*, 10(1): 1–16.

4. A. Lashinsky, 2004, Murdoch's air war, *Fortune*, December 13: 131–138.

5. D. Bank & D. Clark, 2004, Microsoft, SAP teach a lesson: Eat or be eaten, *Wall Street Journal*, June 9: C1, C4.

6. 2004, At BMC, bigger is still better, *Wall Street Journal*, June 16: B9.

7. B. Mascarenhas, A. Kumaraswam, D. Day, & A. Baveja, 2002, Five strategies for rapid firm growth and how to implement them, *Managerial and Decision Economics*, 23: 317–330.

8. 2004, K2 to buy three ski-gear makers as it continues acquisition spree, *Wall Street Journal*, June 16: B4.

9. 2004, MGM Mirage's board votes for deal, *Wall Street Journal*, June 16: B4.

10. A. L. Ranft & M. D. Lord, 2002, Acquiring new technologies and capabilities: A grounded model of acquisition implementation, *Organization Science*, 13: 420–441.

11. J. Gammelgaard, 2004, Access to competence: An emerging acquisition motive, *European Business Forum*, Spring: 44–48.

12. M. Warner, 2002, Can GE light up the market again? *Fortune*, November 11: 108–117.

13. R. J. Aiello & M. D. Watkins, 2000, The fine art of friendly acquisition, *Harvard Business Review*, 78(6): 100–107.

14. G. Cullinan, J.-M. Le Roux, & R.-M. Weddigen, 2004, When to walk away from a deal, *Harvard Business Review*, 82(4): 96–104.

15. T. Vestring, T. Rouse, & S. Rovit, 2004, Integrate where it matters, *MIT Sloan Management Review*, 46(1): 15–18.

16. M. Blyler & R. W. Coff, 2003, Dynamic capabilities, social capital and rent appropriation: Ties that split pies, *Strategic Management Journal*, 24: 677–697.

17. R. A. Weber & C. F. Camerer, 2003, Cultural conflict and merger failure: An experimental approach, *Management Science*, 49: 400–415.

18. S. Zaheer, M. Schomaker, & M. Genc, 2003, Identity versus culture in mergers of equals, *European Management Journal*, 21(2): 185–195.

19. T. Saxton & M. Dollinger, 2004, Target reputation and appropriability: Picking and deploying resources in acquisitions, *Journal of Management*, 30: 123–147.

20. T. Dougherty & E. Stein, 2004, Doomed for failure: Sears + Kmart, *Brandweek*, December 6: 20.

21. Y. Weber & E. Menipaz, 2003, Measuring cultural fit in mergers and acquisitions, *International Journal of Business Performance Management*, 5(1): 54–72.

22. A. K. Bucholtz, B. A. Ribbens, & I. T. Houle, 2003, The role of human capital in postacquisition CEO departure, *Academy of Management Journal*, 46: 506–514.

23. M. A. Hitt, L. Bierman, K. Shimizu, & R. Kochhar, 2001, Direct and moderating effects of human capital on strategy and performance in professional service firms, *Academy of Management Journal*, 44: 13–28.

24. J. A. Krug, 2003, Why do they keep leaving? *Harvard Business Review*, 81(2): 14–15; H. A. Krishnan & D. Park, 2002, The impact of workforce reduction on subsequent performance in major mergers and acquisitions: An exploratory study, *Journal of Business Research*, 55(4): 285–292.

25. D. Lovallo & D. Kahneman, 2003, Delusions of success: How optimism undermines executives' decisions, *Harvard Business Review*, 87(5): 56–64.

26. M. A. Hitt & D. L. Smart, 1994, Debt: A disciplining force for managers or a debilitating force for organizations? *Journal of Management Inquiry*, 3: 144–152.

27. S. Clow, 2004, Vivendi's asset mix poses new problem; CEO may have restored balance sheet but remaining businesses share little crossover, *Wall Street Journal*, May 27: B2.

28. M. L. A. Hayward, 2002, When do firms learn from their acquisition experience? Evidence from 1990–1995, *Strategic Management Journal*, 23: 21–39; M. A. Hitt, J. S. Harrison, & R. D. Ireland, 2001, *Mergers and Acquisitions: A Guide to Creating Value for Stakeholders*, New York: Oxford University Press.

29. J. Pfeffer, 2003, The human factor: Curbing the urge to merge, *Business 2.0*, July: 58.

30. N. P. Varaiya, 1988, The "winner's curse" hypothesis and corporate takeovers, *Managerial and Decision Economics*, 9: 209–219.

31. C. Gopinath, 2003, When acquisitions go awry: Pitfalls in executing corporate strategy, *Journal of Business Strategy*, 24(5): 22–27.

32. K. E. Meyer & E. Lieb-Doczy, 2003, Post-acquisition restructuring as evolutionary process, *Journal of Management Studies*, 40: 459–483; L. Capron, W. Mitchell, & A. Waminathan, 2001, Asset divestiture following horizontal acquisitions: A dynamic view, *Strategic Management Journal*, 22: 817–844.

33. S. L. Gillan, J. W. Kensinger, & J. D. Martin, 2000, Value creation and corporate diversification: The case of Sears, Roebuck & Co., *Journal of Financial Economics*, 55: 103–138.

34. M. F. Wiersema & J. P. Liebeskind, 1995, The effects of leveraged buyouts on corporate growth and diversification in large firms, *Strategic Management Journal*, 16: 447–460.

35. M. Wright, R. E. Hoskisson, & L. W. Busenitz, 2001, Firm rebirth: Buyouts as facilitators of strategic growth and entrepreneurship, *Academy of Management Executive*, 15(1): 111–125.

Your Career

© Mary Kate Denny/Photo Edit

Search a major business news outlet (such as *The Wall Street Journal, Business Week, Fortune,* and *Forbes*) to find a description of a proposed acquisition. Conduct a due diligence study of the proposed acquisition so you'll have the information needed to answer the four basic due diligence process questions: (1) What is the acquiring firm really buying? (2) What is the target firm's stand-alone value? (3) Where are the synergies the acquisition might create? (4) What is the acquiring firm's walk-away offer price? Use secondary or library sources to decide whether the transaction should be completed and the approximate walk-away offer price.

Engaging in this due diligence process will give you a better feel for how this process works in firms using an acquisition strategy. In your career, you will probably work for a firm using an acquisition strategy or for a firm that is an acquisition target. Understanding the process and its outcomes will help you deal with it as an employee. Also, if you are interested in working for a firm using an acquisition strategy or for an investment bank or private equity firm, completing your own "trial" due diligence processes of proposed acquisitions provides some experience that you can apply in a future job. Because it yields insights about acquisitions, practicing the due diligence process now may also benefit you when interviewing with firms using an acquisition strategy.

Acquisitions are one of the most common and most important strategies used by firms in efforts to succeed. The bad news is that many acquisitions fail (the general rule of thumb is that up to 70 percent do not achieve estimated synergies). Many times, acquisitions are not well thought out ahead of time or are the personal mission of CEOs. This chapter addresses many of the pitfalls and remedies associated with acquisitions; this chapter's tool is a road map for navigating the acquisition decision.

Acquisition Analysis Flowchart

```
                    Understand Purpose of
                    Acquisition
                    • Reduce costs
                    • Gain market power
                    • Increase growth
                    • Learn and build capabilities

                         Analyze Opportunity

              Internal Factors                    External Factors

    Strategic        Strengths and       Industry            Identify Acquisition
    Objective        Weaknesses          Attractiveness      Candidates

    Resources        Acquisition Fit     Porter's Five       Soft Issues
                                         Forces              • Culture/fit
                                         Three Cs            • Management

                                                             Hard Issues
                                                             • Price
                                                             • Balance sheet
```

✳ BIZ FLIX

MEET THE PARENTS: ASSESSING THE GREG FOCKER ACQUISITION

Business acquisitions have a striking parallel to a major acquisition in people's lives—marrying into another family. Think of this scene from *Meet the Parents* as a metaphorical look at business acquisitions. Carefully consider the following questions while viewing the scene.

Greg Focker (Ben Stiller) hopes his weekend visit to his girlfriend Pam's (Teri Polo) home will leave a positive impression on her parents. Unfortunately, Jack Byrnes (Robert De Niro), Pam's father, immediately dislikes him. Jack's fondness does not improve after Greg accidentally breaks the urn holding Jack's mother's ashes. Other factors do not help the developing relationship: Greg is Jewish, while Jack is a WASP ex-CIA psychological profiler. These factors blend well to cause the continuous development of stress and stress-related responses of all parties involved.

This scene comes from the "No More Lies" segment near the film's end. Jack says, "Is your name Gaylord Focker?" Jack holds Greg's wrists to feel his pulse. This scene ends after Jack says, "Will you be my son-in-law?" while holding the engagement ring. The film continues to its end after this scene with Jack suggesting to his wife Dina (Blythe Danner) that they meet the Fockers, Greg's parents.

What to Watch for and Ask Yourself
1. Does Jack Byrnes carefully screen the potential acquisition—Greg Focker?
2. Does Jack Byrnes apply due diligence as described in this chapter while assessing Greg Focker?
3. Are there any pitfalls in this acquisition? Recall this chapter's discussion of pitfalls and apply them to this scene.

Mini-Case

Credit Agricole Acquires Credit Lyonnais SA to Become the World's Third-Largest Bank

Credit Agricole started a long-anticipated consolidation of European banks by acquiring Credit Lyonnais SA. Because Credit Agricole is now the third-largest bank in the world (see Table 7.3), this acquisition may force a response from large European rivals such as Barclays Bank of the United Kingdom and Deutsche Bank. Although the acquisition of Credit Lyonnais was within France's border, one significant cross-border deal would force all major players to assess their strategic alternatives. With the expansion of the European Union to include many new Eastern European countries, the scale of banking will become larger.

Because of limited growth opportunities in their mature home markets, each large European bank is looking abroad to expand. Furthermore, many of these banks' largest clients operate across borders in the European Union. These banks will want to follow their clients as they expand to new geographic areas. Currently, Credit Agricole, with its 16 percent holding in BancaIntesa SpA, Italy's largest bank, is the only large bank to own a position in a fairly large European rival.

In addition to Credit Agricole, other European banks such as Deutsche Bank are considering acquisitions as a means of increasing their consumer banking assets. Interestingly, the German government has suggested that Deutsche

TABLE 7.3　Largest Banks by Assets Held

Banks	Assets Held (in Billions)
Citigroup (U.S.)	$1,264.0
UBS (Switzerland)	$1,120.5
Credit Agricole Group (France)	$1,105.4
Mizuho Financial Group (Japan)	$1,080.8
HSBC Holdings (U.K.)	$1,034.2
Deutsche Bank AG (Germany)	$1,014.8
BNP Paribas (France)	$ 989.0
Sumitomo Mitsui Fin 1Grp (Japan)	$ 844.8
Royal Bank of Scotland (U.K.)	$ 806.2
Barclays Bank PLC (U.K.)	$ 791.3

NOTE: Figures for the Japanese banks are as of March 31, 2003. Other figures are as of December 31, 2003, except for the updated information on France's Credit Agricole.

Bank consider acquiring Deutsche Post, the parent of Post Bank. The German government's suggestion surfaced in response to Citibank's analysis of Deutsche Bank as either a takeover target or as a merger partner.

Although acquiring Deutsche Post would increase its consumer banking assets, Deutsche Bank officials think the acquisition price is steep. The price is problematic because Deutsche Post would be difficult to restructure, given Germany's inflexible labor regulations in regard to layoffs of potentially redundant employees. The Post Bank has been considering an IPO that would bring in approximately $7.12 billion. Deutsche Bank has evaluated Deutsche Post's assets and has concluded that a price much beyond $6 billion would be an overpayment. However, Deutsche Post is unwilling to sell to Deutsche Bank unless it receives a larger premium for its assets.

In the United States, the banking industry continues to consolidate through acquisitions. To date, however, although European banks continue to study each other, only Credit Agricole has completed a major acquisition of another bank. Each European country's desire to have its own major bank influences decisions about acquisitions. Thus, only the passage of time will enable us to know how many acquisitions will be completed in the European banking sector.

SOURCES: 2004, Possible bid for Post Bank Recedes, *Wall Street Journal*, May 12: A3; 2004, Finance and economics: That shrinking feeling; German banks, *The Economist*, March 27; 2004, Deutsche Bank CEO calls a takeover or takeover unlikely, *Wall Street Journal*, March 10: B1; Laferty Ltd., 2004, Europe's banks commence mating season, *European Banker*, February: 1; J. Wrighton, 2004, France's Credit Agricole is making its move; Carron faces challenge of turning bank into European power house; regional holders may pose hurdle, *Wall Street Journal*, June 3: C1.

Questions

1. What would be the strategic motivations for a consolidation of large banks in the European Union? (Hint: Examine this chapter's "Focusing on Strategy" for information on other bank acquisitions.)
2. What other issues besides strategic concerns are hindering or motivating banks that are considering acquiring other banks in the European Union?
3. What competitive reactions do you expect to see from the Credit Agricole acquisition of Credit Lyonnais SA?
4. If you were the CEO of Deutsche Bank, what bank would you pursue as an acquisition target and why?

EXPERIENTIAL EXERCISES

EXERCISE ONE: 2004'S BIGGEST ACQUISITIONS AND MERGERS

The following chart lists the biggest combinations of Chicago firms in 2004, according to *Crain's Chicago Business*.

First, use the Internet or a business library to analyze each deal and determine whether it was a merger, an acquisition, or a takeover. Be able to defend your classification based on concepts defined in Chapter 7.

Second, look at the rationale for the combination and classify it using the five motivation categories in Chapter 7. Again, be able to defend your classification.

Third, assess the extent to which the firms did proper target screening, selection, target negotiating, and due diligence. Once again, be able to defend your assessment of each criterion.

Firm #1	Firm #2	Merger, Acquisition, or Takeover	Rationale Category	Screening	Selection	Negotiation	Due Diligence
J. P. Morgan Chase & Co., New York, N.Y.	Bank One Corp., Chicago, Ill.						
Exelon Corp., Chicago, Ill.	Public Service Enterprise Group Inc., Newark, N.J.						
Kmart Holding Corp., Troy, Mich.	Sears, Roebuck and Co., Hoffman Estates, Ill.						
Madison Dearborn Partners LLC, Chicago, Ill.	Boise Cascade Corp., Boise, Idaho						
Tellabs Inc., Naperville, Ill.	Advanced Fibre Communications Inc., Petaluma, Calif.						

Source: *Crain's Chicago Business*, January 24, 2005.

EXERCISE TWO: CAPITAL ONE'S ACQUISITION OF HIBERNIA BANK

Capital One Financial Corp., a McLean, Virginia–based company primarily focusing on credit cards, was at a critical strategic decision point. For some time, Capital One had depended heavily on direct mail and media advertisements to attract new credit card customers. These actions resulted in a significant amount of growth for the firm. However, as the twenty-first century began, Capital One found itself facing increasing competition in what were becoming increasingly saturated markets. Furthermore, Capital One had found gaps in its ability to access some types of customers and to expand product lines. On March 7, 2005, Capital One purchased New Orleans–based Hibernia Corporation for a reported $5.35 billion. At the time, Hibernia was the retail bank leader in Louisiana and also had significant market presence/opportunity in major Texas markets.

Research this acquisition and be prepared to discuss the advantages and disadvantages of integrating these two organizations. Do you think the acquisition will benefit Capital One? Why or why not? Be prepared to justify your answer.

CHAPTER 8

Competing across Borders

Reading and studying this chapter should enable you to:

*Knowledge Objectives

1_
Explain four reasons why firms pursue international strategies.

2_
Understand the two major pressures leading to three dominant international strategies.

3_
Describe the four basic alternative contractual modes for entering international markets and explain the trade-offs for using each mode.

4_
Discuss how three types of advantages affect the decision

about which mode of entering international markets to use.

5_
Explain the three alternative types of foreign direct investment and the strategic basis for each one.

6_
Describe the organizational structures that are used to implement each of the international strategies.

Focusing on Strategy

eBay's International Expansion Strategy

"Today, eBay Inc., as it's now known, has catapulted from its early days as the place to trade Beanie Babies to become the Web's most powerful corporate enterprise in its own right, worth more than $70 billion ... Were eBay a country, its expected gross sales of $34 billion this year would rank as the 59th largest gross domestic product in the world, just behind Kuwait." (Robert D. Hof, *Business Week,* 2004)

In September 1995, Pierre Omidyar launched eBay, an online person-to-person auction or trading forum. eBay receives a fee for a listing and for sales. It competes in markets similar to newspaper classified ads, flea markets, garage sales, and traditional auction houses. Omidyar hoped that the auction community on eBay would reflect the values of openness, honesty, empowerment, and trust. In Omidyar's words, "eBay was founded with the belief that people are honest and trustworthy. We believe that each of our customers, whether a buyer or seller, is an individual who deserves to be treated with respect."

eBay executives worked hard to improve the community and services in order to develop the trust and loyalty needed for its auction business to flourish. Originally, eBay found that serious collectors and small traders were the most active site users. Accordingly, it developed its PowerSellers program to benefit bulk sellers. To expand its opportunities, eBay formed a strategic alliance with AOL in March 1999. This agreement gave eBay a prominent presence across the domestic and international AOL family of brands. eBay also used AOL's brands prominently in its sites to encourage eBay users to use AOL as an Internet service provider.

In 1999, eBay began to expand into international markets. It did so initially in the United Kingdom and Canada by using a greenfield venture (discussed later in the chapter) in these markets. Some German entrepreneurs copied eBay's source code and set up a mirror image of eBay under the name Alandro.de in Germany. However, by the end of 1999, eBay had acquired Alandro.de and renamed the site eBay.de. The firm also started an eBay site in Australia through a joint venture with a leading Internet media company, PBL Online. In February 2000, eBay Japan was launched through a joint venture with NEC. However, Yahoo initiated an auction site in Japan five months earlier through a joint venture with Softbank, a large Japanese Internet company. In 2002, eBay withdrew from Japan's market because Yahoo had an insurmountable lead.

Meg Whitman, CEO of eBay, learned a lesson from the Japanese experience. When considering China as a market opportunity, she invested early to get ahead of the competition. To launch its operations in China, eBay acquired China's Each Net, which eBay renamed eBay Each Net. Although in many parts of Asia, online payment is a novelty, delivery systems are flawed, and theft can be a difficult problem, eBay's China venture has 4.3 million users. Furthermore, eBay is not developing only in Shanghai and Beijing; 52 percent of its users live in largely rural western China. Thus, eBay has extended its geographic reach in China and elsewhere surprisingly quickly and across a vast array of languages and cultures.

eBay's most recent international actions include the acquisition of Baazee.com, Inc., India's largest online auction site, for $50 million and acquisition of Marktplaats.nl, the top classified-listings Web site in the Netherlands. Despite the potential size of India's market, it lags far behind other markets, including China, in Internet usage. However, eBay considers India a huge growth opportunity as it did China; the market is expected to grow as customers become accustomed to shopping and trading online. Currently, India has an estimated 17 million Internet users, compared with 84 million in China and 188 million in the United States. Internet usage is expected to dramatically grow in all three countries.

eBay bought Marktplaats.nl to strengthen its position in the Netherlands, where 70 percent of the population use the Internet, and to learn more about the Internet classified-listing market. Earlier in 2004, eBay purchased a 25 percent position in Craigslist, which offers Web-based classified listings for users in the San Francisco Bay area, New York, Los Angeles and several dozen other cities. Marktplaats.nl will report to eBay Netherlands while operating as a separate business.

Growing approximately 40 percent a year, eBay earned $2.17 billion on gross sales of $24 billion in 2003. Currently, 40 percent of eBay's revenue comes from its international businesses, but it expects relatively more growth from its international operations in the future. Although eBay has expanded rapidly into a number of distinct geographical and cultural markets, the firm must now organize these disparate operations into an overall international strategy as well as structure its organization. To date, eBay has used a number of entry modes: acquisition, joint venture, and greenfield investment. As we've discussed, most of these entries are successful, but some are not (such as the entry into Japan). Meg Whitman has an important challenge in formulating an overall strategy and developing an organization to manage eBay's dispersed international operations.

SOURCES: R. D. Hof, 2004, The Web for the people, *Business Week,* December 6: 18; M. Mangalindan, 2004, eBay buys Netherlands classified-listing site, *Wall Street Journal,* November 11: B11; L. M. Weiss, M. M. Capozzi, & L. Prusak, 2004, Learning from the Internet giants, *MIT Sloan Management Review,* 45(4): 79–84; N. Wingfield, 2004, eBay sets sights on Indian market with acquisition, *Wall Street Journal,* June 23: A3; L. Wozniak, 2004, An on-line cash machine, *Far Eastern Economic Review,* April 29: 66; R. D. Hof, 2003, The eBay economy, *Business Week,* August 25: 125–128.

As "Focusing on Strategy" indicates, expanding international operations is increasingly important to eBay's strategic and financial performance as it arranges transactions between sellers and buyers at its various auction sites throughout the world. The increase in globalization mentioned in Chapter 3 is based on several historical changes in the global business environment. In the first half of the twentieth century, firms wishing to enter new markets were frustrated because of barriers against foreign trade and investments imposed by national governments. After World War I, many countries imposed tariffs and quotas on imported goods that favored local firms; as a result, international trade declined throughout the 1930s. These tariffs and quotas contributed to the severity of the U.S. depression.

However, after World War II, these policies were reversed as major trading powers negotiated reductions in tariffs and quotas and eliminated many barriers to foreign direct investment (FDI). **Foreign direct investment** is a process through which a firm directly invests (beyond exporting and licensing) in a market outside its home country. These negotiations were embodied in the General Agreement on Tariffs and Trade (GATT) and its successor organization, the World Trade Organization (WTO). Furthermore, regional trading agreements such as the European Union, the Mercosur Accord, and the North American Free Trade Agreement (NAFTA) have also relaxed trade and investment barriers among member countries.

Additionally, investments in technology, particularly communications and transportation technologies, are making international transactions more feasible and more profitable by reducing the costs of transactions. Similarly, the rapidly growing use of the Internet has affected international transactions in at least three ways. First, the Internet and associated technologies are facilitating trade in services such as banking, consulting, retailing, and even gambling. For instance, many U.S. companies have outsourced customer service and data entry operations to low-cost-labor countries outside North America, such as India. Second, the Internet makes competition between large and smaller firms more reasonable regardless of the good or service being sold.[1] This means that the amount of investment needed to expand into foreign markets has been substantially reduced. Consider that Internet technology makes it possible for a company in Missouri, Indonesia, or Brazil to create a Web site and compete with a larger business with facilities located in one of the world's larger cities of commerce. Third, the Internet creates a more efficient networking capability among businesses. General Motors, for instance, expects to reduce its purchase order costs significantly through online purchasing by integrating its suppliers and by monitoring inventory of parts ordering and shipping.[2] Have you used the Internet for transactions with companies overseas? Do you use it to explore international Web sites? If so, hasn't using the Internet in this manner changed how you conduct business transactions?

Even though significant trends have fostered growth in international business, the costs and risks of doing business outside a firm's domestic market can be significant. The research literature labels these costs the **liability of foreignness**.[3] As Chapter 4 indicates, a firm must have resources that enable it to overcome these additional costs. In this chapter, we discuss firm-specific resources as well as location advantages that help to overcome these costs.

In summary, international strategies are becoming more widespread because of the environmental and technological changes taking place in the twenty-first

FIGURE 8.1

International Strategy: Motives, Strategic Approach, Mode of Entry, and Structural Implementation

Motives for International Strategies

- Sourcing of resources and supplies
- Seeking to expand or develop new markets
- Competitive rivalry
- Leveraging core competencies and learning

International Strategies

- Multidomestic strategy
- Global strategy
- Transnational strategy

Implementing International Structures

- Geographic-area divisional structure
- Worldwide divisional structure
- Global matrix structure

Modes of Entry

- Exporting
- Licensing
- Franchising
- International strategic alliance and joint venture
- Greenfield venture (wholly owned)
- International acquisition

century.[4] However, firms must still have the resources necessary to formulate and implement a strategy to overcome the continuing costs of the liability of foreign entry. In this chapter, as illustrated in Figure 8.1, we explore the reasons for and types of international strategies that firms use. We begin this important exploration by outlining the motives for using an international strategy. Next, we explore the basic international strategies employed by firms. While reading this chapter, remember that international strategies are sometimes called cross-border strategies. Once a strategy is chosen, managers must choose a mode of international entry. Finally, the firm must choose an organizational structure and accompanying processes to implement the chosen strategy.

Motives for International Strategies

A number of motives drive the use of international strategies. Next, we describe four of the most prominent motives.

Sourcing of Resources and Supplies

Seeking new sources of supply has long been a common reason to engage in international trade. During the Middle Ages, for example, Italy used its political and military strength in Venice, Genoa, and Florence as the foundation for its ability to be a major center of international commerce and banking. During this time, Italy was the major trading link between Europe and Asia. However, after these trade routes were severed by the Turks in 1453, European governments sought new ocean routes to the Far East. This is one of the reasons why the Spanish government backed Christopher Columbus's expedition to sail west from Europe looking for such routes. Inadvertently, as we know, Columbus found new sources of supply in the Americas, a discovery that ultimately led to the colonization of the Americas by European countries. Similarly today, large firms make foreign direct investments largely to reduce the costs they incur to obtain needed supplies. As we explain in "Understanding Strategy," with China's entrance into the WTO, many firms are investing in that country and the seemingly inexhaustible and inexpensive labor. However, as China's markets continue to provide a source of supply, demand for products such as automobiles is growing. Thus, firms also enter China to expand their markets. The motive to expand a firm's potential market is discussed next.

Seeking to Expand or Develop New Markets

As firms mature in their domestic market, they often expand into international markets to increase revenues and profits. This is the case for consumer products giants Procter & Gamble, Unilever, and Colgate-Palmolive. These three firms are using international strategies to expand into a host of countries, including China and India—countries with huge market potential for the firms' products such as toothpaste and detergents. Firms also seek to lower costs of production by developing economies of scale (defined in Chapter 3). International expansion balances a firm's risk. This balance results from the firm's ability to sell in multiple markets, reducing its dependency on sales in any one market.[5] To show the magnitude of international strategies, think of how many of the products you use are made by a nondomestic company. What about your car? Your furniture and stereo system? The clothes you are wearing? For most of us, answering this question clearly highlights the global nature of the world's economy.

Competitive Rivalry

Some businesses enter foreign markets to enhance their ability to compete with major rivals. For example, Coca-Cola and PepsiCo are both aggressively expanding their international operations. Of course, neither firm can allow its competitor to gain a competitive advantage in terms of global markets.[6] Think about this outcome. If either Pepsi or Coke gained a significant advantage in global markets, the additional profitability earned as a result of using that advantage could be used to damage the competitor in the all-important U.S. market. The relationships between earth-moving equipment firms Caterpillar and Komatsu and between photographic firms Kodak and Fuji are similar to the relationship between Coca-Cola and Pepsi. Each firm actively competes against its rival in global markets. This competitive rivalry exists to prevent a competitor from gaining a significant advantage in any one country or region.

Interestingly, other firms pursue international ventures to avoid domestic competition. In the local Japanese automobile market, competition is very intense because of the number of large firms competing in the local market, including Toyota, Honda, Nissan, Mazda, Mitsubishi, Suzuki, Subaru, Isuzu, and Daihatsu. Part of the reason for moving into the international market was the nature of domestic competition. Japanese automakers have largely been successful

understanding strategy:

THE EFFECTS OF CHINA'S DEVELOPING MARKET ECONOMY

The annual increase in gross domestic product (GDP) in China has outpaced all other major economies in the world in recent years. China's GDP averaged over eight percent annual growth for 2000–2003. This phenomenal economic growth, however, has been fueled by "bubble" investments in real estate. One analyst estimated that 80 percent of all Zhejiang province bank loans in 2002 and 2003 were given to real estate ventures. Simultaneously the government is spending huge amounts on building bridges, highways, dams, and power plants to fuel a private economy to make up for underinvestment during prior years.

© REUTERS/Claro Cortes IV/Landov

Manufacturers are suffering chronic electricity shortages, a sign that the economy is growing too quickly. China's growth rate has had an impact beyond its borders as well. One of these effects is the dramatic increase in the global prices of raw materials such as crude oil, cement, and scrap steel. This is a classic case of demand and supply relationships. The supply of a number of raw materials (for example, oil) hasn't increased dramatically, while the demand for oil and its derivative products by China and other nations is definitely increasing.

Chinese regulators recognized that the nation's economy is growing too quickly. This knowledge has motivated regulators to establish policies that reduce the annual growth rate to about seven percent. To reach this goal, the Chinese government increased bank reserve requirements; capped the percentage of debt companies can use to purchase cement, steel and aluminum and fund real estate projects; the government also signaled tighter credit policies for commercial lending. These actions must be implemented carefully because the collapse of China's economy would have severe effects on the world and especially on the regional economies of Japan, South Korea, Taiwan, and Hong Kong that feed China's export growth.

China's entrance into the WTO also facilitated changes in government policies that created entry opportunities in many industries. For instance, China is developing legislation to open the telecommunications market more fully, not only to domestic but also to foreign firms. The law will facilitate the continued breakup of state-run monopolies and induce more healthy competition.

In the auto industry, the problem is just the opposite of the telephone industry. China's highly fragmented auto industry means that none of the Chinese manufacturers have the economies of scale needed to compete on a global basis. Although new policies resulting from China's entrance into the WTO are likely to be burdensome for foreign firms because of the requirement to use a higher percentage of parts made in China, it will foster development of the Chinese automobile industry.

To solidify its changes in policy, China is also developing antitrust laws. However, some of this legislation may be targeted toward large multinationals such as Microsoft, Eastman-Kodak, and Tetra Pack AB, a Swedish packaging company.

The impact of the Chinese economy on firms across the world is strong and visible. As we've described, a large number of firms are using

SOURCES: A. Browne, 2004, China charts a tight course, *Wall Street Journal*, May 18: A17; R. Buckman, 2004, China hurries anti-trust law, *Wall Street Journal*, June 11: A7; K. Chen, 2004, Changes are reshaping China, *Wall Street Journal*, June 8, A13; K. Chen, 2004, Giving credit where credit is due in China, *Wall Street Journal*, June 24: C1, C6; K. Chen, 2004, China crafts telecom law to level playing field, *Wall Street Journal*, May 20: B5; J. Cox, 2004, China pulls reins on its economy, *USA Today*, April 28, B1; D. J. Lynch, 2004, China economy zooms ahead, but growth might be too fast, *USA Today*, April 29: B1, B2; R. McGregor, 2004, China's ruling party to lift role in business, *Financial Times*, June 22: 7.

international strategies to compete in China. Large and small firms and companies from both developed and developing economies (such as India) are interested in competing in China. The effects of the Chinese economy are significant for China's domestic companies as well as for firms across the globe wanting to use international strategies to compete in a huge market with seemingly unlimited opportunities.

in their international ventures. In fact, the "big three" in the United States are now the "big two"—Ford and General Motors, plus DaimlerChrysler, which is owned by Daimler-Benz, a German firm.

Leveraging Core Competencies and Learning

As we discussed in Chapter 4, firms invest heavily to develop core competencies. Once it has developed a core competence that is a competitive advantage in its domestic market, a firm may be able to use that competitive advantage in international markets as well. When the competitive advantage is in R&D, the firm may have the foundation needed to rely on innovation as the source of entry to international markets. We'll speak further to the issue of using innovation to enter new markets in Chapter 10.

Learning is also an important reason for international expansion. Firms often invest in countries that have centers of excellence in industries such as semiconductors. These firms enter international markets to gain access to product and manufacturing process knowledge. For example, large pharmaceuticals firms have formed alliances with foreign partners in order to learn about new drug research that could lead to developing and introducing new products into their domestic market.[7]

We've discussed motives influencing firms to use strategies to compete in international markets. As you would expect, firms can choose from several different strategies to compete in international markets. We discuss these strategies in the next few sections.

International Strategies

Firms consider two important and potentially competing issues when choosing an international strategy—the need for global efficiencies and the need to customize a good or service for a particular host country market.[8] Generally, efficiency increases when the firm can sell its current good or service in multiple international markets. In contrast, the need for customization to serve local, international markets increases when the firm sells a good or service that is adapted specifically to a particular local market.

© Reuters/Landov

Firms seeking global efficiency may decide to locate in countries where their production and distribution costs will be low. For example, a firm may locate in a country with low labor costs. It might also obtain economies of scale by building factories that can serve customers in more than a single country. Alternatively, by broadening their product line in countries they enter, firms can achieve economies of scope (see Chapter 6) and thereby lower their production and marketing costs for related products.

Despite the initial mistranslation of their famous slogan, Kentucky Fried Chicken restaurants have proven very successful in China with over 900 outlets and approximately 250 more opening per year, such as this one—the first drive-through restaurant in Beijing.

In some international settings, firms can be more successful by customizing their products to meet local market tastes and interests. For instance, KFC has adapted its restaurant foods to fit the culture and taste preferences of local markets. KFC offers more fish dishes in Asian countries and less chicken, for example. Language can also present challenges as the following indicates: "Pepsi-Cola went into Taiwan and carefully translated its slogan, 'Come alive with the Pepsi generation.' However, the translation came out as 'Pepsi will bring your ancestors back from the dead.' And, KFC's slogan 'Finger licking good,' in Chinese says, 'Eat your fingers off.'"[9]

As shown in Figure 8.2, the need for global efficiency and the need to satisfy a local host country market's unique needs provide a two-dimensional matrix illustrating the different global strategies. We next describe the three international strategies shown in Figure 8.2.

The Multidomestic Strategy

*
multidomestic strategy

an action plan that the firm develops to produce and sell unique products in different markets

The **multidomestic strategy** is an action plan that the firm develops to produce and sell unique products in different markets. To use this strategy, a firm establishes a relatively independent set of operating subsidiaries in which each subsidiary develops specific products for a particular domestic market. Each subsidiary is free to customize its products' marketing campaign and operating techniques to best meet the needs of local customers. The multidomestic strategy is particularly effective when clear differences between national markets exist; potential economies of scale for production, distribution, and marketing are low; and the cost of coordination between the parent and foreign subsidiaries is high. Because each subsidiary must be responsive to the local market, the parent usually delegates considerable power and authority to managers of host country subsidiaries. Many multinational corporations used the multidomestic strategy during World War II because it was difficult to communicate and transfer technologies. Many European firms also adopted this strategy because of the cultural and language differences they needed to overcome in order to conduct business in each European country. Let's consider a specific firm to demonstrate these points.

The French defense contractor French Thomson-CSF has transformed into a new global defense and aerospace electronics group called Thales SA. Thales has won contracts worldwide by using a multidomestic strategy. It has become a "local

FIGURE 8.2 International Strategies

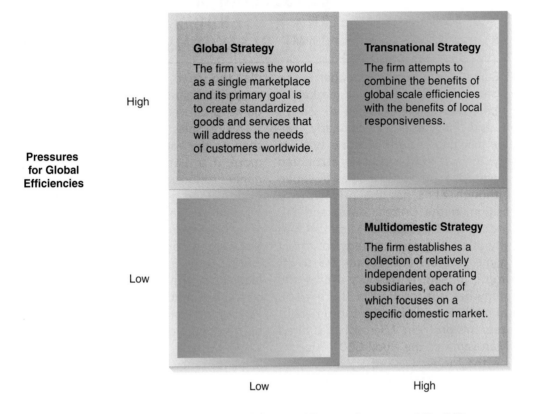

Pressures for Global Efficiencies

High

Global Strategy

The firm views the world as a single marketplace and its primary goal is to create standardized goods and services that will address the needs of customers worldwide.

Transnational Strategy

The firm attempts to combine the benefits of global scale efficiencies with the benefits of local responsiveness.

Low

Multidomestic Strategy

The firm establishes a collection of relatively independent operating subsidiaries, each of which focuses on a specific domestic market.

Low   High

Pressures for Local Responsiveness and Flexibility

player in six countries outside France: Britain, the Netherlands, Australia, South Africa, South Korea, and Singapore."[10] It implemented its strategy using a series of joint ventures with and acquisitions of local players in each of these markets.

The Global Strategy

*

global strategy

an action plan that the firm develops to produce and sell standardized products in different markets

The **global strategy** is an action plan that the firm develops to produce and sell standardized products in different markets. To use this strategy, a firm manages its products from a central divisional office to develop, produce, and sell its standardized products throughout the world. A firm using a global strategy seeks to capture economies of scale in production and marketing as well as economies of scope and location advantage. Because the global strategy requires worldwide coordination, the production and marketing strategies are usually centralized with decisions made at a division headquarters. Mercedes-Benz, a unit of DaimlerChrysler, uses the global strategy to sell its products in many global markets. This strategy is successful for Mercedes-Benz because its products are known for their quality and reliability.[11] However, as discussed in "Understanding Strategy," at times the global strategy leads to difficulties in

understanding strategy:

WHY IS THE SONY PLAYSTATION OUTSELLING MICROSOFT'S XBOX AND NINTENDO'S GAMECUBE VIDEO GAME PLATFORMS?

Nintendo's GameCube, the former leader in the $27 billion-plus video game global market, is struggling because of the success of Sony's PlayStation and PlayStation 2. Similarly, Microsoft Xbox machines have not done well internationally. In fact, Xbox machines accounted for two percent of game console sales in Japan in 2003. Although Xbox has the number two console position in the United States and Europe, behind Sony's PlayStation, Microsoft has had difficulty using its global strategy to attract Japanese game creators and consumers to its game platform. Indeed, Microsoft's use of the global strategy has not resulted in the adaptation to local markets as desired by consumers.

To address this problem, Microsoft has hired Yoshihiro Maruyama as the Xbox CEO in Japan. Maruyama is the former COO of Squar, a video game producer. One of Maruyama's objectives is to persuade game producers in Japan to create games for the Xbox platform.

The lack of sales in the United States in 2003 resulted in Nintendo's reporting a loss for the first time in its history. Apparently, the Japanese firm's game machine and associated games have lost ground in the U.S. market. In other words, Nintendo's international strategy in the United States was not very competitive. In 2002, because it had too many unsold GameCube machines late in the holiday selling cycle, Nintendo had to cut its console price to $99 from $149, which was almost 50 percent less than the price of its rivals, PlayStation 2 and Microsoft Xbox. The lack of console sales harms a firm like Nintendo even more because it tries to make a profit on both its hardware and its software, or video game titles. Without consoles on which to play the video games, sales of the video games dropped dramatically. Nintendo and other video game producers count on the video game or software sales for more of their net income than on the console or hardware sales. Furthermore, if a platform is not selling, major video game producers such as Electronic Arts stop producing video games for that platform.

Ken Kutaragi is the mastermind behind the Sony PlayStation offerings. When Nintendo was the number one video game producer in the world, Sony formed a team under Kutaragi's leadership. The team's charge was to build a system superior to Nintendo's system. In 1994, the PlayStation system beat Nintendo's Super NES to become the world's top home-gaming platform. Later, with a $2.5 billion dollar investment, PlayStation 2 was introduced and captured 75 percent of the worldwide home video game and console market. Through Kutaragi's division's success, Sony's annual revenue increased by $10 billion. The importance of this division is also demonstrated by the fact that in 2002, the division accounted for more than 58 percent of Sony's worldwide operating profits.

Both Microsoft and Nintendo seem to be following global strategies that are centralized and operated mainly from their home countries, the United States and Japan, respectively. Microsoft has not been able to penetrate the Japanese market, which is important because it is Sony and Nintendo's home market. Likewise, Nintendo has not done a good job meeting the competition in pricing and forecasting sales in the U.S. market. These may be symptoms of problems with Nintendo's global strategy because its managers do not understand consumers in markets that are different culturally from their home markets. However, Sony has done well by achieving globally efficient operations and by adapting effectively to demands in foreign markets (such as the United States and Europe). Nobuyuki Idei, Sony's former chairman, was strongly committed to pursuing convergence in music, movies, games, and communications. The Sony PlayStation 2 is an example of this approach; it combines a game platform with the ability to play DVDs and connect to the Internet. Sony's strategy exemplifies the transnational strategy (defined next). Although the transnational strategy is difficult to implement, it is also difficult for competitors to imitate. Having the right strategy is important, but so is implementing it effectively. Sony has demonstrated its ability to effectively formulate and implement its international strategy in the global video game market.

SOURCES: 2004, Business: A serious contest; Video games, *The Economist,* May 8: 73; K. J. Delaney, 2004, Space Invaders: Ads in video games pose a new threat to media industry, *Wall Street Journal,* July 28: A1, A8; P. Dvorak, 2004, Nintendo steers away from the pack, *Wall Street Journal,* May 11: B10; 2004, Nintendo Co.: Weak console sales, firm yen lead to a 51% drop in profit, *Wall Street Journal,* May 28: B6; J. Frederick, 2003, Playing his way to the next level, *Time,* December 1: 84; P. Dvorak, 2003, Nintendo's GameCube sales surge after price cut, *Wall Street Journal,* November 4: B4.

marketing the firm's standardized products to local consumer markets. As we'll see, both Microsoft and Nintendo have had difficulty using the global strategy to sell their video platforms (Xbox for Microsoft; GameCube for Nintendo) outside of their home markets.

The Transnational Strategy

*

transnational strategy

an action plan that the firm develops to produce and sell somewhat unique, yet somewhat standardized products in different markets

The **transnational strategy** is an action plan that the firm develops to produce and sell somewhat unique and somewhat standardized products in different markets. With this strategy, the firm attempts to combine the benefits of global scale efficiencies with the advantages of being locally responsive in a country or geographic region; it requires both centralization and decentralization simultaneously. Ikea, a worldwide furniture producer, employs the transnational strategy. In using this strategy, Ikea relies on standardization of products with global production and distribution, but it also has a system (called "democratic design") through which new designs for local markets are developed and introduced. Democratic design is helping Ikea produce products that meet the tastes of local customers. Ikea is a world leader in furniture production and distribution and is now one of the top furniture retailers in the United States. In fact, ten percent of American homes have at least one Ikea item.[12]

Although the transnational strategy is more difficult to manage and expensive to implement, it is probably the best international strategy to use to facilitate learning. The balance of centralization and decentralization usually results in a corporate culture that promotes transfer of knowledge among subsidiaries. The multidomestic strategy uses a decentralized authority structure. This structure makes it difficult to transfer knowledge across subsidiaries. The global strategy, on the other hand, centralizes decision making, which also hampers new knowledge development. So when using the global strategy, the firm learns less from different host country markets because of its focus on exploiting the firm's current knowledge in each of the markets rather than learning from each market to adapt the products. As suggested in "Understanding Strategy," Sony has managed the PlayStation video game platform well using the transnational strategy.

Modes of International Market Entry

After a firm decides to pursue an international strategy, it must choose a mode of entry. Factors affecting the choice of an entry mode are presented in Figure 8.3.[13] These factors include firm-specific resource advantages, country-specific or location advantages, internal-coordination or administrative advantages, need for control, and resource availability. We begin with an explanation of each mode of entry followed by a discussion of how each potential advantage affects the choice of entry mode.

Entry Modes

Exporting

Perhaps the simplest and most common form of mode of entry is exporting domestic products to a foreign country. **Exporting** is the process of sending goods and services from one country to another for distribution, sale, and service. The advantage of exporting is that the firm can gradually enter an interna-

*
exporting

the process of sending goods and services from one country to another for distribution, sale, and service

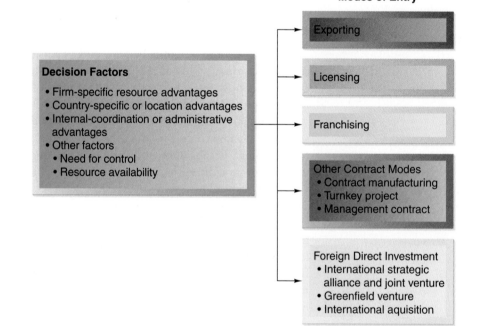

FIGURE 8.3 International Modes of Entry and Decision Factors

Decision Factors

- Firm-specific resource advantages
- Country-specific or location advantages
- Internal-coordination or administrative advantages
- Other factors
  - Need for control
  - Resource availability

Modes of Entry

Exporting

Licensing

Franchising

Other Contract Modes
- Contract manufacturing
- Turnkey project
- Management contract

Foreign Direct Investment
- International strategic alliance and joint venture
- Greenfield venture
- International aquisition

tional market without taking too many risks. Exporting also has the advantage of helping the firm to acquire knowledge about a local market before making large investments. But exporting isn't without problems. Firms exporting their products are vulnerable to tariffs and often encounter logistical challenges in getting products to an international market. Exporting firms also must be aware of possibly being in conflict with local distributors who may want to distribute the firm's products instead.

Licensing

Licensing is the process of entering an international market by leasing the right to use the firm's intellectual property—technology, work methods, patents, copyrights, brand names, or trademarks—to a firm doing business in the desired international market. The firm doing the leasing is the licensor and the firm receiving the license is the licensee. Licensing is popular because it involves little direct cost or risk for the licensor. Electronic Arts successfully uses this strategy as it licenses games worldwide to game platform or hardware producers such as Sony (PlayStation), Nintendo (GameCube), and Microsoft (Xbox). These firms are willing to pay a license fee to Electronic Arts to have rights to the firm's innovative games and titles.[14] Through licensing, Electronic Arts generates revenues and also develops new video games, thereby stimulating further demand for its games and other products. Although licensing has low financial risks, it also provides few opportunities for profit growth. While licensing provides a low-cost means to assess market potential, it also creates dependence on the licensee for exploiting that potential. Another risk is that the licensee can learn the technology and become a competitor of the licensor. Microsoft, for instance, is a software producer and has produced its own video games.

Franchising

Franchising is a special form of licensing and is discussed further in Chapter 9 as a cooperative strategy. **Franchising** is the licensing of a good or service and business model to partners for specified fees (usually a signing fee and a percentage of the franchisee's revenues or profits). The franchisor provides trademarks, operating systems, and well-known products as well as service support such as advertising, specialized training, and quality-assurance programs. McDonald's has developed a successful global franchising system. Pizza Hut, KFC, and Taco Bell have also franchised restaurants worldwide. Benetton uses franchised retail stores to distribute stylish clothing in over 120 countries.

Marriott International has achieved distinction as a franchiser of hotel chains. However, it owns less than three percent of the properties, unlike Hilton and Starwood (St. Regis, Sheraton, and Westin hotel chains), which own more than 30 percent of their properties. One analyst noted that Marriott has "become the industry leader by obsessively whipping its troops into line—not just employees, but hotel owners—while pampering loyal customers and winning bookings away from rivals."[15]

Other Contracting Modes

Contract manufacturing is another popular contractual mode of entry. Large firms in Asia, such as Taiwan Semiconductor Manufacturing Company (TSMC),

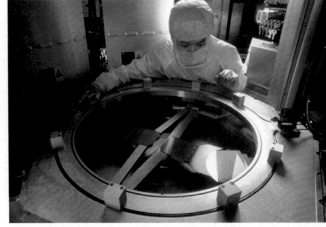

A technician checks production of silicon wafers at the Taiwan Semiconductor Manufacturing Company, which works for clients such as Hewlett-Packard.

manufacture chips for large clients such as Hewlett-Packard (HP). Big Asian contract manufacturers like TSMC are expected to do better than smaller U.S. firms because their cost advantage in Asia has attracted large clients such as HP, that can invest significant amounts of capital thereby enabling the manufacturers to keep their competitive edge. The cost of a new chip plant requires more than $2 billion; "The U.S. share of global chip production is expected to fall from 37 percent this year to 34 percent by 2008, while Asia's rises from 20 to 26 percent."[16]

Similarly, turnkey projects, often construction projects to build large infrastructure items such as coal- or gas-fired electrical power plants, are done on a contractual basis. Management agreements to run such facilities are done on a contractual basis as well.

Approaches to Foreign Direct Investment

With FDI entry modes, the firm has greater control of its destiny in the international market it has chosen to enter. But there is greater risk with FDI investments as well. Next, we discuss three approaches to FDI—strategic alliances and joint ventures, greenfield ventures, and acquisitions.

International Strategic Alliances and Joint Ventures

International strategic alliances represent a cooperative agreement in which home and host country firms work closely together. In the case of a joint venture, "working together" results in creating a separate company to promote the partners' mutual interests (joint ventures and strategic alliances are discussed further in Chapter 9). Firms in emerging economies often want to form international alliances and ventures to gain access to sophisticated technologies that are new to them. This type of arrangement can benefit the non-emerging-economy firm as well, in that it gains access to a new market and doesn't have to pay tariffs to do so (because it is partnering with a local company).[17] However, the non-emerging-economy firm needs to be careful to protect its technologies from being copied by its partner.

Greenfield Venture

In a **greenfield venture**, a firm buys or leases land, constructs a new facility and hires or transfers managers and employees, and then independently launches a new operation (usually a wholly owned subsidiary) without involvement of a partner. The firm maintains full control of its operations with a greenfield venture. More control is especially advantageous if the firm has proprietary technology. Research also suggests that "wholly owned subsidiaries and expatriate staff are preferred" in service industries where "close contacts with end customers" and "high levels of professional skills, specialized know-how, and cus-

*
_____
greenfield venture

a venture in which a firm buys or leases land, constructs a new facility and hires or transfers managers and employees, and then independently launches a new operation (usually a wholly owned subsidiary) without involvement of a partner tomization" are required.[18] The major disadvantage with a greenfield venture launched in an international market is that it takes time to implement and succeed. A lack of experience with and knowledge about the international local market makes it hard for the greenfield venture to have rapid success. Therefore, firms establishing greenfield ventures in international markets need to be patient in order to achieve success with that venture.

International Acquisition

The final FDI entry mode is one in which a firm acquires an existing host country firm. By acquiring a current business, the purchaser gains control over the acquired firm's assets, employees, technology, brand names, and distribution. Therefore, entry is much quicker than by other modes. In fact, acquisitions are the mode used by many firms to enter Eastern European markets. Wal-Mart has entered Germany and the United Kingdom by acquiring local firms.[19]

Using the acquisition entry mode is not without risk. The main risk centers on the fact that when using this entry mode, the acquiring firm often assumes all of the acquired firm's liabilities. Complicating this matter even more is the fact that the firm acquiring a local company may not be fully aware of the conventional practices used to account for liabilities in the acquired firm's market.[20]

We've explored the entry modes available to firms that want to enter international markets. Next we consider the factors influencing the firm's choice of an entry mode, as illustrated in Figure 8.3.

Factors Affecting the Selection of Entry Mode

Firm-Specific Resource Advantages

Firm-specific resource advantages are the core competencies that provide a competitive advantage over a firm's rivals.[21] As we recall from our discussions in Chapter 4, core competencies are often based largely on intangible resources. When the success of a firm's entry into an international market relies on transferring core competencies, an entry mode should be used that involves an equity stake. Therefore, a joint venture, an acquisition, and a greenfield venture represent the best entry mode choices in these cases, because the firm retains more ownership of its competencies. However, if the firm-specific advantage is a brand name, which is protected by law, a licensing or franchising entry mode may be the best choice. As a precaution, a firm needs to be careful in selecting the right licensee because a brand name's reputation can be easily damaged.

Country-Specific or Location Advantages

Country-specific or location advantages are concerned with the desirability of producing in the home country versus locating production and distribution assets in the host country. If country-specific advantages for production are stronger in the home country, it is likely that exporting is the best choice for entering an international market. Such location advantages can be influenced by costs of production and transportation requirements as well as the needs of the intended customers.[22] Many firms, for instance, have located their assets in Turkey because its geographic, religious, linguistic, and cultural ties provide opportunities to enter Central Asian markets of the former Soviet Union as well as markets in the Middle East.[23]

*
_____
country-specific
or location
advantages

advantages that concern the desirability of producing in the home country versus locating production and distribution assets in the host country

However, political risks such as the likelihood of terror or war, unstable governments, and government corruption may discourage making direct investments in a host country. Government policies can also influence the mode of entry. For example, high tariffs discourage exporting and encourage local production through direct investments. Similarly, economic risks such as currency fluctuations may create problems for international investment. If a currency is devalued, so are the assets invested through FDI in that country. Currently the dollar has a lower value than other currencies such as the euro which supports U.S. exports. However, it hurts foreign exporters coming into the United States from countries with a higher-valued currency. Cultural influences may also affect location advantages and disadvantages. If there is a strong match between the cultures in which international transactions are carried out, the liability of foreignness is lower than if there is greater cultural distance.[24]

Internal-Coordination or Administrative Advantages

internal-coordination or administrative advantages

advantages that make it desirable for a firm to produce the good or service rather than contracting with another firm to produce or distribute it

Internal-coordination or administrative advantages make it desirable for a firm to produce the good or service rather than contracting with another firm to produce or distribute it.[25] When a firm outsources the manufacture and distribution of a product, it experiences transaction costs, or the costs of negotiating, monitoring, and enforcing the contract. If these costs are high, a firm may rely on some form of FDI rather than using exporting or contracting (such as licensing or franchising) as an entry mode. Toyota has two advantages that must be maintained internally: efficient manufacturing techniques using a team approach, and a reputation for producing high-quality automobiles.[26] These advantages for Toyota are based on effective management; if Toyota outsourced manufacturing, it would likely lose these advantages. Therefore, Toyota uses some form of FDI (such as greenfield and joint ventures) rather than franchising and licensing for its foreign manufacture of automobiles.

After choosing an appropriate entry mode, the firm must implement its international strategy. Next, we discuss the different organizational structures firms use to implement the multidomestic, global, and transnational international strategies.

Implementing the Multidomestic Strategy

geographic-area divisional structure

a decentralized organizational structure that enables each division to focus on a geographic area, region, or country

The geographic-area divisional structure is used to implement the multidomestic strategy (see Figure 8.4). The **geographic-area divisional structure** is a decentralized organizational structure that enables each division to focus on a geographic area, region, or country.[27] This structure is particularly useful for firms selling products with characteristics that frequently change (such as clothing). The geographic-area structure facilitates managers' actions that tailor the product mix to meet the cultural or special tastes of local customers. However, cost efficiencies are often sacrificed when using the geographic-area structure. Indeed, economies of scale are difficult to achieve using this structure because each country has unique products. The disadvantage of this structure, then, is duplication of resources across each division; for example, each division has its own

FIGURE 8.4

Using the Geographic-Area Divisional Structure to Implement the Multidomestic Strategy

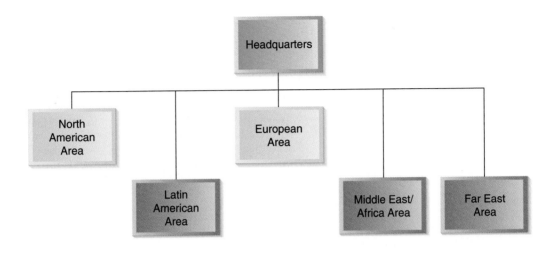

functional marketing specialists and production facilities. Coordination across divisions is also difficult and expensive due to the decentralization.

Implementing the Global Strategy

*

worldwide
divisional
structure

a centralized organizational structure in which each product group is housed in a globally focused worldwide division or worldwide profit center

The worldwide divisional structure is used to implement the global strategy (see Figure 8.5). The **worldwide divisional structure** is a centralized organizational structure in which each product group is housed in a globally focused worldwide division or worldwide profit center.[28] In this structure, the first level of organizational structure below corporate headquarters is that of worldwide product divisions. The global responsibility to develop and manage new products is located in each division. Because a specific division focuses on a single product or product group, division managers are exposed to all aspects of managing products on a global basis. This experience helps managers learn how to integrate the firm's activities to improve manufacturing efficiency and responsiveness—abilities that help the firm adjust production requirements in light of fluctuating global demand. The major disadvantage of the worldwide divisional structure is that it encourages extensive duplication of activities because each division has similar functional skills in marketing, finance, information management, and so forth. Additionally, each product group must develop its own knowledge about the cultural, legal, and political environments of the various regional and national markets in which the various divisions operate. Furthermore, coordination and learning across product groups is difficult. It also results in low responsiveness to specific country needs.

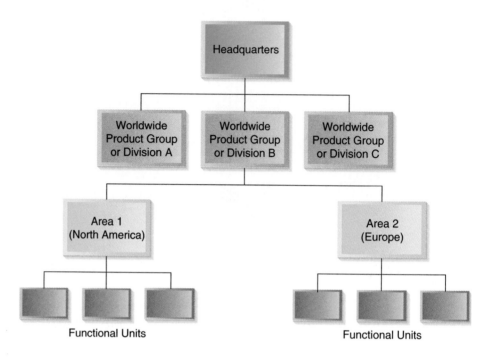

Implementing the Transnational Strategy

global matrix structure

an organizational structure in which both functional and product expertise are integrated into teams so the teams will be able to quickly respond to requirements in the global marketplace

The transnational strategy is usually implemented through a global matrix structure[29] (see Figure 8.6). The **global matrix structure** is an organizational structure in which both functional and product expertise are integrated into teams so the teams will be able to quickly respond to requirements in the global marketplace. The global matrix structure promotes flexibility in designing products and responding to customer needs from different geographical areas. However, it places employees in a position of being accountable to more than one manager. In fact, at any given time an employee may be a member of several cross-functional or product or cross-geographical teams and may find it difficult to be loyal to all of them. Although the global matrix structure gives authority to managers who are most able to use it, the corporate reporting relationships are so complex and vague that it often takes longer to approve major decisions.

When you begin your career, you will likely serve on an international project team with people located in several countries. Don't be surprised if this occurs on your first job. Therefore, international strategies and the organizational structures used to implement them are highly relevant to you.

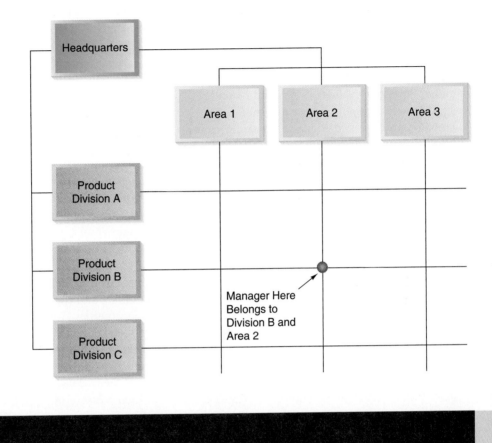

Summary

The primary purpose of this chapter is to examine firm strategies that extend across national borders. In doing so, we examined the following topics:

- The use of international strategies is increasing as firms seek to gain access to new markets and to valuable resources or to reduce their labor costs. The Internet and other technological innovations such as those in logistics are facilitating global business transactions. Reduced regulations and tariffs are also fostering greater opportunities for the use of international strategies.

- International strategies are driven by four major motives: (1) to reduce costs and secure resources; (2) to increase economies of scale and scope and to capitalize on opportunities to secure desirable locations; (3) to respond to pressure by rivals who have moved into regions untapped by others; and (4) to seek learning and other advantages that provide new knowledge from international markets.

- Firms going abroad usually select one of three international strategies. Firms use a **multidomestic strategy** to sell products that are customized to the needs of individual, host country markets. This international strategy works best when decision-making authority is decentralized to each business so it can operate freely in separate regions or countries. The decentralized authority allows the business to adapt its goods and services to the local geographic market. When global markets demand similar characteristics in a good or service, the firm uses a **global strategy** to sell standardized products to global customers with similar needs. Being able to operate efficiently is critical to the success of a global strategy. Finally, a **transnational strategy** combines characteristics of both multidomestic and global strategies in order to respond to pressures for local responsiveness and the need to globally integrate and coordinate operations for efficiency purposes.

- Firms can use several different modes to enter an international market. Entry modes requiring lower asset commitment include international **exporting, licensing,** and **franchising.** These entry modes have less financial risk but also allow less control over operations. They also reduce profit potential, which is shared with the licensee or franchisee. Other contract approaches include contract manufacturers, turnkey projects, and management contracts. These approaches require more investment by the licensee but also have similar advantages of reduced financial investment relative to the previously discussed contract approaches.

- FDI modes include joint ventures or strategic alliances, **greenfield ventures,** and acquisitions. Each FDI entry mode requires more up-front investment, but allows for more control of the venture. A joint venture includes a separate entity for which control is shared with a local partner. A greenfield venture (new wholly owned subsidiary) allows more control and should be used when proprietary technology needs to be protected. An acquisition is more appropriate when speedy entry is important. However, acquisitions often have significant challenges, including the fact that effective due diligence is difficult to conduct in international settings.

- For FDI strategies, significant political and economic risks are encountered. Political risks include terrorism, wars, and outright nationalization of a private firm's assets by the host country. Economic risks include currency fluctuations and devaluations. Commonly, economic risks are accentuated in transition or emerging economies where the economy is less stable. Of course, political and economic risks are often interrelated.

- Implementing international strategies is often complex and can limit international expansion opportunities. The multidomestic strategy requires decentralization and therefore is implemented with a geographic-area divisional structure. The global strategy is implemented with a worldwide divisional structure. The transnational strategy requires both centralization and decentralization, and is commonly implemented with a **global matrix structure.**

Key Terms

country-specific or location advantages 203
exporting 200
foreign direct investment 191
franchising 201
geographic-area divisional structure 204

global matrix structure 206
global strategy 197
greenfield venture 202
internal-coordination or administrative advantages 204
liability of foreignness 191
licensing 201

multidomestic strategy 196
transnational strategy 199
worldwide divisional structure 205

Discussion Questions

1. What are the basic reasons why firms choose to expand their operations internationally by employing international strategies?
2. What are the two primary pressures leading to three main international strategies?
3. What are the four contract-based international entry modes?
4. What major advantages influence the type of entry mode firms choose to enter international markets?
5. What are the three types of foreign direct investment (FDI) and what rationale supports the use of each one?
6. What structures are used to implement the multidomestic, global, and transnational strategies?

Endnotes

1. J. T. Johnson, 2004, Externalization: Changing the shape of business, *Network World*, June 14: 24.
2. G. Rifkin, 2002, GM's Internet overhaul: How the world's largest manufacturer of cars and trucks is using technology to turn itself into a "small" and profitable company, *Technology Review*, October: 62–67.
3. J. Mezias, 2002, How to identify liabilities of foreignness and assess their effects on multinational corporations, *Journal of International Management*, 8: 265–282.
4. J. E. Ricart, M. J. Enright, P. Ghemawat, S. L. Hart, & T. Khanna, 2004, New frontiers in international strategy, *Journal of International Business Studies*, 35: 175–200.
5. N. Capar & M. Kotabe, 2003, The relationship between international diversification and performance in service firms, *Journal of International Business Studies*, 34: 345–355.
6. D. Luhnow & C. Terhune, 2003, Latin pop: A low-budget cola shakes up markets south of the border; Peru's Kola real takes on Coke and Pepsi by cutting frills, targeting bodegas; how plastic leveled the field, *Wall Street Journal*, October 27: A1.
7. K. T. Yeo, 2003, Factors motivating MNCs to set up local R&D facilities: The case of Singapore, *International Journal of Technology Transfer & Commercialisation*, 2(2): 128–138.
8. P. Ghemawat, 2004, Global standardization vs. localization: A case study and model, in J. A. Quelch & R. Deshpande (eds.), *The Global Market: Developing a Strategy to Manage across Borders*, New York: Jossey-Bass, Chapter 8.
9. G. Hoffman, 1996, On foreign expansion, *Progressive Grocer*, September: 156.
10. D. Michaels, 2003, World business (a special report); Victory at sea: How did a French company capture several British naval contracts? Think "multidomestic," *Wall Street Journal Europe*, September 26: R5.
11. P. Wonacott & L. Hawkins Jr., 2003, A global journal report: Saying 'beamer' in Chinese; Western luxury car makers see sales boom in China as newly rich seek status, *Wall Street Journal*, November 6: B1.
12. C. Daniels, 2004, Create IKEA, make billions, take bus, *Fortune*, May 3: 44; E. Brown, 2002, Putting EAMES within reach, *Fortune*, October 30: 98–100.
13. R. G. Javalgi, D. A. Griffith, & D. S. White, 2003, An empirical examination of factors influencing the internationalization of service firms, *Journal of Services Marketing*, 17: 185–202; J. H. Dunning, 1980, Toward an electric theory of international production: Some empirical tests, *Journal of International Business Studies*, 11: 9–31.
14. C. Edward, 2004, Keeping you glued to the couch; In video games, top developer Electronic Arts zaps the competition, *Business Week*, May 27: 58–59.
15. S. Fitch, 2004, Soft Pillows and Sharp Elbows, *Forbes*, May 10: 66.
16. J. Adams, Chip dip in water? *Newsweek*, October 18: E20.
17. J. Bamford, D. Ernst, & D. G. Fubini, 2004, Launching a world-class joint venture, *Harvard Business Review*, 82(2): 91–100.
18. C. Bouquet, L. Hebert, & A. Delios, 2004, Foreign expansion in service industries: Separability and human capital intensity, *Journal of Business Research*, 57: 35–46.
19. J. Levine, 2004, Europe: Gold mines and quicksand, *Forbes*, April 12: 76.
20. K. Shimizu, M. A. Hitt, D. Vaidyanath, & V. Pisano, 2004, Theoretical foundations of cross-border mergers and acquisitions: A review of current research and recommendations for the future, *Journal of International Management*, 10: 307–353; M. A. Hitt & V. Pisano, 2003, The cross-border merger and acquisition strategy: A research perspective, *Management Research*, 1: 133–144.
21. B. Lev, 2004, Sharpening the intangible edge, *Harvard Business Review*, 82(6): 109–116.
22. R. Tahir & J. Larimo, 2004, Understanding the location strategies of the European firms in Asian countries, *Journal of American Academy of Business*, 5: 102–110.

23. E. Tatoglu, K. W. Glaister, & F. Erdal, 2003, Determinants of foreign ownership in Turkish manufacturing, *Eastern European Economics*, 41(2): 5–41.

24. D. Xu & O. Shenkar, 2004, Institutional distance and the multinational enterprise, *Academy of Management Review,* 27: 608–618.

25. T. W. Malone, 2004, Bringing the market inside, *Harvard Business Review*, 82(4): 107–114.

26. S. J. Spear, 2004, Learning to lead at Toyota, *Harvard Business Review*, 82(5): 78–86.

27. A. Ferner, P. Almond, I. Clark, T. Colling, & T. Edwards, 2004, The dynamics of central control and subsidiary anatomy in the management of human resources: Case study evidence from US MNCs in the UK, *Organization Studies*, 25: 363–392.

28. J. Wolf & W. G. Egelhoff, 2002, A reexamination and extension of international strategy-structure theory, *Strategic Management Journal*, 23: 181–189.

29. G. Ietto-Gillies, 2002, *Transnational Corporations: Fragmentation amidst Integration*, New York: Routledge.

Your Career

© Getty Images

Take the opportunity to explore with a professor or one or more managers of firms how the nature of a job in which you are interested has been changed over the last ten years because of increased globalization. What kinds of skills are now needed to succeed in this job? Think about what international location you might prefer if your organization decided to transfer you. Will you need to learn a new language? Explore what cultural attributes are important and which ones you will need to learn in this location. What actions could you take now to increase the likelihood you'll be prepared to work in an international setting?

When devising cross-border strategies, many business leaders fall into predictable biased patterns of behavior, known as blind spots. In the case of global expansion, for example, companies often base their strategies on what has worked in their own countries, without adequate consideration of the expansion territory context. This chapter's tool is designed to help executives break through the blind spots and avoid costly strategic mistakes.

Defending against Blind Spots

Blind Spots
- Overconfidence
- Invalid assumptions
- Representativeness (e.g, using a "comparable known" event and assuming similar outcomes)

Remedies
- Checks and balances
- Extensive data analysis
- Statistical surveys

✳ BIZ FLIX

MR. BASEBALL: LESSONS IN REDUCING THE LIABILITY OF FOREIGNNESS

This chapter emphasized "liability of foreignness" as an important blockage to successful entry into foreign markets. Firms that pursue international strategies need to have cultural sensitivity and cultural awareness for successful, smooth entry. Watch this *Mr. Baseball* scene carefully while considering the following questions.

The New York Yankees trade aging baseball player Jack Elliot (Tom Selleck) to the Chunichi Dragons, a Japanese team. This lighthearted comedy traces Elliot's bungling entry into Japanese culture and exposes his cultural misconceptions, which almost cost him everything—including his new girlfriend Hiroko Uchiyama (Aya Takanashi). After Elliot slowly begins to understand Japanese culture and Japanese baseball, his teammates finally accept him. This film shows many examples of Japanese culture, especially its love for baseball.

This scene is an edited version of the "Welcome to Japan" sequence that appears early in the film. Jack Elliot arrives at Nogoya International Airport, Tokyo, Japan. Yoji Nishimura (Toshi Shioya) meets him and acts as Jack's interpreter and guide. The film continues after this scene with the unfolding adventure of Jack Elliot playing for the Chunichi Dragons.

What to Watch for and Ask Yourself

1. Is Jack Elliot culturally sensitive or culturally insensitive?
2. What cross-cultural errors does he appear to make on his arrival in Japan?
3. What could have been done to decrease Jack Elliot's "liability of foreignness"?

Mini-Case

The Olympic Games: An Opportunity for Growing International Businesses

The Olympic Games took place in Athens, Greece, in 2004. The Games provide a way for outstanding national athletes to compete on an international stage. However, for global firms they are a significant opportunity to increase global brand awareness. Firms such as Coca-Cola, Panasonic, Accenture, and Samsung have the opportunity to market their products worldwide and in specific markets during the Olympic period by using a number of local and regional outlets to establish their global identities.

Likewise, large media firms seek to benefit from the potential advertising revenue associated with the Olympics. NBC, for example, commits significant sums of money to obtain the broadcast rights for the Olympic Games in North America. The network paid $1.27 billion for the broadcast rights of the 2000 Sydney Summer Games and the 2002 Salt Lake City Winter Games. Additionally, NBC agreed to pay $2.3 billion for the broadcast rights of the 2004, 2006, and 2008 Games and an additional $2.2 billion for the 2010 and 2012 Games, even though the sites for these Games haven't been determined. Additional broadcast rights for Europe, Australia, Asia, and the rest of the Americas will go for smaller amounts but will still be large for the local broadcasters in these areas.

NBC's investments seem to be paying off. The network earned $125 million on its 2000 and 2002 broadcasts. For the 2004 Games, NBC used its portfolio of networks (Bravo, CNBC, NBC, MSNBC, and Telemundo) to broadcast on a 24-hour basis in the North American market. The network earned $70 million from its investment to broadcast the 2004 Games, which was $20 million more than NBC expected. Many of the more global firms spend considerable sums to advertise on NBC's outlets because of the broader exposure, including most of North America, during the Olympics.

How can NBC and other local broadcasters pay so much for the broadcast rights to these Games and yet make a profit? Think "international markets" and "international marketing" and you'll have the answer to this question. In terms of the 2004 Games, analysts reported that "The network is trying to sell a record $1 billion worth of advertising across its TV portfolio, including Bravo, USA Network, MSNBC, CNBC, and Telemundo. In addition to recouping its $793 million rights fee plus additional production and promotion costs, NBC sees the Olympics as a prime platform to hype its fall schedule." With this exposure, NBC hopes to keep the momentum going after the Olympics.

The Olympics are managed by the International Olympics Committee (IOC), based in Switzerland. Because of the high cost of running the Olympics, the IOC and national Olympic committees continually search for ways to support the costs. Revenues received from firms for the rights to broadcast the Games are a great help in covering the Games' costs. In addition, the IOC also uses the prestige and the marketing capability of the Games to sell high-profile corporate sponsorships. These sponsorships enable global corporations to capture the status and visibility of being associated with the Games. A worldwide partnership, the most expensive designation, at a recent Games cost $55 million.

The primary advantage of a worldwide partnership with the IOC is that it provides advertising space during Olympic event broadcasts. For instance, Coca-Cola paid $60 million beyond its partnership for television advertising during the 1996 and 2000 Games.

In summary, the Olympic Games represent an opportunity for firms whose markets have become more global to advertise to the world during the two-week period of the Games. People across the world watch these games and global firms seek to advertise their wares in what are increasingly becoming international rather than domestic-only markets.

SOURCES: J. M. Higgins & S. McClellan, 2004, Welcome to the Olympics, *Broadcasting & Cable,* June 7: 1; J. Lafayette, 2004, Peacock Crowing about Olympics, *TelevisionWeek,* August 30: 4; A. Romano, 2004, NBC plans to give local-cable ads an Olympian push, *Broadcasting & Cable,* January 19: 35–36; S. Fatsis & J. Flint, 2003, NBC plans 24-hour coverage of Summer Olympics in 2004, *Wall Street Journal,* February 6: B10; P. McClintock, 2003, Ebersol's got games: NBC Sports chair's pact covers next 5 Olympics, *Daily Variety,* December 17: 7–9; B. Steinberg and Stefan Fatsis, 2003, NBC Olympics bid easily clears bar—GE agrees to pay $2 billion for rights to broadcasts, soaring past competition, *Wall Street Journal,* June 9: B5; R. Thurow, 2004, The two faces of the games, *Wall Street Journal,* August 13: A10.

Questions

1. If you wanted to build your firm's brand image at the Olympics and you were pursuing a global strategy, how would you market your products? Would you market your products differently if you were pursuing a multidomestic strategy? Describe the marketing approaches that you might use in advertising as well as local promotion at the Games.

2. What international strategy (multidomestic, global, or transnational) is NBC using to market in its region in North America (including the United States, Canada, and Mexico)? What are the characteristics of its international strategy?

3. What structure should be used to implement the particular strategy chosen in Question 2? Explain why the structure you chose was the most appropriate.

EXPERIENTIAL EXERCISES

EXERCISE ONE: INTERNATIONAL STRATEGY CHOICES IN PRACTICE

In small groups, discuss the following firms. Based on your familiarity with these firms, how would you classify each firm's international strategy: global, multidomestic, or transnational?

- British Airways
- Procter & Gamble

- Nestlé
- Honda
- L'Oréal

Be ready to defend your choices to the whole class.

EXERCISE TWO: A FRIEND'S MODE-OF-ENTRY CHOICES

A friend from high school has come to you with an exciting proposition. Over the last few years, she has been building a business around a new product she has been perfecting. Her innovations are all patented and have reached a state of sophistication allowing them to provide a high degree of value to a wide range of customers. She commissioned a consulting firm to tell her what she could expect in the way of demand growth over the next ten years. The consultant's report was overwhelming. It charted how this product would grow dramatically in the NAFTA region over the next few years. The product also had the potential to gain wide acceptance outside NAFTA. In fact, in five years, half of the sales revenue could be coming from Europe and Asia. Indeed, future growth in Asia could make that region the single largest market for this product by the tenth year.

On examining your friend's innovation, you noted that it was relatively small and weighed only a moderate amount. It was not perishable and it was relatively easy to make. If not for its patents, it could easily be copied by a good engineer. Your friend knows that you are completing your business degree and that you have been studying alternative ways for firms to enter international markets. She asks you to help her with the advantages and disadvantages of several market-entry alternatives, both those she would consider right away and those she may consider a few years from now.

To make your presentation easy for your friend to understand, you will set out the alternatives in chart form based on your observations of the product and the consultant's report.

	Exporting	Licensing	Contracting	Joint Venture	Overseas Acquisition	Greenfield
Advantages						
Disadvantages						

CHAPTER 9

Creating and Maintaining Alliances

Reading and studying this chapter should enable you to:

*Knowledge Objectives

1_
Define strategic alliances and explain the difference between equity and nonequity alliances.

2_
Explain why firms develop strategic alliances.

3_
Identify business-level strategic alliances and explain vertical and horizontal alliances.

4_
Describe how strategic alliances are used to implement corporate-level strategies.

5_
Explain why strategic alliances represent a common means of entering international markets.

6_
Identify the major risks of strategic alliances.

7_
Explain how strategic alliances can be managed to increase their success.

Focusing on Strategy

All Roads Lead to Joint Ventures in China, the Mother of Emerging Markets

"As China's largest steelmaker gathers steam, Western competitors scramble to come up with a game plan." (O. Brown, *Wall Street Journal*)

As the quote from the *Wall Street Journal* writer suggests, the Chinese economy is one of the healthiest and fastest-growing economies in the world. In fact, analysts predict that between 2040 and 2050, the Chinese economy will become the world's largest market. Because of its size and incredible potential, many firms want to enter and build a major presence in Chinese markets. The importance of these markets is shown by General Motors' announcement in 2004 that it and its Chinese venture partners plan to invest $3 billion by 2007 to expand operations in China. GM earned $437 million in net profit from its Chinese operations in 2003. Still, not all firms earn huge profits in China, partly because there is considerable competition in some sectors of the economy. Additionally, as a nation, China is trying to develop larger local automobile manufacturers. Moreover, China limits foreign ownership of joint ventures in most industries to 50 percent. However, exceptions to the ownership rule may be made when a venture is formed with the intention of exporting what it produces.

In spite of some of these potential hurdles, China is a popular destination for investments by foreign firms. Siemens, the German electronics and engineering company, has developed 45 joint ventures in China and its operations there account for about five percent of the firm's total annual revenues. While Siemens wants to be a major player in the Chinese market, it must compete with joint ventures formed by General Electric and Motorola from the United States and Alcatel from France. Likewise, Korean Air has formed an alliance with China Southern Airlines to enter the Chinese high-growth air traffic market. Demand for flights between Korea and China is strong. An executive for Korean Air stated that China was the company's highest priority destination because of predicted increases in annual demand for air travel of 30 percent and air cargo of 20 percent.

Some Chinese firms are the aggressor in forming alliances. For example, several Chinese steel companies, such as Wuhan Iron & Steel, have formed joint ventures with foreign partners to gain access to raw materials to satisfy Chinese demand. Shanghai's Baosteel Group formed a joint venture with Brazil's top iron ore producer, Vale do Rio Doce SA. Through the joint venture, they are building a steel mill in Brazil. Therefore, the alliances provide Chinese companies with access to resources they need to grow.

SOURCES: K. Bradsher, 2004, Made in India vs. made in China, *New York Times*, http://www.nytimes.com, June 12; A. Ward, 2004, Investing in China: Korean Air pushes into Chinese market, *Financial Times*, http://www.ft.com, June 9; L. Yuan & P. Glader, 2004, Looming battle, *Wall Street Journal Online*, http://www.wsj.com, September 27; K. Bradsher, 2004, GM to spend over $3 billion to expand in China, *New York Times*, http://www.nytimes.com, June 8; J. L. Lee, 2004, China seeks formation of large auto groups, *Wall Street Journal Online*, http://www.wsj.com, May 27; M. Karnitschnig, 2004, Siemens to expand business in China and boost sales, *Wall Street Journal Online*, http://www.wsj.com, May 18; O. Brown, 2004, BHP sets China iron-ore deal, *Wall Street Journal Online*, http://www.wsj.com, March 1.

The popularity of Chinese markets is shown in "Focusing on Strategy." Because of its size and subsequent sales potential, firms from many parts of the world want to enter Chinese markets. "Focusing on Strategy" describes companies entering Chinese markets from North America, Europe, and Asia. It also suggests that Chinese firms are accessing needed resources from Latin America. Combined, these actions emphasize the importance of strategic alliances to firms throughout the world. For example, Siemens has set up 45 joint ventures in China as a means of building a strong presence in Chinese markets. GM entered the Chinese markets with a joint venture as well, and the importance of this market to GM is clear from the amount of profit GM earns from it as well as the $3 billion GM plans to invest along with its Chinese partners. Finally, "Focusing on Strategy" shows that strategic alliances provide a means of accessing resources unavailable inside domestic markets. Chinese firms have developed joint ventures with Brazilian companies that have access to iron ore to obtain more of this resource to meet demands of heavy construction projects ongoing in the Chinese market.

A **strategic alliance** is a relationship between firms in which the partners agree to cooperate in ways that provide benefits to each firm. A strategic alliance is a type of cooperative strategy. A **cooperative strategy** is an action plan the firm develops to form cooperative relationships with other firms. Although firms choose to cooperate with one another rather than compete when using a cooperative strategy such as a strategic alliance, the purpose of doing so is the same in both instances: namely, to develop a competitive advantage.[1] Thus, a cooperative strategy adds to the repertoire of strategies firms use to build competitive advantages that can help them successfully compete in one or more markets.

There are at least two types of strategic alliances—equity alliances and nonequity alliances. In an **equity alliance**, each partner owns a percentage of the equity in a venture that the firms have jointly formed. If a separate business is

*
strategic alliance

a relationship between firms in which the partners agree to cooperate in ways that provide benefits to each firm

*
cooperative strategy

an action plan the firm develops to form cooperative relationships with other firms

*
equity alliance

an alliance in which each partner owns a percentage of the equity in a venture that the firms have jointly formed

*

joint venture

a separate business that is
created by an equity alliance

*

nonequity
alliance

a contractual relationship
between two or more firms
in which each partner
agrees to share some of its
resources or capabilities

created by this alliance, it is often referred to as a **joint venture.** A **nonequity alliance** is a contractual relationship between two or more firms in which each partner agrees to share some of its resources or capabilities.[2]

In previous chapters, we discussed business-level strategies, corporate (product diversification) strategies, and international strategies, which all concern actions the firm takes to compete in markets against other firms operating in them. In this chapter, we explore the use of strategic alliances, the reasons for them, and their different types. We also examine alliances at the business and corporate levels along with international alliances. Finally, we explore the means of managing alliances, including balancing the risks of using such strategies. We begin with the reasons to develop strategic alliances.

Reasons for Developing Strategic Alliances

As suggested in "Focusing on Strategy," strategic alliances are a highly popular strategy used by firms throughout the world. Strategic alliances represent a major trend in global business primarily because of the potential value they provide to partnering firms. They can help firms grow and often provide 20–35 percent of many firms' revenue.[3] Therefore, alliances can have a major effect on the performance of partner firms.[4] They are an important strategy for many reasons. We present some of these reasons in Table 9.1. Before examining Table 9.1, think of reasons you believe would cause firms to form alliances. You likely identified some of the reasons listed in the table and may have included a few others as well. This shows that alliances can be used to help a firm in many ways.

A major reason for firms to engage in strategic alliances is to allow them to enter restricted markets. China provides a prime example; the Chinese government requires foreign firms to form joint ventures with Chinese partners in

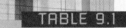

TABLE 9.1

Reasons for Strategic Alliances

- Gain access to a restricted market
- Develop new goods or services
- Facilitate new market entry
- Share significant R&D investments
- Share risks and buffer against uncertainty
- Develop market power
- Gain access to complementary resources
- Build economies of scale
- Meet competitive challenges
- Learn new skills and capabilities
- Outsource for low costs and high quality output

order to enter most Chinese markets. Therefore, GM, Siemens, and Korean Air had to form alliances with Chinese firms to enter and serve Chinese markets. Alliances also can allow a firm to overcome trade barriers to enter a market. In other words, a firm may form a joint venture in a country to produce and market products so it would not have to pay major tariffs on those same products if they were imported.

R&D alliances to facilitate development of new goods and services have become increasingly common. R&D alliances help firms share the costs and risks of developing new products. The success of new products in the marketplace is very low. Therefore, sharing the costs and risks allows individual firms to either invest less in R&D or invest the same amount and increase the number of successes in the market (by introducing more new products, for example). Additionally, partner firms may develop better new-product ideas because by cooperating to integrate resources from each, they can create new and different capabilities.

The value of being able to share costs and risks may be quite significant for firms using international alliances to enter new markets.[5] As we noted previously, risks arise because success with new products is highly uncertain. However, other forms of uncertainty exist as well. For example, entering new international markets presents uncertainty in the form of market demand, government actions, and competitor reactions. Therefore, firms may develop strategic alliances such as R&D alliances to overcome uncertainty and share the risks.[6] Nokia's actions show how this can happen.

Nokia entered the Chinese market in 1996 and by 2001 had seven joint ventures with Chinese companies. In 2004, Nokia announced that it intended to expand its R&D operations in China. Part of the reason is that Nokia experienced a 15 percent revenue decline in the first quarter of the year (see Chapter 3) and felt that it needed to improve the design of its products so they would be more competitive in an intense global market (and, in this market, how a product is designed influences customers' purchases). The CEO stated that China was an important part of Nokia's global R&D network. Nokia also announced that 40 percent of its handsets would be designed at its R&D center in Beijing. So, Nokia is collaborating with Chinese corporations to improve the design of its handsets so they'll be more competitive in global markets, and thereby reduce its risk and uncertainty partly by using the capabilities of its partners.[7]

As suggested by the Nokia example, alliances can provide access to complementary resources. **Complementary resources** are resources that each partner brings to the partnership that, when combined, allow for new resources or capabilities that neither firm could readily create alone. By integrating their complementary resources, partners can take actions that they could not take separately. So, gaining access to complementary resources is a major reason for engaging in strategic alliances.[8] Nokia expects that the complementary resources held by its partners and within its firm can help it create better designs for the products it sells in global markets.

Firms can also use alliances to gain market power. For example, the alliance between Korean Air and China Southern Airlines opened new markets and routes for the Korean airline to serve. In this way, Korean Air increased its market power to compete against its major domestic competitor, Asiana Airlines. It gained market power because of the ability to provide its customers flights into major Chinese markets—an ability already available from its competitor. Market power can be achieved when partners combine their resources to create synergy and when their market share increases as a result of doing so.

At times, firms form alliances to meet competitive challenges. In fact, they may need to gain access to partners' resources to compete effectively. For example, Sematech was formed in Austin, Texas, during the 1980s by a group of U.S. semiconductor firms with the blessing of the U.S. government. It was developed to conduct joint R&D to meet the competitive challenges of foreign semiconductor firms, particularly Japanese businesses at the time. The consortium was so successful that Sematech has a different purpose today, although its general focus remains that of improving knowledge in the semiconductor industry.

Of critical importance is the amount of knowledge a firm holds. In fact, some argue that firms holding greater stocks of knowledge often have a competitive advantage. Because of this, many alliances are formed to gain access to a partner's valuable knowledge. So, a primary reason for developing alliances is to learn from partners, which can contribute to higher performance by the firm.[9] In some cases, firms may attempt to learn from partners in order to explore new areas (such as R&D alliances). In other cases, firms may want to learn from partners in order to know how to better use their current capabilities. For example, large multinational corporations often enter emerging markets to exploit their current technological knowledge. To do so, they must learn the local culture and marketplace. They must also learn how to deal with the foreign government and distributors. This knowledge can be obtained from local partners.[10]

A final reason why firms develop alliances is to outsource an important function or activity of their business. *Outsourcing* (defined in Chapter 4) involves acquiring a capability from an external supplier that contributes to creating value for customers.

As we explained in Chapter 4, outsourcing is a popular trend among U.S. firms. While much outsourcing occurs in manufacturing, outsourcing of information technology, human resources, and other internal staff functions has become increasingly common as well. Outsourcing is commonly used to reduce costs. However, firms also outsource to gain access to special skills for higher-quality output.[11] For example, Ford Motor Company has an alliance with the Pininfarina Group in Italy for the engineering and production of new automobile models, such as the StreetKa. Pininfarina also does design work for Ferrari, product engineering for Jaguar, manufacturing for Mitsubishi, and styling, design, engineering, and production for Peugeot. All of this work resulted in annual revenues for Pininfarina of $826 million in 2003, and revenues are projected to reach $1.2 billion by 2006.[12] Because international outsourcing is believed responsible for exporting jobs to other countries, it is controversial. However, from a strategic management perspective, outsourcing has the potential to help firms successfully implement their strategies and to earn returns for shareholders as a result. You will read more about outsourcing in this chapter's Mini-Case.

Firms form alliances for use at different levels in their hierarchy of strategies. First, we'll explore business-level alliances.

Business-Level Strategic Alliances

There are two types of business-level strategic alliances—vertical and horizontal. Next we explore how a firm can use either type of business-level alliance to help create or maintain a competitive advantage.

Vertical Strategic Alliances

A **vertical strategic alliance** is an alliance that involves cooperative partnerships across the value chain (the value chain was discussed in Chapter 4). A relationship between buyers and suppliers is a common type of vertical alliance. Some firms use vertical alliances to produce their products. Nike uses quite a few vertical alliances to produce many of its athletic shoes. These alliances are a part of the value chain discussed in Chapter 4.

Although contracts are usually written to form them, vertical alliances are most effective when partners trust each other.[13] Trust enables partners to invest less time and effort to ensure that a contract's terms are fulfilled. Trust also helps partners learn from each other in ways that benefit both firms. In fact, when developed and sustained over long periods of time, trust even facilitates the transfer of technological knowledge from buyers to suppliers. When this happens, the supplier is more likely to provide exactly the materials the buyer needs to be successful.[14]

Both partnerships discussed in "Understanding Strategy" were vertical strategic alliances. Pixar provided Disney with creative animation capabilities and Amazon.com provided market channels and distribution of goods for Toys "R" Us. Vertical alliances can be highly important to a firm's success. For example, an estimated 45 percent of Disney's operating income for its film studio during 2000–2005, more than $1.1 billion, came from Pixar films.[15] Therefore, the disintegration of this partnership appears to have potentially serious implications for Disney's performance.

Horizontal Strategic Alliances

A **horizontal strategic alliance** is an alliance that involves cooperative partnerships in which firms at the same stage of the value chain share resources and capabilities. Horizontal alliances are often intended to enhance the capabilities of the partners to compete in their markets. Firms sometimes develop horizontal alliances to respond to competitors' actions or to reduce the competition they face. DaimlerChrysler created equity-based strategic alliances with Mitsubishi and Hyundai with both purposes in mind. In particular, Daimler-Chrysler executives hoped that these alliances would make the firm more competitive in global markets. They expected these alliances to open markets in Asia for DaimlerChrysler products and enable the firm to access technological knowledge with which it could develop and build small autos that are competitive in global markets. However, neither horizontal alliance was successful. Mitsubishi turned out to be a "money pit" into which DaimlerChrysler had to inject much more capital than it originally intended, with no guarantee of earning a return on its investments. The partnership with Hyundai deteriorated, reportedly because of culture clashes and power struggles between the two firms. One DaimlerChrysler manager stated, "The game is over. Strategically, the alliance with Hyundai has fully failed."[16]

understanding strategy:

ENDING FORMERLY GOOD RELATIONSHIPS THAT HAVE GONE BAD

The vertical alliances between Amazon.com and Toys "R" Us and between Disney and Pixar were both highly successful. Toys "R" Us's original effort to reach its market using the Internet failed. However, after creating an alliance with Amazon.com to manage Toys "R" Us Internet sales and distribution, sales blossomed. Likewise, Disney and Pixar formed a vertical alliance to create animated films. Working together, Disney and Pixar developed several highly popular films such as *Monsters, Inc., Toy Story,* and *Finding Nemo.* Yet the partnerships either have been dissolved or are in the process of unraveling. What went wrong?

In Disney and Pixar's case, negotiations to renew the alliance broke down and the former partners each decided to go their own way. The press reported that the two companies could not agree on the distribution of investments and profits between the partners on future projects. Additionally, Pixar preferred to do one film project per year (to maintain the quality) and Disney wanted to develop two per year. Some felt that the breakdown in negotiations could be attributed largely to the egos of the CEOs for the two firms, Michael Eisner (Disney) and Steven Jobs (Pixar).

© Disney/Pixar/The Kobal Collection

In recent years, Disney's efforts to produce animated films have been unsuccessful except for films produced with Pixar. The 13-year relationship between the two firms ended in spring 2004.

In the Amazon.com and Toys "R" Us partnership, the problems are less clear and the reasons for the alliance's failure have not been articulated. However, the relationship between the firms seems to have deteriorated even more greatly than between Disney and Pixar. The seriousness of the problems is shown by the fact that Toys "R" Us filed a lawsuit against Amazon.com claiming that Amazon violated the contractual agreement for exclusivity by allowing other companies selling competitive products to sell their goods on the Amazon.com Web site. Returning the favor, Amazon.com filed a countersuit claiming that Toys "R" Us consistently failed to meet the terms of the agreement. Amazon asked that the alliance be terminated and also requested $750 million in damages. It looks as if there is little hope for salvaging this vertical alliance after four seemingly successful years.

SOURCES: N. Wingfield, 2004, Amazon countersues, seeking to end Toys "R" Us partnership, *Wall Street Journal Online,* http://www.wsj.com, June 29; L. Foster, 2004, Amazon sues to cut Toys "R" Us ties, *Financial Times,* http://www.ft.com, June 28; L. Foster, 2004, Toys "R" Us unit files Amazon lawsuit, *Financial Times,* http://www.ft.com, May 24; 2004, Disney-Pixar public row getting down and dirty, *Houston Chronicle,* February 6: C3; 2004, Insiders say clash of egos drove Disney, Pixar apart, *Houston Chronicle,* February 3: B3; 2004, Dream ends for Disney, Pixar, *USA Today,* http://www.usatoday.com, January 29; D. Fonda, 2003, Eisner's wild, wild ride, *Time,* December 15: 46–47.

Because of dynamic and highly competitive markets, firms often face substantial uncertainty. To buffer against this uncertainty, they frequently form alliances to share the risks (as noted earlier in the chapter). High uncertainty has become increasingly common in many markets in addition to high-technology markets—markets that you would expect to be highly uncertain. For example, markets for banks have become highly competitive as they experience significant change. One response has been to acquire other banks to increase market power. However, compared to acquisitions, alliances can accomplish similar objectives, but with a smaller investment of a bank's financial capital. Of course, care must be taken in horizontal alliances to avoid explicit or tacit collusion.

While explicit collusion is illegal, tacit collusion is more difficult to identify.[17] *Tacit collusion* occurs when firms signal intentions to one another through their actions. The market signaling observed when firms tacitly collude is more likely to occur in concentrated industries with only a few large competitors. For example, Kellogg, General Mills, Post, and Quaker have almost 80 percent of the ready-to-eat cereal market.[18] An example of tacit collusion in this industry would be if most or all of these four competitors took no action to reduce the price of their products when the demand for them declined.[19]

Vertical alliances often have the highest probability of producing positive returns, while horizontal alliances usually are the most difficult to manage and sustain. In particular, vertical alliances in which partners have complementary capabilities and the relationship between the partners is strong are likely to be successful. Horizontal alliances are difficult because often the partners are also competitors. Firms in these alliances must guard against opportunistic actions (being unfairly taken advantage of) by their partners because of the potentially serious implications they might have for the firm's ability to remain competitive. Also, because of the differences between competitors, horizontal alliances are ripe for conflict.

While business-level partnerships are important, corporate-level alliances also can have substantial effects on firm performance. We examine these types of alliances next.

Corporate-Level Strategic Alliances

Corporate-level strategic alliances usually focus on the firm's product line and are designed to enhance firm growth. Corporate-level alliances are particularly attractive because they often have the same purpose as acquisitions, but are much less costly.[20] Corporate-level strategic alliances include those for diversification, for synergy, and for franchising.

Diversification by Alliance

R&D strategic alliances may be formed with the intent to develop new products that serve markets distinct from those that the partners currently serve. Partners operating in different industries may be able to integrate unique knowledge stocks to create products that serve new markets and customers. In this way, the new products add to each partner's current product line. In fact, developing new products for markets different from those served may be difficult for firms without help from partners who have the additional knowledge needed. The knowledge held by a firm can be valuable but also create a *path dependence* whereby it is difficult to learn something new that does not fit with the firm's current knowledge base.[21] Diversification alliances can be especially valuable if the new products developed are related to the current products in some way such that synergy can be created.

However, alliances can also be used to refocus the firm and reduce its level of diversification. Using information technology to build partnerships may be useful for reducing the scope of a firm's product offerings and increasing their specialization.[22] Japanese semiconductor manufacturers Fujitsu, Mitsubishi, Hitachi, and NEC formed joint ventures to consolidate and spin off diversified businesses that were earning poor returns. These actions enabled the firms to refocus on their core business and to give the poorly performing business special management attention. These actions have the potential to increase the performance of the spun-off business and the core firm.[23]

Synergy by Alliance

Strategic alliances at the corporate level between firms can be used to create synergy. Synergy is created in this instance when partners share resources or integrate complementary capabilities to build economies of scope. In fact, a synergistic strategic alliance is similar to a complementary business-level alliance in that both types of alliances are intended to synergistically involve partners with new businesses. A relationship between SBC Communications and EchoStar Communications (DISH Network) is an example of such a corporate-level strategic alliance. In 2004, the phone company's customers were able to sign up for EchoStar TV services by calling SBC sales representatives. SBC has similarly improved its broadband offering by partnering with Yahoo. Thus, SBC has been able to "bundle" other services with its telecommunications services to increase its customer base. These relationships rely on partners' complementary capabilities to create value for each partner's diversified service offerings.[24]

Franchising

One successful franchisor is 7-Eleven.

Franchising is a well-established and successful type of corporate-level strategic alliance. As defined in Chapter 8, *franchising* is the licensing of a good or service and business model to partners for specified fees (usually a signing fee and a percentage of the franchisee's revenues or profits). Franchising allows a firm to expand a successful venture and earn additional returns without taking large financial risks. Franchising has the added advantage of allowing the franchisor to maintain control of its product and business model. Usually, the franchisor establishes tight controls on the actions a franchisee can take with its product and business name.

Many well-known firms franchise. McDonald's, Hilton International, and 7-Eleven all have franchisees operating some of the businesses carrying their name and products. 7-Eleven has found franchising to be a particularly successful strategy, with more than 25,000 stores worldwide and in excess of $3 billion in annual revenues.[25]

For franchising to be highly effective, the partners must cooperate closely. The franchisor must develop and transfer successful programs and means of managing the operation to the franchisee. The franchisee must have the knowledge and capabilities necessary to compete in the local market. And franchisees must provide feedback to the franchisor about activities that work and those that do not. Franchisees should

understanding strategy:

SONY IS USING STRATEGIC ALLIANCES TO REVITALIZE ITS PERFORMANCE

Sony is taking several actions to renew its performance—cutting costs to increase its efficient use of assets as well as forming strategic alliances to develop attractive new products. In 2001, Sony teamed with Ericsson to create a joint venture to build new products. The joint venture had some rough times in overcoming the cultural differences of the Swedish and Japanese firms. The venture developed the GSM mobile telephone that has been popular in the market. Sales of this product exceeded $8 million at the end of 2003.

Sony also has joint ventures with DoMoCo and Samsung. The venture with DoMoCo is intended to develop smart cards for mobile telephones. As a result, it has the potential to develop synergy with the Sony Ericsson venture. Embedding a smart card in a mobile phone could enable it to work as a security device or as a credit card. The intent is to license the technology to mobile phone manufacturers. Analysts believe that this venture has high potential.

Perhaps Sony's most ambitious alliance is the joint venture it formed with Samsung to develop flat-panel displays. Each company agreed to invest $1 billion in the venture and owns 50 percent equity in it. This venture partners Sony with a competitor and is designed to build a competitive advantage. The joint venture may help Sony leverage Samsung's technology and also take advantage of Samsung's market-leading position in the market for flat panel displays. It also allows each firm to control its capital investment and R&D costs.

While none of these corporate-level alliances is risk-free, they help the partners in each balance their risks. Furthermore, if the capabilities of each firm can be successfully integrated, they should be better able to develop a unique and valuable product. Therefore, this appears to be a potentially successful strategy for Sony's turnaround. In addition, the alliances create synergistic diversification for Sony as well as the partner firms.

SOURCES: A. Lashinsky, 2005, Saving face at Sony, *Fortune*, February 21, 79–86; J. Yang, 2004, A savvy strategy for Sony, *Business Week Online*, http://www.businessweek.com, May 4; B. Einhorn, 2004, DoMoCo's "new business model," *Business Week Online*, http://www.businessweek.com, April 19; P. Dvorak, 2004, Sony, Samsung finalize deal for flat-panel joint venture, *Wall Street Journal Online*, http://www.wsj.com, March 8; A. Edstrom, 2004, Signs of life at Sony Ericsson, *Fortune*, http://www.fortune.com, February 10.

also inform the franchisor about the important characteristics of competitors and market conditions in their local markets. Franchising can also enable a franchisor to gain a first-mover advantage without some of the risks involved in being a first mover.[26]

Sony is trying to develop highly related new products using alliances. Each alliance described in "Understanding Strategy" is intended to create synergy. The most ambitious and probably the most important alliance is the joint venture with Samsung, a competitor. This venture has much potential for Sony, particularly with Samsung's technology and its market-leading position in flat panel displays. Interestingly, Sony's alliances with Ericsson and Samsung are both cross-border alliances, the next topic of discussion.

International Strategic Alliances

Cross-border strategic alliances have become the most prominent means of entering foreign markets. One reason is that some countries require that firms form joint ventures with local firms in order to enter their markets. This is the case for most industries in China, as explained in "Focusing on Strategy." Additionally, foreign firms need knowledge and perhaps other resources to understand and compete effectively in the newly entered markets. As noted earlier, even if the Chinese government did not require joint ventures, foreign firms would do well to form them anyway. They could use the alliances to learn about the different culture and characteristics of the market and to develop relationships with distributors and important government units. Also, the trend toward outsourcing to businesses in foreign countries due to their lower labor costs increases the number of cross-border strategic alliances. Therefore, as noted in Chapter 8, entering foreign markets is an attractive option for many firms.[27]

As we explain shortly, all strategic alliances carry risks. However, the use of international strategic alliances, a popular strategy for entering markets or gaining access to special skills and resources, carries some additional risks and potential costs. In the Sony and Ericsson joint venture, the differing cultures of the two companies' workforces created an early barrier to an effective alliance. Different cultures and a lack of trust can hinder the transfer of knowledge or sharing of other resources necessary to make an alliance successful. Top executives warn against making assumptions when moving into new international markets. A firm's products often must be adapted to the local market. This requires close cooperation of local partners. Firms may have to use different distribution channels as they cross into new international markets. For example, Procter & Gamble sells its goods in the United States largely through drugstores and supermarkets (multi-product retailers), but many of its products are sold through more limited-product pharmacies in Europe.[28]

Managing Risks in Strategic Alliances

Each type of strategic alliance (business-level, corporate-level, and cross-border) has its own risks and there may be some generic ones as well. Many strategic alliances fail, even some that were formerly successful as in the case of Disney and Pixar. Estimates of alliance failure range from 50 percent to 70 percent.[29] Given the substantial conflict in the Amazon.com and Toys "R" Us alliance, the risks related to lack of trust are evident. When partners don't trust each other, they are less likely to share resources, particularly the most valuable ones. Without trust, partners also must invest more time and energy (resulting in extra costs) to guard against possible opportunistic behavior by the other firm. As a result, alliances without trust between partners are unlikely to meet their goals.

Of course, all alliances suffer from the potential differences in corporate and national cultures. These differences reflect emphases on separate values and may also lead to communication problems between partners as well as an inability to understand each other's intentions with the alliance. Additionally, because it is impossible to know all of a firm's capabilities before alliances are formed,

China's Sichuan Changhong Electric Company experienced a problematic alliance with Apex Digital in the United States, leading to substantial losses for the firm.

participants in alliances often discover that the partner's competencies are not as strong or complementary as assumed.

Firms also may be unwilling to share important resources as assumed when the alliance was formed.[30] For example, Pixar's market power grew considerably during the time of its alliance with Disney because of the substantial success of their jointly produced animated films, so Pixar likely became unwilling to share its creative talent with Disney, at least under the old arrangement. When the alliance ended, Disney may have needed Pixar more than Pixar needed Disney.

Effectively managing alliances can reduce some of their risks. But it isn't easy to manage the risks of alliances, as evidenced in the demise of successful alliances such as those between Disney and Pixar and between Amazon.com and Toys "R" Us. Some firms use detailed contracts to try to guard against opportunistic behavior by a partner. While a detailed contract can help, it isn't possible to identify and then specify in a contract all partner actions that are acceptable while they cooperate as alliance partners.[31]

In 2004, the leading Chinese manufacturer of television sets, Sichuan Changhong Electric Company, announced a huge loss estimated at approximately $500 million. The loss was attributed largely to declining sales in the United States because of the 25 percent tariffs imposed by the U.S. government and a financial scandal involving its major alliance partner in the United States. The partner, Apex Digital, which supposedly owed Changhong almost $468 million, accounted for much of Changhong's loss. Apex acted as a distributor of Changhong products to such customers as Wal-Mart. Thus, problems with overseas alliance partners can have a substantial negative effect on a firm's performance.[32]

Indeed, the best action that most firms can take is to attempt to develop a trusting relationship. Trust is the best preventive medicine against opportunistic behavior. In addition, trust promotes the sharing of resources and even the willingness to cooperate with and help alliance partners. We emphasize the importance of trust in our discussion of managing alliances.

Managing Strategic Alliances

Given the importance of strategic alliances and their potential effects on firm performance, businesses have started to emphasize the management of alliances as a way to develop a competitive advantage and create value for their shareholders.[33] As a result, firms are even creating units with the responsibility of managing their multiple strategic alliances.[34] The actions required to successfully manage alliances and their outcomes are shown in Figure 9.1.

Selecting partners is the first step in managing alliances to make them successful. If an incompatible partner is selected, the alliance is likely to fail. Furthermore, the firm should understand its partner well enough to ensure that it has the resources desired. An important part of the analysis and selection of a

FIGURE 9.1   Managing Alliances

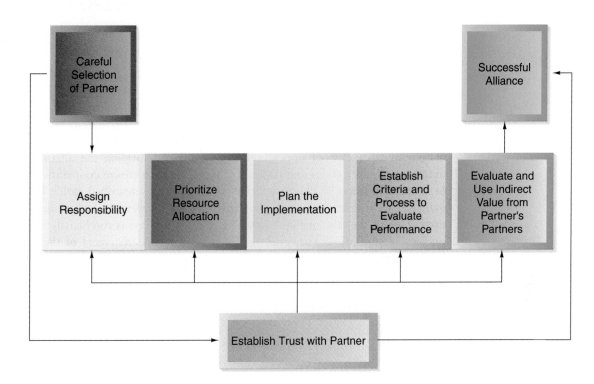

partner is to understand the context in which the partner operates, its competitive landscape, and the institutional forces (such as banks and government policies) with which it must deal (especially for international alliances).[35]

After selecting the partner and starting the alliance, each partner must access the resources desired from the other partner and learn the knowledge needed to successfully use the alliance. If either or both partners fail to achieve their goals, the alliance will fail. To increase the probability of alliance success, then, both partners must provide access to resources and even be willing to help the other partner learn as needed. The willingness to help partners may require extra effort until trust between them grows. Firms should attempt to build trust with the intent of establishing social capital in the alliance.[36] Trust is the base for social capital, which in turn leads to cooperation between partners. Social capital implies that firms will help their partners gain value from an alliance. Of course, the partner is expected to reciprocate. Because of the difficulty in building trust and social capital, firms often form alliances with former partners with whom social capital already exists.

One measure of an alliance's success, in addition to its longevity, is the extent to which knowledge is transferred between partners and integrated into the alliance operations. Integrating separate knowledge sets is important because doing so helps produce synergy and innovation.[37] Thus, alliance managers should invest time and effort to ensure that both partners learn (add knowledge) from the alliance and that their two complementary knowledge stocks are integrated to create value in the alliance.

According to some recent research, firms would do well to pay careful attention to equity investments in the alliances. The failure rate is high in alliances where the foreign investors have a low equity investment. However, the success rate is higher when the foreign investor makes a large equity investment.[38] Obviously, when the equity is high, the investor has an incentive to ensure that the alliance succeeds. Therefore, more effort is also invested to make the alliance work. Additionally, foreign investors are likely to have greater technological and management expertise. Therefore, a higher equity stake encourages them to use more of their expertise to make the alliance successful.

Alliance success also is more likely when alliances are managed to identify and take advantage of opportunities rather than to minimize costs. Alliances formed on the basis of detailed formal contracts with extensive monitoring mechanisms are more likely to fail. Rather, firms should build trust in order to take maximum advantage of opportunities generated by forming the alliance. Such outcomes require careful and dedicated management to ensure cooperative efforts in strategic alliances.[39] The Sony/Ericsson joint venture described earlier has been managed well after some early problems. In fact, the venture lost money in the early stage of the relationship largely because the focus was too heavily weighted on cost minimization. However, realizing the mistake, managers of the venture began emphasizing joint opportunities, creating innovation as explained earlier. The result was a successful turnaround creating value for both venture partners.[40]

In addition to the actions suggested previously, the following steps are recommended as guidelines for effectively managing strategic alliances:

1. Even if the firm has a unit with the overall responsibility of managing its network of alliances, a manager or sponsor should be named for each alliance (and a similar person should be named by the partner). These managers keep each other informed of major alliance activities, resource allocations, and outcomes.

2. The organization should analyze the alliance's priority within its resource allocations and ensure the commitment needed for each alliance to succeed.

3. A clear plan for implementing the alliance should be created and activated after the partners have agreed to the alliance.

4. The means for analyzing the performance of the alliance and distribution of performance outcomes to the partners should be clearly established. Important stakeholders' interests need to be considered when establishing the performance criteria.

5. When evaluating an alliance's value, the partners' partners in other alliances should be considered. The indirect network of partners from other alliances may be of value for future alliances or in providing indirect value through the benefits derived by the firm's partner.[41]

Summary

The primary purpose of this chapter is to explain how a firm can develop and manage strategic alliances to develop or maintain a competitive advantage. In doing so, we examined the following topics:

- A **strategic alliance** is a relationship between firms in which the partners agree to cooperate in ways that provide benefits to each of them. In an **equity alliance**, each partner owns a specified percentage of the equity in a separate venture. These ventures are often called **joint ventures.** In a **nonequity alliance,** a contractual relationship is established between two or more firms for them to share resources or capabilities.

- Firms form alliances for many reasons. Alliances can be helpful for entering new markets (product or geographic), especially those that are restricted (such as by governments). Alliances can be useful for sharing the risks of entering the markets or in developing new products. In some cases, alliances help firms expand their economies of scale and market power. Strategic alliances are often helpful in meeting competitive challenges, especially when they enable firms to gain access to **complementary resources** or learn new capabilities. Finally, strategic alliances have played a major role in the recent outsourcing trend.

- Strategic alliances can be established at the business level. They may be **vertical alliances** across separate primary activities in the value chain or **horizontal alliances** between competitors at the same stage of the value chain.

- Corporate-level strategic alliances include those for facilitating diversification and/or those designed to create synergy. Additionally, franchising is a type of corporate-level strategic alliance.

- International strategic alliances have become highly common for entering new foreign markets. Often, these alliances are used as a means to outsource primary or secondary activities to firms operating in countries with lower labor costs. Although they facilitate learning about new markets, the cultural differences between participating firms make international strategic alliances quite risky.

- While strategic alliances can provide several benefits to the partners, they also carry some potentially important risks. A major risk is the potential for opportunism by one of the partners. There is a high alliance failure rate, often because of differences in corporate or national cultures and due to information asymmetries. Differences in culture may produce conflicts, and information asymmetries can lead to inaccurate assumptions about resources and capabilities held by partners.

- To increase the probability of success, strategic alliances need to be managed. First, firms should take great care in selecting compatible partners that have the resources needed. It is also important to examine the amount of equity used in forming an alliance. After the alliance is formed, the partners should establish trust to ensure the transfer of resources and learning. They should also assign responsibilities within the firm, develop priorities for allocating resources, plan for an alliance's implementation, and develop means for evaluating its performance and distribution of performance outcomes to partners.

Key Terms

complementary resources 220
cooperative strategy 218
equity alliance 218

horizontal strategic alliance 222
joint venture 219
nonequity alliance 219

strategic alliance 218
vertical strategic alliance 222

Discussion Questions

1. What is a strategic alliance and what are the differences between equity and nonequity alliances?
2. Why do firms form alliances? Explain.
3. What are vertical and horizontal business-level alliances?
4. What are corporate-level strategic alliances?

5. Why do firm commonly use strategic alliances to enter international markets?
6. What are the major risks involved in forming strategic alliances?
7. What can firms do to manage strategic alliances in ways that will increase their probability of success?

Endnotes

1. R. D. Ireland, M. A. Hitt, & D. Vaidyanath, 2002, Alliance management as a source of competitive advantage, *Journal of Management*, 28: 413–446.

2. S. S. Lui & H.-Y. Ngo, 2004, Trust and contractual safeguards on cooperation in non-equity alliances, *Journal of Management*, 30: 471–485; T. B. Folta & K. D. Miller,

2002, Real options in equity partnerships, *Strategic Management Journal,* 23: 77–88.

3. M. Schifrin, 2001, Partner or perish, *Forbes,* May 21: 28; M. Gonzales, 2001, Strategic alliances, *Ivey Business Journal,* 66(1): 47–51.

4. M. J. Leiblein & J. J. Reuer, 2004, Building a foreign sales base: The roles of capabilities and alliances for entrepreneurial firms, *Journal of Business Venturing,* 19: 285–307.

5. R. Narula & G. Duysters, 2004, Globalisation and trends in international R&D alliances, *Journal of International Management,* 10: 199–218.

6. R. J. Arend, 2004, Volatility-based effects on shareholder value: Alliance activity in the computing industry, *Journal of Management,* 30: 487–508.

7. Nokia to increase R&D in China in effort to revive market share, *Wall Street Journal Online,* http://www.wsj.com, May 21.

8. M. A. Hitt, M. T. Dacin, E. Levitas, J.-L. Arregle, & A. Borza, 2000, Partner selection in emerging and developed market contexts: Resource-based and organizational learning perspectives, *Academy of Management Journal,* 43: 449–467.

9. P. Dussauge, B. Garrette, & W. Mitchell, 2004, Asymmetric performance: The market share impact of scale and link alliances in the global auto industry, *Strategic Management Journal,* 25: 701–711.

10. F. T. Rothaermel & D. L. Deeds, 2004, Exploration and exploitation alliances in biotechnology: A system of new product development, *Strategic Management Journal,* 25: 210–221.

11. M. J. Mol, P. Pauwels, P. Mattyssens, & L. Quintens, 2004, A technological contingency perspective on the depth and scope of international outsourcing, *Journal of International Management,* 10: 287–305.

12. Andrea Pininfarina: Chief executive, Pininfarina Group, Italy, 2004, *Business Week Online,* http://www.businessweek.com, June 7; G. Edmondson, 2003, A talk with Pininfarina's driver, *Business Week Online,* http://www.businessweek.com, March 3.

13. P. Saparito, C. C. Chen, & H. J. Sapienza, 2004, The role of trust in bank–small firm relationships, *Academy of Management Journal,* 47: 400–410.

14. M. Kotabe, X. Martin, & H. Domoto, 2003, Gaining from vertical partnerships: Knowledge transfer, relationship duration, and supplier performance improvement in the U.S. and Japanese automotive industries, *Strategic Management Journal,* 24: 293–316.

15. B. Orwall, 2004, Can Disney still rule animation after Pixar? *Wall Street Journal Online,* http://www.wsj.com, February 2.

16. G. Edmondson & M. Ihlwan, 2004, Hyundai and Daimler-Chrysler: Driving in different directions, *Business Week Online,* http://www.businessweek.com, May 3; G. Edmondson, B. Bremner, K. Kerwin, & C. Palmeri, 2004, Daimler: Now for the next repair job, *Business Week,* April 26: 58.

17. J. B. Barney, 2002, *Gaining and Sustaining a Competitive Advantage,* Upper Saddle River, N.J.: Prentice Hall.

18. G. K. Price & J. M. Connor, 2003, Modeling coupon values for ready-to-eat breakfast cereals, *Agribusiness,* 19(2): 223–244.

19. Barney, *Gaining and Sustaining a Competitive Advantage,* 351.

20. J. S. Harrison, M. A. Hitt, R. E. Hoskisson, & R. D. Ireland, 2001, Resource complementarity in business combinations: Extending the logic to organizational alliances, *Journal of Management,* 27: 679–699.

21. D. Lei, M. A. Hitt, & R. A. Bettis, Dynamic core competences through meta-learning and strategic context, *Journal of Management,* 22: 547–567.

22. P. J. Brews & C. L. Tucci, 2004, Exploring the structural effects of internetworking, *Strategic Management Journal,* 25: 429–451.

23. J. Yang, 2003, One step forward for Japan's chipmakers, *Business Week Online,* http://www.businessweek.com, July 7.

24. L. J. Flynn, 2003, EchoStar deal lets SBC offer satellite TV in phone bill, *New York Times Online,* http://www.nytimes.com, July 22.

25. J. Wilgoren, 2003, In the urban 7-Eleven, the Slurpee looks sleeker, *New York Times Online,* http://www.nytimes.com, July 13.

26. S. C. Michael, 2003, First mover advantage through franchising, *Journal of Business Venturing,* 18: 61–80; S. C. Michael, 2002, Can a franchise chain coordinate? *Journal of Business Venturing,* 17: 325–342.

27. J. Lu & P. W. Beamish, 2004, International diversification and firm performance: The s-curve hypothesis, *Academy of Management Journal,* 47: 598–609; M. A. Hitt, R. E. Hoskisson, & H. Kim, 1997, International diversification: Effects on innovation and firm performance in product diversified firms, *Academy of Management Journal,* 40: 767–798.

28. C. Hymowitz, 2003, European executives give some advice on crossing borders, *Wall Street Journal Online,* http://www.wsj.com, December 2.

29. D. C. Hambrick, J. Li, K. Xin, & A. S. Tsui, 2001, Compositional gaps and downward spirals in international joint venture management groups, *Strategic Management Journal,* 22: 1033–1053.

30. Hitt, Dacin, Levitas, Arregle, & Borza, op. cit.

31. M. A. Hitt, M. T. Dacin, B. B. Tyler, & D. Park, 1997, Understanding the differences in Korean and U.S. executives' strategic orientations, *Strategic Management Journal,* 18: 159–167.

32. C. Buckley, 2004. Leading Chinese TV exporter has huge loss, *New York Times Online,* http://www.nytimes.com, December 28.

33. Ireland, Hitt, & Vaidyanath, op. cit.

34. J. H. Dyer, P. Kale, & H. Singh, 2001, How to make strategic alliances work, *MIT Sloan Management Review,* 42(4): 37–43.

35. M. A. Hitt, D. Ahlstrom, M. T. Dacin, E. Levitas, & L. Svobodina, 2004, The institutional effects on strategic alliance partner selection in transition economies: China versus Russia, *Organization Science,* 15: 173–185.

36. K. Starkey & S. Tempest, 2004, Bowling along: Strategic management and social capital, *European Management Review,* 1: 78–83.

37. S. Rodan & C. Galunic, 2004, More than network structure: How knowledge heterogeneity influences managerial performance innovativeness, *Strategic Management Journal,* 25: 541–562.

38. C. Dhanaraj & P. W. Beamish, 2004, Effect of equity ownership on the survival of international joint ventures, *Strategic Management Journal,* 25: 295–305.

39. J. H. Dyer & C. Wujin, 2003, The role of trustworthiness in reducing transaction costs and improving performance: Empirical evidence from the United States, Japan and Korea, *Organization Science,* 9: 285–305.

40. J. L. Schenker, 2003, Sony Ericsson posts loss despite sales gain, *New York Times Online,* http://www.nytimes.com, July 16.

41. K. E. Klein, 2004, Fine-tune that alliance, *Business Week Online,* http://www.businessweek.com, February 10.

Your Career

During your career, you will be actively involved in many professional and working relationships. Advancement in your career may partially depend on how you build and maintain these relationships. You might think of these relationships as social capital that can be highly valuable to you. As you progress in your career, you will receive responsibilities to establish and manage many relationships. In some cases, the relationships will be informal, yet important. In other cases, the relationships will be formal and will likely affect not only the performance of the unit that you manage but also the performance of the firm you serve. Some or even many of the formal relationships may be strategic alliances. Because of their importance for firm performance, the way in which you manage these relationships can be critical to the firm. If you manage them well and the alliances are successful, you are likely to receive positive credit and advance in your career. However, as noted, many alliances fail. Therefore, the challenges you face in managing alliances could be significant. Knowledge of the purposes, risks, and means of managing strategic alliances can help you deal positively with these challenges. Careful attention to learning the knowledge contained in this chapter is therefore important. Also, you will want to work to develop the complementary skills (such as communication, negotiation, and human relations) that are linked to successful management of alliances. If you build these skills and integrate them with effective knowledge of strategic alliances (such as the importance of establishing trust), you may have rare and valuable capabilities to manage alliances that will set you apart from others and enhance your career opportunities.

Before forming a strategic alliance, a firm must carefully analyze the supporting logic and rationale. This chapter's tool can be a helpful way to assess whether a proposed alliance makes sense and has a strong likelihood of helping the firm reach its objectives.

Alliance Decision Evaluation Grid

Rationale	A. Relative Importance (1 = low, 5 = high)	B. Support for Alliance (1 = low, 5 = high)	Calculated Attractiveness (A × B)
Gain access to a restricted market			
Develop new goods or services			
Facilitate new market entry			
Share significant R&D investments			
Share risks and buffer against uncertainty			
Develop market power			
Gain access to complementary resources			
Build economies of scale			
Meet competitive challenges			
Learn new skills and capabilities			
Outsource for low costs and high quality output			

Partnerships are a strategic alliance form discussed in this chapter. This scene from *Erin Brockovich* quickly shows you some issues that a firm must consider when entering such an alliance.

Erin Brockovich (Julia Roberts), a single mother of three, needs a job and persuades skeptical attorney Ed Masry (Albert Finney) to hire her. She quickly discovers a potentially large case against Pacific Gas & Electric Company (PG&E) for environmental pollution. Based on a true story, the film has many dramatic and funny moments. Roberts received the 2000 Best Actress Academy Award.

This scene is an edited segment from the "Erin finds out about their new partner" sequence about 90 minutes into the film. Ed Masry has just entered into a partnership with another attorney who has extensive experience in toxic litigation. He had not discussed his idea of the partnership for the PG&E case with Erin. It begins with Erin and Ed Masry discussing the new partner. The film continues after this scene to its dramatic conclusion.

What to Watch for and Ask Yourself

1. Does Ed Masry describe a clear need for entering into this partnership?
2. What strengths does the partnership bring to litigation against PG&E?
3. What type of strategic alliance discussed in this chapter best describes this partnership? Is it a business-level, corporate-level, or international strategic alliance?

Mini-Case

Is Outsourcing Good or Bad for Firms?

Outsourcing has been important to many firms for several years. However, the amount of outsourcing by U.S. firms has increased dramatically in recent years. Furthermore, firms are now outsourcing professional jobs done by white-collar workers; most previous outsourcing involved blue-collar jobs. Because it is affecting a large number of all types of jobs, outsourcing has become a political issue. However, some argue that outsourcing, such as in the automobile industry, will lead to establishing production and sales in foreign countries with growing demand such as China. More broadly, some argue that trade with foreign countries such as China has fostered moves away from past repression toward more economic freedom.

Gateway buys most of the electronic products it sells from low-cost manufacturers in Taiwan and the People's Republic of China. The list of products it buys from these sources includes TVs, DVD players, portable music devices, and digital cameras. Most of these products have become commodity items, as is the case with the personal computer (PC). Even Japanese firms such as Toshiba are outsourcing the manufacture of PCs. While outsourcing to low-cost manufacturers has been common for some time, software development, programming, and even high-technology professional activities such as interpreting medical X rays are more recent examples of work activities being outsourced.

Outsourcing professional activities means that higher-paying jobs are going overseas; this is a political liability for organizations. Yet businesses argue that outsourcing is a necessity to remain competitive in global markets. In fact, managers suggest that outsourcing of important activities not only saves money (by reducing costs) but also increases quality in some cases because those doing the outsourced work are specialists. There are problems, however. Outsourcing firms lose the capability to perform the activity when they outsource it, meaning that it will be difficult and costly to redevelop that capability at a later date, if desired. Additionally, while outsourcing provides flexibility that is important in a dynamic competitive landscape, firms must be careful not to outsource key areas. Managers must also ensure that the firm does not lose a core competence or an activity important for supporting a core competence because of their outsourcing decisions.

As noted earlier, the outsourcing trend has reached Japan. It is also becoming more common in Europe. For example, an estimated 73,000 financial service jobs and 100,000 telecommunications jobs will be outsourced out of Western Europe by 2008.

There are arguments on both sides about outsourcing's costs and benefits. Firms must decide whether outsourcing is positively linked to performance, what to outsource, and to whom. They might have to fend off politicians who may provide incentives not to outsource. In addition, legislation could be introduced that would call for a tax to be levied on imported goods or services that have been developed through outsourcing. The problems related to outsourcing that managers face are complex and the answers may not be simple.

SOURCES: B. Einhorn, 2004, Rebooting Toshiba, *Business Week Online*, http://www.businessweek.com, May 31; C. Matlack, M. Kripalani, D. Fairlamb, S. Reed, G. Edmondson, & A. Reinhardt, 2004, Job exports: Europe's turn, *Business Week*, April 19: 50–51; J. Thotam, 2004, Is your job going abroad? *Time*, March 1: 26–36; P. Lewis, 2004, Gadget wars, *Fortune*, http://www.fortune.com, January 27.

Questions

1. From the perspective of strategic management, what are the costs and benefits of outsourcing?
2. As a manager, what type of information would you gather and what analyses would you conduct to decide whether to outsource an activity?
3. How do you predict that outsourcing from U.S., Japanese, and European firms to China, Taiwan, and India will affect the economies and firms in the three sourcing countries?

EXPERIENTIAL EXERCISES

EXERCISE ONE: INTERNATIONAL FRANCHISING

Franchising is an alliance form that, like most other types of alliances, has an underlying tension between the partners. Managing these tensions can be costly, and opportunism by either party can damage a brand significantly with adverse economic consequences for all the franchisees, not just those involved in the dispute. Keeping franchise relationships smooth becomes particularly challenging when the franchisees are located overseas.

First, go back to the discussion of international licensing in Chapter 8 and note the reasons that international licensing can present particular problems for the licensee. Second, set out each of these concerns and identify how each one would manifest itself in a franchising relationship.

EXERCISE TWO: THE BIOTECH START-UP

You are working as a management consultant for a biotech start-up. The firm is owned and run by its founder, who holds a Ph.D. in biochemistry and has developed some promising drug targets. Several pharmaceuticals firms have expressed curiosity in the drug targets, but they realize that there is a high failure rate between the identification of a drug target and the marketing of a new drug. The owner-entrepreneur has come to you for advice as to what type of relationship would be appropriate for his firm with these large pharmaceuticals firms. He wants to retain control of his firm and its research agenda. However, he recognizes that the drug companies have three things he needs to successfully develop these drug targets. First, his firm is a research firm with no skills in conducting the clinical testing and dealing with the U.S. Food and Drug Administration to get the drug approved. Second, even if the drug is approved, he has no sales force to promote the drug to doctors. And, most important, the drug firms must have free cash, which would be critical to conduct all of the research and testing activities that must occur before the first sale of an

approved drug. Specifically, he has sought your advice on what types of alliances could best serve his many desires and would likely be acceptable to the drug firms as well.

Part 1

Should the entrepreneur consider an equity alliance with a pharmaceuticals firm? This could solve all three problems at once, providing cash and assuring access to the drug firm's well-developed clinical testing and marketing operations. Is it likely that the pharmaceuticals firm would be interested in this type of alliance? Why or why not?

Part 2

Should the entrepreneur consider only an R&D alliance at this time? What would a pharmaceuticals firm likely expect if it set up an alliance for research with the start-up wherein the big firm would be providing most of the cash needed to carry on the research?

Innovating through Strategic Entrepreneurship

Reading and studying this chapter should enable you to:

*Knowledge Objectives

1_
Define innovation, entrepreneurship, and entrepreneurs.

2_
Describe entrepreneurial opportunities and entrepreneurial capabilities.

3_
Understand strategic entrepreneurship and explain how organizations use it.

4_
Describe how firms internally develop innovations.

5_
Explain how firms use cooperative strategies to develop innovations.

6_
Discuss acquisitions as a means of innovation.

7_
Summarize the use of strategic entrepreneurship as a means of innovation and market entry.

Focusing on Strategy

Strategy, Innovation, and Entrepreneurship: The Foundation for Success at Hasbro

"Their relationship . . . is a little bit like Frick and Frack, but it strikes a healthy balance between the creative and strategic needs of a company based on intellectual property that has to compete in the multibillion dollar global toy business." (S. McGowan, *NYSE Magazine*)

This comment describes the relationship between Alan Hassenfeld, chairman of Hasbro, and Al Verrecchia, the firm's CEO. (*Frick and Frack* is a term used to describe what others see as an interesting, sometimes even a bit odd pair of individuals.) Hassenfeld is known as the creative free thinker who is constantly thinking about the "next great toy." With an outward focus on the marketplace and a commitment to understanding children's play needs, Hassenfeld concentrates on bringing his toy industry expertise to the firm's creative processes. Verrecchia, on the other hand, is more inwardly focused and fact-based as he leads the firm's efforts to use current competitive advantages to successfully implement chosen strategies. Concerned with properly exploiting the firm's competitive advantages to continuously improve its profitability, Verrecchia works with everyone in the firm to question what is being done to determine how to do things better. Therefore, Hassenfeld's creative or entrepreneurial focus causes him to be primarily concerned with spotting opportunities to serve children's play needs. Verrecchia's strategic focus directed at exploiting the firm's current competitive advantages in the global toy industry interacts with Hassenfeld's efforts to prepare Hasbro for future success. Hassenfeld's and Verrecchia's combined leadership enables Hasbro to leverage its core brands while innovating to quickly introduce new products to the marketplace. Transformers, G.I. Joe, Playskool, and Trivial Pursuit are some of Hasbro's core brands. Beyblad (a line of spinning tops for boys over age 8), FurReal

Friends (a line of plush toy pets such as Go Go My Walkin' Pup) and VideoNow (a portable, personalized video player for children) are examples of Hasbro's recent product innovations.

History shows that Hasbro innovates through several means. For example, acquisitions during the 1990s gained access to products that were new to Hasbro: Tonka trucks, Kenner's Easy-Bake Oven, and Monopoly and Clue games. In addition to these products, Hasbro also gained innovation skills from these acquired firms.

Hasbro also uses its own innovation skills to develop new products. The well-known line of G.I. Joe toys, the Transformers line, and My Little Pony are examples of innovative products that Hasbro developed itself. The company continues to use its own innovation skills to introduce extensions of some of its products, such as new editions of Monopoly, Scrabble, and Twister games. Although currently reducing its emphasis on cooperative relationships as a means to innovate, Hasbro continues to form partnerships with various companies making popular movies such as *Finding Nemo* and *Shrek 2.* These links work extremely well for Hasbro when the toys and figures it develops based on a film's character are associated with a "hit" movie. However, the fees Hasbro pays to negotiate a tie-in with a movie are often excessive if the movie is not a hit that attracts moviegoers to buy the toys associated with the film.

Although the firm they lead faces challenges from global competitors and from the hot electronic-toy-learning market, Hassenfeld and Verrecchia remain confident that their dual commitment to innovation and the development and use of competitive advantages to exploit the firm's innovations is the key to Hasbro's continuing success. As Verrecchia says, "In this business you look at many, many products. You run the numbers. You do market research. But products get to market because people have a passion for them and pushed them. Those are the ones that tend to be creative and stimulating and appealing."

SOURCES: 2004, Hasbro Inc., *Standard & Poor's Stock Report,* http://www.standardandpoors.com, July 3; S. McGowen, 2004, The game plan at Hasbro, *NYSE Magazine,* January/February: 12–16.

As explained in "Focusing on Strategy," innovation is critical to Hasbro's success. We can see why this might be the case. As children, didn't we want to play with the newest, most creative toys?

Increasingly though, innovation is proving to be vital to the success of virtually all companies. The CEO of Switzerland-based Novartis, for example, believes that his firm's success is largely based on its ability to continuously and successfully innovate.[1] Similarly, the CEO of the large consumer-products firm Alberto-Culver believes that innovation is the secret to maintaining the attractiveness of his firm's brand image with its customers. In his words, "The key to keeping a beauty brand fresh is to innovate with new products, packaging improvements and advertising that reflects current trends and needs."[2] The

CEO of Siemens AG believes that innovation is one of four factors influencing the sustainability of a firm's (including Siemens's) competitive advantages (concern for the environment, financial stability, and a meaningful global presence are the other three factors).[3] In fact, a number of studies found a positive link between innovation and firm performance.[4] These findings corroborate the experiences of the companies mentioned here. And, as is true for many organizations, especially larger ones, Hasbro, Novartis, Alberto-Culver, and Siemens all use three methods to innovate—internal development, cooperative relationships, and acquisitions.

The purpose of this chapter is to explain the use of innovation as a means for firms to enter new markets or to create entirely new markets. United Parcel Service (UPS) relied on its information technology and systems analysis skills to successfully enter a new market—the logistics management or synchronized commerce market (see the "Focusing on Strategy" segments in Chapter 5 and Chapter 6).[5] Essentially, when innovating, companies develop unique and successful solutions to problems facing customers.[6] UPS's logistics customers, for example, can reduce the amount they spend to transport and store their goods.

We discuss several topics in this chapter to describe firms' use of innovation as a means of market entry and market creation. We first define innovation and then describe innovation's relationships with entrepreneurship and entrepreneurs. We also introduce the characteristics and behaviors of entrepreneurs. The case about Oprah Winfrey at the end of the book allows you to study these characteristics and behaviors as you read about the actions of a highly successful entrepreneur. In addition, we explain the concept of strategic entrepreneurship (the pursuit of entrepreneurial opportunities using a strategic perspective). The chapter then describes the three ways firms innovate when engaging in strategic entrepreneurship. After discussing internal innovation, we examine innovation through cooperative relationships and then through acquisitions. We close the chapter with a summary analysis of how firms can create value by successfully using strategic entrepreneurship.

corporate entrepreneurship

an organization-wide reliance on entrepreneurship and innovation as the link to solid financial performance

Our focus in this chapter is on innovation and entrepreneurship in existing organizations. This phenomenon is called **corporate entrepreneurship,** which is an organization-wide reliance on entrepreneurship and innovation as the link to solid financial performance.[7] Thus, our concern is with entrepreneurship and the innovation it spawns within established firms rather than how entrepreneurship is the bedrock for starting new ventures. Courses in entrepreneurship describe how innovation often is the foundation on which new entrepreneurial ventures are built.

Before beginning our discussions of these topics, you should know that uncertainty surrounds innovation. Uncertainty exists when the probability of a certain outcome being achieved is unknown.[8] This means that even when firms do everything the way it should be done, there are no guarantees that what they are doing will lead to innovations. Firms must accept uncertainty when dealing with innovation. Uncertainty does not diminish the value of innovation at all; but, firms can't expect every innovation effort to succeed. But uncertainty isn't uncommon. In fact, many actions that firms take are uncertain in terms of their outcomes. Uncertainty is reduced, however, when the firm successfully follows the steps in the strategic management process.

© Fred Prouser/Reuters/Landov

Innovation, Entrepreneurship, and Entrepreneurs

Innovation

What image comes to mind when you think of innovation? Are you thinking of something new? If so, your thoughts are on target, in that **innovation** is the development of something new—a new good, a new type of service, or a new way of presenting a good or service. Newness sometimes finds a firm creating a new market niche (for example, Subway's creation of the "health-conscious" niche in the fast-food industry) or even redefining an industry. Television shows such as *Cops, America's Most Wanted, In Living Color,* and *American Idol* seem to be redefining parts of the entertainment industry. Who created these shows? Not ABC, CBS, or NBC. Newcomer Fox Television developed and introduced all of these shows. Indeed, some analysts suggest that for the first 15-plus years of its life, Fox has been redefining the television industry as a result of its ability to shape trends through its programming choices (*Cops* and *America's Most Wanted* are early examples of reality TV). Moreover, unlike its counterparts, Fox has managed to create a brand that provides customers with programming that is hip, young, and sometimes outrageous.[9] HBO also has changed the television industry through its original programming such as *The Sopranos* and *Deadwood* among others.

As customers, we are familiar with innovative goods and services. Process and administrative innovations are also important to firms and their efforts to enter new markets, although we may not be aware of them as customers. **Process innovations** are new means of producing, selling, and supporting goods and services. Dell's famous direct-sales model is an example of a process innovation. Before Dell, personal computers (PCs) were sold through storefront retailers. Seeing an opportunity, Michael Dell developed a new process to sell PCs, which was to sell directly to customers rather than indirectly through retailers.

During his time at the helm of General Motors, Alfred P. Sloan, Jr., "invented the very idea of the modern American corporation."[10] An **administrative innovation** is a new way of organizing and/or handling the organizational tasks firms use to complete their work. Sloan's administrative innovation was to break General Motors into smaller divisions that could operate autonomously as long as they met their financial goals. Initially, the divisions focused on different products (Chevrolet, Buick, Pontiac, Oldsmobile, and Cadillac) that were intended to meet customers' different needs (family transportation, sporty performance, luxury, and so forth). Sloan believed that his innovative organizational structure would enable employees to work more independently in each division. Division independence from the direct control of the firm's upper-level managers, he thought, would cause employees in those divisions to be more creative and productive.

Therefore, innovation is concerned with bringing something new into use. As we've described, the newness of an innovation can take the form of a new good;

Fox's innovation of the audience participation singing contest American Idol *has proven to be one of the most successful shows on television.*

*

innovation

the development of something new—a new good, a new type of service, or a new way of presenting a good or service

*

process innovations

new means of producing, selling, and supporting goods and services

*

administrative innovation

a new way of organizing and/or handling the organizational tasks firms use to complete their work a new service; a new process to manufacture, sell, and support a good or service; or a new way of managing and directing how a firm operates. From the perspective of a consumer of an innovation, innovation is all about a new choice.[11]

It is important to recognize that the purpose of innovation is to increase the firm's performance. Of course, this increase is often sought in the form of larger profits. In the words of Kevin Rollins, Dell's CEO, "The key to the whole game is to innovate and make a profit."[12] Recently, firms producing innovative flat-screen televisions based on different technologies such as LCD, DLP, and plasma gas, as well as companies making components for flat screens, earned significant and record profits. Some business analysts believe that the amount devoted to R&D by firms in the flat-panel industry suggests that additional innovations will stimulate still more growth and profitability in the industry.[13]

What helps firms in their efforts to consistently innovate? As we discuss next, entrepreneurship and the entrepreneurs who are its foundation play important roles in a firm's ability to innovate.

Entrepreneurship

★
entrepreneurship

a process of "creative destruction" through which existing products, methods of production, or ways of administering or managing the firm are destroyed and replaced with new ones

Joseph Schumpeter, the famous economist, saw **entrepreneurship** as a process of "creative destruction" through which existing products, methods of production, or ways of administering or managing the firm are destroyed and replaced with new ones.[14] Firms encouraging entrepreneurship are willing to take risks as well as to be creative while trying to outperform competitors.[15] Peter Drucker, a well-known management writer, very directly describes the relationship between innovation and entrepreneurship: "Innovation is the specific form of entrepreneurship, whether in an existing business, a public service institution, or a new venture started by a lone individual."[16]

The processes firms use to innovate are unique to each firm. In "Understanding Strategy," we describe Intel's innovation process. While reading about what Intel did to "produce the world's fastest transistor," notice that the firm's scientists were trying to find a way to creatively destroy existing chips with new ones that have superior functionality.

★
entrepreneurial
opportunities

circumstances suggesting that new goods or services can be sold at a price exceeding the costs incurred to create, make, sell, and support them

The specific focus of entrepreneurship is on discovering and exploiting profitable entrepreneurial opportunities. **Entrepreneurial opportunities** are circumstances suggesting that new goods or services can be sold at a price exceeding the costs incurred to create, make, sell, and support them. Sometimes opportunities are borne out of cold-hard realities. This was the case at Intel as the firm's decision makers concluded that a different type of transistor had to be developed if the PC industry was to continue growing (and Intel along with it!). As we discuss next, entrepreneurs are people in organizations who identify entrepreneurial opportunities and then convert them into successful innovations.

Entrepreneurs

★
entrepreneurs

people who recognize entrepreneurial opportunities and then take risks to develop an innovation to pursue them

Entrepreneurs are people who recognize entrepreneurial opportunities and then take risks to develop an innovation to pursue them. Entrepreneurs are found throughout an organization, meaning that those actually making a firm's good or service are just as capable of being entrepreneurs as are managers and staff personnel.

A number of characteristics describe entrepreneurs. For example, entrepreneurs are optimistic,[17] are highly motivated, are willing to take greater financial responsibility for their projects, accept uncertain outcomes, and are courageous.[18]

understanding strategy:
INTEL'S INNOVATION PROCESS

Moore's Law suggests that the number of transistors (the microscopic, silicon-based switches that process the digital world's ones and zeros) on a chip roughly doubles every two years. This doubling creates more features, increased performance, and reduced cost per transistor. But in the 1990s, it became obvious that the limitations of existing technologies would rather quickly prevent continuing repetition of Moore's Law. Essentially, the problem facing chip manufacturers such as Intel was that as microcircuits continue to shrink while becoming more powerful, they run hotter and hotter, making it impossible to satisfactorily provide cooling. In 2001, Intel's chief technology officer crisply specified the long-brewing problem by noting that Intel's then-current chips "generate about as much heat as a hot plate. Extrapolate recent trends," he suggested, "and in three years the chips will rival a nuclear reactor, in two more years, a rocket nozzle, and in another two years, the sun's surface." What does this mean? According to Intel, a failure to find a radically different way to build chips would bring Moore's Law, and advances in the personal computer (PC) industry as well, to a screeching halt.

Intel had significant resources to face this challenge. First, the firm had built a substantial R&D capability, especially in the form of its stable of scientists and engineers. Supporting these individuals' work is Intel's more than $4 billion annual allocation to R&D. In fact, Intel tends to spend more on R&D during recessions (as was the case during 2000, 2001, and 2002) than it does when the economy is robust, in order to take advantage of opportunities available when competitors are likely to spend less.

Intel's continuing work on the problem with current chip technologies yielded significant results in late November 2001, when the firm announced that its researchers had pioneered an innovative transistor structure and new materials that enabled "dramatic" improvements in transistor speed, power efficiency, and heat reduction. This innovation led to the creation of the TeraHertz chip. This chip runs at least ten times as fast as existing chips without consuming more power or generating additional heat. Real-time voice and face recognition, computing without keyboards, and smaller computing devices with higher performance and improved battery life are examples of the applications the TeraHertz chip is expected to make possible.

How were Intel's researchers able to develop the TeraHertz chip? What process does Intel use to consistently and successfully innovate so it can generate new products such as the TeraHertz chip?

Evidence shows that Intel's innovations, including the ones leading to development of the TeraHertz chip, result from a four-step process: (1) carefully and correctly defining the problem to be solved through innovation, (2) assigning the "right" people to each project, (3) eliminating project-specific barriers between R&D and manufacturing, and (4) balancing autonomy with guidance for each project's researchers.

In terms of the TeraHertz chip, here's how the process worked. First, the limitations of existing technologies were specified as the problem or constraint when it came to continuing to fulfill Moore's Law. To deal with this problem, a performance goal of quickly designing the world's fastest transistor was established. Second, in 1998, a small group of "elite" scientists was formed and assigned to the project. To break down barriers between R&D and manufacturing, the scientists were located adjacent to a full chip-development factory and were encouraged to immediately test new ideas in a "clean room" environment. By quickly developing and testing actual prototypes in the production facility, scientists could immediately determine what did and didn't work. Lastly, Intel's top-level executives resisted the temptation to micromanage the project. This temptation could have been great, given the project's significance to Intel's future. During quarterly review meetings, executives provided feedback to verify that the scientific team's work remained on target.

They also assigned additional personnel to the project who could help solve unexpected problems outside the team's expertise. However, the top-level managers did not try to unduly influence the direction of the group's work.

Intel's scientists continue to work on the TeraHertz chip. However, the firm believes that its four-step innovation process has helped it develop a chip that will prevent the PC industry from grinding to a halt and that has the potential to make Moore's Law a continuing reality. In addition, the firm believes the chip will help it win its marketplace battles with competitors.

SOURCES: 2004, Intel Corp., *Lehman Brothers Equity Research,* http://www.lehmanbrothers.com, July 14; 2003, Intel researchers develop breakthrough transistor technologies to fight power, heat issues in future processors, Intel Home Page, http://www.intel.com, November 5; G. Anders, 2002, How Intel puts innovation inside, *Fast Company,* March: 122–125; 2001, Intel announces TeraHertz transistor breakthrough in chip design, Intel Home Page, http://www.intel.com, November 26.

By responding to the issues in Table 10.1, you'll have some perspective about the degree to which these characteristics describe you.

The characteristics of an entrepreneur certainly describe Thomas J. Watson, Jr. As the CEO of IBM, Watson was an innovator who bet his firm's future when he decided in 1964 to replace all of the firm's existing computer lines with a radically different type of machine called the System/360. Before the introduction of this innovative product line, firms required different software programs for every computer model. In contrast, the System/360 was a family of computers that allowed programs written for one computer to work on

---

TABLE 10.1   Characteristics of Entrepreneurs—Where Do I Stand?

Entrepreneurs are known to have certain characteristics. For each characteristic, rate yourself on a scale of 1–4 with the following scale values:

1 This characteristic does not describe me
2 This characteristic slightly describes me
3 This characteristic accurately describes me
4 This characteristic strongly describes me

Characteristic	Rating
Highly motivated	_____
Very optimistic	_____
Very willing to take responsibility for the outcomes of projects	_____
Consistently view uncertainty as an opportunity	_____
Highly tolerant of ambiguous situations	_____
Highly committed to the importance of innovation	_____
Very willing to tackle tasks, even with insufficient resources	_____

The higher your score is, the greater is the probability that you have many of the characteristics of entrepreneurs.

© Marvin Koner/CORBIS

In the case of IBM CEO Thomas J. Watson, Jr., a risky innovation certainly had its rewards for the company.

another computer in the family. Questioned at the time about his decision to push IBM in this direction, Watson is now thought of as a courageous and brilliant innovator.[19] Entrepreneurs such as Watson make unique connections among seemingly unconnected events and see possibilities others haven't noticed.[20] Of course, these possibilities are actually entrepreneurial opportunities.

After identifying entrepreneurial opportunities, entrepreneurs turn their attention to developing capabilities that will be the basis of the competitive advantages required to make a profit from pursuing the opportunities. This means that identifying entrepreneurial opportunities is a necessary but insufficient step for innovation and subsequently, for corporate success. As we learned in Chapter 4, to successfully exploit opportunities, firms must develop capabilities that are valuable, rare, difficult to imitate, and nonsubstitutable. Capabilities satisfying these four criteria are competitive advantages and are the basis on which entrepreneurial opportunities can be successfully pursued.

Therefore, to innovate and to use innovation as a path to enter new markets, firms must identify opportunities *and* determine how to take advantage of them. As you have probably already determined, identifying opportunities is an entrepreneurial process, while developing the capabilities needed to exploit them is a strategic process. When innovations are exploited, they contribute to maintaining or creating competitive advantages. Both processes are concerned with growth and creating value for customers and wealth for shareholders.

Strategic entrepreneurship is the process of taking entrepreneurial actions using a strategic perspective by combining entrepreneurial and strategic management processes to enhance the firm's ability to innovate, enter new markets, and improve its performance. Strategic entrepreneurship allows the firm to first identify and then exploit entrepreneurial opportunities. Strategic entrepreneurship also helps the firm balance its need to find and exploit tomorrow's "new products" while exploiting its current marketplace successes.

As we said earlier, firms can use strategic entrepreneurship to innovate in three ways. Next, we examine these methods and summarize them in Table 10.2.

*

strategic entrepreneurship

the process of taking entrepreneurial actions using a strategic perspective by combining entrepreneurial and strategic management processes to enhance the firm's ability to innovate, enter new markets, and improve its performance

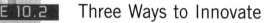

TABLE 10.2 Three Ways to Innovate

Internal Innovation
- Using a firm's own resources and capabilities to innovate

Cooperating to Innovate
- When two or more firms form an agreement to join some of their resources and capabilities to innovate

Acquiring Innovation
- Buying ownership of another firm's innovations and innovation capabilities

Three Ways to Innovate

Internal Innovation

The firm uses its own resources and capabilities when engaging in *internal innovation*. Of the organizational functions around which resources and capabilities are developed, R&D is the most critical to efforts to develop innovations internally. Indeed, in most industries, the battle to innovate and to use innovation to enter new markets begins in R&D labs. In fact, in industries that are highly dependent on innovations for continuing success, such as pharmaceuticals, firms devote large amounts of their total sales to R&D. Novartis, for example, annually allocates at least 15 percent of its sales to support its R&D efforts. At the end of its fiscal year 2004, Hewlett-Packard (HP) had generated $7 billion in sales revenue through internal growth—growth that was being fueled by internal innovations. Impressively, on average, HP created 11 patents per day during its 2004 fiscal year. This performance caused then-CEO Carly Fiorina to suggest that in essence, HP had become an organic growth company.[21] (Organic growth means that a firm is growing primarily through internal means rather than through acquisitions.)

Most of us expect pharmaceutical companies (such as Novartis) and technology firms (such as HP) to be innovative. Sometimes, however, firms we wouldn't necessarily think of as being concerned with innovation do indeed support R&D to develop internal innovations. For example, IHOP Corporation seems to be committed to internal innovations. In fact, IHOP's director of R&D is responsible for introducing new products that attract new customers while retaining the loyalty of current customers.

All companies, including IHOP, develop R&D processes that are unique to them. Think about Intel's four-step innovation process that we explained earlier in "Understanding Strategy." The process at IHOP begins when IHOP's R&D director (or one of his staff members) thinks of a product idea or a company approaches IHOP with a proposal. Armed with only a description of the innovation, IHOP personnel ask at least 100 "screeners" (IHOP customers) if the product is one they want to see IHOP offer and if they believe the new item will blend with the menu. R&D personnel then evaluate the high-scoring items to determine how difficult they would be to make as well as the cost to do so. A different set of screeners is then asked to sample proposed products and react to how they are presented on the menu. Proposed food items surviving this evaluation are test-marketed in a limited number of IHOP units. Responses are then gathered from actual guests and carefully examined to see how well the proposed product is being received. As IHOP's R&D director says, "It's a more involved process than most people think."[22]

While competitors may try to imitate the R&D processes Intel and IHOP are using, it will be difficult for them to do so. The main reason for the difficulty, of course, is that Intel and IHOP are each using unique capabilities in unique ways to internally develop innovations such as Intel's TeraHertz chip and IHOP's stuffed crepes (one of the firm's most recent menu item innovations).

As our descriptions of Intel and IHOP suggest, some innovations are incremental while some are radical. IHOP's new food items are primarily *incremental innovations*, meaning that each one builds on the firm's existing knowledge about foods to extend the breadth and depth of its offerings. Product line extensions such as those we see in laundry detergents (for example, liquid Tide as an extension of Tide powder) are another example of incremental innovations. On the other hand, Intel's TeraHertz chip is a radical innovation. A *radical innovation* results from a technology breakthrough and the creation of new knowledge.

Both incremental and radical innovations have the potential to create value. However, radical innovations may lead to more substantial improvements in a firm's performance. Nonetheless, it is important to understand that incremental innovations can be very profitable (Procter & Gamble's introduction of Crest Whitestrips is an example of a successful incremental innovation). In general, though, the firm can use its current capabilities to successfully exploit incremental innovations and maintain its competitive advantages. In contrast, new capabilities are required to gain full value from radical innovations, thereby creating new competitive advantages.

Firms accept risks when innovating through internal means. The most prominent of these is the fact that internal innovations tend to take a great deal of time to develop to realize commercial successes. This can be a serious issue, because rapid innovation is important to a firm's success. As the chairman and CEO of Charles River Laboratories International says, "Everything in this business is about speed to market."[23]

In the final analysis, firms learn a great deal from their efforts to innovate internally. This is especially true when radical innovations are developed. However, firms also learn from internally created innovations that become product failures. Because of this, some organizations openly celebrate failures and their potential to help improve the firm's innovation ability.

We discuss one firm's commitment to learning from failed innovations in the "Understanding Strategy." While reading about this firm, think of the type of culture required for a firm to support failure. In addition to tolerating failure, the culture needs to be open and receptive to even radically different ideas. Can you envision working in an organizational culture in which failure resulting from carefully designed and executed efforts to innovate is tolerated? Alberto Alessi, head of a design firm in Italy, whose actions are described in "Understanding Strategy," made the following statement: "I have to remind my brothers how vital it is to have one, possibly two fiascoes per year. Should Alessi go for two or three years without a fiasco, we will be in danger of losing our leadership in design."[24]

Innovating by Cooperating

As we noted, firms pursuing internal innovations use their own resources and capabilities to innovate. When an organization partners with one or more other firms to combine two sets of resources and capabilities as the source of innovation, it is labeled *innovating by cooperating*. Strategic alliances and joint ventures are common organizational forms used by partner firms to cooperatively develop innovations.

One reason why firms decide to cooperate on innovation is that it is becoming increasingly rare for a single company to have all the resources and capabilities needed to successfully innovate in today's dynamic marketplaces. Discussing the complexity of continuous innovation, the president and CEO of Unisys observed that, "very few companies have the resources to do everything."[25] From a strategic entrepreneurship perspective, a partnership formed to

understanding strategy:

THE GLORY OF FAILURE!

A key theme in this chapter is that innovation is critical to organizational success. One reason is that increasingly customers want to buy innovative goods and services. In the words of Steven Reinemund, CEO and chairman of PepsiCo, "Innovation is what consumers are looking for." But innovation isn't easily accomplished. In fact, a number of failed efforts almost always precede the introduction of a successful innovation.

Some firms also believe that because they generate valuable insights, innovation failures should be celebrated. Alberto Alessi, who along with his two brothers has converted his family's formerly staid housewares firm into a trend-setting designer firm called Alessi Spa, firmly believes that failed innovations, which he calls fiascoes, should be celebrated as learning opportunities. Of course, Alessi is proud of his firm's innovation successes when it comes to product designs, including those that led to the production of Alessandro Mendini's Anna G. corkscrew and Philippe Starck's Juicy Salif lemon squeezer. But he is equally proud of the Philippe Starck

© Anna Clopet/CORBIS

Hot Bertaa kettle. This product had a few complicated and innovative engineering features on the inside of the kettle that prevented steam from escaping the kettle as water was poured out. Although the features worked well on prototypes, the firm never determined how to retain the functionality of those features when producing the product in large production runs. As is always the case with a failure in this particular company, discussions were held to determine what had been learned from the failure and how those lessons could help in future projects.

The firm's private museum, in which its failed products are displayed, is further evidence of the value Alessi places on innovation failures. Designers meet weekly with Alessi in the museum to talk about new product designs. This setting allows designers to abort new possibilities if the museum already houses a product that failed at least partly because of something that is an aspect of a current design proposal. The publication of a book of the firm's prototypes that failed also highlights Alessi's awareness of what hasn't worked in previous efforts and how those failures can influence positive innovation outcomes in the future.

SOURCES: 2004, Europe's leading speaker bureau, http://www.speakers.co.uk, July 9; D. Brady, 2004, A thousand and one noshes, *Business Week,* June 14: 54–56; I. Wylie, 2001, Failure is glorious, *Fast Company,* October: 35–37.

innovate can involve one partner bringing to the cooperative relationship its capability to identify entrepreneurial opportunities while the other partner brings its capability to exploit opportunities and create competitive advantages. Strategic entrepreneurship is often practiced in relationships between large pharmaceutical companies and more entrepreneurial biotechnology companies. In these instances, the smaller biotechnology company provides its capability to identify entrepreneurial opportunities and develop innovative products in light of them. The larger organization in the partnership commonly has the skills needed to exploit those innovations (such as manufacturing, marketing, and distribution) and form competitive advantages in the marketplace.

An interesting example of innovating by cooperating is the set of relationships between companies and researchers housed in different universities and research centers located throughout the world. For example, Merck has formed partnerships with scientists at more than 100 universities and clinical centers worldwide. Using these partnerships, Merck has developed an early-stage human papillomavirus (HPV) vaccine for the treatment of cervical cancer (which annually kills 200,000 women in the world). Early-stage trial results for the vaccine are very encouraging. In fact, early tests show the vaccine to be 100 percent effective in preventing a viral infection that commonly leads to cervical cancer. Merck is now partnering with university and clinical center scientists to test an extension of the vaccine that targets four types of HPV that cause most cervical cancers. Through the 100-plus partnerships, Merck has access to the results of research that scientists are completing with a sample in excess of 23,000 young women. Merck and its partners are thus cooperating to find ways to successfully bring an innovative medicine to the marketplace.[26]

Cooperating to innovate is not without risk, however. One firm might "steal" its partner's knowledge with the intention of improving its own competitive ability. A second risk is that before the work of a partnership actually commences, there is uncertainty about the true level of skills a partner possesses. Because of risks such as these, a firm needs to be careful in choosing its partner before trying to cooperate to innovate. Also, partnering with others shares the risks so that one firm does not have to shoulder all of the risk. Additionally, partners share the cost of developing the innovation; this can be especially useful when the innovation is expensive to develop.

Innovating through Acquisitions

A firm that acquires a fully developed product from another entity or acquires an innovation capability by buying another company is *innovating through acquisitions*.[27] A firm may do this for several reasons: to add a complementary product to its existing line, to gain immediate access to different markets or market segments, to substitute an acquired firm's superior technology for its own less effective technology, to add talented scientists and innovative personnel to the firm's labor pool, and to achieve firm growth. Clearly, acquiring innovations allows much faster growth compared to cooperative alliances or internal development. During the 1990s, Cisco Systems acquired a number of firms to gain access to their product innovations and often their innovative capabilities. Pfizer recently acquired Pharmacia, largely to improve the ratio between products developed in its combined labs and those that become commercial successes.

As with the other two means of innovating, acquiring innovations isn't risk-free. A key risk is that acquiring innovation may reduce a firm's ability to innovate internally. Indeed, a failure to support R&D as the base for internal innovations can cause bright and talented people to leave a firm. Research evidence that firms acquiring innovations introduce fewer new products into the marketplace highlights the dangers of relying heavily on acquisitions as a means of innovating.[28]

Across time and events, the most successful firms learn how to innovate internally, through cooperative relationships and by acquiring other companies. However, the firm must balance its use of the three innovation methods in ways that will create maximum additional value for customers as well as enhance the wealth of its shareholders. In the final section, we discuss how firms can create this balance by both identifying and exploiting entrepreneurial opportunities.

Innovation and Strategic Entrepreneurship

"I follow a great market that provides an opportunity to satisfy customers and make money."[29] This comment by Thomas Stemberg, founder and executive chairman of Staples, captures the essence of strategic entrepreneurship. As we've discussed, strategic entrepreneurship involves identifying an opportunity and creating innovation to pursue that opportunity to create value for customers and wealth for shareholders. *Business Week* writers also suggested strategic entrepreneurship's importance when presenting its 2004 list of "100 Hot Growth Companies." The common denominator among these companies, the writers claim, is "The ability to find—and then exploit—a sweet spot in the economy."[30] As a result, all firms must be able to use entrepreneurial capabilities to identify entrepreneurial opportunities and to develop innovations in light of them *as well as* to use strategic capabilities to exploit the innovations and opportunities and build competitive advantages.

An important skill is the ability to choose among the alternatives for pursuing an entrepreneurial opportunity: internal innovation, cooperative innovation, and innovation from acquisitions.[31] A central issue in determining whether a firm should pursue an internal venture focuses on its internal skills and abilities. If the firm has a strong set of skills and capabilities to innovate, the targeted innovation should largely remain internal. Firms that have developed strong, intangible capabilities in a specific domain are often in an excellent position to leverage these capabilities through a new internal venture when a related opportunity is perceived.

If firm executives perceive a significant entrepreneurial opportunity that is also important strategically to the firm, but circumstances suggest that the firm does not currently have the skills and capabilities to take advantage of the opportunity, one of the external options (cooperation or acquisition) should be considered.[32] We suggest that a cooperative venture is the appropriate mode of entry choice to facilitate rapid development of the skills needed to take advantage of an opportunity, especially when there is significant uncertainty about whether the technology is available or whether the market will accept the potential prototype good or service. The uncertainty of success suggests that it would be wise to share this risk with partners who have complementary skills that, when combined with those of other partners, would be sufficient to take advantage of the opportunity.

If, on the other hand, the opportunity is less uncertain and more speed is required, an acquisition approach might be more successful. Acquisitions attempt to create value by uniting the complementary innovative resources or capabilities of the acquiring firm and the acquired firm in order to create whole capabilities that did not exist previously. Companies that seek to enhance their technical capabilities with speed and efficiency often target innovative firms with expertise in the area of the perceived entrepreneurial opportunity and complementary R&D capabilities necessary for the acquiring firm to succeed. Cisco has used this approach to acquire new startup firms to speedily build new niche products in the network gear market.[33]

Combining entrepreneurial and strategic skills to successfully innovate and enter new markets is a relatively new concept. But companies that can do so outperform those that cannot. In increasingly competitive markets, the highest returns accrue to companies that can quickly identify entrepreneurial opportunities, innovate, and then use novel capabilities to exploit innovations and develop them into commercial successes.

Summary

The primary purpose of this chapter is to describe how a firm's entrepreneurs can rely on entrepreneurship and strategic entrepreneurship to create innovation as the foundation for entering new markets. In doing so, we examined the following topics:

- **Innovation** is concerned with the creation of newness, especially new products—that is, with bringing something new into use. New goods (such as a medicine that significantly improves a patient's chance of recovering from an illness) and services (such as the ability to purchase low-cost tickets for travel and entertainment among other services from Internet vendors) are commonly used to satisfy consumers' needs. However, for firms, **process innovations** (such as discovering a new way to create value in the primary-activities part of the value chain) and **administrative innovations** (such as developing value-creating methods to operate the firm) are also important. Effective innovation helps firms create value for customers and wealth for shareholders and can be the basis for entering new markets. Innovation helps firms differentiate their goods and services from competitors' goods and services and facilitates organizational efforts to rapidly move products to the marketplace.

- As a process of creative destruction, **entrepreneurship** is an organizational process through which firms innovate. Entrepreneurial firms are willing to take risks and strive to innovate to quickly introduce goods or services to the marketplace.

- **Entrepreneurs** are people who recognize entrepreneurial opportunities and are willing to take risks to develop an innovation to pursue them. Entrepreneurs have certain characteristics, including being highly motivated, tolerant of uncertainty, and willing to take greater financial responsibility for the outcomes attained through their innovation-focused efforts.

- **Entrepreneurial opportunities** are the product of entrepreneurial behaviors while pursuing opportunities results from strategic behavior. The most effective firms rely on strategic entrepreneurship as their source of innovation. **Strategic entrepreneurship** is the process of taking entrepreneurial actions with a strategic perspective. Strategic entrepreneurship is becoming increasingly important for firms trying to innovate and to use innovation as a means of entering new markets.

- Firms use one or more of three means to innovate (increasingly, firms use all three means). Internal innovation takes place when the firm uses its own resources and capabilities to innovate. Each firm develops an innovation process that is unique to it. When that process satisfies the criteria of sustainability discussed in Chapter 4, it can be a source of competitive advantage. Because most firms lack all resources and capabilities required for consistently effective innovation, they also form cooperative relationships such as strategic alliances and joint ventures to innovate. Lastly, firms may acquire specific innovations as well as another firm's innovative capabilities. Each means of innovation has benefits and risks. The most effective firm learns how *and* when to use each means of innovation.

- If a firm finds an entrepreneurial opportunity that fits its skills and abilities, it probably should use an internal innovation process to pursue such an opportunity. Alternatively, if a firm's skills do not currently fit the opportunity, it probably should use one of the external approaches (cooperatively develop the skills or acquire the skills) to pursue the opportunity. The cooperative option is more likely to be successful if there is significant uncertainty about the technology or market because it allows risk sharing. The acquisition approach might be better if the opportunity is more certain because speed to market becomes more important in developing the necessary skills.

Key Terms

administrative innovation 242
corporate entrepreneurship 241
entrepreneurial opportunities 243

entrepreneurs 243
entrepreneurship 243
innovation 242

process innovations 242
strategic entrepreneurship 246

Discussion Questions

1. What is innovation and what is entrepreneurship? Who are entrepreneurs? What is the relationship between entrepreneurship and entrepreneurs?
2. What are entrepreneurial opportunities and entrepreneurial capabilities? Why must a firm have entrepreneurial capabilities as well as entrepreneurial opportunities to use innovation as a means of entering new markets?
3. What is strategic entrepreneurship? Why do firms use strategic entrepreneurship when innovating?
4. How do firms develop innovations internally?
5. How are cooperative strategies used to develop innovations?

6. How do firms use acquisitions as a way to innovate?
7. Is strategic entrepreneurship of increasing importance to firms committed to innovation and to using innovation as a way to enter markets that are new to them? Under what circumstances would you use each of the three approaches (internal innovation, cooperative relationships, and acquisition) to pursue a new entrepreneurial opportunity?

Endnotes

1. J. R. Quain, 2004, From pipeline to lifeline, *NYSE Magazine,* May/June: 13–17.
2. 2004, Brand awareness, 2003, *NYSE Magazine,* January/February, 28–32.
3. 2003, Siemens takes on the 21st century, *NYSE Magazine,* January/February, 26–32.
4. Summaries of these studies can be found in C. E. Hull & J. G. Covin, 2004, Investigating the determinants of innovation mode: Organizational, managerial, and environmental considerations. Working paper, Indiana University.
5. M. Fones, 2004, UPS syncs up, *NYSE Magazine,* March/April: 10–14.
6. A. Overholt, 2002, Mr. Patent, *Fast Company,* June: 59–62.
7. R. D. Ireland, J. G. Covin, & D. F. Kuratko, 2005. A model of corporate entrepreneurship strategy. Working paper, Texas A&M University.
8. F. H. Knight, 1921, *Risk, Uncertainty, and Profit.* Houghton Mifflin (reprint ed.). Chicago: University of Chicago Press.
9. N. Oppenheim, 2004, The big three out-foxed, *Wall Street Journal Online,* http://www.wsj.com, June 11.
10. D. Welch, 2004, Reinventing the company, *Business Week,* March 22: 24.
11. C. Palmeri, 2004, Teach an old sneaker enough new tricks—and kids will come running, *Business Week,* June 7: 92–94.
12. M. Veverka, 2004, Old wounds fester at confab, *Barron's Online,* http://www.barrons.com, June 14.
13. E. Ramstad, 2004, As flat-screen fever heats up, Asia producers offer pure plays, *Wall Street Journal Online,* http://www.wsj.com, June 11.
14. J. Schumpeter, 1934, *The Theory of Economic Development,* Cambridge, Mass.: Harvard University Press.
15. R. Katila, 2002, New product search over time: Past ideas in their prime? *Academy of Management Journal,* 45: 995–1010.
16. P. F. Drucker, 1998, The discipline of innovation, *Harvard Business Review,* 76(6): 149–157.
17. 2004, Rules to live by, and break, Knowledge @ Wharton, http://knowledge.wharton.upenn.edu, June 17.
18. D. Duffy, 2004, Corporate entrepreneurship: Entrepreneurial skills for personal and corporate success, *Center for Excellence,* http://www.centerforexcellence.net, June 14.
19. S. Hamm, 2004, Junior achievement, *Business Week,* June 14: 18.
20. M. M. Crossan, H. W. Lane, & R. E. White, 1999, An organizational learning framework: From intuition to institution, *Academy of Management Review,* 24: 522–537.
21. D. Fuscaldo, 2004, H-P CEO: Will create $7B in organic growth in fiscal '04, *Wall Street Journal Online,* http://www.wsj.com, June 8.
22. J. Connelly, 2004, IHOP stacks up, *NYSE Magazine,* May/June: 33–36.
23. A. Barrett, C. Palmeri, & S. A. Forest, 2004, The 100 best small companies, *Business Week,* June 7: 86–90.
24. I. Wylie, 2001, Failure is glorious, *Fast Company,* October: 35–37.
25. 2004, The power of partnerships, *NYSE Magazine,* May/June: 22–26.
26. 2004, When big pharma and academia unite, *NYSE Magazine,* May/June: 10.
27. Hull & Covin, op. cit.
28. M. A. Hitt, R. E. Hoskisson, R. A. Johnson, & D. D. Moesel, 1996, The market for corporate control and firm innovation, *Academy of Management Journal,* 39: 1084–1119.
29. 2004, Rules to live by.
30. Barrett, Palmeri, & Forest, op. cit.
31. R. E. Hoskisson & L. W. Busenitz, 2002, Market uncertainty and learning distance in corporate entrepreneurship entry mode choice, in M. A. Hitt, R. D. Ireland, S. M. Camp, & D. L. Sexton (eds.), *Strategic Entrepreneurship: Creating a New Mindset,* Oxford, U.K.: Blackwell, 151–172.
32. T. Keil, 2004, Building external corporate venturing capability, *Journal of Management Studies,* 41: 799–825.
33. S. Thurm, 2003, After the boom: A go-go giant of Internet age, Cisco is learning to go slow, *Wall Street Journal,* May 7: A1.

Your Career

In this chapter we have stressed that firms should master strategic entrepreneurship if they wish to use innovation as a means of entering new markets. As we've discussed, firms using strategic entrepreneurship act entrepreneurially while using a strategic perspective. In this context, innovative organizations consistently strive to identify new opportunities and develop the competitive advantages required to exploit those opportunities in the marketplace.

So it should be with your career. Using a strategic perspective, you will want to continuously find ways to add to or update your skill set, with your skill set being your competitive advantage. To do this, you could identify skill-based courses offered by your company. In addition, you could take courses available from educational institutions, either "live" in your local community or "virtually" through online instruction.

A fair question for you to ask would be, "What skills should I try to develop?" The answer to this question is that you want to ensure that the skills you are using to complete your job today are as current as they can be. You want to be able to complete tasks in a manner that is superior to how others complete the same task. The second skill set to develop relates to the skills you will need to be a superior employee (or entrepreneur for yourself) when entrepreneurial opportunities are identified. To do this, you need to continuously anticipate what your company will do in the future to be successful. If you work in the telecommunications industry, for example, what entrepreneurial opportunities result from the convergence among different communications technologies? What skills are necessary to create superior value for a firm pursuing newly identified entrepreneurial opportunities in the telecommunications industry? What can you do now to enhance your skill set to be prepared for future entrepreneurial opportunities?

How might you start today using strategic entrepreneurship to benefit your career? First, revisit your competitive advantages that you identified in response to "Your Career" in Chapter 5. What can you do today to upgrade those competitive advantages? Second, study the industry in which you are working or wish to work. What trends are taking place in that industry? What trends are expected to occur in that industry in the future? Given the known and expected trends, what entrepreneurial opportunities might surface for your firm (or others) to pursue? What skills will you need to help a firm pursue those opportunities? In light of the entrepreneurial opportunities that you believe may surface and the skills you'll need to help firms pursue them, what can you do now to begin developing the skills you'll need in the future? Following these recommended actions across time will increase the probability that you'll have a successful, satisfying career framed around the newness that innovation brings to light.

CEOs need to have some of the key skills associated with entrepreneurship, such as willingness to change and an ability to clearly articulate a long-term vision. That being said, pure entrepreneurs are somewhat of a different breed, as they often find the confines of corporate hierarchies constraining. The last tool of this book is a way to quickly assess whether you would be better suited as a corporate CEO or an entrepreneur.

The Entrepreneurial Mindset Checklist

1. Do I generally enjoy taking chances?	Yes/No
2. Am I more comfortable with an established infrastructure?	Yes/No
3. Do I generally accept the state of situations, rather than try to change them?	Yes/No
4. Do I think that I would prefer a guaranteed base pay over commission?	Yes/No
5. Am I comfortable in situations of high ambiguity?	Yes/No
6. Am I creative?	Yes/No
7. Do I generally rely on the opinions of others to guide my actions?	Yes/No
8. Have I ever brainstormed very carefully about an unmet business need?	Yes/No
9. Do I generally have problems articulating my ideas to others?	Yes/No
10. Do I occasionally have difficulty fitting in, when others all seem comfortable?	Yes/No

Watch the *October Sky* scenes after you have studied the discussion of innovation and strategic entrepreneurship in this chapter. You also can view the scene again as a way of studying this chapter's material.

The film tells the true story of Homer Hickam's (Jake Gyllenhaal) rise from a West Virginia coal-mining town to becoming a NASA engineer. Homer and his friends experiment with building small rockets as a way of winning college scholarships and getting out of working in the coal mines. Hickam's *Rocket Boys* memoir was the basis of the screenplay. This film is an enjoyable, uplifting story of building a better future for yourself.

The scenes are an edited composite of parts of the "Rocket Roulette" and "Splitting the Sky" sequences that appear a third of the way into the film. Although Homer and his friends are not developing a new product for sale, the process they use to develop their rocket has many characteristics of innovation described in this chapter.

What to Watch for and Ask Yourself
1. What aspects of innovation discussed in this chapter appear in these scenes? Does the process Homer and his friends use have the characteristics of "creative destruction" discussed earlier? Why or why not?
2. Is Homer Hickam behaving like an entrepreneur as described earlier in this chapter?
3. Do the scenes show internal innovation or innovating by cooperating? Refer to the earlier discussion in this chapter for details.

Mini-Case

Again Acquiring to Innovate: Is This a Good Thing?

Hammerhead Systems is a startup venture producing gear that moves telecommunications companies' data services to the Internet. Joe Sigrist, CEO of Hammerhead, has noted: "The big guys are realizing they have gaps in their product portfolios—and they're willing to take whatever action necessary to fill them." Sigrist's comment suggests that many large telecommunication firms are acquiring other companies to plug holes in their product lines with innovative new goods and services and to gain access to the innovative capabilities of the acquired firms.

Some analysts believe that it is fair to say in hindsight that the heady days of the tech boom in the 1990s were when a number of companies making equipment for the telecommunications industry, such as Lucent Technologies, Nortel Networks, and Cisco Systems, often spent large sums of money to buy what were actually "dreams." Indeed, a fair number of the companies acquired during this time did not actually possess proven market-based technologies.

But things appeared different in mid-2004. Although acquisitions during the first half of the year (some $6.5 billion) almost equaled the total value of acquisitions in the telecommunications industry in all of 2003 ($7.4 billion), industry analysts viewed most of these acquisitions as "strategic deals" in which large firms were acquiring smaller companies to "get their hands on the technology they needed to roll out the next generation of telecom services." These next-generation services ranged from Internet-based telephony to digital televisions. Examples of favorably viewed acquisitions from the first half of 2004 include Ciena Corporation's purchase of Catera Networks and Internet Photonics, Tellabs' announced $1.9 billion acquisition of Advanced Fiber Communications (AFC), and Lucent's $300 million purchase of software maker Telica. Ciena's acquisitions were intended to accelerate the firm's expansion beyond optical infrastructure products. Tellabs had extended an offer to buy AFC as its basis for moving into the broadband gear market. Lucent purchased Telica primarily to gain access to the firm's innovative capabilities to produce voice over Internet protocol (VOIP) communications systems for next-generation networks.

What created a situation in which the large telecommunications industry equipment makers need to acquire innovation? Reductions in allocations to R&D budgets are a major culprit. Between 2000 and 2004, for example, Lucent's R&D budget dropped 60 percent, Ericsson's fell 55 percent, and Nortel's declined by 45 percent. Perhaps unwisely, these large firms reduced their R&D allocations in order to cut their costs during lean years. Of course, the net result of these declines is that the companies weren't developing innovative products and worse, they were losing their innovative capabilities. In contrast, during the same period, "startups felt they had no choice but to innovate." Therefore,

the stage was set for large companies that lacked internally developed product innovations and had lost part of their innovative abilities to acquire startup ventures and smaller firms with innovative products and innovative capabilities.

Will these acquisitions turn out to be profit-generating transactions? Although it is too early to answer this question, it seems that "The startups being acquired now have real technology to offer—and buyers have real needs, not just blue-sky visions." On the other hand, Lucent paid roughly eight times Telica's earnings to acquire that firm, which is about twice the premium paid in most deals. Paying high premiums for acquired firms makes it more difficult to earn a profit on the transaction. It will be interesting to see over the next several years whether the transactions described in this Mini-Case increase the profitability of the firms acquiring smaller technology companies as a source of innovation.

SOURCES: S. Tully, 2005, The urge to merge, *Fortune,* February 21, 21 & 26; P. Burrows, 2004, Networking titans buy the future, *Business Week,* July 5: 80; 2004, Ciena company history, Ciena Home Page, http://www.ciena.com, July 7; 2004, Lucent Technologies to acquire Telica, Lucent Technologies Home Page, http://www.lucent.com, July 7; 2004, FTC grants early termination of waiting period for Tellabs proposed merger with AFC, Tellabs Home Page, http://www.tellabs.com, July 7.

Questions

1. Using materials in this chapter, do you think it is wise for the larger manufacturers of telecommunications equipment to be acquiring companies? Why or why not?
2. Search the Web sites of Ciena, Lucent, and Tellabs to identify what has happened with the acquisitions mentioned for each company. What does your search suggest about the acquisitions? Do they appear to have been successful? Why or why not?

EXPERIENTIAL EXERCISES

EXERCISE ONE: INSIDE HOT 100 COMPANIES

Chapter 10 mentioned the *Business Week* "Hot 100" list of growth companies. Some of these companies are new, and they are still primarily growing with the firm's original hot product. Others, however, have been around for some time but have successfully developed new goods or services or modified their original hot good or service to enable them to continue to grow.

For this exercise, team up with a partner or two. Each team should investigate one of the following firms to learn how it has earned the title of a hot growth company. Specifically, look for the ways the firm has created an entrepreneurial environment and identify the type of internal innovation approaches it takes.

When each team returns with its information, the class should be able to fill in the following chart.

Firm	What Are the Firm's Innovations or Inventions That Make it "Hot"?	Does the Firm Use Internal Innovation Processes?	Does the Firm Use Strategic Alliances or Joint Ventures?	Does the Firm Engage in Acquisitions to Gain Access to Innovative Capabilities?
Coach				
K-Swiss				
Shuffle Master				
Champs Entertainment				
Urban Outfitters				
Applebee's International				
J. M. Smucker				
Fossil				
Finish Line				
Cheesecake Factory				

Source: Firms listed in *Business Week*, June 7, 2004.

EXERCISE TWO: CORPORATE ENTREPRENEURSHIP THROUGH VENTURING

In this exercise, you will need access to the Internet. First, visit the following Web sites and explore the organizations that have developed them.

- http://www.dow.com/venture
- http://www.motorola.com/ventures
- http://www.intel.com/capital

Second, evaluate the approach to corporate entrepreneurship you have found here. Consider why these firms do not spend the money inside their firm trying to develop strategic entrepreneurship capabilities. Clearly, these are innovative firms, as the story about Intel in this chapter indicates. What entrepreneurial opportunities and benefits might be available through the addition of corporate entrepreneurship to a firm's strategic efforts to enter or create new markets?

CASE STUDIES

Contents

Preparing an Effective Case Analysis

What to Expect from In-Class Case Discussions

As you will learn, classroom discussions of cases differ significantly from lectures. The case method calls for your instructor to guide the discussion and to solicit alternative views as a way of encouraging your active participation when analyzing a case. When alternative views are not forthcoming, your instructor might take a position just to challenge you and your peers to respond thoughtfully as a way of generating additional alternatives. Instructors will often evaluate your work in terms of both the quantity and the quality of your contributions to in-class case discussions. The in-class discussions are important in that you can derive significant benefit from having your ideas and recommendations examined against those of your peers and from responding to challenges by other class members and/or the instructor.

During case discussions, your instructor will likely listen, question, and probe to extend the analysis of case issues. In the course of these actions, your peers and/or your instructor may challenge an individual's views and the validity of alternative perspectives that have been expressed. These challenges are offered in a constructive manner; their intent is to help all who are analyzing a case develop their analytical and communication skills. Commonly, instructors will encourage you and your peers to be innovative and original when developing and presenting ideas. Over the course of an individual discussion, you are likely to develop a more complex view of the case as a result of listening to and thinking about the diverse inputs offered by your peers and instructor. Among other benefits, experience with multiple case discussions will increase your knowledge of the advantages and disadvantages of group decision-making processes.

Both your peers and your instructor will value comments that help identify problems and solutions. To offer relevant contributions, you are encouraged to use independent thought and, through discussions with your peers outside class, to refine your thinking. We also encourage you to avoid using phrases such as "I think," "I believe," and "I feel" when analyzing a case. Instead, consider using a less emotion-laden phrase, such as "My analysis shows. . . ." This highlights the logical nature of the approach you have taken to analyze the case. When preparing for an in-class case discussion, plan to use the case data to explain your assessment of the situation. Assume that your peers and instructor are familiar with the basic facts of the case. In addition, it is good practice to prepare notes regarding your analysis of case facts before class discussions and use them when explaining your perspectives. Effective notes signal to classmates and the instructor that you are prepared to discuss the case thoroughly. Moreover, thorough notes eliminate the need for you to memorize the facts and figures needed to successfully discuss a case.

The case analysis process described here will help prepare you to effectively discuss a case during class meetings. Using this process helps you consider the issues required to identify a focal firm's problems and to propose strategic actions through which the firm can improve its competitiveness. In some instances, your instructor may ask you to prepare an oral or written analysis of a particular case. Typically, such an assignment demands even more thorough study and analysis of the case contents. At your instructor's discretion, oral and written analyses may be completed by individuals or by groups of three or more people. The information and insights gained through completing the six steps shown in Table 1 are often valuable when developing an oral or written analysis. However, when preparing an oral or written presentation, you must consider the overall framework in which your information and inputs will be presented. Such a framework is the focus of the next section.

Preparing an Oral or Written Case Presentation

Experience shows that two types of thinking (analysis and synthesis) are necessary to develop an effec-tive oral or written presentation (see Exhibit 1). In the analysis stage, you should first analyze the gen-eral external environmental issues affecting the firm. Next, your environmental analysis should focus on the particular industry or industries in which a firm operates. Finally, you should examine companies against which the focal firm competes. By studying the three levels of the external environment (general, industry, and competitor), you will be able to iden-tify a firm's opportunities and threats. Following the external environmental analysis is the analysis of

TABLE 1	An Effective Case Analysis Process
Step 1: *Gaining Familiarity*	a. In general—determine who, what, how, where, and when (the critical facts of the case). b. In detail—identify the places, persons, activities, and contexts of the situation. c. Recognize the degree of certainty/uncertainty of acquired information.
Step 2: *Recognizing Symptoms*	a. List all indicators (including stated "problems") that something is not as expected or as desired. b. Ensure that symptoms are not assumed to be the problem (symptoms should lead to identification of the problem).
Step 3: *Identifying Goals*	a. Identify critical statements by major parties (for example, people, groups, the work unit, and so on). b. List all goals of the major parties that exist or can be reasonably inferred.
Step 4: *Conducting the Analysis*	a. Decide which ideas, models, and theories seem useful. b. Apply these conceptual tools to the situation. c. As new information is revealed, cycle back to substeps a and b.
Step 5: *Making the Diagnosis*	a. Identify predicaments (goal inconsistencies). b. Identify problems (discrepancies between goals and performance). c. Prioritize predicaments/problems regarding timing, importance, and so on.
Step 6: *Doing the Action Planning*	a. Specify and prioritize the criteria used to choose action alternatives. b. Discover or invent feasible action alternatives. c. Examine the probable consequences of action alternatives. d. Select a course of action. e. Design an implementation plan/schedule. f. Create a plan for assessing the action to be implemented.

C. C. Lundberg and C. Enz, 1993, A framework for student case preparation, *Case Research Journal*, 13 (Summer): 144. Reprinted by permission of NACRA, North American Case Research Association.

EXHIBIT 1

Types of Thinking in Case Preparation: Analysis and Synthesis

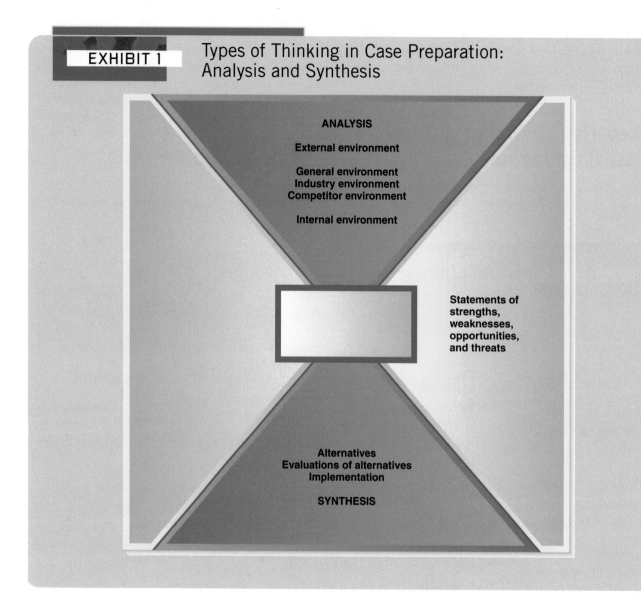

ANALYSIS

External environment

General environment
Industry environment
Competitor environment

Internal environment

Statements of strengths, weaknesses, opportunities, and threats

Alternatives
Evaluations of alternatives
Implementation

SYNTHESIS

the firm's internal environment, which identifies the firm's strengths and weaknesses.

As noted in Exhibit 1, you must then change the focus from analysis to synthesis. Specifically, you must synthesize information gained from your analysis of the firm's internal and external environments. Synthesizing information enables you to generate alternatives that can resolve the problems or challenges facing the focal firm. Once you identify a best alternative from an evaluation based on predetermined criteria and goals, you must explore implementation actions.

Table 2 outlines the sections that should be included in either an oral or a written presentation: introduction (strategic profile and purpose), situation analysis, statements of strengths/weaknesses and opportunities/threats, strategy formulation, and implementation. These sections are described in the following discussion. Familiarity with the contents of your book's ten chapters is helpful because the general outline for an oral or a written presentation shown in Table 2 is based on an understanding of the strategic management process detailed in those chapters. We follow the discussions of the parts of Table 2 with a few comments about the "process" to use to present the results of your case analysis in either an oral or written format.

TABLE 2   General Outline for an Oral or Written Presentation

I. Strategic Profile and Case Analysis Purpose
II. Situation Analysis
- A. General environmental analysis
- B. Industry analysis
- C. Competitor analysis
- D. Internal analysis

III. Identification of Environmental Opportunities and Threats and Firm Strengths and Weaknesses (SWOT Analysis)

IV. Strategy Formulation
- A. Strategic alternatives
- B. Alternative evaluation
- C. Alternative choice

V. Strategic Alternative Implementation
- A. Action items
- B. Action plan

Strategic Profile and Case Analysis Purpose

The strategic profile should briefly present the critical facts from the case that have affected the focal firm's historical strategic direction and performance. The case facts should not be restated in the profile; rather, these comments should show how the critical facts lead to a particular focus for your analysis. This primary focus should be emphasized in this section's conclusion. In addition, this section should state important assumptions about case facts on which your analyses may be based.

Situation Analysis

As shown in Table 2, a general starting place for completing a situation analysis is the general environment.

General Environmental Analysis

Your analysis of the general environment should focus on trends in the six segments of the general environment (see Table 3). Many of the segment issues shown in Table 3 for the six segments are explained more fully in Chapter 3 of your book. The objective you should have in evaluating these trends

is to be able to *predict* the segments that you expect to have the most significant influence on your focal firm over the next several years (say three to five years) and to explain your reasoning for your predictions.

Industry Analysis

Porter's five-forces model is a useful tool for analyzing the industry or industries in which your firm competes. We explain how to use this tool in Chapter 3. In this part of your analysis, you want to determine the attractiveness of the industry or industries in which the focal firm is competing. As attractiveness increases, so does the possibility that your focal firm will be able to earn profits by using its chosen strategies. After evaluating the power of the five forces relative to your focal firm, you should evaluate *how* attractive the industry is in which your focal firm is competing.

Competitor Analysis

Firms also need to analyze each of their primary competitors. This analysis should identify competitors' current strategies, strategic intent, strategic mission, capabilities, core competencies, and a competitive response profile. We explain these items in

TABLE 3	Sample General Environmental Categories

Technological Trends	• Information technology continues to become cheaper with more practical applications. • Database technology enables organization of complex data and distribution of information. • Telecommunications technology and networks increasingly provide fast transmission of all sources of data, including voice, written communications, and video information. • Computerized design and manufacturing technologies continue to facilitate quality and flexibility.
Demographic Trends	• Regional changes in population due to migration • Changing ethnic composition of the population • Aging of the population • Aging of the "baby boom" generation
Economic Trends	• Interest rates • Inflation rates • Savings rates • Trade deficits • Budget deficits • Exchange rates
Political/Legal Trends	• Antitrust enforcement • Tax policy changes • Environmental protection laws • Extent of regulation/deregulation • Privatizing state monopolies • State-owned industries
Sociocultural Trends	• Women in the workforce • Awareness of health and fitness issues • Concern for the environment • Concern for customers
Global Trends	• Currency exchange rates • Free-trade agreements • Trade deficits

Chapter 3. This information is useful to the focal firm in formulating an appropriate strategy and in predicting competitors' probable responses. Sources that can be used to gather information about an industry and companies with whom the focal firm competes are listed in Appendix I. Included in this list is a wide range of publications, such as periodicals, newspapers, bibliographies, directories of companies, industry ratios, forecasts, rankings/ratings, and other valuable statistics.

Internal Analysis

Assessing a firm's strengths and weaknesses through a value-chain analysis facilitates moving from the external environment to the internal environment. Analyzing the primary and support activities of the value chain will help you understand how external environmental trends affect the specific activities of a firm. Such analysis helps highlight strengths and weaknesses (see Chapter 4 for an explanation and use of the value chain).

For purposes of preparing an oral or a written presentation, it is important to note that strengths are internal resources and capabilities that have the potential to be core competencies. Weaknesses, on the other hand, are internal resources and capabilities that have the potential to place a firm at a competitive disadvantage relative to its rivals. Therefore, some of a firm's resources and capabilities are strengths; others are weaknesses.

When you evaluate the internal characteristics of the firm, your analysis of the functional activities emphasized is critical. For instance, if the strategy of the firm is primarily technology-driven, it is important to evaluate the firm's R&D activities. If the strategy is market-driven, marketing activities are of paramount importance. If a firm has financial difficulties, critical financial ratios would require careful evaluation. In fact, because of the importance of financial health, most cases require financial analyses. Appendix II lists and operationally defines several common financial ratios. Included are tables describing profitability, liquidity, leverage, activity, and shareholders' return ratios. Leadership, organizational culture, structure, and control systems are other characteristics of firms you should examine to fully understand the "internal" part of your firm.

Identification of Environmental Opportunities and Threats and Firm Strengths and Weaknesses (SWOT Analysis)

The outcome of the situation analysis is the identification of a firm's strengths and weaknesses and its environmental threats and opportunities. The next step requires that you analyze the strengths and weaknesses and the opportunities and threats for configurations that benefit or do not benefit your firm's efforts to perform well. Case analysts, and organizational strategists as well, seek to match a firm's strengths with its external environmental opportunities. In addition, strengths are chosen to prevent any serious environmental threat from negatively affecting the firm's performance. The key objective of conducting a SWOT analysis is to determine how to position the firm so it can take advantage of opportunities, while simultaneously avoiding or minimizing environmental threats. Results from a SWOT analysis yield valuable insights into the selection of a firm's strategies. The analysis of a case should not be overemphasized relative to the synthesis of results gained from your analytical efforts. You may be tempted to emphasize the results from the analysis in your oral or written case analysis. It is important, however, that you make an equal effort to develop and evaluate alternatives and to design implementation of the chosen strategy.

Strategy Formulation— Strategic Alternatives, Alternative Evaluation, and Alternative Choice

Developing alternatives is often one of the most difficult steps in preparing an oral or written presentation. Development of three to four alternative strategies is common (see Chapter 5 for business-level strategy alternatives and Chapter 6 for corporate-level strategy alternatives). Each alternative should be feasible (it should match the firm's strengths, capabilities, and especially core competencies), and feasibility should be demonstrated. In addition, you should show how each alternative takes advantage of environmental opportunities or protects against environmental threats. Developing carefully thought-out alternatives requires synthesis of your analyses' results and creates greater credibility in oral and written case presentations.

Once you develop strong alternatives, you must evaluate the set to choose the best one. Your choice should be defensible and provide benefits over the other alternatives. Therefore, it is important that both alternative development and evaluation of alternatives are thorough. You should explain and defend your choice of the best alternative.

Strategic Alternative Implementation—Action Items and Action Plan

After selecting the most appropriate strategy (the one most likely to help your firm earn profits), you must turn your attention to implementation-related issues. Effective synthesis is important to ensure that you have considered and evaluated all critical implementation issues. Issues you might consider include the structural changes necessary to implement the new strategy. In addition, leadership changes and new controls or incentives may be necessary to implement strategic actions. The implementation actions you recommend should be explicit and thoroughly explained. Occasionally, careful evaluation of implementation actions may show the strategy to be less favorable than you thought originally. A strategy is only as good as the firm's ability to implement it.

Process Issues

You should ensure that your presentation (either oral or written) is logical and consistent through-out. For example, if your presentation identifies one purpose, but your analysis focuses on issues that differ from the stated purpose, the logical inconsistency will be apparent. Likewise, your alternatives should flow from the configuration of strengths, weaknesses, opportunities, and threats you identified by analyzing your firm's external and internal environments.

Thoroughness and clarity also are critical to an effective presentation. Thoroughness is represented by the comprehensiveness of the analysis and alternative generation. Furthermore, clarity in the results of the analyses, selection of the best alternative strategy, and design of implementation actions are important. For example, your statement of the strengths and weaknesses should flow clearly and logically from your analysis of your firm's internal environment.

Presentations (oral or written) that show logical consistency, thoroughness, clarity of purpose, effective analyses, and feasible recommendations (strategy and implementation) are more effective and are likely to be more positively received by your instructor and peers. Furthermore, developing the skills necessary to make such presentations will enhance your future job performance and career success.

APPENDIX I: Sources for Industry and Competitor Analyses

Abstracts and Indexes

Periodicals

ABI/*Inform*
Business Periodicals Index
EBSCO Business Source Premier
InfoTrac Custom Journals
InfoTrac Custom Newspapers
InfoTrac OneFile
Lexis/Nexis Academic
Public Affairs Information Service Bulletin (PAIS)
Readers' Guide to Periodical Literature

Newspapers

NewsBank—Foreign Broadcast Information
NewsBank—Global NewsBank
New York Times Index
Wall Street Journal/Barron's Index
Wall Street Journal Index
Washington Post Index

Bibliographies

Encyclopedia of Business Information Sources

Directories

Companies—General

America's Corporate Families and International Affiliates
D&B Million Dollar Database (http://www.dnbmdd.com)
Hoover's Online: The Business Network (http://www.hoovers.com/free)
Standard & Poor's Corporation Records
Standard & Poor's Register of Corporations, Directors & Executives (http://www.netadvantage.standardandpoors.com)
Ward's Business Directory of Largest U.S. Companies

Companies—International

America's Corporate Families and International Affiliates
Business Asia
Business China
Business Eastern Europe
Business Europe
Business International
Business International Money Report
Business Latin America
Directory of American Firms Operating in Foreign Countries
Directory of Foreign Firms Operating in the United States

Hoover's Handbook of World Business
International Directory of Company Histories
Mergent International Manual
Mergent Online (http://www.fisonline.com)
Who Owns Whom

Companies—Manufacturers

Thomas Register of American Manufacturers
U.S. Manufacturer's Directory, Manufacturing & Distribution, USA
U.S. Office of Management and Budget, Executive Office of the President, *Standard Industrial Classification Manual*

Companies—Private

D&B Million Dollar Database (http://www.dnbmdd.com)
Ward's Business Directory of Largest U.S. Companies

Companies—Public

Annual reports and 10-K reports
Disclosure (corporate reports)
Mergent's Manuals:
    Mergent's Bank and Finance Manual
    Mergent's Industrial Manual
    Mergent's International Manual
    Mergent's Municipal and Government Manual
    Mergent's OTC Industrial Manual
    Mergent's OTC Unlisted Manual
    Mergent's Public Utility Manual
    Mergent's Transportation Manual
Standard & Poor's Corporation, *Standard Corporation Descriptions* (http://www.netadvantage.standardandpoors.com)
    Standard & Poor's Analyst's Handbook
    Standard & Poor's Industry Surveys
    Standard & Poor's Statistical Service
Q-File

Companies—Subsidiaries and Affiliates

America's Corporate Families and International Affiliates
Mergent's Industry Review
Standard & Poor's Analyst's Handbook
Standard & Poor's Industry Surveys (2 volumes)
U.S. Department of Commerce, *U.S. Industrial Outlook*
Who Owns Whom

Industry Ratios

Dun & Bradstreet, *Industry Norms and Key Business Ratios*
RMA's Annual Statement Studies
Troy Almanac of Business and Industrial Financial Ratios

Industry Forecasts

International Trade Administration, *U.S. Industry & Trade Outlook*

Rankings and Ratings

Annual Report on American Industry in *Forbes*
Business Rankings Annual
Mergent's Industry Review (http://www.worldcatlibraries.org)
Standard & Poor's Industry Report Service
    (http://www.netadvantage.standardandpoors.com)
Value Line Investment Survey
Ward's Business Directory of Largest U.S. Companies

Statistics

Bureau of the Census, U.S. Department of Commerce, *American Statistics Index* (ASI)
Bureau of the Census, U.S. Department of Commerce, *Economic Census* publications
Bureau of the Census, U.S. Department of Commerce, *Statistical Abstract of the United States*
Bureau of Economic Analysis, U.S. Department of Commerce, *Survey of Current Business*
Internal Revenue Service, U.S. Department of the Treasury, *Statistics of Income: Corporation Income Tax Returns*
Statistical Reference Index (SRI)

APPENDIX II: Financial Analysis in Case Studies

TABLE A-1   Profitability Ratios

Ratio	Formula	What It Shows
1. Return on total assets	$$\frac{\text{Profits after taxes}}{\text{Total assets}}$$ or $$\frac{\text{Profits after taxes + Interest}}{\text{Total assets}}$$	The net return on total investments of the firm or The return on both creditors' and shareholders' investments
2. Return on stockholder's equity (or return on net worth)	$$\frac{\text{Profits after taxes}}{\text{Total stockholder's equity}}$$	How profitably the company is utilizing shareholders' funds
3. Return on common equity	$$\frac{\text{Profits after taxes – Preferred stock dividends}}{\text{Total stockholder's equity – Par value of preferred stock}}$$	The net return to common stockholders
4. Operating profit margin (or return on sales)	$$\frac{\text{Profits before taxes and before interest}}{\text{Sales}}$$	The firm's profitability from regular operations
5. Net profit margin (or net return on sales)	$$\frac{\text{Profits after taxes}}{\text{Sales}}$$	The firm's net profit as a percentage of total sales

TABLE A-2   Liquidity Ratios

Ratio	Formula	What It Shows
1. Current ratio	$$\frac{\text{Current assets}}{\text{Current liabilities}}$$	The firm's ability to meet its current financial liabilities
2. Quick ratio (or acid-test ratio)	$$\frac{\text{Current assets – Inventory}}{\text{Current liabilities}}$$	The firm's ability to pay off short-term obligations without relying on sales of inventory
3. Inventory to net working capital	$$\frac{\text{Inventory}}{\text{Current assets – Current liabilities}}$$	The extent to which the firm's working capital is tied up in inventory

TABLE A-3   Leverage Ratios

Ratio	Formula	What It Shows
1. Debt-to-assets	$\dfrac{\text{Total debt}}{\text{Total assets}}$	Total borrowed funds as a percentage of total assets
2. Debt-to-equity	$\dfrac{\text{Total debt}}{\text{Total shareholders' equity}}$	Borrowed funds versus the funds provided by shareholders
3. Long-term debt-to-equity	$\dfrac{\text{Long-term debt}}{\text{Total shareholders' equity}}$	Leverage used by the firm
4. Times-interest-earned (or coverage ratio)	$\dfrac{\text{Profits before interest and taxes}}{\text{Total interest charges}}$	The firm's ability to meet all interest payments
5. Fixed charge coverage	$\dfrac{\text{Profits before taxes and interest} + \text{Lease obligations}}{\text{Total interest charges} + \text{Lease obligations}}$	The firm's ability to meet all fixed-charge obligations including lease payments

TABLE A-4   Activity Ratios

Ratio	Formula	What It Shows
1. Inventory turnover	$\dfrac{\text{Sales}}{\text{Inventory of finished goods}}$	The effectiveness of the firm in employing inventory
2. Fixed-assets turnover	$\dfrac{\text{Sales}}{\text{Fixed assets}}$	The effectiveness of the firm in utilizing plant and equipment
3. Total assets turnover	$\dfrac{\text{Sales}}{\text{Total assets}}$	The effectiveness of the firm in utilizing total assets
4. Accounts receivable turnover	$\dfrac{\text{Annual credit sales}}{\text{Accounts receivable}}$	How many times the total receivables has been collected during the accounting period
5. Average collecting period	$\dfrac{\text{Accounts receivable}}{\text{Average daily sales}}$	The average length of time the firm waits to collect payment after sales

TABLE A-5 — Shareholders' Return Ratios

Ratio	Formula	What It Shows
1. Dividend yield on common stock	$$\frac{\text{Annual dividend per share}}{\text{Current market price per share}}$$	A measure of return to common stockholders in the form of dividends
2. Price-earnings ratio	$$\frac{\text{Current market price per share}}{\text{After-tax earnings per share}}$$	An indication of market perception of the firm; usually, the faster-growing or less risky firms tend to have higher PE ratios than the slower-growing or more risky firms
3. Dividend payout ratio	$$\frac{\text{Annual dividends per share}}{\text{After-tax earnings per share}}$$	An indication of dividends paid out as a percentage of profits
4. Cash flow per share	$$\frac{\text{After-tax profits + Depression}}{\text{Number of common shares outstanding}}$$	A measure of total cash per share available for use by the firm

Notes

1. C. Christensen, 1989, *Teaching and the Case Method,* Boston: Harvard Business School Publishing Division; C. C. Lundberg, 1993, Introduction to the case method, in C. M. Vance (ed.), *Mastering Management Education,* Newbury Park, Calif.: Sage.
2. C. C. Lundberg and C. Enz, 1993, A framework for student case preparation, *Case Research Journal* 13 (Summer): 133.
3. J. Soltis, 1971, John Dewey, in L. E. Deighton (ed.), *Encyclopedia of Education,* New York: Macmillan and Free Press.

The ABL Goes One-on-One with the WNBA

Matthew A. Rutherford
James Madison University

Ann K. Buchholtz
University of Georgia

On the morning of June 23, 1997, Gary Cavalli wasn't sure how he should be feeling. As CEO of the American Basketball League (ABL), he had watched with interest two days earlier when the Women's National Basketball Association (WNBA) began play. Cavalli wasn't sure if he was witnessing the emergence of a new and powerful competitor, or if he was watching the opening games of an ally that would help to promote the sport of women's basketball. One thing was certain: the ABL's business environment was changing rapidly. Cavalli was certain that he must take some type of strategic action to ensure the success of his business.

Although Cavalli knew that immediate action was necessary, he was less sure what that action should be. Should he dig in his heels and fight for the future of his newly formed league? Should he seek to merge or develop a strategic alliance with this new and very powerful competitor? Gary Cavalli had some important decisions to make.

History

In September 1995, a significant transformation occurred in the world of women's sports—the formation of the American Basketball League. This announcement broke new ground in many ways. First, the nation's top female athletes now had an opportunity to play basketball professionally. More important, these players would all be competing in the same league. Traditionally, women players were scattered throughout professional leagues around the world. Gary Cavalli and the rest of the league's founders shared a common vision: "creating a successful league that focuses attention on women as professional athletes and positive role models."[1]

While Gary Cavalli had high hopes for his league, a number of question marks remained. No one knew if a women's professional basketball league could be financially successful in the United States. Was there enough fan interest in the sport of women's basketball

By Matthew A. Rutherford, James Madison University, and Ann K. Buchholtz, Terry College of Business, The University of Georgia. The authors thank Gary Cavalli, Jamelle Elliott, Andy Landers, and three anonymous reviewers for their helpful comments and suggestions. This case is intended as a basis for class discussion rather than to illustrate either effective or ineffective handling of an administrative situation. All individuals and events in the case are real.

to support a full-time league? While several factors appeared to be in the ABL's favor, much work remained to be done.

By the summer of 1996, public interest in women's basketball had reached an all-time high. The women's college game continued to grow in popularity, as ticket sales soared and television exposure expanded. The 1996 Women's NCAA Championship game between Georgia and Tennessee drew the network's second highest television rating for any college basketball game, men's or women's, since 1993. During the 1996 Olympic Games, the United States women's basketball team won the gold medal and impressed many fans with the members' level of play. Both of these developments contributed to the decision by the ABL to start a professional basketball league for women.

The ABL was not the first women's professional basketball league. Between 1976 and 1991, no fewer than six different professional leagues for women's basketball were initiated in North America. While some of these leagues, such as the National Women's Basketball League and the Continental Basketball Association, folded before a single game was played, others allowed women to briefly play professionally in the United States. The most enduring league, the Women's Professional Basketball League, lasted for three seasons before going out of business. Of the eight teams in this league, the most prosperous lost $718,000 during its three years of operation. They lacked capital, failed at marketing, and were unable to design sufficient management controls. As a result of their failure, women who wanted to play professional basketball could only play in the numerous leagues for women that existed in Europe, Asia, the Middle East, and South America. While the quality and pay of these leagues varied greatly, the top professional players in the best leagues were able to sign six-figure deals.

Women's basketball has only recently begun to be considered a serious sport. With the exception of a few early trailblazers like the 1936 "All-American Redheads" who used men's rules and competed against men, most women's basketball teams played a watered-down version of the game. Full-court play was not allowed until 1971, the same year that the 30-second shot clock was instituted. It took 16 more years, until 1987, to have the 3-point field

goal become part of the women's game. As recently as 1991, when the Liberty Basketball Association was formed, women's professional basketball meant lowered baskets, shorter courts, and "unitards" (the LBA folded after one game).

Title IX of the Educational Amendment of 1972 prohibits gender discrimination in high school and college athletics. It has prompted a dramatic increase in the number of females participating in sports. In 1970, 1 in 27 high school girls played a varsity sport; but in 1996, the number was closer to 1 in 3. By the end of the 1990s, more than a half million girls were playing high school basketball. This has led to a higher caliber of player as well as an increase in the public's enthusiasm.

Along with Title IX, a general growth in the public's appetite for televised sporting events fueled the movement for women's professional basketball. By 1996, at least 20 networks carried some sports programming. Many of these networks were targeted at a specific audience, such as the Women's Sports and Entertainment Network (WSEN), which was introduced on December 31, 1994. The public's heightened interest in sports in general led to the creation of a number of new professional leagues, including beach volleyball, women's fast-pitch softball, and men's and women's soccer. Sports fans' insatiable appetite attracted more corporate sponsors and advertisers than ever before, providing the league offices with the necessary capital to begin and maintain a league. For a sample listing of networks carrying sports programming, please refer to Exhibit 1.

The American Basketball League

The ABL consisted of eight teams, all of which were centrally owned by the league. They played their inaugural season from October 1996 through March 1997, the traditional time of year for a basketball league.

Founders

Three entrepreneurs who shared a common interest in women's athletics founded the American Basketball League (ABL) in 1995. Gary Cavalli, Anne

EXHIBIT 1 — Sampling of Networks Carrying Sports Programming

	ABL	WNBA	NBA	Women's College	Men's College
ABC					*
CBS				*	*
NBC		*	*	*	*
FOX					
ESPN		*		*	*
ESPN2		*		*	*
BET	*				
Lifetime		*			
TNT			*		
TBS			*		
SportsChannel	*				
Home Team Sports				*	*
SportSouth				*	*
WGN			*	*	*

Cribbs, and Steve Hams each possessed experience in both sports and business. In addition to their expertise, each founding member shared a common devotion to the game of women's basketball. Mr. Cavalli, who spent eight years as an Associate Athletic Director and Sports Information Director at Stanford University, served as CEO of the ABL. He had been involved in the promotion, production, and management of sports-related events for over 20 years. He also had served in a number of executive positions with several firms, and founded Cavalli and Cribbs, an advertising, public relations, and event management firm.

The Teams

Each ABL team was located in an area known to be supportive of women's basketball, typically this support was derived from the proximity of a highly successful college program. The eight teams were:

Atlanta Glory—Georgia
Colorado Xplosion—Colorado
Columbus Quest—Ohio
New England Blizzard—Connecticut
Portland Power—Oregon
Richmond Rage—Virginia
San Jose Lasers—California
Seattle Reign—Washington

For a graphical representation of the location of ABL teams, please refer to Exhibit 2.

During the ABL's inaugural season, each team consisted of ten players. An effort was made to place popular players where their fan support was strongest. For example, three-time Ohio State All-American Katie Smith was placed with the Columbus Quest, former University of Connecticut star Jennifer Rizzotti was placed with the New England Blizzard, and former University of Georgia star Teresa Edwards was placed with the Atlanta Glory. During the first year, the teams were restricted to having only one foreign player on their rosters. Each of the eight ABL teams played 40 games during the regular season, with the best four teams advancing to the playoffs.

The Players

Eight of the twelve members of the 1996 U.S. Olympic women's basketball team and many of the best recent college graduates played in the ABL.

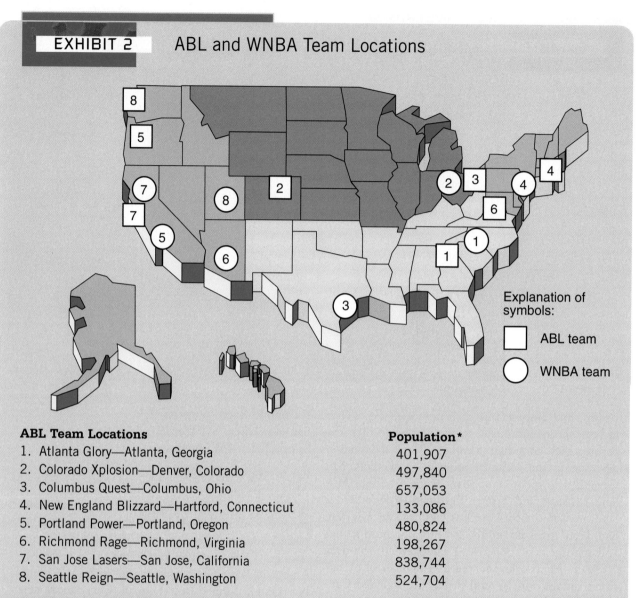

EXHIBIT 2   ABL and WNBA Team Locations

Explanation of symbols:

☐ ABL team

◯ WNBA team

ABL Team Locations	**Population***
1. Atlanta Glory—Atlanta, Georgia	401,907
2. Colorado Xplosion—Denver, Colorado	497,840
3. Columbus Quest—Columbus, Ohio	657,053
4. New England Blizzard—Hartford, Connecticut	133,086
5. Portland Power—Portland, Oregon	480,824
6. Richmond Rage—Richmond, Virginia	198,267
7. San Jose Lasers—San Jose, California	838,744
8. Seattle Reign—Seattle, Washington	524,704

WNBA Team Locations	**Population**
1. Charlotte Sting—Charlotte, North Carolina	441,297
2. Cleveland Rockers—Cleveland, Ohio	498,246
3. Houston Comets—Houston, Texas	1,744,058
4. New York Liberty—New York, New York	7,380,906
5. Los Angeles Sparks—Los Angeles, California	3,553,638
6. Phoenix Mercury—Phoenix, Arizona	1,159,014
7. Sacramento Monarchs—Sacramento, California	376,243
8. Utah Starzz—Salt Lake City, Utah	172,575

*1997 population. *The World Almanac and Book of Facts 1999.*

Shortly after the completion of its first season, the ABL received commitments from the 1997 Naismith Award winner, Stanford University's Kate Starbird, and the Associated Press player of the year, the University of Connecticut's Kara Wolters, for the second season.

Salaries in the ABL averaged $80,000, with a minimum of $40,000 and a maximum of $150,000. Opportunities for endorsements with major sponsors were also possible for league players. However, when players signed with the ABL they were prohibited from playing in any other professional league.

Results of the First Year

The ABL lost over four million dollars during its first year of operation. Although this loss was substantial, it was offset by the infusion of six million dollars from two corporate investors, three million from Phoenix Home Life Mutual Insurance Company, based in Hartford, Connecticut, and three million from a group of investors based in California's Silicon Valley. The two groups purchased significant amounts of equity in the ABL, with the option to buy the operating rights to the New England Blizzard and the San Jose Lasers, respectively. While the ABL continued to own the teams and be responsible for player recruitment, salary negotiations, and the development of sponsorship and broadcast agreements, the team operators handled all front office operations for their team and arranged local advertising and sponsorship contracts. The ABL planned to sell the operating rights of its teams as a major source of new capital.

The attendance projection for the ABL's first year was 3,000 people per game. The final attendance figures were almost 20 percent higher than expected, with a season average of 3,536 tickets sold per game. Tickets to all games were $10, with courtside seats costing $25 to $35.

The number of tickets sold varied by team and by time of year. The New England Blizzard averaged a league high 5,008 per game, and drew a league record 11,873 for one game. The Columbus Quest, holders of the best regular-season record and eventual league champions, drew the smallest crowds, averaging 2,682 per game. Across the league, ticket sales for opening round games were brisk; three

games were sold out, and two others had crowds in excess of 8,700. While attendance decreased during the middle of the season, ticket sales increased again for the last month of the regular season and the playoffs. As of June 1997, the ABL had already sold more season tickets for its second year of play than it had during all of the previous year. Demographic research conducted by the ABL revealed that two-thirds of those attending games were female. Fifty-eight percent of fans were between the ages of 25 and 44, 85 percent had at least a technical or associate's degree, and 51 percent made at least $45,000 per year.

The ABL's televised games appeared on either SportsChannel or Black Entertainment Television (BET). During the regular season, several games were aired on each network, with exposure increasing in the playoffs. SportsChannel carried every game of the ABL's championship series. Sponsors for the initial season were Reebok, Lady Foot Locker, Nissan, and Phoenix Home Life Insurance Company. Reebok, the founding sponsor of the ABL, outfitted four of the eight teams in the league.

The ABL planned several changes for its 1997–1998 season. First, a new team was to be added in Long Beach, California. Second, during the ABL's second season each team's roster would be expanded from 10 to 11 players. Finally, with the addition of a ninth team, the league increased the schedule to include 44 games.

A New Competitor Emerges

Seven months after the formation of the ABL, David Stern, Commissioner of the National Basketball Association (NBA), announced the creation of a second women's professional basketball league. This new league was named the Women's National Basketball Association (WNBA), and was set to begin play in June 1997. Although the NBA's decision to launch the new league was not completely unexpected, many observers questioned whether they would have attempted a league if the ABL had not existed. Whatever their motivation, the NBA's decision to enter changed the competitive landscape of the ABL dramatically.

The Women's National Basketball Association

The WNBA was backed by the National Basketball Association (NBA), which had provided men with a professional league for over 50 years. The WNBA played during the summer months, the traditional off-season for basketball.

The Teams

The WNBA also had eight teams, each of which was owned and operated by the NBA. The teams were:

Charlotte Sting—North Carolina
Cleveland Rockers—Ohio
Houston Comets—Texas
New York Liberty—New York
Los Angeles Sparks—California
Phoenix Mercury—Arizona
Sacramento Monarchs—California
Utah Starzz—Utah

For a graphical representation of the location of WNBA teams, please refer to Exhibit 2.

Each team was located in a city with an NBA franchise, and all teams used the same facilities as the men's league. The teams played 28 games during a ten-week season. By playing in the summer, the WNBA avoided competing for fan interest with professional and college basketball and football, as well as with the ABL.

Sponsors

At the outset, ten corporations in seven different product categories signed contracts with the WNBA to become official marketing partners. They were:

American Express
Bud Light
Champion
Coca-Cola
General Motors
Kellogg USA
Lee Jeans
Nike
Sears
Spalding

Spalding provided the WNBA's distinctive orange-and-oatmeal-colored ball, which was 28.5 inches in circumference. While women at the high school and college level also used the 28.5-inch ball, the ABL chose to use the full-sized 30-inch basketball. Champion was the official outfitter and the exclusive apparel licensee for all eight WNBA teams. Nike, a major sponsor of both the WNBA and the NBA, was the first company to give a female athlete her own shoe contract; the Air Swoopes, named for WNBA star Sheryl Swoopes. Reebok, while not an official marketing partner of the WNBA, also invested in the league by supplying official footwear.

Media Exposure

No new league in the history of athletics received as much initial exposure as the WNBA. During the highly rated NBA playoffs, television ads began airing that promoted the WNBA's slogan "We Got Next" and showcased the league's three biggest stars: Lisa Leslie, Sheryl Swoopes, and Rebecca Lobo. The WNBA negotiated contracts with three television networks to broadcast WNBA games throughout the ten-week season. CBS, ESPN, and Lifetime all agreed to air at least one game each per week. CBS is a national broadcast network, while ESPN is an all-sports cable network, and Lifetime is a cable network that specifically targets women.

Players

The WNBA attracted three of women's basketball's most popular players in Lisa Leslie, Sheryl Swoopes, and Rebecca Lobo. The trio was featured in early league promotions, which aired during the NBA playoffs. Leslie reportedly signed a two-year contract worth one million dollars, and Swoopes and Lobo both signed one-year contracts worth $250,000. While the ABL had 8 of 12 Olympic team members, the WNBA had three of the five starters in Leslie, Swoopes, and Ruthie Bolton-Holifield, and one of women's basketball's most popular players in Lobo.

Salaries in the WNBA tended to be lower for the average player than those offered in the ABL. However, endorsements were potentially easier to secure due to the large number of official league sponsors. Top players, such as Leslie, Swoopes, and Lobo, received contracts above the ABL maximum (although most WNBA players received between $15,000 and $50,000 per year). The WNBA allowed its players to participate in other leagues during the normal winter basketball season.

Initial Results for the WNBA

On Saturday, June 21, 1997, the WNBA began play. While the WNBA had hoped to achieve an attendance level of 4,000 fans per game, initial results were well above expectations. The average attendance for the first week's games was 10,369. Attendance was particularly strong for the opening round of games. For example, the New York Liberty drew an opening-night crowd of 17,780 while games in Houston and Phoenix each drew over 16,000. For a comparison of many of the relevant facts and figures concerning the ABL and the WNBA, please refer to Exhibit 3.

Player Reactions

Having to choose between two professional leagues created some bad feelings among the players who were leery of the NBA's intentions for the WNBA. When the NBA announced its intention to form a women's professional league, they did it as an endnote to a press conference that was called to discuss the sale of the Philadelphia 76ers, one of their men's teams. The fact that the formation of the WNBA was announced as the ABL was sending final contract papers to its committed players also raised eyebrows. Players, who had helped develop the ABL during the time that the NBA had shown virtually no interest in women's basketball, questioned the depth of the NBA's commitment (Bosley, 1996).

The differences in the leagues only underscored the players' concerns. The shorter season and smaller, multicolored ball were interpreted as signs that the women were not to be taken as seriously as the men. Some feared that the WNBA would become an entertaining sideshow, or a ladies' auxiliary, to the NBA. In the words of Teresa Edwards, "Folks are trying to be diplomatic and supportive. But this is war . . . I'm not going to support a ten-week summer league based on filling dates to augment tractor pulls in NBA arenas and give TV networks something more than skydiving and skateboarding" (Jacobs, 1996).

EXHIBIT 3	Quantitative Comparison of the ABL and the WNBA	
	ABL	**WNBA**
Player Salaries:		
Average	$80,000	$30,000[1]
Min–Max	$40,000–$150,000	$15,000–$1,000,000
# of Olympians	8	4
Games per Season	40	28
Weeks per Season	22	10
Size of ball	30"	28.5"
Shot Clock	25	30
Time Periods	Quarters	Halves
Largest Crowd	11,873	17,780[2]
Average Attendance	3,536	9,669

[1]From ESPN.com article.
[2]Through first week of games.

Cavalli's Dilemma

The news for the ABL was both good and bad. On the good side, Cavalli had successfully launched a women's professional basketball league that surpassed the expected attendance numbers and garnered a great deal of enthusiastic fan support. There had been financial losses, but these expenses were an expected part of start-up and they were easily offset by the infusion of new capital. Most importantly, the ABL had won the respect of women athletes by taking a chance on women's professional basketball at a time when the only other logical entrant, the NBA, had shown no interest. On the bad side, the NBA responded to the entry of the ABL by forming a league of its own. The NBA had deep pockets and a marketing machine that far surpassed the resources of the ABL. The intense marketing campaign that surrounded the introduction of the WNBA signaled that the NBA was gearing for battle.

How could the ABL David fight the WNBA Goliath? Was fighting the answer? Should the ABL seek to partner with the WNBA and, if so, what form should this partnership take? What should Cavalli do?

Note

1. ABL press release, 1997.

References

1. Bosley, Don. "It's a court battle." *The Sacramento Bee,* p. D1, June 10, 1996.
2. El-Bashir, Tarik. "So far, winning numbers for Liberty and WNBA." *New York Times,* p. B11, July 1, 1997.
3. Green, Daniel. "Toss up." *Working Woman,* vol. 22, pp. 26–31, April 1997.
4. Hamilton, Joan O.C. "The hoopla over women's hoops." *Business Week,* p. 46, April 10, 1995.
5. Jacobs, Jeff. "Edwards the diplomat paints rosy picture for ABL." *The Hartford Courant,* p. C1, December 16, 1996.
6. Rubel, Chad. "Women's sports in spotlight as corporations become sponsors." *Marketing News,* vol. 29, pp. 2–13, May 22, 1995.
7. Sadomir, Richard. "Sounds of summer: W.N.B.A. to take center court." *New York Times,* p. B13, June 19, 1997.
8. *The World Almanac and Book of Facts 1999.* World Almanac Books, Mahwah, NJ, 1998.
9. WNBA webpage: http://www.wnba.com.

Air India—The Virgin Airways Saga

Sanjib Dutta
ICFAI, Center for Management Research

"We are grateful to AI but as it is a government regulated body, it fails to understand many commercial implications, namely, that to operate two flights a week, we need to create the same infrastructure we require to operate six. This has led to an increase in Virgin's overhead costs as the crew keeps waiting for a week. This way, we will scarcely be able to pass on the envisaged benefits to our customers."

—Mackenzie Grant, Virgin Atlantic's
General Manager (India), in 2000

Introduction

In December 1999, India's national carrier, Air India (AI) signed an agreement with Virgin Atlantic Airways[1] (VA) by which VA would fly three flights on the Delhi–London route on a code-sharing[2] basis with AI. This was hailed as a significant development for the ailing AI. The code-sharing arrangement was expected to trigger a price war in the Delhi–London route where British Airways (BA) was a dominant player. According to the agreement, VA would fly three more flights a week on this route by 2001.

In July 2000, VA started with two flights a week on Thursdays and Saturdays from Delhi. It planned to have a third flight by October 2000. However, until late 2001, VA was still flying two flights. AI did not seem ready to allow VA to fly the third flight because AI too had a flight from Delhi on Monday, the day VA wanted to fly from Delhi. Meanwhile, the Government of India granted rights to BA to fly three more flights per week from Kolkata to London. This was in violation of the bilateral pact signed between Britain and India according to which BA and AI were allowed to fly 16 flights a week to each other's country. BA was already flying 16 flights a week—seven from Delhi, seven from Mumbai and two from Chennai.

In late 2001, VA was severely affected by the downturn in the global aviation industry. VA was finding it difficult to sustain its operations in India with only two flights a week. VA had made it clear that unless it was allowed to increase the number of weekly flights to three, its exit from India would be a distinct possibility.

This case was written by Sanjib Dutta, ICFAI Center for Management Research (ICMR). It is intended to be used as the basis for class discussion rather that to illustrate either effective or ineffective handling of a management situation.

The case was compiled from published sources.

Background Note

AI was registered as Air India International in 1948. Later in 1962, the word *International* was dropped and from March 1994, the airline began functioning as Air India Limited. In 2000, AI's network covered 44 destinations (refer to Exhibit 1). In addition, AI had a code sharing arrangement with a number of foreign airlines. These included Air France, Swiss Air, Bellview Airlines, Austrian Airlines, Asiana Airlines, Scandinavian Airlines, Singapore Airlines, Aeroflot, Air Mauritius, Kuwait Airways and Emirates.

In the late 1990s, as part of its disinvestments program, the Government of India decided to divest its 40 percent stake in AI and began looking for a strategic partner. The strategic partner would take a 40 percent stake with only a 26 percent cap to foreign airlines.

Since it began operations in 1984, VA focused on international routes. After the airline's maiden flight, from London's Gatwick airport to Newark on the outskirts of New York, Richard Branson[3] added several luerative routes to his kitty. Until 1999, VA's route network in the Asian region included Heathrow–Tokyo–Heathrow, Heathrow–Hong Kong–Heathrow and Heathrow–Shanghai–Heathrow. The airline had code-sharing agreements with Continental Airlines, Malaysian Airlines, and British Midland. In the late 1990s, Branson was targeting the lucrative Delhi–London route. Every year an estimated 0.3 million passengers traveled from Delhi to London, which was nearly 40 percent of the total outbound traffic from India. The only available direct route codes were held by BA and AI. As a result, passengers were forced to take circuitous routes offered by airlines like Emirates and Royal Jordanian, which made them wait for hours at distant airports.

Branson's efforts to woo AI started in 1997. He said, "Air India was once famous for its service and I'd like to think that as well as competing with Air India we can share with it our experience of making Virgin Atlantic the success it is today." Analysts felt that AI would learn from VA's innovation in hospitality. VA was the first airline to offer a TV monitor with every seat (in every class). It offered in-flight beauty therapy including the services of masseurs, ice-cream cones during in-flight movies and a chauffeured motorcycle service to airports. Also in the offering were e-mail and Internet services. Upper-class passengers were provided laptop power leads with every seat, and headsets to reduce noise in the cabin.

Besides commercial cooperation on cargo services, yield management, and product development, the arrangement with Branson would give AI's staffers access to cabin crew training. However, analysts felt that once VA started its operations, it would be an all-out fight to lure passengers and AI would be the

EXHIBIT 1	AI's Network
India	Ahmedabad, Amritsar, Bangalore, Calcutta, Chennai, Delhi, Goa, Hyderabad, Kochi, Kozhikode, Mumbai, Thiruvananthapuram
UK	London
Europe	Paris
Asia Pacific	Tokyo, Osaka, Bangkok, Hong Kong, Kuala Lumpur, Singapore and Jakarta
Gulf & Middle East	Doha, Abu Dhabi, Bahrain, Jeddah, Kuwait, Muscat, Riyadh, Dhahran and Dubai
USA & Canada	New York and Chicago
Africa	Nairobi and Dar-es-Salaam

worst sufferer. As VA promised to offer tickets at 15 percent less than BA, a Delhi-London VA ticket would be cheaper than AI's.

The Deal

In 1999, the Ministry of Civil Aviation of India said that it was willing to consider an agreement between VA and AI that would benefit both carriers. The agreement was to include a code-sharing arrangement or sharing of AI flight quotas. The entry of VA on the London–India routes was likely to bring down the fares on the sector.

In December 1999, VA signed an agreement with AI to fly three flights a week on a code-sharing basis between Delhi and London from July 2000. The arrangement with AI was for five years. To facilitate code-sharing, each agreed to fly three flights a week and scale back the large number of original planned flights. As such, VA scaled back the number of flights that it had originally planned so that AI would fly three flights a week as well by 2001.[4] VA and AI would share seats on each other's routes and VA would operate flights to the UK on routes not covered by AI. VA would also fly on days that were not flown by AI. Under the terms of the agreement, flights would carry both VA and AI flight numbers, and both airlines would sell seats on those services in competition with one another. Said Branson, "Launching flights between the UK and India has always been an ambition of mine. It is a very potent route and currently I see a lack of capacity on this route, which has decreased tourist flow between the two countries. I think between the two airlines—Air India and Virgin—we will be able to improve the route."

According to some analysts, the Government of India was interested in forging an alliance with VA because of the group's interests in entertainment, music, telecom, insurance and financial services. Branson had raised hopes of further investments in publishing, holiday homes and telecom. He said, "This is just the beginning. We will study the Indian market and see what business is best suited for the market and for us and proceed accordingly. We will see where we can make a difference." AI had been in the red for a long time and was hoping that the

VA venture would improve its bottom line. Said Branson, "We are paying a significant amount to AI under the code-sharing agreement, though I would not like to reveal the amount. Let me assure you: Air India can make a few millions."

However, Air India officials felt that more than the financial gains, it was the partnership that mattered and the move would bring in fresh traffic to the country. Besides traffic, VA's arrival could also mean reduction in airfares. Said Branson, "Our upper class and premium class as we call them are as competitively priced as the first-class and business-class fares of other airlines respectively. Except, of course, we give more services such as limousines, manicures, beauty treatments, etc., to every passenger on board. As for our economy class, our priority is to fly it at full capacity and hence the pricing is whatever it takes to get the customer. Hence, since we will be competing with Air India, too, despite this agreement, the pricing and services will be competitive."

VA's arrival was also expected to improve AI's services and even bring about a reduction in the fares depending on the market conditions. Said M. P. Mascarenhas, the then Managing Director of AI, "We will have to compete and hence we will have to perform, even if it means fare reduction." Analysts felt that a possible fare reduction would have an adverse effect on the bottom line of AI. Responded Mascarenhas, "I don't think it would because it would increase traffic and improve the overall situation. You see, now, between the two airlines, there will be services all days of the week."

Analysts felt that with the AI-VA code-sharing agreement, other carriers such as Thai Airways and Cathay-Pacific, which were asking for more flights, would pressurize the Government of India for code-share arrangements with AI in lieu of more flights.

Who Will Rule the Delhi–London Skies?

Analysts felt that with the entry of VA, the Indian skies would see some fierce price wars between VA and BA. Branson said that VA's first-class fares would be equivalent to the business-class fares of

BA and that the economy fare would be 30–50 percent cheaper than BA's. If BA brought down ticket prices as it had done in May 2000, VA would fly for less, Branson said. Since BA had proposed a fare of about Rs 27,000 on the Delhi–London sector, Branson said VA would file an application with the Government of India for a lower fare. At the same time, VA would respect the Government's sentiments on fares, since it was a regulated market, Branson said.

In June 2000, VA announced that it would start its operations in India in July with a bi-weekly service—Wednesdays and Fridays from London and Thursdays and Saturdays from Delhi. VA planned to launch a third weekly flight around October. The airline would offer low introductory fares. Mackenzie Grant, VA's general manager for India, said the initial fare was still being worked out and that it would be difficult to give a comparison with competing airlines.

Analysts felt that VA would give BA some stiff competition, not only in terms of fares, but also with its array of services such as sleeper seats, massage services and lounge facilities. Said one, "Virgin's entry will certainly be a boost to services between India and Europe. The airline has a high quality product." Branson promised VA fare would be extremely competitive. Analysts felt that competitive pricing would mean that VA would price its Delhi–London flight for less than Rs 25,000, which was approximately the AI fare. AI feared there would be an exodus of its already dwindling passenger list.

Meanwhile, BA was bracing itself to meet the VA challenge on the Delhi–London sector. The airline announced direct daily services between London and Delhi from October 30, thereby increasing capacity by 25 percent on this sector. For this, the airline suspended its twice-weekly service to Calcutta and terminated its five-times-a-week service from Delhi to Dhaka from October 30. The changes were made as part of a renewed bilateral agreement between the U.K. and India signed in February 2000.

On July 5, 2000, VA dropped a bombshell. It slashed its introductory airfare from the normal Rs 42,598 to Rs 31,000 for a return ticket on the busy London–Delhi route. But just before VA's entry into Indian airspace, BA also announced a special economy-class fare: a Rs 27,635 round trip ticket. According to analysts, consumers were at last getting the benefits of a liberalised competitive sector.

In July 2000, BA won the right to three more flights per week between India and Britain, drawing an immediate protest from VA. According to BA's South Asia manager Alan Briggs, under a special arrangement outside a bilateral aviation agreement, the Government of India had given BA permission to fly three times a week to the eastern city of Calcutta. Under the bilateral pact, which was renewed in February 2000, BA and AI were each allowed to fly 16 times a week to each other's home country. AI used 10 of its 16 weekly flight entitlements on the route. BA used all 16 of its flight entitlements, with seven flights a week to Delhi, seven to Mumbai and two to Madras. BA had been lobbying since 1993 to increase the number of its flights to India.

The End of the Honeymoon?

By October 2000, VA was to start its third code-sharing flight as per the agreement with AI. In addition to the Rs 100 million per flight per annum that AI got from VA, the third flight would fetch AI Rs 300 million per annum. However, till late 2001, VA was flying only two flights a week. Also, there was no progress on the remaining three flights that VA was entitled to fly from 2001. This seemed to be the bone of contention between VA and AI. VA officials were particularly unhappy that BA was granted rights to fly three additional flights per week from Kolkata to London against the prevailing norms. What seemed particularly strange was that there was no commercial agreement or code-sharing agreement for any of these additional frequencies. Commenting on the Government of India's Ministry interest in BA, a leading business magazine in India wrote, "The needle of suspicion automatically points to vested interests in the Ministry and their sudden penchant for BA."[5]

By December 2000, it became clear that VA would have to wait a bit longer for final clearance from AI to commence the third code-sharing flight on the India–London sector. While VA officials claimed that they would start the third code-sharing flight within a reasonable period of time following clearances from Indian authorities, AI officials said that nothing was being planned as yet. Said a VA official, "The ball is in the court of AI and the Indian Government. The day we get the permission, we will start the service in a reasonable time period, which will allow us to relocate aircraft and crew to commence the third flight. Further, the airline will be only too happy to serve other destinations in India."

Some analysts said that while VA was keen to operate the third flight on Sundays from London with a Monday departure from Delhi, AI was opposed to this proposed flight, as the Indian carrier also had a Delhi to London flight on Monday morning. VA was willing to schedule its flight at 2 P.M., ensuring a gap of more than six hours between its flight and AI's London flight. But this was not acceptable to AI, which pointed out that according to the agreement signed between VA and AI, VA was to operate flights only on those days when AI did not operate services to London.

A VA official said that the delay in granting permission to VA to operate the third flight on the sector was proving to be financially disastrous for AI. However, despite these problems, VA said it was interested in code-sharing with AI to other cities such as Chennai, Bangalore, Hyderabad and Ahmedabad.

In late 2001, VA was in some trouble because of the downturn in the transatlantic aviation business and shrinking revenues. VA announced a 20 percent reduction in operations, grounded five of its aircraft and pruned the workforce by 1200 to tide over one of the worst crises for the international aviation business in the aftermath of the U.S. attacks.[6] Having already announced a 20 percent reduction of activities, the airline seemed unable to sustain its operations in India with just two flights a week. Said Paul Smitton, general manager–India, VA, "Two flights each from Delhi is not a viable proposition in the long run. At least three or more flights makes the business viable as it would enable us to get more traffic and meet economies of scale from our operations here." He added, "No airline can sustain loss making regions for long. And this time round, we will wait for just months and not years before making a decision." Analysts felt that VA was likely to review its strategy for its fledgling unprofitable Indian operations. During its short stay in India, VA had already notched up losses on the Delhi–London sector and industry sources ruled out the chances of VA breaking even unless the number of flights increased from the current level. VA officials have indicated to the Government of India that VA may have to pull out of India if the frequency of operations was not increased.

VA informed the Government of India that it had agreed to provide AI with income worth Rs 100 million per annum for each flight on the basis of the understanding that a third flight would be allowed on schedule. VA also said that it had hired an Indian crew for three flights and spent money on publicity, as it was confident its number of flights would be increased. It informed the Government of India that it would have to pull out of India if the third flight was not cleared. In October 2001, the Government of India ordered a full review of the code-sharing pact.

What remained to be seen was whether the much-hyped AI–VA alliance would be sustainable in the long run.

Questions for Discussion

1. Air India's code-sharing arrangement with Virgin Atlantic was expected to benefit the ailing Air India. However, by the end of 2001, relations between Air India and Virgin Atlantic deteriorated and Virgin Atlantic threatened to pull out of India. Explain why the Air India–Virgin Atlantic code-sharing arrangement failed to have the desired effect.
2. "Tie-ups between major airlines have become a key part of the global aviation strategy in the late 1990s. They range from mere code-sharing arrangements and joint frequent flyer programs to alliances." Discuss.

Notes

1. UK's second biggest airlines after British Airways.
2. Code-sharing is an arrangement between two airlines, ranging from mere allocation of space on each other's flights to a closer relationship, which may even involve profit sharing. One example of a common code-sharing agreement is that between Air India and Singapore Airlines on the Singapore–Los Angeles route. As Air India does not fly to LA, it has a code-share with Singapore Airlines, wherein it undertakes to fill a certain number of seats every week on Singapore Airlines.
3. Chairman of Virgin Atlantic Airways.
4. Under the terms of the U.K./India air services agreements, both Indian and British airlines had the right to operate 16 flights per week. Air India operated only ten of their permitted total, while BA operated all of the U.K.'s frequencies.
5. *Business India*, September 4–17, 2000.
6. On September 11, 2001, terrorists attacked the World Trade Center in the United States.

America Online–Time Warner Merger: Why It Failed

Deepak Vahsist
Srikanth G.
ICFAI Business School Case Development Center

"Just merging the two organizations has a lot of challenges. The potential pitfalls and opportunities for disagreements exceed whatever benefits could be gained."[1]

—Ted Turner, Founder–CNN

Introduction

On January 10, 2000, America Online (AOL) and Time Warner (TW) announced a strategic merger to create the world's first fully integrated media and communications company for the Internet century. Time Warner was the traditional media business company and AOL was the 'new media' Internet company. The merger was touted as the "merger of equals" creating a "Clicks and Mortar" company which envisaged a convergence of Internet growth and the traditional profit levels. When the merger was initially announced, Internet and online companies were popular investments with fast track growth in revenues, albeit small. AOL had an excellent track record of harnessing the Internet into profits by virtue of their business model. Time Warner, on the other hand, tried hard to develop a successful Internet venture that never really worked well. Together AOL and the Time Warner had the potential to cross promote and cross exploit their assets and resources to become a media behemoth.[2] The merger also offered the potential of more interactive services, like ordering a movie, a meal or an outfit on the same set that brought favorite television shows.[3]

America Online

America Online was widely regarded as the biggest, richest and the one of the most successful companies in the world because the company figured out how to make money banking on the Internet—by charging the consumers a monthly subscription to sign up on their Internet services and at the same time charging companies to advertise their services.[4]

America Online was founded as Quantum Computer Services in 1985. When the company changed its name to AOL in 1994, it already had around a million subscribers and was listed on the stock market. In its early years, it was almost brought down by the problem of introducing unlimited access for a fixed monthly fee. As usage increased, the company found itself having widespread capacity problems. The consumers complained that they could not get their connections to work.

The problem was solved by a deal with MCI-WorldCom, leading to an investment in an extended Internet backbone, and a merger with rival CompuServe. AOL further consolidated its position in 1998 with its acquisition of Netscape, the Internet browser company, for $4.21 billion, a deal that jolted rival Microsoft.[5] Under the agreement, Netscape shareholders received 0.9 of an AOL share for each of their Netscape shares. The deal allowed AOL to distribute Netscape's Internet browser software. Consequently, AOL came to own two of the most heavily used sites on the Internet. It also became one of the most important companies in the computer software industry and the main rival to Microsoft's market dominance,[6] since it now had access to Netscape's browser software.

E-commerce made up nearly one-third of the revenues of AOL. It had commercial deals to market everything from General Motors cars to computers with Compaq and Gateway. While more than 24 million subscribers paid AOL a monthly fee of about $20 (depending on the pricing plan) to access the Internet, there were an additional 2.8 million people subscribing to its CompuServe subsidiary, and 4.4 million international members.[7]

AOL's basic strategy was to market and use the unrestricted and global Internet reach as the suburbs of its online services. Mr. Case, Chief Executive at AOL, always held the opinion that the "online business was less about technology than about consumer marketing."

AOL's potential weakness was its lack of access to the high-speed Internet services over television cables, which its rivals AT&T and Microsoft had. These high-speed, broadband networks were expected to open the way to the digital distribution of new services for interactive entertainment, information and e-commerce through everything from desktop computers and handheld devices to television sets. AOL recognized that despite its presence as the nation's largest Internet Service Provider (ISP), with nearly 40 percent of the market, its ability to become the country's number one ISP hinged heavily on its ability to use cable TV's network for delivering super fast video and data. Early on, AOL had long been banking on the open access to the telephone networks that were the "common carriers" by law. However, the cable TV networks were "proprietary" networks that were controlled by their owners themselves. The company had lobbied extensively in the past for "open access" in the cable networks with the Federal Trade Commission (FTC). In 1999, AOL went in for a strategic partnership with DirecTV, Hughes network systems, Philips Electronics, and Network Computer Inc., a subsidiary of Oracle, to develop an interactive television service and to extend AOL's services on to television. The company already had agreements with regional telephone companies, Bell Atlantic in the eastern United States, and the SBC Communications in the south-central United States, to provide high speed DSL[8] access. Together they developed an interactive Internet television services known as AOL TV—a part of the AOL's "AOL Anywhere"[9] campaign.

In the 1990s, broadband access was a major driver behind growing instances of mergers and acquisitions. America Online first announced its plans to acquire Time Warner in 2000. With the regulations not favoring its campaign for an "open-access" regime, AOL was in danger of losing its customers due to its inability to provide high-speed access to AOL. What actually drove AOL's strategic acquisition was the fact that Time Warner's cable network was the second largest in the United States. And with premier holdings such as *Time*, *People*, *Fortune*, and *Sports Illustrated* magazines, Warner Brothers, Warner Music, the WB network, and 13 million strong subscribers, Time Warner was an attractive target for AOL. AOL's Chairman Mr. Steven Case said that the convergence of AOL's Internet services and Time Warner's entertainment and news production could create "an integrated consumer space" with the combined entity simultaneously producing content and providing high speed Internet access. "We don't want AOL to be a place people go through to get someplace else," explained

Mr. Case, who became the Chairman of AOL Time Warner combined. "We want to be able to create an integrated consumer space. That's why ultimately, the ownership of media brands will be important."[10]

Time Warner

Time Warner was the traditional media company having products ranging from rolling news station CNN and TV's *Friends* to *Time* magazine and a movie-making history. In the ten months since the merger plan was announced, its stock market value rose from $88.3 billion to $112.6 billion. Time Warner was itself a result of two previous giant mergers. The first was between Time, Inc. and Warner Communications in 1989. Both Time, the publisher of *Time* magazine, and Warner, which included Bugs Bunny among its stars, had a history stretching back 75 years. The second megamerger came with Turner Broadcasting in 1996, which saw CNN founder Ted Turner joining the group as deputy chairman.[11]

Time Warner expected that the merger with AOL would help the company to build up its digital media ventures. The company said that it had always been at the forefront of technological innovation. In 1975 the company pioneered the satellite broadcasting services, with the launch of the HBO television network in the United States. It also built considerable fiber-optic cable networks in the United States. It was one of the key players in the launch of DVDs and also had the "CDNow" e-commerce site in its product portfolio.[12] However, the company's attempt to establish its own Internet hub never materialized a CNN news site, and its "Pathfinder" network failed to create a significant impact in the Internet media. The company invested $500 million in 1999 as part of its efforts to boost its Internet venture before opting for a merger with AOL. Ted Turner, Vice President of Time Warner, commented, "It's not easy to build an AOL."[13]

But the merger with America Online was expected to catapult Time Warner into the Internet big league and place it in a strategic position to capitalize on the growth of broadband delivery of television and Internet at home. And, if content was required for the successful exploitation of the new information technologies, then Time Warner could bring to AOL a vast array of household names from the media and entertainment industries.

The Merger

America Online and Time Warner announced their merger on January 10, 2000. The combination of Time Warner and America Online was the largest merger in the corporate history of the United States, for a total value of $183 billion on the day the announcement was made. Of this, America Online offered $166 billion in stock and undertook to assume another $17 billion in debt. It was also the first time that a corporate behemoth created by the Internet used its high valuation to acquire an old media Fortune 500 company. The new AOL Time Warner became the fourth largest company in the United States in terms of market valuation ($350 billion) after Microsoft, General Electric, and Cisco Systems.[14] In terms of market capitalization, AOL was nearly twice as much as Time Warner, but its shareholders got only a 55 percent stake in AOL Time Warner.

By virtue of the merger, while AOL converted a substantial portion of its paper value into the acquisition of real assets, Time Warner shareholders received a 71 percent premium on the prevalent market price of $64.75, i.e., about $110 per share that AOL offered (1.5 shares of the AOL Time Warner for every share held, AOL shareholders got a one-on-one share swap). The AOL shares were up 19 percent and the Time Warner shares gained by 12 percent.[15] Analysts stated that AOL hugely overvalued Time Warner in the deal and that in the long run, depreciation and the debt payments could dent the earnings of the merged company.[16] Despite being the major partner, AOL was expected to contribute only 20 percent of the new company's earnings. There were also doubts whether AOL could keep up with its high profit historical growth rate because of its bulky acquisition.

In general however, the analysts touted the merger as positive in almost every area the two companies could touch together, and with the combined company having the potential to become a front-line player for existing businesses, such as Internet access, e-commerce and advertising-driven content. AOL Time Warner was poised to become a dominating player in new businesses in areas such as broadband cable access, digital music distribution and interactive television (Exhibit 1).

"If the integration is successful (not a given, certainly), we believe that the market will ultimately value the company less as a collection of disparate media and Internet properties and more as the dominant platform supporting consumer interactivity, a platform around which other services will eventually standardize," a Merrill Lynch report read.[17]

The AOL Time Warner combination also had an amiable power-sharing setup. Bob Pittman, President of AOL, was to oversee the company advertising and subscription based businesses (with its 128 million subscribers and 2001 earnings of $30.2 billion, AOL, Time Inc., Turner Broadcasting, Time Warner Cable, Home Box Office, and the Warner Brothers' Television Network contributed 60 percent to 70 percent of total revenues in 2001). Dick Parsons was to head the studio businesses that generated 2001 revenues of $13.4 billion that included Warner Bros., New Line Cinema, and Warner Music Group. The two met regularly to hammer out policy on budgets, Web strategies and agreements on technologies. In 2001, *Time* magazine was selling over 100,000 subscriptions a month via AOL, while Time Warner was also promoting AOL by sending AOL disks along with its magazines spanning 40 million households. The company also planned to launch a new personal finance portal on AOL using Time Warner's CNNfn cable, *Fortune* and *Money* magazine content.[18] "We can look at opportunities together, instead of just pieces of the opportunity," said Pittman.

When AOL first announced the merger in 2000, Time Warner President Mr. Richard Parsons described it as "a pivotal moment in the unfolding of the Internet age." "Traditional media assets have a vibrant future if they can be catapulted into the

EXHIBIT 1	Groups under AOL Time Warner

I.	America Online	29 million subscribers, dominated the consumer online access market
II.	Time Warner Cable	Second largest U.S. cable operator pushing digital services and broadband Web access to 21 percent of U.S. Households.
III.	Time, Inc.	Publisher of 40 magazines, including *Time, Sports Illustrated, Fortune,* etc.
IV.	HBO	Largest premium cable network with 37 million subscribers
V.	Warner Bros.	Ranks third among movie studios
VI.	WB Television Network	—
VII.	New Line Cinema	No. 9 ranked studio
VIII.	Warner Music Group	—
IX.	Turner Broadcasting Group	Cable TV top networks including CNN, TBS, and TNT
X.	Time Warner Trade Publishing	Parent company of Warner Books and Little, Brown

SOURCE: Benefits of AOL Time Warner merger.

Internet age," added Mr. Steven Case.[19] In 2000, AOL had a profit of $1.2 billion against revenues of $6.89 billion. During the period, its earnings from advertisements and e-commerce grew by 95 percent to $609 million.[20]

The AOL-TW merger put up a strong performance in 2001 with AOL subscribers surpassing the 29 million mark with new additions of 2 million subscribers in the first quarter. Mr. Jerry Levin, CEO of AOL-TW, said, "Our businesses are working together as one, unified organization to deliver shareholder value over the near- and long-term."[21] AOL also drove in a considerable increase in the net traffic to *People, Time, Sports Illustrated*, and CNN through Netscape and other AOL flagships. According to a report from Media Metrix, Time Warner sites attracted nearly 23 million first-time visitors in March 2001, an increase of 69 percent from the previous year and a 10 percent increase over February.[22]

Merger Blues

The merger faced stringent resistance from consumer advocacy groups such as the Consumer Unions, Consumer Federation of America, Media Access Project, and competitors in the media and the Internet players, such as Disney and NBC. They wanted AOL-TW to open up its cable lines to all ISPs and allow the rival entertainment companies access to Internet customers. Also, AOL had been a strong advocate of open access to the cable broadband platform. Its interests were expected to change if the merger was allowed since Time Warner owned 20 percent of the cable network in the United States. The impending merger came under the scrutiny of the Federal Communications Commission (FCC) and the FTC for possible anti-trust violations. The critics contended that if the merger were allowed to go through, AOL Time Warner would be able to use its high-speed cable to promote its own content websites and e-commerce applications. Hence, they wanted the FTC to recommend that AOL Time Warner agree to non-discriminatory access for competing ISPs (Internet Service Providers). Critics of the merger also wanted the FTC to guarantee that AOL-TW would treat other content providers, including all web sites, equitably. They wanted these policies extended to next-generation devices, including television set-top boxes and interactive TVs, which were expected to play a major role in delivering high-speed digital content in the future. These groups also asked the FTC to sever the ties between AOL-TW and AT&T (the nation's largest cable provider) that could otherwise give them control of more than half of all cable TV households in the country. However, Mr. Steven Case and Mr. Gerald Levin, CEO of AOL and Time Warner respectively, said that the merger was very much in the public interest, as it would provide them with "next generation branded content." The merger was approved by the FCC subject to the condition of Time Warner allowing other high speed ISPs other than AOL access to its systems; AOL-TW had to ensure that its Instant Messaging service could operate easily with at least three other rival services enabling the customers to exchange e-mails, and that AOL-TW was to sever all relations with the rival AT&T, which had a 25 percent stake in Time Warner. Under FTC guidelines, access to other ISPs and access to broadband services were addressed to ensure that other broadband operators got the same leverage as AOL. The European Commission also chipped in by disallowing AOL Time Warner to buy out EMI, a leading music company in the UK[23] and any further deals with Bertelsmann, AOL's European partner.[24] By the time the merger was finally approved by the FCC on January 11, 2001, the combined market capitalization of the merger was already on the decline. AOL's share prices had dropped almost 50 percent.

The FTC finally approved the merger on January 11, 2001. From the time the merger was first declared to the FTC approval, AOL's share price had dropped from $73 to $37.50 and it resulted in the major proportion of the expected premium to the Time Warner shareholders vanishing. As the Internet bubbles burst, Yahoo! Scrip lost 89 percent while Amazon.com plummeted 87 percent.

It was also a big challenge to blend in the two cultures and to redefine the corporate culture—one that could effectively tap the synergy between the twenty-something executives at AOL with the Time Warner graybeards. According to a study by KPMG, 83 percent of the 700 mergers between 1996 and 1998 failed to boost the share prices due to poor execution.[25]

In 2002, AOL-TW announced that a sluggish advertisement sector could cause the results of its America Online Internet division to fall below anticipated figures. When the merger was first announced, AOL with its phenomenal growth trajectory had promised to "super-charge" the growth at Time Warner. However, falling advertising revenues and failure to create an impact with the broadband customers was hampering the company. AOL had a 20 percent share in the online advertisement sector and with the sector facing a 6 percent decline, its revenues came under pressure and fell by 40 percent. AOL expected its advertising revenues to fall by nearly 50 percent as majority of the deals signed during the dot-com boom came to an end[26] in 2003. America Online division got just 492,000 new subscriptions in the second quarter of 2002 nearly half of what the analysts expected. Its earnings for 2002 were about £1.1 billion, down from £1.7 billion in 2001.[27]

During 2002, AOL also lowered its earnings by about $193 million due to an accounting miscue at its Internet division relating to improperly booked advertisement revenues between September 2000 and June 2002. The company came under investigation from the U.S. Justice Department and the SEC (Securities and Exchange Commission). Revenues fell at AOL even as Time Warner reported an overall growth of six percent (Exhibit 2). The company reported a profit of $57 million, compared to a loss of $997 million in 2001. However, shareholders were finding it difficult to ignore AOL's problems. "Investors want to see evidence that one division can help enhance the other, which is what the merger was supposed to be all about," said one media analyst.[28] The company also set off speculation when it reported that Mr. Steven Case, the architect of the merger, had floated the idea of spinning off the America Online Internet division.[29] It was around the same time that AOL Time Warner came up with a new strategy to keep its AOL division afloat by shifting its focus on selling premium add-on services. It was seen as a make or break effort to determine if AOL could contribute to the company's future growth even as competition from telecom and cable companies made it difficult for AOL to sell its broadband services. AOL was also facing a SEC investigation into its accounting irregularities that took place around the time of the merger with Time Warner in 2001.[30]

EXHIBIT 2

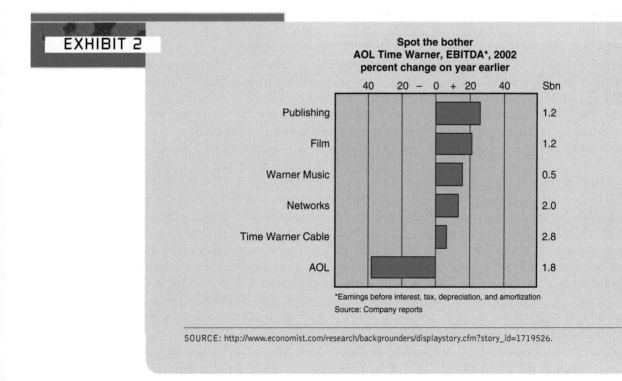

Spot the bother
AOL Time Warner, EBITDA*, 2002
percent change on year earlier

Publishing		1.2
Film		1.2
Warner Music		0.5
Networks		2.0
Time Warner Cable		2.8
AOL		1.8

*Earnings before interest, tax, depreciation, and amortization
Source: Company reports

SOURCE: http://www.economist.com/research/backgrounders/displaystory.cfm?story_id=1719526.

In 2002, AOL came under an investigation by the U.S. Justice Department and the SEC for its dubious accounting practices employed by the company to falsely inflate its revenues in 2000 and 2001 to prop up its share value for the Time Warner takeover. A report in the *Washington Post* highlighted a series of anomalies in the company's accounting policies. In one instance, AOL had converted a legal settlement with Britain's Wembley into an advertising sales deal. In another, it booked revenue from advertising sold for online auctioneer eBay and then had renegotiated long-term contracts to be able to recognize revenue more quickly.[31] AOL Time Warner acknowledged that its online division might have improperly accounted for advertisement revenue worth around £31.7 million.[32]

In 2002, the company also came under investigation by the U.S. authorities given their continual upbeat assessment of the company earnings predictions. Fourteen top executives at AOL Time Warner, including Chairman Steven Case and Chief Executive Richard Parsons, made nearly $256 million profit by selling their shares between February and June 2001 even as they insisted that the company would meet its target.[33] The stock prices fell nearly 70 percent over the year 2002.

The company also faced critical leadership problems as most of the top executives who engineered the merger left. Mr. Gerald Levin, the CEO of the merged company, resigned in 2001 and left the company in 2002. David Colburn, Head of Business Affairs, and Mr. Robert Pittman, Chief Operating Officer at AOL Time Warner, left in 2002 amidst deteriorating performances and continual Justice Department and SEC investigations into AOL's accounting malpractices.[34]

Time Warner had been traditionally using EBITDA—operating income before amortization of intangible assets—to size up its profitability. In 2002, the AOL Time Warner merger disclosed an asset impairment charge of $54.24 billion due to new accounting rules—the largest in U.S. corporate history. Under the new rules, goodwill—the premium payable for an acquisition over and above the actual cash value of the tangible assets acquired—was no longer to be written off gradually over the 40-year period. Instead, the company had to constantly weigh in the effects of the value of their investments in the acquired company and write off any depreciation in the subsequent valuation. The loss at AOL Time Warner was primarily due to a sharp decline in the company's stock price, which fell by nearly half since the merger was first announced.[35]

In 2003, AOL posted an operating income of $663 million against a loss of $32.7 million in 2002. On a consolidated basis, full year AOL's revenues declined 5 percent. Operating income before depreciation and amortization increased to $1.5 billion from a loss of $32.0 billion in 2002. On December 31, 2003, the AOL service had 24.3 million members in the United States, a decrease of 2.2 million for the year. In the fourth quarter, a decrease of 830,000 subscribers was offset partially by an increase of 431,000 members in retention programs. The AOL service in Europe had nearly 6.4 million members (in 2003) that remained flat on a year-on-year (an increase of only 91,000 from September 30, 2003). A growth in America Online's subscription revenues was more than offset by a decline in advertising and other revenues. Subscription revenues grew by five percent largely due to increase at AOL Europe, which benefited to the extent of $240 million due to favorable foreign currency exchange rates and higher pricing. Subscription revenues within the United States were flat, reflecting a year-over-year increase in broadband subscribers, offset by a decline in U.S. narrowband membership. Advertising revenue was down by 40 percent due to expiration of a majority of prior-period contract sales of over $550 million. Other revenues declined 61 percent[36] (Exhibit 3).

Mr. Steven Case, Chairman of the AOL Time Warner merger and the last of the AOL executives, also resigned in 2003. He said that the shareholders "continued to focus their disappointment with the company's post-merger performance" on him personally.[37] He stayed on as a Director of the company with joint responsibility for corporate strategy. Mr. Case admitted that "a lack of leadership at the heart of AOL had hurt the online division after its merger with Time Warner" and that aggressive financial targets had caused a myopic view on short-term profits that had undermined services to the AOL customers.[38] Deutsche Bank termed Case's departure as a "minor positive" and said that the

EXHIBIT 3

Three Months and Full Year Ended December 31:

	Three Months Ended December 31.		Full Year Ended December 31.	
Revenues:	**2003**	**2002**	**2003**	**2002**
AOL	$ 2,156	$ 2,322	$ 8,600	$ 9,094
Cable	2,003	1,837	7,699	7,035
Filmed Entertainment	3,378	2,875	10,967	10,040
Networks	2,168	2,080	8,434	7,655
Publishing	1,633	1,592	5,533	5,422
Intersegment Eliminations	(434)	(461)	(1,668)	(1,932)
Total Revenues	$ 10,904	$ 10,245	$39,565	$ 37,314
Operating Income:				
AOL	$ 109	$(33,351)	$ 663	$(32,742)
Cable	377	(10,138)	1,531	(9,012)
Filmed Entertainment	341	322	1,173	962
Networks	545	611	1,809	1,839
Publishing	261	294	664	881
Corporate	(111)	(123)	(458)	(426)
Intersegment Eliminations	(3)	10	(17)	(56)
Total Operating Income	$ 1,519	$(42,375)	$ 5,365	$(38,554)
Operating Income before Depreciation and Amortization:				
AOL	$ 301	$(33,139)	$ 1,507	$(31,957)
Cable	797	(9,806)	2,992	(7,799)
Filmed Entertainment	417	392	1,465	1,232
Networks	602	681	2,027	2,032
Publishing	347	397	955	1,155
Corporate	(102)	(115)	(424)	(398)
Intersegment Eliminations	(3)	10	(17)	(56)
Total Operating Income before Depreciation and Amortization	$ 2,359	$(41,600)	$ 8,505	$(35,791)

Year Ended December 31, 2003

	Operating Income before Depreciation and Amortization	Non-cash Impairments of Goodwill and Intangible Assets	(Gains)/Losses from Asset Disposals	Adjusted Operating Income before Depreciations and Amortizations
AOL	$ 1,507	$ —	$ —	$ 1,507
Cable	2,992	—	—	2,992
Filmed Entertainment	1,465	—	(43)	1,422
Networks	2,027	219	—	2,246
Publishing	955	99	29	1,083
Corporate	(424)	—	—	(424)
Intersegment elimination	(17)	—	—	(17)
Total	$ 8,505	$ 318	$ (14)	$ 8,809

Year Ended December 31, 2002

	Operating Income before Depreciation and Amortization	Non-cash Impairments of Goodwill and Intangible Assets	(Gains)/Losses from Asset Disposals	Adjusted Operating Income before Depreciation and Amortization
AOL	$ (31,957)	$ 33,489	$ —	$ 1,532
Cable	(7,799)	10,550	(6)	2,745
Filmed Entertainment	1,232	—	—	1,232
Networks	2,032	—	—	2,032
Publishing	1,155	—	—	1,155
Corporate	(398)	—	—	(398)
Intersegment elimination	(56)	—	—	(56)
Total	$ (35,791)	$ 44,030	$ (6)	$ 8,242

SOURCE: http://www.timewarner.com/investors/quarterly_earnings/2003_4q/pdf/release.pdf.

move "fully opens the door to selling or spinning off AOL at some point down the road, though we would expect to see major cost cuts . . . before that would be given serious consideration."[39]

AOL Time Warner also went in for a series of debt-reduction measures by planning to offload its non-core asset business areas. In 2002, the company planned to sell off its book division in order to pay off some of its debts amounting to £16 billion. The sale was expected to raise only £200 million but was seen largely as its efforts to reduce its debt and send out positive signals to the shareholders.[40] The company completed that sale of its DVD and CD manufacturing and distributing business in October 2003 for $1.05 billion.[41] On November 24, 2003, it also sold its Warner Music Group (WMG) including its music operations business and music publishing business for a consideration of $2.6 billion to an investor group led by Thomas H. Lee Partners, Edgar Bronfman, Jr.'s Music Capital Partners, Bain Capital and Providence Equity Partners. Under the terms of the agreement, Time Warner retained the option of buying back up to 15 percent of the stake any time during the next three years and under certain circumstances, up to 19.9 percent.[42] Dick Parsons, Time Warner Chairman and CEO, said, "The transaction has enabled us to reach our net debt target nearly a full year ahead of time, and we intend to deploy the proceeds of this sale toward high-growth, high-return opportunities both inside and outside our company." At the end of 2003, the company had a debt of $22.7 billion, down from $25.8 billion in December 2002.

Endnote

On October 16, 2003, the AOL name was finally dropped and the company again reinstated itself to being the erstwhile Time Warner. Its stock ticker symbol was reinstated to TWX in 2003. The company posted a profit of $638 million in last quarter 2003. In 2004, Time Warner's market capitalization stood at $76,439,341,326. Its pre-merger market cap was $75,912,718,365 in 2000. Effectively, during the four-year merger, AOL Time Warner lost nearly all of the worth of AOL in the deal. And the original Time Warner shareholders held only 44.76 percent of the share in the new company. Hence, of the total worth of the company, they had a claim of only $34,214,249,178. Time Warner's initial promise of windfall gains for its shareholders from the merger had ended up in a loss of nearly $42 billion.

Notes

1. Turner counts costs of AOL disaster, http://www.media.guardian.co.uk/city/story/0,7497,889289,00.html, February 5, 2003.
2. AOL: The first Click and Mortar company, http://www.newsearch.bbc.co.uk, October 11, 2000.
3. AOL Time Warner merger could net consumers more and less, http://www.cnn.com/2001/TECH/compuling/01/11/aol.tw.merger, January 11, 2001.
4. AOL: The company that grew up, http://news.bbc.co.uk/hi/english/business, October 11, 2000.
5. Ibid.
6. Final hurdle for AOL, http://news.bbc.co.uk/hi/english/business, March 17, 1999.
7. Ibid.
8. Digital Subscriber Line—A high speed internet access medium.
9. The new AOL service software saved the subscribers' address books in AOL's servers rather than their hard disks. AOL said that this would enable users to access AOL's products and features from multiple locations and multiple devices.
10. A Mass Medium for Main Street, http://www.crab.rutgers.edu/~goertzel/aolwarner.htm, January 11, 2000.
11. Time Warner: An Internet Blue chip, http://news.bbc.co.uk/hi/english/business/newsid_597000/597405.stm, October 11, 2000.
12. Ibid.
13. How blind alleys led Old Media to New, http://www.cronkite.pp.asu.edu/russo/readings.html#TWAOL2, January 16, 2000.
14. AOL buyout Time Warner: Merger frenzy sweeping corporate America, http://www.wsws.org/articles/2000/jan2000/merg-j14.shtml, January 14, 2000.
15. AOL and Time Warner confirm Merger, http://news.bbc.co.uk/hi/english/business, January 10, 2000.
16. Op. cit., AOL buyout Time Warner: Merger frenzy sweeping corporate America.
17. Analyst Bullish on AOL–Time Warner merger, http://news.com.com/2100-1023-237207.html, February 23, 2000.
18. Show Time for AOL Time Warner, http://www.businessweek.com/2001/01_03/b3715001.htm, January 15, 2001.
19. A Mass Medium for Main Street, http://www.crab.rulgers.edu/~goertzel/aolwarner.htm, January 11, 2000.
20. AOL's billion dollar profits, http://news.bbc.co.uk/hi/english/business/newsid_843000/843838.stm, July 20, 2000.
21. AOL–TW reports strong growth, http://www.isp-planet.com/news/2001/aollw_q1.html, April 19, 2001.
22. Ibid.
23. AOL–Time Warner: Conditions of the Deal, http://news.bbc.co.uk/hi/english/business/newsid_1113000/1113492.stm, January 12, 2001.

24. AOL Time Warner: Timeline of the merger, http://news.bbc.co.uk/hi/english/business/newsid_1113000/1113599.stm, January 12, 2001.

25. Op. cit., Show Time for AOL Time Warner.

26. Hundreds of Jobs to go at AOL as revenues fall, http://media.guardian.co.uk/advertising/story/0,7492,855124,00.html, December 6, 2002.

27. AOL warns on revenue, http://www.media.guardian.co.uk/city/story, September 9, 2002.

28. AOL recasts hits Time Warner revenue, http://www.media.guardian.co.uk/city/story, October 24, 2002.

29. Case moots AOL Time Warner Demerger, http://www.media.guardian.co.uk/city/story, October 29, 2002.

30. AOL pins revival hope on add-on services, http://www.media.guardian.co.uk/city/story, December 3, 2002.

31. U.S. Justice Department to investigate AOL, http://www.media.guardian.co.uk/city/story, August 1, 2002.

32. Question mark hangs over £32 Million of AOL ad revenue, http://www.media.guardian.co.uk/city/story.

33. A Steal, http://www.economist.com, October 24, 2002.

34. Senior AOL Time Warner executive quits, http://www.itweek.co.uk/News/1133744, July 19, 2002.

35. AOL Time Warner reports biggest loss in U.S. history, http://it.asia1.com.sg/newsarchive/04/news008_20020426.html, April 26, 2002.

36. http://www.timewarner.com/investors/quarterly_earnings/2003_4q/pdf/release.pdf.

37. Case Quits AOL Time Warner, http://www.media.guardian.co.uk/city/story, January 13 2001.

38. AOL boss admits to lack of leadership, http://www.media.guardian.co.uk/city/story, October 2, 2002.

39. A new AOL Time Warner, http://www.atnewyork.com/news/article.php/1568551, January 13, 2003.

40. AOL Time Warner brought to the books.

41. http://www.timewarner.com/investors/quarterly_earnings/2003_4q/pdf/release.pdf.

42. http://media.aoltimewarner.com/media/press_view.cfm?release_num=55253823.

Apple Computer, Inc.: iTunes and iPod

Jeff Berrong
Marilyn Klopp
Max Mishkin
Jimmy Pittman
Adrian Ray
Robert E. Hoskisson
Arizona State University

"This will go down in history as a turning point for the music industry," said Apple Computer CEO Steve Jobs. "This is landmark stuff. I can't overestimate it!"[1] Jobs was referring to the April 28th, 2003 debut of Apple's iTunes Online Music Store, the first legal online music service to have agreements with all five major record labels. Though only initially available for Macintosh users, iTunes sold over a million songs by the end of its first week in operation. Not only could iTunes quite possibly change the nature of the music industry, it could also add greatly to Apple's revenues by way of promoting the purchase of the iPod—a portable digital music device that can store downloaded iTunes songs. In 2003, Apple's net income was $6.9 billion and Jobs hopes that this new capability will spur higher sales (for financial information see Exhibit 1). To succeed, however, Apple must beat the competition on a number of levels. iTunes faces stiff competition from new and existing online music download services both legal and illegal. On the hardware side, the iPod also faces competition from a variety of lower-priced substitutes. Apple's innovative ability and the quality of its marketing strategy will likely determine the outcome of the company's foray into the music business.

Early Company History

On April 1, 1976, Steve Jobs and Stephen Wozniak began the partnership that would eventually become Apple Computer. Both electronics gurus, Jobs and Wozniak had known each other since high school and had worked together previously on other projects.[2] In early 1976, Wozniak had been working on combining video monitors with computers. His idea was to invent a user-friendly computer that ordinary consumers could buy. Wozniak, who worked for Hewlett-Packard (HP) at the time, decided to approach his employer with his idea. HP, however, did not see a future for personal computers (PCs) and soundly rebuffed him. At that point, Steve Jobs told his friend Wozniak that they should go into business together and sell computers themselves.[3]

This case is intended to be used as the basis for class discussion rather than to illustrate either effective or ineffective handling of an administrative or strategic situation. We appreciate the direction of Professor Robert E. Hoskisson in the development of this case. Reprinted by permission of Robert E. Hoskisson, Arizona State University, and team members: Jeff Berrong, Marilyn Klopp, Max Mishkin, Jimmy Pittman, and Adrian Ray.

EXHIBIT 1	Apple's Financial Performance: Consolidated Balance Sheets (In millions, except share amounts)		

	September 27, 2003	September 28, 2002
ASSETS:		
Current assets:		
Cash and cash equivalents	$ 3,396	$ 2,252
Short-term investments	1,170	2,085
Accounts receivable, less allowances of $49 and $51, respectively	766	565
Inventories	56	45
Deferred tax assets	190	166
Other current assets	309	275
Total current assets	5,887	5,388
Property, plant, and equipment, net	669	621
Goodwill	85	85
Acquired intangible assets	24	34
Other assets	150	170
Total assets	$ 6,815	$ 6,298
LIABILITIES AND SHAREHOLDERS' EQUITY:		
Current liabilities:		
Accounts payable	$ 1,154	$ 911
Accrued expenses	899	747
Current debt	304	—
Total current liabilities	2,357	1,658
Long-term debt	—	316
Deferred tax liabilities and other non-current liabilities	235	229
Total liabilities	2,592	2,203
Commitments and contingencies		
Shareholders' equity:		
Common stock, no par value; 900,000,000 shares authorized; 366,726,584 and 358,958,989 shares issued and outstanding, respectively	1,926	1,826
Deferred stock compensation	(62)	(7)
Retained earnings	2,394	2,325
Accumulated other comprehensive income (loss)	(35)	(49)
Total shareholders' equity	4,223	4,095
Total liabilities and shareholders' equity	$ 6,815	$ 6,298

(continued)

EXHIBIT 1 Apple's Financial Performance *(continued)*
Consolidated Statements of Operations
(In millions, except share and per share amounts)

Three fiscal years ended September 27, 2003	2003	2002	2001
Net sales	$ 6,207	$ 5,742	$ 5,363
Cost of sales	4,499	4,139	4,128
Gross margin	1,708	1,603	1,235
Operating expenses:			
Research and development	471	446	430
Selling, general, and administrative	1,212	1,109	1,138
Restructuring costs	26	30	—
Purchased in-process research and development	—	1	11
Total operating expenses	1,709	1,586	1,579
Operating income (loss)	(1)	17	(344)
Other income and expense:			
Gains (losses) on non-current investments, net	10	(42)	88
Unrealized loss on convertible securities	—	—	(13)
Interest and other income, net	83	112	217
Total other income and expense	93	70	292
Income (loss) before provision for (benefit from) income taxes	92	87	(52)
Provision for (benefit from) income taxes	24	22	(15)
Income (loss) before accounting changes	68	65	(37)
Cumulative effects of accounting changes, net of income taxes	1	—	12
Net income (loss)	$ 69	$ 65	$ (25)
Earnings (loss) per common share before accounting changes:			
Basic	$ 0.19	$ 0.18	$ (0.11)
Diluted	$ 0.19	$ 0.18	$ (0.11)
Earnings (loss) per common share:			
Basic	$ 0.19	$ 0.18	$ (0.07)
Diluted	$ 0.19	$ 0.18	$ (0.07)
Shares used in computing earnings (loss) per share (in thousands):			
Basic	360,631	355,022	345,613
Diluted	363,466	361,785	345,613

SOURCE: Table drawn from http://www.sec.gov/.

EXHIBIT 2

Selected Apple Product Releases

1976	Apple I
1977	Apple II
1980	Apple III
1983	Lisa
1984	Macintosh
	Graphical user interface (GUI)
1986	Macintosh Plus
1987	Macintosh II
1991	Macintosh Quadra
	PowerBook 100
1994	PowerMac 6100
1997	PowerBook G3
1998	iMac
1999	iBook
2001	iTunes
	iDVD
	iPod
2003	iLife suite
	iTunes 4 (online music store w/200,000 downloadable songs)

SOURCE: Information drawn from http://www.apple-history.com.

Their first computer, the *Apple I,* was built in Jobs' parents' garage (see Exhibit 2). Known as a "kit computer," the original Apple consisted merely of a circuit board and did not even have an exterior casing. It was intended to be sold to hobbyists only. Jobs called the computer an "Apple" in honor of his days working at an orchard while seeking enlightenment, and because neither he nor Wozniak could come up with a better name.[4] The *Apple I* received mixed responses from hobbyists and the duo decided it was time to expand the market for personal computers by building a more attractive and useful machine, the *Apple II.*[5]

Growth

After taking on new partners to fund expansion plans, the company officially became Apple Computer, Inc. in early 1977.[6] Within months, the recapitalized company introduced the *Apple II,* the first computer to come with a sleek plastic casing and color graphics.[7] Annual sales increased dramatically to $10 million and the company began to grow quickly in size, adding thousands of employees.[8] On December 12, 1980, Apple became a public company. On the first day of trading, its share price increased from an initial $22 offering to $29.[9] By the end of the year, Apple reached $100 million in annual sales.[10] The fledgling company, however, was about to receive some very experienced competition. In 1981, IBM released its first personal computer. IBM's sheer size ensured its domination of the young PC market. Steve Jobs realized that Apple would have to move fast in order to remain a viable company. Over the next few years the company released several new computer models, most notably the *Apple III* and the *Lisa.* Neither of these models sold particularly well.

In 1983, Jobs recruited Pepsi-Cola CEO John Sculley as Apple's president and CEO. Jobs hoped that this change would bring more structure and organization to the young company.[11] Apple's biggest computer achievement, the Macintosh, was soon to come. After initially opposing it, Jobs had personally taken on the task of developing the Mac, which became the first PC featuring a graphical interface and a mouse for navigation. Apple first debuted the now-famous Macintosh computer with a riveting January 1984 Super Bowl commercial. The memorable commercial featured an Orwellian *1984* world filled with stoic human zombies, all watching a large-screen image of "Big Brother." A young woman rushes into the room and dramatically destroys the screen. Apple used this *1984* imagery to depict IBM's computer dominance being destroyed by the new Macintosh.[12] After a few enhancements that made the Mac easy to use for publishing, and a marketing strategy that concentrated on universities, the new computer began to sell very well, pushing Apple's fiscal 1984 sales to an unprecedented $1.5 billion.[13]

Shake-Up

By 1985, however, Jobs and Sculley began to disagree over the direction they wanted the company to take. After Jobs' attempt to remove Sculley failed, Jobs left Apple in May to start his own new business, NeXT Computers. Meanwhile, Microsoft benefited from Apple's poor negotiation of a contract that cleared the way for successive versions of the Windows operating system to use graphical user interface (GUI) technology similar to that of the Mac. With this agreement, "Apple had effectively lost exclusive rights to its interface design."[14]

In 1990 Microsoft released Windows 3.0, the first universal software that could run on nearly every PC, regardless of the manufacturer. Though Apple's worldwide sales had reached over $7 billion by 1992, Apple soon found itself fighting an uphill battle against the movement toward standardized software. While more and more businesses and consumers wanted compatible operating systems, Macintoshes still ran exclusively on Mac OS, a system not available to other computers. By 1993, Apple's board of directors decided it was time to replace Sculley as CEO. Apple moved through two CEOs over the next five years. During this time, Apple partnered with IBM and Motorola to produce the PowerPC chip, which would run the company's new line of PowerMacs, allowing them to outperform computers powered by Intel microprocessors.[15] Despite this and Apple's attempts to reorganize, losses mounted in 1996 and 1997. In December 1996, Apple acquired NeXT, Steve Jobs' other company, with the plan of using its technology as the basis for a new operating system. After being gone for more than a decade, Jobs had returned to the company he had originally co-founded with Wozniak.

Jobs Returns

One of the first problems Steve Jobs moved to fix was the ongoing dispute between Apple and Microsoft over the Windows graphical user interface (GUI). Microsoft not only paid an undisclosed amount to Apple, but also made its Office 98 suite compatible with Macintoshes.[16] Jobs then proceeded to change the company's sales strategy in 1997 to encompass direct sales—both online and by phone. In a flurry of product releases, Apple introduced the new generation of PowerMacs, PowerBooks, and the highly anticipated iMac and iBook, which were less expensive computers aimed at the low-end computer market. After an entire year without showing a profit, the first quarter of 1998 began three years of profitable quarters for Apple.[17]

After rejoining Apple, Jobs stated that he wanted to transform the company by making the Mac "the hub of your digital lifestyle." To do this, Apple introduced iLife in 2002, a software suite including applications such as iPhoto, iMovie, iTunes, and eventually the iPod. With the advent of Napster and peer-to-peer music sharing, Apple saw a way to capitalize on the emerging trend of cheap music downloads by creating a legal online music distribution network. iTunes would be the key to exploiting this market. Once downloaded by way of iTunes, music could then be transferred only to the iPod (due to encryption). Apple adopted a limited strategy of giving away iTunes through a short-term promotion with PepsiCo products in order to encourage the sales of the iPod. For the first quarter of 2004, iPod sales comprised $256 million of Apple's $2 billion in total sales[18] (see Exhibit 3 for Apple 10Q Report). With iTunes, Apple has quite possibly revolutionized the distribution of music.

MP3 Technology

The MPEG-1 Layer III (MPEG Audio Layer III) or MP3 has a recent but detailed history.[19] The MP3 is an audio segment of the MPEG industry. This is the major format in which digital music exists. This official industry standard was set by the ISO (Industry Standards Organization) in 1992. The patents regarding this technology belong to Fraunhofer Gesellschaft (FLG), a German company. MPEG-1 is a low-bandwidth video compression, the same type as that used over the Internet. The MPEG-1 Layer III is an audio-only compression component that came from the MPEG-1.

The MP3 originated in Germany in 1987 at the Fraunhofer Institute Integrieste Schaltungen. At the time it was known as Eureka project EU147. Professor Dieter Seitzer of the University of Erlangen came up with an algorithm that was known as the IPO-MPEG Audio Layer 3. In January 1998, Moving

EXHIBIT 3 — Apple Computer, First Quarter Fiscal 2004 10Q Report

Net Sales

Net sales and Macintosh unit sales by operating segment and net sales and unit sales by product follow (net sales in millions and unit sales in thousands):

	Three Months Ended		
	12/27/03	**12/28/02**	**Change**
Net Sales by Operating Segment:			
Americas net sales	$ 924	$ 738	25%
Europe net sales	519	351	48%
Japan net sales	157	139	13%
Retail net sales	273	148	84%
Other segments net sales (a)	133	96	39%
Total net sales	$ 2,006	$ 1,472	36%
Unit Sales by Operating Segment:			
Americas Macintosh unit sales	378	377	0%
Europe Macintosh unit sales	240	202	19%
Japan Macintosh unit sales	77	71	8%
Retail Macintosh unit sales	73	46	59%
Other segments Macintosh unit sales (a)	61	47	30%
Total Macintosh unit sales	829	743	12%
Net Sales by Product:			
Power Macintosh net sales (b)	$ 398	$ 292	36%
PowerBook net sales	399	235	70%
iMac net sales	251	356	(29)%
iBook net sales	221	216	2%
Total Macintosh net sales	1,269	1,099	15%
Peripherals and other hardware (c)	499	218	129%
Software (d)	149	88	69%
Service and other sales (e)	89	67	33%
Total net sales	$ 2,006	$ 1,472	36%
Unit Sales by Product:			
Power Macintosh unit sales	206	158	30%
PowerBook unit sales	195	101	93%
iMac unit sales	227	298	(24)%
iBook unit sales	201	186	8%
Total Macintosh unit sales	829	743	12%
Net sales per Macintosh unit sold (f)	$ 1,531	$ 1,479	4%
iPod unit sales	733	219	235%
iPod net sales	$ 256	$ 81	216%

SOURCE: Table drawn from http://www.sec.gov/.

Picture Exports Group (MPEG) became established as a subcommittee of ISO/IEC (International Standards Organization/International Electrotechnical Commission). The patent for the MP3 came to Fraunhofer in April 1989 in Germany and on November 26, 1996, the MP3 got its patent in the United States. Since then, there has also been the development of MPEG-2. The MPEG-2 is a high-bandwidth audio and video compression format that is the standard for DVDs. In September 1998, Fraunhofer began to try to market his MP3 encoders and decoders to independent developers. Due to the use of the algorithm used in the MP3, which Fraunhofer had patented, developers would have to apply to Fraunhofer for a license.

Beginning in February 1999, the MP3's popularity had increased and numerous MP3 players began to appear on the market. The evolution of personal audio devices has come a long way, from the Walkman to the portable CD to the MP3 player. Now there are numerous Internet sites that offer MP3 music.

iTunes: Apple's Online Music Store

Apple ventured into the market of legal downloads with the introduction of its iTunes Music Store.[20] iTunes offers thousands of downloads at a specified price without requiring a subscription or monthly fees. Originally offered exclusively on Apple's own Mac, iTunes can now be installed on PCs as well. The idea behind iTunes is to provide a solution to the illegal pirating of music and software from rival sources such as Kazaa.

iTunes offers its users a selection of over 500,000 songs, with new songs being continually added. Something can be found from just about every genre of music. Users can perform a search by type of music, artist name, or title of track or album. Each song available can be previewed without making a purchase. If someone decides to buy, he or she has the option of purchasing the entire album, or just the song itself. Each song is 99 cents and a complete album starts at $9.99. Downloads can be made not only to a Mac or PC, but also directly to an iPod. All new song additions are encoded in AAC format, which many say is superior to MP3, although iTunes does still carry the MP3 format on some of its older selections.

Once songs are downloaded, they are stored into a digital music library. As this collection grows, this list of songs can be arranged in many different ways. Songs can be arranged by personal rating, artist, or genre. This feature allows for a customizable playlist for playback or burning onto a CD. iTunes also has playlists arranged by celebrities. Users can read remarks from these celebrities on their song selections as well as purchase songs directly from their list.

iTunes also contains many downloads other than just music. Audiobooks, ranging in price from $2.95 to $15.95, can also be downloaded. iTunes has a collection of over 5,000 audiobooks, including many different language lessons. Also available are downloadable versions of public radio shows.

Many parents make use of the allowance accounts on iTunes. For example, parents can set up an account with a certain predetermined spending limit. The child can then make as many downloads as the money in the account allows. Accounts can be set up to refresh on a monthly basis. For those with multiple children, different accounts can be made so that each child has his or her own spending limit. An alternative to setting up accounts would be the purchase of gift certificates. These gift certificates are available in different denominations and can be sent electronically through e-mail.

iTunes has been a huge success since its inception. In its first week of existence, the number of downloads from iTunes surpassed the one million mark. This feat is amazing considering that at the time of iTunes' introduction to the market downloading was only available for the Mac. In addition, at that time Mac users comprised less than five percent of U.S. computer users.[21] When iTunes was introduced for the PC, sales increased even more rapidly. iTunes downloads for the PC reached the one million mark in three days, less than half the time it took for the Mac version. But the success of iTunes is not measured in number of downloads sold per day or week. After paying royalties, iTunes makes little off the sale of music downloads, approximately ten cents per song. iTunes is used as a means to boost the sales of iPods, which generates a substantial profit per sale. Apple saw a 140 percent increase in the sale of iPods when compared to the previous year before the launch of iTunes.[22]

Suppliers

Record Labels

One key component of success is the relationship that iTunes has with each respective record label. iTunes has agreements with all 5 major labels (BMG, EMI, Sony Music Entertainment, Universal, and Warner Bros.) as well as more than 200 independent labels.[23] These agreements allow iTunes to sell the music owned by these labels and pay the record label each time a song is downloaded. This deal would be considered a reseller agreement, meaning that Apple is not licensing content from these labels, but rather buying it wholesale and re-selling it to consumers.[24] Apple gets to keep its share, while the portion the label receives must be divided among many parties including artists, producers, and publishers. In 2003, labels were projected to earn approximately $33.8 million from sales on iTunes.[25] Although this figure may seem small compared to the number of record labels, it is still far greater than receiving nothing from the millions of illegal downloads that have nearly crippled the music industry.

iTunes Competitors

Since the October 2003 launch of iTunes.com for Windows, Apple has faced a multitude of competitors. Two of these control over 85 percent of the music downloading market both legally and illegally. During the late 1990s, the emergence of music sharing came about with Napster, a freeware program offering free downloads using peer-to-peer transfers. Peer-to-peer transfers mean the users connect directly with other users, without the need for a central point of management.[26] Napster has recently become a subscription service like iTunes. Kazaa, the industry dominator in music and media downloads, was created in 2002. It is based in Australia and Kazaa's services are provided free to the public.

Napster

In May 1999, 19-year-old Shawn Fanning created Napster and the online music revolution, while studying at Northeastern University. The name Napster came from his Internet "handle" he had used as a programmer. He created a type of software that allowed music fans anywhere to "share" MP3s in one forum. This software creation led to the ever-growing controversy of the availability of MP3s on the Internet. As the explosion of music sharing came about in the late 1990s, Napster's servers were overloaded with millions of requests a day for media downloads. Artists found this new "sharing" forum to be nothing more than continuous copyright violations. Fanning soon became the target for their animosity and became one of the most disliked people in the music industry. During the first year of service, Napster was obtaining more than 250,000 new users a week, while maintaining a free service.[27]

During 2000, Napster was in and out of court and was finally slated to shut down on July 26, 2000. The decision was reversed two days later on July 28, 2000.[28] In 2001, Konrad Hilbers, a 38-year-old German, became CEO of the rapidly declining music file-sharing site Napster. In June 2001, Napster had over 26 million users, but growth was declining fast, going from 6.3 billion minutes used a day to 2.2 billion minutes used a day. On March 7, 2002, Napster closed its servers, while opting to implement a fee-based service to comply with Federal Judge Marilyn Patel's decision. On June 3, 2002, Napster filed for Chapter 11 bankruptcy in an effort to secure court-ordered protection from creditors. This move was part of the overall financial restructuring strategy of Bertelsmann AG, which was proceeding with its takeover of the once popular file-sharing system. By July 2003, Roxio, Inc. had taken over Napster and was planning a Napster 2.0 launch, which became a legal paid service, by Christmas 2003 and was successful.[29]

Currently Napster 2.0 is online with content agreements from five major record labels and hundreds of independent labels. Napster 2.0 currently uses WMV files for downloading which is proprietary to Microsoft. WMV file encoding falls in between MP3 and AAC (MP4) in terms of quality. Prices are $0.99 a song or $9.95 for an entire album. Currently, Napster has a selection that only carries three out of ten songs currently queried for on the Internet. This means that Napster is only licensed to sell 30 percent of the songs users on the Internet want.[30] Through a restructuring and quality legal representation, Napster finally has a legal base that is expected to stand.

Kazaa

Sharman Networks Limited was founded in January 2002 as a private limited company. Kazaa Media Desktop and Kazaa Plus are products of Sharman Networks. Sharman Networks develops and markets world class Internet applications and is the owner of Kazaa, the world's leading seek-and-find media application. Sharman Networks is a privately owned company that makes millions by soliciting companies to advertise on its software. Kazaa Media Desktop currently has over an 80 percent market share of music file downloads on the Inter-

net. The attached graph shows usage of bandwidth at Cornell University of all data moving inbound and outbound from 2002 (see Exhibit 4). As is illustrated, Kazaa makes up a large portion of college Internet traffic. Being Australian-based has kept the RIAA away for the time being but the recording industry is in legal pursuit of Kazaa and its owner Sharman Networks. Sharman has been in constant legal battles in both the United States and Australia over the Australian Digital Media Act.

Kazaa Media Desktop is a program littered with spyware and ad-based programs that "infect" consumer systems, unless the consumer upgrades to a platinum service for a one time fee of $29.95, which would block the ads. The program is available in a multitude of languages which goes along

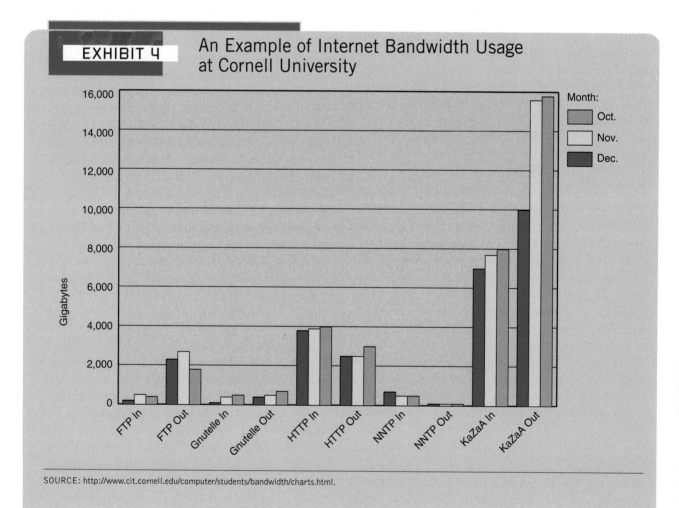

EXHIBIT 4 An Example of Internet Bandwidth Usage at Cornell University

SOURCE: http://www.cit.cornell.edu/computer/students/bandwidth/charts.html.

with the company's world-wide advertising strategy, which is clearly working. To illustrate, over two million new subscribers were added from the week of February 29, 2004, to March 6, 2004.[31]

Sharman's CEO Nikki Hemming argues that "More than 60 million consumers worldwide see file sharing on the Internet as the most convenient, efficient, and enjoyable way to get digital entertainment." Sharman is far from the clear when it comes to its legal battles in 2004 and beyond. The company struggles to maintain its dominance in the music sharing industry as the RIAA is winning the battle in making music downloads legitimate.

RealNetworks, Inc.

RealNetworks through its RealPlayer Music Store is apparently seeking to start a price war with Apple by dropping the price to $0.49 a song and $4.99 compared to Apple's price of $0.99 and $9.99, respectively. However, analysts indicate that Real-Networks is pricing below the cost of purchasing the music from the record companies. As part of its battle to reduce Apple's market share, RealNetworks also recently launched technology called Harmony which will allow RealNetworks users to translate songs purchased from RealPlayer Music Store into a format that can be played on iPod, Apple's portable music player. It also allows Real-Networks music to be played on Microsoft formats as well. Apple has suggest that it will respond legally, but RealPlayer has suggested that it has not broken any laws.[32]

Other Competitors

Wal-Mart, the world's largest retailer, "fired a shot heard across the Internet" on March 24, 2004 with the launch of its own online music store, with 88-cent downloads—11 cents cheaper than Apple. Other companies slated to start their own music sharing business are Virgin and Sony.[33] Microsoft and Yahoo have both signaled that they will start selling music online in late 2004.[34]

Differentiation

iTunes service has many similarities and differences to its closest competitors. First and foremost, iTunes is 100 percent legal, which makes using its service morally correct. iTunes is on the cutting edge in song format, being the first company to utilize the AAC (MP4) format, which carries the highest compression ratio, while maintaining the best song quality. AAC (or Advanced Audio Compression) is among the new formats for file compression and is being fused with the new audio standard for quality MP4. However, Apple's own FairPlay digital-rights-management (DRM) system is a computer code bound to each downloaded track or album that carries instructions on how the music may be used. For example, FairPlay allows unlimited CD burns of single tracks but doesn't allow songs bought through iTunes to be played on devices other than iPod or to be traded on file-swapping networks. While anyone can use AAC—it's an open standard, after all, and widely available for licensing—Fair-Play puts a barrier between Apple and the rest of the online music community because iTunes downloads can play only on iPods.[35] Kazaa and Napster predominantly use MP3 and WMV, respectively. Although Kazaa uses MP3 it does not have a standard media format on its service.

iTunes software is compatible on all Mac and Windows operating systems, while Napster is only compatible with certain versions of Windows. Kazaa operates on all versions of Windows, but neither Napster nor Kazaa are compatible with Apple's Macintosh format. iTunes software offers live stream radio stations 24 hours a day, which both Napster and Kazaa do not. It also has a 10-band equalizer for customizing your music. iTunes does, however, lack the CD burning software that comes with Napster for free.

Both iTunes and the new legal version of Napster have extremely similar pricing at $0.99 a song. However, Napster offers a premium service for $9.95 a month and Kazaa has a completely free service. Despite the staggering success of Apple iTunes Music Store in just four months, illegal music sharing and downloading is still ahead of the legitimate music services, but losing ground quickly. This is where iTunes must market itself and show the strengths that it offers that the others do not offer. Apple is doing so accordingly by giving away millions of free songs with Pepsi to try to get the market away from the illegal services. Napster has yet to react with a similar marketing campaign.[36] iTunes is building an image for itself as a premium quality music retailer by offering top of the line files and software at a market price. This is a main focus in its efforts to differentiate itself from the competitors.

Hardware

Apple's Digital Music Player, the iPod

The wildly popular iPod was one of Apple's most successful product releases of 2003. The iPod comes in the small or mini form (see Exhibit 5).[37] The mini iPod holds 1000 songs while the small iPod holds 3700, 5000, or 10,000 songs depending upon the gigabytes (GB) or storage size available (15, 30, or 40 GBs). The battery life for both the small and mini is 8 hours. Both products also have skip protection for up to 25 minutes. The mini and small also have accessories that include headphones, AC adapter, and FireWire cable.

Major Competitors

Some of the iPod's major competitors include: Rio Karma, Dell Digital Jukebox DJ, Samsung Napster YP-910GS, and the Gateway Jukebox Player DMP-X20 (see Exhibit 6).[38] Some of the differences from the iPod include a longer battery life for these competitors such as a 16-hour battery life for the Dell MP3 player. The weight also varies from one competitor to the next ranging from 7.7 ounces to 5.5 ounces. (For a detailed list of the major competitors' specifications, see Exhibit 7.)

Marketing

Apple's recent marketing endeavors have earned it awards, product sales, and a devoted base of customers, both new and old. In fact, Apple has been awarded *Advertising Age*'s 2003 Marketer of the Year for its upbeat, original, and most importantly,

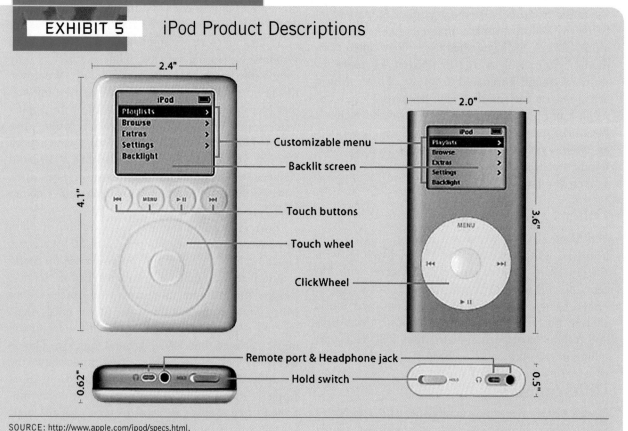

EXHIBIT 5 iPod Product Descriptions

2.4"
4.1"
0.62"

2.0"
3.6"
0.5"

Customizable menu
Backlit screen
Touch buttons
Touch wheel
ClickWheel
Remote port & Headphone jack
Hold switch

SOURCE: http://www.apple.com/ipod/specs.html.

EXHIBIT 6   Products of Competitors to iPod

Creative Nomad
Jukebox Zen NX (20 GB)

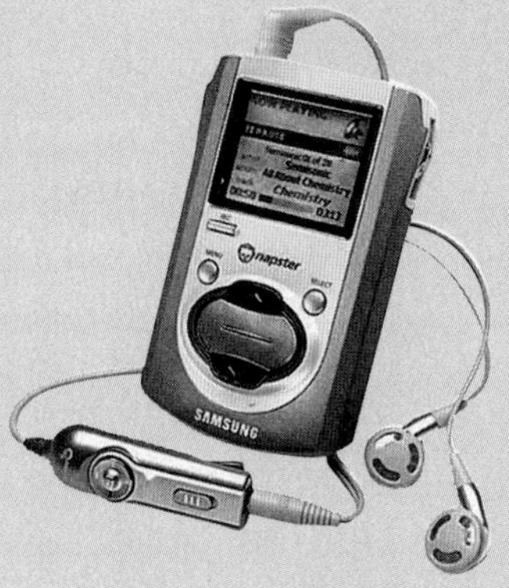

Samsung Napster
YP-910GS (20 GB)

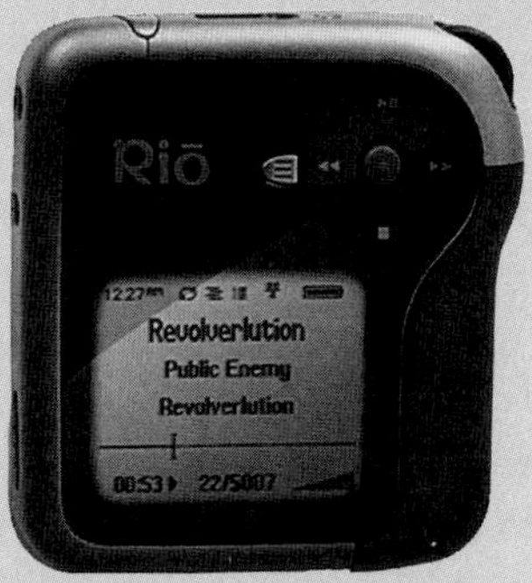

Rio Karma (20 GB)

iRiver iHP-120

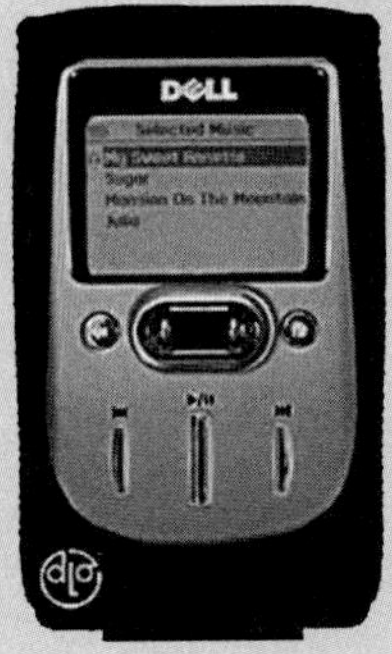

Dell Digital Jukebox
DJ (20 GB)

Gateway Jukebox Player
DMP-X20 (20 GB)

SOURCE: http://reviews.cnet.com/4520-6497-5093864.html.

memorable advertisements for both its iPod and iTunes.[39] Apple has been hailed as one of the best marketers of 2003 by many different sources, and has had a reputation over the years of being a brand that can gain customers through its well thought out and carefully executed marketing strategies. Marketing is indeed one of Apple's strengths and the company continues to develop new advertising ideas and strategies for each new product it introduces.

Apple has focused more on the advertisement of its iPod rather than the actual iTunes website. Because most of Apple's profit comes from sales of the highly profitable iPod, it has been the focus of the campaign. In almost all ads, however, it is mentioned that the iPod is to be used with Apple's iTunes digital music store. All marketing tactics employed by Apple focus on the consumer. Although embraced by the younger generation, the marketing strategies used by Apple are effective with the older

EXHIBIT 7 Details of Products of Competitors to iPod

Product name	Creative Nomad Jukebox Zen NX (20 GB)	Samsung Napster YP-910GS (20 GB)	Rio Karma (20 GB)	iRiver iHP-120	Dell Digital Jukebox DJ (20 GB)	Gateway Jukebox Player DMP-X20 (20 GB)
Basic Specs						
Product type	Digital player	Digital player / recorder / radio	Digital player	Digital player / voice recorder / radio	Digital player / voice recorder	Digital player / voice recorder / radio
PC interface(s) supported	Hi-Speed USB	Hi-Speed USB	Hi-Speed USB	Hi-Speed USB	Hi-Speed USB	Hi-Speed USB
Flash memory installed	8 MB	Info unavailable	Info unavailable	Info unavailable	Info unavailable	Info unavailable
Storage capacity	20 GB	20 GB	20 GB	20 GB	20 GB	20 GB
Digital formats supported	MP3	MP3	MP3	MP3	MP3	MP3
Weight	7.2 oz	6 oz	5.5 oz	5.6 oz	7.6 oz	7.7 oz
Resolution	132 × 64	Info unavailable	160 × 128	Info unavailable	160 × 104	160 × 128
Battery technology	Lithium ion	Lithium polymer	Lithium ion	Lithium polymer	Lithium ion	Lithium ion
Mfr estimated battery life	14 hour(s)	10 hour(s)	15 hour(s)	16 hour(s)	16 hour(s)	10 hour(s)
Software included	Creative MediaSource	Drivers & Utilities	Drivers & Utilities	Drivers & Utilities	Drivers & Utilities	Drivers & Utilities

SOURCE: http://reviews.cnet.com/4520-6497-5093864.html.

generation as well.[40] The tactics that Apple has employed to reach its consumer focus on energy, fun, and freedom. Many contend that Apple ads make people want Apple products right away, and that those who have Apple products are included in a group that is different, maybe even more elite, than those who do not have Apple products.[41] Apple's marketing and design appeals to consumers across generations and international boundaries.[42] Apple's successful marketing technique is not luck, however. Its success lies in a carefully thought out plan.

Marketing Plan

The plan begins with design of the product.[43] In an industry of low profit margins and cost cutting, Apple takes a different approach to the design of its products. While competitors are doing everything they can to keep costs down, Apple does what it can to make its product different. The beginning of this differentiation comes with design. Design is important for all Apple products, especially the iPod. Great care was taken in its design because the iPod is not simply an item that sits on the top of a desk (as a PC would). Instead, it is an accessory—an accessory with a use.[44] Therefore, consumers are attracted to its sleek, modern design. It appeals to their need for a high-tech product that looks high-tech.

Next, Steve Jobs is essential to the public relations and promotional aspect of Apple, especially with the iPod.[45] Steve Jobs is an expert when it comes to talking with the press, maintaining relationships with magazine editors, and continually creating new relationships.[46] Because of his dynamic, high-energy personality, he is not usually without a new idea that he is energetic about, and is always ready and willing to share it to gain exposure. He maintains relationships with the media well and has been called the "public face and champion of the brand."[47] In fact, in 2003, more than 6,000 iPod and iTunes stories ran in major publications worldwide.[48] In the first eight months of 2003, Apple had only spent $19 million on iPod and iTunes marketing combined.[49] The majority of iPod's press coverage came from people writing about this new phenomenon in the digital music industry.

Third, Apple has garnered major success for iPod and iTunes by way of strategic partnerships with other well-known brands. Apple has created marketing agreements with America Online, Pepsi, Volkswagen of America, and Burton Snowboards.[50] A new partnership created with Hewlett-Packard in January 2004 will give the iPod a major boost in sales to the Windows community (for more information on Apple's relationships with these companies, please see the "Strategic Agreements" section).[51] By affiliating itself with different brands, Apple gains consumer confidence. If one customer is loyal to Pepsi, for example, that customer may be more likely to purchase an iPod or iTunes as a result of the fact that a brand that he or she trusts, Pepsi, is endorsing the Apple brand and new technology. Also, Apple gains exposure through marketing partner advertisements.

Finally, Apple has spent $293 million in capital expenditures on 73 Apple retail stores. Almost 14 million people visited these stores in 2003, according to Apple.[52] Apple philosophy behind the stores is brand exposure. Apple believes that the more people who can touch an Apple product and see what it can truly do with their own eyes, the greater the potential market share.[53]

Advertising Campaign, 2003

Apple's most successful advertising campaign for iTunes and the iPod occurred in 2003. In these ads, dancing black silhouettes were featured against a brightly colored background of bold yellow, purple, orange, green, or bright pink.[54] The silhouettes were featured one at a time on the television screen or were pictured alone on outdoor and print ads. The silhouettes were equipped with an iPod in hand and ear buds in ears and are pictured dancing (Exhibit 8). In the television ads, the silhouettes danced energetically, alone with only their iPod, to songs with

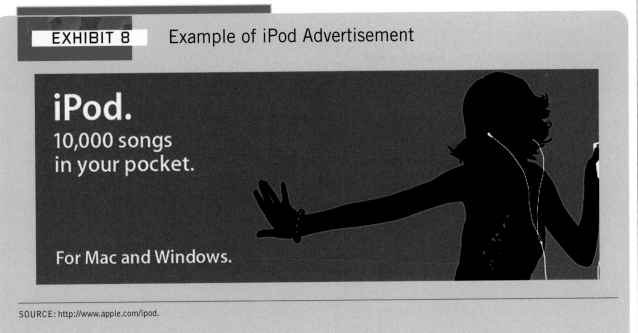

EXHIBIT 8   Example of iPod Advertisement

iPod.
10,000 songs
in your pocket.

For Mac and Windows.

SOURCE: http://www.apple.com/ipod.

hip-hop or edgy rock themes such as "Hey, Mama" by the Black Eyed Peas, or "Are You Gonna Be My Girl" by Jet.[55] The iPod, in Apple's signature stark white color, pops out against the black silhouettes and brightly colored backgrounds. At the end of the ad, the words *iPod and iTunes for Mac or Windows* were shown. In the print ads, the black silhouette is featured in the middle of a dance move, again with the bright background and white iPod. Apple has invested in new print advertising endeavors, especially in music magazines, to promote iTunes and iPod. Apple spent $1.5 million to advertise in *Rolling Stone,* $1.4 million to advertise in *Entertainment Weekly,* and $212,400 to advertise in *Spin* magazine in 2003.[56]

Apple has begun to advertise the iPod mini, its newest hardware endeavor, by using the same black silhouette ad campaign. Usually the ads are done in a two-page spread in print with a cardboard insert of four mini iPods protruding from the seam of the magazine. The mini iPods are true to size and are just another way that Apple is exercising its philosophy of making the product design available to consumers any way it can.

The black silhouette advertisements (television, outdoor, and print) are well liked by all age groups. Although they appeal mainly to 25–29-year-olds, 50–64-year-olds also gave the ads a positive rating

(Exhibit 9, information only available for age groups shown).[57] One reason that the ads appeal to all age levels and nationalities is because the silhouettes do not illustrate age or race. Therefore, any consumer may be able to imagine himself or herself as the dancing silhouette. This marketing strategy has had wide appeal, largely due to its simplicity and energy, which all consumers can relate to. Put simply, the ads "transcend age and nationality—they are about an Apple state of mind."[58]

Strategic Agreements

Hewlett-Packard

Apple's latest agreement will help the company to delve deeper into the mainstream Windows market.[59] In January 2004, HP and Apple agreed to join forces in the iPod revolution. Beginning in the summer of 2004, HP will begin to sell iPods, coated in its signature blue, under a new HP name.[60] The iPod will still look the same, however, and "Everyone will (still) know it's an iPod."[61] In return, HP, the world's second largest computer maker, will preinstall the iTunes music jukebox on all HP desktops and laptops beginning in the summer of 2004.[62]

HP did consider launching its own digital player and online music service.[63] However, at the Con-

---

EXHIBIT 9 Summary of Results for Ad Track, *USA Today*'s Weekly Consumer Survey (Focus: iPod)

Subjects interviewed: consumers familiar with the Apple iPod silhouette ads

Like the ads "a lot"	19%	Average:	21%
Consider the ads "very effective"	20%	Average:	21%

Age group selections:
Ages 25–29
  Like the ads "a lot"   29%
Ages 50–64
  Like the ads "a lot"   19%

SOURCE: T. Howard, "Ads for iPods Offer Big Music Gift in Small Package," *USA Today,* January 5, 2004.

sumer Electronics Show in Las Vegas in January 2004, HP CEO Carly Fiorina stated, "We looked at the music space and said, 'There's a great digital music player and a great music store out there, so it's logical for us to partner.'"[64] For the first time, a company who usually packages Windows software on its PCs will be packaging an Apple program (the iTunes online music service) on its PCs. The deal stipulates that Apple will not co-brand iPods for any other PC company, however.[65] Apple will be able to distribute the iPod throughout HP's large retail network, which is likely to bring in more customers for Apple. This, in turn, is likely to bring more customers to the iTunes Music Store as well.

Apple's motivation for the deal was that the company wants to reach more Windows users through the iPod and iTunes. HP brings many Windows customers into the picture, so the partnership seems like a profitable deal on both ends of the agreement.[66] The exposure to Windows users is not only good for iPod and iTunes, but also for Apple as a brand, whose computers are "limited to a niche of less than 5 percent of the worldwide PC market share."[67]

Pepsi

In October 2003, Apple and Pepsi-Cola North America announced a promotion to legally give away 100 million free songs to Mac and Windows users from the iTunes Music Store.[68] This promotion has been deemed historic by many because there had never been an agreement so large between an established brand and a digital online music seller.[69] This agreement helped to solidify the success of the online music selling business, and gives excellent exposure to Apple's iTunes and iPod.

The agreement stated that beginning on February 1, 2004, 100 million winning codes would be placed under the caps of Pepsi, Diet Pepsi, and Sierra Mist.[70] Pepsi would package 300 million bottles in the promotional iTunes wrapping, however, making one in three customers a winner.[71] The campaign began with a Super Bowl ad on February 1, 2004, and ran until March 31, 2004. The winning codes were redeemable for one free song at the iTunes Music Store. Winners could choose from any of the 400,000 songs available on the site.[72] Pepsi paid Apple for the songs downloaded by the win-

ners. Apple gained exposure to customers by way of winners visiting iTunes.com and redeeming the code for a song. Apple hoped that the promotion would encourage people who might not have been to the iTunes site before to try it, and hopefully return for business.

Pepsi and music have always been synonymous in the advertising world. Steve Jobs supported the promotion wholeheartedly. He said, "This historic promotion to legally give away 100 million free songs will go down in history as igniting the legal download market. Pepsi has marketed their products through music for generations, and this is going to be another one that is remembered for decades."[73]

On the Pepsi side, the promotion very much complemented its advertising strategies. Through the promotion, Pepsi hoped to capitalize on the iPod and iTunes popularity, and hoped to target consumers that were users (or potential users) of Apple's music community. Pepsi had long integrated music as part of its platform with advertisements featuring Michael Jackson, Madonna, Shakira, and Beyoncé.[74] The Apple agreement complemented Pepsi's ongoing music advertising initiatives, and would benefit Pepsi as well as Apple.

America Online

America Online (AOL) and Apple entered into an alliance in October 2003 to integrate AOL Music and iTunes.[75] AOL is the world's leading interactive services company, with more than 25 million U.S. members.[76] AOL Music, one of the most popular music destination sites on the web, reaches the largest audience of online music fans in the world.[77] Each month, AOL music reaches 16 million unique users through programming, products, and services that make it possible to "discover, experience, listen to and buy music online."[78] At AOL Music, AOL members can preview songs, videos, and concerts (live) before they are released anywhere else.[79]

Now, AOL will feature links to the iTunes Music Store next to an artist that it is featuring, playing, writing an article about, etc., if the artist has music available at the iTunes website. The purpose of the deal was to unite "the number one music destination site, AOL Music, with the number one music download site, Apple's iTunes Music

Store, to bring the customers the most complete on-line digital music experience," according to Jonathan Miller, Chairman and CEO of America Online.[80] The deal integrates and gives exposure to the two biggest music providers, and both companies can expect to gain from the deal.

Volkswagen

In early 2003, the iPod was promoted with Volkswagen of America. Volkswagen (VW) offered a free iPod to customers who purchased a 2003 hardtop Beetle 10. The ad campaign was aptly named "Pods Unite."[81] The deal brought iPod enthusiasts (and people who just wanted to learn more about the iPod) into the Volkswagen stores, and both products benefited from the advertisement. For three months, iPods were shown in Volkswagen showrooms.[82] Also, the Volkswagen sold iPod connectivity wiring and a cradle for the iPod to be used in the new VW Beetle.[83] Because both brands are known for unique design, it is likely that the promotion brought in consumers that highly value the design aspect of a product, whether it is a car or a digital music player.

Burton Snowboards

In January 2004, Burton announced that it would be making and soon releasing a snowboarding/snow-skiing jacket made especially for use with the iPod (Exhibit 10). The jacket has a built-in iPod control electronic system on the sleeve of the jacket, so that the iPod can be operated without having to remove gloves, dig in pockets, or fumble with zippers.[84] The iPod rests in a protected chest pocket in the inner lining of the jacket. As of March 2004, both the men's and women's versions of the jacket have sold out.[85] This is a further attempt by Apple to place a product into the hands of those who use

EXHIBIT 10 Complementary Product Advertised with iPods

SOURCE: http://www.burton.com/Burton/gear/products.asp?productID=728.

iPods, and will create exposure for the iPod by way of young snowboarders and skiers showing off and wearing the special jacket.

Future Opportunities and Challenges

Apple's newest technology for music computer files, AAC-encoded files, may pose a problem for Apple. Currently, iTunes are in both the MP3 format and the AAC format. Any and all new songs that Apple adds to iTunes will be in the AAC format. Apple has now set the technology so that any AAC-encoded songs (the new standard) downloaded from iTunes will not play on any other device than the iPod. This may boost sales of their product, but may also anger iTunes users who have been able to use their own non-iPod players with iTunes downloads. However, it must be noted that each time iTunes users download a song, they make a 99-cent investment in Apple and their music collection. Each time they download a song, this is an incentive to stay with their iPod rather than change to a different brand of digital music player, especially if their investments (songs) will not play on a competitor's brand.[86] However, the competitive threat by current competitors, and new entrant RealNetworks and other potential entrants such as Microsoft and Yahoo, are likely to be problematic as Apple moves forward.

The entertainment industry is rapidly changing. There have been technology gurus who have predicted that in the future all home entertainment will be downloadable, and physical discs and tapes will be obsolete. Apple may have a future in developing an online marketplace where one can buy movies, videos, video games, or other forms of media entertainment. With the success of iTunes and iPod will likely come additional competitors besides those already in the market. Apple will have to continue to be the leader in the market through innovation and differentiation in order to remain successful.

Notes

1. Leonard, Devin, "Songs in the Key of Steve," *Fortune,* April 28, 2003.
2. Ibid.
3. apple-history.com, http://www.apple-history.com/frames/.
4. Ibid.
5. Kimmel, Leigh, "Apple Computer, Inc.: A History," 1998, http://www.geocities.com/Athens/3682/applehistory.html.
6. Ibid.
7. apple-history.com.
8. Apple Computer History Weblog, http://apple.computerhistory.org.
9. Kimmel.
10. Apple Computer History Weblog.
11. apple-history.com.
12. Ibid.
13. Apple Computer History Weblog.
14. Quoted in apple-history.com.
15. Ibid.
16. Ibid.
17. Ibid.
18. Apple Computer, 1st Quarter Fiscal 2004 10Q Report.
19. Section information adapted from "History of the MP3 and How Did It All Begin?" http://www.mp3-mac.com/Pages/History_of_MP3.html.
20. Section information adapted from http://www.apple.com/itunes.
21. Hardy, Phil, "Apple Launches Windows Based iTunes . . .," *Music & Copyright Magazine,* October 29, 2003.
22. Ibid.
23. "History of the MP3 . . ."
24. Cohen, Warren, http://www.rollingstone.com/news/newsarticle.asp?nid=18075.
25. "How Does Kazaa Work?" 2003, http://www.sharmannetworks.com/content/view/full/83.
26. "Napster's History," 2001, http://w3.uwyo.edu/~pz/nap2.htm.
27. "The History of the Napster Struggle," 2001, http://www.theneworleanschannel.com/news/457209/detail.html.
28. "Napster 2.0 to Launch by Christmas," 2003, http://www.roxio.com/en/company/news/archive/prelease030728.jhtml.
29. Ibid.
30. "Napster 2.0 Review," 2004, http://www.breakdownindustries.com/archives/000032.html.
31. "Kazaa Usage Map," 2003, http://tools.waglo.com/kazaa.
32. Wingfield, Nick, "Price War in Online Music," *Wall Street Journal,* August 17, 2004.
33. Salkever, Alex, "Byte of the Apple, Digital Music: Apple Shouldn't Sing Solo," *Business Week Online,* March 24, 2004.
34. Wingfield.
35. Ibid.
36. "Apple iTunes Music Store Review," 2004, http://www.breakdownindustries.com/archives/000028.html.
37. Section adapted from http://www.apple.com/ipod/specs.html.
38. Section adapted from CNET Reviews, http://www.reviews.cnet.com/html.
39. Cuneo, A., "Apple Transcends as Lifestyle Brand," *Advertising Age,* December 15, 2003.
40. Howard, T., "Ads for iPods Offer Big Music Gift in Small Package," *USA Today,* January 5, 2004.
41. Ibid.

42. Cuneo.
43. Ibid.
44. Salkever, A., "Apple + HP = iPod Forever," *Business Week Online,* January 14, 2004.
45. Cuneo.
46. Ibid.
47. Ibid.
48. Ibid.
49. Ibid.
50. Arango, T., "McDonald's Spins Billion-Song iTunes Giveaway," *The New York Post,* November 6, 2003.
51. Evans, M., "Partnership with HP Gives Apple Extra Push for iTunes and iPod: Deeper into Windows," *National Post's Financial Post & FP Investing,* January 9, 2004.
52. Cuneo.
53. Ibid.
54. Howard.
55. Ibid.
56. "Teen Marketing: Teen Targets," *Adweek,* October 27, 2003.
57. Howard.
58. Ibid.
59. Evans.
60. Wong, M., "HP Deal Latest Boost for Apple iPod," *Associated Press Online,* January 10, 2004.
61. Ibid.
62. Ibid.
63. Evans.
64. Wong.
65. Salkever., "Apple + HP = iPod Forever"
66. Wong.
67. Ibid.
68. "Apple and Pepsi to Give Away 100 Million Free Songs," *PR Newswire,* October 16, 2003.
69. Ibid.
70. Ibid.
71. Arango.
72. "Apple and Pepsi to Give Away 100 Million Free Songs."
73. Ibid.
74. Ibid.
75. "Apple and America Online Announce Online Music Alliance," *PR Newswire,* October 16, 2003.
76. Ibid.
77. Ibid.
78. Ibid.
79. Ibid.
80. Ibid.
81. Wong.
82. Ibid.
83. Ibid.
84. Ibid.
85. http://www.burton.com/Burton/gear/products.asp?productID=730.
86. Kidman, A., "Online Move Unstoppable in Movies, Music," *The Australian,* September 16, 2003.

Avid Technology, Inc.

Philip K. Goulet
Alan Bauerschmidt
University of South Carolina

"I think that any company that is very successful can be a victim of its own success," proclaimed David Krall in the fall of 2000 as he pondered Avid Technology's past performance. He was Avid's third CEO in almost as many years. Poor financial performance led the board to replace a company founder in 1996 with a successful outside executive from a large, high-tech company to turn Avid around. However, results were slow in coming, causing the board to replace him three years later with Krall, one of the company's divisional chief operating officers.

The burden of a second attempt at a turnaround was squarely placed on the shoulders of the 39-year-old Krall, a relatively young man with only four years experience in one of the company's divisions. Krall had a history as an innovator. He won the Harvard Business School Entrepreneur of the Year Award for one of his inventions: a backup battery for laptop computers for which he received a patent, and he navigated Digidesign, a division of Avid, to strong performance while the overall company suffered poor results. Avid's board was counting on the entrepreneurial Krall to orchestrate the strategic renewal the company desperately needed.

Avid Technology, Inc. was the quintessential high-tech success story. Sales grew rapidly following the company's first product shipment in late 1989. Avid achieved high growth rates and accolades from customers and industry analysts by applying digital technology to processes used to manipulate pictures, graphics, and sound in the creation of movie films, television programming, and news broadcasts. In effect, Avid built "a better mousetrap" in the way moving pictures, graphics, and sound were captured, edited, and then reproduced for an audience's viewing and listening pleasure.

However, by 1995 sales growth began to slow. New management was brought in by the end of 1996 to turn Avid's fortunes around and place the company, once again, on a profitable growth path. The return to Avid's stellar past, though, was a tumultuous one. The new management team, which had been in place for three years, made several strategic decisions to turn the company around. However, their efforts failed to achieve sustainable results, and they soon lost the confidence of the company's board. Their departure was indicative of Avid's failure to find the strategic prescription for the problems that plagued the company.

By decisively replacing top management for a second time, the board sent a strong signal to the company's newest management team that nothing short of Avid's immediate turnaround was expected. Understanding what had happened to Avid over the past few years was the urgent task now facing Krall. The new CEO had to determine what the prior two CEOs had done, or not done, that turned Avid's fortunes so quickly. And, more important, Krall had to determine a new course of action to return the company to its glorious past.

Reprinted by permission of Philip K. Goulet, University of South Carolina, and Alan Bauerschmidt, Moore School of Business, University of South Carolina.

Company Overview and History

Located within the high-tech metropolitan area of Boston, Massachusetts, Avid Technology produced systems to digitally capture, edit, and distribute media in the forms of movie films, television programming, and news broadcasts. The company was an industry leader in several markets. This was accomplished by providing products that improved the productivity of film editors. Traditional analog technology required the capturing of moving pictures, graphics, and sound on magnetic tape, the cutting and splicing of this tape to edit picture sequences, and the duplication of this tape for distribution. Digital technology captured moving pictures, graphics, and sound in the form of binary codes recognizable by computers. Editing these digitized pictures, graphics, and sound sequences therefore became a process similar to editing a word processing file (which consists of digitized text)—a mouse is used to cut and paste the pictures, graphics, and sound into the desired sequence on the computer. The resulting movie film, for example, is a computer file of digitized pictures, graphics, and sound. Digital technology enabled editors to manipulate moving pictures, graphics, and sound in a faster, more creative, and less costly manner than that of traditional analog, tape-based systems. It also provided editors with greater capabilities for creating special effects. Editing and creating the special effects in the new *Star Wars* series, as an example, was accomplished through the use of Avid products. Similarly, Avid systems were employed by producers to achieve the visualization of Gary Sinise (Lieutenant Dan Taylor) as a double amputee in the movie *Forrest Gump*. Moreover, unlike analog film which shows wear and tear after 15–25 showings, no quality is lost in digital films.

Avid also developed computer systems for digital editing in newsrooms, which helped create content for television news programs. Additionally, the company developed digital audio systems for professional use. Avid's products were used worldwide in film studios, network, affiliate, independent, and cable television stations, recording studios, advertising agencies, government and educational institutions, and corporate video departments. Corporate uses included video applications by real estate firms to display property listings and by professional sports teams, such as the Green Bay Packers, to analyze game plays.

Avid was founded in 1987 by William Warner, who left his position at Apollo Computer, Inc., a manufacturer of computer systems, to pursue his revolutionary idea of digitizing moving pictures and sound onto computer disk to enhance the ability to edit stored images and sounds. In 1988, Curt Rawley, former president of Racal Design Services, a designer of printed circuit boards, and Eric Peters, former engineer at Apollo Computer and Digital Equipment Corporation (now Compaq Computers), joined Warner in his vision.

The three entrepreneurs developed Media Composer, the product upon which the new company was launched. Product shipment began in the fourth quarter of 1989. Sales grew rapidly, rising from $1 million in 1989 to $7 million, $20 million, and $52 million in 1990, 1991, and 1992, respectively.

To finance the company's growth, Avid went public in 1993 (NASDAQ: AVID), generating additional capital of $53 million. In the same year, sales more than doubled to $113 million. The company rose to the fifth position in *Inc.* magazine's list of "100 Fastest Growing Small Public U.S. Companies" and ranked ninth on *Fortune*'s list of "100 Fastest Growing American Companies." Rapid growth continued, with Avid recording revenues of $204 million in 1994 and $407 million in 1995, an 81 percent and 100 percent increase over the prior year, respectively. Through 1995, Avid was achieving its objectives to quickly gain market share and develop a leadership position in its markets. However, sales growth following 1995 slowed, with revenues increasing only five percent to $429 million in 1996, ten percent to $471 million in 1997, and two percent to $482 million in 1998. In 1999, revenues decreased for the first time in the company's history, dropping six percent to $453 million. Exhibit 1 provides a consolidated statement of operations and Exhibit 2 a consolidated balance sheet for the company. Avid grew to about 1,700 employees by the end of 1999.

A key factor in Avid's rapid sales growth was its ability to establish a channel for international sales during its earliest days. Avid established sales offices in seven different countries by 1993, and by 1999 it had offices in 20 different countries. Sales outside North America quickly grew from 11 percent of revenues in

EXHIBIT 1

Avid Technology, Inc. Consolidated Statement of Operations for the Periods Ending 1989–2000

Financial Data in $ Millions
except per share data

	1989	1990	1991	1992	1993	1994	1995	1996	1997	1998	1999	2000
Net Revenues	0.9	7.4	20.1	51.9	112.9	203.7	406.6	429.0	471.3	482.4	452.6	476.0
Cost of Sales	0.5	3.4	9.6	23.7	54.1	99.9	198.8	238.8	221.5	190.2	205.9	234.4
Gross Profit	0.4	4	10.5	28.2	58.8	103.8	207.8	190.2	249.8	292.2	246.7	241.6
Operating Expenses	2.1	6.3	10.5	24.7	55.7	87	185.2	220.5	219.7	242.6	246.9	229.8
Nonrecurring Costs	0	0.6	1	0.9	0	0	5.5	29	0	28.4	14.5	0
Amort. of Acquired Assets	0	0	0	0	0	0	0	0	0	34.2	79.9	66.9
Other Inc. <Expense>	0	0.1	0.1	0	1.5	1	1.4	3.4	8.1	8.6	3.5	3.7
Income Taxes	0	0	0	1.2	0.9	4.8	8.6	–17.9	11.8	–0.8	46.4	5
Net Income <Loss>	–1.7	–2.8	–0.9	1.4	5.5	13	15.4	–38	26.4	–3.6	–137.5	–56.4
Net Income <Loss> per Common Share	–0.57	–0.84	–0.27	0.29	0.38	1.1	0.77	–1.8	1.08	–0.15	–5.75	–2.28
Common Stock Value												
High	n/a	n/a	n/a	n/a	27.16	43.50	48.75	25.88	38.00	47.75	34.25	24.50
Low	n/a	n/a	n/a	n/a	16.00	20.50	16.75	10.13	9.00	11.06	10.00	9.38

NOTE: Nonrecurring costs primarily relate to write-offs resulting from restructuring and/or acquisitions. Amortization of acquired assets relates to the Softimage acquisition.
SOURCE: Avid annual reports/10Ks 1993–2000.

EXHIBIT 2

Avid Technology, Inc. Consolidated Balance Sheet for the Years Ending 1998–2000

Financial Data in $ Millions

	1998	1999	2000
Assets			
Cash & marketable securities	111.8	72.8	83.2
Accounts receivable, net	89.8	76.2	90.0
Inventories	11.1	15.0	21.1
Other current assets	29.0	12.6	11.7
Total current assets	241.7	176.4	206.1
Property, plant & equipment, net	35.4	32.7	26.1
Other assets	209.6	102.9	34.2
Total assets	486.7	312.0	266.4
Liabilities & stockholders' equity			
Accounts payable	24.3	24.0	28.8
Other accrued charges	75.4	61.8	56.2
Deferred revenues	22.9	20.3	24.5
Total current liabilities	122.6	106.1	109.5
Long-term debt	13.3	14.2	13.4
Other	60.5	23.8	5.7
Stockholders' equity			
Common stock	0.3	0.3	0.3
Additional paid-in-capital	349.3	366.6	359.1
Retained earnings	14.3	−128.1	−197.8
Treasury stock	−68.0	−66.5	−15.6
Deferred compensation	−3.8	−1.9	−4.8
Cumulative translation adjustment	−1.8	−2.5	−3.4
Total stockholders' equity	290.3	167.9	137.8
Total liabilities & stockholders' equity	486.7	312.0	266.4

SOURCE: Avid annual reports/10Ks 1998–2000.

1990 to 42 percent in 1992 and 51 percent by 1999, with Avid selling to over 75 foreign markets. European sales showed the most promise, representing approximately 87 percent of total international sales. Sales from the Asian region were disappointing, but were expected to generally improve as the economy of the region, especially that in Japan, came out of recession.

Avid's Markets

Avid served three markets. Avid's primary market as a source of company revenues was the film, television, and related industries. The film and television industries came to recognize digital technology as state-of-the-art, and Avid Technology as the leader in this technology. Exhibit 3 provides a sample listing of films and television programs that were created using Avid products. The estimated $1 billion film industry was a rapid adopter of new technology and thus quickly migrated from analog to digital products, giving Avid more than an 80 percent share of the market segments it served in this industry.

On the other hand, the $2 billion television industry was still predominantly tape-based, as was the $900 million audio industry. These industries represented a significant growth opportunity for the company. The $985 million corporate and institutional video industry was also predominantly tape-based, with Avid holding the leadership position in the digital segment (Avid's total industry share was 13 percent, versus all other digital-based competitors who comprised 27 percent). Thus, the company saw an opportunity for significant growth in this industry as well.

Avid's secondary market as a source of company revenues was the $350 million news broadcast industry. Although the company had focused on this market since 1993, its efforts to gain a strong foothold in the news broadcast industry were less successful than its efforts in the film and television industries. A key factor was the cost of the large, integrated systems these customers required, which ran into the millions of dollars. In addition, Avid did not offer products that could perform all the functions required in the highly complex process of news broadcast creation. To satisfy the diverse needs of news broadcast customers, the company's products required bundling with digital or analog products made by other vendors.

Further, this industry was still predominantly analog-based. Its migration from an analog to a digital format was significantly influenced by the high switching costs involving capital outlays and personnel training, as well as the perceived risks associated with systems that may have an unwieldy mix of both analog and digital devices. However, news broadcast firms were expected to more readily make the transition to digital technology as their expensive analog equipment reached replacement age.

Other factors limiting Avid's performance in this industry were the company's relative size and experience compared to competitors such as Sony. When making high-cost investments reaching and exceeding one million dollars in highly critical areas of their operations, news broadcast firms relied heavily on suppliers with financial stability, past performance, and long-lasting relationships. As a result, Avid, a small high-tech company (i.e., less than $500 million in sales) and a relative newcomer to the industry, realized that establishing a strong presence in this market would take time.

EXHIBIT 3 Films and Television Programs Created Using Avid Products (sample listing only)

Films	Television Programs
Lethal Weapon 4	Ally McBeal
Lost in Space	Frasier
The Perfect Storm	Friends
Star Trek: Insurrection	Just Shoot Me
Titanic	Survivor II
The X-Files Fight the Future	Veronica's Closet

NOTE: 85 percent of films made in the U.S. in 2000 were edited on Avid systems. 95 percent of prime-time television programs in 2000 were edited on Avid systems.

SOURCE: Avid Technology, Inc. public documents; The Boston Globe, 4/30/01.

Avid's tertiary market as a source of company revenues was the retail consumer market. The company entered this market in 1994. The retail consumer includes individuals who, for example, edit home videos or photos on their personal computers. Several firms were producing products to serve the home market, yet no one firm had yet emerged as the market leader.

Avid competed in this market with its Avid Cinema product. Avid Cinema was created by the company as an easy-to-use video software package for the retail consumer. Individuals with videotapes of school plays, sporting events, weddings, birthdays, and family get-togethers, for example, could use Avid Cinema to add special effects, songs from favorite CDs, and professional-looking titles to these tapes, turning them into entertaining movies. Avid Cinema had received strong industry reviews. It was named a finalist in 1999 for best digital video product by the editors of *Popular Photography Magazine* and *DigitalFocus,* the leading digital imaging newsletter publishers, and, in 1998, it was nominated for Best of Comdex Fall 1998 and won Best New Product at Retail Xchange (both industry trade shows).

Because this market was still in its infancy, sales to retail consumers were expected to remain modest over the next few years. However, Avid realized that the retail consumer market had great sales potential once the individual gained an understanding of and appreciation for digital editing technology as a standard home-computer application. More excitement was being generated by this market as the cost for high-quality digital cameras (a product that enhanced the utility of Avid Cinema) fell under $500, and computer retailers such as Best Buy and CompUSA began reporting that digital cameras were one of their fastest moving electronic/computer accessories.

Product Development

Avid's first product, Media Composer, was designed specifically for the film and television industries. Indeed, the company's rapid growth was largely attributed to the market's acceptance of this initial product. Although Avid offered other products to the film and television industry, Media Composer remained its key product offering by contributing the most to both revenues and company profits.

Avid was dedicated to new product development. The company maintained a consistent level of R&D activity approximating 17 percent of sales, which mirrored its industry average. In addition, Avid engaged in several acquisitions to purchase leading technology in the form of existing products and capabilities that the company believed complemented its existing in-house technology. Exhibit 4 identifies Avid acquisitions that provided the company product diversification and sales growth. As a result of these acquisitions, Avid was able to develop a presence in the news broadcast industry (with systems installations at CBS, NBC, CNN, CNBC, and the BBC, for example), as well as the audio and special effects markets. Avid also formed alliances with other firms to help develop new technologies (see the "Strategic Alliances" section).

Avid's products could be classified into six general categories: video and film editing products, audio products, digital news gathering systems, newsroom computer systems, graphics and special effects products, and storage systems. The company offered numerous products that ranged widely in cost and target market. For example, Avid Symphony, a sophisticated film editing system, cost $150,000 and was designed for professional editors. On the other hand, Avid Cinema cost $139 and was marketed to nonprofessionals—retail consumers using personal computers.

Establishing Industry Standards

As a pioneer in digital technology, Avid took the lead in developing and promoting open industry standards. The company released into the public domain the platform of basic digital technology it developed and applied to specific product creations. This platform, or basic standards observed in the creation of digital media products, became known as Open Media Framework (OMF). OMF grew into a cooperative effort involving more than 150 leading manufacturers of digital products. Products based on OMF standards were compatible with other OMF-based media products (whether graphics,

EXHIBIT 4   Avid Acquisitions[1] ($ in millions)

Year	Company	Revenues	Cost	Description
1993	Digital Video Applications Corp.	n/a	$4.6	Developed video editing and presentation software products targeted for sale to nonprofessional video editors.
1994	Basys Automation Systems (newsroom division)	$26[2]	$5[2]	Developed newsroom automation systems.
1994	Softech Systems			Developed newsroom automation software.
1995	Digidesign, Inc.	$39	$205	Leading provider of computer-based digital audio production systems for the professional music, film, broadcast, multimedia, and home recording markets.
1995	Elastic Reality	$12[3]	$45[3]	Developed digital image manipulation software.
1995	Parallax Software			Developed paint and compositing software.
1998	Softimage	$37	$248	Leading developer of 3D animation, video production, 2D cel animation, and compositing software.
2000	The Motion Factory	n/a[4]	$2.3[4]	Developed 3D media for games and the Web.
	Pluto Technologies International			Developed newsroom storage and networking products.

[1] Represents significant acquisitions from 1993 to 2000.
[2] Combined totals for Basys Automation Systems and Softech Systems acquisitions.
[3] Combined totals for Elastic Reality and Parallax Software acquisitions.
[4] Combined totals for The Motion Factory and Pluto Technologies International acquisitions.
n/a data not available.

NOTE:

1. Digital Video Applications Corp. was acquired to give Avid a presence in the nonprofessional video market as well as enhance its existing market capabilities.

2. Basys Automation Systems (newsroom division) and Softech Systems were acquired to provide Avid access to the news broadcast industry.

3. Digidesign, Inc. was acquired to give Avid a leadership position in the digital audio market.

4. Elastic Reality and Parallax Software were acquired to form Avid's graphics and effects group; the companies developed a range of image manipulation products that allow users in the video and film postproduction and broadcast markets to create graphics and special effects for use in feature films, television programs and advertising, and news programs. The Softimage acquisition significantly strengthened Avid's capabilities and market presence in these areas.

5. The Motion Picture Factory was acquired to enhance Avid's gaming and Web capabilities.

6. Pluto Technologies International was acquired to diversify its product offerings for the news broadcast industry.

SOURCE: Avid annual reports, public documents, and on-site interview with company representative; *Computer Reseller News* (10/31/94), *Newsbytes News Network* (3/31/95), *The Boston Herald* (10/22/98 and 6/30/00), *CCN Disclosure* (9/10/00).

video, audio, animation, or text), allowing different products from different vendors to be used simultaneously during the production process.

Avid understood the advantages of releasing its basic digital technology to firms providing competing as well as complementary products. These open standards resulted in increased development of innovative digital media technology and products, with more firms producing complementary as well as competing products. This increased the speed in which industries migrated from analog to digital technology. Additionally, by establishing industry standards, Avid ensured that its products would be compatible with complementary products of other firms. This increased the utility of Avid products. However, by making its basic digital technology available to other firms, Avid lost the ability to distinguish itself in this respect from competitors.

Strategic Alliances

To enhance its competitiveness, Avid engaged in several alliances with other technology firms. They included both horizontal and vertical alliances and were designed to address specific needs of the company. For example, Avid products were originally designed to operate solely on Apple computers. However, during the 1990s personal computer (PC) manufacturers began to erode product performance differences between Apple and IBM-compatible computers. As a result, Apple's market share dropped, causing some industry experts to question the continued viability of Apple. Avid realized the risk of being dependent on Apple technology to run its software and thus entered into a vertical alliance with Intel to develop the technology necessary to migrate the company's software to PC-based systems. This pact also included Intel taking a subsequent 6.75 percent ownership stake in Avid in 1997, providing the company $14.7 million in cash to help fund the process. By 1994, Avid began shipping comparable products on both Apple and PC platforms and continued to migrate and develop additional products to and for PC-based systems. Consequently, Avid reduced the uncertainty connected with being dependent on Apple, while at the same time making its products available to a wider market of both Apple and PC users.

Another partnership formed by Avid was the 1993 vertical alliance with filmmaker George Lucas and his Lucas Film and Lucas Digital groups. This agreement allowed for cooperation on the development of an extended line of special-effects products for the film industry. Avid provided software and hardware, and Lucas provided design specifications. Avid also entered into a partnership with Ikegami Tsushinki Co., Ltd., in 1994 to develop the world's first full-motion, digital-based camera.

More recent arrangements included Avid's 1998 acquisition of Softimage, a Canadian company located in Montreal. Although criticized by some industry analysts for not meeting product development deadlines and maintaining product quality, Softimage was recognized as a leader in 3D software designed to generate special effects in movies and advertisements using Microsoft operating systems. Softimage was formerly a division of Microsoft and was considered a fringe competitor of Avid. As part of the $248 million acquisition that included $128 million in goodwill, Microsoft took a 9.1 percent ownership stake in Avid. Changing the relationship with Microsoft from competitor to part-owner effectively aligned Avid with one of the most powerful firms in the technology industry.

In 1998, Avid also entered into a horizontal strategic alliance with Tektronix. This agreement resulted in a joint venture between the two competitors. Avid and Tektronix were able to identify mutual needs in responding to competition in the news broadcast market. Tektronix, a diversified organization with revenues of $2 billion, had advantages in the areas of digital storage technology as well as in its network of news-broadcast-industry customers. Although Avid produced digital storage devices, it conceded that the storage devices produced by Tektronix were more widely accepted by the industry. In addition, being relatively new to the news broadcast industry, Avid had yet to develop its customer network on par with that of Tektronix. Further, the market would perceive Avid to have greater financial stability if it partnered its operations with those of a larger firm. At the same time, Tektronix conceded that Avid's digital editing products were superior to its own.

The joint venture was called Avstar. Each partner took a 50 percent ownership position in the venture and, in 1999, each contributed an initial $2 million in cash and assets. Through Avstar, Avid and Tektronix planned to combine their competencies in both digital editing and storage technology, while further enhancing innovation and product development in the news broadcast market. Together, they expected to more quickly grow market share in this industry, while reducing the risk each would face if it sought to develop the market on its own.

Avid Management

From its founding in 1989 through 1995, Avid co-founders held the position of CEO. Initially, William Warner held the position until 1991, before leaving to start another, noncompeting company. Subsequently, Curt Rawley held the position until 1995. They both answered to a board of directors chaired by the general partner of Greylock Management Corporation, a venture capital firm that played a significant role in the company's initial equity funding. These co-founders led Avid through a period of remarkable growth and success.

However, Avid's initial objectives to gain market share and develop a position of industry leadership eventually took their toll on company profitability. Lack of strong controls to monitor growth resulted in large write-downs in 1996 of various assets, including obsolete inventories and uncollectable receivables. At the same time, sales growth slowed, thus exacerbating the impact of insufficient controls on the company's bottom line.

Slowing sales and decreasing profits during this period led Avid's board of directors to recognize the need for a new management team that could institute the functional competencies necessary to halt the company's deteriorating financial performance. As a consequence, emphasis shifted from being a market-share-driven firm to one seeking balanced growth with increased profitability. The board decided that an "outside" individual with proven experience running a large technology firm in a highly competitive environment was needed to provide the leadership necessary to guide Avid through these trying times.

In 1996, Bill Miller, 53, a seasoned executive in the technology industry, was hired to turn the fortunes of Avid around. As former chair and CEO of Quantum Computers, Miller had proven his ability to direct a large technology company in a highly competitive industry—the computer hard-drive industry. Under Miller's leadership, Quantum grew from $1.1 billion in revenues to $3.4 billion in five years.

Miller's responsibilities as Avid's new CEO included implementing the controls necessary to reduce the company's cost structure and reestablishing Avid as a profitable growth company. Understanding the need for Avid's quick turnaround, the board provided Miller with a high level of authority. He was granted CEO-duality status by being appointed to the positions of both CEO and chair of the board. The remaining eight board members were all nonexecutive directors.

Avid Attempts a Turnaround

Miller was excited about Avid's prospects and competitive staying power, saying that "in a world in which media can be used for virtually any message and delivered across the airwaves, a cable, or a computer network, we intend to continue to provide the tools that people use to tell their story." The proliferation of television channels alone signaled to Miller future potential for Avid, as he exclaimed, "the average cable household will soon have 90 channels, and with the fast spread of digital signals, that number may increase very quickly. More channels mean more programming to edit with software like Avid's."

However, Miller also recognized that Avid had outgrown the capabilities of its management, and that market leadership had to be paired with superior profitability. As a result, he began his tenure by building a new management team. This included hiring a new CFO to establish necessary financial control systems to decrease costs. Inventories and accounts receivable were significantly reduced, from $63.4 million and $107.9 million in 1995, respectively, to $9.8 million and $79.8 million in 1997, respectively. These efforts improved the company's cash flow, while reducing risks associated with inventory obsolescence and the collectibility of receivables. The turnaround entailed streamlining the organization, staffing reductions of approximately 70 positions, and discontinuance of development and sale of certain products. The total one-time cost to the company was $15.8 million.

In addition to shaping a new management team, Miller began to make significant changes in operations in an effort to boost company growth and profitability. One such change involved the company's product distribution channels. During Miller's tenure, Avid developed stronger relationships with firms that could distribute its products to a broad base of commercial and retail customers. As this channel grew, Avid was able to reduce its direct sales (in-house) activities to only key accounts that required a significant amount of time during the sales and post-sales process. Avid was thus able to take advantage of its indirect channel members' (independent distributors, value-added resellers, and dealers) well-developed networks to commercial and retail accounts, while reducing overall operating expenses relating to in-house sales and marketing activities. Sales through indirect channel members (as opposed to the direct, in-house sales function) grew from 50 percent of total annual sales in 1996 to 85 percent in 1999.

The company also focused on its customer support function, by expanding resources and restructuring the function to increase customer satisfaction. For example, Miller increased training for his support staff, which helped improve its ability to fix a problem on the first service call from under 50 percent to over 90 percent, while reducing the period of time customers waited for technical help to about two minutes (*Forbes*, 1998).

Under Miller's leadership, Avid worked toward realizing its mission statement of becoming the leading provider of powerful digital content creation tools used to "entertain and inform the world." The company sought to focus on and expand its presence in its existing digital media markets. The company also targeted new markets and continued to drive and support open industry standards.

However, the benefits of Miller's restructuring were short lived. The Softimage acquisition, Miller's most significant strategic action while running Avid, and perhaps the most important single transaction in the company's history, was more difficult for the company to digest than originally expected. Additionally, sales growth and profits remained elusive three years into Miller's tenure as Avid's chief executive. In 1999, Avid recorded revenues of $452.6 million, a six percent decrease from 1998, and a net loss of $137.5 million—the company's worst performance in its ten-year history. Further, from 1998 to 1999, cash and marketable securities decreased from $111.8 million to $72.8 million; the current ratio decreased from 2:1 to 1.7:1, and long-term debt as a percentage of equity increased from 4.6 percent to 8.5 percent (see Exhibit 1 for the consolidated statement of operations and Exhibit 2 for the consolidated balance sheet).

This resulted in the board of directors once again taking action by replacing top management. In late 1999, Bill Miller, CEO and chair of the board, and Clifford Jenks, president, both resigned. A few months later in early 2000, William Flaherty, CFO under Miller, resigned. The company stated that its business plan was no longer achievable given rapid changes in the market. As a result, the board determined that another thorough restructuring was necessary to position the company for future growth and profitability.

Krall, who was COO of Avid's Digidesign division, was appointed to the position of CEO in April 2000. The Digidesign division had been a bright spot for Avid, as it achieved record sales and operating income while the company as a whole was underperforming expectations. In making these changes, though, the board eliminated the company's CEO-duality status. The board chair position (also held by Miller during his reign) was filled by Robert Halperin, a non-executive board member. Krall was the only executive on the now six-member board. The restructuring also entailed an 11 percent reduction in staff. About 200 jobs were terminated at a $10 million cost to the company. Avid expected the restructuring to reduce forward costs by $20 million annually. The company also announced that it would discontinue the development and sale of a limited number of existing products. The recent Softimage acquisition was, for the most part, spared of any significant restructuring and allowed to continue operating as a relatively autonomous division of the company.

The Competitive Landscape

Avid benefited from introducing digital technology to the film and television industries. The company's success was achieved by providing superior digital products as a substitute for traditional analog products. The new digital technology was originally developed and marketed by small, innovative firms, many of which had since failed or been acquired by Avid or other firms in an attempt to establish industry leadership.

However, competition was intensifying. As digital technology became more firmly established, competition was expected from some of the big, well-entrenched analog firms that were beginning (or expected to begin) to produce their own digital products. These firms, such as Sony and Panasonic, were much larger than Avid and had significantly greater financial, technical, distribution, support, and marketing resources to bear on any strategic decision designed to take away the leadership position Avid held in digital technology. Avid also expected to face competition in one or more of its markets from computer manufacturers, such as IBM, Compaq, and Hewlett-Packard, and software vendors, such as Oracle and Sybase. All of these firms had announced their intentions to enter some or all of the company's target markets, specifically the broadcast news and special effects markets. Exhibit 5 provides further information on key competitors.

Krall's Dilemma

"We revolutionized the digital content industry," said Krall. "We build the best content creation tools in video, film, 3D, and audio; 85 percent of films

---

EXHIBIT 5   Key Competitors* (excluding music production markets)

Company Name	Sales F/Y 2000 ($ millions)
Digital (direct competition)	
• Adobe	$ 1,266
• Alias/Wavefront (subsidiary of Silicon Graphics)	2,331**
• BTS (subsidiary of Philips Electronics)	35,253**
• Discreet Logic (subsidiary of Autodesk)	936**
• Kinetix (subsidiary of Autodesk)	936**
• Lightworks USA (subsidiary of Tektronix)	1,103**
• Media 100	73
• Panasonic (subsidiary of Matsushita)	63,470**
• The Grass Valley Group (subsidiary of Tektronix)	1,103**
Analog (indirect competition)	
• Sony	63,607
• Matsushita	63,470
• Tektronix	1,103***

*Includes video and film production and postproduction markets, broadcast news market, and graphics and special effects market; does not include the music production and postproduction markets.

**Annual sales represent that of the parent company's total operations; most subsidiaries represent acquisitions by larger firms as a means to enter Avid's markets.

***Tektronix annual sales at the time of the 1998 joint venture with Avid were $2.1 billion. The decrease from 1998 to 2000 is due to divestitures of certain businesses in 1999 and 2000.

SOURCE: Avid annual reports, public documents, and on-site interview with company representative; individual company 10K/10F filings.

made in the U.S. actually utilize Avid tools." Additionally, Avid equipment is used to edit 95 percent of prime-time television programs. The company had established a leadership position in several markets by applying new technology in a timely fashion to meet emerging customer needs. However, for Avid to remain a leader, it was necessary to maintain an accurate understanding of customer needs, technological advancements, and competitive dynamics in the markets it served.

Krall and the new management team he needed to build faced many challenges. Concern existed over the slowed rate of growth in company revenues and the staggering losses. Some industry analysts viewed the purchase of Softimage as a signal for investors to "wait and see," wondering whether the sheer magnitude of Avid's first cross-border acquisition was too much for the company to manage. Krall acknowledged that "it's easy for expenses to get ahead of revenues," and indicated that "the company's first goal was to bring expenses back in line (with company revenues)." He also noted that the company's "second goal was to lay the foundation for growth in the future." Meanwhile, Avid risked competition from major international firms, such as Sony and Panasonic, that were attracted to opportunities offered by digital technologies the company pioneered. Avid's ability to compete effectively against these well-established firms would be severely tested.

Krall had nearly four years experience working for Avid prior to his appointment as CEO, first as the Digidesign division's director of program management and then later as the division's vice president of engineering and, eventually, COO. His strong technical background, with BS and MS degrees from MIT and an MBA from Harvard, as well as his company and industry knowledge would all come to bear on the strategic decisions he would have to make to turn Avid around.

During his first year as CEO, the proactive Krall announced a new focus on Internet-related editing products and once again set Avid on an acquisition track. In 2000, Avid purchased Pluto Technologies International Inc. and The Motion Factory Inc. for an aggregate $2.3 million. Pluto Technologies specialized in storage and networking products for the news broadcast industry, and The Motion Factory specialized in interactive games for the Web. These were Avid's first acquisitions since its 1998 acquisition of Softimage. Krall also oversaw an alliance with Intel and Microsoft to develop products for creating interactive digital television.

Krall finished his first year with Avid on a modestly successful note. Avid's 2000 revenues were up five percent from 1999, and, although the company incurred a net loss of $56 million, it was significantly less than the $137 million loss incurred in 1999.

As Avid's now experienced CEO entered 2001, he had to reevaluate his first-year decisions and determine what new strategic actions, if any, should be made to ensure Avid's successful turnaround. With competition intensifying, Krall knew he had to act fast. His strategic decisions to further diversify the company into the Internet, gaming, and digital television markets as well as make further commitments to the news broadcast market would have to be weighed against the company's performance in 2000. Krall had to assess whether he had addressed the causes of the company's past performance problems. Another downturn in Avid's financial performance would not only result in further turmoil within the company and investment community, but even jeopardize the company's ability to survive as an independent entity. In a keen sense of humor, the youthful Krall stated, "If you look at Avid's history, it has roughly had a new CEO every three years. One could guess that perhaps I've got two years left on my clock."

References

Avid 10K Reports, 1998–2000.

Avid 10Q Reports, 3/31/98, 6/30/98, 9/30/98, 3/31/01.

Avid Annual Reports, 1993–2000.

Avid Business Overview, Prudential Securities Technology Conference, Fall 1998.

Avid on-site interview with company official, 12/29/98.

Avid: Leadership & Vision, 1998.

Avid: NAB '98 Avid Teaser, 1998.

Avid Prospectus, 3/1/93.

Avid Prospectus, 9/21/95.

Avid: The Corporate Overview, 8/14/98.

Avid Web page, http://www.avid.com, various press releases 1998–2001.

Broadcasting & Cable, Glen Dickson. Avid makes new friends in Las Vegas: Forms alliances with Hewlett-Packard and Panasonic, 4/17/96, p. 12.

Broadcasting & Cable, Glen Dickson. Avid's turnaround man; No matter how good the technology, Krall sees execution as key, 10/9/00, p. 81.

Business Wire. Softimage enters agreement with Microsoft to develop tools and middleware for Xbox, 5/15/01.

CCN Disclosure. Avid acquires Pluto, expanding its broadcast and post-production product line-up, 9/10/00.

CNBC on-air interview with Bill Griffith, 10/20/00.

Computer Reseller News. Avid Technology to acquire Digidesign in a stock-swap merger worth about $205 million, 10/31/94, p. 231.

DTV Business. Avid, Microsoft, Intel alliance, 4/17/00.

Film + Television, first quarter 1998, volume 2, issue 1.

Forbes, Anne Linsmayer. The customer knows best, 8/24/98, pp. 92–93.

Newsbytes News Network, Avid Technology acquired two software companies, Elastic Reality and The Parallax Software Group, for $45 million, 3/31/95.

The Boston Globe, Anthony Shadid. Technology & Innovation: Fast forward; there's no firm more avid for digital film technology, 4/30/01, p. C2.

The Boston Herald. Avid's acquisition posted losses, 10/22/98, p. 48.

The Boston Herald. Avid acquires The Motion Picture Factory, 6/30/00, p. 30.

The Wall Street Journal. Avid agrees to buy Softimage unit from Microsoft, 6/16/98, Sec. B, p. 7.

The Wall Street Journal. Avid Technology Inc. staff to be trimmed 11% under restructuring plan, 11/11/99, Sec. B., p. 23.

The Wall Street Journal. Best Buy Co.: December sales rose 21% on strong DVD purchasing, 1/7/99, Sec. A., p. 15.

The Wall Street Journal. Computers: Cheaper PCs start to attract new customers, 1/26/98, Sec. B., p. 1.

The Wall Street Journal. The Internet; advancing the film: For those who want to beam photos over the Internet, digital cameras may be the way to go, 3/22/99, Sec. R., p. 6.

The Wall Street Journal. Technology: CompUSA net rises 44% as revenue jumps 22% to $1.46 billion, 1/29/98, Sec. A., p. 10.

The Wall Street Transcript. CEO interviews, 47(12), 12/29/1997.

TV Technology, Jay Ankeney. A summertime trip to Avid, 6/27/98, volume 16, no. 15, p. 31.

China Kelon Group (A): Diversify or Not?[1]

Justin Tan
Creighton University

Paul Beamish
The University of Western Ontario

As the leader in the Chinese home electrical appliance industry, China Kelon Group (Kelon) was the number one manufacturer of refrigerators in China. The company's entrepreneurial founder, chief executive officer (CEO), and chairman, Mr. Pan Ning was facing a significant turning point: With his retirement rapidly approaching, Mr. Pan Ning was anxious for Kelon to establish itself as a professionally managed company, while still maintaining its strength as a performer/player in the electrical appliance industry.

The Chinese refrigerator market had become increasingly competitive. Domestic manufacturers dominated the market and aggressively sought means to increase sales. They had conducted research and improved their production technology to guarantee quality products and have expended significant effort to extend their sales network and enhance after-sales service. However, as the urban market matured and became saturated, demand increasingly relied on replacement needs. Thus, firms had been forced to cut price to gain sales, and price wars had broken out, hurting profit margins. Facing a saturated market, the Kelon Group, which had avoided product diversification attempts, decided to move into the air conditioner market. How could Kelon, a well-established yet still vulnerable township enterprise, make use of its existing facilities and networks to enter this market? Additionally, entry into another market represented a major reorientation for Kelon, which traditionally had pursued a focused strategy and avoided diversification into other businesses. Could the management of Kelon handle it? Most important, could Kelon make a smooth transition from an entrepreneurial firm toward a professionally managed one at the same time as its charismatic leader was facing retirement?

The Birth of a Legend

The Kelon Group started in 1984 as a non-state township enterprise[2] in Shunde County in Guangdong province in South China. It was founded as the Pearl River Refrigerator Factory with Mr. Pan Ning as its director. Legend had it that the founders of Kelon wanted to travel outside the farming town to large cities. However, in order for them to get travel authorization and have their expenses reimbursed by the township government, they had to find some official business. They applied to visit refrigerator factories in order to develop some industry know-how. Upon their return, the government officials told them they needed to actually develop a prototype within six months. In desperation, they bought one from Hong Kong and used reverse engineering to build the first hand-made refrigerator, which is still on display in Kelon's headquarters.

At that time, there had been severe shortages in the Chinese economy and the company was able to seize this opportunity to enter the market. Kelon produced up to 20,000 refrigerators annually. In reflecting on the environment, the company's marketing vice president said: "The main task of our sales people was to turn away customers politely when we could not keep up with the demand." In October 1985, the central government was about to designate selected companies to make refrigerators. As the only candidate outside the state system, Kelon invited delegates to hold the meeting in its hometown. It became the last firm on the list of officially approved refrigerator manufacturers.

From 1987 to 1991, competition increased; Kelon began to develop its own corporate culture and improve its quality of management, importing machinery and technologies from overseas. Through hard work and investments, the Rongsheng brand refrigerator produced by Kelon group became a national brand and earned the reputation as the quality leader in the China market.

By the early 1990s, Kelon had become an exemplar of economic reform. The company received a surprise visit by Chinese leader Deng Xiaoping, the only non-state enterprise ever to receive such an honor. When the nearly 90-year-old Deng inspected Kelon's automated assembly line and entered its elegant headquarters in a rural town in Southern China, he asked other Chinese top government officials, "Are you sure this is a township enterprise?"

Two major events shaped Kelon. The first was the fall of a leading Chinese refrigerator manufacturer that was once Kelon's model. This company started to push out sub-standard products when demand exceeded supply, eventually ruining its reputation and leaving the market. This incident became Kelon's turning point and led to Kelon's motto: "Winning by top quality." Ever since, Kelon has monitored its production quality with an almost religious obsession.

The second major incident for Kelon was a failed strategic alliance with General Electric (GE). In the early 1990s, more and more foreign companies tried to enter the China market by cooperating with domestic companies. At that time, GE from America approached Kelon to form a strategic alliance. However, GE demanded that it retain Kelon's original top management team and control 51 percent of Kelon's major shares. While the township government was anxious to push the high profile deal through, Mr. Pan and his deputies threatened to resign if Kelon lost majority control. They wanted to build a national name brand.

These disagreements led to the failure of the merger between the two companies. However, the inexperienced Kelon executives realized the importance of governance structure and ownership, which was an unexplored concept in a state-centered economy. They formed an equity relationship with the township government, whereby the government oversaw the firm mainly through exercising voting rights rather than through arbitrary and administrative interference, which was still common in China. The founding members also learned the value of a recognizable brand name. With that intangible asset, Kelon could leverage itself for favorable positions.

Partly due to the GE experience, Kelon realized the importance of working with foreign companies. In 1992, following the success of its RongSheng refrigerator, the Kelon group formulated a strategy to diversify into the freezer market through cooperation with the Japanese Sanyo Group. It also established a subsidiary in Japan. In 1998, Kelon reached a long-term agreement with Whirlpool, through which Whirlpool would become the original equipment manufacturer (OEM) for Kelon and make Kelon brand washing machines. In turn, Kelon would become Whirlpool's OEM in the near future to make Whirlpool brand air conditioners (AC). The deal marked the entry of Kelon into the washing machine market.

In recent years, Kelon had made a major transition from focusing on internal growth toward merger and acquisition in order to expand. In 1996, Kelon expanded its production capacity by acquiring two struggling companies, one in Northeast China and another in Southwest China.

Using Hong Kong as a gateway to the global market, Kelon decided to list on the Hong Kong Stock Exchange. It had permission from the Chinese government to issue H-shares in Hong Kong. On July 23, 1996, under the name Guangdong Kelon Electrical Holding Co. Ltd., Kelon became the first refrigerator producer and first non-state firm to issue H-shares on the Hong Kong Stock Exchange. From that point, Kelon continued to improve its management and production.

As it entered the 1990s, Kelon faced several major transformations. First, it shifted from being production oriented to being marketing oriented. Second, with the diversification into the freezer and air conditioner markets, Kelon had begun selling multiple products rather than a single product. Third, previously a township enterprise, Kelon became a public company, which added accountability to stockholders into its goals and mission. Kelon had also shifted its focus from internal growth to a focus on both external and internal growth. Finally, the vision to become a global giant also meant that Kelon was aiming to expand domestically *and* internationally.

Kelon had received more than 140 state, provincial, and international awards. It was the only manufacturer in China to have been awarded ISO 9001, ISO 14001 and MRP II Class A accreditation simultaneously. From 1993 to 1997, it was the frontrunner in national AC quality evaluations.

By 1998, Kelon had a total of 8,530 employees. Among them were 397 middle- and high-level managers, 389 low-level managerial staff, 642 research and development (R&D) personnel and 425 marketing persons; this represented 21 percent of the total labor force, a ratio that was higher than the industry average. The top management team was mainly made up of the founders who composed a highly respected and effective team. The total capital in 1998 was RMB6 billion. Profit in 1998 was RMB600 million.

In 1998, Kelon was among the top ten firms in terms of market share in the AC market, and Kelon air conditioners were widely considered to be a high-end brand with superior product quality. Kelon's founder was widely viewed as a legendary Chinese entrepreneur and one of the most influential executives in the Chinese electrical appliances industry. Mr. Pan Ning had built Kelon Group in a small farming town, and he possessed only an elementary school education. Yet he was awarded an honorary doctoral degree by a British university in 1998. Many senior executives from Chinese state-owned enterprises had engaged in questionable business practices; Mr. Pan would be retiring honorably to a quiet, yet comfortable private life in his hometown.

The Chinese Market

China was one of the largest markets in the world with a total population of approximately 1.3 billion. It also represented the largest air conditioner and refrigerator market in the Far East. The population of China had increased steadily, and its overall economy had also improved greatly. According to the National Bureau of Statistics, China achieved 7.8 percent economic growth in 1998. The development of the urban economy had resulted in the growth of the middle-income class. In major cities, the share contributed by the middle classes to total consumer sales had increased from 35 percent in 1992 to 65 percent in 1997.

Having satisfied their basic needs, these people were beginning to look for a better quality of life and for more sophisticated products like air conditioners. Thus, the growth of the middle-class population was expected to generate more demand. There was also a trend toward owning more than one air conditioner per family; however, many urban residents had already made such purchases. Thus consumer demand had become somewhat flat. The economic situation in rural areas was also expected to improve. According to a state information center report, the rural market was growing by 20 percent or more each year. Higher purchasing power provided a great potential for the development of the home appliance industry.

Market conditions in China were improving. Transforming from a planned to a market economy, the Chinese government in this transitional period spent considerable effort on maintaining order in the market.

To create a stable and favorable environment in order to attract domestic and foreign investment, regulations and rules were established and many reforms were carried out. Also, past restrictions on foreign investors were lifted. The Chinese government was also concerned with the possible negative impact of a totally free market. To prevent destructive price competition in the market, a pricing law was passed on May 1, 1998. This legislation stated that an enterprise was not allowed to launch an unreasonable pricing strategy (e.g., cut prices dramatically) that would affect the stability of the market, lead to unhealthy competition, or damage the interests of the country and other enterprises.

For manufacturers, such legislation showed clearly that there was a limit on aggressive pricing. If they were to successfully compete in the market, manufacturing firms would have to focus on growing brand loyalty, providing high-quality products, and providing value-adding services.

Some large manufacturers had unique advantages in the Chinese market. The Chinese government has chosen several companies to receive government assistance to support their operations. At the same time, the technological advantages for foreign corporations were diminishing. Since China adopted the Open Door Policy (in 1978), many foreign investors had established operations there, mostly in the forms of joint ventures and acquisitions. They usually brought along advanced technology, which allowed domestic manufacturers to learn from them and improve their own technology and efficiency.

The Chinese appliance industry has gone through several major stages of development. The first stage, in the 1980s, was characterized by rapid demand growth and massive imports of refrigerator technology and production lines. This phenomenon was repeated in the early 1990s by AC manufacturers. The second stage, from the late 1980s to the early 1990s, was characterized by smooth growth. Companies in the industry as a whole shared and benefited from industry growth and attractive profitability. Although there were several major price wars and many less competitive companies faded out, the industry experienced high growth. Since the mid-1990s, industry competition has intensified. Companies had directed their strategic thrust toward brand loyalty, quality, and service, although price-cutting continued to be widespread. To remain competitive, major companies had devoted increasing attention to building distribution networks.

In recent years, the Chinese home appliance industry underwent a major consolidation. This was true in both the white appliance industry, which included refrigerators, air conditioners, freezers, washers/dryers, dehumidifiers, electrical cooking devices, etc., and in the black appliance industry, which included television sets, VCRs, and other home entertainment products. Many small firms that lacked economies of scale, quality, distribution network, and R&D capabilities exited. As a result, industry concentration was high. In 1997 for instance, the combined market shares of the top five producers in major markets were: 70 percent for refrigerators, 60 percent for ACs, 64 percent for freezers, and 56 percent for washers.

The foreign corporations now have diminished advantages in terms of brands. In the home electrical appliances market, domestic manufacturers have made continuous improvements in brand building, product quality, service, corporate image, and product range. Domestic brands are now widely recognized by consumers, and the market is no longer dominated by imports. Consumers have become more receptive to domestic brands. Domestic brand sales have increased from 64.6 percent in 1995 to 81.6 percent in 1997 and have become leaders in the market.

The global greenhouse effect may create an advantageous position for the appliance industry in China. Many people in China have become more environmentally conscious. Refrigerators and air conditioners emit gases that are detrimental to the ozone layer, and thus do not fit with this green culture. In order to meet the changing needs of their customers, manufacturers have begun to produce environmentally friendly appliances and predict that this will be a trend in the industry.

The housing reform that the Chinese government planned to carry out in 1998 was also expected to have an impact on the appliance industry. Many restrictions had been abolished, and private developers were allowed to enter the real estate market. In recent years, the market had been growing rapidly and a large number of houses had been built. This could potentially generate more demand for air conditioners and refrigerators. Finally, these industries were happy to see improvement in the electricity supply in China. Refrigerators and air conditioners require much electricity to operate. In the past, there were always power shortages in the villages and sometimes even in the cities. With recent technological developments, the situation was much improved.

The Chinese Refrigerator Industry

The Chinese refrigerator industry was started in 1954. During the ensuing 40 years, foreign brands tried to gain market share but made little progress. Starting from the early 1980s, there was a growing demand for household electrical appliances, including household refrigerators. During that time, supply could not meet demand, so many new entrants were attracted to the industry, including domestic and foreign companies. In 1988, the industry entered the first fast-growth stage. At the same time, there was a relatively high level of inflation in the country, and the production and sales volume of refrigerators peaked. The total production was 7.55 million units, the largest quantity in the world. From 1989 to 1992, the industry entered the adjustment stage, where price wars became widespread. From 1992 onwards, most members in the industry placed emphasis on technology.

During this period, it was popular for foreign companies to buy stocks—or even an entire corporation—in China, such that the local names were discontinued. Nonetheless, the refrigerator market was still dominated by local Chinese brands.

In order to remain competitive, the refrigerator producers went through a transition from importing technology and production lines to developing their own technology. In addition to emphasizing quality control, the manufacturers also gave more attention to developing a distribution network and improving customer service.

The industry also went through a consolidation. In 1997, the market share of the top ten brands increased from 85 percent in 1996 to 92 percent and for the top five brands, 70 percent, compared to 65 percent. The small group of dominant companies were comparable in size, and actions taken by any one of them would generate a quick reaction by the others. Moreover, their significant market share constituted a large entry barrier to new entrants. In 1997, there were no new brands that could expect to enter the top ten in the industry. As well, fewer potential entrants were expected in the future.

The market in China was not a united one. Different companies dominated in different regions. The government had no intention of uniting the market. In addition, the effectiveness of the state-owned distribution system gradually declined as the number of small collective and individual stores increased.

Manufacturers also began to market their products directly or indirectly to secondary and tertiary cities to tap the refrigerator market. As of June 1998, four local companies controlled more than 70 percent of the market in the Chinese refrigerator industry; Kelon accounted for 18 percent.

At the early development stage of the Chinese refrigerator market, the imported brands were able to attract customers, even without promotion or advertising. This was because of the low technology level of domestic producers and consumer fascination with foreign products. However, these producers could not hang on to their business. In 1997, the market share of imported brands was less than one percent. High prices and lack of sales networks and after-sales service were likely to continue to restrict the penetration of these brands in China.

Major appliance manufacturers from North America, Europe, and Japan, such as Matsushita (National/Panasonic), Sharp, Hitachi, Toshiba, Sanyo, Mitsubishi, ElectroLux, Siemens, and Whirlpool, had all established presence through joint ventures, starting in the 1980s. These producers were the market leaders in the industry. With more capital, these companies had sufficient volume and achieved economies of scale.

With adequate in-depth domestic market knowledge after being in China for a decade or more, the major appliance manufacturers had built sales networks. Moreover, their joint ventures had benefited from access to more advanced technology, management skills, and human resources gained in different cultures. These companies were mainly focused on the high-end market.

The Challenges

The competition in the Chinese refrigerator and AC markets had become increasingly intense. With profit margins in the refrigerator market continuing to decline, Kelon had moved to the AC market. Yet such a shift required significant cash inflow to the AC division, and this infusion had not yet been forthcoming from the revenue-producing refrigerator division. The company was also struggling with the choice of building a unified sales force versus two separate ones. Apparently, the AC market was more service intensive than that of refrigerators.

Additionally, escalating competition was expected in the urban market. Many industry experts predicted that the rural market had the largest market potential. According to a survey among 100 urban households, 73 percent of them owned a refrigerator and 12 percent owned an air conditioner, but the percentage was only eight percent and 1.2 percent in the rural households. This ratio was extremely low compared to other developed countries. The question faced by Kelon top management was whether external factors were favorable for Kelon to "go rural." How should Kelon develop its strategic plan to manage this diversified company and to capture the rural market? Should Kelon reposition its brand or use another brand to enter the rural market? What different approaches should Kelon use to sell refrigerators and air conditioners in the rural market? More fundamentally, moving into different product and geographical markets represents major strategic transition and reorientation. Histori-cally, Kelon's founding members had resisted the temptation of over-expansion and diversification in order to maintain the strategic flexibility associated with an entrepreneurial firm. As a result, Kelon group may not have the capability, skills, and corporate culture that would support a major transformation. On the other hand, in order to revitalize itself and grow beyond a local entrepreneurial firm, a major innovation and reinvention would be crucial for further growth. These were all critical issues for a Kelon top management team that was also facing CEO succession.

Notes

1. This case has been written on the basis of published sources only. Consequently, the interpretation and perspectives presented in this case are not necessarily those of China Kelon Group or any of its employees.
2. Township enterprises operate outside the state plan and control. They were established and controlled by the township governments. Neither state-owned nor privately owned, they embodied a form of community property so that, in theory, the property belonged to all who lived within the jurisdiction of the local government. This left township governments with the strongest claim over profits from these firms, which soon became their major source of revenue through levies and revenue-sharing arrangements. There was no independent legal system to guarantee property rights, and the overall structure of political power may have lacked legitimacy, but contingent upon the existing governmental structure, property rights of township enterprises appeared unambiguous. Township governments in China significantly assisted their companies in securing production factors, accessing infrastructure, arranging marketing channels, and getting higher-level government ratifications if needed.

The Richard Ivey School of Business gratefully acknowledges the generous support of The Richard and Jean Ivey Fund in the development of this case as part of the RICHARD AND JEAN IVEY FUND ASIAN CASE SERIES.

CNN and September 11th, 2001: Management in a Crisis

Nisa Lewites
Polytechnic University

Background

Before September 11th, 2001, the press was writing about CNN's obituary. Having built its reputation and audience on breaking events such as the Gulf War, the network had suffered an identity crisis in the absence of a solid, globe-straddling story. CNN had slipped in its position and influence in recent years, and internal dissension and widespread personnel upheavals had demoralized its staff and diminished its influence. Then, the unthinkable occurred.

The events of September 11th have driven viewers back to CNN in droves—and to the same hard-charging frontlines of CNN that truly put it on the map during the Gulf War. CNN handled the crisis beautifully. But, while CNN may have returned to its element, it still faces high expectations and an uncertain future going forward. As Eason Jordan, CNN's chief news executive, put it, "nobody is going to say, 'Why wasn't somebody else there?' but they will say, 'Why wasn't CNN there?'" This, coupled with the increasing competition from other cable news networks such as Fox and MSNBC, will challenge CNN's ability to stay on top. This case attempts to look at the factors that led to a successful management of a crisis, and to determine if these factors will be enough to drive success going forward.

Overview of CNN

CNN was formed in 1980 by Ted Turner as the first 24-hour cable news network. After being sold to Time Warner, CNN is now part of Turner Broadcasting System, Inc., which is now owned by AOL Time Warner. In addition to other entertainment networks, Turner operates all of the networks in the CNN News Group. According to recent ratings, CNN is the most watched 24-hour news network. Along with CNN Headline News and CNN International, it is the world's only global, 24-hour news network, reaching more than a billion people worldwide.[1] CNN also has a network of websites around the world, which generate more traffic than any other news competitor.[2] CNN's culture has been characterized as "speedy" and run "with a profit motive in mind."[3] It currently has its world headquarters at its facilities in Atlanta. Many of the sales and marketing teams are based in New York, and many perform these functions across all of the Turner Broadcasting properties. CNN has 3,800 staffers worldwide with 300 correspondents outside of the United States and bureaus at 43 locations throughout the world (30 outside the United States). (See Exhibit 1.)

Impact of September 11

Location, Security

Unlike many companies that were written about after September 11th, none of CNN's offices were directly affected by the events of September 11th, so there was no need to relocate employees, or change business operating procedures. However, like other media companies, CNN needed to deal with the threat of anthrax and beef up security procedures at its headquarters and bureaus around the world. In addition, CNN's reporters in Afghanistan are at risk in the middle of the fighting. Nic Robertson has reported from Afghanistan throughout the coverage so far but was forced to move from Kabul to Kandahar after officials of the ruling Taliban told him they could not guarantee his safety. "They told me in no other terms, that should there be an attack, the mob will rule and nothing will be able to be done," Mr. Robertson said. "One official told me: 'The crowd will set upon you and pull you apart into so many pieces no one will be able to identify you from a piece of meat.'"[4] Obviously, CNN is trying to protect its reporters as much as possible, but this takes time and increased communication.

Organizational Structure

Part of CNN's strength in responding to September 11th is its organizational structure. CNN has journalists and bureaus around the world—more than any other network. CNN has doubled its number of employees to 75 in Central Asia and the Middle East, including 40 in Pakistan and 15 in Afghanistan.[5]

CNN also has a very strong rights-gathering department. It acquired some of the best amateur video taken during the first hours of the attacks, and Nic Robertson was the first and, for a while,

only television correspondent reporting from anywhere in Afghanistan. Footage from Afghanistan is exclusive to CNN—an agreement by broadcasters and cable networks to share footage does not extend to foreign images, so many of CNN's competitors have had to settle for reporting from Pakistan.

Leadership

Walter Isaacson, who was recently named Chairman and Chief Executive of CNN News Group, has stepped up to a leadership role in the crisis. "It helped us regain our focus," Mr. Isaacson said of the attacks. "It's injected a note of real seriousness. And the things we think of doing to chase ratings now pale in comparison to the importance of doing this story seriously and reliably . . . I think this has been a wake-up call to the public and to all of us in the news business that there are certain things that really matter more than the latest trivial thing that can cause a ratings boost."

Mr. Isaacson also issued a memo while the ruins of the WTC were still smoking. In it, he directed CNN reporters to balance their coverage, to supply the context for the American bombing raids, and to beware of being used by Taliban propagandists.[6] He said: "As we get good reports from Taliban-controlled Afghanistan, we must redouble our efforts to make sure we do not seem to be simply reporting from their vantage or perspective. We must talk about how the Taliban are using civilian shields and how the Taliban have harbored the terrorists responsible for killing close to 5,000 innocent people . . . you want to make sure people understand that when they see civilian suffering there, it's in the context of a terrorist attack that caused enormous suffering in the United States . . . do not forget it is that country's leaders who are responsible for the situation Afghanistan is in now."

Rick Davis, CNN's head of standards and practices, noting that it may be difficult for the correspondents to reiterate these points clearly each time there is new footage, suggested language to the anchors in a separate memo.[7] In fact, CNN has assembled a group of senior executives since the attacks to decide if breaking developments should be aired or not if they are both provocative and of questionable news value.[8]

EXHIBIT 1

CNN Holdings by Business Unit[19]

Broadcast Properties

CNN

CNN/U.S., the world's leading 24-hour global news and information television network and the flagship of the CNN News Group, pioneered 24-hour television news when it launched on June 1, 1980. CNN/U.S. provides its audience with in-depth, live coverage and analysis of breaking news events. CNN/U.S. also offers a full range of programs covering the latest in business, weather, sports, entertainment, health and science news, as well as topical, in-depth interviews.

CNN Headline News

CNN Headline News, cable television's most successful brand extension, updates more than 76 million households on today's news constantly, 24 hours each day. CNN Headline News provides the top stories about health, technology, weather, entertainment, the environment, sports, travel and money as well as breaking or "just in" news. The network is broadcast from a state-of-the-art "in the round" studio at CNN's world headquarters in Atlanta and is designed especially for viewers who want relevant and comprehensive news in a way that suits the urgency of their schedules. Teams of at least four anchors interact to deliver fast-paced, lively and engaging news, using the best resources of the CNN News Group.

CNN International

CNN International (CNNI) is the world's only global, 24-hour news network. CNNI can be seen in more than 151 million television households in 212 countries and territories worldwide through a network of 23 satellites. In September 1997, CNNI launched a regionalization strategy that has led to five separately scheduled channels to date: CNN International Europe/Middle East/Africa, CNN International Asia Pacific, CNN International South Asia, CNN International Latin America, and CNN International USA.

CNNmoney

CNNmoney, the financial network, delivers comprehensive business news 24 hours each weekday. By utilizing the unmatched resources of the CNN News Group, including its 42 bureaus and almost 900 broadcast affiliates worldwide, CNNmoney provides up-to-the-minute business news coverage from Wall Street and throughout the world. CNNmoney offers viewers a broad range of business, financial and consumer news, giving small investors and professionals alike financial news that goes beyond the numbers to deliver informative and credible analysis.

CNN/*Sports Illustrated*

CNN/*Sports Illustrated,* a joint venture of CNN and *Sports Illustrated,* is a 24-hour sports network offering complete coverage of the world of sports, with

(continued)

EXHIBIT 1

CNN Holdings by Business Unit *(continued)*

in-depth reporting and live coverage of breaking news and press conferences. The network combines the unmatched newsgathering resources of CNN with expert analysis and unique commentary from *Sports Illustrated*'s stable of writers, editors, and reporters. This unique combination allows CNN/*Sports Illustrated* to offer unmatched journalism, analysis, and commentary.

CNN en Español

The 1997 debut of CNN en Español represented the most successful launch in the history of Latin American pay television. The network delivers international and regional news produced, written and presented by Latin Americans for Latin Americans in Spanish. CNN en Español currently reaches more than 10 million households in Latin America and a growing population in the United States. CNN en Español's Mexico feed features a Mexico-specific newscast and the *Infocinta* CNN ticker, continually updated with news headlines, stock and financial data, sports scores and local time and weather information.

CNN Airport Network

CNN Airport Network, a subsidiary of Turner Private Networks, Inc., is the only live, satellite-delivered television service broadcast to waiting air travelers across the United States. CNN Airport Network can be seen in more than 1,600 gates and other viewing areas in 35 major U.S. airports, representing more than 400 million passenger enplanements annually. CNN Airport Network delivers national and international news, live breaking events, entertainment, weather, sports, business, and lifestyle features. CNN Airport Network International can also be seen in more than 80 viewing areas at Amsterdam's Schiphol Airport. CNN Airport Network's Web site provides weather updates, flight tracking and city guides, as well as other useful travel information.

CNNRadio

CNNRadio is a full-service network, providing its more than 1,900 worldwide affiliates with the latest information in news, sports, and business. Utilizing CNN's 42 bureaus worldwide, CNNRadio offers an unmatched menu of audio clips and reports in closed-circuit feeds. CNNRadio is based in CNN's world headquarters in Atlanta with personnel, including radio-only correspondents, located at the CNN bureaus in Washington, D.C., Los Angeles, and New York. CNNRadio programming is distributed exclusively for radio broadcast in the United States by Westwood One and has received the 1999 Radio Television News Directors Association's (RTNDA) highest award, the Edward R. Murrow Award for Overall Excellence in Network Radio, and the Murrow Award for Best News Series.

CNNRadio Noticias

CNNRadio Noticias provides radio affiliates in the United States and throughout Latin America with the latest news, sports, business and entertainment news in Spanish. CNNRadio Noticias airs live hourly newscasts and Internet-delivered

(continued)

EXHIBIT 1

CNN Holdings by Business Unit *(continued)*

news resources via the exclusive "A La Carta" Web site, produced using the worldwide resources of CNN en Español and the CNN News Group.

CNN Newsource

CNN Newsource is the world's most extensively syndicated news service, comprised of more than 650 network affiliates and independent television stations throughout North America. In addition to live correspondent reports from the scene of Breaking news stories, CNN Newsource affiliates receive 17 news feeds each weekday and 12 news feeds each weekend day of local, national and international news, weather, sports, medical, business, lifestyle and entertainment stories, along with graphics and special franchise pieces to enhance their local news programs. CNN Newsource's more than 200 international affiliates receive three news and feature feeds each day.

CNN+

CNN+ is the first CNN-branded local language news channel operated and controlled outside of Atlanta. The 24-hour Spanish-language news channel is based in Madrid and is produced by Compania Independiente de Nocias de Television (CINTV), a company held 50 percent by Turner Broadcasting International and 50 percent by Sogecable, owner of Canal Plus España and Canal Satélite Digital (CSD).

CNN Turk

CNN Turk is the second CNN-branded, local-language news service operated and controlled outside of Atlanta. CNN Turk is a joint venture owned by Turner Broadcasting International and Turkey's Dogan Media Group.

n-tv

Based in Berlin, n-tv is Germany's only national news and business channel. Time Warner has a 49.79 percent equity stake in n-tv; Handelsblatt and Nixdorf are the other principal shareholders.

The CNN Web Sites

CNN is responsible for the award-winning news site CNN.com, as well as three other U.S.-based Web sites and the distribution of CNN news content via platforms such as mobile phones. In addition to CNN.com, the U.S.-based sites include CNNfn.com, the financial news Web companion to CNNfn; CNNfyi.com, an educational site for students and teachers; and CNNSI.com, the sports news Web companion to CNNSI. The collective CNN sites include eight international sites and are among the world's leading news and information destinations. The CNN sites rank No. 1 in Gross Usage Minutes among all online news sites. CNN's Web sites are updated continuously from production centers worldwide.

The eight international sites are: CNN.com.br, the Portuguese-language news and information site serving Brazil and Latin America; CNN.co.jp, CNN's

(continued)

EXHIBIT 1 CNN Holdings by Business Unit *(continued)*

Japanase-language news and information site serving Japan; CNN.de, CNN's German-language news and information site serving Germany; CNN.dk, CNN's Danish-language news and information site serving Denmark; CNNenEspanol .com, CNN's Spanish-language news and information site serving Latin America; CNNItalia.it, CNN's Italian-language news and information site serving Italy; CNN.com Europe, CNN's English-language news and information site reporting news that impacts Europe; and CNN.com Asia, CNN's English-language news and information site reporting news that impacts Asia.

Use of Technology

Another of CNN's strengths has been their news gathering technology. The videophone has enabled CNN to get live footage to viewers from the remotest of places. Small, portable and costing only $7,500, videophones—which can send pictures over circuits normally used to transmit audio—are transforming the way reporters can do their jobs. Conventional satellite equipment is normally too heavy for one reporter to transport and videophones can be set up or dismantled in minutes, usually by one reporter. It comes with its own batteries, or can be operated off another small power source such as a cigarette lighter outlet in a car. It is also noiseless and inconspicuous, which are key advantages in this war. "You're not lugging equipment that catches people's attention," said Nic Robertson, CNN correspondent in Afghanistan, "you can put this in a backpack." He added, "I truly believe this equipment is the future."

However, Eason Jordan, CNN's chief news executive, said the technology doesn't change reporters' ethical responsibilities. "We're not spies, we're professional journalists," he said. "We're committed to acting properly with this or without it. We still have to do what's prudent and responsible."

New versions of the videophone are expected to improve on the jerky pictures. Clearly, managing the audience's expectations will be a challenge for CNN. Viewers tend to forget that the celebrated pictures of bombs falling on Baghdad in the Persian Gulf War, which put CNN on the map, weren't on air for 24 hours after the war started; the first days' reports were radio or live accounts from reporters on the phone.

Costs

Besides the costs of physical operations, there has been a clear economic impact on CNN in handling the increased costs of news coverage since September 11th. CNN's budget is already about $700 million annually vs. NBC and ABC with $400 million and $500 million, respectively. One analyst estimates that these budgets will need to increase by 25 percent to 35 percent over the next few years to create new bureaus abroad, boost technology, and widen coverage.[9] Eason Jordan, CNN's chief news executive, says that CNN has raised its incremental spending by about ten times since the crisis erupted, noting that "money is not a big concern at a time like this."[10] Of course, AOL Time Warner, CNN's parent company, has pledged that CNN will have unlimited funds to cover the war on terrorism, but there is only so long that a for-profit entity can do this.

Another option is for the networks to pool some of the news coverage costs. Indeed, this has been in discussion for some time and may heat up again as the networks weigh the financial challenges ahead of covering the story on the war on terrorism. Recent discussions, however, show that CNN may not be part of these cooperative efforts. CNN is also exploring ways to squeeze more out of its existing overhead. In the wake of layoffs earlier this year, CNN is asking its field staffers to do more than one job: camera operators, for example, would be asked to report, edit, and even write in addition to shooting pictures.[11]

Revenues

The cost issue raises a clear problem for profitability since ad revenues were weak before the attacks and continue to get weaker since them. Immediately following the attacks, CNN was unable to capitalize on an audience that rose to ten times normal levels, averaging 3.4 million viewers per day,[12] because it declined to run any commercials until September 17 at 6 a.m.[13] Since then, CNN has been trying to convince advertisers to pay higher rates because of the larger audience. It has presented syndicated research suggesting the most desirable, higher-income viewers are more likely to accept a faster return to normal commercial activity in news shows, and it has sold more inventory it usually keeps on reserve.[14] Larry Goodman, president for sales and marketing at CNN, said that "For us to go out there and say 'Resume business as usual,' sounds self-serving but President Bush has made that almost a daily mantra: 'Let's get back to our normal lives' . . . this story is going to be with us for a while, in one incarnation or another."[15] Therefore, the ad sales staff asserts that advertisers who withdraw to the sidelines to wait it out may gravely harm companies dependent on the sales stimulation that ads can provide. Despite these efforts, negotiating where ads can or cannot run further complicates the sales environment and requires additional resources. At the end of this year, CNN will still likely be at a net loss but that may have more to do with overall economic conditions than the events of September 11th. (See Exhibit 2.)

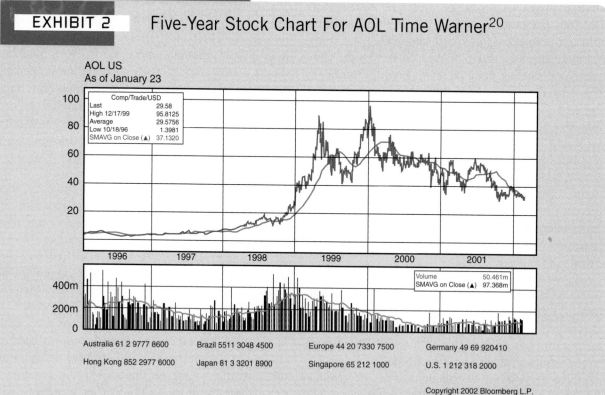

EXHIBIT 2   Five-Year Stock Chart For AOL Time Warner[20]

AOL US
As of January 23

Comp/Trade/USD	
Last	29.58
High 12/17/99	95.8125
Average	29.5756
Low 10/18/96	1.3981
SMAVG on Close (▲)	37.1320

Volume 50.461m
SMAVG on Close (▲) 97.368m

Australia 61 2 9777 8600   Brazil 5511 3048 4500   Europe 44 20 7330 7500   Germany 49 69 920410

Hong Kong 852 2977 6000   Japan 81 3 3201 8900   Singapore 65 212 1000   U.S. 1 212 318 2000

Copyright 2002 Bloomberg L.P.
G384-120-0 23-Jan-02 23:07:22

Global Strategy

CNN has always been a global company, having staff around the world, many in highly-visible positions. Chris Cramer runs CNN International Networks. He believes that "our strength has been in our global coverage. We have 43 bureaus around the world and 300 journalists outside the United States. So when it came to deploying correspondents to cover this story, CNN was ahead of many networks. Plus, our journalists are very experienced." He also indicated that, unlike other media organizations, the global nature of CNN has given it a huge responsibility to report in a balanced and non-propogandist manner.[16] "We listen and report all sides," he said, "We do not have an agenda and are not propagandists for any government. Our coverage reflects this, which is why we have the audiences and business partnerships that we do." In fact, he continues, this is how CNN sees itself: "as a global network that just happens to be based in Atlanta—not a U.S. network that is broadcast internationally. This distinction is at the very core of what CNN is all about."[17]

That may be true from an editorial perspective; however, from a business perspective it is clear that the staff in the United States has the best handle on what is happening in offices around the world. For example, according to one ad sales executive at CNN, "the U.S. sales staff knows what inventory is available for bundling worldwide, while the European offices in London are only selling inventory for Europe." This may suggest a disconnect between the editorial and business sides of CNN's global operations.

It remains to be seen whether the global nature of the operations will have any impact from the events of September 11th. It is clear that the United States has become a more global culture now—with more recognition and understanding of what is happening in other parts of the world. Therefore, CNN may need to become even more global in nature to address these new needs.

Innovation Strategy

What is next for CNN? No one is certain how long the interest in the terrorist attacks and the war will last. What happens when this is over? If history is a guide, interest in wars tends to wane after the first few months, so executives at the company need to be thinking about how to innovate and continue to grow. One area where this seems to be occurring is new distribution technologies. CNN's web and wireless sites have become even more important now, as more people logged on in the hours and days following the terrorist attacks to receive up to the minute reports. After news of the crisis hit, officials at CNN.com rushed to triple its computer capacity and streamline its web pages to make them smaller. Mitch Gelman, CNN.com's executive producer, said "within ten minutes, we were unable to serve the volume of requests. On a normal day, we can easily service up to six million visitors." The site saw record traffic, hitting nine million page views an hour since the tragedy occurred. "We've never seen anything like this," said Gelman; "the last time things got this busy on the Web site was when people were hungry for 2000 election results." The Internet community rushed to fill the void and offered assistance. For instance, a company in Italy and several businesses in the United States put their excess Internet capacity at CNN's disposal.[18]

Conclusion

Obviously, we cannot yet fully understand the long-term impact on CNN from the events of September 11th—in terms of management practices, structure, technology and innovation. However, it is crucial to begin by exploring emerging trends and to learn from them.

From an organizational and product perspective, it appears that there is a "back to basics" model whereby leadership is top-down and the focus is on core competency. On the other hand, the resilience of a network-like structure is also clearly in evidence, whereby reporters and anchors need to make decisions that will affect the entire network. If CNN is to thrive and remain competitive, they will need to capitalize on this bipolar organization. They will need to continue to innovate by trusting staff on the front lines who are using new technologies, while top management makes speedy decisions on policy.

Notes

1. Turner Broadcasting Systems Overview, http://www.aoltw.com/about/companies/turnerbroad.html.
2. Turner Broadcasting Systems Overview, http://www.aoltw.com/about/companies/turnerbroad.html.
3. Alongkorn Parivudhiphongs, "CNN Chief Relishes a Challenge," *Bangkok Post,* November 6, 2001.
4. Bill Carter, "CNN Returns to Its Element but Faces High Expectations," *The New York Times,* September 19, 2001.
5. Alongkorn Parivudhiphongs, "CNN Chief Relishes a Challenge," *Bangkok Post,* November 6, 2001.
6. Dorothy Rabinowitz, "Neutral in the Newsroom," *Wall Street Journal Interactive,* November 6, 2001.
7. Dorothy Rabinowitz, "Neutral in the Newsroom," *Wall Street Journal Interactive,* November 6, 2001.
8. Doug Young, "U.S. Network News Divisions Grapple with What to Air," Reuters, October 25, 2001.
9. Tom Wolzien, media analyst at Sanford C. Bernstein & Co.
10. Joe Flint and Sally Beatty, "U.S. Television Networks Run Up Significant Costs to Cover Attacks," *The Wall Street Journal Europe,* September 19, 2001.
11. Joe Flint and Sally Beatty, "U.S. Television Networks Run Up Significant Costs to Cover Attacks," *The Wall Street Journal Europe,* September 19, 2001.
12. Bill Carter, "CNN Returns to Its Element but Faces High Expectations," *The New York Times,* September 19, 2001.
13. Bill Carter, "CNN Returns to Its Element but Faces High Expectations," *The New York Times,* September 19, 2001.
14. Sally Beatty, "Covering Terrorism Is Costly for U.S. Television Networks," *The Wall Street Journal, Europe,* November 6, 2001.
15. Stuart Elliott, "News Organizations Try to Dispel the Notion That Ads and Bad News Don't Mix," *The New York Times,* October 26, 2001.
16. Alongkorn Parivudhiphongs, "CNN Chief Relishes a Challenge," *Bangkok Post,* November 6, 2001.
17. Alongkorn Parivudhiphongs, "CNN Chief Relishes a Challenge," *Bangkok Post,* November 6, 2001.
18. P. J. Huffstutter, Dave Wilson, and Christine Frey, "News Web Sites Clogged in Aftermath," *Los Angeles Times,* September 12, 2001.
19. AOL Time Warner Website, January, 2002.
20. Source: Bloomberg.

Colorado Creative Music

Rachel Deane Canetta
Joan Winn
University of Denver

. . . I was a good musician, so I thought, what better thing to start than a music company?

Darren Skanson, lead artist and CEO of Colorado Creative Music (CCM), settled into his flight on Friday, March 9, 2001. He was heading to New Smyrna Beach, Florida, where he would perform at the Images arts festival. As lead artist, Darren had been traveling all over the country performing light classical guitar and selling his line of CDs. As CCM's biggest money machine, Darren was performing 40 two-to-three-day weekends a year. As CEO, Darren's concerns were increasing. He was being pulled in too many directions. He realized that he couldn't continue to travel and perform as much as he had been and still manage the growth of his record label. While he waited for the plane to take off, he thought about how to turn the nightmare that his company had become into the dream that he believed it could be.

Darren Curtis Skanson

I've always been a performer; music was in our household from very early on. When I first saw what a musical group, a band, can do to an audience—just the excitement and the adulation that they received—that moment changed my life. I said, "I want to do that."

Darren Curtis Skanson was born and raised on a farm seven miles outside of Fertile, a small town of about 800 people in the northwestern part of Minnesota. Darren's father was an elementary school teacher, and his mother was a piano teacher and a teacher's aide. Darren was the oldest of four boys.

Darren's passion for music began at an early age. Some of his earliest memories were of singing with his brother Brant in church at the age of four. Darren traced his dream of being a rock star to watching the crowd respond to a high school band performance.

I was in seventh or eighth grade and one of my best friends, a tenth-grader, was playing with a bunch of seniors. They played a pep rally for a sporting event, and the school all comes down and gets together. Everyone came out of the bleachers and went up to the stage and, you know, it was a pretty strong experience. . . . The first night that I ever played live with a band on stage and got a similar response just reinforced it.

Reprinted by permission of Rachel D. Canetta, IMBA, and Joan Winn, University of Denver.

© 2001 by Rachel Deane Canetta and Joan Winn of the University of Denver. Published in *Entrepreneurship Theory and Practice,* 26(3) Spring 2002. Funding for preparation of this case was provided by the John E. and Jeanne T. Hughes Charitable Foundation Entrepreneurship Education and Awareness Grant and the Daniels College of Business at the University of Denver. This case is intended to stimulate class discussion rather than to illustrate the effective or ineffective handling of a managerial situation. *All events and individuals in this case are real, but some names may have been disguised.* Additional company information is available at http://www.ccmbiz.com.

With the encouragement of his parents, Darren went to Moorhead State University, graduating with a BA in music in 1989. This education helped him discover the intellectual and emotional aspects of music. Darren had originally intended to get a Music Industry degree, which required a minor in business. But during his senior year, the music took over, and he ended up without enough business courses to fulfill the minor. Darren regretted that now, "but you know when you are 22 years old you don't really foresee the future very well. You see the ideals and not the practicalities."

Just out of college, Darren began performing as lead guitarist in a heavy metal band called Mata Hari. The band toured the United States playing in small venues and opening for bigger bands in larger venues. After four years Darren was frustrated. The band had only produced one CD, and the band members did not want to move to a place that was more conducive to making a break in heavy metal. They had been living and performing out of Fargo, North Dakota, which was not a hotbed for performing artists. When Jack, the lead singer, left the band to get married, Darren was ready to call it quits and break up the band.

In March 1993, Mata Hari's last stretch of a tour put the group in Denver. Darren liked Denver and looked for an excuse to stay. He found an ad in the newspaper soliciting a guitarist for a Classical–New Age duo called Watson and Company. Darren's classical training gave him the courage he needed to call and set up an audition. He got the job, which turned out to be a major turning point in his musical career.

Malcolm Watson, a classical violinist, was making his living by performing at arts festivals around Colorado and selling his CDs. Darren and Malcolm produced Watson and Company's third CD. Darren's college friend, Jennifer, was hired to serve as Watson and Company's booking agent. She began booking the duo nationwide, and within a year Watson and Company's sales increased from $100,000 a year to a quarter of a million dollars.

Darren believed that there were ways to capitalize on the knowledge the team had about the arts festivals. He saw arts festivals as a strong distribution venue that could be utilized more fully. Additionally, Darren's vision was to sign on other artists in a way that kept them tied in so that they could not just absorb the knowledge and leave. Discouraged that Malcolm wanted to move more slowly, Darren and Jennifer decided to end their relationship with Watson.

Jennifer began booking other artists, taking a percentage of their sales. Darren wanted to move beyond booking artists to forming a company that would manage and promote artists. His vision was to record, produce, and sell his own music as well as the music of a cohesive group of artists that would comprise a unique record label and distribution company. Jennifer was helpful as a booking agent, but Darren's vision of a viable business venture differed from hers. Jennifer was not the person Darren was looking for in a business partner.

Colorado Creative Music

I've always been a very driven person, and I got tired of waiting or depending on other people to get things done. I was always the spearhead in getting stuff done in every other organization or business relationship I was in.

Darren started Colorado Creative Music in January 1995. Working solo, Darren produced two CDs and sold them at the arts festivals that Jennifer booked for him. He did this on his own for two and a half years, and as sales grew and doing business got more complicated he began to see a need for bringing others on board.

In June 1997, Darren's cousin Ted, a business school student at St. Cloud State University in Minnesota, contacted him about doing a business internship. Darren and Ted began writing down everything about how the business was run. "We started transferring the knowledge to my cousin, and then into processes." At the end of Ted's internship, Darren tried to find someone who could continue the work Ted had begun, with hopes of fine-tuning the processes into a workable set of operational systems. In early 1998, Darren hired Ryan, a young musician who was familiar with the music industry, to continue documenting processes and also to help with equipment repairs and recordings. By summer, CCM was so busy that Darren started to look for someone to take over some of the day-to-day operations, like filling and mailing orders and handling the bookkeeping. In late fall he hired Andy Harling, a classical guitarist, to help with the day-to-day office work and the maintenance of instruments and equipment. When Ryan left CCM to go back to school to finish his music degree, Andy inherited the task of examining the day-to-day processes to make CCM operate more efficiently.

Soon after Andy was hired, Jennifer, who had continued to act as Darren's booking agent, had openings for two shows that had been left vacant by a musician who had cancelled at the last minute. Darren was already booked for other gigs, but felt it was important to find another artist to do the shows. Darren quickly recorded a CD of Andy's repertoire, duplicated it in-house, and sent Andy out to do the two gigs. To Darren's excitement, Andy was successful. But now that Andy had actually gone out and done an arts festival under Darren's direction, Andy had valuable knowledge of how to capitalize on arts festivals. Darren felt there was a risk that Andy could leave and become his competitor. Recognizing this as an opportunity, Darren signed Andy to a recording contract. Andy's first full CD with CCM was launched as Andrew Thomas Harling.

As Andy's responsibilities expanded into more and more performing, CCM needed someone else to help answer telephones and fill orders. Amy was hired in August 2000 as Andy's assistant.

Darren's growing company required more space, so Darren moved CCM from his one-bedroom office and recording studio to a large rental house. A large laundry room in the basement was transformed into a well-organized mailroom; a spare bedroom served as an office. Darren built a workbench for repairing equipment and turned another room in the basement into a nearly soundproof recording studio. The garage served as a warehouse, with all inventory and equipment neatly organized on labeled shelves and workbenches.

The Performance Music Recording Industry and the Digital Revolution

What used to be a quarter of a million dollar piece of gear ten years ago, say in the late 80s, you can get now for five thousand dollars, and the quality is just as good, maybe even better.

Traditionally, the record industry was the exclusive domain of five or six major record labels. These major labels had large staffs, big budgets, and huge distribution. The cost of recording and pressing vinyl was very high. In the early 1980s, a professional recording studio could cost several million dollars. Although most performances were recorded on tape, editing was virtually non-existent. Music was typically recorded onto a multi-master track. This was then mixed down to a half-inch tape called the master. The master was then transferred to vinyl. In order to cut anything, the half-inch tape had to be physically spliced with a razor. Because of the high cost of recording and of pressing in vinyl, a company had to produce a minimum of about five thousand copies of any given album just to cover fixed expenses. The costs and difficulty of building a major record label kept industry competition in the hands of a few established companies.

With the digital revolution came the compact disc. The cost of digitally recording and burning a CD was significantly less expensive than creating copies from a vinyl or tape master. In 2000, a professional recording studio could be assembled for about $5,000. In addition, the hardware and computers used to edit music were affordable, even for the spare-room hobbyist. The ability to edit music and manipulate it via computer became far more comprehensive than in the past. Not only was digital recording and editing cheap, CDs were cheap to duplicate, even in small quantities. Kashif (1996) estimated that 500 CDs cost between $1.90 and $3.63 per CD to duplicate. A production run of 2,000 CDs would bring the cost down to under $1 per unit.

Unlike vinyl or tape masters, digital recordings could be duplicated without deterioration of the master disc. A musician could create a master CD on his own home computer, design and print attractive labels, and duplicate 500–1000 without investing in expensive equipment or contracting with a professional studio. The size and weight of compact discs made storage and shipping cheap and convenient, thus opening the music recording and distribution industry to an uncountable number of players in even remote locations.

Production costs represented only part of the total cost picture to launch a recording. Major recording labels invested heavily in marketing, promotion, distribution, royalties, and "image" building, often exceeding $1 million. On the other end of the spectrum, "anyone with talent and a business perspective can start their own virtual reality or vanity label . . ." (Wacholtz, 2001).

With the availability of cheap production equipment and easy access to Internet marketing and distribution, the industry became fragmented and distinct segments appeared. Music production companies, or labels, generally fell into four categories, or levels. Exhibit 1 gives some examples of the labels within these categories.

The "first tier companies" consisted of the major labels such as Columbia, BMG, EMI, and Sony Music. These labels had national, or even international, distribution. Typically, they had more than 100 artists under contract, representing a broad array of musical styles. They did not tend to focus on just one genre. CCM did not really compete with major labels, and Darren Curtis Skanson didn't want to position himself to compete directly with classical guitarists such as Christopher Parkening and John Williams, whose music was produced by Sony's Classical Division.

Independent labels were the next largest segment of the industry. Many of these companies were managed by a musician/artist, but larger independents were run by professional managers. Independent labels had anywhere from 10–100 artists under contract. Some of these labels may have been comparable in size to some of the major labels, but independents tended to focus on one or two genres of music. Narada, whose focus was New Age music, was a typical example of a successful independent label. Another producer of New Age music was

EXHIBIT 1   Record Label Company Categories

Major Labels Over 100 artists	Independent Labels 10–100 artists	Micro-Labels 2–10 artists	Vanity Labels 1 artist
Sony	Soundings of the Planet (inspirational/healing)	Etherian (meditative)	Bob Culbertson
Columbia	Narada (New Age)	Evol Egg Nart (rock/pop)	Lisa Lynn Franco
BMG	Higher Octave Metal (New Age)	Cuneiform Records (progressive jazz)	Watson and Company
EMI	Metal Blade Records (heavy metal)	CCM (light acoustic)	Lao Tizer
Giant Records	Rhino Records (compilations)		Esteban Ramirez
Warner Brothers	W.A.R. (punk, rock, & reggae)		
Elektra Records	Windham Hill (light classical & easy listening)		
Atlantic Records			

NOTE: Hustwit lists over 1000 major and independent labels. This table illustrates CCM's perceived competitor and/or partner labels. [Hustwit, Gary (1998) *Releasing an Independent Record*, Rockpress Publishing Company.]

Higher Octave. Metal Blade Records was an independent label that focused on heavy metal. Rhino Records focused on re-releasing compilations. Soundings of the Planet produced several easy-listening and classical offerings that directly competed with CCM. Some of the larger independent labels had national distribution, but most were regional or specialty distributors.

The next tier of recording companies were known as the "micro-labels." These labels typically had fewer than ten artists under contract, and tended to be more tightly focused than the independent labels. The micro-labels had small staffs, and the owner/manager was often the lead artist. Micro-labels seldom had formal distribution systems, relying on direct sales to fans and wholesale to clubs and specialty retailers. Because of the size of these labels and the small distribution networks they commanded, they existed only because of the low costs involved in digital recording. Etherian was an established micro-label that competed directly with Colorado Creative Music.

The most specialized segment of the music industry consisted of the vanity labels. These labels were created by independent artists who wanted to record and sell their own music. They were usually one-person operations with no formal distribution. These artists relied on direct sales to concert-goers and loyal fans. Musicians such as Bob Culbertson, Lisa Franco, Watson and Company, Peruvian Bands, and Lao Tizer are examples of artists on vanity labels that had been successful at direct selling at arts festivals.

While it was fairly common for a vanity label to move up to micro-label status, it was quite uncommon for a micro-label to move up to the independent label level. Soundings of the Planet was one example of a record label that was able to do this. It was virtually unheard of for an independent to compete at the major label level, although some independent labels had been acquired by major label companies.

Marketing and Promotion

A key element in recorded-music sales was getting music heard. In general people didn't want to buy music they had not heard. The major labels used their established relationships with prominent radio stations for tremendous leverage in getting new music played on prime-time programs. Command of distributors and capital to produce in large quantities allowed major record labels to offer new recordings for sale at the same time that radio stations gave the music airplay. Music was a fashionable business, and sales were heavily correlated to good timing.

The radio stations' primary relationship was with the major labels, so independents, micro, and vanity labels had to rely on other means of getting their music heard. Many bands on these smaller labels relied on touring and performing. Big Head Todd and the Monsters (Giant Records), Phish (Warner Brothers), and Widespread Panic (Capricorn Records) found their fame through the college circuit, performing and selling their music all over the country. Musicians who recorded their music on vanity labels often played small local venues, such as bars, coffee houses, and bookstores.

Because getting music heard was so essential, there were promotional companies that specialized in getting music airplay. These companies called stations to negotiate airplay, promotional giveaways, and interviews. While many independent labels might have had the funding for this, smaller labels could rarely afford such extensive promotional campaigns.

Distribution

Most recorded music was distributed through major distributors and "one-stops" (see Exhibit 2). Major distributors contracted with large chain stores like Tower Records, Sam Goody, Barnes and Noble, and Borders Books and Music. It was very difficult for small record labels to use a major distributor because of the large order requirements and risky payment policies that had become standard for the industry. These distributors generally operated on a 60–90 day turnaround with full return. This meant that if a CD sold, the producer would typically be paid two or three months later. In addition, all those CDs that didn't sell were returned to the label or producer. Major distributors also wanted large quantities of inventory. A label might have to front the money for 40,000 CDs, which required a large

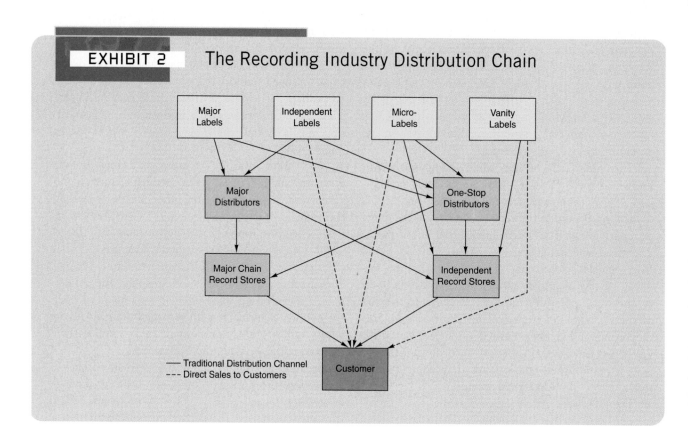

EXHIBIT 2 The Recording Industry Distribution Chain

—— Traditional Distribution Channel
--- Direct Sales to Customers

amount of working capital, with no guarantee that the CDs would sell.

One-stops started out mainly to service independent music stores like Joe's Records on the corner. These one-stops allowed stores to buy in smaller quantities than from a major distributor. One-stops would sometimes carry music from major labels, but were similar to an independent label in that they tended to specialize in one type of music.

From Musician to Entrepreneur

I started this business because I was a good guitar player, so I thought a music company is perfect. But what you need to start a business—to be an entrepreneur—is different than being a guitar player. So I had to learn not to concentrate so much on the musical end of things, and instead to concentrate on the entrepreneurial things. That was a huge shift that started with Acoustitherapy. That is really where that whole process began, *when I said I don't need to make guitar music, I can make any kind of music, I just have to look at it as a businessman, not a musician.*

Darren Skanson soon realized that the physical work involved in setting up a studio was much easier than building and managing a business. His music degree did not prepare him for the tasks of marketing and promoting his music, nor did it provide a framework for creating a workable system of operations and control.

When Darren began Colorado Creative Music out of his bedroom in 1995, he did everything himself. He was his own accountant, desktop publisher, database manager, newsletter editor, website designer, and copywriter. Early on, he started transferring his stack of arts festival contacts from three-by-five notecards to a computerized database. By 1997 he switched to a computerized accounting system.

Using only his own savings to finance the company, Darren was concerned about keeping overhead low and expenses down (see Exhibit 3). To save on

| EXHIBIT 3 | CCM Income Statements | | | |

Year ending:	2000	1999	1998	1997
Income				
GIG sales	$ 181,451.92	$ 148,839.76	$ 145,721.78	$ 129,445.25
Wholesale	12,238.83	19,556.04	17,587.02	10,887.02
Mail & phone orders	11,442.24	2,928.72	3,148.00[a]	0.00[a]
Website sales	6,419.35	760.50	0.00	0.00
Other	1,758.79	1,417.89	3,714.98	1,259.59
Total Sales	213,311.13	173,502.91	170,171.78	141,591.86
Other income	3,302.92	2,750.09	4,329.00	1,527.28
Total Income	216,614.05	176,253.00	174,500.78	143,119.14
Cost of goods sold	22,034.33	23,311.38	36,468.62	36,226.52
Gross Profit	$ 194,579.72	$ 152,941.62	$ 138,032.16	$ 106,892.62
Expenses				
Advertising Expense	$ 10,422.83	$ 4,388.71	$ 11,432.35	$ 4,110.43
Automobile Expense	0.00	2,279.01	1,644.83	4,016.88
Bad Check Expense	156.00	583.14	416.99	1,072.50
Bank Service Charges	5,320.39	4,790.75	3,070.60	2,509.47
Commissions	32,861.14	31,333.92	30,283.59	27,828.66
Dues and Subscriptions	10.00	0.00	0.00	397.45
Depreciation Expense	0.00	5,820.00	0.00	0.00
Equipment Rental	491.14	0.00	0.00	0.00
Furniture and Fixtures	0.00	0.00	329.95	656.84
Insurance	2,344.79	2,655.51	2,109.19	1,173.00
Interest Expense	631.96	0.00	0.00	0.00
Licenses and Permits	0.00	0.00	218.00	327.09
Miscellaneous	580.37	1,077.27	1,462.62	2,282.64
Parking Expense	308.75	661.00	348.00	258.00
Payroll	15,515.76	6,660.29	5,150.64	0.00
Payroll Expenses/Taxes	3,143.38	11,671.74	0.00	0.00
Postage and Delivery	6,432.22	2,321.22	1,626.06	2,150.97
Printing and Reproduction	4,691.82	1,818.19	4,414.28	7,409.34
Professional Fees[b]	29,719.26	2,242.50	217.10	1,145.00
Rent and Storage Fees	14,080.45	13,368.07	9,973.29	2,174.75
Repairs and Maintenance	2,531.25	1,863.00	3,217.77	2,229.01
Royalties	17,283.39	8,848.99	1,776.91	746.57
Shipping	3,776.97	3,257.89	2,804.05	2,345.05
Subscriptions	80.95	443.18	472.76	0.00
Supplies	13,142.81	7,343.05	5,343.78	8,247.67
Taxes	4,744.94	4,678.58	7,961.01	6,796.28
Telephone	4,399.22	5,269.83	4,860.00	4,754.38
Travel & Entertainment	16,156.64	23,889.21	17,759.91	19,092.13
Utilities	1,461.29	1,262.04	511.78	244.92
Total Expenses	$ 190,287.72	$ 148,527.09	$ 117,405.46	$ 101,969.03
Net Income	$ 4,292.00	$ 4,414.53	$ 20,626.70	$ 4,923.59

[a]Included with wholesale.
[b]This includes payments to backup musicians at live performances and an independent music consultant to direct the production of the *Classica* and *A Christmas Story* CDs.

time, Darren would purchase rolls of stamps and postage packages according to their weight. This sometimes resulted in overpostaging some packages. Stamps and address labels were affixed by hand, since CCM didn't have enough mail orders to warrant purchasing an automated postage system. As mail order demand grew, the wastefulness of the system became significant.

Promotion was most effective at arts festivals, but Darren understood the need for retail distribution to increase sales. He approached some retailers himself, but found that it was an onerous and time-consuming task.

I tried to take care of it myself, going out there trying to get CDs into stores, but it's too big a job for me. I have too many things pulling me into too many other directions. I actually hired a sales guy in the summer of '98, and he turned out to be worthless. He basically didn't do anything; he took the money and didn't do anything—the employer's nightmare. Then I tried friends who wanted to do it part time, but that didn't work out either.

Then we hooked up with one of the "one-stops" here in Colorado. Basically what a one-stop does is they have a huge catalog of stuff. If the demand is there, the stores will ask the one-stop, "Do you have any Darren Curtis Skanson CDs?" The thing we ran into with that is we had some Barnes & Noble stores calling the one-stop to get our stuff, but the one-stop put such a markup on the CDs that B&N didn't want to buy from them. He's got to make money too, that I understand, but B&N would call us wanting to get more CDs and we'd tell them, "That's great, but we're doing business with John over there at USA One-Stop. Just give him a call and he'll set you up." Then they call us back, and tell us that John is charging them a ridiculous amount for the CDs wholesale, and they say, "We don't want to deal with John, we want to deal with you." And you're back to where you started from.

In 1999, feeling overwhelmed with the tasks of running a business, Darren outsourced the accounting function and made a list of tasks and systems that needed to be codified (Exhibit 4). He also began reading books on entrepreneurship, searching for a way to organize Colorado Creative Music and to make it more profitable.

Creating a Sustainable Enterprise

Darren wanted Colorado Creative Music and Darren Curtis Skanson to become identifiable names, with enough demand to make distribution through large book and record stores feasible. He envisioned a promotional spot on the evening news, with thousands of people watching, and then heading out to buy his CD in a store. He wanted someone browsing the shelves to see a Darren Curtis Skanson CD, recognize him from the newscast, and buy it.

I think you always start with a vision, and of course that vision was to record, produce, and sell my own music. And that of course still is a major part of CCM. Your vision always changes. I'm amazed at how much your vision changes as you learn and grow as a business person.

Darren's early success in selling his and Andy's recordings led him to realize the potential for profitability and growth that the digital revolution had opened up. He knew enough about the music industry to be wary of labeling himself "New Age" or "classical" or "folk," competing with established artists. He decided to call his own music "light classical," and position CCM as a company that handled a portfolio of artists, each with a distinctive light acoustic style.

The first step in "branding" CCM was a promotional catalogue that could be handed out to people who approached his sales table at arts festivals and shopping malls. He enclosed the catalogue with every sale and offered it for free on CCM's website.

CCM's first catalogue was a small brochure. With the addition of new CCM offerings, Darren felt the need for an upgrade that would portray a high-quality image. He was able to reproduce an attractive catalogue for about 12 cents apiece. He was pleased with the appearance of catalogues, but he wasn't sure how to manage them as inventory or how to decide how many to produce at one time. He didn't want a box of 1,000 old catalogues on

EXHIBIT 4

Colorado Creative Music Task List

Research and Development

Musical
1. Song writing
2. Arranging
3. Pre-production
4. Recording, producing, engineering
5. Mastering

Books to read:
Zen and the Art of Motorcycle Maintenance—Persig

Market
1. CCM R+D Worksheet
2. Artwork

Books to Read:
Positioning: the Battle for Your Mind—Reis/Trout
22 Immutable Laws of Branding—Reis

Operations

Accounting

Fulfillment

Maintenance
1. Instruments and gear
2. Office equipment

Gear Preparation for Shows

Duplication

Inventory Management

Database Management

Design

Brand Marketing

Live Performance
1. Malls
2. Arts festivals
3. Concerts

Website
Essential elements

Books to Read:
Front-Page 2000 for Dummies
Software to know:
Front-Page 2000

Publicity
1. Airplay: Radio, TV, Internet radio
2. Live Interviews: Radio, TV
3. Print Press: Reviews, features, events listings

Sales

Direct
1. Live performance
2. 800 #
3. Website
4. Mail-order catalogue
5. After sale: Thank you letter

Direct letters from database
Direct response

Books to Read:
Guerrilla Marketing—Levinson

Indirect
Traditional
1. Chain music stores
2. Chain book stores
3. Independent music stores

(continued)

EXHIBIT 4   Colorado Creative Music Task List *(continued)*

Research and Development

Books to Read: *(continued)*
The New Positioning—Trout
Guerrilla Marketing—Levinson
Kotler on Marketing—Kotler

Operations

Books to Read:
The E-Myth—Gerber

Software to know:
Quickbooks 2000 Pro
Microsoft Access
Microsoft Works
Microsoft Word 2000

Brand Marketing

Promotions
1. In store
2. Contests
3. Sponsoring
4. Give-away

E-Mail
Monthly newsletter

Books to Read:
Guerrilla Marketing—Levinson

Software to Know:
Aureate Group Mail

Sales

Non-Traditional
1. Retail chains
2. Catalogues
3. Gift stores
4. Independent book stores
5. Health, massage, yoga, tai chi, day care
6. Christian: chains and independents

hand when he needed to add a new product to the order form. The company was adding two new titles a year, which made sales and inventory increasingly difficult to manage.

By December 2000, CCM had four product lines, and a total of eleven different records. The four product lines (or brand names) were Darren Curtis Skanson, Acoustitherapy, Andrew Thomas Harling, and Music for Candles.

Darren Curtis Skanson

Darren described this line of music as "Light Classical Guitar." This product line was marketed as a more gentle and intimate approach to classical music, positioned against more purist classical guitarists such as John Williams and Christopher Parkening. Darren has released five titles under this brand name. *Peace, Earth, and Guitars* was released in September 1995. Due to the success of this title, CCM released *Peace, Earth, and Guitars, Volume II* in January 1997. Darren's next title was a Christmas album, *Angels, Guitars, and Joy*, released in October 1996. *Classica* was released in May 2000; *A Christmas Story* was released in November 2000. These last two releases featured a cello backup to Darren's solo guitar, in an effort to broaden Darren's audience appeal.

Acoustitherapy

This line of records was Darren's response to what many customers wanted from instrumental music. Customers specifically wanted acoustic instrumental music that was slow, soft, and soothing. Darren collected music from various artists who wrote original music and performed on a variety of acoustic instruments. *Relaxation* and *Regeneration* were released in September 1997. *Gentle Passion* was released in October 1998, and in July 2000 *World Meditations* was released. Acoustitherapy was marketed as soft and soothing music for the mind, body, heart, and soul.

Andrew Thomas Harling

Andy's debut CD, *The Road to the Soul*, was a combination of traditional melodies and new compositions written by modern classical guitarists. A second CD was in the making, to be released by August 2001.

Music for Candles

CCM engineered and produced a CD called *Starry Night* for the vanity label Music for Candles. In 2001, CCM carried this product in its catalogue under a distribution contract with the Music for Candles artists. Darren hoped to produce and distribute CDs for other labels to expand CCM's catalogue offerings and promote CCM's name recognition.

Pushing the Products

Darren knew that he needed to understand his customers and cater to their tastes. He had noticed that the people who approached him at the arts festivals and shopping malls where he sold his CDs were generally white, middle-class adults, mostly mid 40s to 60-year-old women whose children were grown. These people expressed their delight in meeting Darren personally, and often asked for his autograph. Phone orders appeared to be coming from a similar demographic, with callers enthusiastic about talking with Darren personally when they placed an order for one of his recordings. Darren was careful to keep this personal touch and sent regular e-mails to his growing list of fans.

Darren understood quickly that these people were not classical music enthusiasts, but rather drawn to his music for its blend of soft acoustic sounds and familiar classical tunes. He chose his music offerings carefully, trying to maintain a distinction between himself and other artists. He knew that his company would need to offer a variety of titles to gain the sales volume he needed to compete for retail space.

Darren had an easy time selling his CDs in local music and book stores, but had not been able to set up distribution beyond his home state. Out of town, Darren relied on live performances to sell his recordings. For these shows (arts festivals, shopping malls, and concerts), he set up a pricing structure that he hoped would encourage the purchase of more than one CD (see Exhibit 5). Darren wanted to encourage an impulse buy with customers that were harder to reach on a regular basis.

With regular appearances at two local upscale malls, Darren's pricing structure appeared to create some saturation. Many customers were returning

CCM Pricing Structure for Recorded Compact Discs, 2000 Sales

At live shows	Mail, e-mail, and 800 number orders
1 CD $17.00	$16.00 per CD
2 CDs $28.00	$1.75 shipping and handling per CD
3 CDs $38.00	$17.75 Total per CD
4 CDs $47.00	
5 CDs $55.00	(no mail-order discount for multiples)
6 CDs $62.00	
7 CDs $68.00	

fans who already had all his CDs. For this reason he changed the price at local mall performances to $17 per CD, with no discounts for multiple purchases. Darren's rationale was clear: "If we are going to be playing at these places over and over again, we can't be shooting ourselves in the foot by selling five CDs at a great price, then when the customer comes back, he or she has everything. We might even be too late on that. We may have shot ourselves in the foot already."

Darren was also concerned that Jennifer was not finding many new venues for him, preferring to book him at the regular shows and festivals where he already had a strong presence. Traveling around the country gave him exposure to a wider customer base, but he was afraid that bookings at the same shows year after year limited his ability to reach a broader market. As he brought more musicians on board, Darren believed that he could produce music that would appeal to a broader audience. By rotating artists, each performer would be able to do different festivals each year, minimizing the saturation problem.

In addition to festival and shopping mall distribution, Darren wanted to be able to offer his CDs in retail outlets nationwide. He knew he couldn't compete with the major labels, but he did not know how to break into the traditional industry distribution networks. From some of his reading on entrepreneurship, Darren concluded that it was important to think in terms of company "saleability" as a measure of business success, even though selling CCM to a major label was not his ultimate goal. He felt he could build a stronger, more focused business if he thought of CCM in terms of its attractiveness as a potential acquisition or investment. That meant that he needed to build enough volume for CCM products to be sold nationally through traditional distribution channels. Major labels expected sales of 15,000 copies of a recording in one year before they would consider offering a contract. This was the benchmark that Darren set for himself.

Darren's Dilemma

The major dilemma is that we have built the backbone of our company on direct sales, whether it is at the gig, in the mall, or in the back end (800 number, website, mail order). That has been a very profitable thing for us, but as I discovered this last Christmas, I only have so many hours of performance in me to be out there direct selling—which is the engine that drives all of the other back-end sales.

Darren realized that he had a long way to go in getting national distribution. By the end of 2000, Colorado Creative Music had sold over 30,000 Darren Curtis Skanson CDs, but that number included all five Darren Curtis Skanson titles over six years. Over a seven-month period, CCM sold 4,100 units of his CD *Classica* that was released in May 2000. Most of these were from direct sales, stemming from Darren's tireless efforts as performer, publicity agent, promoter, and salesman.

Darren started to list his goals and think about his options:

1. To create a profitable record label with a complementary range of artists.
2. To position Darren Curtis Skanson to compete with artists on a recording label on a par with Sony Classical. This required selling records in stores through traditional distribution methods.

3. To create a product line, such as Acoustitherapy, that was saleable, and use the funds to work toward accomplishing goals 1 and 2.

Feeling strongly that something was missing in his efforts to make CCM and his music more successful, Darren began researching and reading books about marketing and positioning. He was searching for a way to position Acoustitherapy and Darren Curtis Skanson against the competition.

One of the better books I found was The E-Myth *by Michael Gerber. He talks about thinking about a business as a franchise. You can be successful if you can define everything in your business, like a franchise does, like McDonald's does. They say, cook these fries for three minutes at x number of degrees and plop them out there and leave them in the drainer for 30 seconds. It's the same thing with me. The thing I need to concentrate on now is my promotion and publicity processes. How do you promote a record? It should be a fairly simple process, but I should have a process for it.*

When Darren began thinking of CCM as a franchise, he thought in terms of having a system into which he could plug other artists. He felt that by putting Andy into the systems that he had tried and tested, he was franchising the company. As he fine-tuned these processes, Darren started seeking out other artists that he felt would fit well into the system. Darren wanted to train each artist to sell in a way that would allow them to focus their energies on performing without having to worry about the business end of things. Darren had already compiled a procedures manual that included checklists for equipment necessary to take to a show, settings for the soundboard and speakers, and even a script for making sales. Darren saw his main weakness in the area of marketing.

I had always thought that the better-quality product always wins. So I had to be a better guitar player, I had to be faster, and all those things. When I read those books I realized that quality matters, but it is not near as important as the position that you own in the mind of whomever. If you say classical guitar *to someone, most people would say "Andrés Segovia," and then they'd say "John Williams" or "Christopher Parkening."*

There's an implicit ranking, a product ladder in people's minds. There is no way that I will compete—EVER compete—with those people. It doesn't really matter if I'm a better musician. The reality or the truth makes no difference. In people's minds, truth and perception become melded. So I need to work on the image, the perception in people's minds, of the CCM label and the artists it employs.

Having been bitten by this marketing mindset, Darren became driven in his pursuit of product positioning and image creation. He began formulating a worksheet for positioning CCM products and documenting a process for publicity. He created a system for writing press releases that included information on the timing and frequency of sending press releases. Darren purchased a nationwide publicity database to help prepare in advance for every trip. Even with all of these new ideas being put into action, Darren was still traveling about 40 weekends a year to perform at arts festivals and shopping malls where the largest portion of direct sales could be made. Most phone, mail, and e-mail orders were still directly related to Darren's arts festival appearances. Although website (Internet) sales increased threefold in 2000, this was still a small portion of overall direct sales.

In December 2000, when Darren was playing a ten-day stint at a shopping mall in Denver, the reality of Darren's limitations began to set in. He began feeling the pains of tendonitis in his left elbow, and soon after Christmas he realized he had a significant problem. His plan to put out two new Darren Curtis Skanson CDs in order to ride a wave of recent publicity would have to be put on hold.

With the harsh realization that Darren could not continue to keep up his previous performance pace, he knew he needed to find other musicians to drive sales. In January 2001, he began to formulate some ideas for growing the label that would take some of the pressure for performance off him.

First he decided to produce only one new Darren Curtis Skanson CD, and instead produce a second Andrew Thomas Harling CD. Darren felt that if Andy had another CD he would be in a better position to take over some of the bigger arts festivals that Darren had been doing himself.

To compensate for the fact that CCM would produce only one Darren Curtis Skanson CD (which might not be released until November), Darren knew he had to do something different to attract a bigger crowd of listeners. He decided to look for violists or violinists to play with him when he played larger Colorado festivals, capitalizing on the success of the cello-enhanced *Classica*. He transcribed the cello harmonies from the *Classica* CD into a score for viola and violin and auditioned musicians who would make a commitment to do a certain number of shows. He found musicians, set up rehearsals, and sold more CDs at their first show together than Darren had sold alone the previous year with the initial release of *Classica*.

Darren also began actively searching for other artists who would fit well with the CCM label. He began negotiations with a pianist and a violinist, but both eventually broke down. The pianist wanted 50 percent ownership of CCM, which made Darren nervous.

The Next Step

In order for us to get legitimate, and our product lines to be legitimate in the "standard music industry," we have to have distribution through retail stores. It's just how the music business machine works. That's the distribution dilemma. Of course personally, I would like Darren Curtis Skanson the brand name to be courted by Sony Classical because we've sold 15,000 of my next CD through established chains. And they'd be calling and asking who Darren Curtis Skanson is, saying that they want to sign him. And we could say, "Well, CCM has his contract and we would let him go for x number of dollars," or whatever deal you negotiate.

I guess in a nutshell the dilemma is this, in order to (a) grow the company or (b) sell the product lines to an entity larger than CCM, those entities want to see your sales in traditional outlets. But in order to get it into those outlets, you either have to commit to huge product run, or be satisfied with pounding away at it, or just incrementally working your sales up. I would love to get bigger distribution because bigger distribution

means bigger sales, but I can't handle huge distribution without a bigger base of performers and a bigger push for publicity. In the short term, making direct sales is good for cash flow, it's good for the bottom line, it's good for the business, but in the long term, in order to turn any one of our product lines into something bigger than just making direct sales, you have to make a significant amount of sales through the established music business machine, which is record stores.

I think ultimately one-stops and distributors is the way you have to go, that's the way the whole industry works, but I don't believe that I can do that myself. That is going to have to be someone's job. If it means hiring a guy part time to start, it's just going to have to be his responsibility—that is, all he does is chase that down.

Darren was caught in a chicken-and-egg dilemma. He knew that CCM needed more sales to be attractive to the retail distributors, and he needed retail distribution to increase sales. Unless he could produce more CDs, Darren's festival performances would not yield the sales volume he needed to keep CCM profitable. Even if he produced another Darren Curtis Skanson CD, he was not sure that it would sell if he could not actively promote it himself. Until his elbow healed, his performance schedule would have to be curtailed.

As CCM's lead performer, Darren had hoped to turn over the sales and managerial functions to others. Now he was forced to rethink his role. Darren knew that he still wanted to perform, but it was clear that he could not keep up his current performance schedule. Should he work harder to get other musicians on board to tour and publicize the CCM name while he acted as master manager and coach? Should he hire a sales manager or focus his energies on getting CCM's products into retail outlets himself? Should he concentrate on recording-studio activities to increase CCM's product offerings and try to push the catalogue sales, which had higher profit margins? Would hiring an experienced marketing manager help Darren uncover new arenas for growth? Could a new salesperson free up Darren to explore alternative performance venues? Or were his talents best directed at refining the CCM "system" and managing the recording studio?

Darren felt that his company was at a crossroads. His first love was music, and he loved to perform, but he knew that his personal satisfaction hinged on building a profitable company. He understood that growth and profitability were directly tied to maintaining and building CCM's customer base. As the plane started its descent into the Orlando airport, Darren tried to ready himself for the performance weekend ahead. But visions of CCM as a sought-after label were not far from his mind. He wished he could build a business as easily as he could serenade a crowd.

References

Hustwit, G. (1998). *Releasing an Independent Record,* 6th Edition. San Diego, California: Rockpress Publishing Company.

Kashif (1996). *Everything You'd Better Know about the Record Industry.* Venice, California: Brooklyn Boy Books.

Wacholtz, L. E. (2001). "The New Music Business: Internet Entrepreneurial Opportunities in the Performing Arts," *Proceedings of the 2001 USASBE/SBIDA National Conference.* Orlando, Florida, August.

The Crowne Inn: A Classic Case of a Family Business in Turmoil

Todd A. Finkle
University of Akron

Case Description

The primary subject matter of the case concerns the succession of a family-owned business. Secondary issues examined include contracts, personality conflicts, valuations, and ethics. The case has a difficulty level that is appropriate for senior level undergraduate students and is designed to be taught in a 1-hour and 20-minute period. Students are expected to spend at least four hours of outside preparation for the case.

Case Synopsis

In early 2001, Barbara Johnston and her four sons were negotiating with Barbara's son Bruce for the rights to own the family-owned business, The Crowne Inn. After Bruce's father retired from the business in 1995, Bruce made an oral agreement with his parents to pay off the mortgage of their house ($23,500), pay their medical costs, and pay $500 cash per month for the rest of their lives in exchange for the future profits from the business. The company was structured as an S-corporation with Bruce's father owning 100% of the stock. The stock of the company remained with the parents, until their death, upon which the stock would pass to Bruce without remuneration.

In 1997 Bruce's father, Harvey, passed away and the stock moved into Barbara's name. The decision focus of the case takes place in 2001 where Barbara and her four sons were negotiating with Bruce to acquire the stock of the bar. The family's attorney, Bobby Free, devised three possible solutions to the problem: (1) have Bruce pay a lump sum, (2) have Bruce pay a smaller lump sum and $500 per month, or (3) sell the business outright to an outside party.

Bruce stated that he would pay a lump sum of not more than $60,000 to his mother. The family was unsure whether this was a fair offer. And if not, what was a fair offer? The family was also unsure if the lump sum method was the best way to handle the problem. Furthermore, would Bruce be willing and/or able to pay a higher lump sum? The real challenge was solving the family crisis without alienating Bruce and his family. Barbara was looking to her sons and her attorney for an answer to this complicated, nerve-racking family crisis.

Introduction

It was a clear cool fall day in late 2000 when Barbara Johnston, a retired nurse, was confronted with one of the biggest challenges of her life. Her son Bruce had entered her dilapidated house, threw down his keys and blurted out the following:

Reprinted by permission of Dr. Todd A. Finkle, The University of Akron.

You are all plotting behind my back. You are trying to bankrupt and steal the bar away from me. Well, you can have the keys to my house, car, and the lousy bar. But you will lose your son and two grandchildren forever.

No one wanted the bar. I made the bar what it is today. If I leave, the business will collapse and then you will have nothing. I have already talked to the employees and they will all walk out. After this is over, I am going to disown this whole family. I have had it with all of you!!

Barbara's family was on the verge of being torn apart . . . over the family's largest asset, a bar called The Crowne Inn located in Kansas City, Missouri. Since the death of her husband Harvey in 1997, Barbara had problems with Bruce's inability to meet his previously agreed upon oral agreement to take care of her. On the day of his father's retirement in 1995, Bruce made an oral agreement to pay off the second mortgage of his parents' house ($23,500), give them $500 in cash per month, and pay their health insurance and medical bills for the rest of their lives. He made this oral agreement in front of his parents and their attorney, Bobby Free. However, despite repeated warnings from Free, Harvey refused a formal written contract. As a result of the agreement, Bruce received all of the proceeds from the bar.

After five years, Bruce had not lived up to his agreement with his parents. The family was trying to work out a deal with Bruce's lawyer and accountant to sell him the business. The family's attorney, Bobby Free, devised three possible solutions to the problem: (1) have Bruce pay a lump sum, (2) have Bruce pay a smaller lump sum and $500 per month, or (3) sell the bar outright to an outside party.

Bruce stated that he would pay a lump sum of not more than $60,000 to his mother. The family was unsure whether this was a fair offer. And if not, what was a fair offer? Also, was the lump sum method the best way to handle the problem? Furthermore, would Bruce be willing and/or able to pay a higher lump sum? Previously, he told his older brother Karl that he refused to pay $75,000. He stated that he would be better off going into business with someone else rather than pay $75,000.

The real challenge was solving the family crisis without alienating Bruce and his family. Furthermore, Bruce only had one good relationship with his four brothers, Karl. Barbara was looking to her sons and her attorney for an answer to this complicated, nerve-racking, family crisis.

The Johnston Family

Born in Kansas City in 1934, Barbara Johnston grew up in a lower middle class Lutheran family and was a by-product of the Depression. Despite her challenging upbringing, Barbara was a gregarious, warm, friendly, family-oriented woman.

During her junior year in high school, she fell in love with a senior named Harvey Johnston. Harvey married Barbara four years after she graduated from high school. The marriage proved to be very tumultuous, but produced five healthy boys and six grandchildren. Most of the boys had similar personality characteristics as their father, which included a very high need for independence, an extremely strong work ethic, and an entrepreneurial flair. The oldest son, Karl, a twice-divorced 47-year-old, was currently married (Caren). Karl was a street-smart, successful entrepreneur who owned a 3M dealership in Seattle, Washington. He had grown the business to over $1.5 million in sales in four years. His salary, not including the profits from the business, was around $85,000 a year.

Her second son, Cal (Jessica), had been married for 22 years. His marriage produced three children: Jason, Jennifer, and Jim. Cal was a religious, optimistic, and successful 45-year-old cardiologist who lived in Kansas City. Of the five brothers, Cal was the most financially successful. His independent medical practice had sales of $1,000,000 with an annual net income of $250,000.

The middle child, Bruce (Sharon), had been married since 1985 and had two children, Albert and Bob. Bruce and Sharon were currently running the family business, The Crowne Inn. Bruce enjoyed partying with his friends from the bar. Bruce and Sharon worked at the bar and made a combined salary of $84,000 (1999), not including the profits from the bar. (See Exhibit 1.)

Year	Bruce	Sharon	Bar's Net Income Pre Tax	Totals
1997	$53,500	$20,000	$ (500)	$73,000
1998	60,000	20,000	3,440	83,440
1999	62,000	22,000	6,450	90,450
2000	64,000	24,000	6,500	94,950

The fourth son, Tyler, was a single (never married), 40-year-old dentist living in Las Vegas, Nevada. He was a hard working free spirit who enjoyed his freedom and convertibles. His dental practice was very successful and he made approximately $100,000 a year.

Danny, the last son, was also single (37 years old). He was extremely creative and enjoyed working with his hands. He had just started his own entertainment company that specialized in decorations for holidays and special events.

The Crowne Inn

Harvey and Barbara Johnston were married in 1952. Before their marriage, Johnston's father, Norm, realized that his son needed a profession to support his new wife. Norm approached his 22-year-old son and asked him what profession he wanted to enter. After some thought, Johnston stated that he wanted to start his own bar. The loose, free lifestyle appealed to him.

Before opening the bar, Johnston asked his best friend, Leo Smith, if he wanted to be his partner. Smith had been bartending with Johnston for the past two years and enjoyed it so he agreed. Smith also had more experience in the bar business so it was a good match. He was a warm, friendly man who was married with one daughter.

In 1952 Johnston and Smith took out a $10,000 loan and started a bar called Leo and Harvey's in downtown Kansas City. The bar was structured as an S-corporation where both Johnston and Smith owned 50 percent of the stock in the company.

After seven years of moderately successful business, they made a decision to move the business to the northeastern part of Kansas City. The downtown area had become increasingly dangerous with an increase in crime and an increase in the number of homeless people. The new location had fewer competitors, less crime, and a better clientele. The partners purchased the land and building and moved into the new location in 1959, renaming the bar The Crowne Inn.

The Crowne Inn was unique from other bars because it was patterned after the Old West. Old wooden barrels lined the front of the building. The building itself was made of wood boards and signs were placed all over the front of the building that ranged from "Dance Girls Wanted" to "Whisky Served Here" to "Coldest Beer in Town." On the top of the building was a 7-Up sign.

At the entrance of the smoke filled bar there was a shiny, dark stained, wooden bar with ten swinging stools for customers. A pair of small swinging doors led to the back of the bar where a small cooler held mugs, cans, and bottles of beer and wine. There were five taps: one for Champagne, Cold Duck, Miller High Life, and two for Budweiser (their best selling beer). On the other side of the bar were a small grill, refrigerator, office, and cooler for kegs and cases of beer. A limited supply of hard alcohol and food items were also for sale behind the bar.

The Crowne Inn differentiated itself from other bars in a number of ways. First, the bar had a very homey atmosphere with approximately 15 tables and a total capacity of 70 people. This gave customers the ability to converse without all the hassles (e.g., fights, loud music) of a typical bar. The bar also served lunch (hamburgers, hot dogs, chili dogs, and chips) and snacks (Slim Jims, beef jerky, bags of peanuts). The bar initially had a pool table and color TV; however, they dropped the pool table due to fights.

The historic ambiance of the bar was enhanced through the shellacking of historic newspaper clippings on the walls. Actual articles on the Japanese surprise attack at Pearl Harbor, the sinking of the *Lusitania,* and the D-Day invasion were all exhibited on the wall. The bar was also full of historic relics, which included old menus, beer trays, political buttons, and beer cans. Jim Beam bottles (novelty bottles filled with whiskey) were also located all over the bar.

The Crowne Inn's busiest times were weekdays for lunch (11–1 PM), happy hour (5–7 PM), and weekend evenings (8–1 AM). Business professionals made up the largest segment of customers at lunch. During the late afternoon and evenings the customers were primarily local blue-collar workers.

Johnston and Smith worked alternating two-week shifts: day (10 AM–6 PM) and evening (6 PM–2 AM). As their business slowly grew, so did their families. Smith eventually had four girls and moved into a beautiful four-bedroom house, while Johnston had five boys, moved into a small three-bedroom house, and struggled to pay his bills.

Transitional Years

In 1981, Harvey bought out Smith's stock in the company for $50,000 cash. At the age of 28, Karl joined the business full-time. Karl brought a new ambiance to the bar. He had a high level of energy, creativity, and numerous innovative ideas to enhance the sales of the bar. One of the first things that he did was add a large cooler that contained over 80 imported beers from all over the world. He also created an advertising campaign in the local entertainment papers, bought a popcorn machine, a stereo system, and a VCR to play movies. These ideas along with Karl's jovial personality bolstered

sales and changed the culture of the bar from a primarily neighborhood blue-collar establishment to a younger, trendier 25- to 40-year-old crowd.

By late 1982, Karl had grown weary of the long hours, drunks, and low pay. Furthermore, he had recently been married and his wife, Jessica, wanted him to leave the bar business. Despite the rise in sales of the bar to $125,000, he was not making as much money as he had hoped. He quit the bar and moved to San Diego, California.

Turnaround

By late 1982, Johnston's middle son, Bruce, started working part-time for the bar; however, Harvey still worked the majority of the hours. In 1984, Karl returned from San Diego as a divorcé and started working at the bar again. Karl and Bruce came up with some innovative ideas to increase sales. They started selling warm roasted peanuts at 75 cents a bowl and ice-cold pints of imported beer on tap (e.g., Guinness, Heineken, Bass Ale). They also started selling pickles, inserted video games, a pinball machine, a jukebox CD player and a big screen television.

After two years of working together, sales had increased to $185,000. Despite the increased success of the bar, Karl decided to quit. He had been robbed twice at gunpoint, including one time where the robbers took all of the money and jewelry from the customers. He also got remarried and his second wife, Judy, was pushing him to get out of the bar business. Karl and Judy moved to San Diego at the end of 1986.

By the end of 1986, Bruce was working full-time with his father. Bruce continued his entrepreneurial flair over the next ten years. One of his most innovative moves was a strategic alliance with an Italian restaurant across the street, called Pappa's Pizza. The take out or dine in restaurant consisted of tasty Italian food. Since the bar did not serve food (besides snacks) in the evenings, it was an ideal strategy to allow people to order food from Pappa's Pizza and bring it into the bar. This strategy beefed up sales for both businesses.

Bruce also had promotional events where guest DJs would come in and play music. One of his most innovative special events was Crownewood. Crownewood was held every year on the night of the Oscars. Customers would vote on which stars would win. If they guessed correctly, they would win prizes. Other events focused on sporting events. For example, free chili was served during Monday Night Football.

These activities combined with advertising in the local entertainment paper, *Rebel,* attracted two new market segments, the college crowd and young urban professionals. The Crowne Inn had transformed itself from a primarily blue-collar neighborhood bar into one of the most progressive bars in Kansas City. As a result, the Johnstons increased their prices and sales. Under Harvey and Bruce's tenure, the sales of the bar increased from $145,000 in 1984 to $200,000 in 1994 (four percent increase in sales a year). (See Exhibit 2.)

EXHIBIT 2

The Crowne Inn Sales from 1982–2000

Year	Sales
1982	$125,000
1983	135,000
1984	145,000
1985	165,000
1986	185,000
1987	170,000
1988	175,000
1989	180,000
1990	185,000
1991	190,000
1992	192,500
1993	197,500
1994	200,000
1995	225,000
1996	250,000
1997	295,000
1998	326,000
1999	346,000
2000	366,000

One of the keys to Bruce's success in turning around the bar was his girlfriend, Sharon, who he eventually married in 1985. Sharon was a very savvy businessperson with a very strict authoritarian management style with tight controls. This was in contrast to Harvey and Bruce's laid-back personalities, which led Sharon to take control of the bar.

Failure of the Oral Agreement

In 1994, after 42 years of running the bar, Harvey was ready to retire. Harvey had emphysema, diabetes, and was obese. He approached his sons to see who wanted the bar. Bruce was the logical person to purchase the bar since he had been running it successfully for the past 11 years.

On the day of his father's retirement, Bruce made an oral agreement with his parents. In exchange for the future proceeds from the bar, Bruce made an oral agreement to pay off the $23,500 left on the second mortgage of his parents' house, give them $500 in cash per month, and pay for their health insurance and medical costs for the rest of their lives. Harvey refused to have a written contract. Harvey remained the president of the company and owned all of the stock. If he passed away, the stock would move into his wife's name. After they both passed away, the stock would then pass on to Bruce. The remainder of the estate's assets would then be divided among the other four siblings. The estimated amount of the remainder of the estate in 2001 was $50,000 (house), $80,000 (cash and securities), automobile ($10,000), and miscellaneous ($5,000).

Bruce had paid his parents' health care premiums with the most inexpensive policy up until his father's death in 1997. By 1998, when Barbara was eligible for Medicare, Bruce did not pay for any of her health care costs, which included Medicare ($46 per month) and medications ($300 per month). Cal ended up paying for the medications, which caused resentment from Cal and his wife. Barbara paid for her Medicare.

From 1994–1998, Bruce paid his mother $500 per month; however, he treated her as an employee. Therefore, taxes were deducted from her paycheck of $500, which resulted in a final sum of approximately $400. Bruce did pay $500 cash for one year, but in 2000 he treated his mother as an employee again. Furthermore, Barbara often complained that Bruce missed paying her on time (fifth of the month). However, Barbara stated that after a phone call to Bruce, he always paid her by the end of the month. She insisted that he never missed a payment. To make matters worse, the bar's accountant was also Bruce and Barbara's personal accountant.

In April 2000, Bruce told his mother that she owed $10,000 in taxes for the tax year 1999. He stated that she owed this because she cashed in $15,000 in stock (initial cost basis of $1,352 in 1965) to refurbish parts of her house. Barbara's total income and taxes paid for 1999 can be seen in Exhibit 3.

Bruce and Sharon recommended that Barbara take out a $10,000 loan for the taxes that she owed. This was done within a 24-hour period of

time. When Barbara informed her sons about this, they were suspicious. They decided to obtain a copy of the financial statements of the bar from 1997–1999. In October 2000, Danny requested a copy of the financial statements from Bruce. Bruce vehemently refused, stating that Danny was not a shareholder in the bar so he could not receive a copy of the financials. The next day Danny and Barbara visited Bruce's accountant and demanded a copy of the financial statements for the past three years. The accountant reluctantly gave copies to Barbara. (See Exhibits 4, 5, and 6.)

The next day the accountant called Barbara to inform her that she would be receiving a refund of approximately $6,482 from her taxes. Bruce and Sharon both went ballistic. They charged over to Barbara's house and threatened to disown her and the family:

> You have no right looking into our personal financial situation. You are trying to steal the bar away from us! You are taking away my kids' education money.

The following day Bruce and Sharon showed up unannounced at Barbara's house with an unsigned contract (see Exhibit 7). Under duress, they took Barbara to see their attorney and placed pressure on her to sign the contract. After this, they quickly went to see Barbara's attorney, Bobby Free. There was a sense of urgency on the part of Bruce and Sharon to get the contract signed immediately. Free could tell by the look on Barbara's face that she was under duress. Danny showed up at Free's office and they stated that they needed time to examine the contract before they would allow her to sign anything.

Everyone left, but the turmoil continued. Danny updated the brothers and they determined that something had to be done about the situation. This had gone on for too long.

The Bar Industry in 2001

In 2001, the bar industry was in its mature stage of the industry life cycle. The sales of alcoholic beverages in the United States had increased from $90.5 billion in 1998 to $96.1 billion in 1999. Packaged alcohol consumption increased from $44.7 to $48.7 billion while alcoholic drinks increased from $45.8 to $47.4

EXHIBIT 3

Barbara Johnston's Sources of Income and Tax Summary for the Tax Year 1999

Source of Income	Amount
Taxable Interest	$ 2,294
Dividends	2,752
Cashed in Stock (Capital Gain)	13,648
Taxable Pension	5,778
Taxable S-Corp Income (Bar)	2,299
Total Income	$26,771
Adjusted Gross Income	26,771
Standard Deduction	5,350
Personal Exemptions	2,750
Taxable Income	18,671
Total Federal Tax	$ 2,576
Total State Tax	942
Total Tax	$ 3,518

EXHIBIT 4 — Income Statement for the Crowne Inn 1997–1999

	1997 $	1997 % Sales	1998 $	1998 % Sales	1999 $	1999 % Sales
Sales	$295,621	—	$326,352	—	$345,669	—
Cost of Goods Sold	$156,100	52.80%	$157,231	48.18%	$174,139	50.38%
Gross Profit	$139,521	47.20%	$169,121	51.82%	$171,530	49.62%
Operational Expenses						
Advertising	$ 8,318	2.81%	$ 8,277	2.54%	$ 5,777	1.67%
Bank Charges	$ 892	0.30%	$ 1,094	0.34%	$ 1,592	0.46%
Insurance—General	$ 9,762	3.30%	$ 7,024	2.15%	$ 11,555	3.34%
Payroll—General	$ 94,951	32.12%	$ 96,027	29.42%	$ 98,383	28.46%
Professional Expense	$ 1,083	0.37%	$ 1,424	0.44%	$ 2,341	0.68%
Repairs and Maintenance	$ 2,096	0.71%	$ 9,211	2.82%	$ 1,687	0.49%
Taxes—Other	$ 7,813	2.64%	$ 23,312	7.14%	$ 27,308	7.90%
Utilities	$ 7,011	2.37%	$ 7,689	2.36%	$ 6,883	1.99%
Other	$ 5,678	1.92%	$ 7,882	2.42%	$ 6,369	1.84%
Total SG&A Expense	$137,604	46.55%	$161,940	49.62%	$161,895	46.84%
Operating Profit	$ 1,917	0.65%	$ 7,181	2.43%	$ 9,632	2.79%
Depreciation Expense	$ 1,753	0.59%	$ 2,353	0.72%	$ 2,086	0.60%
Interest Expense	$ 664	0.22%	$ 1,387	0.43%	$ 1,096	0.32%
Pretax Profit (Loss)	($ 500)	−0.17%	$ 3,441	1.05%	$ 6,451	1.87%

billion during the same time period. A recent survey of 434 colleges polled by the Higher Education Research Institute found that beer drinking in 2000 had decreased from the previous year by a half percentage point.

Over the past few years the industry has seen numerous changes. One of the more popular trends was the increasing amount of import liquors and import beer from all over the world. Another trend was the increase in sales of micro brewed beer. Many bars have also increased the number of movies/videos, video games, and billiards available to customers.

Technology was also having an affect on the bar industry. Leisure time has been down 25 percent over the past ten years due to the introduction of the Internet, digital television, and game consoles. Sixty percent of the bars in the United States cur-

rently have access to the Internet. Finally, there was the increasing liability associated with owning a bar due to the implementation of the .08 alcohol intoxication limit in most states.

Local Environment and Competition in 2001

Kansas City was the home of pro baseball's Kansas City Royals and pro football's Kansas City Chiefs. The city was split in two by the Missouri River. There was a Kansas City, Kansas, and a Kansas City, Missouri. Two million people currently live in the metropolitan Kansas City area.

The cost of living index for Kansas City was 98.6 on a U.S. scale = 100. This was significantly lower than other high cost areas like San Francisco,

EXHIBIT 5 — The Crowne Inn: Balance Sheet 1997–1999

	1997	1998	1999
Cash & Marketable Securities	$ 6,280	$ 5,359	$ 8,118
Inventory	$ 6,250	$ 7,325	$ 6,785
Total Current Assets	$ 12,530	$ 12,684	$ 14,903
Property, Plant, & Equipment	$ 80,790	$ 82,315	$ 86,467
Less: Accumulated Depreciation	$ 60,791	$ 63,144	$ 69,384
Total Net Fixed Assets	$ 19,999	$ 19,171	$ 17,083
Total Assets	$ 35,529	$ 31,855	$ 31,986
Accounts Payable	$ 5,146	$ 3,183	$ 3,456
Sales & Income Tax Payable	$ 1,460	$ 1,481	$ 1,827
Total Current Liabilities	$ 6,606	$ 4,664	$ 5,283
Long Term Liabilities	$ 14,045	$ 11,872	$ 9,085
Total Liabilities	$ 20,651	$ 16,536	$ 14,368
Common Stock or Owner's Equity	$ 6,000	$ 6,000	$ 6,000
Retained Earnings	$ 5,878	$ 9,319	$ 11,618
Total Equity	$ 11,878	$ 15,319	$ 17,618
Total Liabilities and Owner's Equity	$ 32,529	$ 31,855	$ 31,986

EXHIBIT 6 — The Crowne Inn Cash Flow Summary 1997–1999

	1997	1998	1999
Total Sales	$ 295,621	$ 326,352	$ 345,669
Total Purchases	$ 156,100	$ 157,231	$ 174,139
Increase (Decrease) in Inventory	$ 820	$ 1,075	($ 540)
Cash Available after Purchase	$ 156,920	$ 158,306	$ 173,599
Uses of Cash:			
Operating Expenses per Income Statement	$ 137,604	$ 161,940	$ 161,896
Interest Expense	$ 664	$ 1,387	$ 1,096
Principal Payments (Loan Additions)	($ 14,045)	$ 2,173	$ 2,787
Assets Additions	$ 16,917	$ 1,525	
Other Decreases (Increases)	$ 2,282	($ 1,942)	($ 3,532)
Cash Flow	($ 157)	($ 921)	$ 2,759
Beginning Cash	$ 6,437	$ 6,280	$ 5,359
Ending Cash	$ 6,280	$ 5,359	$ 8,118
Cash Flow Increase (Decrease)	($ 157)	($ 921)	$ 2,759

EXHIBIT 7 **Contract Proposed by Bruce**

AGREEMENT

This agreement made and entered into this 11th day of November, 2000, by and between Barbara A. Johnston, hereinafter referred to as Seller and Bruce S. Johnston, hereinafter referred to as Buyer:

WITNESSETH:

WHEREAS, Seller is the owner of a majority of the Stock in The Crowne Inn, Inc.; and

WHEREAS, Buyer desires to buy the Seller's stock, and to purchase all of the Seller's interest in the real and personal property where The Crowne Inn conducts business; and

WHEREAS, the parties had previously agreed to a monthly payment for the purchase of Seller's stock which agreement the parties wish to codify herein.

NOW THEREFORE, in consideration of the mutual promises and covenants contained herein, the parties agree as follows:

1. That seller shall sell to Buyer, and the Buyer shall buy from Seller, the real and personal property where The Crowne Inn, Inc. conducts its business. The parties agree that subsequent to this Agreement, all of the documents will be prepared, to effectuate said transfer, including a deed to the real property and bill of sale to all personal property and both parties shall execute such necessary documents. The consideration for this transfer shall be the sum of $50,000.00, which the Buyer shall pay forthwith even though the transfer documents shall not be prepared until after the date of this Agreement.

2. That Buyer shall continue to pay to Seller, the sum of $500.00 per month, for the remainder of her life, said payment being the consideration for the present transfer of all of the Seller's stock in The Crowne Inn, Inc. Seller shall, immediately upon receipt of said funds, execute any and all documents necessary to transfer all of Seller's interest in the stock in The Crowne Inn to Buyer.

IN WITNESS WHEREOF, the parties hereto have entered in this Agreement the day and date first above written.

_____
Barbara A. Johnston, Seller

_____
Bruce S. Johnston, Buyer

which had an index of 179.8. Wages for most occupations were close to the national average in the United States. Furthermore, out of 180 metropolitan areas surveyed by the National Association of Home Builders, Kansas City ranked fourteenth in housing affordability during the fourth quarter of 2000.

The Crowne Inn was located on the northeast side of Kansas City (Clay County) about five miles from downtown. The surrounding area was a combination of both residential and commercial properties.

The total number of households in the surrounding area with the same zip code was 12,800 with a population of 31,500. The median age, household income, and household size were 43, $37,786, and 2.3. Most of the people owned their houses while only 30 percent of the households had children.

The primary competitive advantage for The Crowne Inn was its location. Several businesses, two major universities, a medical school, and two major hospitals were located within a five-mile radius. In addition to the local residential market, this added an additional 30,000 people.

There were five competitors located within a one-mile radius. However, the Crowne Inn had its niche. Its reputation was a homey place where you could relax, get good food and drinks, and have quiet conversations.

The Decision

Barbara and her sons had to determine a final resolution with Bruce. It was quite evident that Bruce was unable to meet his oral obligations. Their attorney came up with three alternatives. First, they could sell the bar outright to Bruce and receive a lump sum. This would allow Bruce to pay off all of his future financial obligations to his mother in one lump sum. Second, they could have Bruce pay a smaller sum and continue with payments of $500 per month. Or third, they could sell the bar to a third party.

Karl and Bruce discussed an appropriate way to deal with the problem. Karl communicated to his family that Bruce wanted to pay a lump sum of not more than $60,000. Furthermore, it became increasingly evident that Karl was now on Bruce's side. He was not looking at the situation from an objective viewpoint. Karl insinuated that Bruce had done nothing wrong. Bruce stated to Karl:

I am not willing to go above $60,000. If you want me to pay more than that I will go into business with the owner of Pappa's Pizza. We have been talking about opening a new pizza/bar in one of the fastest growing segments of the city, the East. This area is dangerous. We have been robbed three times in the last three years. If we move, this would put The Crowne Inn out of business.

The family, excluding Karl, Bruce, and Sharon, met over Christmas and discussed their next move. They were unsure whether or not the $60,000 was a fair offer. They were also uncertain as to how they would determine a fair lump sum. Bruce had previously sent Karl a letter outlining all of the money that he had spent on his parents over the years. In the letter he stated that he had given his parents $98,275 over the past five years. He insinuated that he had already paid for the bar. (See Exhibit 8.)

Danny asserted that $60,000 was a ridiculously low offer. In 1999, the bar had sales of $346,000 and Bruce and Sharon made $84,000 plus the profits from the bar. Danny stated that they should pay $175,000. Danny also had a great idea:

We need to determine the average life expectancy for a person in Barbara's age group. Once we do this we can determine a fair offer.

EXHIBIT 8

Money Bruce Spent on His Parents since 1995

5 years at $500/month	$30,000
Mortgage on House	23,500
Extra Money given at X-Mas for 5 years	4,000
Cost of Insurance	30,000
Lawn & Snow Care at House	3,000
Repair Bills Paid	2,000
New Furnace and Air Conditioner	4,800
Personal Tax CPA Costs	975
TOTAL	$98,275

EXHIBIT 9

Life Expectancy Table for Females

Age	Life Expectancy (Years)
10	68.6
20	59.8
30	50.2
40	40.6
50	31.4
60	22.9
65	19.0
66	18.2
67	17.5
68	16.8
69	16.0
70	15.4
80	9.1
90	4.7
100	2.5
110	1.3
120	0.6

SOURCE: Health Care Financing Administration (HCFA), *State Medical Manual 1999*, #3258.9 (HCFA Transmittal No. 64).

According to the tables she had a life expectancy of 17.5 years; however, due to her past health problems (e.g., heart condition), her life expectancy was 14.5 years. (See Exhibit 9.)

As the holidays came to an end, Karl, Cal, Tyler, and Danny had a number of questions. Was the lump sum method the best way to handle the problem? If so, was the $60,000 offer fair? If this was not a fair offer, what was fair? Furthermore, would Bruce be willing and/or able to pay a higher lump sum? He had earlier told Karl that he was unwilling to pay $75,000. As they sat around pondering the situation, their mother was thinking:

I do not want to lose my son and grandchildren over this bar. It is not worth it. However, Bruce made an oral agreement to take care of me.

Cycle and Carriage versus Parallel Importers of Mercedes-Benz Cars

Khai S. Lee
National University of Singapore

Introduction

Cycle and Carriage (C&C) was a leading company that was listed on the Singapore Stock Exchange and was 25.98 percent owned by Jardine Strategic Holdings Limited. The company was a premier motor vehicle distributor with operations in Singapore, Malaysia, Australia, and New Zealand. It distributed exclusively brands such as Mitsubishi, Proton, and Kia in Singapore. The company also had a five-year contract with DaimlerChrysler to be its exclusive distributor for the Mercedes-Benz line of cars in Singapore starting from January 1, 2001.

For five decades prior to 2001, C&C had been the sole distributor of Mercedes-Benz cars in Singapore. As the sole distributor, C&C had invested heavily in promotions, sales, and after-sales services to build up the premium brand image and consumer demand for Mercedes-Benz cars in Singapore. The company had been so successful in its market development efforts that Mercedes-Benz cars were the all-time best-selling luxury cars in Singapore. As of 2000, Mercedes-Benz cars made up 11 percent of the total car population of around 400,000, behind only Toyota (16.8 percent), Honda (13.0 percent), and Nissan (12.1 percent).[1] In both 1999 and 2000, despite the economic downturn, Mercedes-Benz held about 6.5 percent of the market for new cars, which stood at about 38,500 and 58,000 respectively (see Exhibit 1).

However, the Mercedes-Benz line of premium cars also faced severe competition from parallel importers in Singapore. In 2000, for instance, over 23 percent of all parallel-imported cars in Singapore were Mercedes-Benz cars.[2] That is to say, out of every four cars parallel-imported into Singapore, approximately one was a Mercedes-Benz car.

When Success Breeds Parallel Imports

C&C's success in developing the market for Mercedes-Benz cars was also the source of the parallel-importing problem. The Mercedes brand was prestigious and well known for its product quality. The market demand for Mercedes-Benz cars was substantial, with many Singaporeans aspiring to own one. The "Merc," as it was widely referred to, was a symbol of success. The demand for Mercedes-Benz cars was so strong that, at one stage, buyers had to endure a waiting period of up to 18 months for delivery of purchases. This was despite the fact that even the cheapest model could

---

Reprinted by permission of Dr. Lee Khai Sheang, NUS Business School, National University of Singapore.

EXHIBIT 1

Breakdown of Top Ten Brands of New Cars Registered

Brand	1999	%	2000	%
Nissan	7,632	19.8	12,041	20.7
Toyota	7,147	18.6	9,854	17.0
Hyundai	2,003	5.2	5,608	9.7
Honda	3,751	9.7	5,578	9.6
Mitsubishi	4,566	11.9	4,870	8.4
Mercedes-Benz	2,491	6.5	3,738	6.4
BMW	1,872	4.9	2,523	4.3
Mazda	1,305	3.4	1,928	3.3
Ford	1,106	2.9	1,545	2.7
Proton	1,196	3.1	1,501	2.6
Others	5,413	14.1	8,912	15.3
Total	38,482	100.0	58,098	100.0

NOTE: Tax-exempted cars excluded.
SOURCE: Land Transport Authority, http://www.lta.gov.sg.

cost at least S$200,000 then (depending on the prevailing price of the Certificate of Entitlement)! It was reported that C&C typically made between S$40,000 and S$50,000 for each Mercedes-Benz car sold.[3]

Only rich and affluent Singaporeans could afford Mercedes-Benz cars at such prices, although they had a wide appeal across all segments of the local driving public. All these facilitated the parallel importation of Mercedes-Benz cars into Singapore. Furthermore, there were no artificial barriers to the importation and distribution of cars in Singapore. In fact, the local authorities were simplifying import regulations for the independent importation of cars so as to encourage competition in the market. For instance, car importers previously had to obtain certain documents from the car manufacturers to obtain permission from the local authorities for the imported cars to enter Singapore. Following complaints that it was becoming difficult to get documents from manufacturers who were eager to protect their authorized distributors in Singapore, the local authorities amended the import rules so that car importers needed only to prove that the vehicle was roadworthy for local use by first registering the new car in a country that had the same or higher safety and emission standards than the local standards, and later deregistering the vehicle, to obtain permission to import.[4] Finally, given that Mercedes-Benz cars were a globally distributed brand, it was likely that the cars could be sourced without much difficulty from other markets.

The occurrence of parallel importing was therefore ironic in that it brought with it both good and bad news for C&C. The fact that parallel importing occurred signaled that C&C had done a great job of developing the market for the Mercedes-Benz line of cars. There was probably no other place in the world where the unit sales of Mercedes-Benz cars was comparable to that of Japanese makes such as Toyota, Nissan, and Mitsubishi. At the same time, this very success also sensitized potential entrants to the market opportunity in the parallel importation of Mercedes-Benz cars, which led to the erosion of the market share held by C&C.

Certificate of Entitlement and Cost of Cars

To prevent overcrowding on the roads, the Singapore government had introduced the Vehicle Quota System on May 1, 1990, to regulate the growth of the local vehicle population, so that traffic volume could be controlled. Since then, anyone wishing to purchase a vehicle would have to first obtain a Certificate of Entitlement (COE) from the Land Transport Authority. This allowed them to own a specified type of vehicle for ten years. The number of COEs released by the government each month therefore limited the sale of vehicles every month.

To obtain a COE, prospective vehicle owners had to bid for one in a monthly sealed-bid auction. Bidding for a COE took place under five categories: (i) cars 1600 cc and below, (ii) cars above 1600 cc, (iii) cargo vehicles and buses, (iv) motorcycles, and (v) an open category. The successful bidder of a COE in a particular category entitled the owner to purchase a vehicle belonging to that category only. COEs from the open category, however, could be used to purchase any vehicle type.

The price of the COE was determined by the bid of the lowest successful bidder. When the system was first put in place in May 1990, the prevailing premium started at around S$1,000 for a small car. Since then, COE prices had fluctuated between an all-time low of S$50 (January 1998) and a princely premium of S$110,500 (December 1994) for the mere right to own a vehicle. COE prices were driven mainly by the demand for vehicles, which was in turn highly dependent on the state of the economy. Prices of COEs could rocket or nosedive in accord with stock market indices, which were a leading indicator of how the economy fared. On average, COE prices for cars above 1600 cc, into which Mercedes-Benz cars fell, for the year 2000 was S$38,756.

The total vehicle population at the end of 2000 stood at 692,807. The government allowed this figure to grow at a rate of three percent per annum. Thus the number of COEs released by the government was determined by the projected number of vehicles to be deregistered and taken off the road that year in addition to the three percent increase in vehicle population. The total number of COEs re- leased was divided proportionately among the five categories according to the category's share of the total vehicle population.

The basic cost of a car comprised its open market value (OMV), a registration fee of $140, an additional registration fee of 140 percent of OMV, a customs duty of 31 percent of OMV, a three percent goods and services tax on the OMV and customs duty, and the COE cost. The OMV was set by customs on import. Exhibit 2 illustrates the basic cost structure of several popular models in Singapore.

The Parallel Importer's Strategy: "Equal but Better"

Most of the parallel importers of the Mercedes-Benz cars were small independent operators who could afford to import only a few units of luxury cars at any one point in time. However, because of the substantial profit margin and strong demand, the market was sufficiently attractive for the parallel importers despite the low sales volumes of each of these parallel importers.

In order to attract sales for the parallel-imported Mercedes-Benz cars, the parallel importers followed a standard formula of offering a package that was "equal but better" compared to that offered by C&C. This meant that for the same price charged by C&C, consumers were offered a Mercedes-Benz car with upgraded features and accessories. Alternatively, for the same Mercedes-Benz car with standard product features as those offered by C&C, the parallel importers charged a lower price. Considering that parallel importers typically made around S$10,000 on each car sold,[5] and slightly more for luxury cars, a Mercedes-Benz car from a parallel importer could cost up to S$30,000 cheaper than one from C&C.

However, not every potential buyer of the Mercedes-Benz car would choose to purchase from parallel importers despite the better value offered on the parallel-imported Mercedes-Benz car. Some buyers still preferred to buy Mercedes-Benz cars directly from C&C. This was because such buyers perceived C&C, the authorized distributor, to be better equipped to provide reliable sales and after-sales services. Hence, to these buyers, the ease of

EXHIBIT 2

Basic Components of Car Cost (S$)

	Mercedes Benz E200ML Auto 1998 cc	BMW 318IA/4DR 1895 cc	Honda Accord Auto 1997 cc	Toyota Corona GLI A 1587 cc	Nissan Sunny 1.6 A 1597 cc
Average OMV	46,855	30,979	29,696	25,367	16,280
Custom Duty (31% OMV)	14,525	9,604	9,206	7,864	5,047
GST (3%)	1,841	1,217	1,167	997	640
ARF (140% OMV)	65,597	43,371	41,574	35,514	22,792
Registration Fee	140	140	140	140	140
COE	34,930	34,930	34,930	35,468	35,468
Total Basic Cost	163,889	120,242	116,712	105,349	80,366
Selling Price	206,000	167,000	123,988	111,988	89,500
Difference	42,111	46,758	7,276	6,639	9,134

SOURCE: Land Transport Authority, http://www.lta.gov.sg; Motor Traders' Association, http://www.mta.org.sg.

mind that came from the knowledge that their Mercedes-Benz car was imported and supported by C&C was well worth the premium charged.

On the other extreme, there were consumers who preferred the parallel imports. These consumers valued the lower cost, extra features, and shorter waiting period offered by the parallel importers. The parallel importers thus appeared to be catering to a segment of consumers who had hitherto been neglected by C&C. Interestingly, parallel importers of the Mercedes-Benz cars were able to thrive despite efforts by C&C to counter them. In fact, the parallel importers never intended to compete head-on with the authorized distributor. As a director of a company that parallel-imported Mercedes-Benz cars testified, "It doesn't make sense to fight with a giant [like C&C]. All we can do is to be more competitive and provide better prices."[6]

The Defenseless Giant

Concerned with the strides parallel importers were making, C&C took several steps to counter parallel importing. It warned in local newspaper advertisements in 1996 that warranties other than those that it issued would not be honored. However, this tactic backfired when the Land Transport Authority in Singapore announced that it understood from DaimlerChrysler, the German manufacturer of Mercedes-Benz cars, that these cars carried a worldwide warranty against manufacturing defects.

It had also been rumored that C&C, through aggressive pricing, might price the parallel-imported Mercedes-Benz cars out of the market. This rumor arose because the company adopted a low price for the E-series Mercedes Benz cars, pricing them at S$15,000 less than what a parallel importer would charge,[7] when they were first launched in the Singapore market. Such a deep price cut would be effective in deterring parallel imports, as evidenced by the experiences of other authorized distributors in tackling parallel imports into their markets.[8] However, one wondered if C&C would be willing to follow such a low price strategy over an extended period of time. This was because a reduction in profit margins that ran into tens of thousands of dollars per car would result in an astronomical cost for such an aggressive action. Indeed, C&C responded to the rumors that the low price offer was only for an introductory period, and denied engaging the parallel importers in a price war.

The parallel importers appeared not too concerned that C&C would try to wipe them out by a price war. They had correctly anticipated that a price war would hurt C&C's profitability even more. As one parallel importer pointed out, C&C would lose substantially more by cutting its profit margins as it sold thousands of Mercedes-Benz cars every year. The parallel importers were therefore of the view that there was little that C&C could do to counter the parallel importation of the Mercedes-Benz line of cars. As one parallel importer declared, "The parallel imported Mercedes is here to stay, especially when there is a long queue at Cycle and Carriage."

C&C was perhaps more successful in preventing parallel imports by fleet users. A deal by a local taxi operator to buy a fleet of 30 Mercedes-Benz cars from a parallel importer for a pioneer upmarket taxi service fell through. The taxi operator eventually bought the fleet of Mercedes-Benz cars directly from C&C. According to some sources, C&C managed to prevent the parallel importation of the fleet of Mercedes-Benz cars by urging its principal in Germany to block the import of the fleet into Singapore.[9] This was also the view shared by several parallel importers, who believed that C&C had pressured the German principal to trace and stop the supplier in Europe. However, C&C denied that it had engaged in such activities. Others found it strange that the German principal would act against the parallel import of this particular fleet of Mercedes-Benz cars, given that it had not acted against other parallel imports, especially by independent motor traders.

Guess Who's Laughing All the Way to the Bank?

C&C adopted a high price strategy and positioned Mercedes-Benz cars as a premium good to the more affluent segment of the market, consisting of consumers who were willing to pay extra for the after-sales services provided by an authorized distributor. Thus, it gave the parallel importers an opportunity to cater to those consumers who were more "budget conscious" and did not mind doing without such services. In return for getting the car at a cheaper price and also ahead of others in the queue, these consumers were willing to risk forgoing maintenance services provided by C&C and/or bearing the uncertainty of the availability of warranty services. Being the sole distributor, C&C had a monopoly on all authorized service centers for Mercedes-Benz cars in Singapore.

C&C refrained from staging a price war to drive out the parallel importers as it had more to lose in terms of profitability vis-à-vis the parallel importers. C&C sold thousands of cars every year in contrast to the limited number of cars brought in by individual parallel importers. This perhaps explained why C&C had yet to carry out any formal price discounting programs against the parallel importers. C&C's options in deterring parallel imports were limited. The company could only resort to threats like negative advertising, withdrawal of warranty services, and/or discriminating against parallel imports in terms of maintenance services provided. However, these actions had met with limited success in deterring parallel imports.

Thus far, no substantive market actions had been observed to be taken by DaimlerChrysler against the parallel importation of Mercedes-Benz cars into Singapore, other than periodic full-page advertisements proclaiming that C&C was the sole authorized distributor for the Mercedes-Benz line of cars in Singapore.

Loss of Exclusive Distributorship

On January 1, 2001, DaimlerChrysler terminated the exclusive distributorship status of C&C in Singapore for the Mercedes-Benz line of cars, which C&C had held for five decades. C&C retained the rights to retailing (but not to wholesaling) and provision of after-sales services in Singapore for a period of five years, after which the agreement was to be renewed annually. Market talk had it that the decline in sales of the Mercedes-Benz line of cars over the past few years had spurred DaimlerChrysler to take over the wholesale and import functions from C&C. Previously in 1995 and 1996, Mercedes-Benz cars had a market share position second only to Toyota.[10] Mercedes-Benz was sixth in position in terms of new car sales at the time of takeover. Yet others speculated that DaimlerChrysler intended to introduce the Chrysler brand through the same distributors as those that distributed the Mercedes-Benz brand so as to utilize the "large and grossly under-utilized Chrysler manufacturing capacity in Thailand."[11] A new joint-venture company—DaimlerChrysler Singapore—was set up to handle the import and wholesaling of Mercedes-Benz cars, of which C&C had a 24.9 percent stake, while the rest of the stake was held by DaimlerChrysler.

Notes

1. Figures from the website of the Land Transport Authority at http://www.lta.gov.sg.

2. According to the *Business Times (Singapore)* (Grey importers yet to make their mark, January 31, 2001, p. 17), in 2000, 430 units of all Mercedes-Benz cars and 1,842 units of all cars sold in Singapore were parallel imports. Therefore the quoted figure of 23 percent was based on 430 as a percentage of 1,842.

3. *Global News Wire* 2001. Outlook. February 19.

4. *The Straits Times (Singapore)* 2000. Easing of import rules: continental car price dip likely. May 25.

5. *Business Times (Singapore)* 2001. Grey importers yet to make their mark. January 31.

6. *The Straits Times (Singapore)* 1996. Co-exist, not confront, urge parallel importers. August 16.

7. *The Straits Times (Singapore)* 1995. C&C's new E-class Mercedes-Benz is priced lower. December 14.

8. *Business Times (Singapore)* 1998. Overtaking the "grey" bikes. April 9.

9. *The Straits Times (Singapore)* 1996. Parallel imports: Copyright owners fight back. August 12.

10. *Business Times (Singapore)* 1996. Toyata overtakes Merc as best-seller in S'pore. January 9; *Business Times (Singapore)* 1997. Toyota zooms past Merc to retain best-selling spot. January 8.

11. Kulwant Singh, Nitin Pangarkar, and Gaik Eng Lim 2001. *Business strategy in Asia: a casebook.* Singapore: Thomson Learning, p. 192.

The Enron Debacle

Trenton Beau Page

Introduction

Over the course of a decade, Enron went from a normal utility company, loaded with hard assets, to the icon of the New Economy. However, as with many things in the New Economy, the firm's success was not all that it appeared to be. Increasing levels of debt led to worries about liquidity, which led the company to hide the problem. When it could no longer hide the problem ethically, it found ways to bend the rules. And then the company collapsed under the weight of its own complex financial dealings.

On Tuesday, January 29, 2002, Stephen Cooper, the managing partner of Zolfo Cooper LLC, was named interim CEO and chief restructuring officer of Enron Corp.[1] His job was to clean up the mess created by Enron's ex-executives, which promised to be a very formidable task. Not only was the fall of Enron the largest bankruptcy in history,[2] but there were also many issues involving the unprincipled, and possibly illegal, actions of the former management.

This case considers the issue of Enron's ethics, especially how executives' unethical behavior affects the company's chance to survive bankruptcy. A short history of the company is given, which leads into a detailed description of the events that led to the company's bankruptcy—along with a detailed look at the write-offs that brought much of the financial problems to light, the web of partnerships that brought it all down, and the failure of the company's auditor, Arthur Andersen. The effect of all this is then detailed through the liquidation of company assets and how it affected the future business of the company, as well as how the bankruptcy and the scandal has affected the industry and economy as a whole. As such, the case reflects Enron's situation as well as its competitors in 2002. Lastly, this case examines some of the obstacles that stood in Enron's way to recovery.

History

Enron was created by the merger of Houston Natural Gas and InterNorth in July 1985.[3] The CEO of Houston Natural Gas, Kenneth Lay, became chairman and CEO of the combined company in February 1986. On April 10, 1986, the company changed its name to Enron.[4] Enron was created to take advantage of the deregulation of the energy industry that occurred during the mid-1980s. Mr. Lay tried to create the largest pipeline in the nation to have leverage in Washington as Congress deregulated the industry.[5]

In 1987, as a result of oil traders in New York overextending the company's accounts by close to $1 billion, Enron began to form services to help mitigate the risk involved with things as varied as gas, oil, and advertising space. In 1988, the firm

This case is intended to be used as the basis for class discussion rather than to illustrate either effective or ineffective handling of an administrative or strategic situation. Reprinted by permission of Robert E. Hoskisson, Arizona State University, and Trenton Beau Page.

opened offices in England, its first overseas office, to take advantage of privatization of the power industry in that country. In the same year, at a gathering of executives, the company announced its strategic shift from focusing solely on regulated pipeline markets to focusing on unregulated markets in addition to regulated ones.[6] In 1989, Enron hired its one-time consultant Jeffrey Skilling, who later rose to become the CEO. The company also hired Andrew Fastow, who worked closely with Mr. Skilling and eventually rose to become the company's chief financial officer. The two of them started a program named Gas Bank, through which buyers could lock in long-term supplies at fixed prices.[7]

Enron expanded south in Latin America in 1992 through its purchase of Transportadora de Gas del Sur. Its international expansion continued with the construction in 1993 of a power plant in England.[8] The company's international strategy was initially successful, but just a few years later, beginning in 1996, it would find itself in a very disturbing situation. In 1996 it began the construction of the Dabhol Power project in India. The 740-megawatt power plant, which was budgeted for $3 billion, was supposed to open the way for a strong Enron presence in India. Instead, thanks to an overly involved government bureaucracy and Enron's "cowboy operating style,"[9] the project was troubled from the start. When the first phase of the plant opened in 1999, the electricity produced cost four times the expected amount, and Enron's reputation in India was destroyed.[10]

In June 1994 the firm began trading electricity.[11] It expanded its commodities-trading business to England in the following year.[12] The company's trading business, under the name Enron Capital & Trade Resources, was run by Jeffrey Skilling. Under his leadership, this unit of the company grew until it contributed 90 percent of the firm's profits.[13] One event that helped fuel this amazing performance was the creation of the EnronOnline website. The website, which quickly became the largest e-business site in the world, made it easier and faster to purchase the many commodities that Enron traded. In recognition of this success, Mr. Skilling was promoted to president and chief operating officer in December 1996.[14] Mr. Skilling's finance wizard, Andrew Fastow, was promoted to CFO in 1998.[15]

Starting in 1997, Enron began to swiftly expand its business. It further increased its electricity holdings by purchasing Portland General Electric Co., a Portland, Oregon, utility. It also began to offer energy management services through its newly formed Enron Energy Services unit. It diversified into the water utility business in 1998 by purchasing Wessex Water, a firm based in England that was made the starting point for Azurix, which Enron spun off beginning in 1999. The company also formed its now-defunct broadband unit in 1999, believing it to be a promising new market.[16]

The year 2000 was a successful one for the now-large energy trader. Its annual revenues reached $100 billion, and the Energy Financial Group named it the sixth largest energy company in the world, based on market capitalization.[17] On August 23, 2000, Enron's stock price hit a high of $90.56, the highest it would ever be.[18] The company was well respected, and was named by *Fortune* magazine the twenty-second best company to work for in December of that year; it also was named the top company for "Quality of Management" and second best for "Employee Talent."[19] For its astounding abilities as a market maker, and its many innovative achievements, Enron would be named *Fortune* magazine's "Most Innovative Company in America" for the sixth year in a row in February 2001.[20] On December 13, 2000, Enron announced that Jeffrey Skilling would succeed Kenneth Lay as CEO and president of Enron effective February 12, 2001.[21]

Enron's House of Cards

Regardless of its early success, things quickly began to unravel for the company. The first surprise was Mr. Skilling's resignation on August 14, 2001, just six months after he became CEO.[22] He cited only personal reasons for his departure, although he later admitted that the falling stock price (which was at $42.93 when he resigned) had affected his decision.[23] Kenneth Lay reassumed the position of CEO, a position he had held for 15 years before being succeeded by Mr. Skilling.[24] When asked about Mr. Skilling's departure, Mr. Lay said:

There are absolutely no problems that had anything to do with Jeff's departure. There are no accounting issues, no trading issues, no reserve issues, no previously unknown problem issues. The company is probably in the strongest and best shape that it has ever been in. There are no surprises. We did file our 10-Q a few days ago. And, if there were any serious problems, they would be in there. If there's anything material and we're not reporting it, we'd be breaking the law. We don't break the law.[25]

Despite questions about the company's health and its falling stock price, few expected the next bombshell. On October 16, 2001, Enron announced that it would take a $1.01 billion charge to its earnings, giving the company a $618 million loss in the third quarter (write-offs discussed later in more detail).[26] The company also announced in a conference call that there would be a $1.2 billion write-down of equity,[27] which resulted from a decision to buy back 55 million shares that had been part of its dealings with LJM2, a partnership that will be discussed in greater detail later in this case.[28] Mr. Lay described the write-offs as part of an effort to "find anything and everything that was a distraction and was causing a cloud over the company."[29] Part of the charge to earnings was a $35 million charge involving the partnerships run by Andrew Fastow (discussed later in more detail).

After this announcement, the outlook for Enron became much darker. On October 22, Enron announced that the Securities and Exchange Commission was beginning an informal probe into the company's related party transactions. On October 31, Enron announced that the SEC had upgraded its probe to a formal investigation to determine if the partnerships were involved any illegal activity.[30] At the same time Moody's, the debt-rating service, lowered Enron's debt rating from Baa1 to Baa2, just two steps above noninvestment grade. Enron would default on billions of dollars of debt if its rating fell to junk status.[31]

To avoid any further reductions in its debt rating, Enron searched for a partner to infuse money into the company. On November 8, 2001, Enron and Dynegy, a smaller competitor, announced that they were in negotiation for Dynegy to buy Enron. At the same time, Dynegy would inject $1.5 billion into Enron. Dynegy, which was about one-fifth the size of Enron, was negotiating a price between $7 billion and $8 billion in stock, about one-tenth the amount Enron had been worth just 15 months before.[32]

The same day the talks were announced, Enron reduced its earnings for the previous four years, back to 1997, by $586 million as a result of improper accounting involving Mr. Fastow's partnerships (see Exhibits 1, 2, and 3).[33] Enron said that it should have consolidated the Chewco and JEDI partnerships into its financial reports in November 1997, instead of in 2001; the LJM1 partnerships should have been consolidated in early 1999 (descriptions of these partnerships appear later in the case).[34]

On November 9, just one day after announcing that Dynegy and Enron were in merger talks, the

EXHIBIT 1	Overview of Financial Statements						
	1997	1998	1999	2000	2001.I	2001.II	2001.III
Reported net income	$ 105	$ 703	$ 893	$ 979	$ 425	$ 404	$ (618)
Restated net income	$ 9	$ 590	$ 643	$ 847	$ 442	$ 409	$ (635)
Reported debt	$6,254	$7,357	$8,152	$10,229	$11,922	$12,812	$12,978
Restated debt	$6,965	$7,918	$8,837	$10,857	$11,922	$12,812	$12,978

SOURCE: Enron Corp. Website, http://www.enron.com/corp/investors, SEC Filings, November 8, 2001.

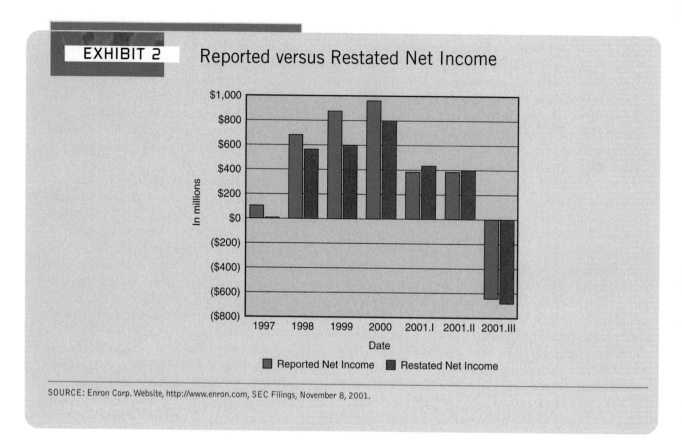

EXHIBIT 2 — Reported versus Restated Net Income

In millions

1997 | 1998 | 1999 | 2000 | 2001.I | 2001.II | 2001.III

Date

■ Reported Net Income   ■ Restated Net Income

SOURCE: Enron Corp. Website, http://www.enron.com, SEC Filings, November 8, 2001.

two companies announced that Dynegy would purchase Enron. The merger would create a company with annual revenues over $200 billion and assets worth $90 billion. Enron's shareholders would have owned 36 percent of the combined company, Dynegy, Inc. Dynegy would have given Enron $1.5 billion to help with its liquidity problems in the short run.[35]

Unfortunately for Enron, more bad news was coming. On November 28, the credit rating agencies lowered Enron's debt rating to junk status. As a result, $3.9 billion worth of debt immediately came due.[36] Dynegy immediately called off the merger.[37] Four days later Enron filed for Chapter 11 bankruptcy protection.[38] Overall, the company was approximately $40 billion in debt.[39]

The main catalyst for the events that brought Enron down was the October 16 announcement of write-offs. The write-offs drew attention to the fact that there were questionable dealings going on at Enron. Almost immediately after the announcement, the business press questioned the propriety of the related-party dealings mentioned.[40] The result of the write-offs for Enron was a downward spiral into bankruptcy.

The Write-Offs

The write-offs were divided into three categories. The first was a $287 million write-off involving Azurix Corp., a water company that had been spun off from Enron in 1999 and then repurchased in March 2001 for $983 million.[41] Azurix was formed to make a profit in the private water market, selling water and wastewater services to cities worldwide. Unfortunately for the company, the growth in the industry was too slow, and its stock, which at one point reached $20 per share, was trading at around $8 per share when Enron repurchased the company.[42] At the time of the write-offs, Azurix had announced its intention of withdrawing from a contract in Argentina that was supposed to supply water services to 2.5 million people.[43] According to the company, the write-offs reflected the planned divestiture of some service-related businesses in North and South America.[44]

EXHIBIT 3 Reported versus Restated Debt

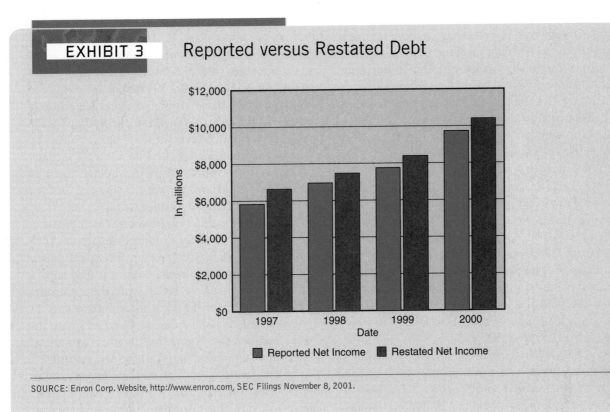

SOURCE: Enron Corp. Website, http://www.enron.com, SEC Filings November 8, 2001.

The second part of the write-offs was $180 million related to the company's broadband operations. The company had formed its broadband unit after buying Portland General Electric, an Oregon utility company that had a fiber-optic network in the Pacific Northwest. In July 2000, Enron announced a deal with Blockbuster to release videos on-demand to paying customers. However, the deal was never realized and Blockbuster withdrew in March 2001.[45] The write-offs resulted from "restructuring Broadband Services, including severance costs, loss on the sale of inventory and the . . . reduced value of Enron's content services business."[46]

The last section of the write-offs was the $544 million charge related to investments (and their devaluation) made by Enron. This charge included a write-off of $35 million related to the "early termination" of some partnerships that involved Andrew Fastow, the company's chief financial officer.[47] This write-off, a small amount compared to the $544 million total, received the attention of many people, since it raised conflict-of-interest questions.

As the next section explains, the partnerships were ultimately responsible for Enron's failure.

The Partnerships

Because of the cost of financing and the effect that debt can have on a company's credit rating, many companies have used off-balance-sheet accounting. The partnerships that Enron created, at least originally, involved finding outside investors willing to provide at least three percent of the equity of the partnership so that it could be treated as a separate entity from Enron. These partnerships would then invest in a specific project, spreading some of the risk away from the parent corporation. Plus, any debt incurred by the partnership was kept off Enron's balance sheet, because it was considered a separate entity.[48] Keeping the debt off the balance sheet helped preserve Enron's credit rating at investment grade.

As Enron grew, Mr. Skilling and others wanted to hurry the process of forming these partnerships. As a result of the required negotiations with outside investors, partnerships can take months to form. Enron's growth was based on fast trading and deal making in the short term, meaning that they needed the partnerships to be formed quickly. To hurry the process, Andrew Fastow, then the vice-president of finance, and Mr. Skilling wanted to create partnerships that would be partly owned and run by Enron employees. With obvious conflicts of interest, they were unable to find any investors willing to become involved with such a scheme.[49]

Then, in 1997, an opportunity developed. Back in 1993, Enron had formed a joint venture for energy investments with California Public Employees Retirement System (CaLPERS) named the JEDI for Joint Energy Development Investments. Enron wanted to form another joint venture with CaLPERS named JEDI II, but the pension fund managers would agree only if the fund was reimbursed for its investment in the first JEDI. Enron bought back the CaLPERS stake in JEDI for $383 million.[50] At the time, Enron's debt levels were becoming extremely high, causing concern for its executives. Instead of consolidating JEDI at that time, Enron's executives decided to keep it out of the financial reports by having CaLPERS's share purchased by an outside entity, Chewco Investments.[51]

Mr. Fastow designed Chewco, named after a character in a *Star Wars* movie, to appear to be independent of Enron, while in actuality it was run by an Enron employee. This employee, Michael Kopper, would run the partnership, even though he would remain an employee of Enron. Chewco was backed by several hundred million dollars of loan guarantees. Commercial banks loaned money to Chewco as well as to two other small entities connected to Mr. Kopper. The two smaller entities provided the three percent outside equity required for Chewco to be considered a separate entity from Enron.[52] This partnership kept more than $700 million of debt off Enron's balance sheet.[53]

The success of Chewco led to the formation of more such partnerships, the best known being the LJM Cayman and LJM2 partnerships involving Mr. Fastow. LJM Cayman LP was created in June 1999, followed four months later by LJM2 Co-Investment LP; Mr. Fastow ran and partly owned both of them. LJM Cayman was supposed to protect the value of a portfolio of volatile telecommunications assets.

LJM2 was designed to do the same thing, but for other risky investments.[54] The two partnerships were involved in billions of dollars' worth of hedging transactions. While LJM Cayman raised only $16 million, LJM2 raised $394 million, showing the growing reliance that Enron placed on such partnerships.[55] By the year 2000, these partnerships were providing over 40 percent of the company's pretax income of approximately $1.4 billion.[56] The partnerships also spawned many offshoots, such as Raptor and Talon, which were to protect various investments the company made.

One of the largest concerns with such partnerships is the potential for conflicts of interest. The conflict results when a company officer, who has a fiduciary responsibility to the company, also runs a partnership that makes deals with the company. Would such a person find, as one company memorandum stated, that his interests "aligned" with investors because the "economics of the partnership would have significant impact on [his] wealth"?[57] Mr. Fastow made, according to the company, more than $30 million from running these partnerships.[58] The question is, did his interests always align with those of Enron's shareholders? Based on information found in company documents, there was at least one occasion when LJM2 renegotiated a deal that saved millions of dollars of Enron's expense. In September 2000, LJM2 invested $30 million in Raptor III, an additional partnership involved in writing put options on Enron stock at a set price for six months. After only four months, however, LJM2 approached Enron with the intent to settle early, giving LJM2 a $10.5 million profit. If the partnership had waited the full six months, it would have had to buy Enron shares at a loss of $8 per share.[59]

These partnerships eventually became the cause of Enron's downfall. Investors and analysts lost confidence in the company when the extent of its self-dealing was discovered. In addition, there were questions regarding the legality of the transactions since Enron did not disclose the existence of Chewco to the SEC until it restated its earnings in November.[60] As a result, investors withdrew their support, which caused the stock price to plunge and raised questions about the legitimacy of the company's audits. Thus, some of the focus on the fall of Enron shifted toward its auditor, Arthur Andersen.

Arthur Andersen

Arthur Andersen, the smallest of the Big Five accounting firms, was Enron's auditor at the time the partnerships were formed, as well as during the bankruptcy. Enron later found a different auditor.[61]

When the SEC announced at the end of October that it would investigate Enron for possible improprieties, an Arthur Andersen partner decided to destroy many documents related to Enron and the auditor's knowledge of Enron's partnerships.[62] Although the partner who did this was fired, the company itself was strongly punished for his actions. Almost all (approximately 160) of the company's largest accounts left and found new auditors.[63] The international operations of the company were dissolved and individual units merged with other auditors. The domestic operations experienced difficulty finding a single merger partner, and instead merged parts of their business with KPMG and Deloitte & Touche separately.[64]

On March 14, 2002, the Justice Department unsealed a criminal obstruction-of-justice indictment against Arthur Andersen.[65] Along with the indictment, Arthur Andersen's role in the Enron debacle has brought increased scrutiny and bad press for the entire accounting profession.[66] The role of Arthur Andersen in these events has raised an important question. If Arthur Andersen had done its audits faithfully, many of the questionable acts of Enron's executives might have been stopped in their infancy instead of causing the failure of the company. If the auditors had done what they were supposed to, would Enron have had to file for bankruptcy, and thus have to sell the majority of its assets to pay its creditors?

Bankruptcy and Restructuring

As a result of Mr. Fastow's partnerships, Enron was able to hide a large amount of debt for several years. When the partnerships were belatedly disclosed to the public, the sheer audacity of such a violation of ethical behavior destroyed public confidence in the company. Thus, its credit rating fell and a large portion of that debt came due. Faced with such an enormous amount of debt, Enron had no choice but to file for bankruptcy; it would never have been able to pay off its creditors. However, company executives believed that it would be able to restructure the firm and reemerge as a viable company, thus creating value for its creditors. Accordingly, Kenneth Lay unveiled a restructuring plan for the company in December. Under this plan, Enron would sell between $4 billion and $6 billion of its assets, sell its energy-trading business, and emerge from bankruptcy protection in one year.[67] After filing for bankruptcy, Enron followed this plan by liquidating many of its largest assets to focus on its core business, as well as find money to pay its many creditors. The following is a short description of the liquidation efforts.

Energy-Trading Operation

At one point, Enron's North American wholesale natural gas and electricity trading business generated 90 percent of the company's profits.[68] After filing for bankruptcy, however, it became just another non-core business to sell. On January 11, 2002, Enron announced that it had sold its North American trading business to UBS Warburg, an investment banking group.[69] According to the terms of the sale, Enron would still receive 33 percent of the profits generated by the business for the next ten years. However, UBS Warburg retained the option, after three years, to buy one-third of Enron's royalties, thus giving Enron a 22 percent royalty. UBS could then buy another 11 percent at a later date, and the remaining 11 percent again later.[70] In accordance with the agreement, Enron transferred its wholesale energy-trading operation, which included a staff of about 800 people and the computer systems and hardware that once made up EnronOnline to UBS Warburg.[71]

EnronOnline, which was launched in November 1999, handled 548,000 transactions in the year 2000, with a gross value of $336 billion. It accounted for 74 percent of the North American volume of natural gas traded in 2000 and "helped to practically double daily transactions."[72] In 2002, however, the EnronOnline.com web address led to UBSW energy.com, the energy trading web site of UBS Warburg.

Enron Wind

Enron Wind was a profitable business unit of Enron. In 2001, it earned approximately $750 million in revenues.[73] Although Enron Wind was not included as part of Enron's bankruptcy proceeding, it was still considered an asset that must be sold to generate cash. According to Stanley Horton, chairman and CEO of Enron Global Services, the business unit that ran Enron Wind, "While Enron Wind has historically been a good business with solid returns, its future growth requires more capital than we can justify under current circumstances."[74] As a result, Enron sold its wind unit to General Electric Co. on February 20, 2002, for approximately $250 million. Per the agreement, Enron Wind filed for bankruptcy, and GE bought its assets. The total value of the deal, including debt and other considerations, was approximately $400 million.[75]

Azurix Assets

Azurix Corporation, a water company formed after Enron's purchase of the British water utility Wessex Water was spun off and later repurchased by Enron. As discussed previously, it experienced problems in Argentina, and was largely unprofitable. Even before declaring bankruptcy, Enron began to sell Azurix assets. It sold Azurix North America Corp. and Azurix Industrials Corp. to American Water Works, Inc. on November 7, 2001, for $141.5 million cash.[76]

More importantly for Enron, on March 26 it announced the sale of Wessex Water, one of the company's largest international assets. YTL Power International, a Malaysian utility company, purchased Wessex Water for 544.6 pounds, the equivalent of $776.4 million. YTL also assumed $991 million of debt from Azurix, which was very beneficial for Azurix creditors. According to Michael Anderson, Azurix chairman, "The terms of the sale . . . will allow us to retire substantially all of our debt."[77]

Dabhol Power Co.

Dabhol Power, which built and operated a 740-megawatt power plant in India, was never profitable. Enron, which owned 65 percent of the project, offered its stake for sale at $1 billion. Analysts believed that Enron might not even receive $300 million.[78] The sale of the project was not moving very quickly, however, at the time of this writing. Bidders for the assets and Enron found it difficult to agree on many points of the sale, including the length of time allowed for the bidders to examine the company's fi-

nancial records.[79] Enron was concerned that it would not receive any money from the sale, but that all of the proceeds would go to the lenders. For this reason, Enron was not overly cooperative, and the lenders were considering a possible takeover of the assets.[80]

Enron Europe

Enron Europe Ltd., which included Enron Capital & Trade Resources, Enron Gas & Petrochemical Trading, and Enron Power Operations, sold its assets to pay its many creditors. The accounting firm of PricewaterhouseCoopers was appointed the administrator for Enron's European operations; the firm's task was to sell assets and unwind trading positions to be able to repay creditors. The firm said it expected to recover somewhere between $750 million and $1 billion, and that creditors might receive back 20 to 25 percent of the debt issued to Enron Europe.[81] As a result of this, Enron will have few assets left on the continent.

Other Foreign Assets

Although still subject to approval by the bankruptcy court, on March 29, 2002, Enron announced that it had sold its turbines, generators, and an unfinished power plant in Spain for $315 million to Iberdrola S.A., Spain's second-largest electricity company. The turbines and generators were located in Cadiz, Spain; Schenectady, New York; and Rotterdam, Netherlands.[82]

Enron Broadband

Enron did not sell its broadband unit; it shut it down. Enron Broadband was once a highly-touted business unit that was expected to earn a large amount of money in the future. However, after a failed deal with Blockbuster (discussed earlier), Enron Broadband began to deteriorate. It made $2.1 million in revenue in 2001, but its monthly operating expenses were $2.5 million. The broadband unit was expected to sell its 18 existing contracts for approximately $491,000.[83]

Effect on Economy and Industry

Once investors recovered from the shock of the bankruptcy, they immediately began searching for other companies that might cause them similar troubles. No company was considered too large, strong, or well-run to avoid scrutiny. Even General Electric, one of the most admired companies in the world, was criticized for having financial reports that were too opaque.[84] Huge conglomerate Tyco, in the past acclaimed for its constant, significant growth, lost $50 billion in market capitalization when investors decided that its financial reports were not transparent enough. Stalwarts such as Disney, Cisco, and AOL Time Warner were all similarly punished, although not as drastically.[85] Enron's unprincipled actions reverberated throughout the economy as companies were scrutinized for any resemblance to the fallen energy giant.

The industry most strongly affected by Enron was the natural gas utility and electricity trading industry. The three companies that most resembled Enron, and that have thus been most affected by Enron, also happened to be very close geographically. For these reasons, resemblance and proximity, Dynegy Inc., Williams Corp., and El Paso Corp. are also examined.

Dynegy Inc.

Dynegy Inc. was a global energy merchant similar to Enron at its peak. Formed by Chuck Watson in 1985 under the name NCG Corp., the company was incorporated in 1991 and was renamed Dynegy when it went public in 1995.[86] As a gas marketer and trader, it grew to be one of the largest energy suppliers in the United States, with operations in the United Kingdom as well as in continental Europe. Dynegy almost merged with Enron, but pulled out after signing the papers (see earlier discussion).[87] The Houston-based company's 2001 net income was $648 million, up 29 percent from the year before, on sales of over $42 billion, which were up 43 percent.[88]

Dynegy's primary businesses were Marketing and Trade, Midstream Services, Illinois Power, and Global Communications. The Marketing and Trade unit focused on marketing and trading natural gas and power and was one of the largest such units in its industry. It was also a leading producer of electricity. Dynegy owned or controlled approximately 19,000 MW of generating capacity. In 2000, it produced and sold 138 million MW hours of power. At the time of this writing its sales were approximately 11 billion cubic feet of natural gas per day. Midstream Services produced and marketed natural gas liquids. It owned an interest in 14,000 miles of pipelines, as well as an interest in 33 natural gas processing facilities. Illinois Power was an energy delivery company in Decatur, Illinois, with 650,000 electricity and natural gas customers. Global Communications was a broadband marketing and trading operation. It had 16,000 miles of broadband in the United States and 5,100 miles in Europe.[89]

On May 8, 2002, the Securities and Exchange Commission announced that it would proceed with an investigation into Dynegy's finances. This announcement followed a similar announcement one month earlier of an informal probe into the same thing. Dynegy made a multiyear natural gas transaction called Project Alpha to reduce taxes and increase cash flow. While the project did increase cash flow, it did not affect net income because of some related trades. After the announcement the company's stock fell sharply, and it was anticipated that the company's credit rating would be downgraded to noninvestment status as a result.[90] The superficial similarities of this circumstance to the off–balance-sheet financing of Enron likely affected the way it was treated by investors as well as credit rating agencies.

Williams

Two brothers, Miller and David Williams, founded Williams Brothers in Fort Smith, Arkansas, in 1908. In 1919 they moved the company's headquarters to Tulsa, Oklahoma, where it remained. The company changed its name to Williams in 1997.[91] It was advertised that Williams "connects businesses to energy, delivering innovative, reliable products and services."[92] Williams' net loss for 2001 was $477.7 million, down 191 percent from 2000, on revenues of $11,034.7, which were up 15 percent from the previous year.[93]

Williams was separated into two business units: Williams Gas Pipeline and Williams Energy. Williams Gas Pipeline supplied natural gas throughout the midwestern and western United States and Canada. The company owned over 26,000 miles of interstate pipelines and provided 16 percent of the natural gas used in the United States.[94] The Williams Energy unit is further divided into four units: Energy Marketing and Trading, Exploration and Production, Mid-stream Gas and Liquids, and Petroleum Services. The Energy Marketing and Trading unit marketed and traded power and natural gas products both domestically and abroad. The Exploration and Production division was the tenth largest natural gas producer in the United States with 3.3 trillion cubic feet in reserves. The division produced 560 million cubic feet per day. Williams Midstream Gas and Liquids gathered and processed natural gas. It controlled 11,300 miles of gathering pipeline as well as 14,300 miles of transportation pipeline. Petroleum Services refined and transported petroleum. It owned a 9,100-mile transportation pipeline, as well as two refineries with the capacity to process 227,000 barrels per day.[95] The company also had similar assets in Argentina, Canada, Lithuania, Venezuela, and the United Kingdom.[96]

As with Dynegy, Williams had its credit rating pressured since Enron's bankruptcy. On May 8, 2002, Moody's Investors Service warned that the company's debt rating might be cut to the lowest investment-level rating. This would depend partly on how Moody's evaluated the company's liquidity and its attempts to mitigate debt.[97] Of course, these are the same maneuvers that Enron was trying to hide from the world through its off–balance-sheet partnerships, poor liquidity, and high debt levels. It appeared that the debt rating services were watching energy utilities more closely as a result of Enron.

El Paso Corp.

El Paso Corp. was based in Houston, Texas, having been formed there in 1928 by Paul Kayser. It was created to supply the city of El Paso with natural gas, since El Paso was the only city in Texas that was not receiving natural gas. The company's original name was El Paso Natural Gas, but it changed to El Paso Corp. in 2001.[98] It was a global company that supplied energy around the world. The company had a net income in 2001 of $93 million, down almost 93 percent from the previous year, on sales of over $52 billion, which were up approximately 17.5 percent.[99]

El Paso Corp. was divided into six different units: Production, Midstream Group, Pipeline, Global Networks, Merchant Energy Group, and Global LNG. Production focused on exploration and the produc-

tion of natural gas. It was the fifth largest producer of natural gas in the United States, with over six trillion cubic feet of natural gas reserves. Midstream Group provided services such as processing, compression, and transmission to natural gas producers throughout the southern United States and the Gulf of Mexico. It controlled 24,000 miles of pipeline. The Pipeline unit transmitted natural gas across the United States. It owned or controlled approximately 48,550 miles of pipeline. The Global Networks group provided broadband service in the southwestern United States, mostly in the state of Texas. El Paso's Merchant Energy Group was in charge of generating and marketing power worldwide as well as trading power, oil, and other market derivatives, much like Enron at its peak. The last business unit, Global LNG, transported and stored liquid natural gas (LNG) worldwide. Global LNG had terminals on the East Coast of the United States with a combined capacity of 20 billion cubic feet and could transport as much 752 billion cubic feet per year.[100]

At the end of May 2002, El Paso announced that it was cutting about half of its energy trading personnel. This was an attempt to bolster its balance sheet amid the increased investor and creditor scrutiny that resulted from the Enron scandal. This announcement, which was probably the most dramatic retrenchment move by an energy company trying to reassure markets, caused the company's stock price to fall by 23 percent in the hours after the announcement.[101]

Restructured Company

The question that remained after observing the general trend of Enron's asset liquidation, was: "What will be left?" According to the company's December restructuring plan, the resulting company would be focused around energy assets such as "pipeline and power assets, exploration and production operations, and various services related to gas storage and power stations."[102] One and a half months later, acting CEO Stephen Cooper said the new company would be "dedicated to movement of natural gas and generation of electricity."[103] On May 3, 2002, Stephen Cooper met with creditors in New York and outlined his proposal about what this new company could look like.[104]

Mr. Cooper's plan involved the creation of a new company, with the working title of OpCo Energy Co. This company would have about $10.8 billion worth of hard assets such as pipelines, power plants, and electricity distribution throughout North and South America.[105] The main properties of the company would be Portland General Electric Co. and Elektro, a Brazilian electric utility, as well as various smaller pipeline assets throughout the two continents. Portland General Electric was, according to an earlier agreement, supposed to be sold to Northwest Natural Gas Co., but the deal could be broken to establish OpCo Energy. Mr. Cooper had not said whether or not he planned to buy back Northern Natural Gas Co. from Dynegy.[106] Northern Natural Gas Co. was the largest asset Enron owned before the bankruptcy, but it was seized by Dynegy Inc. after the merger agreement failed. Enron retained the right to repurchase the pipeline until June 30, 2002.[107]

OpCo Energy would employ approximately 12,000 employees, down from 23,000. Mr. Cooper said that he expected approximately 2,000 employees of bankrupt companies would be laid off over time, while the remaining 9,000 would be hired by those companies that bought Enron's remaining assets.[108]

The new company would have revenues of $1.3 billion in the year 2003.[109] The company's pro forma net income was estimated to be $243 million in 2002, $352 million in 2003, $450 million in 2004, and $503 million in 2005.[110] OpCo Energy Co. would closely resemble the company that Kenneth Lay originally ran back in the early 1990s.

Many steps were necessary for the formation of the new company. It first would have to be approved by the company's creditors, who had the power to reject the plan and force a liquidation of all the company's assets. If it obtained the approval of the creditors, the proposal would then have to be approved by the bankruptcy court. The reason for this was that Enron was trying to circumvent some of the hassle of bankruptcy by creating the company and then selling it. According to this plan, creditors would have first choice, either taking a share in the company or a portion of the proceeds of the sale. Afterward the company would no longer be subject to the bankruptcy proceedings, and would, theoretically, leave its Enron past behind.

This was a novel approach, but under the circumstances, it might have been allowed.[111]

The reason creditors and the courts might allow this unconventional proposal was because it could create the most value for the creditors. Mr. Cooper stated that "[the creditor's] goal, to maximize value, is consistent with ours. I'm confident that we will be able to make a case for value maximization by adopting this approach."[112] This proposal could have created the most value for creditors because of a glut of assets in the market that lowered prices, meaning that liquidation would not raise as much money as it normally would. A significant factor in the glut of assets in the market was Enron, however. As a result of its unethical behavior, other companies were being watched more closely and credit standards were tightened. Many energy firms had to sell assets similar to those Enron needed to sell.[113] In fact, the Enron bankruptcy, especially the reasons behind it, had a powerful effect on the industry and on the economy as a whole.

Challenges

Enron became a tainted name. Everything connected to Enron was perceived as being polluted. UBS Warburg assured itself that it would have no legal liability for the misbehavior of Enron's trading business, but new revelations involving the California energy crisis and Enron's role could have implicated some of the employees that UBS hired to run the business. So the history of the trading business continued to haunt it.[114] Any company that could survive the bankruptcy proceedings—whether sold out of bankruptcy as Mr. Cooper had proposed, or if some core assets survived the proceedings to become a company—would be affected by the reputation Enron left behind. Three obstacles that would need to be overcome were Congress's investigation into the possibly illegal behavior of some executives, new revelations about Enron's role in the California energy crisis, and the extant widespread distrust of the company.

The Investigation in Congress

Starting in January, Congress established many committees to investigate Enron, its bankruptcy, and its possible illegal actions. The Senate Governmental

Affairs Committee looked at possible regulatory failures as well as possible violations of the law by Enron officials. The Justice Department investigated possible illegal actions by Enron employees. The Labor Department and the Senate Commerce Committee investigated Enron's retirement plan and funds.[115]

The investigation in Congress produced a letter that was written August 15, 2001, by Enron vice-president, Sherron Watkins. Ms. Watkins wrote a letter to Kenneth Lay telling him that the company was engaged in some very questionable accounting practices that could cause the company to "implode in a wave of accounting scandals."[116] She spoke with Mr. Lay the next day, but his response to her charge was to have the company's law firm, Vinson & Elkins, conduct an internal investigation—a move she counseled against because the law firm was a party to a number of the partnerships. The investigation found that there was nothing improper, although there was a "serious risk of adverse publicity and litigation."[117]

One major concern of Congress was Enron's 401(k). Many Enron employees held most of their retirement funds in company stock. Prior to the bankruptcy procedure, there was a lockdown—a time period in which employees could not sell Enron stock. By that time, Enron stock had lost approximately 70 percent of its worth, which continued to fall during the lockdown. Enron matched employees' contributions to the 401(k) with company stock, but it was criticized because employees were not allowed to sell this stock until they reached the age of 50. The fall of Enron's stock caused many employees to lose large amounts of their retirement funds, and resulted in considerable outrage in the press and in Congress.[118]

In Congress, most of the executives refused to testify, citing their Fifth Amendment right. However, Congress considered the possibility of bringing criminal charges against former top executives such as Mr. Lay, Mr. Skilling, and Mr. Fastow.[119]

California Energy Crisis

While Congress investigated possible illegal practices by Enron executives, new information was discovered that implicated Enron in questionable practices during the California energy crisis of 2000–2001.

Internal company memos released May 6, 2002, outlined a system by which electricity traders abused the deregulated California power market to make extra profits. It appeared that the company used false claims of energy demand to create excess demand in the market, thus it could sell power at a higher-than-advertised price. Two of the memos also indicated that Enron was not the only major energy supplier in the market to use such practices.[120]

This new information was an indication that the problems at Enron ran very deep. As discussed in a previous paragraph, many of these same traders worked for UBS Warburg, and their past followed them. Such evidence made it difficult for investors to believe that anything related to Enron could be trusted. For example, John Olson, a Houston energy analyst, said this about OpCo Energy: "Clearly, anybody looking at this set of assets, given its pedigree, where they came from, would be sifting through this with a fine-toothed comb."[121]

Distrust

Besides the September 11 tragedy, the most negative event affecting the stock market in 2001 and 2002 was the Enron debacle. The effect of the firm's bankruptcy and subsequent accounting scandal has been dubbed "Enronitis."[122] The public outcry that resulted from the mishandling of employees' 401(k) plans lends an eye of distrust on the future activities of the company's managers. The constant mention of Enron in the press, whether related to Arthur Andersen's troubles or the Congressional investigation, was a constant reminder to the public of the sordid past of the company. The company also became a focus of efforts to reform everything from the accounting industry to pension funds and executive compensation.[123] According to CEO Stephen Cooper:

There has not been, at least in my experience, any situation which has generated as much attention and has provided such a platform relative to this particular set of dynamics ... This has become the lightning rod, literally—because I've felt the lightning.[124]

In what appeared to be an eerily prophetic statement, Ms. Watkins wrote Mr. Lay that if Enron collapsed because of the accounting problems, "the business world will consider the past successes as nothing but an elaborate accounting hoax."[125] As shown earlier, Ms. Watkins was correct; everything associated with Enron was looked at with distrust.

Enron, to become and survive as OpCo Energy, needed the public to disregard any connection between the company it is trying to become and the company that it was. As stated in a draft of OpCo's business plan, "The success of OpCo as a going concern will depend on its ability to separate reputationally from Enron."[126] The company needed to find a way to overcome its ethical failures of the past to become a successful entity in the future.

Notes

1. Enron Corp. Website, 2002, Enron names Stephen F. Cooper interim CEO . . . , http://www.enron.com/corp/pressroom/releases/2002, January 29.
2. *The Economist,* 2001, Leaders: Wasted energy; Enron's bankruptcy, December 8, pp. 13–14.
3. Ibid.
4. B. Gruley & R. Smith, 2002, Anatomy of a fall: Keys to success left Kenneth Lay open to disaster, *Wall Street Journal Online,* http://www.wsj.com, April 26.
5. Ibid.; W. Zellner & S. Forest, 2001, The fall of Enron, *Business Week,* December 17, pp. 30–36.
6. HoustonChronicle.com, 2002, Enron timeline, http://www.houstonchronicle.com, January 17.
7. D. Barboza & J. Schwartz, 2002, Fastow: The financial wizard tied to Enron's fall, *The New York Times Online,* http://www.nytimes.com, February 6; HoustonChronicle.com, 2002, Enron timeline, http://www.houstonchronicle.com, January 17; J. Roberts & E. Thomas, 2002, Enron's dirty laundry, *Newsweek Online,* http://www.msnbc.com/news, March 6.
8. HoustonChronicle.com, 2002, Enron timeline, http://www.houstonchronicle.com, January 17.
9. M. Kripalani, 2001, Enron switches signals in India, *Business Week Online,* http://www.businessweek.com, January 8.
10. Ibid.
11. HoustonChronicle.com, 2002, Enron timeline, http://www.houstonchronicle.com, January 17; J. Roberts & E. Thomas, 2002, Enron's dirty laundry, *Newsweek Online,* http://www.msnbc.com/news, March 6.
12. HoustonChronicle.com, 2002, Enron timeline, http://www.houstonchronicle.com, January 17.
13. M. Pacelle & R. Smith, 2002, UBS emerges as winning bidder for Enron energy-trading unit, *Wall Street Journal Online,* http://www.wsj.com, January 14; W. Zellner, 2001, We built a heck of a business, *Business Week Online,* http://www.businessweek.com, August 24.
14. HoustonChronicle.com, 2002, Enron timeline, http://www.houstonchronicle.com, January 17.
15. D. Barboza & J. Schwartz, 2002, Fastow: The financial wizard tied to Enron's fall, *The New York Times Online,* http://www.nytimes.com, February 6.
16. HoustonChronicle.com, 2002, Enron timeline, http://www.houstonchronicle.com, January 17.
17. Ibid.
18. S. Forest, 2001, Jeffrey Skilling's surprising split from Enron, *Business Week Online,* http://www.businessweek.com, August 15.
19. Enron Corp. Website, 2000, Enron named #22 of "100 Best Companies to Work for in America," http://www.enron.com/corp/pressroom/releases/2000, December 18.
20. Enron Corp. Website, 2001, Enron named most innovative for sixth year, http://www.enron.com/corp/pressroom/releases/2001, February 6.
21. Enron Corp. Website, 2000, Enron announces promotion of Jeff Skilling to CEO . . . , http://www.enron.com/corp/pressroom/releases/2000, December 13.
22. S. Forest, 2001, Jeffrey Skilling's surprising split from Enron, *Business Week Online,* http://www.businessweek.com, August 15.
23. Ibid.; W. Zellner, 2001, We built a heck of a business, *Business Week Online,* http://www.businessweek.com, August 24.
24. S. Forest, 2001, Jeffrey Skilling's surprising split from Enron, *Business Week Online,* http://www.businessweek.com, August 15.
25. S. Forest, 2001, Enron's Ken Lay: "There's no other shoe to fall," *Business Week Online,* http://www.businessweek.com, August 24.
26. J. Emshwiller & R. Smith, 2001, Enron posts surprise 3rd-quarter loss after investment, asset write-downs, *Wall Street Journal Online,* http://www.wsj.com, October 17.
27. P. Eavis, 2001, Still no clarity at Enron, *TheStreet.com,* http://www.thestreet.com, October 16.
28. R. Smith & J. Emshwiller, 2001, Enron CFO's tie to a partnership resulted in big profits for the firm, *Wall Street Journal Online,* http://www.wsj.com, October 19.
29. J. Emshwiller & R. Smith, 2001, Enron posts surprise 3rd-quarter loss after investment, asset write-downs, *Wall Street Journal Online,* http://www.wsj.com, October 17.
30. J. Emshwiller & R. Smith, 2001, SEC elevates Enron financial inquiry to the level of formal investigation, *Wall Street Journal Online,* http://www.wsj.com, November 1.
31. J. Emshwiller & M. Schroeder, 2001, Moody's downgrades Enron's debt, maintains review; stock drops 10%, *Wall Street Journal Online,* http://www.wsj.com, October 30.
32. R. Sidel & R. Smith, 2001, Dynegy holds talks to buy Enron, inject $1.5 billion to shore up firm, *Wall Street Journal Online,* http://www.wsj.com, November 8.
33. J. Emshwiller, R. Smith, R. Sidel, & J. Weil, 2001, Enron reduces profits for 4 years by 20%, citing dealings with officers' partnerships, *Wall Street Journal Online,* http://www.wsj.com, November 9.
34. Enron Corp. Website, 2001, http://www.enron.com/corp/investors, SEC Filings, November 8.
35. Enron Corp. Website, 2001, Dynegy and Enron announce merger agreement, http://www.enron.com/corp/pressroom/releases/2001, November 9.

36. G. Zuckerman & J. Sapsford, 2001, Lobbying kept agencies from issuing warnings, *Wall Street Journal Online*, http://www.wsj.com, November 29.

37. Enron Corp. Website, 2001, Enron announces notification by Dynegy of merger termination . . . , http://www.enron.com/corp/pressroom/releases/2001, November 28.

38. R. Smith & M. Pacelle, 2001, Enron units seek bankruptcy protection . . . , *Wall Street Journal Online*, http://www.wsj.com, December 3.

39. E. Bellman, 2002, Sale of Enron's power unit in India could take years, *Wall Street Journal Online*, http://www.wsj.com, February 1; M. Pacelle, M. Schroeder, & J. Emshwiller, 2001, Enron unveils a one-year restructuring plan . . . , *Wall Street Journal Online*, http://www.wsj.com, December 13.

40. J. Emshwiller & R. Smith, 2001, Enron posts surprise 3rd-quarter loss after investment, asset write-downs, *Wall Street Journal Online*, http://www.wsj.com, October 17.

41. *Weekly Corporate Growth Report,* 2001, Enron to acquire Azurix for 1.59 times revenue, March 26, p. 11240.

42. Ibid.; M. Powers, 2000, Azurix's free-falling numbers push Mark out the door, *ENR*, September 4, 245(9), p. 15.

43. Reuters, 2002, Enron unit Azurix gives up Argentine water contract, http://www.reuters.com, March 7.

44. Enron Corp. Website, 2001, Enron reports recurring third quarter earnings . . . , http://www.enron.com/corp/pressroom/releases/2001, October 16.

45. R. Smith, 2002, Blockbuster deal shows Enron's inclination to all-show, little-substance partnerships, *Wall Street Journal Online*, http://www.wsj.com, January 17.

46. Enron Corp. Website, 2001, Enron reports recurring third quarter earnings . . . , http://www.enron.com/corp/pressroom/releases/2001, October 16.

47. J. Emshwiller & R. Smith, 2001, Enron posts surprise 3rd-quarter loss after investment, asset write-downs, *Wall Street Journal Online*, http://www.wsj.com, October 17.

48. J. Emshwiller & R. Smith, 2002, Murky waters: A primer on the Enron partnerships, *Wall Street Journal Online*, http://www.wsj.com, January 21.

49. J. Emshwiller & R. Smith, Minutes from a 1997 meeting reveal Enron brass were in partnership loop, *Wall Street Journal Online*, http://www.wsj.com, February 1.

50. J. Leopold, 2002, Skilling, Fastow wooed fund for JV that led to Chewco, *Wall Street Journal Online*, http://www.wsj.com, February 26.

51. J. Emshwiller & R. Smith, Minutes from a 1997 meeting reveal Enron brass were in partnership loop, *Wall Street Journal Online*, http://www.wsj.com, February 1.

52. Ibid.

53. J. Emshwiller, 2002, Enron records show Lay was briefed on some aspects of questionable deals, *Wall Street Journal Online*, http://www.wsj.com, February 25.

54. J. Emshwiller & R. Smith, Minutes from a 1997 meeting reveal Enron brass were in partnership loop, *Wall Street Journal Online*, http://www.wsj.com, February 1.

55. J. Emshwiller & R. Smith, 2001, Enron posts surprise 3rd-quarter loss after investment, asset write-downs, *Wall Street Journal Online*, http://www.wsj.com, October 17; R. Smith & J. Emshwiller, 2001, Enron CFO's tie to a partnership resulted in big profits for the firm, *Wall Street Journal Online*, http://www.wsj.com, October 19.

56. J. Emshwiller & R. Smith, Minutes from a 1997 meeting reveal Enron brass were in partnership loop, *Wall Street Journal Online*, http://www.wsj.com, February 1.

57. J. Emshwiller & R. Smith, 2001, Enron posts surprise 3rd-quarter loss after investment, asset write-downs, *Wall Street Journal Online*, http://www.wsj.com, October 17.

58. J. Emshwiller & R. Smith, Minutes from a 1997 meeting reveal Enron brass were in partnership loop, *Wall Street Journal Online*, http://www.wsj.com, February 1.

59. J. Emshwiller & R. Smith, 2002, Murky waters: A primer on the Enron partnerships, *Wall Street Journal Online*, http://www.wsj.com, January 21; R. Smith & J. Emshwiller, 2001, Enron CFO's tie to a partnership resulted in big profits for the firm, *Wall Street Journal Online*, http://www.wsj.com, October 19.

60. J. Emshwiller, R. Smith, R. Sidel, & J. Weil, 2001, Enron reduces profits for 4 years by 20%, citing dealings with officers' partnerships, *Wall Street Journal Online*, http://www.wsj.com, November 9.

61. K. Brown & H. Sender, 2002, Enron's board fires Arthur Andersen . . . , *Wall Street Journal Online*, http://www.wsj.com, January 18.

62. J. Wilke, J Weil, & A. Barrionuevo, 2002, Andersen ex-party pleads guilty . . . , *Wall Street Journal Online*, http://www.wsj.com, April 10.

63. K. Blumenthal & C. Bryan-Low, 2002, International Paper drops Andersen . . . , *Wall Street Journal Online*, http://www.wsj.com, April 9.

64. K. Brown, C. Bryan-Low, & S. Ascarelli, 2002, Andersen takes a step toward breaking up its U.S. operations, *Wall Street Journal Online*, http://www.wsj.com, April 5; S. McBride, 2002, Search for Andersen ties turns into a free-for-all, *Wall Street Journal Online*, http://www.wsj.com, April 4.

65. J. Wilke & N. Kulish, 2002, Indictment by Justice Department puts Arthur Andersen's fate on line, *Wall Street Journal Online*, http://www.wsj.com, March 15.

66. For example, C. Bryan-Low, 2002, Auditors still perform nonaudits despite concerns about conflicts, *Wall Street Journal Online*, http://www.wsj.com, April 3; M. McNamee & H. Timmons, 2002, PwC: Sharing the hot seat with Andersen?, *Business Week Online*, http://www.businessweek.com, February 15; J. Whitman, 2002, For competence, accounting gets a "D" in poll of businesses, *Wall Street Journal Online*, http://www.wsj.com, April 9.

67. M. Pacelle, M. Schroeder, & J. Emshwiller, 2001, Enron unveils a one-year restructuring plan . . . , *Wall Street Journal Online*, http://www.wsj.com, December 13.

68. M. Pacelle & R. Smith, 2002, UBS emerges as winning bidder for Enron energy-trading unit, *Wall Street Journal Online*, http://www.wsj.com, January 14.

69. Enron Corp. Website, 2002, Enron announces successful bidder for wholesale trading operation, http://www.enron.com/corp/pressroom/releases/2002, January 11.

70. Enron Corp. Website, 2002, Enron releases details of UBS Warburg agreement, http://www.enron.com/corp/pressroom/releases/2002, January 15.

71. M. Pacelle & R. Smith, 2002, UBS emerges as winning bidder for Enron energy-trading unit, Wall Street Journal Online, http://www.wsj.com, January 14.

72. Enron Corp. Website, 2001, 2000 Annual Report, http://www.enron.com/corp/investors, p. 9.

73. R. Frank, 2002, GE could buy wind-turbine unit of Enron for about $250 million, Wall Street Journal Online, http://www.wsj.com, February 20.

74. Enron Corp. Website, 2002, Enron to sell wind assets to General Electric Company, http://www.enron.com/corp/pressroom/releases/2002, February 20.

75. R. Frank, 2002, GE could buy wind-turbine unit of Enron for about $250 million, Wall Street Journal Online, http://www.wsj.com, February 20.

76. Enron Corp. Website, 2001, Azurix Corp. closes sale of Azurix North America, http://www.enron.com/corp/pressroom/releases/2001, November 7.

77. E. Portanger, 2002, YTL Power buys Wessex Water from Enron for $776.4 million, Wall Street Journal Online, http://www.wsj.com, March 26; C. Prystay, 2002, YTL Power will purchase Enron's British water unit, Wall Street Journal Online, http://www.wsj.com, March 27.

78. E. Bellman, 2002, Sale of Enron's power unit in India could take years, Wall Street Journal Online, http://www.wsj.com, February 1.

79. S. Jegarajah & H. Kumar, 2002, Disagreement over proceeds delays sale of Dabhol Power, Wall Street Journal Online, http://www.wsj.com, March 10.

80. J. Slater, 2002, Dispute over proceeds halts sale of Enron's Dabhol plant, Wall Street Journal Online, http://www.wsj.com, April 10.

81. W. Lambert, 2002, Enron's creditors may get 20–25% of debt back, but total is unknown, Wall Street Journal Online, http://www.wsj.com, February 18.

82. K. Chu, 2002, Iberdrola bids $315 million for Enron's foreign assets, Wall Street Journal Online, http://www.wsj.com, March 29.

83. Dow Jones Newswires, 2002, Federal judge allows shutdown of Enron's broadband network, Wall Street Journal Online, http://www.wsj.com, March 11.

84. D. Brady, 2002, GE: More disclosure, please, Business Week Online, http://www.businessweek.com, February 18.

85. N. Byrnes, 2002, Paying for the sins of Enron, Business Week Online, http://www.businessweek.com, February 11.

86. Yahoo! Finance Website, 2002, Business Description—Dynegy, http://www.yahoo.marketguide.com, April 11.

87. Enron Corp. Website, 2001, Dynegy and Enron announce merger agreement, http://www.enron.com/corp/pressroom/releases/2001, November 9; Enron Corp. Website, 2001, Enron announces notification by Dynegy of merger termination . . . , http://www.enron.com/corp/pressroom/releases/2001, November 28.

88. J. Sapsford & P. Beckett, 2002, Dynegy addressed cash-flow fears with complex accounting tactics, Wall Street Journal Online, http://www.wsj.com, April 3.

89. Dynegy Inc. Website, 2002, Dynegy Fact Sheet, http://www.dynegy.com/downloads/DynegyFactSheet.pdf, January.

90. H. Hovey, 2002, Dynegy dn 18% after SEC launches formal investigation, Wall Street Journal Online, http://www.wsj.com, May 8.

91. Williams Website, 2002, Our history and culture, http://www.williams.com/information, April 8.

92. Williams Website, 2002, Williams fact sheet, http://www.williams.com/information, April 8.

93. Williams Website, 2002, 2001 Fourth quarter earnings, http://www.williams.com/investors, April 8.

94. Williams Website, 2002, Stats, http://www.williams.com/gaspipeline, April 10.

95. Williams Energy Website, 2002, About Williams Energy, http://www.williamsenergy.com/about, April 10.

96. Williams Website, 2002, Businesses, http://www.williams.com/businesses, April 10.

97. C. Richard, 2002, Moody's warns Williams Companies debt rating may be cut, Wall Street Journal Online, http://www.wsj.com, May 8.

98. El Paso Corp. Website, 2002, Our history, http://www.elpaso.com/about, April 11.

99. El Paso Corp. Website, 2002, 2001 Annual report, http://www.elpaso.com/investor, 67.

100. El Paso Corp. Website, 2002, Our business portfolio, http://www.elpaso.com/portfolio, April 8.

101. C. Cummins, 2002, El Paso will trim trading floor, restructure amid investor fears, Wall Street Journal Online, http://www.wsj.com, May 30.

102. M. Pacelle, M. Schroeder, & J. Emshwiller, 2001, Enron unveils a one-year restructuring plan . . . , Wall Street Journal Online, http://www.wsj.com, December 13.

103. R. Smith, 2002, Acting Enron CEO voices optimism about possibility of salvaging firm, Wall Street Journal Online, http://www.wsj.com, January 31.

104. HoustonChronicle.com, 2002, Cooper outlines Enron reorganization proposal, http://www.houstonchronicle.com, May 3.

105. Ibid.; L. Goldberg, 2002, Enron offers unorthodox revival plan, HoustonChronicle.com, http://www.houstonchronicle.com, May 3.

106. L. Goldberg, 2002, Enron offers unorthodox revival plan, HoustonChronicle.com, http://www.houstonchronicle.com, May 3; HoustonChronicle.com, 2002, Cooper outlines Enron reorganization proposal, http://www.houstonchronicle.com, May 3; R. Smith & M. Pacelle, 2002, Enron will try to reorganize itself as a small firm with a new name, Wall Street Journal Online, http://www.wsj.com, May 2.

107. Enron Corp. Website, 2002, Enron enters into settlement on procedural dispute with Dynegy, http://www.enron.com/corp/pressroom/releases/2002, January 3.

108. HoustonChronicle.com, 2002, Cooper outlines Enron reorganization proposal, http://www.houstonchronicle.com, May 3.

109. Ibid.

110. R. Smith & M. Pacelle, 2002, Enron will try to reorganize itself as a small firm with a new name, *Wall Street Journal Online,* http://www.wsj.com, May 2.

111. L. Goldberg, 2002, Enron offers unorthodox revival plan, HoustonChronicle.com, http://www.houstonchronicle.com, May 3.

112. R. Smith & M. Pacelle, 2002, Enron will try to reorganize itself as a small firm with a new name, *Wall Street Journal Online,* http://www.wsj.com, May 2.

113. Ibid.

114. K. Kranhold & M. Pacelle, 2002, UBS finds itself in the spotlight as owner of Enron trading unit, *Wall Street Journal Online,* http://www.wsj.com, May 8.

115. M. Schroeder & T. Hamburger, 2002, Democrats try to make hay of Enron fall as Lieberman calls hearings on collapse, *Wall Street Journal Online,* http://www.wsj.com, January 3.

116. W. Zellner, 2002, A hero—and a smoking gun letter, *Business Week Online,* http://www.businessweek.com, January 28.

117. Ibid.; M. Schroeder & J. Emshwiller, 2002, Enron employee told Lay last summer of concerns about accounting practices, *Wall Street Journal Online,* http://www.wsj.com, January 15.

118. *Wall Street Journal Online,* 2002, Taking stock in Enron, http://www.wsj.com, January 24.

119. M. Orey, 2002, Enron's fall spurs call for charges, *Wall Street Journal Online,* http://www.wsj.com, February 12.

120. M. Benson & B. Lee, 2002, FERC to probe strategies used by energy traders, *Wall Street Journal Online,* http://www.wsj.com, May 8; M. Golden, 2002, Enron memo: Traders discussed strategies with other cos, *Wall Street Journal Online,* http://www.wsj.com, May 7; K. Kranhold & R. Smith, 2002, Documents say two other firms took part in Enron power scheme, *Wall Street Journal Online,* http://www.wsj.com, May 9.

121. L. Goldberg, 2002, Enron offers unorthodox revival plan, HoustonChronicle.com, http://www.houstonchronicle.com, May 3.

122. E. Wahlgren, 2002, "Enronitis": A disease—and a cure, *Business Week Online,* http://www.businessweek.com, February 6.

123. For example, A. Barrett, 2002, Corporate America gets slammed, *Business Week Online,* http://www.businessweek.com, March 4; M. Schroeder, 2002, Bush supports businesses in debate over changing options accounting, *Wall Street Journal Online,* http://www.wsj.com, April 10.

124. Dow Jones Newswires, 2002, New CEO says saving Enron not an impossible job, *Wall Street Journal Online,* http://www.wsj.com, March 6.

125. W. Zellner, 2002, A hero—and a smoking gun letter, *Business Week Online,* http://www.businessweek.com, January 28.

126. R. Smith & M. Pacelle, 2002, Enron will try to reorganize itself as a small firm with a new name, *Wall Street Journal Online,* http://www.wsj.com, May 2.

Building a Sustainable, Profitable Business: Fair Trade Coffee (B)

Jan van der Kaaij
Robert Hooijberg
International Institute for Management Development

Stumbling into the Market

After meeting Frans at Utrecht railway station, Nico pondered his side of the bargain. The Third World Shops had limited capacity, so Nico had to find a way to increase the market share of fair trade coffee with limited marketing resources. Nico's dream was to mainstream fairly traded coffee.

Frans and Nico had already decided on a brand name: Max Havelaar—a name derived from a famous and partially autobiographic Dutch novel written in 1860 by Eduard Douwes Dekker. Douwes Dekker was a progressive civil servant who worked on the island of Java, Indonesia, and who tried to prevent the many wrongdoings against the locals. As he saw the futility of his efforts, he set about writing a novel called *Max Havelaar*, under the pseudonym Multatuli.

Getting Started

Starting off as no more than an average consumer, Nico carefully studied coffee retailing in the Netherlands. As the beans for most brands were processed and distributed by the main coffee-roasting companies, it soon became clear to him that he needed their cooperation to get Max Havelaar onto the supermarket shelves.

His initial talks with the main coffee-roasting companies such as Douwe Egberts, de Drie Mollen, and Marvelo—supermarket chain Albert Heijn's own coffee-roasting company—were disappointing. They had grave doubts about his ability to supply fair trade coffee without quality and logistics hiccups. The risk for their brands was simply too big in their eyes. Therefore, the initial idea of launching Max Havelaar as a hallmark was abandoned. Max Havelaar needed to become a brand in its own right to penetrate the market and to demonstrate what market research had shown: between seven percent and 15 percent of consumers were prepared to pay a premium price for fairly traded coffee.

Convincing Albert Heijn

After a year of business planning, fundraising, and research, Solidaridad (an innovative Dutch interchurch foreign aid organization for Latin America)

Jan van der Kaaij (PED 2002) prepared this case under the supervision of Professor Robert Hooijberg as a basis for class discussion rather than to illustrate either effective or ineffective handling of a business situation.

was ready to launch the Max Havelaar brand in 1987. Nico organized meetings with supermarkets to get the brand into their stores. Again he was surprised by the response: Albert Heijn—the biggest retailer in the Netherlands, with an overall share of 30 percent—was impressed with the business plan that Solidaridad had put together. It agreed in principle to work with Max Havelaar, but not as a brand—as a private label with a fair trade hallmark!

After his initial surprise and irritation over lost effort and wasted time had passed, Nico changed his plans back to the original idea of launching a hallmark. But by the time he was ready and commitments had been made, the game had changed once again. Under pressure from Sara Lee/Douwe Egberts, and after a high-level meeting between executives, Albert Heijn decided to withdraw from the plan to launch a fair trade private label containing the Max Havelaar hallmark.

The Taste of Success

Again Nico had to find an alternative. After much searching and talking, he succeeded in striking a deal with Neuteboom, a small coffee-roasting company that wanted to re-enter the supermarket channel. Finally, on November 15, 1988, the fair trade Neuteboom coffee with a Max Havelaar hallmark was launched.

Meanwhile, the traditional brand owners, encouraged by market leader Douwe Egberts (69 percent market share), tried to further neutralize the Max Havelaar initiative by publicly announcing a program that would ensure more income for the coffee growers in the future. However, many journalists understood the political intent of this program and were cynical in their articles. This provided Max Havelaar with much positive free publicity, and after a successful launch event, the first orders started coming in.

Other smaller coffee-roasting companies followed the example of Neuteboom, and the market share of the Max Havelaar hallmark steadily grew to a stable 2.7 percent (all brands together) in the Netherlands.

In 1996 a significant milestone was reached in the Netherlands: Albert Heijn launched its own private label with a Max Havelaar hallmark, Café Honesta. And Albert Heijn became proactive: In 1997 it started to work closely with Solidaridad and coffee farmers in Guatemala to create a code of conduct aimed at social, environmental, and quality aspects of coffee farming.

Payoff for the Coffee Farmers

A Hard Battle with the Coyotes (local middlemen)

It took much perseverance and smart innovation for the new UCIRI (Union of Indigenous Communities in the Istmo Region) cooperative to drive the coyotes out of business. For instance, setting up a cooperative-owned bus service between the villages torpedoed one of the profitable coyote scams—the monopoly of public transport was broken. The cooperative also opened shops, where villagers could buy basic household goods, to further reduce dependency on the coyotes.

It was a long and hard battle but finally, after 1992, the violence decreased and many coyotes were forced into bankruptcy and consequently moved to other regions.

Improved Living Conditions

The cooperative succeeded in setting up schools, its own processing facility, a health center, public transport, and downstream logistics. Furthermore, it set up an agricultural school independent of the Mexican government. The Centro de Educacion Campesina (CEC) was the only agricultural secondary school in the region. The program was based mainly on the realities and practicalities of peasant life. Students learned how to better understand and cope with the mountainous environment, its vegetation, soil types, and animal life. In addition, participants studied sustainable methods of agriculture for coffee as well as for corn, black beans, and soybeans, for example. Each year 25 young men and women enrolled in the CEC program to be trained in farming and management—knowledge they willingly shared with their communities upon their return.

Feeding Other Initiatives

The UCIRI struggle, experience, and infrastructure allowed several new organizations to emerge. For instance CEPCO, or the Oaxacan State Coffee Producers Network, was founded in 1989 in the midst of a severe crisis in Mexico's coffee industry. CEPCO was formed through the efforts of more than 20,000 small coffee producers from community and regional organizations throughout the state of Oaxaca. It was part of the National Network of Coffee Producer Organizations (CNOC), which to date had organized 71,219 of Mexico's 290,514 coffee farmers.

The UCIRI concept was also quickly and successfully copied in other countries, such as Nicaragua, Colombia, Honduras, and Guatemala. For instance, Prodecoop in Nicaragua sold its first container of coffee to a fair trade organization in 1991, after the rebel government was toppled. Since then, Prodecoop has grown to ship more than 50 containers a year supplied by the 71 farmer cooperatives in the organization. Fair trade proceeds helped this cooperative by providing the necessary economic stability for it to develop itself.

Many other countries followed. Fairly traded coffee became a global commodity.

Quality as Key

A key issue to solve was the quality of the coffee beans. With the creation of a hallmark, consumers expected to be able to buy a consistent quality of coffee from fair trade importing organizations. And since these fair trade organizations were paying a premium for the coffee beans, they expected top quality beans from their suppliers. So UCIRI needed to implement a standard quality assurance process. In addition, it obtained certification for its organic coffee production program from Naturland, a globally accredited certification institute for organic produce.

Much effort was put into the installation of a de-stoning, peeling, and packing facility—with the Max Havelaar logo proudly painted on the outside wall.

UCIRI Flourishes

With the opening of a new roasting facility in 2001, another goal was achieved. Further forward value chain integration became possible. In 2002 the cooperative sold approximately 100 tons of roast and ground coffee and 150 tons of soluble coffee in the Mexican market under its own UCIRI brand.

By 2003 a total of 53 communities in Mexico were members of the cooperative. It was a flourishing enterprise. To enter, farmers had to subscribe to the principles and rules of the cooperative, which went

© Éric St-Pierre

The UCIRI plant with the Max Havelaar logo on the wall

beyond mere coffee farming practices. For instance, members could not own a bar or tavern and were not allowed to grow marijuana or other drugs. The cooperative had a very democratic organization model with elected and rotating management (see Exhibit 1).

Overall the model worked very well. As Cliserio Villanueva Solana, the 2003 president of UCIRI in the community of Guadalupe, stated:

We don't have many difficulties here because the members decide for themselves our course of action . . . each has his say, and whatever our individual opinions, we decide together what is best for all of us. Here there is democracy, equality and respect for ourselves and each other.

Expanding the Distribution Concept

The Max Havelaar team worked hard to transfer the concept to other European countries to achieve their objective of "mainstreaming fair trade" by increasing market volume. Max Havelaar became the model that labeling initiatives all over the world followed. Between 1991 and 1995, Max Havelaar was launched in the majority of European markets (see Exhibit 2). The biggest success was in Switzerland, where the two biggest retailers, Migros and Coop, soon embraced the initiative an eight percent market share was achieved.

To coordinate the certification of fair trade products internationally, an organization called

EXHIBIT 1

EXHIBIT 1   The UCIRI Organization Model

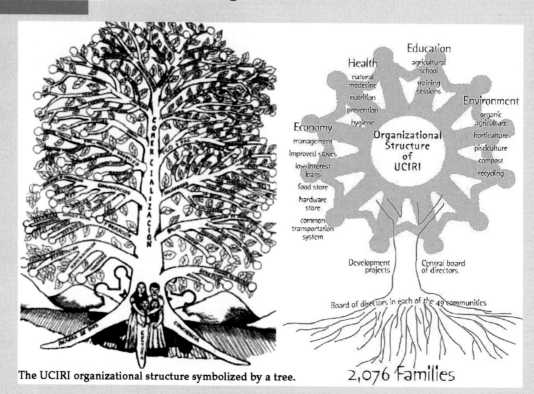

The UCIRI organizational structure symbolized by a tree.

The cooperative has a clear organizational structure and responsibilities are shared. Each of the approximately 2,300 member families of UCIRI has a representative in the local community. This representative must participate in the village's monthly general assembly. The village assembly has its own board of directors, who in turn administers and organizes committees on topics such as organic agriculture, health care, transportation, and projects specific to a given community.

Once a month, each of the participating villages must also send two representatives to the central general assembly where during two days problems are discussed and decisions of a more general nature are made. At the end a report is distributed and each delegate is responsible for sharing this information with all cooperative members in his or her community. The central board of directors is elected by the representatives of each village every three years.

SOURCE: UCIRI.

FLO (Fair Trade Labeling Organizations International) was set up in Bonn, Germany, in 1992. Ten years later, the FLO sourced their coffee from 185 cooperatives around the globe (see Exhibit 2). By 2003 FLO had grown to become a worldwide Fairtrade Standard Setting and Certification Organization, enabling more than 800,000 producers and workers in 41 countries to benefit from labeled fair trade.

A Stagnating Market Share

Despite the predicted market share of at least seven percent, consumers did not vote with their wallets as anticipated in the market research. Fair trade coffee did not have the hoped-for impact. So in 1998, the concern at Max Havelaar was growing. Max Havelaar had failed to become a serious player in a market dominated by global companies,

EXHIBIT 2 Expansion of Cooperatives and Fair Trade Labeling Organizations

Cooperatives

Country	No. of Cooperatives	Country	No. of Cooperatives
Central America	**90**	**Africa**	**23**
Costa Rica	1	Cameroon	1
El Salvador	3	Congo	2
Guatemala	15	Ethiopia	1
Honduras	20	Rwanda	1
Mexico	36	Tanzania	6
Nicaragua	15	Uganda	12
Caribbean	**9**	**Asia**	**6**
Dominican Republic	2	East Timor	1
Haiti	7	Indonesia	1
		Papua New Guinea	3
		Thailand	1
South America	**57**	**Total**	**185**
Bolivia	17		
Brazil	3		
Colombia	18		
Ecuador	1		
Peru	14		
Venezuela	4		

SOURCE: Fair Trade Labeling Organizations International (FLO), 2003.

Fair Trade Labeling Organizations

Country	Organization	Year of Introduction
Netherlands	Max Havelaar Netherlands	1988
Belgium	Max Havelaar Belgium	1991
Switzerland	Max Havelaar Switzerland	1992
Germany	TransFair	1993
Luxembourg	TransFair-Minka	1993
France	Max Havelaar France	1993
United Kingdom	Fairtrade Foundation	1994
Austria	TransFair	1994
Italy	TransFair	1995
Denmark	Max Havelaar Denmark	1995
Sweden	Föreningen för Rattvisermarkning	1997
Ireland	Irish Fair Trade Network	1998
Finland	Reilun Kaupan Edistami-syhdistys	1999

SOURCE: Roozen, Nico and Frans van der Hoff. *Fair Trade, Het verhaal achter Max Havelaar koffie, Oké-bananen en Kuyichi-jeans.* Amsterdam, Van Gennep, 2001.

and because of the price it guaranteed the farmers, there was not a lot of money for additional marketing efforts (see Exhibit 3 for 2001 figures). The market share for Max Havelaar coffee in the Netherlands had been stable for a number of years, hovering just below the three percent mark (refer to Exhibit 4 for market shares of the big three coffee roasters).

On top of this, margins were under extreme pressure as world coffee prices started to drop heavily in 1999 (see Exhibit 5).

In fall 2001 Max Havelaar called a meeting with the brand owners to discuss the future strategy. Nico was uncertain what to do next to achieve his 1985 objective: mainstreaming fair trade coffee.

EXHIBIT 3   Coffee Price Breakdown Based on Dutch Market Figures

Kilogram prices in 2001	Market		Max Havelaar	
Retail price	€ 6,48	100%	€ 7,88	100%
VAT (6%)	€ 0,36	6%	€ 0,44	6%
Max Havelaar—license cost	€ —	0%	€ 0,20	3%
Margin for distribution, coffee roasting, storage, transportation, financing, and margin for importers and roasters	€ 5,04	78%	€ 3,76	48%
FOB price	€ 1,08	17%	€ 3,48	44%
Breakdown of raw material cost (FOB)				
Export duties	€ 0,04	1%	€ 0,16	2%
Cost of local processing, financing, transport, and other trade-related costs	€ 0,72	11%	€ 0,72	9%
Gross income farmers	€ 0,32	5%	€ 2,60	33%

Basis of calculation:
- Pricing based on standard Dutch coffee blend ("roodmerk koffie") consisting of one-third robusta and two-thirds arabica beans.
- FOB (free on board) is the price paid for the coffee ready for shipment.
- 100 lb = 45.36 kg
- Average world market prices arabica (New York) per 100 lb: US$54.84
- Average world market prices robusta (London) per 100 lb: US$23.31
- Average Max Havelaar prices arabica per 100 lb: US$126.00
- Average Max Havelaar prices robusta per 100 lb: US$108.00
- Currency: 2001 average dollar-price: €1,117
- Yield from green beans to roasted beans: 1,19
- Fictitious transport cost correction: US$7.00
- The gross farmer income concerns "unorganized" farmers on the free market; Max Havelaar farmers are part of a cooperative that together decides on payout and allocations for investments.

SOURCE: Dutch Max Havelaar Foundation.

EXHIBIT 4 Market Share Leaders in Three Countries

Big Three Coffee Roasters	Country	Market Share
Nestlé (Nescafé, Nespresso)	UK	51%
Philip Morris (Altria/Jacobs)	Sweden	53%
Sara Lee (Douwe Egberts)	Netherlands	69%

SOURCE: Oxfam Briefing Paper. "Europe and the Coffee Crisis: A Plan for Action." Spring 2003.

EXHIBIT 5 Dropping Coffee Prices (International Coffee Organization/ICO)

ICO Indicator Prices by Year in New York (U.S. cents/lb)

Year	Price
1997	163.04
1998	126.27
1999	106.48
2000	94.58
2001	58.86
2002	57.02

10-Year Monthly Averages of ICO Indicator Prices in U.S. Cents per lb

Year	Jan	Feb	Mar	Apr	May	Jun	Jul	Aug	Sep	Oct	Nov	Dec
1993	58.14	57.32	54.76	51.38	54.18	54.54	60.61	67.69	71.64	67.78	70.03	71.50
1994	69.17	72.37	76.11	81.19	108.42	127.91	191.44	181.53	202.39	185.64	168.12	149.14
1995	152.08	152.24	162.73	159.59	155.96	141.66	132.71	141.70	124.76	120.02	117.99	99.57
1996	100.33	110.50	105.89	107.09	110.24	105.79	99.97	102.73	96.52	98.56	97.14	90.04
1997	100.03	121.89	137.47	142.20	180.44	155.38	135.04	132.63	132.51	121.09	118.16	130.02
1998	130.61	130.78	119.93	119.66	114.23	103.84	97.32	101.25	95.82	95.01	98.26	100.73
1999	97.63	92.36	89.41	85.72	89.51	86.41	78.21	77.22	71.94	76.36	88.22	95.63
2000	82.15	76.15	73.49	69.53	69.23	64.56	64.09	57.59	57.31	56.40	52.18	48.27
2001	49.19	49.39	48.52	47.31	49.38	46.54	43.07	42.77	41.17	42.21	44.24	43.36
2002	43.46	44.30	49.49	50.19	47.30	45.56	44.70	42.79	47.96	50.79	54.69	51.68

NOTE: The 1994 and 1997 price peaks were caused by the bad harvests in Brazil.

SOURCE: ICO website, http://www.ico.org, November 2003.

Flowernet mbH Case Study

Professor Dr. Erich Frese
University of Cologne

Professor Dr. Michael Lubatkin
University of Connecticut

During the late 1980s, Dibrell Bros. Inc. of Virginia, a tobacco wholesaler, faced an industry characterized by high uncertainties, limited growth opportunities, and increasing regulations. As a result, Dibrell was looking to diversify, and they favored the flower industry for a number of reasons. First, the products are similar—both are seasonal commodities, and tobacco is semi-perishable while flowers are perishable—so Dibrell felt that they could apply their management know-how. Second, the five to ten percent annual growth in consumption of fresh flowers was expected to remain stable or increase in the future. With improving handling methods, faster delivery and worldwide expansion of growers, the flower industry was becoming increasingly global.

Flowernet mbH, a family-owned, German-based wholesale cut flower distributor, was seen as an excellent candidate for acquisition because of its strong hold on the international import/export markets. Dibrell management also believed that its own well-developed multinational network of distribution and import locations could expand Flowernet's capacity to handle greater physical volumes. Finally, Flowernet—also an international trader with a decentralized management style—offered Dibrell access to an industry for diversification not directly affiliated with the tobacco industry, but similar in organization style and process. On the surface, the acquisition seemed logical and consistent with Dibrell's goals.

On July 1, 1987, Dibrell Bros. acquired 54.5 percent of the equity interests in Flowernet for a purchase price of $10.7 million. At the same time, Dibrell agreed to purchase the remaining shares of the company by 1991.

In the beginning of 1992, Dibrell purchased the final shares of Flowernet. However, Flowernet was not performing as Dibrell had forecasted when the initial purchase decision was made a few years before. Indeed, in 1988, Flowernet incurred its first loss in 12 years. Also, Flowernet was not reaping any cost efficiencies from its association with Dibrell's tobacco business, nor was it able to take advantage of Dibrell's distribution connections. Dibrell decided to postpone any changes for at least another year—after all, it had purchased the final shares of Flowernet stock only a few months prior, and the company could still strengthen under its new ownership.

Near the end of 1992, however, Dibrell began to seriously reevaluate its investment in Flowernet. These issues compelled Dibrell executives to seriously

Reprinted by permission of Professor Dr. Erich Frese, University of Cologne, and Professor Dr. Michael Lubatkin, University of Connecticut.

question the future of the subsidiary, its own administrative practices that allowed Flowernet to operate fully autonomous of Dibrell's policies and procedures, and capabilities of Flowernet's management. Dibrell officers, therefore, requested a review and redevelopment of Flowernet's strategic approach to the flower business. Dibrell also reaffirmed its desire to assist Flowernet with the addition of any necessary financial or managerial resources.

The Flower Industry

Before World War II, the flower industry consisted only of family-run, local businesses. Loyalties between supplier and retailer controlled much of the local business activity. International transport and worldwide shipping increased only when jet travel became widely available for transport during the sixties.

Within the last few years, a continued growth in demand of about ten percent per capita has graced the industry, but the number of growers has also increased rapidly. The industry structure has not changed much and there remains little vertical integration. Since most businesses in the industry are family owned, they have frequently been passed down through the generations and still act as the family's only source of income. Nearly 90 percent of the companies in the industry are firms like these, operating from a single location. Accordingly, the competition for survival is tough and the exit barriers are high.

By 1990, cut flowers account for approximately $30 billion annually in retail sales in the western world. Market shares per company are difficult to determine due to fragmentation into numerous local markets. The market share of the ten largest companies combined does not even account for ten percent of the total annual sales.

Country involvement, however, discloses useful information on the industry. Holland is the biggest exporter, selling to more than 60 percent of the market and hosting the central flower auctions. Columbia and Kenya, developed in recent years, possess ideal climates and are becoming important exporters. They offer unusual flower varieties and produce during the European off-season.

Cut flowers, however, are a highly perishable product, causing distribution and storage difficulties for everyone in the industry. Flowers must be delivered as soon after cutting as possible and must be kept cool continuously to ensure freshness. The normal transport temperature should be between five and ten degrees Celsius. However, some flowers must be stored above 12 degrees Celsius, while others require much lower temperatures.

The freshness factor is only one of the major problems for transportation. General costs of distribution are also high, especially in international trading where air transport can exceed 50 percent of the landed costs. Growers outside the European

| EXHIBIT 1 | Top Importing/Exporting Countries in 1990 |

Exporters (millions of U.S. $)		Importers (millions of U.S. $)	
Holland	1,970	Germany	1,072
Columbia	280	U.S.	340
Israel	218	France	316
Italy	144	U.K.	294
U.S.	70	Holland	164
Spain	50	Switzerland	145
Kenya	45	Japan	118
France	23	Italy	101

Community who export to the E.C. have extremely high costs due to longer transport routes and tariff barriers, which can be as much as 15 to 20 percent of the final cost. Imported flowers, therefore, tend to be more expensive for the importer whether or not the quality is higher. Finally, companies frequently require space at short notice for late or unexpected orders. When this is needed, transport costs increase even more.

Additional obstacles to the international flower industry are the culture-specific preferences for types of flowers, composition of bouquets, etc., making overall international demand extremely difficult to forecast and satisfy.

Clearly, quality and price are the primary competitive factors in the industry. Little can be done by an individual company to achieve significantly lower transport costs or higher quality. Each company must utilize the same transport methods, and the same natural resources.

Distribution channels differ by country, but normally follow the path below:

Grower to Import/Exporter to Wholesaler to Retailer

The Dutch flower auctions (or markets) are the buying and selling center of the industry—the hub of distribution. Holland hosts three major auctions at which the growers sell their products to wholesalers, import/export brokers, or retailers. Japan also holds auctions, but it hosts hundreds of small auctions that sell directly to the retailer. Indeed, every country operates somewhat differently. The role of the importer/exporter is therefore very complicated, since it must learn to deal with all levels of the distribution chain in various countries.

Great seasonality, due to various holidays and growing seasons, creates huge fluctuations in demand and pricing. During the five major flower holidays (Christmas, Mother's Day, All Saints' Day, Easter, Valentine's Day), demand will augment 20 or 25 times the average quantity sold on the normal weekend. Usually, storage and transportation facilities become overcrowded during the holidays, but remain underutilized the rest of the year. Pricing can never be predetermined, since quantity and quality of the available flowers—and demand for them—is quite volatile. As would be expected, the bargaining power of the growers and traders changes significantly during the holiday seasons when demand greatly exceeds supply.

Flowernet

Flowernet was founded by Peter Kaner in Augsburg, Germany, in 1925 as a wholesale cut flower distributor. The business was simply to sell cut flowers to retailers as a wholesale distributor. In 1945, Flowernet began to import flowers from neighboring countries to sell in the area around Augsburg, in southern Germany. The new business activity prospered, and in 1956 Flowernet opened its first subsidiary in San Remo, followed by a second in Nice during the same year.

Upon retirement, Peter Kaner passed on the management of Flowernet to his son, who opened ten additional wholesale branches in Germany. Walter Kaner had dreams of expanding the company even further. He was a competent, dynamic individual, and so under his direction the company entered a period of extreme growth.

Beginning in the sixties, Walter Kaner established 42 profit centers (including one group wholesale profit center and three production units) in 19 countries and fully engaged Flowernet in the business of importing and exporting fresh cut flowers.

Walter Kaner had neither children nor heirs to take over his position, so in 1987 at the age of 64, Kaner decided to sell his shares of Flowernet to Dibrell. With the retirement of Walter Kaner in 1988, the flower industry lost an outstanding entrepreneur.

Strategy

Kaner pursued the goal to place Flowernet as the largest international flower trader through continual development of new products and new markets, as well as to achieve a return on equity of about six percent.

Flowernet is active in the wholesale business, import and export business, as well as the marketing of fresh cut flowers for selected producers. After only a short-lived endeavor as breeder, Flowernet retreated from the backward integration. It now focuses on the multilevel trading of fresh cut flowers and tries to fulfill the individual customer's special demands. In order to offer a wide selection of cut flowers with exceptional quality, Flowernet uses many suppliers and growers from many countries.

Similar to most enterprises in the cut flower sector, Flowernet is a typical middle-sized family-operated enterprise. The goals and strategies of the Flowernet group have never been recorded or fixed in writing, but resided in the mind of its dominating leader.

Wholesale Business

Flowernet controls about 23 percent of the wholesale sector in Germany and it has served as an efficient cash generator. Its wholesale business is located around ten branch offices in southern Germany, in large urban areas. Every branch office employs numerous drivers who deliver the fresh cut flowers directly to the customers—mainly retail shops—and are responsible for on-site sales with certain minimum price structures. The sales drivers play the significant key role in the success of the wholesale business for Flowernet. Close personal ties between the customers and the sales drivers are just as essential for successful business as a superior delivery service compared to the services of the competitors. It is essential to guarantee a flexible yet reliable tour schedule, which provides the retail stores with fresh cut flowers and beats the competition.

The Dutch corporations, which do not have local branches, have recently gained in market shares of up to five percent over the last few years. Their drivers come directly from the auctions in Holland and offer their products directly to the southern German retail shops. The drivers do not return to Holland until the flowers are gone. Any surpluses are relieved by price dumpings.

Import and Export Business

Flowernet's worldwide import and export business is operated through 36 profit centers, 21 located throughout Europe, nine in the United States and Canada, two in Asia (Thailand and Japan), one in South America (Columbia), and three in Africa. Most profit centers have mainly the role of importers, and with the exception of Holland and Columbia, the profit centers are market leaders in their respective regional markets.

The world export market for flowers is dominated by Columbia and the Netherlands, with shares reaching 10 percent and 60 percent, respectively. However, Flowernet holds only a marginal position in these markets. Their division in Aalsmeer, Holland, involves strictly import activities, and the performance of its division of Bogota has been poor. A significant portion of Flowernet's purchases in Holland falls into the hands of Flowernet's North American divisions. For the rest of the units, the imports from Holland account for only 17 percent of the overall purchased volume.

The import and export divisions supply their customers with a wide variety of performances and services. Flowernet tries to distinguish itself from other suppliers through its voluminous selection, customer-oriented service, and partially exclusive offers of the highest quality flowers from various countries. In addition, Flowernet is known for its exceptional delivery service—even for small quantities. Generally, the customers have a choice between sample selections, preselected boxes, and finished bouquets. The elaborate customs and transport formalities are performed by Flowernet, and even the transportation risk is accepted by the divisions of the Flowernet Group, who purchase the merchandise on a job basis from the growers.

The customers are generally wholesalers and other importers as well as a small number of larger retail store chains and supermarkets. With the exception of the wholesalers—where Flowernet possesses a large supplying potential—customer loyalty is virtually non-existent. The supermarkets are frequently employing professional purchasing managers who are difficult and powerful negotiating partners. The wide selection of fresh cut flowers does not give Flowernet a competitive edge with the supermarkets due to the fact that these customers order only a small variety in very large numbers. Conclusively, the pricing is the only significant competitive parameter for this customer group.

The average number of customers for each of Flowernet's units tends to exceed its competitors and runs between 100 and 500. However, the ten largest customers seldom constitute more than 40 percent of the turnovers for any single unit. Furthermore, every salesman in the local units services between 20 and 50 customers, staying in close contact more than once a day, mainly by telephone. Salesmen need to be supplied with the current updates on availability, pricing, and quality of the products.

In the past, the import divisions have failed to create long-term cooperative alliances with the growers. The growers are confronted with the difficulty of uncertain weather conditions and this often conflicts with scheduled purchases of their customers. Also, the fresh cut flowers still need to be put on the market even in times of low demand. Only flower traders with a strong international presence are able to alleviate these critical situations for the growers and assist them to minimize exceptional losses. Strategic concepts to utilize this cooperative potential are, however, not supported by the corporate headquarters in Augsburg.

The general dilemma confronting the import division is the fact that they are dealing with a perishable good which cannot be stored for any expansive amount of time, while their customers order on short-term basis and demand immediate delivery. Because demand is very difficult to predict, the import division often has to hold too much in inventory, which then must be sold at lower prices and sometimes to customers with poor creditworthiness. At the same time, the profit centers in Europe have experienced a wide range of customer complaints over the last few years with regard to the quality and the delivery services. Over 50 major customers have cancelled their business activities with Flowernet since 1988.

Production and Exclusive Marketing for the Growers

The third and smallest business for Flowernet encompasses the exclusive marketing for the production of certain growers through its own marketing companies, Kenya Flowers and Flower Service in Frankfurt. The contractual arrangements between both corporations with the respective growers can be cancelled within one year. Flower Service distributes exclusively carnations from a Spanish grower to the Flowernet group. Kenya Flowers, on the other hand, sells the entire production of two large Kenyan enterprises. The marketing of their products is very successful, because the products are generally available earlier than products from other countries, with comparative quality. Employees of Kenya Flowers perform the quality inspection directly on-site at the growers in Kenya. The flowers are then selected and specifically packaged for the various wholesalers.

Flowernet's own attempt to produce flowers was short-lived and not successful. Their objective has been to reduce the number of outside suppliers and to provide reliable, quality-conscious sources to supply the Flowernet group. However, the capital costs of entry were high and the production units in Spain, Israel, and Ecuador suffered substantial losses, and subsequently were liquidated in 1988. The cause of the failed attempt included a lack of expertise and general know-how. Poor cuttings, wrong fertilizer, insufficient watering, and poor treatment of the harvest were common experiences, as was a reduction of flexibility in the selection of products for the corporation.

Organizational Structure

The highly decentralized organization structure of Flowernet has hardly changed since the large growth rates recorded in the 1960s. Due to the large presence of an ownership-oriented mentality, nearly all activities reveal a very low level of standardization and formalities. The corporate headquarters is superior to a wholesale enterprise with ten branch offices located in southern Germany. The activities of the 36 legally independent import and export divisions as well as the two marketing units are only loosely coordinated. (See Exhibits 2, 3, and 4.)

Two directors manage the headquarters of the Flowernet group in Augsburg with 17 employees. The first managing director is responsible for the cut flower business and the central purchasing department; the second is responsible for financing, personnel and administration. The managing directors are supported in their efforts by four specialists for purchasing and transportation, controlling, accounting and finance, and personnel management. The managing and control span of the first managing director encompasses the 42 profit center managers and is extremely broad, which makes an effective support and integration of the units nearly impossible.

The wholesale branch offices operate mostly as autonomous profit centers. Only the financial activities are handled by the headquarters in Augsburg.

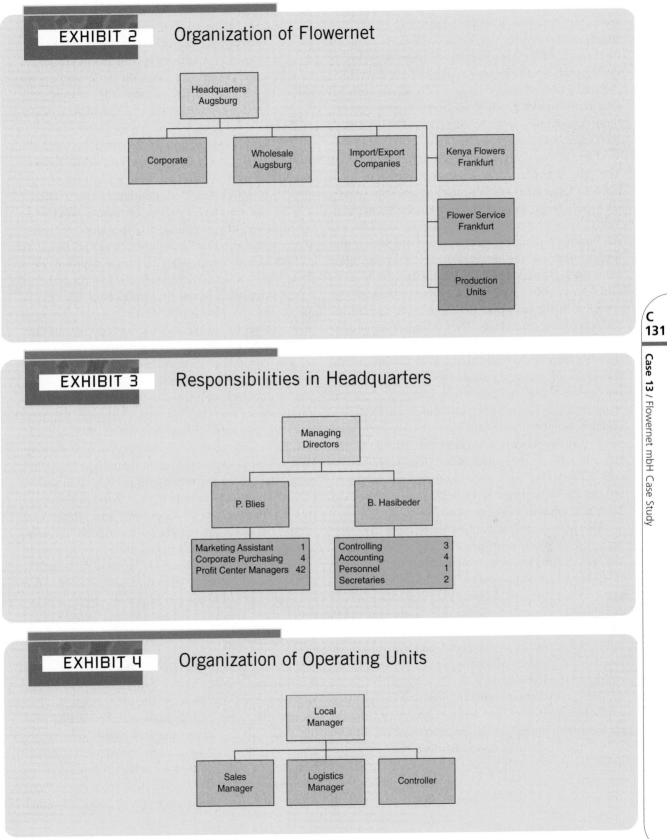

EXHIBIT 2   Organization of Flowernet

Headquarters
Augsburg

Corporate

Wholesale
Augsburg

Import/Export
Companies

Kenya Flowers
Frankfurt

Flower Service
Frankfurt

Production
Units

EXHIBIT 3   Responsibilities in Headquarters

Managing
Directors

P. Blies

B. Hasibeder

Marketing Assistant   1
Corporate Purchasing   4
Profit Center Managers 42

Controlling   3
Accounting   4
Personnel   1
Secretaries   2

EXHIBIT 4   Organization of Operating Units

Local
Manager

Sales
Manager

Logistics
Manager

Controller

In contrast, the branch offices are completely responsible and independent concerning their own supply and turnover decisions. In the Netherlands the branch office has over 14 different suppliers at its disposal, which sometimes also deliver directly to the customers of the wholesaler. Unlike the general dominant market position of Dutch-grown flowers, these constitute only 40 percent of Flowernet's wholesale business.

Each delivery van is managed as a profit center. The drivers purchase the flowers at their branch office at a fixed price—derived from the branch office's own purchasing price including a specific markup. The driver's purchasing price describes more or less the bottom negotiating price between the driver and the customer. If the driver achieves a higher price from the retailers, he receives 20 percent of the additional gain. Although the drivers are responsible for the sales of the cut flowers, they are not responsible for purchasing or storage. They inform the manager of the expected orders of the customers and activate the concrete purchasing activity. If in the aftermath, the expected turnovers could not be achieved, the burden lies entirely on the branch office. The only financial consequences facing the drivers are in the respective variations over and above the bottom sales price. If the product is sold below this price level, the risk still falls on the branch office. The incentive system of Flowernet, therefore, encourages the drivers to sell smaller quantities at higher prices rather than large quantities at moderate price levels.

The import and export business units are each regarded as profit centers under the supervision of the local managers, who assume complete responsibility for all financial results. The profit center managers are entitled to acquire a capital share of 20 percent at maximum. There are numerous sales managers, a logistics manager, and a controller under the authority of the profit center manager. In smaller and midsized units the controller is in charge of the logistics as well.

All profit centers operate independently; they can select their suppliers and customers principally on their own and negotiate the respective conditions in an autonomous fashion. Because the units are generally in relatively strong competitive nature to one another, suppliers and the general conditions are normally considered secret and not generally disclosed. Joint group deliveries contribute only five percent to the overall purchasing volume. On average, each profit center has roughly 150 to 350 different, mostly small suppliers at its disposal. Consequently, there is a critically large amount of low-value single orders, especially during the flower holidays between the months of October and June.

The only coordination of activities between the individual profit centers can be found in the areas of purchasing and controlling, where the central purchasing office in Augsburg coordinates the purchasing for the business units in Germany. Worldwide coordination of purchasing activities does not exist. Sometimes the central headquarters forced the units to purchase flowers from a group supplier, even though the local units drew attention to the fact that it was impossible to sell the products or only possible to sell the products with exceptional losses in their respective markets. This was similar for the supply of flowers from their own production units.

The corporate headquarters keeps contact with the existing group suppliers—especially for complaints and reclamations—and identifies potentially interesting growers and traders. Although the local units are provided with up-to-date market information on weather conditions in the production countries, seasonal expectations on quantity and quality of the various flower types, and packaging methods, this information exchange mainly flows in the direction of headquarters to local units and seldom vice versa. The only indications on the traded varieties, quantities, qualities, and prices are provided mainly through the local auctions. A worldwide information network system with suppliers, traders, and customers to utilize the price/quantity trade-offs between the individual markets does not exist.

Distribution

The central quality criteria for the performance of the Flowernet group is the freshness of the traded and delivered flowers to their customers. The shorter the time period between the cutting and the delivery, the larger the customer's advantage. The competitiveness of imported flowers in comparison to locally grown flowers is highly dependent on the time span of the transportation from their origin to the end user. Experience has shown Flowernet that distribution by means of the international flower auctions is time intensive, and could be circumvented through direct deliveries to wholesalers and retailers. This is very critical for extremely perishable flowers and also for time-sensitive orders.

In the wholesale business, Flowernet has roughly 60 delivery vans, which mainly supply the retail shops. Although the retail stores encompass the major portion of the customers in southern Germany, the recent trend reveals a strong shift in the distribution channels in favor of the supermarkets. Until now it has only randomly occurred that customer-specific packaging in boxes was performed by the suppliers or growers, which burdens the branch offices with time- and cost-intensive repackaging processes.

The distribution capacities in the form of sales drivers, cooled delivery vans, and storage facilities are ascribed to the demand peaks during the five flower holidays. Another consideration is the universal increase in transportation congestion, which demands a higher use of resource utilization when specific delivery schedules must be met. During normal weekends the turnovers could easily be doubled without additional adjustments of capacity.

In sight of the strategic positioning of Flowernet's wholesale business, the increasing level of reclamations by the retailers—nearly three percent of the turnover in 1992—weighs heavy in the eyes of the management. The considerable losses due to overcapacity also shows the necessity of distributional reorganization.

The import/export business units are all situated in the direct vicinity of international airports, because most of the flowers are now transported by air freight. The air freight cost amounts to nearly 50 percent of the sales price to the wholesalers. Delayed departures and holdovers or mistakes in reloading during stopover flights can create expansive losses. The time-consuming process of clearing the flowers is dealt with by the employees of Flowernet. The shipments are cleared immediately upon arrival, often at night or on weekends. The goods are delivered either directly to the customers or, if necessary, stored in Flowernet's own intermediate cooling facilities. With a perishable item such as fresh cut flowers, it is crucial to guarantee that the cooling chain is not interrupted. Even in the import/export units, Flowernet has to maintain large overcapacity.

The customers of the import/export units have increasingly complained about insufficient quality of the delivered merchandise, which can be traced back to problems in the storaging and/or transportation. Occasionally, the merchandise was already of poor quality even prior to shipping from the growers. Because the Flowernet employees rarely do not carry out on-site quality control inspections at the growers, these reclamations arise further on down the value-added chain.

Personnel

Presently, the company has about 550 employees, where the smallest profit center has only four employees, and the largest—Frankfurt or New York—employs between 25 and 30. Approximately 100 people are employed in the ten branches in the wholesale business.

Walter Kaner viewed the employees as the company's major asset. Only by means of strong customer-oriented and qualified employees at all hierarchical levels could the Flowernet group secure and increase its efficiency in the ever-increasing international competition. This is especially crucial for the profit center managers. A mismatch at this level can cost the company dearly.

Roughly only one-third of the employees of the wholesale business work in the administration and receive a fixed monthly income. The other two-thirds—managers and sales drivers—are paid primarily on commission, so that overhead cost can remain flexible and decrease if business developments dwindle.

In the import/export units, about 70 percent of the employees are salesmen, who generally have commission-based or bonus-based salaries. The other 30 percent are drivers of the cooling vans and administrative personnel. The personnel costs are by far the largest fraction of the overhead costs of these units.

A profit-sharing plan for the profit center managers provides them with 15 percent of the pretax profit in addition to their fixed income. With newly founded branch offices or with restructuring of existing ones, the profit sharing is implemented when the actual loss is less than the expected loss. After numerous years of successful enterprising, the profit managers can acquire a maximum of 20 percent of capital shares.

Fulfilling the responsibility of a profit center manager requires motivated individuals willing to work 12- to 18-hour days and weekend shifts prior to the flower holidays. The managers must also possess strong communicative abilities and a fluent command of various languages.

In the wholesale branch offices, the managers are constantly trained and furthered in their career development. Roughly ten trainees participate in intensive programs where they visit flower markets and important suppliers, inform themselves on new products and markets, and glide through the different functions in the ten branch offices. The other profit centers do not yet have such trainee programs.

A large problem for the profit centers is the relatively low level of loyalty and job satisfaction among the employees and the consequential high fluctuation. The turnover rate is about two and a half years. Reasons for the high turnover include the long working hours, the partially poor-paying positions, and the relatively difficult relationship with the main office. Many managers feel insufficiently supported and often unjustly criticized. In the last three years, Flowernet has lost seven acting managers who have become independent and have taken as many as 50 employees along with them.

Finance

Historically, Flowernet's major concerns centered on traded volume, number of customers and suppliers, and range of products. Profit goals and other financials were deemed unnecessary. Nonetheless, the company kept financial track of operations with annual financial statements, and monthly reports consisting of profit and loss statements and balance sheets. Exhibit 5 provides an overview of the development of Flowernet prior to being acquired.

The loss in 1988 is primarily the result of the liquidation of some recent investment in production units. Exhibit 6 explains the loss in further detail.

Dibrell Brothers, Incorporated

Dibrell Brothers of Virginia was founded in 1873 as a partnership in tobacco leaf purchasing and processing. It was incorporated in 1904. Today, Dibrell is involved in tobacco purchasing, processing, and packing for the cigarette industry with plants located in 23 countries around the world.

Employing 2,750 full-time people in its tobacco segment, Dibrell blends different grades of tobacco for various companies including Philip Morris, RJR Nabisco, and Japan Tobacco. Dibrell and its affiliates comprise the second-largest leaf tobacco dealer group in the world.

Dibrell entered the export flower industry in fiscal year 1987 with the purchase of majority interest in Flowernet. Later that same year, Dibrell acquired a 70 percent interest in Baardse, another exporter of fresh cut flowers. Baardse purchases primarily from the Dutch flower auctions, a market in which Flowernet is weak. Close to 1,200 people are employed in Dibrell's flower businesses. The central offices of Flowernet and Baardse are both located in Europe where the majority of the activity takes place. Additional branches are located throughout Europe and in numerous countries worldwide. Dibrell continues to invest in and expand its global tobacco businesses through additional mergers within the tobacco industry as well. Before 1990, Dibrell was engaged in home ice cream freezer and retail flower businesses. These investments were liquidated in 1990.

Finance

Dibrell is a publicly owned company that has, over the years, achieved many of its strict financial expectations, generally pleasing its stockholders. Dividends have increased, as well as operating profit and ROE. Net sales also have steadily increased throughout the past five years at a compounded annual rate of 18 percent and passed the $1 billion market in 1991. Of particular importance to the company is its ability to maintain an above average ROE, nearing 20 percent in four of the past five years—higher than the industry average. Net income reached $30 million in 1992. Unfortunately, Flowernet's recent losses and poor performance have not met Dibrell's standards and threaten the ability of Dibrell to maintain its financial goals.

Dibrell's tobacco operations accounted for two-thirds of the company revenues in both 1991 and 1992. The foreign tobacco markets yielded 61 percent of 1991 and 70 percent of 1992 tobacco revenues. Dibrell's flower businesses accounted for the remaining one-third of company revenues, although they accounted for only 11 percent of

the 1992 profit. The majority of flower revenue is generated in Europe.

Management Strategies

Historically, the company has attributed its success to the high volume that it achieves in the tobacco business and to its willingness to enter joint ventures, strategic alliances, etc. to pool resources, thereby optimizing capacity utilization.

Dibrell is wary of the future of the tobacco industry, especially in the United States. Two-thirds of the growth in the tobacco segment has been in South America, and this is where the company expects future growth. Dibrell is maintaining its area of specialization—"American Blend" tobacco—which is in growing demand on the worldwide market. Dibrell has a strong presence in the areas considered to be the best and lowest cost production areas for tobacco. South America, for example, has the proper climate for growing the best tobacco. Negative publicity such as health warnings, legal restrictions, etc. are most prominent in the United States. For these reasons, Dibrell will concentrate its future outside North America, while maintaining its present hold there. The company plans to target South America, Asia, and Africa as the markets most likely to develop.

Dibrell's goals for the future include differentiation in both industries—tobacco and cut flower—through customer orientation, maintenance of decentralized management in world operations, backward integration in the tobacco industry, further development outside the United States, and diversification.

The Tobacco Industry

Environment

In June 1988, analysts cited three positive trends in the tobacco industry. The first noticeable trend was the growth in the worldwide cigarette market reacting to the declining dollar, better-quality products, and the breaking up of certain national monopolies such as in France, Spain, and Japan. With the combination of these elements, the American cigarette companies were expected to increase worldwide unit sales. Second, American tobacco profit margins (not unit sales) were improving annually (January

1988: 14–15 percent without federal excise taxes). Particularly within the cigarette companies, there was also an accelerating rate of excess cash flow generation. The final trend was the declining corporate tax rate in 1987 and 1988 in the United States.

In spite of these trends, stock prices were falling. In 1988, unit sales volumes were decreasing; media and the first liability lawsuits against the cigarette manufacturers created an uncertain future. Taxes were raised on all tobacco products. By 1991, other regulations threatened the industry as well—including the airline smoking ban on intracontinental flights. As a precaution, many tobacco companies began investing excess cash in nontobacco businesses. Expansion to the newly opened overseas markets—where no negative industry reputation existed—was also favored. A wave of merger activity penetrated the industry.

Nevertheless, tobacco profits remained favorable and increasing. It was later shown that cigarettes will sell regardless of rising prices. This pricing flexibility allowed prices to increase, exceeding cost inflation. Because of that and the highly automated, more efficient processing and curing methods, profits grew even as unit sales decreased. Smokers began purchasing nonbrand cigarettes as well, opening a new market for cigarette manufacturers.

This combination of factors created an uncertain future for tobacco companies—on the one hand, the industry was reacting well to a maturing market, but on the other hand, uncontrollable environmental factors strongly threatened the future of the industry.

For more information about the International Tobacco and Cigarette Markets, please refer to the attachment at the end of the case, which presents a summary of remarks made in a recent interview by a top executive at R.J. Reynolds Tobacco GmbH.

Tobacco Processing Market

There are many aspects to the tobacco industry—tobacco growing, tobacco stemming and redrying, tobacco processing, cigarette manufacturing, etc.

There are more than 100 grades of flue-cured tobacco in the United States—rated by the quality of the stalk and the chemical components, as well as other criteria. The cigarette manufacturers specify blends and grades of tobacco before inspecting the various products available. In the United States, tobacco is sold at auctions. In other countries, it is sold through a variety of other arrangements. Manufacturers normally purchase from many different sources to achieve the mix they desire.

The various companies selling tobacco must rely on historical relationships with manufacturers and excellent service in order to secure customers and differentiate between other growers. There is very little practical difference since it is a basic commodity market—all competitors have the same machinery, the same natural resources, and virtually the same mix of tobacco.

Beginning in the late 80s, a move to consolidate the great number of companies in this business helped to reduce competition and yielded, by 1990, only these four major U.S. players (a reduction from approximately 50 to four major U.S. tobacco processors, all of whom engage in various other aspects of the industry in addition to processing [import/export, growing, etc.])—Dibrell Brothers, Universal Corporation, Standard Commercial, and A.C. Monk and Company. This rapid transformation in the industry arose from the increasing costs of machinery, the difficulties of competing with larger companies, and many other basic changes affecting the tobacco industry as a whole. This occurred at the same time as the tobacco companies' move to invest in nontobacco operations.

Today, these four companies comprise most of the business done in the United States and a substantial portion of the overseas processing business. They all sell to each of the major cigarette manufacturers, who bid on the products and distribute their purchasing decisions among them. No formal contracts exist, but certain lasting relationships do develop (e.g., between Dibrell and Philip Morris) that allow for a dependable and consistent exchange.

Attachment

Discussion with Mr. Stoltenberg, R.J. Reynolds Tobacco GmbH Cologne, Germany

December 6, 1994

I. The International Tobacco Trading Market

The present tobacco trading market is dominated worldwide by four major corporations, which engross nearly 80 percent of the entire traded volume: Universal Corporation, Dibrell Brothers (merging with A.C. Monk & Company to become Dimon Corporation), Standard Commercial, and the Zimbabwe-based Intabex Corporation. Smaller-sized corporations such as Austrian or BAT have significant market shares only in certain national or local markets.

Purchasing in the tobacco trading market can be categorized into four different types:

1. *Contractual cultivation* is when the tobacco traders have contract farmers at their disposal, where quantitative and qualitative minimum purchasing quotas are fixed. This arrangement is mainly to protect the smaller family-owned enterprises, which still dominate the overall picture of tobacco culturing. The European Union prescribes such arrangements for its tobacco traders. Contractual cultivation can be found in Italy, France, Germany, a few Eastern European countries, and Brazil.

2. Large *auctions*, where the buying teams of the large tobacco traders compete against one another for the goods under the supervision of the industry purchasing managers, dominate the scene in the United States of America, Canada, some countries in South America, and Zimbabwe.

3. In Turkey and Greece the dealers purchase—generally through a local agent—directly from the farmers without the binding requirements of long-term contractual agreements (so-called *free purchasing*).

4. Finally, some countries; such as, Japan, Korea, and Bulgaria, have *government monopolies* for the tobacco-growing sector, which are difficult negotiating partners and place exceptional stipulations on the international dealers.

The tobacco that is yet to be sold is generally classified into more than 160 different qualities. Recent developments reveal a trend toward placing certain processing facilities in the immediate vicinities of the tobacco crops, such as removal of foreign objects and sand, as well as leaf selection (picking), automated stripping, etc.

The market for unprocessed tobacco is to the most extent globalized; that is, there is a large interdependency between the different national markets. The large tobacco traders have therefore scattered their buying and sales activities in over 20 countries in every continent. In the course of the concentration process, the traders could extend their market power versus the smaller tobacco growers. The tobacco trade reveals a highly intensified global competitive nature—merely in the partial capital–intensive tobacco processing, we can discover long-term horizontal cooperation.

II. International Cigarette Market

Over 90 percent of all the tobacco on the world market falls into the hands of the cigarette industry, making the cigarette manufacturers the largest customer group to the tobacco traders. Similar to the trading level, we can detect a significant concentration process among the cigarette manufacturers as well. Only a few suppliers—mainly Philip Morris, BAT, and R.J. Reynolds—signify a representable global market presence. Moreover, there are voluminous numbers of competitors with sizable regional concentration. With only a few exceptions, these corporations concentrate (until now) on cigarette manufacturing and do not pursue a strategy of vertical integration on the value-added chain.

The cigarette manufacturers operating on a worldwide scale operate several large production facilities, where the various brands and/or tastes are produced for the respective global regions, such as Europe and the United States. Distribution of license production for defined regions is common. Regional R&D teams in Europe and the United States constantly watch the current market trends and develop success-promising locally tailored product innovations. Purchasing as well as blend selection are determined in general by the regional expert teams.

III. Relationship between Tobacco Traders and Cigarette Manufacturers

The relationship between the internationally active tobacco traders on the one hand and the cigarette manufacturers on the other are generally marked by long-term, very close and personal ties. Global sourcing is a commonly strong characteristic for the cigarette manufacturers when it comes to purchasing preprocessed raw tobacco.

1. The prevalent approach is for the tobacco trader to receive an order from the cigarette manufacturer specifying detailed raw qualities and specifications for the packaging. Therefore, the core of all traders' businesses consists of order bookings.

2. A less common approach is for the cigarette manufacturer to purchase the desired raw tobacco directly on the world market and to negotiate the respective conditions of sale.

3. At the so-called bidding (such as Indonesian bidding in Bremen or Cameroon bidding in Paris) the manufacturers place secret bids, which are fulfilled if they make the highest bid.

For each brand, every manufacturer has a preference as to which raw tobacco is used and a relatively constant quantity of it. It is not unusual for each cigarette brand to have a mixture of 30 to 50 different qualities of raw tobacco, which can strongly vary for the different countries in which it is sold. Due to the long-term relationships between the manufacturers and the tobacco traders—which includes frequent and intensive personal and technical know-how transfer—the traders are equipped with the necessary, voluminous customer-specific know-how. Provided with this knowledge and the fairly stable demand on quantity and quality of the tobacco, the tobacco traders can plan their purchasing activities efficiently and avoid accumulating high quantities of hard-to-sell stocks. Nevertheless, large speculations are still risked in the attempt to profit on acute interregional price and quantity trade-offs.

General Motors and AvtoVAZ of Russia

Michael Moffett
Thunderbird

Andrew Inkpen
Thunderbird

To compete on technology, you have to spend on it, but we have nothing to spend. Were there a normal economic situation in the country, people wouldn't be buying these cars.

—Vladimir Kadannikov, Chairman,
AvtoVAZ of Russia

There are 42 defects in the average new car from AvtoVAZ, Russia's biggest carmaker. And that counts as the good news. When the firm introduced a new model last year, a compact salon called the VAZ-2110, each car came with 92 defects—all the fun of the space station Mir, as it were, without leaving the ground.

—"Mir On Earth," *The Economist,*
August 21, 1997

In June 2001, David Herman, President of General Motors (GM) Russia, and his team arrived in Togliatti, Russia for joint venture negotiations between GM and OAO AvtoVAZ, the largest automobile producer in Russia. GM and AvtoVAZ had originally signed a memorandum of understanding (MOU)—a non-binding commitment—on March 3, 1999, to pursue a joint venture in Russia. Now, nearly two years later, Herman had finally received GM's approval to negotiate the detailed structure of the joint venture (JV) with AvtoVAZ to produce and sell Chevrolets in the Russian market.

The Russian car market was expected to account for a significant share of global growth over the next decade. Herman was increasingly convinced that if GM did not move decisively and soon, the market opportunity would be lost to other automakers. Ford, for example, was proceeding with a substantial JV in Russia and was scheduled to begin producing the Ford Focus in late 2002 (it was already importing car kits). Fiat of Italy was already in the construction phases of a plant to build 15,000 Fiat Palios per year beginning in late 2002. Daewoo of Korea had started assembly of compact sedan kits in 1998 and were currently selling 15,000 cars a year.

However, Herman also knew that doing business in Russia presented many challenges. The Russian economy, although recovering from the 1998 collapse, remained weak, uncertain, and subject to confusing tax laws and government rules. The Russian car industry seemed to reel from one crisis to another. The second largest automobile producer, GAZ, had been the victim of an unexpected hostile takeover only three months ago. GAZ's troubles had contributed to GM's fears over the actual ownership of AvtoVAZ itself. In addition, AvtoVAZ had been the subject of an aggressive income tax evasion case by Russian tax authorities in the summer of 2000. Finally, from a manufacturing point of view, AvtoVAZ was far from world class. AvtoVAZ averaged 320 man-hours to build a car a stark comparison against the 28 hours typical of Western Europe and 17 hours in Japan.

Further complicating the situation was a lack of consensus within different parts of GM about the Russian JV. GM headquarters in Detroit had told Herman to find a third party to share the risk and the investment of a Russian JV. Within Adam Opel, GM's European division, there were questions about the scope and timing of Opel's role. Prior to becoming GM's vice president for the former Soviet Union, Herman had been chairman of Adam Opel. He had been forced out of Opel after growing disagreements with Lou Hughes, vice president of GM's international operations, the unit that oversaw Opel. Hughes wanted Opel to lead the development of three global auto platforms, whereas Herman wished to keep Opel focused on recovering its once dominant position in Germany and Western Europe. Now, Herman needed Opel's support for the Russian JV and had to convince his former colleagues that the time was right to enter Russia. As he prepared for the upcoming negotiations, Herman knew there were many more battles to be fought both within GM and in Russia.

General Motors Corporation

General Motors Corporation (U.S.), founded in 1908, was the largest automobile manufacturer in the world. GM employed more than 388,000 people, operated 260 subsidiaries, affiliates, and joint ventures, managed operations in more than 50 countries, and closed the year 2000 with $160 billion in sales and $4.4 billion in profits.

John F. "Jack" Smith had been appointed Chairman of GM's Board of Directors in January 1996, after spending the previous five years as President

and Chief Executive Officer. Taking Jack Smith's place as President and CEO was G. Richard "Rick" Wagoner, Jr., previously the director of strategic and operational leadership within GM. GM's International Operations were divided into GM Europe, GM Asia Pacific, and GM Latin America, Africa, Middle-East. GM Europe, headquartered in Zurich, Switzerland, provided oversight for GM's various European operations including Opel of Germany and the new initiatives in Russia.

Although the largest automobile manufacturer in the world, GM's market share had been shrinking. By the end of 2000, GM's global market share (in units) was 13.6 percent, with the Ford group closing quickly with a 11.9 percent share, and Volkswagen a close third at 11.5 percent. Emerging markets, like that of Russia, represented so-called "white territories" which were still unclaimed and uncertain markets for the traditional Western automakers.

The Russian Automobile Industry

The Russian auto industry lagged far behind that of the Western European, North American, or Japanese industries. Although the Russian government had made it a clear priority to aid in the industry's modernization and development, inadequate capital, poor infrastructure, and deep-seated mismanagement and corruption resulted in outdated, unreliable, and unsafe automobiles.

Nevertheless, the industry was considered promising because of the continuing gap between Russian market demand and supply and because of expected future growth in demand. As illustrated in Exhibit 1, between 1991 and 1993 purchases of cars in Russia had grown dramatically. But this growth had been at the expense of domestic producers, as imports had garnered most of the increase in sales, largely because of a reduction in automobile import duties. With the reduction of import duties in 1993, imports surged to 49 percent of sales and Russian production hit the lowest level of the decade. Domestic producers reacted by increasing their focus on export sales, largely to former Commonwealth of Independent States (CIS)

EXHIBIT 1   The Russian Automobile Industry, 1991–2000 (units)

Russian Production	1991	1992	1993	1994	1995	1996	1997	1998	1999
AvtoVAZ	677,280	676,857	660,275	530,876	609,025	684,241	748,826	605,728	717,660
GAZ	69,000	69,001	105,654	118,159	118,673	124,284	124,339	125,398	125,486
AvtoUAZ	52,491	54,317	57,604	53,178	44,880	33,701	51,411	37,932	38,686
Moskovich	104,801	101,870	95,801	67,868	40,600	2,929	20,599	38,320	30,112
KamAZ	3,114	4,483	5,190	6,118	8,638	8,935	19,933	19,102	28,004
IzhMash	123,100	56,500	31,314	21,718	12,778	9,146	5,544	5,079	4,756
DonInvest	0	0	0	0	321	4,062	13,225	4,988	9,395
Other	14	14	6	7	1	41	3,932	3,061	1,307
Total	1,029,800	963,042	955,844	797,924	834,916	867,339	985,809	839,608	955,406
Percent change	−6.6%	−6.5%	−0.7%	−16.5%	4.6%	3.9%	13.7%	−14.8%	13.8%
Russian Exports	411,172	248,032	533,452	143,814	181,487	144,774	120,551	67,913	107,701
Percent of production	39.9%	25.8%	55.8%	18.0%	21.7%	16.7%	12.2%	8.1%	11.3%
Imports into Russia	26,649	43,477	405,061	97,400	69,214	54,625	42,974	62,718	55,701
Percent of sales	4.1%	5.7%	49.0%	13.0%	9.6%	7.0%	4.7%	7.5%	6.2%
Auto Sales in Russia	645,277	758,487	827,453	751,510	722,643	777,190	908,232	834,413	903,406
Percent growth	17.5%	9.1%	−9.2%	−3.8%	7.5%	16.9%	−8.1%	8.3%	

SOURCE: http://www.just-auto.com, February 2001.

countries. Exports ranged between 18 percent and 56 percent of all production during the 1991–1995 period.

With the reimposition of import duties in 1994, the import share of the Russian marketplace returned to a level of about seven to ten percent. Domestic production began growing again and fewer Russian-made cars were exported. Unfortunately, just as domestic producers were nearly back to early-1990s production levels, the 1998 financial crisis sent the Russian economy and auto industry into a tailspin. Domestic production of automobiles fell nearly 15 percent in 1998. Auto sales in Russia as a whole fell eight percent. The industry, however, experienced a strong resurgence in 1999 and 2000.

Russian auto manufacturing was highly concentrated, with AvtoVAZ holding a 65 percent market share in 2000, followed by GAZ with 13 percent, and an assorted collection of what could be called "boutique producers."[1] Although foreign producers accounted for less than two percent of all auto manufacturing in Russia in 2000, estimates of the influx of used foreign-made cars were upwards of 350,000 units in 2000 alone.

Although much had changed in Russian in the 1990s, much had also remained the same. In the Russian automobile market, demand greatly exceeded supply. Russians without the right political connections had to wait years for their cars. Cars were still rare, spare parts still difficult to find, and crime still rampant. It was still not unusual to remove windshield wipers for safekeeping from cars parked on major city streets. Cars had to be paid for in cash, as dealer financing was essentially unheard of as a result of the inability of the Russian financial and banking sector to perform adequate credit checks on individuals or institutions. And once paid for, most Russian-made new cars were full of defects to the point that repair was often required before a new car could be driven.

AvtoVAZ

It's mind-blowingly huge. The assembly line goes on for a mile and a quarter. Workstation after workstation. No modules being slapped in. It's piece by piece. The hammering is incessant. Hammering the gaskets in, hammering the doors down, hammering the bumpers. On the engine line a man seems to be screwing in pistons by hand and whopping them with a hammer. If there's a robot on the line, we didn't see it. Forget statistical process control.

—"Would You Want to Drive a Lada?"
Forbes, August 26, 1996

AvtoVAZ, originally called VAZ for Volzhsky Avtomobilny Zavod (Volga Auto Factory), was headquartered approximately 1,000 kilometers southeast of Moscow in Togliatti, a town named after an Italian communist. The original auto manufacturing facility was a JV (in effect, a pure turn-key operation) with Fiat of Italy. The original contract, signed in 1966, resulted in the first cars produced in 1970. The cars produced at the factory were distributed under the *Lada* and *Zhiguli* brands and for the next 20 years became virtually the only car the average Russian could purchase.

AvtoVAZ employed more than 250,000 people in 1999 (who were paid an average of $333 per month), and produced 677,700 cars, $1.9 billion in sales, and $458 million in gross profits. However, the company had a pre-tax loss of $123 million. AvtoVAZ was publicly listed on the Moscow Stock Exchange. The Togliatti auto plant, with an estimated capacity of 750,000 vehicles per year, was the largest single automobile assembly facility in the world. It had reached full capacity in 2000. But the company developed only one new car in the 1990s and had spent an estimated $2 billion doing so.

In the early 1990s, following the era of Perestroika and the introduction of economic reforms, AvtoVAZ began upgrading its technology and increasing its prices. As prices skyrocketed, Russians quickly switched to comparably priced imports of higher quality. As a result, AvtoVAZ suffered continual decreases in market share throughout the 1990s (see Exhibit 1), although it still dominated all other Russian manufacturers.

The financial crisis of August 1998 had actually bolstered AvtoVAZ's market position, with the fall of the rouble from Rbl 11/$ to over Rbl 25/$. Imports were now prohibitively expensive for most Russians.

It's cynical to say, but in the case of a devaluation, the situation at AvtoVAZ would be better. There would be a different effectiveness of export sales, and demand would be different. Seeing that money is losing value, people would buy durable goods in the hopes of saving at least something.

—Vladimir Kadannikov, Chairman
of the Board, AvtoVAZ, May 1998

In recent years, AvtoVAZ senior management had been discussing the development of a more modern car that could be exported to developed countries. This car, called the Kalina, would require an investment of as much as $850 million. AvtoVAZ Chairman Vladimir Kadannikov had stated publicly that he hoped commercial production of the Kalina could begin by 2004. He had also indicated that he was receptive to the Kalina being produced in a joint venture with an outsider automaker.

AvtoVAZ also suffered from tax problems and was called a "tax deadbeat" by the Russian press. In July 2000 the Russian Tax Police accused AvtoVAZ of tax fraud. The accusations centered on alleged under-reporting of automobile production by falsifying vehicle identification numbers (VINs), the basis for the state's assessment of taxes. The opening of the criminal case coincided with warnings from the Kremlin that the new administration of President Vladimir Putin would not tolerate continued industry profiteering and manipulation from the country's *oligarchs,* individuals who had profited greatly from Russia's difficult transition to market capitalism. AvtoVAZ denied the charges and less than one month later, the case was thrown out by the chief prosecutor for tax evasion. A spokesman for the prosecutor's office stated that investigators had found no basis for the allegations against Avto-VAZ executives.

AvtoVAZ Ownership

One of the primary deterrents to foreign investment in Russia had been the relatively lax legal and regulatory structure for corporate governance. Identifying the owners of most major Russian companies was extremely difficult.

Although much about the ownership of Avto-VAZ remained unclear, it was believed that two different management groups controlled the majority of AvtoVAZ shares. One group was led by the current Chairman, Vladimir Kadannikov, that held 33.2 percent of total shares through an organization he controlled, the All-Russian Automobile Alliance (AVVA). A second group, represented by a Mr. Yuri Zukster, controlled 19.2 percent through a different organization, the Automobile Finance Corporation (AFC). A Russian investment fund, Russ-Invest,

held 5 percent, with the remaining 42.6 percent under "undisclosed" ownership.

AvtoVAZ itself held an 80.8 percent interest in Kadannikov's AVVA Group, an investment fund. AVVA, in turn, held a 33.2 percent interest in Avto-VAZ (see Exhibit 2 for an overview of the complex relationships surrounding AvtoVAZ). AVVA itself was in some way influenced, controlled, or owned in part, by one of the most high-profile *oligarchs* in Russia, Boris Berezovsky.

In 1989, prior to the implementation of President Boris Yelstin's economic reforms, Boris Berezovsky, a mathematician and management-systems consultant to AvtoVAZ, persuaded Vladimir Kadannikov to cooperate in a new car distribution system. Berezovsky formed an automobile dealer network, LogoVAZ, that was supplied with Avto-VAZ vehicles on consignment. LogoVAZ did not pay for the cars it distributed (termed "re-export" by Berezovsky) until a date significantly after his dealer network sold the cars and received payment themselves. The arrangement proved disastrous for AvtoVAZ and incredibly profitable for Berezovsky. In the years that followed, hyperinflation raged in Russia, and Berezovsky was able to run his expanding network of businesses with AvtoVAZ's

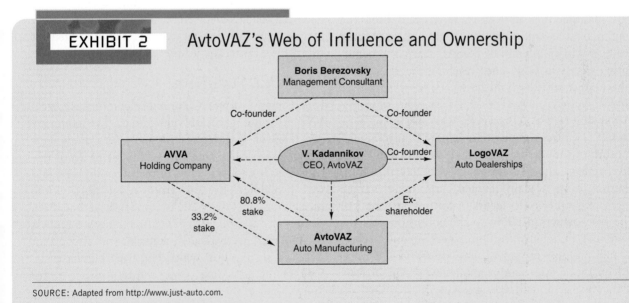

EXHIBIT 2 AvtoVAZ's Web of Influence and Ownership

SOURCE: Adapted from http://www.just-auto.com.

cash flow. (Mr. Berezovsky has admitted to the arrangement, and its financial benefits to him. He has also pointed out, correctly, that under Russian law he has not broken any laws.) LogoVAZ was also one of the largest auto importers in Russia.

In 1994, the Russian government began privatizing many state-owned companies, including AvtoVAZ. Boris Berezovsky, Vladimir Kadannikov, and Alexander Voloshin, recently appointed Chief of Staff for Russian President Vladimir Putin, then formed AVVA. The stated purpose of AVVA was to begin building a strong dealer network for the automobile industry in Russia. AVVA quickly acquired its 33.2 percent interest in AvtoVAZ, in addition to many other enterprises. AVVA frequently represented AvtoVAZ's significant international interests around the world.

By 2000, Berezovsky purportedly no longer had formal relations with AVVA but many observers believed he continued to have a number of informal lines of influence. In December 2000, AVVA surprised many analysts by announcing that it was amending its charter to change its status from an *investment fund* to a *holding company*. Auto analysts speculated that AVVA was positioning itself to run AvtoVAZ, which had reorganized into divisions (car production, marketing and sales, research and development).

Share ownership anxiety had intensified in November 2000 when the second largest automobile manufacturer in Russia, GAZ, had been the victim of a hostile takeover. Beginning in August 2000, Sibirsky Alyuminiy (SibAl) started accumulating shares in GAZ until reaching the 25 percent plus one share threshold necessary for veto power under Russian law. The exact amount of SibAl ownership in GAZ, however, was unknown, even to GAZ. Current regulations required only the disclosure of the identity and stake of stockholders of five percent equity stake or more. Only direct investors were actually named, and those named were frequently only agents operating on behalf of the true owners. Adding to the confusion was the fact that frequently the "nominees" named represented multiple groups of ultimate owners. The inadequacy of information about ownership in Russia was demonstrated by GAZ's inability to actually confirm whether SibAl did indeed have a 25 percent ownership position.

Rumors surfaced immediately that AvtoVAZ could be next, and the threat could arise from the Samara Window Company (abbreviated as SOK), AvtoVAZ's largest single supplier. Many industry players, however, viewed this as highly unlikely.

"Besides Kadannikov, the brass at AvtoVAZ tend to keep a low profile, but they still rank among Russia's elite executives, and they are independent," said an official of a foreign supplier in Russia. *"SOK may be powerful with AvtoVAZ, and AvtoVAZ may find SOK highly useful, but I doubt SOK ever could impact AvtoVAZ strategy, and I think SOK ultimately plays by rules set by AvtoVAZ."*

—"Domino Theory: AvtoVAZ
following GAZ falling to new owner?"
http://www.just-auto.com, December 12, 2000

Management of AvtoVAZ also felt they had an additional takeover defense, which strangely enough arose from their history of not paying corporate taxes. In 1997, as part of a settlement with Russian tax authorities on $2.4 billion in back taxes, AvtoVAZ gave the Russian tax authorities the right to 50 percent plus one share of AvtoVAZ if the firm failed—in the future—to make its tax payments. AvtoVAZ management now viewed this as their own version of a poison pill. If the target of a hostile takeover, management could stop paying taxes and the Russian government would take management control, defeating the hostile takeover.[2]

AvtoVAZ Suppliers

Unlike many former Communist enterprises, AvtoVAZ was not vertically integrated. The company depended on a variety of suppliers for components and subassemblies and an assortment of retail distributors. It had little control over its suppliers, and was prohibited by law from retail distribution. In recent years, AvtoVAZ's supplier base had been continually consolidated. The three biggest suppliers to AvtoVAZ were DAAZ, Plastik, and Avtopribor (see Exhibit 3), all of which had been purchased by SOK in the preceding years. *Sok* in Russian means "juice," but in the auto sector in Russia, the English-language joke was that SOK was SOKing-up the supplier industry.

EXHIBIT 3 — AvtoVAZ Suppliers Owned or Controlled by SOK

Supplier	Location	Parts
Avtopribor	Vladimir	clusters for instrument panels, gauges, speedometers
Avtosvet	Kirzhach	connectors, exterior and interior lights, reflectors, signals
DAAZ	Dimitrovgrad	electronics, lights, moldings, wheels
Osvar	Vyazniki	exterior and interior lights, reflectors, signals, warning lights
Plastik	Syzran	foam, plastics, sealants
Syzranselmash	Syzran	chemicals, headliners, sun visors, window lifters

SOURCE: http://www.just-auto.com.

Starting from a relatively small base, SOK had grown from a small glass window factory to a diversified enterprise of roughly $2 billion sales in 1999, with businesses that included bottled water, building construction, medical equipment, plastic parts and windows, and most recently, AvtoVAZ's largest supplier and retailer. Although SOK officially purchased only 8,000 cars per year for distribution from AvtoVAZ, it was purportedly selling over 40,000 cars per year. The difference was rumored to be cars assembled by SOK from kits exchanged with AvtoVAZ. AvtoVAZ, often short of cash, frequently paid taxes, suppliers, and management in cars.

Dealerships and Distribution

In the early 1990s hundreds of trading companies were formed around the company. Most trading companies would exchange parts and inputs for cars, straight from the factory, at prices 20 percent to 30 percent below market value. The trading companies then sold the cars themselves, capturing significant profit, while AvtoVAZ waited months for payment of any kind from the trading companies. The practice continued unabated in 1996 and 1997 because most of the trading companies were owned and operated by AvtoVAZ managers. Russian law did not prevent management from pursuing private interests related to their own enterprises.

Crime was also prevalent on the factory floor. Mobsters purportedly would enter the AvtoVAZ factory and take cars directly from the production lines at gunpoint. Buyers or distributors were charged $100 at the AvtoVAZ factory gates for protection. To quote one automobile distributor, "They were bandits. Nevertheless, they provided a service." By the fall of 1997 the intrusion of organized crime became so rampant that Kadannikov used Russian troops to clear the plant of thugs.

International Activities

AvtoVAZ was actually a multinational company, with significant international operations in addition to significant export sales.

As illustrated in Exhibit 4, in 1991 AvtoVAZ was exporting over 125,000 cars per year to the countries of the Soviet state. With the deconstruction of the old Soviet Union, sales plummeted to the now CIS countries as a result of the proliferation of weak currencies from country to country, as well as the imposition of new import duties at every border to Russia of 30 percent or more.[3] In the late 1990s, sales were essentially zero. Similarly, sales in the Baltic countries of Latvia, Lithuania, and Estonia had also essentially disappeared.

Brazil has been the site of substantial AvtoVAZ activity in the past decade, with starts and stops. AvtoVAZ had originally flooded the Brazilian market in 1990 with imports when the government

	1991	1992	1993	1994	1995	1996	1997	1998	1999
Baltic countries	8,392	3,895	3,325	590	8,832	2,648	1,101	716	487
CIS countries	126,440	42,900	19,644	4,491	1,601	1,074	962	108	331
Elsewhere	269,936	271,763	280,593	196,696	175,161	129,957	94,303	68,689	49,957
Total exports	404,768	318,558	303,562	201,777	185,594	133,679	96,366	69,513	50,775
Total sales	674,884	673,821	656,403	528,845	607,279	680,965	736,000	599,829	677,669
Export percentage	60%	47%	46%	38%	31%	20%	13%	12%	7%

NOTE: Figures indicate number of units sold.
SOURCE: http://www.just-auto.com.

of Brazil had opened it to imports. Despite 85 percent import duties, deeply discounted Ladas and Nivas sold well. However, in 1995, the Brazilian government excluded AvtoVAZ from a list of select international manufacturers which would be allowed much lower import duties. AvtoVAZ then withdrew from the Brazilian market. In November 2000, AvtoVAZ concluded the negotiation of an agreement with a Brazilian entrepreneur, Carlos de Moraes, for his company, Abeiva Car Imports, to begin assembly of Nivas in 2001. The target price, 17,000 Brazilian reais, about $8,900, would hopefully make them affordable for Brazilian farmers.

In the past decade, AvtoVAZ has exported to a variety of European countries as well, including Germany, Portugal, Spain, the United Kingdom, and Greece. These sales have typically been small special-order models of the Niva (diesel engines, Peugeot gas engines, etc.). Continued issues surrounding quality and reliability, however, had pushed the company toward an emerging market strategy. It was hoped that low-income markets such as Egypt, Ecuador, and Uruguay would reignite the export potential of the company. GM's strategy was based on extreme low prices to successfully penetrate local markets. (See Appendix 1–4.)

Foreign Entry into Russia

GM interest in Russia extended back to the 1970s when Opel had proposed shipping car kits to Moscow for assembly. The plan foundered because of GM concerns about quality control. In 1991, GM renewed its interest in Russia, once again opening talks with a number of potential JV partners. But after more than a decade, few deals had materialized.

In December 1996 GM opened a plant in Elabuga, Tatarstan, in a JV with Yelaz to assemble Chevrolet Blazers from imported kits (complete knockdown kits or CKDs). The original plan had been to ramp up production volumes rapidly to 50,000 units a year. But the operation struggled. One problem was the product; the Blazers were two-wheel drive with 2.2-liter engines. The Russian consumer wanted the four-wheel-drive version widely sold in the United States, typically powered by a 3-liter engine. A second problem was the origin of the kits. The CKDs were imported from Brazil and most Russians did not have a high degree of respect for Brazilian products.

In September 1998 operations were suspended as a result of the Russian financial crisis. Only 3,600 units had been assembled. An attempt was made to restart assembly operations in 1999, this time assembling Opel Vectras, but when it became apparent that the market for a vehicle costing $20,000 would not succeed in the needed volumes, the JV's assembly operations were closed. GM still had over 200 Blazers in inventory in January 2001 and was attempting to close out the last vestiges of the operation.

EXHIBIT 5   Foreign Auto Producers in Russia

Foreign Manufacturer	Russian Partner	Auto Model	Target Price Range	Capacity per year	Expected Startup
Daewoo (Korea)	Doninvest	Compact	$6,000–$8,000	20,000	1998
BMW (Germany)	Avtotor	523,528	$36,000–$53,000	10,000	2000
Renault (France)	City of Moscow	Megane	$8,500–$13,500	100,000	1998
Ford (USA)	Bankirsky Dom	Focus	$13,000–$15,000	25,000	2002
Fiat (Italy)	GAZ	Palio, Siena	$7,000–$10,000	15,000	2002
GM (USA)	AvtoVAZ	Niva, T3000	$7,500–$10,000	75,000	2002

There were a number of foreign automobile producers in various stages of entry into the Russian marketplace, as summarized in Exhibit 5. Daewoo of Korea, which had made major volume achievements in a number of former Eastern Block countries such as Poland, had begun assembly of compact sedan kits in 1998, and had quickly reached a sales level in Russia of 15,000 units in 1999. Similarly, Renault of France had followed the kit assembly entry strategy with the Renault Megane in 1998, but had only assembled and sold 1,100 units by end of year 1999.

Others, like Ford Motor Company of the United States, had announced JVs with Russian manufacturers to actually build automobiles in Russia. The Ford Focus, priced on the relatively high side at $13,000 to $15,000, was planned for a production launch in late 2002. The facility planned was to produce 25,000 cars per year. The Russian government had given its blessing to the venture by allowing the elimination of import duties on imported inputs as long as the local content of the Focus reached 50 percent within five years of startup (2007 under current plans). Ford was already importing the Focus to begin building a market, but in the early months of 2001, sales were sluggish.

Fiat of Italy was potentially the most formidable competitor. Fiat planned to introduce the Fiat Palio and Fiat Siena into the Russian marketplace through a JV with GAZ in 2002. Although the planned capacity of the plant was only 15,000 cars per year, the Fiat Palio was considered by many auto experts as the right product for the market. The critical question was whether Fiat could deliver the Palio to the market at a low enough price. In its negotiations with the Russian government, Fiat announced its intentions to make the Palio a true Russian-made automobile which would quickly rise to over 70 percent in local content. If Fiat could indeed achieve this, and there were many who believed that if anyone could it was Fiat, then this would be the true competitive benchmark.

Renewed Interest

For most Russians, price was paramount. The average income levels in Russia prevented automobile pricing at Western levels. As seen in Exhibit 6, prices over the past few years had dropped as a result of the 1998 financial crisis. For 2001, analysts estimated that almost the entire market in Russia was for cars priced below $10,000. Given that the average Russian's salary was about $100 per month, cars remained out of reach for the average Russian.

In a September 2000 interview, David Herman summarized GM's viewpoint on pricing and positioning:

We could not make an interesting volume with a base price above $10,000. Such a vehicle would feature few specifications—ABS [anti-lock braking systems] and airbags plus a 1.6-liter 16-valve engine. But, if the car costs $12,000, it is only $2,000 less than certain foreign imports, and this gap may be too small to generate enough sales to justify a factory. We knew we could make a vehicle cheaper with AvtoVAZ, but we need to ensure the price advantage of T3000 imports over competitive models is closer to $7,000 than $2,000.[4]

EXHIBIT 6

Russian Auto Market Shares by Price

Price Range	1998		1999	
	Seg	Cum	Seg	Cum
Below $5,000	3%	3%	85%	85%
$5,001–$10,000	65%	68%	12%	97%
$10,001–$15,000	15%	83%	1%	98%
Above $15,000	17%	100%	2%	100%

NOTE: Seg = segment, cum = cumulative.
SOURCE: General Motors.

GM had originally considered the traditional emerging market approach of building complete cars in existing plants and then disassembling them by removing bumpers, wheels, and other separable parts, shipping the disassembled "kit" into Russia, and reassembling with local labor. The disassembly/assembly process allowed the automobile to be considered domestically produced by Russian authorities, thereby avoiding prohibitive import duties. The market assessment group at GM, however, believed that Russian buyers (as opposed to customs officials) would see through the ruse and consider the cars high-quality imports. But marketing research indicated the opposite: Russians did not want to buy cars reassembled by Russians. The only way they would purchase a Russian-made automobile was if it was extremely cheap, like the majority of the existing AvtoVAZ and GAZ product lines, which retailed for as little as $3,000 per car. GM, realizing that it could not deliver the reassembled Opel to the Russian marketplace for less than $15,000 per car, dropped the kit proposal.

GM's marketing research unveiled an additional critical element. Russians would gladly pay an additional $1,000 to $1,500 per car if it had a *Chevrolet* label or badge on it. This piece of research resulted in the original proposal that David Herman and his staff had been pursuing since early 1999: a two-stage JV investment with AvtoVAZ that would allow GM to both reach price targets and position the firm for expected market growth. In the first stage, GM would co-produce a four-wheel-drive sport utility vehicle named the Lada Niva II (VAZ-2123). The target price was $7500 and plant capacity was to be 90,000 cars. The Niva II would be largely Russian-engineered and, therefore GM would avoid many of the development costs associated with the introduction of a totally new vehicle. The Lada Niva I had originally been introduced in 1977 and updated in new models in 1990 and again in 1996. It had been a successful line for AvtoVAZ, averaging 70,000 units per year throughout the 1990s.[5] Since the Niva II was largely Russian-engineered, GM would bring capital and name to the venture.

The second stage of the project would be the construction of a new factory to produce 30,000 Opel Astras (T3000) for the Russian market. Herman's proposal was for AvtoVAZ to use a basic Opel AG vehicle platform as a pre-engineering starting point. Pre-engineering represented about 30 percent of the development cost of a vehicle. The remaining 70 percent would be developed by AvtoVAZ's 10,000 engineers and technicians who worked at a much lower cost than Opel's engineers in Germany. Herman's Russian Group estimated that even if GM and AvtoVAZ used AvtoVAZ's factory to build the existing Opel Astra from mostly imported parts and kits from Germany, the resulting price tag would have to fall to between $12,500 and $14,000 per car. This was still considered too expensive for substantial economic volumes. Using the Russian engineering approach, the car would be cheaper, but still fall at the higher end of the spectrum, retailing at about $10,000 per car. As seen in Exhibit 5, this would still put the higher-priced Chevrolet in the lower end of the foreign-made market.

By no means was there consensus within GM and Opel about the viability of the proposed JV. One concern was that as a result of the cash shortage at AvtoVAZ and the slow rate of negotiation progress, in order to build test-models of the new Niva, AvtoVAZ had to use 60 percent of the old Niva's parts. Although many of the consumers that tested the Niva II ranked it above all other Russian-built cars, the car was rough riding and noisy by Western standards. One Opel engineer from Germany who safety-tested the Niva II and evaluated its performance declared it "a real car, if primitive." Heidi McCormack, General Director for GM's Russian operations, believed that with some minor engineering adjustments, better materials for the interior construction, and a new factory built and operated by GM, the quality of the Niva II would be "acceptable."

GM management was pleased AvtoVAZ appeared willing to contribute the rejuvenated Niva to the JV. "That's their brand new baby," said McCormack. "It's been shown in auto shows. And here's GM, typical big multinational, saying, 'Just give us your best product.'"[6] But in the end, AvtoVAZ's limited access to capital was the driver. Without GM, AvtoVAZ would probably take five years to get the Niva II to market; with GM the time could be cut in half.

Negotiations

Negotiations between AvtoVAZ and GM had taken a number of twists and turns over the years, involving every possible dimension of the project. The JV's *market strategy, scope, timing, financing,* and *structure* were all under continual debate. GM's team was led by David Herman.

Herman had been appointed Vice President of General Motors Corporation for the former Soviet Union in 1998. Starting with General Motors Treasury as an attorney in 1973, Herman had extensive international experience, including three years as GM's Manager of Sales Development in the USSR (1976–1979), and other Managing Director positions in Spain (1979–1982), Chile (1982–1984), and Belgium (1986–1988). These were followed by Chief Executive positions for GM (Europe) in Switzerland and Saab Automobile. From 1992 to 1998, Herman had been Chairman and Managing Director of Adam Opel in Germany. Herman's departure from Opel in Germany was purportedly the result of losing a highly publicized internal battle over the future strategic direction of Opel. Herman had argued that Opel should focus on developing product for the domestic market, while others in the organization argued that Opel should focus on "filling the pipeline for GM's ambitions in emerging markets." Many have characterized his new appointment as head of GM's market initiatives in Russia as a Siberian exile. Herman's parents were Belorussian and he had studied Russian at Harvard. In addition to Russian and English, he was also fluent in German and Spanish.

Market Strategy

Back in Detroit, the JV proposal continued to run into significant opposition. GM President Rick Wagoner continued to question whether the Russian market could actually afford the Opel-based second car, the Opel T3000. Wagoner wondered whether the second phase of the project should not be cut, making the Niva the single product which the JV would produce. This could potentially reduce GM's investment to $100 million.

A further point of debate concerned exports sales. As a result of the 1998 financial crisis in Russia, a number of people inside both GM and AvtoVAZ pushed for a JV which would produce a car designed for both Russian sales and export sales. After 1998 the weaker Russian rouble meant that Russian exports were more competitive. If the product quality was competitive for the targeted markets, there was a belief that Russian cars could be profitably exported. As a result, Herman expanded his activities to include export market development. The working proposal now assumed that one-third of all the Chevrolet Nivas produced would be exported. The domestic market continued to be protected with a 30 percent import duty against foreign-made automobiles, both new and used.

Herman brought AvtoVAZ senior management to the Detroit auto show in the spring of 2000 to meet with GM President Rick Wagoner and Vice Chairman Harry Pearce. The meetings went well. In March 2000, however, GM announced an alliance with Fiat. A key element of the alliance involved GM acquiring 20 percent of Fiat's automotive business. GM paid $2.4 billion using GM common stock for the 20 percent stake, which resulted in Fiat owning 5.1 percent of GM. In June 2000, GM and Fiat submitted a joint bid for Daewoo, which was part of the bankrupt Daewoo *chaebol*. The bid was rejected. Herman returned to Russia, once again slowing negotiations until any possible overlap between GM and Fiat ambitions in Russia were resolved.

Timing

In the summer of 1999, AvtoVAZ had formally announced the creation of a JV with General Motors to produce Opel Astras and the Chevrolet Niva. However, this announcement was not confirmed by GM. Later in 1999, GM's European management, primarily via the Opel division, lobbied heavily within GM to postpone the proposed Chevrolet Niva launch until 2004 to allow a longer period of economic recovery in Russia. Upon learning of this, Kadannikov reportedly told GM to "keep its money," that AvtoVAZ would launch the new Niva on its own. The two sides were able to agree on a tentative 2003 launch date.

Financing

In May 2000 Herman's presentation of the JV proposal of Wagoner and Pearce in Detroit hit another roadblock: the proposed $250 million investment was considered "too large and too risky for a market as risky as Russia—with a partner as slippery as AvtoVAZ."[7] Wagoner instructed Herman to find a third party to share the capital investment and the risk, as GM would not risk more than $100 million itself. Within three months Herman found a third party—the European Bank for Reconstruction and Development (EBRD). EBRD was willing to provide debt and equity. It would lend $93 million to the venture and invest an additional $40 million for an equity stake of 17 percent.[8] (See Appendix 6.)

The European Bank for Reconstruction and Development was established in 1991 with express purpose of fostering the transition to open market-oriented economies and promoting private and entrepreneurial ventures in Eastern Europe and the Commonwealth of Independent States (CIS). As a catalyst of change the Bank seeks to co-finance with firms that are providing foreign direct investment (FDI) in these countries in order to help mobilize domestic capital and reduced the risks associated with FDI. Recent economic reforms and the perceived stability of President Putin's government had convinced the EBRD's senior management that conditions were right.

GM management knew that $332 million would be insufficient to build a state-of-the-art manufacturing facility. However, given that AvtoVAZ contributions would include the design, land, and production equipment, $332 million was believed to be sufficient to launch the new Niva. The planned facility would include a car body paint shop, assembly facilities, and testing areas. AvtoVAZ would supply the JV with the car body, engine and transmission, chassis units, interior components, and electrical system.

Structure

A continuing point of contention was where the profits of the JV would be created. For example, AvtoVAZ had consistently quoted a price for cement for the proposed plant which was thought to be about ten times what GM would customarily pay in Germany. Then, just prior to the venture's going before the GM Board for preliminary approval for continued negotiations, AvtoVAZ made a new and surprising demand that GM increase the price the JV would pay AvtoVAZ for Niva parts by 25 percent. (Vladimir Kadannikov demanded to know where the profits would be, "in the price of the parts each side supplied to the joint venture or in the venture itself?").[9] When Herman warned them this would scuttle the deal, AvtoVAZ backed off. After heated debate, the two parties now agreed that they would not try to profit from the sale of components to the JV.

The structure for the management team and specific allocation of managerial responsibilities had yet to be determined. Although both sides expected to be actively involved in day-to-day management, GM had already made it clear that management control of the JV was a priority for going forward. GM also wanted to minimize the number of expatriate managers assigned to the venture. AvtoVAZ saw the JV as an opportunity for its managers to gain valuable experience and expected to have significant purchasing, assembly, and marketing responsibilities. AvtoVAZ expected GM to develop and support an organizational structure that ensured technology transfer to the JV. AvtoVAZ knew that in China GM had created a technical design center as a separate JV with its Chinese partner. The specific details as to how GM might be compensated for technology transfer to Russia remained unclear. Finally, the issue of who would control the final documentation for the JV agreement had yet to be agreed.

The JV would be located on the edge of the massive AvtoVAZ complex in Togliatti. It would utilize one factory building which was partially finished and previously abandoned. The building already housed much equipment in various operational states, including expensive plastic molding and cutting tools imported from Germany in the early 1990s which AvtoVAZ had been unable to operate effectively but could not resell.

Progress

Again, primarily out of frustration with the pace of negotiations, AvtoVAZ announced in January 2001 that it would begin small-scale production of a SUV under its own Lada brand. Herman once again was able to intervene. Herman promised GM's Board that AvtoVAZ would actually build no more than a few dozen of the SUVs "for show." The two sides also continued to debate whether AvtoVAZ would be allowed to sell the prototypes of the new Niva that AvtoVAZ planned to build (approximately 500). GM was adamant, according to long-standing policy, that these should not find their way to the marketplace. AvtoVAZ countered that this was routine for Russian manufacturers and served as a type of "test fleet."

Finally, on February 6, 2001, Herman presented the current proposal to GM's board in Detroit. After heated debate, the board approved the proposal. The possibility of entering a large and developing market, with shared risk and investment, was a rare opportunity to get in early and develop a new local market. According to Rick Wagoner, "Russia's going to be a very big market."

> We'll sell it in former Soviet Union, and eventually export it and because of the cost of material and labor in Russia, we should reach a price point which gives us a decent volume. That will give us a chance to get a network and get started with suppliers and other partners in Russia in a way which I hope will make us amongst the leaders.[10]

David Herman had gained the approval of the General Motors Board to pursue and complete negotiations with AvtoVAZ. The negotiations themselves, however, represented an enormous undertaking, and both GM and AvtoVAZ had many issues yet to be resolved. The two sides at the negotiating table in June included David Herman and Heidi McCormack of GM Russia and Vladimir Kadannikov and Alexei Nikolaev representing AvtoVAZ.

Notes

1. Other Russian auto manufacturers included KAMAZ, Roslada, SeAZ, IzhMash, and DonInvest.
2. The Russian government was not, however, anxious for this series of events to unfold. It would also mean that AvtoVAZ would be entering an 18-month period in which it paid no taxes whatever to the government if the option were exercised by the Tax Police.
3. AvtoVAZ did attempt to restart CIS sales in 1997 with the introduction of hard-currency contracts. The governments of Uzbekistan, Byelorussia, and Ukraine, however, forbid residents from converting local currency into hard currency for the purpose of purchasing automobiles (in two cases, specifically the product of AvtoVAZ). AvtoVAZ accused the authorities in these countries of working in conjunction with Daewoo of Korea, who had production facilities in Uzbekistan and the Ukraine, to shut them out.
4. "Exclusive Interview: David Herman on GM's Strategy for Russia," http://www.just-auto.com, September 2000.
5. One of the primary reasons for the success of the Niva was the poor state of Russian roads. The four-wheel-drive Niva handled the pot-holed road infrastructure with relative ease.
6. Gregory L. White, "Off Road: How the Chevy Name Landed on SUV Using Russian Technology," *Wall Street Journal,* February 20, 2001.
7. *Wall Street Journal,* February 20, 2001.
8. The willingness of EBRD to invest was a bit surprising given that two of its previous investments with Russian automakers, GAZ and KamAZ, had resulted in defaults on EBRD credits. A third venture in which EBRD was still a partner (20 percent equity), Nizhegorod Motors, a JV between Fiat and GAZ, had delayed its car launch from late 1998 to the first half of 2002.
9. *Wall Street Journal,* February 21, 2001.
10. "David Herman on GM's Strategy for Russia," http://www.just-auto.com, September 2000.

OAO AvtoVAZ Profit and Loss Statement, 1996–1999

(Thousands of roubles)	1996	1997	1998	Jan–Oct 1999
Net sales less VAT	23,697,167	26,255,183	9,533,172	33,834,987
Less cost of goods sold	(18,557,369)	(21,552,999)	(7,650,161)	(25,998,011)
Gross profits	5,139,798	4,702,184	1,883,011	7,836,976
Gross margin	21.7%	17.9%	19.8%	23.2%
Less sales & marketing expenses	(638,739)	(497,540)	(168,381)	(603,170)
Operating income	4,501,059	4,204,644	1,714,630	7,233,806
Operating margin	19.0%	16.0%	18.0%	21.4%
Interest	—	—	—	—
Dividend income	3,366	3,392	159	8,749
Income on asset disposal	3,084,203	23,052,035	2,516,466	4,115,346
Loss on asset disposal	(3,935,990)	(21,718,864)	(3,430,751)	(5,716,732)
Income from core business	3,652,638	5,541,207	800,504	5,641,169
Non-operating income	400,185	372,340	69,415	252,713
Non-operating expenses	(1,136,225)	(1,033,305)	(299,123)	(1,124,448)
Income for period	2,916,598	4,880,242	570,796	4,769,434
Less income tax	(682,556)	(1,166,911)	(77,268)	(1,112,039)
Disallowable expenses	(409,906)	(7,069,333)	(251,574)	(1,674,947)
Net income	1,824,136	(3,356,002)	396,490	1,982,448
Return on sales (ROS)	7.7%	−12.8%	4.2%	5.9%
In U.S. dollars				
Exchange rate (roubles/U.S. $)	5.6	6.0	9.7	24.6
Net sales	$4,231,636,964	$4,375,863,833	$982,801,237	$1,375,405,976
Gross profits	917,821,071	783,697,333	194,124,845	318,576,260
Income from core business	652,256,786	923,534,500	82,526,186	229,315,813
Income for period	520,821,071	813,373,667	58,844,948	193,879,431
Net income	325,738,571	(559,333,667)	40,875,258	80,587,317

SOURCE: AvtoVAZ.

AvtoVAZ Product Prices by City (February 2001, in roubles)

Code	Model	Type	Tolyatti	Moscow	St. Petersburg
21060	Lada Classic	1976 sedan	84,100	86,500	90,100
2107	Lada Classic	1982 sedan	86,700	91,700	94,400
21083	Lada Samara	1985 3-door hatch	111,900	117,500	115,800
21093	Lada Samara	1987 5-door hatch	112,200	119,700	115,800
21099	Lada Samara	1990 sedan	122,500	132,000	132,600
21102	Lada 2110	1996 sedan	146,500	150,700	151,700
21103	Lada 2110	1997 station wagon	161,100	164,800	162,300
21110	Lada 2110	1999 5-door hatch	157,200	161,900	168,900
2112	Lada Samara II	2001 3-door hatch	167,300	168,600	168,300
2115	Lada Samara II	1997 sedan	143,000	153,700	149,600
21213	Lada Niva	1997 SUV	103,500	111,300	111,100
Average (roubles)			126,909	132,582	123,582
Exchange rate (roubles/U.S. $)			30.00	30.00	30.00
Average (U.S. $)			$4,230	$4,419	$4,111

SOURCE: AvtoVAZ.

Russian Demographics and Economics, 1993–2005

Indicator	1993	1994	1995	Actual 1996	1997	1998	1999
Real GDP growth (%)	−8.7%	−12.7%	−4.1%	−3.5%	−0.8%	−4.9%	3.2%
GDP per capita (U.S. $)	1,135	1,868	2,348	2,910	3,056	1,900	1,260
Consumer price index (%chg)	875%	308%	198%	48%	15%	28%	86%
External debt (bill U.S. $)	112.7	119.9	120.4	125.0	123.5	183.6	174.3
Foreign direct investment (bill U.S. $)	na	0.5	0.7	0.7	3.8	1.7	0.8
Population (millions)	148.2	148.0	148.1	147.7	147.1	146.5	146.0
Unemployment rate (%)	5.3%	7.0%	8.3%	9.3%	10.8%	11.9%	12.5%
Wage (U.S. $/hour)						0.63	0.36
Exchange rate (roubles/U.S. $)	1.2	3.6	4.6	5.6	6.0	9.7	24.6

(continued)

APPENDIX 3 Russian Demographics and Economics, 1993–2005 (continued)

Indicator	2000	2001	Estimates 2002	2003	2004	2005
Real GDP growth (%)	5.8%	3.5%	4.0%	4.0%	4.5%	4.2%
GDP per capita (U.S. $)	1,560	1,760	1,970	2,170	2,390	2,610
Consumer price index (%chg)	21%	17%	14%	12%	11%	8%
External debt (bill U.S. $)	160.6	171.2	176.8	182.8	186.2	188.8
Foreign direct investment (bill U.S. $)	2.0	4.0	5.7	6.5	6.5	6.5
Population (millions)	145.4	145.1	144.8	144.5	144.2	143.2
Unemployment rate (%)	10.8%	10.1%	10.1%	9.8%	9.2%	9.1%
Wage (U.S. $/hour)	0.44	0.52	0.60	0.70	0.80	0.90
Exchange rate (roubles/U.S. $)	28.4	30.5	32.0	33.5	35.0	36.0

SOURCE: Economist Intelligence Unit, February 2001.

APPENDIX 4 Foreign Automobile Manufacturers & Russian Partners in Russia

Manufacturer/ Partner	Model	Price Range Low	High	Capacity per year	Startup
Daewoo	Compact sedan	$6,000	$8,000	20,000	1998 Assembly
Doninvest					
BMW Group	523 & 528 models	$36,450	$53,010	10,000	2000 Assembly
ZAO Avtotor					
Renault	Clio Symbol	$8,500	$9,000	$100,000	1998 Assembly
City of Moscow	Megane	$13,500	$16,000	3,000	2002 Assembly
Ford Motor Co	Focus	$13,000	$15,000	25,000	2002 Staged
ZAO Bankirsky Dom	to >50% local in 5 yrs				
Fiat SpA	Palio	$9,000	$10,000	10,000	2002 Production
OAO Gaz	Siena	$10,000	$11,000	5,000	
General Motors	New Niva	$7,500	$10,000	75,000	2002 Production
OAO AvtoVAZ	Astra T3000	$10,000	$12,000		

SOURCE: Compiled by authors.

APPENDIX 5 Russian Automobile Sales Forecasts by Scenario, 2000–2008 (millions)

Scenario	2000	2001	2002	2003	2004	2005	2006	2007	2008
Optimistic	1.317	1.387	1.439	1.498	1.538	1.560	1.615	1.650	1.710
Moderate	1.045	1.131	1.232	1.288	1.315	1.368	1.483	1.500	1.570
Pessimistic	1.017	1.090	1.099	1.125	1.145	1.153	1.174	1.191	1.135

SOURCE: http://www.just-auto.com, September 2000. Average annual growth rates by Scenario: 3.3%, 5.2%, and 1.4%, respectively.

EBRD's Commitment to the GM-VAZ Joint Venture, Russia

The EBRD proposes to provide financing for the construction and operation of a factory to manufacture and assemble up to 75,000 Niva vehicles in Togliatti, Russia.

Operation Status: Signed   **Board Review Date:** 28 March 2000

Business Sector: Motor vehicle manufacturing Portfolio Classification: Private sector

The Client: General Motors—AvtoVAZ Joint Venture is a closed joint-stock company to be created under Russian law specifically for the purpose of carrying out the project. Once the investment is complete, AvtoVAZ (VAZ) and General Motors (GM) will hold an equal share in the venture. GM is currently the world's top automotive manufacturer with production facilities in 50 countries and 388,000 employees worldwide. VAZ is the largest producer of vehicles in Russia, having sold approximately 705,500 (over 70 percent of the Russian new car market) in 2000.

Proposed EBRD Finance: The EBRD proposes to provide up to 41 percent of the financing of the venture in a combination of a loan of US$100 million (€108 million) and an equity investment of US$40 million (€43 million). The loan includes interest during the construction phase. Up to US$38 million of the loan may be syndicated after signing to reduce EBRD exposure.

Total Project Cost: US$338 million (€365 million)

Project Objectives: The construction and operation of a factory to manufacture and assemble up to 75,000 Niva vehicles per annum in Togliatti, Russia.

Expected Transition Impact: The transition impact potential of this transaction stems primarily from the demonstration effects associated with the entrance of a major Western strategic investor into the Russian automotive market. The fact that this investment has two well-known partners who are investing equally in the joint venture adds both to the visibility and the potential of the project. This complex project is one of the largest examples of foreign direct investment in post-crisis Russia in a period when many foreign investors are still adopting a wait and see approach. The use of Russian design and engineering skills together with the introduction of Western technologies, methods and processes and the related development of skills are further key sources of positive demonstration effect, especially given the huge modernization needs of the Russian automotive sector. Other suppliers and client companies will also benefit from technological links or training programs with the joint venture.

Environmental Impact: The project was screened B/1, requiring an audit of the existing facility and an analysis of the impact associated with the joint venture (JV). While typical environmental issues associated with heavy manufacturing are present at the main AvtoVAZ facility, there have been no prior operations at the site of the proposed JV. Potential liabilities arising from historic soil and ground water pollution were addressed as part of the due diligence, and no significant levels of contamination have been identified. The engine for the new Niva will meet Euro II (Russian market) and Euro IV (European market) standards for vehicle emissions. All vehicles will be fitted with catalytic converters. Safety standards for all vehicles will meet EU and GM standards in full. On formation, the JV will adopt GM management and operations systems and GM corporate practices for all aspects of environment, health and safety and will be in compliance with all applicable EU and best international environmental standards.

SOURCE: http://www.ebrd.com/english/opera/psd/psd2001/483gm.htm.

Gold Star Properties: Financial Crisis

Joseph J. DiStefano
International Institute for Management Development

In November 2000, after weathering the worst of the Asian financial crisis, Joseph, Zhang Jinfu, financial director of Gold Star Properties, was conferring with William Cheng, the managing director of the company, prior to the executive directors' meeting scheduled for the next day. They had developed a strategy for stretching the firm's scarce cash to meet the requirements for operations and debt repayment in the coming months. Now they had to sell their approach to the technical director and their other colleagues on the executive board.

Background

Gold Star Properties had started as a small construction company during the early growth period in Hong Kong back in the early 1970s. Gold Star enjoyed steady success over the next three decades and grew in size and reputation. By the 1990s it was a sizable organization with a very good reputation in the construction industry in Hong Kong. As it had grown as a main contractor, Gold Star had outsourced most of its work to smaller subcontractors, which had grown along with Gold Star. The

most valuable assets of the company were its staff of experienced engineers and quantity surveyors.

Decision to Diversify in Property—and Its Aftermath

As the company built its financial success and took part in the boom of the mid-1990s in Hong Kong, the directors decided to diversify the company's activities from the core business of construction by making related investments in a wide range of properties throughout mainland China. As the People's Republic of China had opened up to investment and economic development, Gold Star had developed good relationships with key government officials when it took on several construction contracts in the mainland, starting with the expansion of factories and related infrastructure (such as the toll road) in the Guangdong area adjoining Hong Kong.

Between 1994 and 1997, largely employing funds borrowed from Hong Kong–based financial institutions, the company made property investments, primarily in Shanghai, Beijing, Chengdu, Chong-

Professor Joseph J. DiStefano prepared this case as a basis for class discussion rather than to illustrate either effective or ineffective handling of a business situation.

The cooperation of an anonymous business executive is gratefully acknowledged. Names of people, companies, and mainland cities have been disguised.

ching, and Hainan. Unfortunately, immediately after this investment expansion, the Asian financial crisis struck with full force, starting with Thailand's devaluation in mid-1998. This hit the property industry particularly hard and most of the companies in which Gold Star had recently invested were struggling to make ends meet. To make matters worse, the banks that had been so generous loaning capital in boom times were now calling in loans. Gold Star was servicing debt of HK$800 million,[1] which the banks indicated they would not roll over when it matured in the coming months. In order to survive, Gold Star turned its attention back to its core business in construction.

However, by 2000 the construction business was in rapid decline as large projects left over from the boom were being completed and planned construction was put on hold. Competition was fierce and had driven margins down to around three percent. With such small margins, the company was struggling to maintain its operations and still repay its debt. Joseph, Zhang Jinfu had failed in his attempts to convince Gold Star's bankers to roll over the maturing loan. He had also sought, in vain, new funds. Many of the foreign banks, particularly those from Japan whose head offices were having serious problems of their own, had called in their loans and pulled out of Hong Kong. In addition to causing crises for their own customers, this development, combined with the general decline, meant that capital was in short supply. Gold Star, with its own financial performance deteriorating, was therefore forced to find alternative sources of cash.

Decision to Divest

In early 2000, with the company feeling the cash squeeze and the situation projected to worsen by mid-year, William Cheng, in discussion with Joseph's predecessor, had decided to divest its investments in a power plant in Chongching, a prized entertainment complex in Chengdu, and a five-star hotel in Shanghai. The executive committee approved the sale, which was expected to generate about HK$900 million. They planned to use the proceeds to increase working capital and repay the matured debt. Since the end of the first quarter of 2000, Gold Star had been trying to close the deals

and realize the proceeds from the sales. But between the bureaucracy of the mainland officials and the market slump, the company had been unable to recover the money. Halfway through the final quarter of the year William and Joseph met again to assess the probabilities of getting the cash by year-end. Despite the good relationships they had with the mainland officials, they were not optimistic. So they concluded that it was time to decide how to deal with the crisis, which they expected to peak in the first quarter of 2001.

The People

William Cheng joined Gold Star Properties in 1998 as managing director. He was from China, had a civil engineering degree and was experienced in construction. He was hired for a combination of his knowledge of the industry and his experience with senior PRC officials.

Joseph, Zhang Jinfu, had adopted the English name of Joseph when he started traveling in the West in the early 1990s. He had joined Gold Star in January 2000 as assistant finance director and took over as director when his predecessor resigned in September. Prior to coming to Hong Kong, he had earned his doctorate in engineering at Shanghai Jiao Tong University and joined The Industry Investment Corporation of China as a project director. Two years later he was promoted to deputy divisional director. In 1994 Joseph joined The Industry Bank of China and gained experience in finance. In 1996 he transferred to the bank's international business department, where he took charge of the credit division and was responsible for client lending and borrowing from foreign banks. He moved to Hong Kong in late 1999.

Eric Osborne, the technical director, was from England. He was an experienced architect with an exceptional knowledge of the engineering aspects of construction. He was the longest-serving member of the executive committee, having joined the company 20 years earlier. He had earned a strong reputation in Hong Kong as a man of exceptional integrity and technical expertise.

The other two directors were both from Hong Kong and had joined the company about the same time in 1990. One was responsible for sales and marketing; the other was head of the project managers,

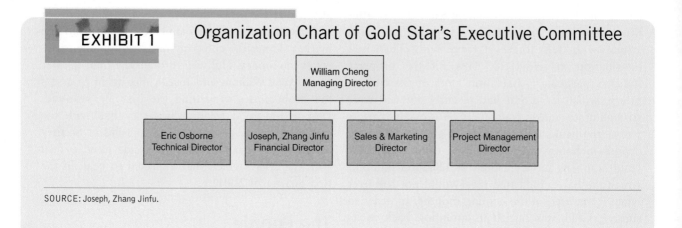

EXHIBIT 1 — Organization Chart of Gold Star's Executive Committee

William Cheng
Managing Director

- Eric Osborne
Technical Director
- Joseph, Zhang Jinfu
Financial Director
- Sales & Marketing
Director
- Project Management
Director

SOURCE: Joseph, Zhang Jinfu.

who were the company's representatives responsible for managing the budgets and schedules at each construction site. (Refer to Exhibit 1 for the organization chart of the executive committee of Gold Star.)

The Meeting and Eric Osborne's Reactions

The day before the executive committee was scheduled to meet, William asked Joseph to join him in his office to discuss how to deal with the situation. Both agreed that while working on obtaining the cash from the divestment of the assets, they must place financial stability and continuous operation of the company as their top priorities. They reached consensus on three general principles:

1. Try to balance paying off the debt service and making subcontractor payments.
2. Avoid triggering the banks calling in their loans: as far as possible, meet the demands of those that were most likely to do so.
3. Use the company's good relationships with subcontractors to help resolve the cash shortage by, as far as possible, deferring payments to those with whom they had the best relationships and who they also thought were in better financial shape than others.

The next day William laid out the priorities he and Joseph had developed and explained the thinking behind them to the executive committee. Joseph was taken aback by the way the meeting went, noting:

I was really surprised by Eric's reaction. He asked one question after another to both William and me, acting as if he knew little about the precarious position we were facing. Eric said that he knew that our financial performance from 1998 wasn't great, but it hadn't affected our project bidding.

Joseph described Eric's position in the meeting.

He said that if we needed more working capital, then we needed to do more contract work. He proposed that we should put first priority on completing projects on time, because doing so was the only way to get more contracts. He strongly demanded that we pay our subcontractors according to the contract schedules, because he worried about possible penalties resulting from work delays. He was convinced that otherwise there would be negative impacts in future contract bidding.

William and Joseph explained that most of the subcontractors had excellent long-term relations with Gold Star and that they needed to use those relationships now:

We told him that we thought some delay in payments wouldn't cause them to stop or slow work because they valued their relationship with us. We emphasized that the subcontractors should believe that their help to Gold Star would bring more business to them in the future.

The project management director added that Gold Star had lent money to some of these subcontractors in the past, when they couldn't get working capital from the banks. "These people don't forget favors like that," he stressed.

Joseph tried to provide more financial data to Eric to underline the seriousness of the situation:

I told him that the bankers were already very nervous and if we defaulted on the debt service they would be very upset. But I wasn't sure that he really heard me.

When Eric finally realized that the other directors supported William's strategy, he turned to Joseph again and pressed for clarity on how much money he could use to pay subcontractors in the following months before the cash from the divestment of assets arrived.

Joseph replied:

Here's a cash flow projection that I prepared so we can plan how to proceed. But remember, we might adjust the fund allocations differently as time goes on. We need to treat the bankers and the subcontractors dynamically, based on the actual situation at any given time.

Obviously frustrated and dissatisfied with Joseph's response, Eric started to get angry. "If you can't give me a fixed number month by month, then how can I do my work?" He ended his remarks with repeated exclamations about the importance of

his credibility with the subcontractors and his subordinates. Joseph and the others were silent in the face of his intensity.

William stepped in:

Look, Eric, I appreciate your feelings, but we are facing an extremely difficult situation. I hope that you will give us your full effort in helping to resolve the crisis together.

Eric paled and did not reply. As the meeting came to a close, William summarized the situation again and reiterated the three principles. He closed by asking all the directors not to disclose the situation to their subordinates in order to avoid further instability. All except Eric promised to maintain the confidentiality. Ominously, once again Eric remained silent.

The meeting ended and the directors returned to their respective offices. But it was clear to Joseph that Eric had not joined the consensus. He wondered why his colleague who had been so important to the firm's development was being so reluctant to help at this time of crisis. And he wondered what he and William could do to get his cooperation.

Note

1. The Hong Kong dollar was pegged to the US$ at the rate of HK$7.799 = US$1.

Harlequin Enterprises: The MIRA Decision[1]

Ken Mark
Rod White
Mary Crossan
The University of Western Ontario

During June 1993, Harlequin management was deciding whether or not to launch MIRA, a new line of single-title women's fiction novels. With the increased popularity of single-title women's fiction, Harlequin's leading position as the world's largest romance publisher was being threatened. While Harlequin was the dominant and very profitable producer of *series* romance novels, research indicated that many customers were reading as many *single-title* romance and women's fiction books as series romances. Facing a steady loss of share in a growing total women's fiction market, Harlequin convened a task force in December 1992 to study the possibility of relaunching a single-title women's fiction program. Donna Hayes, vice-president of direct marketing, stated:

Industry trends reveal that demand for single-title women's fiction continues to grow while demand for series romance remains stable. Our strengths lie in series romance . . . but by any account, launching MIRA will still be a challenge for us. How do we successfully launch a single-title women's fiction program?

Tentatively named "MIRA," Harlequin's proposed single-title program would focus exclusively on women's fiction. Management hoped MIRA's launch would provide the opportunity to continue Harlequin's history of strong revenue growth.

Hayes, leader of the MIRA team, knew this was a significant decision for Harlequin. Several years earlier an attempt at single-title publishing—Worldwide Library—had failed. Before going to her executive group for approval, Hayes thought about the decisions the company faced if it wished to enter single-title women's fiction publishing: What were the growth and profitability implications if Harlequin broadened its scope from series romance to single-title women's fiction? What fundamental changes would have to be made to Harlequin's current business model? Did the company have the necessary resources and capabilities to succeed in this new arena? If the company proceeds, how should it go about launching MIRA?

The Publishing Industry[2]

Apart from educational material, traditional single-title book publishing was typically a high-risk venture. Each book was a new product with all the risks attendant on any new product introduction. The risks varied with the author's reputation, the subject matter, and thus the predictability of the market's response. Among the numerous decisions facing the publisher were selecting manuscripts out of the thousands submitted each year, deciding how many copies to print, and deciding how to promote the book.

Insiders judged one key to success in publishing was the creative genius needed to identify good young authors among the hundreds of would-be writers, and then publish and develop them through their careers. Years ago, Sol Stein of Stein and Day Publishers had commented: "Most successful publishers are creative editors at heart and contribute more than risk capital and marketing expertise to the books they publish. If a publisher does not add value to what he publishes, he's a printer, not a publisher."

Traditional single-title publishers allowed distributors 50 percent margins (from which the retailer's margin would come).[3] Some other typical costs included royalty payments of more than 12 percent, warehouse and handling costs of four percent, and selling expenses at 5.5 percent. Advertising generally required six percent and printing costs[4] required another 12 percent. The remainder was earnings before indirect overhead. Typically, indirect overhead accounted for two percent of the retail price of a book. Because of author advances, pre-publication promotion and fixed costs of printing, break-even volumes were significant. And if the publisher failed to sell enough books, the losses could be substantial. Harlequin's core business, series romance fiction, was significantly different from traditional single-title publishing.

Harlequin Enterprises Limited

The word romance and the name Harlequin had become synonymous over the last half-century. Founded in 1949, Harlequin began applying its revolutionary approach to publishing—a packaged, consumer-goods strategy—in 1968, shortly after acquiring the publishing business of U.K.-based Mills & Boon. Each book was part of an identifiable product line, consistently delivering the expected benefit to the consumer. With a growth rate of 25 percent per year during the 1970s, Harlequin became the world's largest publisher of women's series romance fiction. It was during this time that Torstar, a newspaper publisher, acquired all of Harlequin Enterprises Ltd.

Over the years, many book publishers had attempted to enter Harlequin's segment of the industry. All had eventually withdrawn. Only once had Harlequin's dominance in series romance fiction been seriously challenged. The "romance wars" began in 1980 when Harlequin took over U.S. distribution of its series products from Simon & Schuster (S&S), a large U.S.-based single-title publisher with established paperback distribution. Consequently, S&S began publishing series romance fiction under the Silhouette imprint. After several years, a truce was negotiated between Harlequin and S&S. Harlequin acquired Silhouette, S&S's series romance business, and S&S got a 20-year deal as Harlequin's sole U.S. distributor for series fiction.

During the late 1980s and early 1990s, growth in the series market slowed. Harlequin was able to maintain revenues by publishing longer and more expensive series products and generally raising prices. However, as shown in Exhibit 1, global unit volume was no longer growing.

Harlequin's Target Market and Products

Harlequin books were sold in more than 100 international markets in more than 23 languages around the world. Along with romance fiction, Harlequin participated in the series mystery and male action-adventure markets under its Worldwide Library and Gold Eagle imprints. Harlequin had an estimated 20 million readers in North America and 50 million readers around the world.

EXHIBIT 1 Total Unit Sales (in '000s)

Year	1988	1989	1990	1991	1992	1993
Operating Revenue	$344,574	$326,539	$348,358	$357,013	$417,884	$443,825
Operating Profit	$48,142	$56,217	$57,769	$52,385	$61,842	$62,589
Total Unit Sales	202	191	196	193	205	199

With a median age of 41, the Harlequin romance series reader was likely to be married, well educated, and working outside the home. More than half of Harlequin readers spent at least three hours reading per week. Harlequin series readers were brand loyal; a survey indicated four out of five readers would continue to buy Harlequin books in the next year. Larry Heisey, Harlequin's former chief executive officer and chairman, expanded on the value of Harlequin's products: "I think our books are so popular because they provide relaxation and escape. . . . We get many letters from people who tell us how much these books mean to them."

While Harlequin had advertised its series product on television, current marketing efforts centered on print media. Harlequin advertised in leading women's magazines such as *Cosmopolitan, Glamour, Redbook, Good Housekeeping,* and general interest magazines such as *People.* The print advertisement usually featured one of Harlequin's series products and also promoted the company's brands.

Romance Series Product: Well Defined and Consistent

Under the Harlequin and Silhouette brands, Harlequin published 13 different series with 64 titles each month. Each series was distinctly positioned, featuring a particular genre (e.g., historical romances) or level of explicitness. Isabel Swift, editorial director of Silhouette, discussed the different types of series books published by Harlequin:

Our different lines deliver different promises to our readers. For example, Harlequin Temptation's tagline is sassy, sexy and seductive, *promising that each story will deliver a sexy, fun, contemporary romance between one man and one woman. Whereas the Silhouette Romance title, in comparison, is a tender read within a framework of more traditional values.*

Overall, the product portfolio offered a wide variety of stories to capture readers' interests. For the positioning of Harlequin's series, see Exhibit 2. Sold in more than a dozen countries, Harlequin had the ability to publish series books worldwide. The average retail price of a Harlequin series novel was $4.40,[5] significantly less than the $7 retail price for the typical single-title paperback novel, and much less than the $15 to $25 for longer, hardcover titles by best-selling authors.

Harlequin's series romance product was fundamentally different from that of traditional single-title publishers: content, length, artwork size, basic formats, and print were all well defined to ensure a consistent product. Each book was not a new product, but rather an addition to a clearly defined product line. Unlike single-title books, Harlequin's series products had a common format. They measured 105 millimeters by 168 millimeters and fit neatly into specially designed racks located primarily in supermarkets and drugstores. Most product lines were 192 to 256 pages in length; some were up to 304 pages in length. Cover designs differed slightly by product line and country, but the look and feel were similar (see Exhibit 3).

Harlequin provided prospective series romance authors with plot, style, and book length guidelines. However, crafting the stories still demanded skill and work. As David Galloway, chief executive officer of Torstar, Harlequin's parent company, and the former head of Harlequin, observed:

The books are quite simply good stories. If they weren't, we wouldn't be getting the repeat purchases we do. A lot of writers think they can dash off a Harlequin, but they can't. We've had

EXHIBIT 2   Harlequin/Silhouette Series Positioning Scales

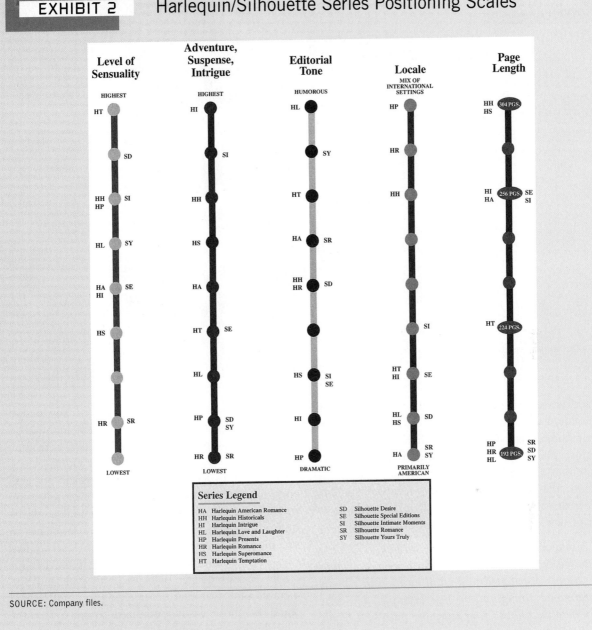

Level of Sensuality

HIGHEST

HT
SD
HH / HP — SI
HL — SY
HA / HI — SE
HS
HR — SR

LOWEST

Adventure, Suspense, Intrigue

HIGHEST

HI
SI
HH
HS
HA
HT — SE
HL
HP — SD / SY
HR — SR

LOWEST

Editorial Tone

HUMOROUS

HL
SY
HT
HA — SR
HH / HR — SD
SI / SE
HS
HI
HP

DRAMATIC

Locale

MIX OF INTERNATIONAL SETTINGS

HP
HR
HH
SI
HT / HI — SE
HL / HS — SD
HA — SR / SY

PRIMARILY AMERICAN

Page Length

HH / HS — 304 PGS.
HI / HA — 256 PGS. — SE / SI
HT — 224 PGS.
HP / HR / HL — 192 PGS. — SR / SD / SY

Series Legend

HA	Harlequin American Romance	SD	Silhouette Desire
HH	Harlequin Historicals	SE	Silhouette Special Editions
HI	Harlequin Intrigue	SI	Silhouette Intimate Moments
HL	Harlequin Love and Laughter	SR	Silhouette Romance
HP	Harlequin Presents	SY	Silhouette Yours Truly
HR	Harlequin Romance		
HS	Harlequin Superomance		
HT	Harlequin Temptation		

SOURCE: Company files.

submissions from Ph.D.'s in English who can certainly write but they can't tell a story.

To ensure that a consistent product emerged, Harlequin's editors assessed many elements including plot, story line, main character(s), setting, percentage of romance in the plot, level of realism, level of fantasy, sensuality, social and/or individual problems, happy ending, and reading impact. Even though many different authors contributed to series romance, Harlequin's editors ensured a consistent finished product, satisfying the needs of their loyal series romance readers. The consequences of this uniformity were significant. The reader was buying a Harlequin novel, and advertising promoted the Harlequin brands rather than a particular book or author.

Bookstores were not the primary channel for series romance novels. Most retail purchases were

EXHIBIT 3   Typical Harlequin Series Romance Products

SOURCE: Company files.

made at supermarkets and drugstores. But many Harlequin customers got the product delivered to their home every month through Harlequin's direct mail service. The standardized size and format made warehousing and distribution more efficient. In addition, the product's consistency enabled standing order distribution to retail. As Pam Laycock, director of new product development, explained:

> *A major contributor to our success as a series publisher is our standing order distribution. Each series is distributed to a retail location in a predetermined configuration—for example in a series where we publish four titles per month, a retailer may take six copies per title and this level of distribution is generally agreed upon and maintained for the entire year. This approach enables us to more accurately predict monthly print quantities and achieve significant print cost effectiveness.*

Orders (and sales) for conventional single-title books were not as predictable. Another significant difference was that series romance books, as part of Harlequin's standing order distribution plan, were displayed on retail shelves for four weeks. Harlequin's

distributors then removed and returned any unsold books, and replaced them with the next month's offerings. By comparison, single-title books were typically displayed from 6 to 12 months or more.

Harlequin's series romance business did not generate or even encourage best-sellers. "Best-sellers (in series romance) would ruin our system," a Harlequin insider stated. "Our objective is consistency in volume. We have no winners and no losers." Unsold books could be returned to the publisher for credit. A consequence of Harlequin's even and predictable sales was that order regulation and returns could be more easily optimized to maximize the contribution to profits.

A comparison of Harlequin's series business model and the operations of traditional "one-off" publishers is presented in Exhibit 4.

With a consistent quality product, standing orders, predictable retail traffic patterns, and the ability to produce and deliver books at low costs, Harlequin had achieved great success. Harlequin's series romance business had consistently earned a return on sales of 15 percent. As shown in Exhibit 5, this figure compared favorably with larger traditional publishers.

EXHIBIT 4

Comparing Harlequin's Series Business Model and a Traditional Publisher's

	Harlequin Series	Single-Title Publisher
Editorial	Emphasizes consistency within established guidelines	Requires separate judgment on potential consumer demand for each manuscript
Rights	Uses standardized contract	Can be a complex process, involving subrights, hard/soft deals, advances, and tying up authors for future books
Author Management	Less dependent on specific authors	Vulnerable to key authors changing publisher
Production	Uses consistent format with focus on efficiency	Emphasizes package, size, and format—cost control secondary
Marketing	Builds the imprint/series	Builds each title/author
Distribution	Supermarkets, drugstores, mass merchandisers, big-box bookstores	Bookstores (all types)
	Large direct mail	Book clubs and mass merchandisers
Selling	Emphasizes servicing, rack placement, and order regulation	Cover, in-store placement, critical reviews, special promotional tactics (e.g., author signings)
Order Regulation/ Information Systems	Utilizes very sophisticated shipping and returns handling procedures	Historically has not received much attention, and hence, is not as sophisticated

Loriana Sacilotto, director of retail marketing, explained why Harlequin outperformed other traditional single-title publishers:

> There are a variety of reasons why other publishers do not achieve the same margins we enjoy. The main reason is that they are broad in their publishing focus whereas we focus on women's fiction. They don't have the same reader recognition, trust and relationships. We invest in it.

Harlequin Business System
The Global Author–Editor Team

Harlequin had established a strong level of reader trust and brand equity by consistently delivering quality content. Editors in three acquisition centers in Toronto, New York, and London were responsible for working closely with 1,300-plus authors to develop and publish more than 1,000 new titles annually. In addition to the work of its regular writers, Harlequin received approximately 30,000 unsolicited manuscripts per year. Typically, about 100 of these were accepted in any given year.

Series authors received royalties of 13 percent of retail book price. Harlequin's typical series authors had more than 100,000 of each of their books distributed worldwide.

Harlequin's series romance product focused solely on *front-list* sales. In the publishing world, front-list sales referred to the first print runs of a book supporting its initial market launch. *Back-list* referred to books reprinted and reissued years after the book's initial run (generally to support an author's subsequent books). Harlequin's series romance novels—unlike a traditional publisher's single-title books—were not available on back-list. However, Harlequin retained these rights.

Printing was a highly competitive business and Harlequin subcontracted its requirements. Costs per series book were typically $0.44 per book compared

EXHIBIT 5 Comparison of Harlequin's Performance with Traditional Publishers—1993 (in millions of dollars)

	Harlequin[a]	Simon & Schuster[b]	Harper/Avon[c]
Sales Revenue	417.8	1,929.0	1,210.4
Operating Profit	61.8	218.4	160.8
Identifiable Assets	319.2	2,875.8	2,528.0
R.O.S.	14.8%	11.3%	13.2%
R.O.I.A.	19.4%	7.6%	6.4%

[a]Canadian dollars
[b]U.S. dollars (Cdn$1.20 = US$1)
[c]Australian dollars (Cdn$0.80 = AUD$1)

to the competitors' average costs of $0.88 per single-title soft cover book.

Distribution, Selling, and Promotion

With its standing orders, Harlequin's distribution costs per book were $0.18, with selling expenses at an average of $0.09 per book. Because it was the dominant player in series romance, Harlequin had relatively low advertising and promotion costs—about $0.22 per book.

In Canada, Harlequin had its own distribution. Elsewhere in the world, independent distributors were employed. In the United States, Pocket Books, the sales division of Simon & Schuster, a large traditional publisher, handled Harlequin's series romance books. Supermarkets, drugstores, discount department stores, and mass merchandisers accounted for 70 percent of retail sales. Specialty big-box bookstores like Barnes and Noble and other chains and independent bookstores accounted for the remainder of retail sales. Globally Harlequin's products were in over 250,000 retail outlets. Eighty thousand of these outlets were in North America; almost 50,000 of these were supermarkets and drugstores. Harequin's series products were in 70 percent of supermarkets but only 55 percent of bookstores. In Europe, kiosks and tobacconists accounted for the largest proportion of retail outlets.

The direct channel handled direct-to-reader book sales. Harlequin's "Reader Service" book club was an important source of sales and profits. Investing in advertising to acquire readers, this direct mail operation offered frequent Harlequin readers the possibility of purchasing every book the company published, delivered right to their doorstep. In the United States, six books were sold through the book club for every ten sold at retail. Furthermore, a book sold through the book club yielded Harlequin the full cover price, whereas a book sold at retail netted the company approximately half the retail price, and required advertising, distribution costs, and the acceptance of returns from retailers.

Rise of Single-Title Romance

The proliferation of titles and authors during the "Romance Wars" had resulted in the emergence of single titles as a significant factor in the women's romance fiction market. Exhibit 6 provides the sales breakdown for romance novels.

In an attempt to capitalize on readers' growing appetite for single titles, Harlequin launched Worldwide Library in 1986, its first single-title publishing program. This move also gave Harlequin's more accomplished series authors another outlet. Laycock commented:

Several authors who began their writing careers with Harlequin writing series romance wanted broader opportunities—opportunities that they saw in the single-title women's fiction publishing arena. Prior to the launch of Worldwide Library,

Harlequin didn't have publishing opportunities to meet the desires of these authors. As a result, authors would seek out competitive publishers to support their single-title works.

By 1988, Worldwide was shut down as a result of several problems. "Worldwide could never decide if it was a romance program, a women's fiction program, or a general fiction program," a Harlequin insider commented. Exhibit 7 illustrates a list of typical titles published at Worldwide.

With the shutdown of Worldwide Library, popular authors moved to other publishers. As shown in Exhibit 8, other publishers continued to exploit the popularity of single-title romance novels.

Eager to find ways to grow its publishing business, Harlequin's management re-examined the publishing market. A broader analysis revealed that although Harlequin's series romance had captured well over 80 percent of the North American series romance market by 1990, Harlequin's estimated share of the North American *women's fiction* market was only about five percent. Exhibit 9 provides a breakdown of the women's fiction market.

There was substantial overlap in the readership of series romance fiction and other fiction. Mark Mailman, vice-president of market research and analysis, added:

> One compelling reason to get into single-title publishing is that when we look at our research on customers, they're reading 20 Harlequin books and 20 single-title books from other publishers. We have an opportunity to take a greater share of that market.

Harlequin's Single-Title Task Force

Faced with slow or no growth in series romance, a Harlequin task force convened in 1992 to study

EXHIBIT 6 — Romance Novel Sales in North America (millions of units)

	1985	1986	1987	1988	1989	1990
Harlequin series romance	77	79	80	82	83	85
Other romance series publishers	12	12	13	13	14	14
Single-title romance books by other publishers	72	79	86	94	102	112
Total romance books	161	170	179	189	199	211

EXHIBIT 7 — Range of Worldwide Titles (1987)

Book Title	Type/Genre	Unit Sales Data	Harlequin Series Author?
Longest Pleasure	Romance	304,000	Yes
Quarantine	Horror	62,000	No
Eve of Regression	Psychological Thriller	55,000	No
War Moon	Suspense	72,000	No
Illusion	Psychological Suspense	35,000	No
Dream Escape	Romance	297,000	Yes
Alien Planet	Science Fiction	71,000	No

EXHIBIT 8	Monthly Single-Title Romance Output Analysis, North American Market

Single Title Romance by Category:	1985	1989	1991
Contemporary	2	6	12
Historical	22	37	43
Regency	6	8	17
Total	**30**	**51**	**72**
By Publisher:			
Zebra (Kensington Publishing)	5	15	21
Bantam/Dell	2	2	8
Diamond	0	0	4
Harper Paperbacks	0	0	3
Avon	4	5	6
Jove	2	2	4
Leisure Books	3	3	5
NAL/Signet	6	7	8
Pocket Books (Simon & Schuster)	1	6	3
Ballantine/Fawcett, Onyx, SMP	4	7	7
Warner Books/Popular Library	3	4	3
Total	**30**	**51**	**72**

SOURCE: Company files.

EXHIBIT 9	North American Women's Fiction Market Size Estimate, 1993 (as a percentage of overall segment sizes in US$ millions)

	General Fiction	Romance	Mystery	Sci-Fi	Total Fiction
Total Segment Size	2,222	1,220	353	476	4,271
Estimated Women's Fiction Share of Segment	60%	100%	60%	38%	69%

the feasibility of launching a new women's fiction single-title program. To begin, they examined why Worldwide had failed and concluded that overall lack of success was attributable to: editorial parameters that were too broad; less than optimal North American retail distribution; very few Worldwide titles distributed through the direct-to-reader channel; global support for the program was not timely and universal; the selection of au-

thors and titles was unsuccessful. The task force report stated:

In the past few years, sell-through efficiencies in the supermarket channels are not as great as the sell-through efficiencies in both mass merchandisers and bookstores. The more efficient retailer knew that the consumer was spending her discretionary reading dollar to buy a diversity of ro-

mantic reads, including those that had previously been thought of as mainstream.

Since a single-title strategy requires a single-title solicitation from the sales force and more expensive single-title packaging, two of Harlequin's strategic lynchpins of our earlier decades have to be rethought (for single-title): standing order program and same format production. However, Harlequin can still capitalize on its global base and its ability to distribute widely to points of purchase that women visit on a regular basis.

MIRA Launch Decision

The task force was preparing its recommendation for MIRA, Harlequin's proposed women's fiction single-title program. The addition of single titles would make a welcome contribution to overhead costs. Currently, indirect overhead costs per series novel were $0.09 per book. Because infrastructure was already in place, it was estimated that MIRA novels would not incur additional indirect overhead costs. Printing costs for single-titles were expected to be $0.71 per book (350 pages on average). Estimated advertising and promotional costs for new single titles were six percent of (the higher) retail price.

Author Management

In the single-title market, authors were categorized into three groups, based on their sales potential:

brand new, mid-list, and best-seller (see Exhibit 10). Depending on the author group royalties, sales and promotional support varied. Best-selling authors were expected to sell more than a million books. Publishers were known to sign established authors for up to a five-book contract with large advances. It had not been determined whether MIRA should follow suit. In addition to author advances, typical royalties per MIRA-type book were estimated to be 13 percent of the $6.75 retail price.

A Different Format

Women's fiction books were expected to have many differences from well-defined series romance books. Unlike series romance, topics would cover a broader range of segments including general fiction, science fiction, and mystery. Women's fiction books would be longer in length: 100,000 to 400,000 words compared with a series romance book length of 75,000 words. Naturally, book sizes would be bigger in terms of page length: from 250 to 400 pages versus a norm of 192 to 304 pages for series romance.

Distribution

Harlequin had a strong distribution network for its series romances through supermarkets, drugstores, and discount department stores. Single-title women's fiction novels required more mainstream distribution focusing on retail bookstores. In addition,

EXHIBIT 10	General Industry Contract Terms for Fiction Category by Author Group		
	Brand New Author	**Mid-List Author**	**Best-Selling Author**
Advance	$10,000 to $30,000	$80,000 to $200,000	$1 million to $5 million
Royalties	5% to 13%	8% to 15%	10% to 17%
Overseas publishing schedule	Within 18 months	Within 12 months	Simultaneous
Overseas publishing markets	Major markets	All markets	All markets
Minimum distribution	30,000 to 80,000	100,000 to 400,000	>1 million
Promotional support per book	Possibly some support (up to $50,000)	Support ($100,000)	Very strong support (more than $300,000)

SOURCE: Industry sources and casewriter estimates.

standing order distribution, a hallmark of Harlequin's series romance business model, would have to be abandoned in favor of relying on orders generated by the distributor's sales force for single-titles.

Success in the United States would be key for MIRA, and in this market, Harlequin relied upon Simon and Schuster's sales force. Since S&S was a major single-title publisher, Harlequin did not know how much support MIRA would be afforded. Harlequin was considering offering better margins to the distributors than those it offered for series romance distribution. Expenses for single-title distribution were expected to be $0.27 per book.

MIRA books would rely more heavily upon distribution through bookstores when distributed through the same channels as the series product. Retailers would be encouraged to shelve MIRA books separately from the series offering. The more intensive selling effort for single titles would require four percent of the single-title retail price. The new single-title program planned to offer $3.38 in margin to the distribution channel for single-title books (50 percent of the typical retail price of $6.75) versus $2.42 for series books (45 percent of the $4.40 suggested retail price).

Acquiring Single-Title Rights

Harlequin subsidiaries in some countries were already buying rights to publish single titles. By launching MIRA Harlequin could negotiate better global-author deals. The task force report added: "By acquiring mainstream titles through a central acquiring office, the collective clout of Harlequin could create the likelihood of better-selling mainstream titles marketed by all countries in the global enterprise."

Harlequin's author and editor relationships remained strong, so much so that many series authors were enthusiastic about maintaining a long-term relationship with a trusted editor as they pursued their break-out mainstream book. With MIRA, these authors could remain loyal to Harlequin.

How Best to Proceed

There were many issues to be resolved prior to any launch of MIRA. Most pressing was the question of whether Harlequin had the resources and capabilities to succeed in its new women's fiction segment.

Certainly there were elements of its series business model that could be transferred to the broader women's fiction market. But what were the gaps? What else did Harlequin need?

Hayes had a several options if MIRA was launched. Several established best-selling authors had begun their writing careers with Harlequin and had moved on to writing single-title books. These authors had established reputations. Harlequin could approach one or more of these authors to sign with MIRA/Harlequin. Such an arrangement would involve a multi-book contract and substantial advances. While risky, this approach would ensure that MIRA's launch attracted attention.

A different, seemingly less risky alternative was to tap into Harlequin's extensive back-list collection and reissue a selection of novels by current best-selling authors currently signed with rival single-title publishers. The physical size of the book and page length could be extended to 250 pages from 192 by adjusting format. In addition, a new, MIRA-branded cover could be produced to repackage the books. Coincident with the launch of this back-list, Harlequin's editors would cultivate and develop existing series authors, encouraging them to write single-title books for MIRA.

Returning to the strategic dilemma that Harlequin faced, Swift commented on the challenge of successfully launching MIRA:

Our biggest challenge is the requirement to publish on a title-by-title basis. Every new book will have to stand on its own, with its own cover, a new marketing plan and possibly even an author tour. Can we as a company develop the flexibility to remain nimble? How patient should we be in waiting for success? Given Worldwide's poor results, how should we approach this challenge?

Notes

1. To protect confidentiality, all financial information within this case study has been disguised.
2. This section is adapted from the Richard Ivey School of Business #9A87M002, Harlequin Enterprises Limited—1979, Peter Killing.
3. All amounts are a percentage of the suggested retail price.
4. Numbers are for the typical paperback. Hardcover books cost more to produce, but as a percentage of their higher retail price, printing costs were roughly the same proportion.
5. All amounts in Cdn$ unless otherwise specified.

Kikkoman Corporation in the Mid-1990s: Market Maturity, Diversification, and Globalization

Norihito Tanaka
Kanagawa University

Marilyn L. Taylor
University of Missouri at Kansas City

Joyce A. Claterbos
University of Kansas

In early 1996, Mr. Yuzaburo Mogi, president of Kikkoman Corporation, faced a number of challenges. Analysts indicated concern with Kikkoman's slow sales growth and noted that the company's stock had under performed on the Nikkei Exchange in relation to the market and to its peers for several years. Throughout the world, ongoing changes in taste preferences and dietary needs presented threats to the company's traditional food lines. The company marketed its branded products in 94 countries and had to consider which products and markets to emphasize as well as which new markets to enter. As Mr. Mogi described the company's focus, ". . . we are now concentrating on further enhancing our ability to serve consumers in Japan and overseas. The basic keynotes of this effort are expansion of soy sauce markets, diversification, and globalization."

In Japan, Kikkoman had long dominated the soy sauce market, and its mid-1990s market share position of 27 percent was well beyond the ten percent of its next closest competitor. However, its share of the soy sauce market had continued to decline from its high of 33 percent in 1983, falling from 28 percent in 1993 to 27.2 percent in 1994. Further, although the company's worldwide sales had increased slightly overall from 1994 to 1995, sales of soy sauce in Japan had decreased over one percent during that period.

Reprinted by permission from the *Case Research Journal*. Copyright 2001 by Norihito Tanaka, Marilyn L. Taylor, and Joyce A. Claterbos and The North American Case Research Association. All rights reserved.

The authors express deep appreciation to Kikkoman Corporation, which provided encouragement to this study, including access to the U.S. manufacturing and marketing facilities in addition to time in the corporate offices in Japan. The authors also gratefully acknowledge the support for this study provided by the Japanese Department of Education and the Institute for Training and Development in Tokyo. Quotes and data in this case study were drawn from a variety of personal interviews in the United States and Japan, company documents, and public sources. Documents and public sources appear in the list of references at the conclusion of the case.

The U.S. market had provided significant opportunity in the post–World War II period. However, the company's U.S. market share for soy and other company products was essentially flat. In addition, three competitors had built plants in the United States beginning in the late 1980s. Mr. Mogi was aware that Kikkoman's choices in the U.S. market would provide an important model for addressing higher income mature markets.

With a market capitalization of nearly ¥160 billion,[1] Kikkoman Corporation was the world's largest soy sauce producer, Japan's nineteenth largest food company, and also Japan's leading soy sauce manufacturer. The company was the oldest continuous enterprise among the 200 largest industrials in Japan. The company began brewing shoyu, or naturally fermented soy sauce, in the seventeenth century and had dominated the Japanese soy industry for at least a century. The company held 50 percent of the U.S. soy sauce market and 30 percent of the world market. Kikkoman had 13 manufacturing facilities in Japan and one each in the United States,

Singapore, and Taiwan. The company was one of the few traditional manufacturers to successfully establish a presence worldwide. (Exhibits 1 and 2 have the locations of and information on the company's principal subsidiaries. Exhibits 3 and 4 list the consolidated financial statements.)

Kikkoman in Japan

The Beginnings in Noda

In 1615, the widow of a slain samurai warrior fled 300 miles from Osaka to the village of Noda near Edo (now called Tokyo). With her five children, the widow Mogi embarked upon rice farming and subsequently began brewing shoyu, or soy sauce. The quality of the Mogi family's shoyu was exceptional almost from its beginnings. At the time, households produced shoyu for their own use, or local farmers made and sold excess shoyu as a side enterprise to farming. As more people moved to the urban areas in the seventeenth and eighteenth centuries, there

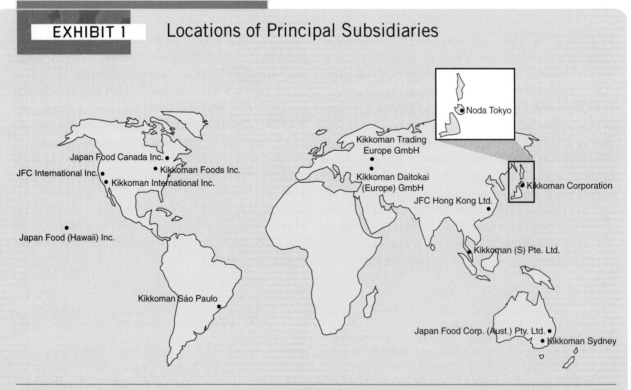

EXHIBIT 1 Locations of Principal Subsidiaries

Japan Food Canada Inc.
JFC International Inc.
Kikkoman Foods Inc.
Kikkoman International Inc.
Japan Food (Hawaii) Inc.
Kikkoman São Paulo
Kikkoman Trading Europe GmbH
Kikkoman Daitokai (Europe) GmbH
JFC Hong Kong Ltd.
Noda Tokyo
Kikkoman Corporation
Kikkoman (S) Pte. Ltd.
Japan Food Corp. (Aust.) Pty. Ltd.
Kikkoman Sydney

SOURCE: "Flavors That Bring People Together," Kikkoman Corporation Brochure, 1994.

EXHIBIT 2   Consolidated Subsidiaries as of FY 1995

Subsidiary	Country	Paid-In Capital ((¥)m/$m)	Kikkoman Equity (%)
Japan Del Monte	Japan	900	99.7
Mann's Wine	Japan	900	100.0
Pacific Trading	Japan	72	66.7
Morishin	Japan	30	66.7
Kikkoman Foods, Inc.	United States	US$6	100.0
Kikkoman International	United States	US$3.5	92.6
JFC International	United States	US$1.2	98.0
Kikkoman Trading Europe	Germany	DM1.5	75.0
Kikkoman Pte	Singapore	S$7.5	100.0
Kikkoman Trading Pte	Singapore	S$.4	100.0
Tokyo Food Processing	United States	US$.02	100.0
Hapi Products	United States	US$.05	100.0
Rex Pacific	United States	US$1.5	100.0

SOURCE: Table 4: Consolidated Subsidiaries, UBS Securities Limited, May 28, 1996, as reported by *Investext*.

was increased demand for non-home production. Households developed preferences for the product of a particular brewer. (See Appendix A: The Making of Soy Sauce.)

Shoyu had come to Japan with the arrival of Buddhism in the sixth century. The teachings of Buddhism prohibited eating meat and fish. Residents of the Japanese islands turned from meat-based to vegetable-based flavorings. One of the favorites became a flavorful seasoning made from fermented soy beans. A Japanese Zen Buddist priest who had studied in China brought the recipe to Japan. The Japanese discovered that adding wheat gave the sauce a richer, more mellow flavor.

Over the eighteenth century, Noda became a major center for shoyu manufacturing in Japan. Shoyu's major ingredients, soybeans and wheat, grew readily in the rich agricultural Kanto plain that surrounded Noda. The trip to the major market of Edo took only one day on the Edo River. The various shoyu-producing families in the Noda area actively shared their knowledge of fermentation. The Mogi family and another Noda area family, the Takanashi family, were especially active in the industry. By the late eighteenth century, the two families had become interrelated through marriage. Their various enterprises made considerable investment in breweries, and family members began ancillary enterprises such as grain brokering, keg manufacture, and transportation.

Japan's Shoyu Distribution System and Industry Structure

Japan's neophyte and fragmented shoyu industry had two distribution systems during this time. In the rural areas, the shoyu breweries sold their products directly to households. In the cities, urban wholesalers distributed shoyu, vinegar, and sake. The wholesalers purchased bulk shoyu and established their own brands. The wholesalers controlled pricing, inventory, distribution, and marketing knowledge. They would distribute branded shoyu only on consignment. During the 1800s, the wholesalers formed alliances that gave them near monopolistic power over the Tokyo market. As the shoyu manufacturers

EXHIBIT 3 Consolidated Profit and Loss Statement ((¥)m)

	1989	1990	1991	1992	1993	1994	1995
Sales	195,851	196,925	206,861	211,671	203,491	200,976	203,286
COGS	117,062	118,808	122,872	124,882	118,504	117,809	119,656
Gross profit	78,789	78,117	83,989	86,789	84,987	83,167	83,629
Gross profit margin (%)	40.2	39.7	40.6	41	41.8	41.4	41.1
SG&A expenses	71,227	71,876	74,181	76,019	74,320	72,689	72,836
SG&A exp. (%)	36.4	36.5	35.9	35.9	36.5	36.2	35.8
Operating profit	7,562	6,240	9,807	10,769	10,666	10,477	10,792
Operating margin (%)	3.9	3.2	4.7	5.1	5.2	5.2	5.3
Net non-op. income	−572	−1,042	−1,564	−1,895	−2,282	−2,197	−2,305
Recurring profit	6,990	5,197	8,243	8,873	8,384	8,280	8,487
Recurring margin (%)	3.6	2.6	4	4.2	4.1	4.1	4.2
Net extraordinary income	181	1,165	1,317	59	108	1,434	−1,177
Pretax profit	7,170	6,363	9,559	8,932	8,493	9,714	7,310
Tax	3,327	3,299	4,726	5,178	4,597	4,157	3,569
Tax rate (%)	46.4	50.7	49.4	58	54.1	42.8	48.8
Minority interest	56	78	37	34	1	−52	46
Amortization of consol. dif.	0	0	−35	1	5	0	−314
Equity in earnings	1,097	1,464	1,188	1,245	887	1,002	996
Net profit	4,697	4,694	6,166	4,928	4,688	6,614	4,447
Shares outstanding (m)	169.08	169.71	169.97	178.61	187.62	187.77	197.2
EPS	27.8	27.7	31.3	25	23.8	33.5	22.6
EPS change (%)	80	−0.4	13.3	−20.2	−4.9	41	−32.8
Cash flow per share	20.8	46.5	48	41.9	44.4	58.5	46.8
Average exchange rate (yen/US$)	137.96	144.79	134.71	126.65	111.20	102.21	94.06

SOURCES: Table 9: UBS Securities Limited, May 28, 1996; The World Almanac, 1998 (original source: IMF).

became more efficient, they found it impossible to lower prices or make other adjustments to increase their market share.

The Mogi and Takanashi families took several steps to counteract the wholesalers' dominance. The Takanashi family had diversified into wholesaling some years prior and were part of the wholesalers' alliance. One Mogi family intermarried with a wholesaler's family—a traditional strategy in Japan for cementing strategic alliances. In addition, the Mogi and Takanashi families worked to increase brand recognition and dominance. In 1838, Mogi Saheiji applied for and received the shogunate's recognition of his family's premier brand, named Kikkoman. He aggressively promoted the brand by sponsoring professional storytellers and sumo wrestlers, embossing paper lanterns and umbrellas with the Kikkoman trademark, and putting ornate

EXHIBIT 4	Consolidated Balance Sheet ((¥)m)					
	1990	**1991**	**1992**	**1993**	**1994**	**1995**
Current Assets	81,611	88,092	89,705	103,152	105,220	107,339
Cash and deposits	13,254	17,570	18,261	28,826	36,381	37,366
Accounts receivable	43,579	44,661	44,503	46,009	44,246	44,439
Securities	315	1,012	1,316	3,310	3,306	3,307
Inventories	21,769	21,300	22,484	21,469	18,579	19,258
Fixed assets	94,631	97,999	105,231	113,940	112,183	119,411
Tangible assets	52,087	53,254	59,276	67,649	65,795	72,684
Land	11,768	12,011	11,910	15,156	15,613	11,540
Investments	26,371	29,597	31,771	33,051	34,083	35,006
Total Assets	177,583	187,316	195,955	218,561	218,805	228,308
Liabilities and Owner's Equity						
Current liabilities	48,040	52,626	54,014	50,272	46,663	63,400
Short-term borrowings	18,846	18,908	19,046	17,462	14,838	15,741
Fixed liabilities	58,374	58,850	62,351	85,532	85,143	71,710
Long-term borrowings	4,457	4,549	4,723	3,274	3,091	2,312
Bonds and CBs[a]	26,565	26,346	26,231	46,170	44,776	29,921
Minority interest	1,223	1,166	1,157	1,103	1,024	427
Total liabilities	107,638	112,643	117,522	136,909	132,832	135,538
Shareholders' equity	69,945	74,673	78,434	81,651	85,973	92,770
Total Liabilities and Equity	177,583	187,316	195,955	218,561	218,805	228,308

[a]There were two CBs issued Jan. 90 exercisable at ¥1,522. The other two were issued July 93 and were exercisable at ¥969. With the share price at approximately ¥100, the total dilution factor was about 18 percent, with 80 percent of that dependent on the two CBs exercisable at ¥969. Of 228 ((¥)m) in 1995, about 170 belonged to the parent (i.e., Japan Corporation) company.

SOURCE: Nikkei Needs as reported in Table 12: Consolidated Balance Sheet, UBS Securities Limited, May 28, 1996.

gold labels from Paris on his Kikkoman shoyu kegs. In the latter part of the nineteenth century, Kikkoman shoyu won recognition in several world's fairs.

In reaction to depressed market prices and fluctuating costs of inputs, a number of the Noda shoyu brewers formed the Noda Shoyu Brewers' Association in 1887. The association purchased raw materials, standardized wages, and regulated output quality. The members' combined efforts resulted in the largest market share at the time, five to ten percent of the Tokyo market, and widespread recognition of the high quality of Noda shoyu.

Noda brewers, and especially the Mogi and Takanashi families, began research and development activities early. The Japanese government encour-

aged the Noda shoyu brewers to conduct research in the recovery and processing of the two by-products of shoyu manufacture, shoyu oil and shoyu cake. In the early 1900s, the association began to fund a joint research and development laboratory.

The Shoyu Industry in the Twentieth Century

In 1910, there were still 14,000 known makers of shoyu in Japan. However, a number of changes led to consolidation. Manufacturing shifted from a small-batch, brewmaster-controlled production process to a large-batch, technology-controlled process. Mogi families in Noda invested in modernized plants, and a fifth-grade Japanese geography reader featured a state-of-the-art Kikkoman facility. A national market also developed, thanks to the development of a railway system throughout most of the country. In addition, consumer tastes shifted to the Tokyo-style shoyu produced by eastern manufacturers such as the Noda Shoyu Brewers' Association.

Consumers also began to purchase shoyu in smaller glass bottles rather than in the traditional large wooden barrels that sometimes leaked and were expensive to build and difficult to store. Raw materials also became more expensive as the brewers increasingly sought higher-quality imported soybeans (from Manchuria, China, and Korea) and salt (from England, Germany, and China). The association members controlled costs by purchasing in bulk and demanding high-quality materials from suppliers.

The Noda Shoyu Company: 1918–1945—A Family Zaibatsu[2]

In 1918, seven Mogi families and a related Takanashi family combined their various enterprises into a joint stock holding company called the Noda Shoyu Company. The merger was in reaction to the market upheaval caused by World War I. The new company was a small zaibatsu with nearly a dozen companies in manufacturing fermented grain-based products, transportation, and finance. Unlike early shoyu manufacturing where ownership, management, and operations were clearly separated, the Mogi and Takanashi families owned, managed, and operated their firm. Initially, the family produced 34 different brands of shoyu at various price points. The Kikkoman brand had a history of heavy promotion for over 40 years, greater Tokyo market share, and a higher margin than the company's other brands. The Kikkoman brand became the company's flagship brand. The new corporation continued its long-standing emphasis on research and development and aggressively pursued new manufacturing processes, increased integration, and acquisition of other shoyu companies.

After the Mogi-Takanashi coalition, the company aggressively pursued a strong nationwide sole agent system and direct distribution. The combined company also continued Kikkoman's well-known advertising activities. Kikkoman had carried out the first newspaper advertising in 1878. In 1922, the company carried out the firm's first advertising on the movie screen.

During the 1920s, the company aggressively modernized with machines such as hydraulic presses, boilers, conveyors, and elevators. The company's modernization efforts were emulated by competitors, and the results were increased supply and heightened industry competition. The changes brought about by increased automation led to severe labor unrest. One particularly long strike against the Kikkoman company in the late 1920s almost destroyed the participating labor union. After the strike ended, Kikkoman rehired about a third of the striking employees. The company centralized and reorganized the work processes to accommodate improved technology, restructured work practices, and established methods to monitor and reward workers for their performance. However, the company also established efforts to improve the identity of the workers with the company. Internal communications carried the message that all employees were members of one family, or ikka, united in a common purpose, i.e., the production of shoyu. The Noda Shoyu Company was also heavily involved in the city of Noda and supported many of its cultural and charitable activities as well as the local railroad, bank, town hall, cultural center, library, fire station, elementary school, hospital, recreation facilities and association, and much of the city's water system.

Kikkoman's International Activities

Kikkoman's initial export activities began in the late seventeenth century with Dutch and Chinese traders. The Dutch began to export shoyu to Holland and the rest of Europe, while the Chinese served the southeast Asian markets. The shoyu brewers relied on agents for these early export transactions. During the nineteenth century, one Mogi patriarch opened a factory in Inchon, Korea. Demand for the increasing export, marketing, and direct investment continued to come primarily from Japanese and other peoples living abroad whose traditional cuisines called for shoyu. In 1910, the Noda city brewer's international activities were recognized when the Japanese government selected

Noda shoyu to appear in a public relations publication introducing Japan's industries overseas.

Noda Shoyu Company continued to expand internationally between World War I and World War II. Acquisition of raw materials from abroad continued. The company added a manufacturing facility for shoyu and miso in Manchuria and two shoyu factories in North America. Other facilities in Japan were expanded or updated to support increasing international sales.

The company established sales offices in China and Korea to market shoyu, miso, and sake. By the late 1930s, the company exported ten percent of its output, about half to the Asian region—especially Korea, China, and Indonesia—and half to Hawaii and California. Almost all of the exports were the Kikkoman brand and were sold through food import/export firms to the company's traditional customers.

Post–World War II Kikkoman in Japan

At the end of World War II, Kikkoman operated only in Japan. Activities elsewhere had been closed. To meet the need for capital, Kikkoman issued publicly traded stock in 1946, reducing family ownership markedly. (Exhibit 5 shows the changes in ownership from 1917 to 1993.) The post–World War II period brought a number of social changes to Japanese society. Japanese families began the change to nuclear rather than extended-family formation. Food tastes changed leading, among other trends, to a decline in per capita consumption of shoyu. Compared with other industries, demand for soy sauce grew very slowly. In 1942, demand for soy sauce in Japan was 1.7 times greater than in 1918. Demand in the 1960s was expected to be 2.2 times greater than that in 1918. However, modernization led to increased output.

Kikkoman had received considerable recognition for its advertising efforts prior to World War II. After the war, the company began to market even more aggressively in Japan. These efforts included establishing the company's strong nationwide distribution system throughout Japan; mounting aggressive activities in marketing research, advertising, and consumer education; and changing to a new and more Western image. As a result of Kikkoman's marketing efforts, the company's market share rose sharply. (Exhibit 6 shows the national output of shoyu and the company's market share from 1893 to 1994.) By 1964, the company officially changed its name to Kikkoman Shoyu and in 1980 became

| EXHIBIT 5 | Noda Shoyu Company and Kikkoman Corporation Ownership |

Shareholder Name	Holdings (% of total shares or assets)			
	1917	1925	1955	1993
Mogi-Takanashi-Horikiri brewing families	100%[a]	34.6%	15.0%[b]	2.3%
Senshusha Holding Company		62.0%	3.1%	3.4%
Insurance and banking companies			9.9%[c]	20.5%[c]
All others		3.6%	71.1%	73.6%

[a]Eight holdings ranging from 1.4 percent to 29.3 percent.

[b]Five holdings ranging from 1.5 percent to 4.4 percent.

[c]In 1955 and 1993, including Meiji Mutual Insurance Co, Mitsubishi Trust Bank; in 1955, including Kofukan Foundation and Noda Institute of Industrial Science; in 1993, including, Nitsuit Trust Bank, Nippon Life Insurance, Sumitomo Trust, and Yasuda Trust.

SOURCES: W. Mark Fruin, *Kikkoman—Company, Clan, and Community* (Cambridge, MA, Harvard, University Press, 1983), pp. 98, 121, 249; *Japan Company Handbook*, Toyo Keizai, Inc., 1993, p. 207.

EXHIBIT 6

National Output and Company Market Share of Shoyu (in kiloliters)[a]

Year	National Output (Japan)	Noda Shoyu Share
1893	230,360	3.5%
1903	317,500	4.5%
1913	430,435	6.1%
1923	624,764	5.1%
1933	576,026	10.1%
1943	680,955	12.0%
1953	822,179	14.1%
1963	1,051,730	21.4%
1973	1,277,887	31.4%
1983	n.a.	33.0%
1993	n.a.	28.0%[c]
1994	1,323,529[b]	27.2%[c]

[a]I kiloliter = 264 gallons.

[b]Derived from Kikkoman's production of 360,000 kl and its 27.2 percent market share. Residents of Japan consumed about 2.6 gallons of soy sauce per capita yearly. In contrast, U.S. citizens consumed about 10 tablespoons.

[c]As reported by UBS Securities Limited, May 28, 1996, in *Investext*. This source also reported that demand for soy sauce was flat in Japan and production between 1984 and 1994 had declined about 5.1 percent.

SOURCE: W. Mark Fruin, *Kikkoman—Company, Clan, and Community* (Cambridge, MA, Harvard University Press, 1983), pp. 40–41.

Kikkoman Corporation. The word *Kikkoman* is a combination of "kikko" (the shell of a tortoise) and "man" (10,000). It was taken from an old Japanese saying, "A crane lives a thousand years and a tortoise 10,000 years." (Implying, in other words, "May you live as long!") In essence, the Kikkoman brand connotes a long-lasting living thing. Kikkoman had become well-known for its advertising skill in Japan and had found that the word *Kikkoman* was easy for Americans to pronounce.

The company also diversified its product line using its expertise in shoyu manufacture, fermentation, brewing, and foods marketing. This diversification included a 1963 venture to market Del Monte products in Japan. In 1990, the company bought the Del Monte assets and marketing rights for the Del Monte brand name in the Asia–Pacific region. (Exhibit 7 shows Kikkoman Corporation's product lists as of 1949, 1981, and 1993.) Kikkoman's R&D expertise led to activities in biotechnology and products such as enzymes, diagnostic reagents, and other biologically active substances used to test for microorganisms in water samples in hospitals, food processing factories, and semiconductor plants. The company also developed a number of patents at home and overseas. The company became involved in both the import and export of wines. It also undertook activities in food processing machinery. In spite of the diversification, Kikkoman's domestic sales were still about 55 percent soy-sauce related.

In the 1990s, soy sauce continued as a perennial favorite in Japan's cuisine, although demand was essentially flat. Among the remaining 3,000 shoyu companies in Japan, Kikkoman produced 360,000 kl in Japan, or about 27 percent of the country's output (Exhibit 6). The company faced price pressures

1949	1981	1994
Kikkoman Brand	**Kikkoman Brand**	**Kikkoman Brand**
soy sauce, sauce, memmi, and tsuyu (soup bases)	soy sauce, mild soy sauce (lower salt, 8%), light color soy sauce (usu-kuchi), teriyaki barbecue marinade and sauce, Worcestershire sauce, tonkatsu sauce, memmi and tsuyu (soup bases), sukiyaki sauce, instant soy soup mix, instant osumono (clear broth soup mix)	soy sauce, mild soy sauce (lower salt, 8%), light color soy sauce (usu-kuchi), teriyaki sauce, Worcestershire sauce, tonkatsu sauce, memmi (soup base), sukiyaki sauce, sashimi soy sauce, lemon flavored soy sauce, mirin (sweet rice wine), Aji-Mirin, plum wine, instant miso (soybean pasta) soups, egg flower soup mixes, rice crackers, tofu, neo-genmai (puffed brown rice), genmai soups, oolong tea, tsuyudakono (soup base), ponzu soy sauce, soy sauce dressing, oyster sauce, bonito stock
Manjo Brand	**Manjo Brand**	**Manjo Brand**
mirin (sweet rice wine), sake, shochu, whiskey	mirin (sweet rice wine), shochu, plum wine	triangle, komaki
	Yomonoharu Brand	**Yomonoharu Brand**
	sake	
	Del Monte Brand	**Del Monte Brand**
	tomato ketchup, juice, puree, paste, chili sauce, Mandarin orange juice	tomato ketchup, juice, fruit drinks, Mandarin orange juice
	Disney Brand	
	fruit juice (orange, pineapple, grape), nectar (peach, orange)	
	Mann's Brand[a]	**Mann's Brand**
	wine and sparkling wine, brandy	koshu, koshu (vintage), zenkoji, blush, brandy
	Higeta Brand	
	shoyu, tsuyu, Worcestershire sauce	
	Ragu Brand	
	spaghetti sauces	

(continued)

EXHIBIT 7 Kikkoman Corporation Products and Product Lines
(continued)

1949	1981	1994
	Kikko's Brand	
	tomato ketchup	**Beyoung**
	Monet Brand	protein powder, wheat germ
	cognac	**Imported wines**
		aujoux, chateau tatour, borie-manoux, franz reh and sohn, pol roger

[a]The company established its Mann Wine subsidiary in 1964.

SOURCES: W. Mark Fruin, *Kikkoman—Company, Clan, and Community* (Cambridge, MA, Harvard University Press, 1983), pp. 275–276; "Flavors That Bring People Together," Kikkoman Corporation Brochure, 1994.

---

especially on its base product of soy sauce, mainly due to the competitive pressures at the retail level in Japan and the aggressive introduction of private brands. Sales in the Del Monte line also decreased in the early 1990s. To improve performance, Kikkoman began to reduce its product line from a high of 5,000 items to an expected eventual 2,500. One bright spot was the growth in wines and spirits. In addition, Kikkoman also introduced successful new soy sauce related products in 1993, 1994, and 1995 in the form of two soup stocks and Steak Soy Sauce. Profit increases in the early 1990s came primarily from higher-priced luxury products. (Exhibits 8 and 9 display the parent company financial statements.) The company recognized that continuing success in its mature domestic market would depend on continuous development of new applications and variations of its older products as well as development of new products.

EXHIBIT 8 Parent Company Revenues by Product Line ((¥)m)

	1994	1995	Percent Change	1996E	Percent Change
Soy sauce	74,666	73,843	−1.1	75,000	1.6
Food	15,091	16,310	8.1	18,500	13.4
Del Monte	24,692	19,857	−19.6	19,000	−4.3
Alcohol	24,993	25,925	3.7	27,000	4.1
Others	4,159	4,285	3.0	4,500	5.0
Total	143,601	140,220	−2.4	144,000	2.7

SOURCE: Table 5: UBS Securities Limited, May 28, 1996, as available on *Investext*.

EXHIBIT 9   Parent Company Balance Sheet ((¥)m)

	1993	1994	1995
Current assets	78,463	81,805	80,749
Fixed assets	88,007	86,029	89,599
Total	166,802	168,000	170,348
Short-term liabilities	33,469	32,033	46,762
Long-term liabilities	79,898	79,527	66,567
Equity	53,434	56,440	57,019
Total liabilities and equity	166,802	168,000	170,348

SOURCE: Table 11: UBS Securities Limited, May 28, 1996, as reported by *Investext*.

Kikkoman in the United States in the Post–World War II Era

U.S. Market Potential

The various Mogi family branches and Noda Shoyu Company had expanded company efforts beyond Japan since the early 1800s. By the end of World War II, the various family enterprises and the Noda Shoyu Company had ended all activities outside Japan. Japanese expatriates living in various countries and other peoples whose traditional cuisine used shoyu comprised the company's primary pre–World War II markets. In 1949, Kikkoman started to export soy sauce, mainly to the United States. In the 1950s, consumption of soy sauce began to decline in Japan. Noda Shoyu Company made the decision to invest heavily in expanding the international sales of Kikkoman brand shoyu to overseas markets. Prior to World War II, Noda Shoyu's major overseas markets were Asia and Hawaii. After the war, the company decided to focus on the mainland United States because (1) political and economic conditions in Asia were very unstable, (2) the Japanese community in Hawaii had relearned shoyu brewing during World War II, and there were many small Hawaiian shoyu breweries that would have made competition intense in that market, and (3) the United States had a healthy and rapidly growing economy.

Several changes in the U.S. market made that market attractive to Noda Shoyu Company. First, Americans who had been in Asia during or just after World War II developed a taste for Japanese goods, including food. Second, the company expected that as Asians in the United States became more Americanized, their consumption of traditional foods including soy sauce would decline. Third, American eating habits were shifting to more natural foods and to food that could be prepared quickly. Noda Shoyu Company moved to target both Asians and non-Asians in its marketing efforts.

During the 1956 U.S. presidential elections, Noda Shoyu bought air time to advertise Kikkoman brand products. Yuzaburo Mogi, son of the head of the company's planning department, urged this move to U.S. television advertising.

U.S. Distribution Activities

During the years immediately after World War II, Japanese companies in general relied on a small group of internationalized and entrepreneurial Japanese and Japanese-American individuals. Sale of food products in the United States involved a complex distribution system with heavy reliance on food brokers as promoters to local wholesalers and retailers. Food brokers required careful training by a knowledgeable sales team in how to use the product, especially where the product was unusual or unfamiliar to consumers. Food brokers marketed the product to wholesalers and large retailers, took orders for the product, and relayed the orders to the manufacturer or, in the case of foreign manufacturers, the manufacturer's agent. The manufacturer or agent then made delivery of the product to the wholesaler or retailer and handled all billing and accounts, paying the broker a commission for his/her marketing representation. The food broker was an important link between the manufacturer and the wholesaler or retailer. Food brokers were evaluated based on their ability to persuade retailers and wholesalers to carry products and to feature them prominently.

In 1957, the company formed Kikkoman International, Inc. (KII), a joint venture between Noda Shoyu Company in Japan and Pacific Trading of California. KII was incorporated in San Francisco to serve as the marketing and distribution center for Kikkoman products in the United States. Most of the products were produced by Noda Shoyu Company, but some were purchased from other manufacturers and sold under the Kikkoman label.

Over the next ten years, sales grew 20 to 30 percent a year. In 1960, the Safeway grocery store chain agreed to have some of its stores carry Kikkoman soy sauce. Noda Shoyu opened regional sales offices for KII in Los Angeles (1958), New York City (1960), Chicago (1965), and Atlanta (1977). Retail marketing activities included in-store demonstrations, advertising campaigns in women's magazines that emphasized soy sauce use in American cuisine, and limited television commercials. The company used brokers as their distribution channels to supermarkets and wholesalers for the small oriental retail stores. The company encouraged food brokers through contests and training. For the food service and industrial market segments, the company carried out industrial magazine ad campaigns and special educational programs. The company also formed partnerships with the American Veal Manufacturers' Association and the Avocado Association to feature Kikkoman soy sauce in their product advertisements.

Other major international companies had to modify their products for the United States. However, Kikkoman marketed the same soy sauce in the United States as in Japan. The company's experience in its campaign to "westernize" soy sauce for the Japanese market applied to the campaign in the United States. In the United States, Kikkoman provided traditional, low-sodium preservative-free, and dehydrated soy sauce. The company also marketed tailor-made sauces, other food extracts, and agents.

Exploration of Potential U.S. Manufacturing Capacity

As early as 1965, Kikkoman Corporation began to explore the possibility of manufacturing in the United States. However, the company determined that sales in North America were insufficient to support the economies of scale required for a minimum efficient scale production facility. Instead, in 1968 Kikkoman Corporation contracted with a subsidiary of Leslie Salt Company of Oakland, California, to bottle the Kikkoman soy sauce shipped in bulk from Japan and to blend and bottle teriyaki sauce, a major ingredient of which was soy sauce. These bottling efforts constituted Kikkoman's first post–World War II manufacturing efforts in the United States. Bottling in the United States reduced customs and tariff costs. However, moving goods back and forth from the United States and Japan added considerably to the company's costs. In the mid 1980s, Japan imported 95 percent and 88 percent of its soybeans and wheat, respectively. The United States was Japan's major source of supply. Transportation of raw materials (e.g., soybeans and wheat) to Japan was between five percent and 20 percent of preproduction costs; transportation costs of brewed soy sauce from Japan to the United States was 25 percent of production costs. Various import/export restrictions and tariffs increased the risk and expense of importing raw materials to Japan and exporting finished goods to the United States.

The North American market was potentially much larger than the Japanese market, and Kikkoman had a greater share of the North American market than the company had in Japan. Yuzaburo Mogi hired a Columbia University classmate as a consultant, and the company formed a team to work with him to consider a U.S. plant. By 1970, the analyses, in spite of higher U.S. labor costs, favored construction of a U.S. manufacturing facility. As Yuzaburo

Mogi put the company's motivation, "We made a decision to go after the American consumer."

Selection of Walworth, Wisconsin

The team considered over 60 potential sites in the east, west, and midwest. The team chose the midwest because of its central location and crop production. Ultimately, the team selected a 200-acre dairy farm site in Walworth, Wisconsin. Walworth provided the best fit with the five criteria established by the company: (1) access to markets (proximity to Milwaukee and Chicago, as well as the geographic convenience of a midway point between the east and west coasts made shipping relatively efficient); (2) ample supplies of wheat and soybeans (soybeans came from Wisconsin, wheat from North Dakota, and salt from Canada); (3) a dedicated workforce; (4) a strong community spirit; and (5) an impeccable supply of water. Kikkoman also appreciated Wisconsin's emphasis on a clean environment.

Walworth, Wisconsin, was situated about two hours northwest of Chicago and about one hour west of Milwaukee. A community of about 1,100, Walworth was surrounded by some of the most productive farmland in the United States. The area included a number of other smaller communities whose economies depended primarily on farming and summer vacation home residences. The company hired a local consultant, lawyer Milton Neshek, who ultimately became general counsel of Kikkoman Foods, Inc. Mr. Neshek described the original reaction to Kikkoman's purchase of prime farmland as mixed, "with a small faction on the town board opposed to the company coming in." Yuzaburo Mogi described the opposition as strong. Residents of the small, rural, close-knit farming community expressed concerns about the impact of a large, especially foreign, corporation in a small community, potential inflation of land values, and the possibility of industrial pollution.

One of Neshek's partners, Thomas Godfrey, visited Kikkoman facilities in Noda City, Japan. "When Kikkoman called me in 1971," said Godfrey, "and asked me to create a Wisconsin corporation for them so they could make soy sauce, I didn't even know what the hell soy sauce was. Nobody else around here did either." Walworth's plant manager, Bill Wenger, recalled his introduction to the company. In 1972, he was stationed with the U.S. Marines in Hawaii. His mother sent a newspaper clipping about the soy sauce plant, suggesting that it might be a good place to begin his return to civilian life. Wenger and his wife didn't know what soy sauce was either, but his wife went to the local grocery store and bought a bottle. As Wenger described it, the purchase was ". . . some horrible local Hawaiian brand. She brought it home and opened it. We looked at one another and said, '*@& . . . , this stuff is terrible.' " Another of the three American production managers employed at the plant had a similar tale. The production manager said, "The first year I worked here, we never had any soy sauce in my home. My wife wouldn't buy it, wouldn't even allow it in the house. I finally brought home a bottle and put it on some meatloaf. Now we use it on just about everything. I put it on peaches. And we even have a local minister who puts it on his ice cream . . . I do too. It's good."

No other Japanese-owned manufacturing facility had been constructed in the United States at the time. Neshek's partner, Godfrey, visited Noda because as he put it, "I had to see for myself what it was they were talking about. I had to make sure the factory wasn't going to pollute the air and water and stink up the place." Local Kikkoman representatives met with organizations such as the local Grange, Farm Bureau groups, church groups, Rotary, and ladies' clubs. Wisconsin's governor, Patrick Lucey, came to one of the seven town meetings held to discuss the plant and explain the state's role and position. Yuzaburo Mogi described the process as "removing the fears of the local people and local council about the building of the new factory." The company was able to convince area residents that Kikkoman would not pollute the environment and would use local labor and other resources. The final vote of the county zoning board was 53 for, 13 against. The town board declined to oppose the zoning board's action. Among other issues, Kikkoman put a great deal of effort into reducing potential pollution. In talking about this process of "nemawashi," or root tending, Mr. Mogi emphasized the importance of a prosperous coexistence between the company and the local community. He said,

"We've been doing business in Noda for 360 years. We learned a long time ago that to survive you need to coexist with the surrounding community."

Opening the New Plant

In January 1971, Kikkoman executives along with Japanese, Walworth, and Wisconsin officials held a ceremonial groundbreaking on the 200-acre site. A Cleveland, Ohio, design and construction firm built the plant. Other American companies, many located in the region, built many of the critical components. The initial investment in the 10,000-kiloliter facility was $8 million, and the plant was finished just in time to avoid the 1973 American embargo on the sale of soybeans to Japan. Kikkoman's Walworth plant was the first Japanese investment in production capacity in the United States in the post–World War II period and the first plant Kikkoman built outside Japan after World War II. Opening ceremonies included dignitaries and officials from Wisconsin, Kikkoman, Japan, and the United States. The 700 invited guests heard the texts of telegrams from the Japanese prime minister and President Richard Nixon. President Nixon referred to the plant as a ". . . visionary step (that) will mean meaningful trade relations and balance of trade and will enhance further friendships between our two countries."

From its opening in 1972 through the mid-1990s, the company expanded the Walworth facility eight times to 500,000 square feet. Kikkoman invested in facilities or equipment every year with production increasing eight to ten percent per year. Originally, the plant produced two products, soy sauce and teriyaki sauce. In the mid-1990s, the plant produced 18 products, including regular and light soy sauce, teriyaki steak sauce, sweet and sour sauce, and tempura dip. All but one used a soy base. The company had been very careful about pollution, treating its wastewater carefully so that there was no threat to nearby popular Geneva Lake. The Walworth town clerk said, "There's no noise, no pollution. I live about three-quarters of a mile from them, and once a day, I get a whiff of something that's like a sweet chocolate odor. It's no problem." The company marketed the plant's output in all 50 states plus Canada and Mexico. Soy sauce was shipped in many varieties, including bottles ranging from five to 40 ounces, one- to five-gallon pails, and sometimes in stainless steel tank trucks for large customers. McDonald's, for example, used soy sauce in one of the Chicken McNuggets condiments.

Management of the Walworth Plant

The company maintained a state-of-the-art laboratory at the Walworth facilities. However, plant management pointed out that the most accurate test during production was the human nose. "Our people have worked with the product for so long, a whiff can tell them something is not quite right," said one Kikkoman director. The venture was described as "a prime example of the best combination of Japanese and American business and industrial savvy." As the plant's general manager, Michitaro Nagasawa, a Ph.D. in biochemistry from the University of Wisconsin, put it, "The productivity of this plant is the highest of all our plants. . . . It's an exceptional case in Kikkoman history. We took the sons and daughters of farmers, trained them and taught them about total quality management. They were raw recruits with no experience in making soy sauce. People with farm backgrounds are very diligent workers. They will work seven days a week, 24 hours a day if necessary. They understand what hard work is."

The plant opened with 50 employees. Originally, 14 Japanese Kikkoman employees and their families came to Walworth to train employees and get the plant functioning. The Japanese families scattered in groups of two or three to settle in Walworth and various nearby communities. Local women's community organizations "adopted" the Japanese wives, formed one-to-one friendships, and helped the Japanese wives become acclimated to the communities, including learning to drive, using the local supermarkets, and hiring baby-sitters for their children. The Japanese husbands joined local service clubs. "That helped achieve an understanding between the Americans and Japanese and helped them to assimilate faster. It exposed Japanese people to a farming town that had had no Asian people before," noted Bill Nelson, Kikkoman Foods vice president. Kikkoman established the practice of rotating its Japanese employees back to Japan after an average of five years in the United States. In the mid-1990s, only seven Japanese families remained in the Walworth area, still spread throughout the local communities.

Community Contributions

Kikkoman Foods, Inc., was an active and contributing member of the community. The company donated time and funds on three levels. At the local level, the company established Kikkoman Foods Foundation in 1993. The foundation, which was to be ultimately funded at the $3 million level, was formed to support area charitable activities. The company supported as many as 30 local projects a year, including college scholarships for area students, local hospital activities, a vocational program that assisted people in developing employment-related skills, and a nearby facility that preserved circus-related items. As Walworth's town clerk put it, "They sponsor just about everything—Community Chest (an organization similar to the United Way), Boy Scouts, Girl Scouts, all the way down the line. They're very good neighbors." The clerk treasurer from a nearby town said, "You see their name in the paper almost every week, helping out some organization."

At the state level, Kikkoman Foods, Inc., supported the University of Wisconsin educational system, established up to four Beloit College scholarships to honor Governor Lucey at his alma mater, and funded a Mogi Keizaburo scholarship at the Milwaukee School of Engineering. Members of the board of directors served on several public service boards and commissions. At the national level, Kikkoman Corporation, through its U.S. subsidiary Kikkoman Foods, Inc., supported Youth for Understanding exchange programs. At the fifth anniversary celebration, Kikkoman's chairman reported that the plant had developed better than had been anticipated. At the tenth anniversary celebration of the Kikkoman plant, the local Walworth paper reported, "In the ten years that Kikkoman Foods, Inc., has been located here, it has become an integrated part of the community. The company has truly become a part of the Walworth community, and not only in a business sense." In 1987, reflecting Kikkoman's contributions, Wisconsin's govenor appointed Yuzaburo Mogi as Wisconsin's honorary ambassador to Japan.

Kikkoman's Japanese–American Management in the United States

In the mid-1990s, Kikkoman operated its U.S. activities through two subsidiaries, Kikkoman Foods, Inc. (KFI), and Kikkoman International, Inc. (KII). KFI owned and operated the Walworth manufacturing plant. KII in San Francisco, California, undertook marketing responsibilities, including wholesaler and distributor activities throughout the United States. The boards of directors for both subsidiaries had several members from the parent corporation but were primarily Americans from among local operations officers or local Walworth citizens (for KFI) or the broader U.S. community (for KII). The KFI board met as a whole once a year and rotated the site of its annual stockholders' meeting between Japan and Wisconsin. An executive committee met monthly to consider operational decisions. The executive committee included Yuzaburo Mogi, who attended two to three meetings in the United States every year, and the head of Kikkoman Corporation's International Division. The remaining members of the executive committee included American and Japanese officers from the U.S. corporation. The KII board operated in a similar manner but met only in the United States.

Yuzaburo Mogi believed that a long-term commitment was essential for international success. A 1961 alumnus of Columbia University's Graduate School of Business, Mr. Mogi was the first Japanese to graduate from a U.S. university with an MBA degree. In the years following graduation, he worked in various departments at Kikkoman, including accounting, finance, computers, long-range planning, and new product development. In time, he took on other roles, including member of Kikkoman's board of directors (1979), managing director of the company (1982), executive management director (1989), and executive vice president (1994). The seventeenth generation of his family to brew soy sauce, Mr. Mogi had become Kikkoman's president in early 1995. He explained his view regarding the necessity of a long-term perspective: "We should do business from a longer range viewpoint. It will be very difficult to expect fruitful results in the short run under different and difficult circumstances. Failure will be inevitable in foreign countries if one proceeds with a short-range view. In fact, it took Kikkoman 16 years to become established in the United States."

Of the five senior managers at the Walworth facility, three were Japanese and two were American. The plant manager, the finance manager, and the laboratory manager were Japanese. It was expected that these three positions would continue to be Japanese appointments. One American manager described the situation: "We know we will only attain a certain level, but that's OK, though. I can accept that. Soy sauce has been made in Japan for centuries. It's their product, their technology. They have the history, the research."

The general manager, i.e., plant manager, was the most senior person in authority at the plant and was responsible directly to headquarters in Japan. The appointment would be a person who had been with the company for many years. The finance manager's position required someone who was familiar with Japanese accounting systems and who was steeped in the Japanese emphasis on long-range profits. Japanese corporate headquarters controlled their foreign branches through their accounting and finance sections.

Mr. Mogi explained the Japanese appointment to the position of laboratory manager: "The production of soy sauce is very sophisticated. Normally, we recruit graduates with a master's degree in Japan who have gone to universities that have specialized programs in soy sauce production. In America, there is no university that teaches soy sauce production techniques, so it is difficult to promote Americans into general manager positions." As Dr. Magasawa, general manager at the Walworth plant, put it in explaining the discriminating tastes the Japanese have developed since childhood, "The sensory system, passion, feeling, or sensitivity can't transfer. That is based on just experience. Our vice president is a kind of god in this plant because he recognizes (even) a slight difference . . . I don't have that. That's why I can't be manufacturing vice president. I am a general manager—nothing special. I am a biochemist (with) 39 years at Kikkoman, mostly in research."

Decisions at the Walworth plant, when possible, were made by consensus. KFI vice president Bill Nelson described the plant management as American in content and Japanese in style, with decisions arrived at from the bottom up and most matters of importance needing a consensus of employees. "It's hard, really, to get at because of the fact that nothing . . . here should run in an American style or a Japanese style or what have you. It was just simply— let's see what happens when you have both parties participate," he said. Nelson gave the example of an idea for changing summer working hours to start at 7 A.M. instead of 8 A.M. so that workers could leave earlier and enjoy more daylight. It was, Nelson, pointed out, unusual for a company to even entertain the idea. Nelson explained the process: "Instead of simply exploring it on a management level, here we started the process by asking individual employees what personal inconvenience would be experienced if the hours were changed."

Milton Neshek observed that Japanese management and the middle management at the Walworth plant worked well together with long-range budgeting and strategic planning carried out by the Japanese executive team. He described the situation: "Our 30 employees feel like part of our family. That makes management more responsive to employees. Decisions, whenever possible, are made by consensus." The fact that the plant has no labor union was no surprise to Nelson. As he put it, a union "has never been an issue here."

Yuzaburo Mogi summarized Kikkoman's approach to its U.S. operations and, in particular, its Walworth plant as a five-point approach:

Kikkoman has been successful doing business in the United States by adapting to American laws, customers, and most importantly, its culture . . . (An) important matter to consider, especially when establishing a manufacturing plant in a foreign country, is the maintenance of what has come to be called "harmony" with society and the local community. A foreign concern should try to prosper together with society and the local community. . . . It is important to try to localize the operation . . . (Our) . . . first commitment is the employment of as many local people as possible. Second we try to participate in local activities . . . trying to be a good corporate citizen (in Wisconsin) and contributing to society through our business activities. Third, we have been trying to avoid the so-called "Japanese village" . . . by advising our people from Japan not to live together in one single community, but to spread out and live in several separate communities in order to become more familiar with the local people. Fourth, we try to do business with American companies. The fifth commitment is our practice of delegating most authority to local management in order to better reflect local circumstances. Through this process we are better able to make the most responsible decision. If we have an opinion, for example, we discuss it with other members at a local meeting in our American plant before reaching a decision. Kikkoman attempts to avoid a remote-control situation with letters or telephone calls from Japan. . . . If we have an opinion, we discuss it with other members at a local meeting in our American plant before reaching a decision.

The plant did encounter intercultural issues, however. For example, plant manager Bill Wenger pointed out, "Communication can be a problem sometimes. The language barrier is one reason. Then there's the problem of saving face. If a mistake is made, the Japanese tend to cover up for one another so the person who made the mistake doesn't lose face."

The company was a popular local employer in Walworth. Local unemployment was phenomenally low at two percent, but the Walworth plant had over 1,000 active applications on file for the plant's total 136 positions. However, turnover among plant employees was negligible. "No one quits unless it is a move by a spouse. Our absenteeism is minimal and as for tardiness—we just don't have it. We offer competitive wages and good benefits . . . employees feel like part of our family," said general counsel Neshek. Company officials stated that they paid about ten percent more than the state average of $9.71 per hour, and employees did not have to contribute to the cost of their health insurance. As the company's vice president Shin Ichi Sugiyama put it, "In management, our primary concern is always the employee." The employees reported, "We feel like they listen to us. Our opinion counts, and we have the ability to make change, to better the company."

Mr. Sugiyama pointed out that the Walworth plant's productivity and quality had been about equal to that of Japanese plants. Productivity improved following the plant opening and by 1993 was actually the best of all the company's plants.

The U.S. Market in the 1990s[3]

U.S. Demand in the 1990s

After the opening of the Walworth plant, Kikkoman's U.S. sales growth slowed somewhat. However, Ken Saito, Kikkoman's brand manager for the midwest, summarized the company's hopes: "Americans are more adventurous than Japanese when it comes to trying new foods. That's why we have developed some products only for the American market. But most Americans still are not familiar with how to use soy sauce." Thus, the company developed a number of non-oriental recipes that call for soy sauce and other Kikkoman products, for example, teriyaki chicken wings and Pacific Rim pizza with sweet and sour sauce, beef and chicken fajitas, and grilled salmon with confetti salsa flavored with "lite" soy sauce. Kikkoman clearly expected Americans to increasingly use soy sauce for applications beyond oriental foods and expected significant growth in the company's base product in the United States. According to Saito, "We figure the market in the United States will increase 100 times in the next decade." Kikkoman marketing coordinator, Trisha MacLeod, articulated the goal as ". . . to get consumers to realize soy sauce is the oldest manmade condiment, and that it can also be used in meatloaf, barbecue—across the spectrum."

MacLeod pointed out, "Americans eat a lot more soy sauce than they realize." However, America's per capita consumption was barely ten tablespoons, translating into $300 million in North American sales. In contrast, Japanese per capita consumption was about 10.5 quarts per person, which translated into about $1.4 billion in annual sales in Japan.

The population of Asian immigrants and families of Asian descent was projected to grow significantly in the United States. The California population increased 127 percent to 2.8 million during the 1980s. The total population of Asian–Americans in the United States was estimated at 7.3 million in 1990, up 108 percent over the 1980s. Asian people represented the traditional mainstay market for oriental foods. Asians had higher income and educational levels than any other ethnic group in the United States. However, each country represented a different cuisine, and the different Asian ethnic groups required different marketing approaches. Asian populations had spread throughout many parts of the United States, and retail outlets were learning how to highlight and display oriental foods to spur sales. Restaurants greatly influenced American food-buying habits. One industry executive observed that almost all U.S. restaurant kitchens in the 1990s had soy sauce. A 1996 National Restaurant Association study indicated that ethnic foods were increasing in popularity. Thus, oriental food manufacturers and distributors expected that oriental food sales would increase sharply.

Some information in the mid-1990s suggested strong and increasing popularity for oriental foods. U.S. sales of oriental foods had slowed considerably. The most recent aggregate information regarding the demand for oriental food in the United States in the mid-1990s is shown in Exhibit 10.

By the late 1980s, consumers began to indicate dissatisfaction with canned entrees, at $81 million in sales the second largest subcategory of oriental foods. Sales of this subcategory had declined as much as ten percent (1991 to 1992) and showed no signs of abating. Competition was intense, with a third of all products sold on the basis of feature, price, and/or display promotion.

U.S. Major Competitors

Kikkoman's two major competitors in the United States were Chun King and LaChoy. Both companies made soy sauce by hydrolyzing vegetable protein. This European derived method was faster and less expensive than the six-month fermentation process Kikkoman used. By 1971, Kikkoman had surpassed Chun King in supermarket sales of soy sauce, becoming number two in the American marketplace. In 1976, Kikkoman outsold LaChoy brand soy sauce and became the number one retailer of soy sauce in the United States, a position it continued to hold in the mid-1990s. However, the company faced strong competitors in the oriental foods category and in the sauces and condiments subcategory.

The new consumer focus was on oriental food ingredients that individuals could add to home-cooked dishes. "People are cooking more oriental foods at home," said Chun King's vice president of marketing, "Over 40 percent of U.S. households stir-fry at least once a month. Sauces are an opportunity to get away from the canned image." Indeed, sauces were the only growth area on the oriental food category, with 1992 sales rising 11 percent over the previous year. Rivals Chun King and LaChoy were flooding the oriental foods aisle in American supermarkets with new products. LaChoy had about 40 percent of the shelf products in oriental foods, and Chun King had about 20 percent.

However, there were more changes than just new products. In the early 1990s, LaChoy and Chun King had revved up their marketing efforts under new ownership. LaChoy was owned by ConAgra's Hunt-Wesson division. Among other initiatives, ConAgra, a major U.S. food company, hired a new advertising firm for LaChoy.

A Singapore-based firm purchased Chun King in 1989 and brought in a new management team. As one observer put it, "The brand had really been neglected as part of Nabisco (its previous owner). It was just a small piece of a big pie." The new management team introduced a line of seasoned chow mein noodles and another of hot soy sauces. The firm's marketing plan included consumer promotions and a print ad campaign in women's magazines. Chun King's 1992 oriental food sales were estimated at $30 million. In mid-1995, ConAgra purchased Chun King from the Singapore company and added the brand to its Hunt-Wesson division. ConAgra was no stranger to the Chun King brand. The large U.S. competitor had purchased Chun King's frozen food line in 1986 from Del Monte. It was expected that Hunt-Wesson would eventually

EXHIBIT 10

U.S. Oriental Food Sales ($000,000)

Year	1992	1993	1994
Sales	$275	$305	$301

SOURCE: Information Resources, Inc., Chicago, IL.

consolidate manufacturing but continue to aggressively advertise the two brands separately. As a Hunt-Wesson executive put it, "They're both established leaders in their field, and they both have brand strength."

LaChoy advertised itself as "the world's largest producer of oriental foods created for American tastes." The company led the oriental foods category with sales (excluding frozen) of $87 million in 1992 and $104.4 million in 1994. Its products included chow mein noodles, bamboo shoots, sauces, and miscellaneous foods. About $28 million of the 1992 sales came from sauce and marinade sales. La-Choy's manager of corporate communications indicated that the Chicago-based firm planned no increase in marketing spending in reaction to the new Chun King initiatives. However, the company did plan to advertise two new lines—Noodle Entrees and Stir-Fry Vegetables 'N Sauce. The company expected to expend most of its marketing support for the latter product line, a set of vegetables in four sauces formulated for consumers to stir-fry with their choice of meat.

Kikkoman and Other Competitors

Kikkoman remained the one bright spot in the oriental food category of sauces and marinades. Kikkoman controlled $63 million of the $160 million sauces/marinades segment and supported its position with a moderate amount of advertising—$3.2 million in 1992, about the same as 1991. In its major product lines, Kikkoman controlled about two-thirds of the California market and had about one-third market share in other major U.S. sales regions. The company was test-marketing a new line of sauces for addition to the consumer's own vegetables and meat.

Kikkoman also had to consider recent moves by several other competitors. Yamasa Shoyu Co., Ltd., Japan's second-largest soy sauce maker, had announced plans to build a factory in Oregon in mid-1994. This multigenerational company was founded in 1645 in Choshi City, Japan. Estimates on the cost of the Oregon factory ranged from $15 million to $20 million, and the plant was expected to eventually employ 50 workers. Yamasa intended to produce soy sauce for the U.S. market by using soybeans shipped from the midwest. It took Yamasa

four years to select the final site for its new plant. The company produced a number of products in addition to soy sauce, including other food and drugs made from biological raw materials such as soybean protein and wheat starch.

Hong Kong–based Lee Kum Kee was a producer and importer of Chinese-oriented sauces and condiments. Lee Kum Kee had opened a sauce manufacturing plant in Los Angeles in 1991 to keep up with rising U.S. demand and to reduce dependence on imports, thus avoiding payment of import duties, which could be as high as 20 percent. The company was a Hong Kong subsidiary of one of Japan's leading soy sauce brewers. Lee Kum Kee retailed its sauces in big supermarket chains in all 50 states. Historically, the company imported its soy sauce through an independent U.S.-based importer of the same name. The U.S. importer also imported about 40 other food products, mostly marinades, curries, and sauces from the East. Lee Kum Kee found its sales propelled by the population doubling of Americans of Asian or Pacific Island descent.

Competitor San-J International of the San-Jirushi Corporation of Kuwana, Japan, built a soy sauce plant in Richmond, Virginia, in 1988. Hawaiian competitor Noh Foods of Hawaii innovated a line of oriental dried seasonings and powdered mixes. In reaction, other manufacturers, including Kikkoman, produced copycat products. Noh Foods distributed its products in the United States, Europe, and Australia through distributors and trade show activities.

Kikkoman's International Position

The Kikkoman Vision

In the mid-1990s, Kikkoman manufactured in four countries and marketed its brand products in over 90 countries. (Exhibit 11 shows the comparison of domestic and non-Japan sales and operating profits.) Of the company's 3,200 employees, over 1,000 were in international subsidiaries, and only five percent of those were Japanese. The company saw at least part of its mission as contributing to international cultural exchange. Yuzaburo Mogi explained,

EXHIBIT 11

Consolidated Results FY 1995 ((¥)m)

	Domestic	Non-Japan
Sales	162,426	40,860
Operating Profit	6,640	4,152
Operating Margin	4.0	10.1

SOURCE: Table 7: UBS Securities Limited, May 28, 1996, as reported by *Investext*.

Kikkoman believes that soy sauce marketing is the promotion of the international exchange of food culture. In order to create a friendlier world, I believe we need many types of cultural exchanges. Among these, there is one that is most closely related to our daily lives—the eating of food. Soy sauce is one of the most important food cultures in Japan. Hence, the overseas marketing of soy sauce means the propagation of Japanese food culture throughout the world.

As one U.S. scholar who had studied the company extensively in the 1980s put it, "There is an evident willingness on the part of Kikkoman to experiment with new products, production techniques, management styles, and operational forms in the international arena." Yuzaburo Mogi put it similarly when he said, "It should be understood that adjustment to different laws, customs, and regulations is imperative, instead of complaining about those differences."

Kikkoman in Europe

Kikkoman began its marketing activities in Europe in 1972. Kikkoman found Europeans more conservative and slower to try new tastes than Americans. The firm found Germany the least conservative and opened restaurants there in 1973. By the early 1990s, the company had opened six Japanese steak houses in Germany. The restaurants gave their customers, over 90 percent of whom were non-Asian,

the opportunity to try new cuisine. The Kikkoman trading subsidiary in Germany was the company's European marketing arm. Said the managing director for Kikkoman's European marketing subsidiary located in Germany, "Germany and Holland are big business for us, as both countries are very much into interesting sauces and marinades." Kikkoman's managing director of Europe made it clear that he had aggressive plans to grow sales both by increasing the sales of soy sauce as well as extending the markets in which the company operated. The massive ready-made meal business in both the United States and Europe had huge potential for Kikkoman. The firm would need to market to end consumers at the retail level as well as to food manufacturers.

The company established its second overseas manufacturing facility in 1983. This facility supplied soy sauce to Australian and European markets. By the early 1990s, Kikkoman had about 50 percent of the Australian soy sauce market. The United Kingdom brand debut occurred in 1986, and the 1992 U.K. market was estimated at one billion pounds. In 1993, the firm opened a 25,000-square-foot warehouse in London. With $1.66 billion (U.S.) in sales, Kikkoman had come a long way with "just" soy sauce. Overall, analysts noted that the United States had experienced about ten percent annual growth in soy sauce demand and expected Europe to expand similarly.

Kikkoman in Asia

In Asia, the company opened a production facility in Singapore in 1983 and incorporated a trading company in 1990. Industry observers expected the company to enter the soy sauce market in China in the near future. In addition, other Asian countries offered various opportunities in sauces, condiments, and foods.

Kikkoman—The Challenges

The company the Mogi family had headed for nearly 400 years confronted a number of challenges on the global stage in the latter part of the 1990s. Kikkoman executives realized that the company's future could depend primarily on its mature domestic market. The multigeneration family firm would have to change its image as a maker of a mature product. As Mr. Mogi stated, "We . . . take pride in our ability to contribute to the exchange of cultures by using some of the world's most familiar flavors. We are now concentrating on further enhancing our ability to serve consumers in Japan and overseas. Kikkoman continues as a company that is proud of its heritage, but nevertheless willing and able to adapt to the constantly evolving requirements of our customers and markets."

Notes

1. In early 1996, the exchange rate was about 95 yen per U.S. dollar. Thus, in U.S. dollars, Kikkoman's market value was about $1.7 billion. Sales at year end 1995 for the consolidated company were 203 billion yen, or slightly less than $2 billion. (See Exhibits 2 and 3 for consolidated financial data and Exhibits 8, 9, and 11 for parent company and domestic versus non-Japan revenues plus other selected financial information.)

2. *Zaibatsu:* Industrial and financial combines dissolved by occupation fiat after World War II, but which have reemerged as somewhat weaker entities. Some of these *zaibatsu* have developed into large conglomerates such as Mitsubishi. However, they should be distinguished from *keiretsu* (of which Mitsubishi is also one of the largest). *Keiretsu* are informal enterprise group-based associations of banks, industrials, and so forth.

3. Information on the market and competitors was drawn primarily from InfoScan.

References

Allen, Sara Clark. "Kikkoman, a Good Neighbor in Wisconsin," *Business,* Tuesday, June 11, 1996.

Bergsman, Steve. "Patience and Perseverance in Japan," *Global Trade,* Vol. 109, Issue 8 (August 1989), pp. 10, 12.

Campbell, Dee Ann. "Del Monte Foods to See European Foods Business," *Business Wire,* April 17, 1990.

Demestrakakes, Pan. "Quality for the Ages," *Food Processing,* Vol. 70, No. 6 (September 1996).

"Fireflies Help Kill Germs," *Times Net Asia,* January 1, 1996.

Forbish, Lynn. "Grand Oriental Celebration Held for Opening of Kikkoman Foods," *Janesville Gazette,* June 18, 1973.

Forrest, Tracy. "Kikkoman: A Way of Life," *Super Marketing,* January 28, 1994.

Fruin, W. Mark. *Kikkoman: Company, Clan, and Community* (Cambridge, Massachusetts: Harvard University Press, 1983).

Hewitt, Lynda. "Liquid Spice," *Food Manufacture,* February, 1993, p. 23.

Hostveldt, John. "Japan's Kikkoman Corp. Brews Success Story in Walworth," *Business Dateline: The Business Journal—Milwaukee,* Vol. 3, No. 31, Sec. 3 (May 19, 1986), p. 17.

"In-Store: Happy New Year's Feast" (Article on Kikkoman's In-Store Promotion), *Brandsweek,* Vol. 37 (January 1, 1996), pp. 14–15.

Jensen, Debra. "Kikkoman Executive Lauds Wisconsin, Lucey," *Gazette,* January 13, 1989, p. 1B.

Jensen, Don. "A Stainless Success Story," *Kenosha News,* Business Section, August 1, 1993.

Jensen, Leah. "Kikkoman Spices Up Walworth's Quality of Life," *Janesville Gazette,* January 21, 1984.

Kikkoman Corporation: Flavors That Bring People Together (Company Brochure).

Kinugasa, Dean. "Kikkoman Corporation," 1979 (Private Translation by Norihito Tanaka and Marilyn Taylor, 1994).

LaChoy's Homepage (http://www.hunt-wesson.com/lachoy/main/mission/).

LaGrange, Maria L. "RJR Sells Del Monte Operations for $1.4 Billion," *Los Angeles Times,* Vol. 108, Issue 297, September 26, 1989, p. 2.

Mogi, Yuzaburo. "*Masatsunaki Kokusai Senryaku*" (Tokyo, Japan: Selnate Publishing Co., Ltd., 1988—in English Translation).

Mogi, Yuzaburo. "The Conduct of International Business: One Company's Credo—Kikkoman, Soy Sauce and the U.S. Market" (Available from Company).

Ostrander, Kathleen. "Kikkoman's Success Tied to Proper Blend," *Business Datelines (Wisconsin State Journal),* March 1, 1992, p. 29.

Plett, Edith. "Kikkoman Foods Marks Fifth Year," *Janesville Gazette,* January 26, 1979.

Redman, Russell. "Hunt-Wesson Acquires Chun King," *Supermarket News,* Vol. 45, No. 19 (May 8, 1995), p. 101.

SBA Homepage, Wisconsin Gallery.

Schoenburg, Lorraine. "Governor Supports Kikkoman," *Janesville Gazette,* September 14, 1989.

Shima, Takeshi. "Kikkoman's Thousand-Year History," *Business JAPAN,* January, 1989, p. 65.

"The Joy of Soy: How a Japanese Sauce Company Found a Happy Home in Walworth, Wisc.," *Chicago Tribune Magazine,* January 31, 1993, p. 13.

Wilkins, Mira. "Japanese Multinational in the United States: Continuity and Change, 1879–1990," *Business History Review,* Vol. 64, Issue 4 (Winter 1990), pp. 585–629.

Yates, Ronald E. "Wisconsin's Other Brew," *Chicago Tribune Magazine,* January 31, 1993, p. 14.

In addition to personal interviews in Tokyo, Walworth, Wisconsin, and San Francisco, information and quotations were also drawn from these references. This list is part of a much broader set of sources that the authors consulted.

APPENDIX A: The Making of Soy Sauce

The Chinese began making jiang, a precursor of soy sauce, about 2,500 years ago. The most likely story of soy sauce's origins relates how Kakushin, a Japanese Zen priest who studied in China, returned to Japan in the middle of the thirteenth century and began preparing a type of miso, or soybean paste produced through fermentation, that became a specialty of the area. By the end of the thirteenth century, the liquid was called *tamari* and sold commercially along with the miso. Experimentation with the raw ingredients and methods of fermentation began. Vegetarianism also became popular in Japan during this time, and people were eager for condiments to flavor their rather bland diet. Soldiers also found the transportability of the seasonings useful.

Soy sauce evolved from tamari and miso by adding wheat to the soybean fermentation mash. The Japanese modified the shoyu to include wheat to gentle the taste so that it did not overwhelm the delicate flavors of Japanese cuisine. Most households made their shoyu during the slack time in agricultural cycles. Families harvested grains in the fall and processed them into mash. The mash fermented beginning in October–December to January–March when the shoyu was pressed from the mash.

Regional differences among the soy sauces developed depending upon the mix of soybean, wheat, and fermentation techniques. Even in the last decade of the twentieth century, there were hundreds of local varieties of soy sauce available commercially in Japan.

Produced in the traditional way, soy sauce was a natural flavor enhancer. In the latter part of the twentieth century, ingredient-conscious consumers shied away from artificial flavor enhancers. Soy sauce responded to the challenge of finding ingredients to flavor foods. For vegetarian manufacturers, the "beefy" taste provided by the soy sauce without any meat extract was highly desirable.

There were two methods of manufacturing soy sauce—the traditional fermentation processed used by Kikkoman and the chemical method.

Soy Sauce through Fermentation— Kikkoman's Traditional Method

Kikkoman's process was the traditional one and involved processing soy and wheat to a mash. Kikko- man had developed an inoculum of seed mold that the company added. The seed mold produced a growth, the development of which was controlled by temperature and humidity. The resulting mash (koji) was discharged into fermentation tanks where selected microorganism cultures and brine were added. The product (moromi mash) was aerated and mixed, then aged. During this process, enzymes formed in the cells of the koji and provided the characteristics of the brewed sauce. The soybean protein changed to amino acid, and the enzymatic reaction that occurred between the sugar and amino acids produced the taste and color. Enzymes changed the wheat starch to sugars for sweetness, and a special yeast developed changing some of the sugars to alcohol. Fermentation changed other parts of the sugars to alcohol that produced tartness. The brewing process determined flavor, color, taste, and aroma. The brine added to the koji mixture stimulated the enzymes and produced the reddish brown liquid mash. This process resulted in umami—or flavor-enhancing—abilities, as well as the brewed flavor components. The final mash was pressed between layers of cloth under constant pressure. After a pasteurization process to intensify color and aromas, the shoyu was filtered again and bottled. There were no flavorings, coloring, additives, or artificial ingredients in the product. According to produce developers, these complex flavors were not present in brewed soy sauce.

Chemically Produced Soy Sauce

Nonbrewed soy sauce could be made in hours. Soybeans were boiled with hydrochloric acid for 15 to 20 hours. When the maximum amount of amino acid was removed from the soybeans, the mixture was cooled to end the hydrolysis action. The amino acid liquid was then neutralized, mixed with charcoal, and finally purified through filtration. Color and flavor were introduced via varying amounts of corn syrup, salt, and caramel coloring. The resulting soy sauce was then refined and bottled.

Oprah Winfrey—The Story of an Entrepreneur

A Neela Radhika
A Mukund
ICFAI Center for Management Research

"Oprah Winfrey arguably has more influence on the culture than any university president, politician, political or religious leader, except perhaps the pope."

—*Vanity Fair* Magazine, in 1994

"She (Oprah) may be uncomfortable talking about it (money), but when it comes to making it, she sure knows what she's doing."

—*Fortune* Magazine, in March 2002

The Mad Cow Controversy— A Talk Show Queen in Trouble

In mid-1996, Oprah Winfrey, one of the world's most well-known media personalities and the host of *The Oprah Winfrey Show*, was entangled in a major controversy. The controversy arose because of statements made by Oprah and Howard Lyman (a founder member of the Humane Society of the United States) during an episode of *The Oprah Winfrey Show* telecast on April 16 1996.[1] The show, based on the theme "Dangerous Food," talked about mad cow disease[2] and the threat it supposedly posed to beef consumers in the United States.

On the show, Lyman blamed the practice of feeding rendered livestock (protein derived from cattle remains) to cattle for the outbreak of the disease in Europe, which resulted in the death of over 1.5 million cattle and 20 people in 1996. Lyman's statements suggested that beef consumers in the United States could also contract the human form of mad cow disease as a similar practice of feeding livestock was followed in the United States. On the show, Oprah swore that she would never eat a hamburger again in her life.

In May 1996, some cattle producers filed a $10.3 million suit against Oprah and Lyman in the Texas state court, under the Texas False Disparagement of Perishable Food Products Act,[3] claiming business disparagement, negligence, and defamation. They said Oprah created fear regarding the consumption of beef, when she vowed that she would never again eat a burger in her life. David Mullin, an attorney representing cattle producers, said, "The message of the show was never meant to be where opinions are shared. The show was meant to be scary."

The cattle producers claimed that Oprah knowingly aired false and defamatory comments about the threat of mad cow disease in the United States.

This case was written by A Neela Radhika, under the direction of A Mukund, ICFAI Center for Management Research (ICMR). It is intended to be used as the basis for class discussion rather than to illustrate either effective or ineffective handling of a management situation.

The case was compiled from published sources.

The show reportedly had a devastating impact on cattle prices and sales in the United States. Prices fell to a ten-year low within a week of the show, causing losses exceeding $12 million to the cattle producers. However, Chip Babcock, Oprah's attorney, claimed that the show in question was fair and did not suggest that beef was unsafe. Commenting on the decline in cattle prices following the show, Oprah's attorneys said that the decline in prices was due to factors such as drought and oversupply.

Oprah soon aired a second show on mad cow disease, with cattle industry representatives on the discussion panel to arrive at a balanced perspective on the issue. Commenting on this, Bill O'Brien, a co-owner of the Texas Beef Group, said, "I do not think it repaired the damage. She did not go on the program and eat a hamburger before the world." In February 2000, a federal court dismissed the suit against Oprah, stating that though Oprah's show melodramatized the issue, it did not give false information to defame cattle producers. The court also acquitted Lyman, stating that his statements, though strongly stated, were based on established facts.

The issue attracted media attention all over the world, highlighting Oprah's immense popularity and influence over her viewers. Oprah, with a business empire worth over $1 billion in 2002, was unarguably the most successful female media personality ever. How this lady overcame her disturbed, troubled childhood and several other problems to become so popular and successful is essentially a story of her entrepreneurial and leadership skills.

Oprah's "Rags to Riches" Journey

The "talk show queen," Oprah was born out of wedlock to Vernon Winfrey and Vernita Lee on January 29, 1954, in Kosciusko, Mississippi. Named Orpah Gail Winfrey, she became Oprah after Orpah was misspelt in her school records. Her parents separated when she was very young. Following this, she was sent to live with her grandmother, Hattie Mae Lee, on a small farm. Hattie laid the foundation of Oprah's career when she taught her to read the Bible. At the age of three, Oprah spent hours reading Bible stories to the animals on the farm. Hattie also taught her many lessons about God and faith.

These lessons inspired her (at that tender age itself) to become strong and help people in need. She believed that she had a higher calling and she was sent to "do good" to others.

Public speaking skills were evident in Oprah right from her childhood. In 1957, at less than four years of age, Oprah recited sermons from the Bible at her local church. Oprah loved the attention and applause she received after her recitals. Oprah was an intelligent child who reportedly asked her teachers to advance her to higher grades.

At the age of six, Oprah was sent to live with her father in Nashville, Tennessee. Her father and her stepmother, Zelma, noticed her interest in reading and encouraged her by buying more books. Her voracious reading helped her always stay ahead of her classmates.

Later that year, she was sent to her mother in Milwaukee. Oprah led a few painful years of her childhood at her mother's. She was sexually abused by her male relatives and acquaintances. These experiences had a profound effect on her and she turned into a promiscuous and problematic teenager. Her mother tried to admit her to a home for troubled teens, but as the home was full, Oprah was sent to live with her father again. The shift to her father's place was a turning point for Oprah. It reportedly put her life back on track. Oprah referred to the reunion with her father as "my saving grace."

Oprah said that her father was a tough taskmaster, insisting on hard work and discipline. This attitude helped her improve herself in all aspects. In Oprah's words, "As strict as he was, he had some concerns about me making the best of my life, and would not accept anything less than what he thought was my best."

Oprah's father encouraged her to participate in various competitions. Participation in such activities helped her develop her self-confidence and improved her communication skills. Oprah organized and directed a series of presentations (especially on *God's Trombones*, written by James Weldon Johnson) at various local churches. Oprah used these presentations to raise funds to buy new robes for the youth choir of her church. She actively participated in Sunday church activities and spoke frequently in church. She also worked hard at her studies and, as a result, won a scholarship to attend

Tennessee State University, where she specialized in Speech Communications and Performing Arts.

In 1971, at the age of 17, Oprah got her first broadcasting job. She worked as a part-time radio announcer for WVOL radio station (targeting mainly African Americans) in Nashville. In 1972, she won the Miss Black Tennessee title. In 1973, after graduating from Tennessee State University, she joined WTVF-TV in Nashville as a reporter. In 1976, she joined WJZ-TV, a major affiliate of ABC,[4] in Baltimore, as a news anchor. She worked at WJZ-TV until 1983. During her tenure at WJZ-TV she got a chance to host a talk show.[5] She was the co-host for *People Are Talking*, a popular talk show in those days.

In 1984, Oprah moved to WLS-TV Chicago (an affiliate of ABC) to host a local TV talk show, *A.M. Chicago*. Oprah deviated from the general talk-show format, referred to as "report-talk." She introduced a new format, referred to as "rapport-talk," which involved back and forth conversation between the host and the audience. Oprah's show became an instant hit with women, mostly in the 30–50 age group. According to analysts, Oprah's show was a success because the conversational mode formed the basis of "female bonding." Many of the people in her audience felt that Oprah had made the talk show more personal and confessional.

By the end of the year, the talk show became very successful. As a result of the show's success and Oprah's increasing popularity, the show was renamed The Oprah Winfrey Show and its duration was increased from 30 minutes to one hour. In 1986, the show went national and became the country's number one talk show within one year of being nationally syndicated.

During the mid-1980s, Oprah began her acting career with a role in Steven Spielberg's *The Color Purple* (1985). For her performance in the movie, Oprah was nominated for Oscar and Golden Globe Awards in the category of Best Supporting Actress. Her performance in her second movie, *Native Son* (1986), also won applause from critics.

Oprah's love for acting and her desire to offer quality entertainment led to the establishment of Harpo Productions Inc. (Oprah spelt backward). With Harpo, Oprah became the third woman, in U.S. history to own a movie production studio (the pioneers were Mary Pickford and Lucille Ball). In October 1988, Harpo Productions acquired the ownership and production rights of The Oprah Winfrey Show from ABC. This made Oprah the first woman in the history of TV to own and produce her own talk show.

In 1992, Oprah got engaged to Stedman Graham, a former basketball player and a public relations executive, with whom she had been living since 1986. During the late 1980s and 1990s, Oprah won many awards and garnered recognition for her work in TV and films. In 1994, she was included in the TV Hall of Fame (see Exhibit 1 for details of the awards won by Oprah).

For over a decade, Oprah's talk show, like other talk shows, focused on dysfunctional families and their problems. However, in 1994, Oprah announced a change in her program format. She decided to stop the "dysfunctional group" based shows, and began focusing on positive shows that inspired people to rise above their limitations and achieve their dreams. The aim of this new format was to "entertain, enlighten, and empower" the millions of viewers that watched the show across the world.

The new format thus offered direction, advice, and help to people through "entertainment mixed with therapy." Oprah introduced Dr. Phil McGraw (a renowned psychologist) as a weekly guest on the show, to help guests and the audience gain insights into their problems. Thus, while other talk shows continued to focus on entertainment and shock value, Oprah's shows (and her various ventures) helped change lives for the better.

The Oprah/Harpo Empire

During the 1990s, Oprah expanded her business into many areas besides the television. She entered various fields such as publishing, music, film, health and fitness, and education. In 1994, Oprah's initiatives for the protection of children against abuse were rewarded when then U.S. President Bill Clinton signed the Oprah Bill, a new law designed to protect children against abuse.

In 1996, Oprah headed the list of Forbes' highest-paid entertainers with earnings of $171 million,

EXHIBIT 1   Awards Won by Oprah

Year	Award
1971	Crowned Miss Fire Prevention, Nashville, TN
1971	Won Miss Black Tennessee pageant
1987	Daytime Emmy (Outstanding Talk/Service Show Host, *The Oprah Winfrey Show*)
1988	International Radio and Television Society, Broadcaster of the Year; youngest recipient
1989	Daytime Emmy (Outstanding Talk/Service Show, *The Oprah Winfrey Show*)
1991	Daytime Emmy (Outstanding Talk/Service Show Host, *The Oprah Winfrey Show*)
1991	Daytime Emmy (Outstanding Talk/Service Show, *The Oprah Winfrey Show*)
1991	NAACP Image (Outstanding News, Talk or Information Series, *The Oprah Winfrey Show*)
1992	Daytime Emmy (Outstanding Talk/Service Show Host, *The Oprah Winfrey Show*)
1992	Daytime Emmy (Outstanding Talk/Service Show, *The Oprah Winfrey Show*)
1993	Daytime Emmy (Outstanding Talk/Service Show Host, *The Oprah Winfrey Show*)
1993	Daytime Emmy (Outstanding Children's Special, *Shades of a Single Protein*, ABC After-School Special)
1994	Daytime Emmy (Outstanding Talk/Service Show Host, *The Oprah Winfrey Show*)
1994	Daytime Emmy (Outstanding Talk/Service Show, *The Oprah Winfrey Show*)
1995	Daytime Emmy (Outstanding Talk/Service Show Host, *The Oprah Winfrey Show*)
1995	Daytime Emmy (Outstanding Talk/Service Show, *The Oprah Winfrey Show*)
1996	George Foster Peabody Individual Achievement Award
1996	Daytime Emmy (Outstanding Talk/Service Show, *The Oprah Winfrey Show*)
1997	People's Choice Award, Favorite Female Television Performer
1997	Daytime Emmy (Outstanding Talk Show, *The Oprah Winfrey Show*)
1997	NAACP Image (Outstanding News, Talk or Informational Special, *Dinner with Oprah: A Lifetime Exclusive—Toni Morrison;* shared award)
1997	NAACP Image (Outstanding News, Talk or Informational Series, *The Oprah Winfrey Show: Oprah's Book Club—Dinner with Maya Angelou;* shared award)
1998	People's Choice (Favorite Female Performer in a TV Series, *The Oprah Winfrey Show*)
1998	Daytime Emmy (Lifetime Achievement; presented by the National Academy of Television Arts and Sciences)
1998	Daytime Emmy (Outstanding Talk Show Host, *The Oprah Winfrey Show;* tied with Rosie O'Donnell)
1999	National Book Foundation's 50th Anniversary Gold Medal (for influential contribution to reading and books)
2001	Woman of the Century Award from *Newsweek*
2002	Emmy (Bob Hope Humanitarian Award)

SOURCE: http://www.eonline.com.

beating even celebrities such as Steven Spielberg, Michael Jackson, Arnold Schwarzenegger, and Jim Carrey. In September 1996, Oprah launched Oprah's Book Club on TV, which was aimed at inculcating and encouraging reading among people. Oprah's Book Club was a great success; most of her fans chose to read the books that were selected by Oprah for the book club. Reportedly, sales of all the books selected for the club increased substantially (on an average, by ten times) and found a place in the bestseller lists.

Harpo Films Inc., Oprah's film production division signed a long-term agreement with ABC Television Network in the mid-1990s to produce the *Oprah Winfrey Presents* series of telefilms. Some of the major projects under the *Oprah Winfrey Presents* banner were *Amy and Isabelle, Tuesdays with Morrie, David and Lisa, The Wedding,* and *Before Women Had Wings.* Oprah even acted in some of these telefilms (such as *The Women of Brewster Place, Before Women Had Wings,* and *There Are No Children Here*) and recorded critical acclaim for her performance. The telefilms venture met with reasonable success and generated $4 million in revenues in 2001.

Oprah also signed an exclusive agreement with the Walt Disney Motion Picture Group in the mid-1990s to produce feature films for Disney. The first film produced by the Harpo group for Disney was Touchstone Pictures' *Beloved,* in which Oprah played the lead role.

By the end of the 1990s, Oprah had reportedly become one of the very few people in the world who were recognized immediately by their first name alone. She had become so popular that in 1998, she was voted the second most admired woman in the United States, next only to President Clinton's wife, Hillary Rodham.

In November 1998, the Harpo Group launched Oxygen Media LLC in partnership with Geraldine Laybourne's GBL LLC, an entertainment company, and Carsey Werner Mandabach (CWM) LLC.[6] Harpo had a 25 percent stake in Oxygen. Oxygen media, aimed at women, was an integrated media company, which combined the advantages of both cable television and the Internet. Geraldine Laybourne was the chairman and CEO of Oxygen Media. The company's cable network featured a range of programs that included talk shows, music, health, news, comedy, movies, cartoons, and sports.

Oprah Goes Online, the first program featured on the Oxygen cable network, was a 12-episode course on using the Internet. Oprah also produced and hosted the show *Use Your Life* on Oxygen Media. Oxygen media's websites included http://Oxygen .com, http://Oprah.com, http://ThriveOnline.com, and http://Trackers.com. Oprah's website, http:// www.oprah.com, which offered the latest information regarding *The Oprah Winfrey Show* (and later the Angel Network and *O* Magazine), was reportedly viewed over seven million times every month in 1999 and received more than 2,000 e-mails every day.

Oprah's popularity and ratings had surged ahead of other talk show hosts including veterans such as Phil Donahue (the pioneer of talk shows), Regis Philbin (*Live with Regis*), Kelly Ripa (*Kelly*), Sally Jessy Raphael, Jerry Springer, and David Letterman (see Exhibit 2 for details of popular TV personalities in the United States from 1993 to 2000). The Harpo empire entered the magazine business in early 2000. By 2002, Oprah headed Harpo Inc., Harpo Production Inc., Harpo Video Inc., Harpo Films Inc., and Harpo Studios Inc. as the Harpo Group's chairman.

In April 2000, Harpo Entertainment and Hearst Magazines (United States) jointly launched *O* Magazine in New York City. The magazine was positioned as a personal growth guide for women in the 21st century. *O* addressed various aspects of a woman's life such as her inner well-being, fashion, health and fitness, relationships, self-discovery, books, home design, and food among others. The magazine, targeted at women between 25 and 49 years of age, was circulated across the country. Speaking about *O,* Oprah, who was also its editorial director, said, "I believe you are here to become more of yourself, to live your best life. The magazine will present articles and stories of other people to help women look at their lives differently."

Columns in *O* included "Live Your Best Life," "Make Your Dreams Come True" (a step-by-step planning guide), "Tell it Like It Is" (by Dr. Phil), "Dream Big" (a profile of a person who took steps to live out his/her dream), and "My Journal" (profile of a celebrity's intimate thoughts).

O was reportedly the most successful startup in the magazine industry. In 2001, its revenues amounted to over $140 million. According to

EXHIBIT 2 Favorite TV Personalities—Ranks (Based on Harris Poll)

	1993	1994	1995	1996	1997	1998	1999	2000	2001
Drew Carey	*	*	*	10	6	8	1	3	1
Regis Philbin	*	*	*	*	*	*	*	2	2
Oprah Winfrey	2	2	3	3	3	1	2	1	3
David Letterman	6	6	4	5	7	*	*	6	4
Ray Romano	*	*	*	*	*	*	*	7	5
Jay Leno	*	8	10	10	8	6	*	7	6
Bill O'Reilly	*	*	*	*	*	*	*	*	7
Kelsey Grammer	*	*	8	8	9	5	5	5	8
Katie Couric	*	*	*	*	*	*	*	*	9
Rosie O'Donnell	*	*	*	8	5	6	8	9	10

*Not rated in that year.

SOURCE: http://www.harrisinteractive.com.

Favorite TV Personality among Different Groups (Based on Harris Poll)*

Gender-Based

Men	Drew Carey
Women	Oprah Winfrey

Age-Based

Age 18–24	Drew Carey
Age 25–29	David Letterman
Age 30–39	Drew Carey
Age 40–49	Regis Philbin
Age 50 and over	Regis Philbin

Race-Based

White	Regis Philbin
African-American	Drew Carey
Hispanic	David Letterman

*The Harris Poll was conducted (online) in the U.S. between December 20, 2001, and January 1, 2002. The sample size of the poll was 2,098 adults from a cross-section of audiences across the country.

SOURCE: http://www.harrisinteractive.com.

Cathleen Black, President, Hearst Magazines, most successful magazines took nearly five years to become as profitable as O did in only two years. Analysts noted that though the market was down and many magazines had posted losses in 2001, O's advertising revenues increased by 43 percent over its revenues in 2000. O's paid-up circulation amounted to an estimated 2.5 million copies, which was more than that of leading magazines such as *Vogue* or *Martha Stewart Living*. O targeted the premium segment, which had an average income of $63,000 and patronized premium brands such as Lexus, Coach, and Donna Karan (which were key advertisers for *O*).

Oprah described *O* as a personal growth manual and took an active part in the content development of the magazine. Analysts remarked that *O* was a reflection of Oprah's personality. The success of *O* was primarily attributed to Oprah's popularity. Commenting on the high revenues earned by the magazine in terms of advertising revenue, Black said, "Advertisers have unanimously responded to the powerful presence of Oprah. The magazine is a new voice for a new time—a lifestyle magazine with heart and soul."

However, Oprah's talk show continued to be her biggest success, generating revenues of over $300 million annually. The show was aired in over 107 countries in the world and was watched by 26 million people in the United States itself. It remained the number one talk show in the daytime slot for 16 years, despite competition from over 50 rivals. According to Bob Iger, President, Walt Disney, the Oprah show contributed significantly to the company's profits (Walt Disney's ABC Network syndicated *The Oprah Winfrey Show* in many major markets). The show appealed primarily to women in the age group of 30 to 50 years. Since most of the audience was from the middle class, the show attracted huge advertising revenues from companies such as Wal-Mart, Procter & Gamble, and Sears.

Oprah—The Entrepreneur

Despite the fact that she was the owner of a huge business empire, Oprah reportedly did not even know how to read a balance sheet and did not follow any corporate models. She had declined offers from many companies such as AT&T, Intel, and Ralph Lauren to be on their boards, stating that "she did not understand what she would do on their boards." Oprah was once reported to have hoarded $50 million in cash, which she called her personal "bag-lady fund," as she was afraid of investing in the stock market, being totally ignorant about it.

Interestingly, she did not like being referred to as a businesswoman. Commenting on her "ignorance" of doing business the "usual" way, she said, "If I called a strategic-planning meeting, there would be dead silence, and then people would fall out of their chairs laughing."

According to analysts, Oprah was not in the "business of business," she was in the "business of soothing souls." The kind of intimacy Oprah enjoyed with her audiences was something that reportedly no other talk show host had ever achieved. Oprah's message, "You are responsible for your own life," acted as her unique selling proposition (USP) just like "convenience" and "everyday low prices," the USPs of McDonald's and Wal-Mart, respectively.

The Harpo empire, however did not function purely on Oprah's personal skills. She had put in place a team that dedicatedly worked toward keeping the business running. Dennis Swanson[7] and Jeff Jacobs,[8] President, Harpo Group, contributed greatly to Oprah's success as a talk show host as well as a businesswoman over the years. Explaining Oprah's business, Jacobs said, "We bet on ourselves. We are an intellectual property company, and our partners (ABC, Hearst, Oxygen) are distributors. Core content is developed here and has never left our home base."

Jacobs said that controlling content was a difficult task as Oprah was not only the chief content creator but also the chief content itself. For instance, every issue of *O* sported a "bold and winning" picture of Oprah on its cover page; in her columns in *O*, she gave details of her personal life such as her battle against abuse, her triumph over adversity, and her attempts at losing weight. She also discussed her painful experiences as victim of child abuse and racism. Commenting on the content, Oprah said, "I bring all my stuff with me."

Analysts felt that Oprah's life was central to her "brand." They believed that by making herself and her struggle against adversity the central theme of her messages, she successfully touched the American psyche and motivated Americans to become self-reliant. Oprah won the audience's trust by sharing her personal experiences with them on daytime TV to help them deal with their problems and become accountable for their own lives. This strategy reportedly kept Oprah ahead of her competitors.

Analysts believed that Oprah was reluctant to lose control of her brand because she was aware of its power. Oprah consistently refused requests from major companies to use her name on their products, such as perfumes, clothing, books, and food. One of Oprah's friends remarked that everybody wanted "a part of Oprah's brand" but she was not ready to cede control over it.

Analysts said that though some of her competitors (such as Martha Stewart) had lent their name to various products, Oprah firmly refused to do so. Since many of the products marketed by celebrities had failed in the market, analysts felt that Oprah was right in refusing to dilute her "brand equity."

Oprah was also against taking the Harpo Group public; she held 90 percent of the Harpo Group herself. She claimed that by selling her name or a part of her business, she would be "selling herself." In Oprah's words, "If I lost control of the business, I would lose myself or at least the ability to be myself. Owning myself is a way to be myself." This clearly indicated how the lady perceived her businesses and the extent to which her businesses were based on Oprah herself.

Analysts felt that Jacobs's business acumen also contributed greatly to Harpo's success. Oprah and Jacobs were rather an odd pair to be running a business as both had very different management styles. According to analysts, Oprah followed a management-by-instinct technique and took all her decisions on the basis of her gut feelings, while Jacobs believed in careful planning and execution. While Jacobs described Harpo's strategy as multi-purposing the content in various media, Oprah explained it as reaching out to a larger audience (through different media) to help people better their lives. However, the success of Harpo Group made it evident that the relationship worked.

According to company sources, Jacobs acted as Oprah's strategic advisor and dealmaker. In Oprah's words, "He is a piranha and that is a good thing for me to have." Remembering his meeting with Jacobs and his commitment toward Oprah, Iger said, "I remember being put off initially, but Jeff Jacobs has one thing in mind: his client. And he serves her very well."

Despite his many contributions to the company, Jacobs preferred to remain in the background, and referred to himself as a "behind-the-scenes guy." Besides being the president of Harpo, he also acted as Oprah's personal agent, making her deals and

agreements. This arrangement resulted in a saving of over 25 percent on Oprah's income, which would have gone in payments to agents and managers. Commenting on the financial success of Oprah, Jacobs said, "We understand it is not just how much you make but how much you keep."

Oprah was known for taking sudden decisions on the basis of gut-feeling. Oprah decided to launch O's first international edition (in early 2002) when watching a documentary on Africa, which showed some women in a beauty parlor in Nairobi reading *True Love* and *Hello* magazines. Commenting on this, Oprah said, "I thought, 'African women have no business sitting in a beauty shop reading *Hello* and *True Love*.'" Soon after, she launched O in Africa!

Interestingly, Oprah's business decisions (based on her gut feelings) were often successful. Her decision to run the table of contents of O on page 2 was not common business practice. Most publishers placed it in the middle of the magazine so that readers had to go through a couple of advertisements in search of the table of contents. This practice aimed at benefiting advertisers, but Oprah, in her own words, wanted to "put the readers first."

The fact that O was an instant success proved Oprah's decision right. Commenting on the magazine's success, Oprah said, "I am most proud of the magazine, because I did not know what I was doing." Media reports claimed that O, which was mostly developed by Oprah, reflected her ability to balance practicality and preaching. Analysts believed that Oprah knew that such balance would sell—and it did. According to them, this was the same strategy that made her talk shows such a success. Oprah maintained a balance between the issues or persons she chose for her show. For example, if one day she discussed the entertainment industry with a celebrity, the very next day she examined a grave issue such as the problems of women in Afghanistan.

Reportedly Oprah followed the same "balanced" approach with her finances also. Though she did not track her costs closely, she was aware of their magnitude and was sure to draw the strings when necessary. For instance, when Oprah found that the production costs of her show amounted to $50 million annually (which was double the expenditure incurred by other day-time talk shows), she called up Doug Pattison, Harpo's CFO, and said,

"That is okay, but that is also enough. I think we can keep it at $50 million."

As far as her employees were concerned, Oprah paid them well and expected quality for money. Reportedly, she did not care about ratings as long as her shows and magazines achieved their objectives. Commenting on this, she said, "Ratings go down when we do an Oprah's Book Club show, but that does not matter. We are getting people to read." Thus, Oprah did not pressure her employees to achieve ratings; instead she emphasized creativity and quality. According to her employees, Oprah took care that her staff did not measure its success on the basis of media reports. She showered praises on her staff once a project was completed; but when that project was recognized by the world and won ratings or awards, her staff received no special treatment from her. In words of Kate Forte, President, Harpo Films, "But if it wins big ratings or awards, the boss is mum. It is her reminder that we should not do anything for the external reward."

Though there was great demand for Harpo-produced movies and television films, Oprah did not bend her rules to exploit that demand. According to Iger, though Disney wanted Harpo to produce more films, Oprah's standards and rules limited Harpo's output to one film per year. Commenting on this, Iger said, "Just because there is a buyer does not mean she is a seller."

Oprah's business decisions were based largely on trust (she referred to this as taking "leaps of faith"). It was reported that she asked only one question before she made a decision—"Can I trust you?" Commenting on this, Nancy Petersman, Executive Vice President, Allen & Co (investment banking firm), said, "It is all about character with Oprah. We investment bankers do the same sort of thing—try to figure out what people are made of—but with Oprah, it is like someone is looking into your soul."

Trust and control over the project were major factors in Oprah's decision-making process. Hearst succeeded in winning Oprah's assent for O, despite competition from AOL Time Warner and Conde Nast, by winning Oprah's trust. Hearst promised her that the magazine would reflect her values and would work toward translating her message into the written word. To ensure this, Hearst entrusted Oprah with the total editorial control of the magazine.

It was the same story with Oprah's investment decisions. Geraldine Laybourne, the co-founder of Oxygen, won Oprah's trust by telling her that she was planning a cable network aimed at providing intent and service to women. The idea appealed to Oprah (in fact she had something similar in her mind) and on an impulse, she invested $20 million in the project and also transferred certain rights to *The Oprah Winfrey Show* library. In return, she received a 25 percent stake in Oxygen Media.[9]

Oprah—Serving the People

Since Oprah had been a victim of child abuse, she constantly raised the issue in her show and made constant efforts to protect children from such abuse. In 1991, she demanded that the government pass a new law (The National Child Protection Act) against child abuse. Oprah even testified before the Senate Judiciary Committee of the United States to help them establish a database of convicted child abusers in the United States. In December 1993, Oprah's efforts were rewarded when the Oprah Bill (The National Child Protection Act) was made a law.

On principle, Oprah donated at least 10 percent of her annual earnings to charity during her adult life. Reportedly, most of these donations were made anonymously. However, in the 1990s, Oprah made such donations openly. She reportedly donated millions of dollars to institutes of higher education (Spelman College, Morehouse College, and Tennessee State University) and established scholarships, which helped hundreds of students.

In September 1997, Oprah launched Oprah's Angel Network to encourage people to extend their help to those in need. Oprah asked her audience to help the less fortunate by donating their spare change to the Angel Network. By 2000, the Angel Network received more than $3.5 million in spare change, which was used to give scholarships to poor students and fund humanity homes. In April 2000, the Angel Network announced the Use Your Life Award for people who "made others' lives better." The award, which carried a cash prize of $100,000, was given every Monday on *The Oprah Winfrey Show*.

Oprah was chosen to host the interfaith prayer service held at New York City's Yankee Stadium on September 23, 2001, to mourn the victims of the

September 11 terrorist attacks on the World Trade Center. Rudy Giuliani, mayor of New York City, believed that Oprah was the only national personality who had the ability to host such a profoundly religious service that involved people from different faiths. Oprah lived up to his expectations; her service both comforted and inspired mourners. (See Exhibit 3 for a picture of Oprah at the prayer service and a few other glimpses into her life.)

She said that "loved ones turn to angels after death and are always near to the people's hearts." Oprah reminded the people that hope, prayer, and love never die and asked them to use every moment of their lives to create a deeper meaning to their lives and to find out what really matters. According to an article published in April 2002, Oprah had become an icon of "church-free spirituality" and a spiritual guru to her over 22 million devoted viewers. Her influence was such that the *Wall Street Journal* even credited Oprah with introducing a new technique of interpersonal communication, "Oprahfication" (i.e., "public confession as a form of therapy").[10] This technique became so popular that a magazine even used Oprah as a verb: "I did not want to tell her, but she Oprah'd it out of me." Reportedly, this technique also became popular with politicians, who began holding "Oprah-style" town meetings to understand their constituents.

The Other Side of Oprah?

Not surprisingly, Oprah had many critics. Over the years, many of her personal as well as business-related policies had been criticized. Though employees at Harpo agreed that the pay and benefits offered by the company were exceptional compared to industry standards, some criticized the strict rules and regulations enforced. They said that Oprah forced her employees to sign a lifelong confidentiality agreement, which bound them from making any revelations about Harpo in their lifetime. In a lawsuit filed by a former employee against the company, Harpo was described as a "narcissistic workplace."

Some employees even criticized Oprah for being a tough taskmaster who drove her employees hard to meet her expectations. A former Harpo employee described the environment at Harpo as "an environ-ment of dishonesty and chaos," and said, "everyone undermines everybody else to get more access to Oprah, and I think she encourages it."

Oprah accepted the fact that she gave her employees a tough time. However, regarding the confidentiality agreement, Oprah said, "You would not say it is harsh if you were in the tabloids all the time." Oprah did not respond to other criticism about the work culture at Harpo.

Oprah's decision to invest in Oxygen Media also tarnished her reputation. In 2001 it was reported that the message boards on Oxygen Media offered links to websites featuring sexual content (Oprah banned such stuff on her talk show in the initial years itself). This was attributed to the alliance between Oxygen Media and ThriveOnline, a women's health site. Though Harpo's spokesperson defended Oprah by saying that Oprah was away on a vacation and was ignorant of these aspects of Oxygen Media, some people suspected Oprah of permitting such material on the website.

Some sections of Oprah's audiences criticized her spirituality shows such as *One Way to Live* and *Remembering Your Spirit*. They said that in the early 21st century Oprah had become more of a "preacher woman" than a confidante and a friend. Some viewers even felt that Oprah was a hypocrite. They said that while she preached about the need to disregard material things and focus on the spiritual aspects of life, *O* featured advertisements of luxury items from companies such as BMW, Louis Vuitton, and Lancome, earning huge revenues for Harpo. They even criticized Oprah for keeping the ticket price for her popular *Live Your Best Life* series of shows as high as $185.

Other controversies (such as the one surrounding the mad cow disease issue) added to Oprah's negative publicity. However, they failed to do any major damage to her popularity. Such was her popularity that even the critics were shocked when she announced (in 2001) her decision to quit the show in the near future. Oprah explained, "I am sick of people sitting in chairs stating their problems. Then we roll the videotape, then we have our experts on the topic. I truly do not know what to replace it with. As soon as I do, I am pulling those people from their chairs." She added, "I am in the 'what's next?' phase of my career."

EXHIBIT 3   A Few Glimpses into Oprah's Life and Career

1. Miss Black Tennessee, 1972   2. News Reader, 1976   3. Talk Show, 1986

4. Oprah's Debut Movie, 1985   5. An Oprah Telefilm   6. The First Harpo Movie

7. Oprah's Book Club, 1996   8. Angel Network, 1997   9. *O* Magazine

10. Talk Show, 2002   11. Oprah at the Show   12. Hosting the Prayer Service in New York

SOURCE: http://www.oprah.com (2–8), http://www.girlpower.gov (1), http://www.google.com (9–12).

The Show Goes On

Much to the delight of her fans, Oprah changed her mind, and in mid-2002, renewed her contract for the show till 2006. Media reports mentioned that this was typical of Oprah, as she generally changed her decisions rather easily. Though Oprah renewed the contract, she said that she was exploring the options she had after exiting the show. However, she was quick to add that she would not leave TV.

Analysts remarked that if Oprah did leave the show in the future, her options were unlimited. A few analysts even said that with the kind of influence and power she had, she could even some day become the President of the United States!

However, Oprah's story was not about power and influence; rather, it was about ability and the determination to leverage entrepreneurial and personal skills to make it big. According to analysts, the most remarkable aspect about Oprah was the way she dealt with the success, wealth, and fame she acquired through the years.

It was reported that with the passage of time, Oprah was evolving, becoming more adaptive, stronger, deeper, and more spiritual. Her admirers believed that Oprah's confidence and belief in herself was growing as well—something that was the key to her success, first as a talk show host, then as a businesswoman, and perhaps most importantly, as a compassionate human being.

Questions for Discussion

1. Explore the reasons underlying Oprah's phenomenal success as a talk show host. What personal and interpersonal skills made her the "Queen of Souls"?

2. Examine Oprah's growth as a businesswoman and discuss her entrepreneurial and leadership skills. Do you think the gut-based decision-making style of Oprah is appropriate in the present business scenario? Do you think Oprah would have been more successful as a businesswoman if she based her decisions on sound reasoning and analysis? Justify your answer.

3. Describe the initiatives taken by Oprah to serve society. How far did Oprah's popularity help her succeed in her philanthropic ventures? To what extent was Harpo's performance influenced by Oprah's service initiatives?

4. Briefly comment on the criticisms leveled against Oprah. In light of the fact that *The Oprah Winfrey Show* was Oprah's flagship product, do you think her decision to retire from the talk show will be a good move for the Harpo group? Justify your answer.

Notes

1. The discussion panel comprised Oprah Winfrey (Host), Howard Lyman (Executive Director, Humane Society, U.S.), Gary Weber (Representative, National Cattlemen's Beef Association) and Dr. Will Hueston (Representative, United States Department of Agriculture).

2. Mad cow disease, scientifically called "Bovine Spongiform Encephalophy" (BSE), is a nervous system disorder. The major symptoms of the disease in cattle are belligerence, poor coordination, confusion, and death. According to medical analysts, the disease (in cows) became an epidemic due to the modern farming practices adopted by cattle ranchers, such as feeding cows with rendered livestock. The mad cow disease is linked with a variant of Creutzfeldt-Jakob disease (CJD) found in beef-consuming human beings. This variant is incurable and fatal. It kills its victims by filling their brain with microscopic spongy holes.

3. Under this Act, people can be held liable if they make false and disparaging statements regarding perishable food products.

4. ABC, a subsidiary of Walt Disney Company, is one of the leading broadcasting companies in the U.S. It broadcasts through a network of more than 230 affiliate stations across the U.S. It also owns over 60 radio stations and ten TV stations in all the major markets of the country.

5. A talk show is an interactive session between two or more people. Such shows generally involve interaction between a host, guest(s), and the audience.

6. CWM LLC is one of the major independent production studios in America, distributing programming content in over 175 countries.

7. Dennis Swanson was the head of WLS-TV, Chicago. He appointed Oprah as a talk show host and convinced her that she could succeed even though she was overweight and an African American. Such was his belief in Oprah's capability that he ran her show opposite Chicago's number one talk show hosted by Phil Donahue. Within one month, Oprah's show replaced Donahue's in ratings.

8. Jeff Jacobs was an entertainment lawyer in Chicago. He helped Oprah handle legal formalities regarding her contracts. However, by 1986 he convinced Oprah to establish her own company instead of lending her talent to outsiders. This led to the formation of Harpo Entertainment Inc, in which Jacobs was given a five percent share. He joined Harpo as president in 1989. In recognition of his contribution to the company, Jacobs's stake in the company was increased to ten percent later on.

9. In March 2002, it was reported that Oprah regretted her decision to impart certain rights to *The Oprah Winfrey Show* library to Oxygen Media. She felt that by doing so, she had traded her soul. To undo this mistake, Oprah acquired her rights back and in return she accepted to do a special program on Oxygen Media, *Oprah After the Show.*

10. http://www.christianitytoday.com, April 1, 2002.

Singapore International Airlines: Strategy with a Smile

Kannan Ramaswamy
Manesh Modi
American Graduate School of International Management

Mr. Cheong Choong Kong, the CEO of Singapore International Airlines (SIA), put away his papers as the SIA Megatop circled to land at Changi International Airport in Singapore. He could see the magnificent lights of the city as it prepared for the much-awaited arrival of the new millennium just two weeks away. Singapore had promised a spectacular show because it would be among the first countries to welcome the New Year. Mr. Kong was returning from meetings in London with Mr. Richard Branson, CEO of Virgin Atlantic Airways. The two companies had been exploring the potential for a formal equity alliance. While he was happy with the performance of the company under his leadership, he knew that much remained to be done. The next sequence of strategic moves would be crucial in cementing SIA's meteoric rise.

SIA had managed to weather the storms of declining traffic and yields especially in the Asian region. The regional economies had been showing signs of a nascent recovery. However, the economic recovery was by no means complete. For example, Japan was still unsteady and the other Asian tigers were tentative at best. Some of the quintessential sources of competitive advantage for SIA were increasingly coming under fire. Labor costs had been showing a remarkable upward trend, growing along with the prosperity of Singapore itself. Specialized labor was difficult to find locally, and when available proved to be much more expensive than before. This could not have happened at a worse time since the main competitors were showing signs of cost-based competition and the customer was increasingly attracted to low fares. This posed a dilemma for SIA, which had traditionally relied on Singaporean personnel for most of its operations. Looking overseas for specialized talent, although not new for SIA, could have strong political and economic ramifications that had not been fathomed as yet.

Competitors had been quick to copy many of the remarkable service innovations pioneered by SIA. The avenues for tangible differentiation that SIA had used in the past to set itself apart had soon become the norm. Every major air carrier now offered a choice of meals in economy class, innovative entertainment options in the cabins, and all the trappings of luxury that used to be the sole domain of SIA. Of particular concern was the increasing competition from international carriers headquartered in neighboring countries such as

Thai Airways, Cathay Pacific, Malaysian, and Qantas. These carriers had learned to duplicate some of the key features of SIA's competitive strategy from recruitment to in-flight service and fleet management. Thus, there were fewer and fewer avenues left for SIA to distinguish itself from the others. This placed growing pressure on the firm to refine its differentiation strategy.

In the international markets, alliances had become a way of life. It was probably the only reasonable way to realize global aspirations. After weighing these factors for a considerable time, SIA had recently joined the well-acclaimed Star Alliance. It was also pursuing numerous other partnerships with other carriers as well as exploring direct investment options as a means of growth in overseas markets. While this positioned SIA to take advantage of the booming markets for travel in Europe and the United States, it raised concerns among SIA's loyal clientele. There was some apprehension about the ability of the other partners to be able to live up to the standards that SIA had set. Should there be significant differences in service quality across network partners, some feared that SIA's sterling reputation and brand image in the airline industry could be tarnished. There was indeed a lot riding on the partnerships that SIA had entered or might enter in the near future.

The International Airline Industry

The airline industry had traditionally remained fragmented primarily due to the limiting effects of national and international regulations. Enforced in the form of landing rights and associated competitive constraints, even large airline companies had only been able to develop dominance over their own regional markets at best. With the exception of the United States, dominant national flag carriers, typically owned by the national governments, had remained the only international representatives of their countries. However, the competitive dynamics in this industry had started to change dramatically in recent years. Deregulation, privatization, and the advent of new technologies have started to reshape the industry on a global level.

The United States deregulated its airlines in 1978 and had since witnessed heightened competition and aggressive jockeying for market position. Europe entered the throes of a similar escalation of competition following the creation of the European Union and the disbanding of country-specific barriers to free market competition among air carriers. In Asia, deregulation occurred in fits and starts with some major regions allowing greater access to foreign carriers. For example, India, a regional market of some significance, announced that it would privatize its state-owned airline company. It had already allowed its traditionally domestic airline to compete against its international air carrier in many of the regional markets comprising neighboring countries. Japan made major strides in deregulation after selling off its shares in the then state-owned Japan Airlines and permitted All Nippon Airways to serve international markets. In Latin America, many of the smaller national flag carriers were privatized. Countries such as Mexico and Argentina infused significant levels of market competition in their airline industries by removing anti-competitive barriers and privatizing their national airlines Mexicana and Aerolineas Argentinas.

The trend seemed certain to gain further momentum and open skies might be closer to reality than ever before. The major European nations were already in discussions with the United States to implement an open Trans-Atlantic market area where landing rights would be determined by free market forces rather than regulatory policy. Open skies agreements are bilateral agreements between countries that agree to provide landing and take-off facilities for air carriers originating in any of the partner countries. Such an agreement does not have the typical restrictions related to landing rights that are determined on a city-pair basis. For example, Singapore and the United States had signed an open skies agreement under which a Singapore carrier could travel to any destination city in the United States and vice versa. (Exhibit 1 provides a list of countries that negotiated open skies agreements with the United States.)

The twin trends of privatization and deregulation resulted in an increasingly global approach to strategic positioning in this industry. Although most large carriers still retained their regional dominance,

EXHIBIT 1

U.S. Open Skies Agreements as of 1999

Americas	Asia/Pacific	Europe	Middle East
Aruba	Brunei	Austria	Jordan
Canada	Malaysia	Belgium	United Arab Emirates
Chile	New Zealand	Czech Republic	Bahrain
Costa Rica	Pakistan	Denmark	
El Salvador	Singapore	Finland	
Guatemala	Taiwan	Germany	
Honduras	South Korea	Iceland	
Dutch Antilles	Uzbekistan	Italy	
Nicaragua		Luxembourg	
Panama		Netherlands	
Peru		Norway	
		Romania	
		Sweden	
		Switzerland	

SOURCE: U.S. Department of State.

many forged alliances with other leading carriers to offer seamless services across wider geographic areas. These alliances made most of the larger airline companies *de facto* global organizations. With increasing geographic reach and decreasing regulatory barriers, many of the regions were witnessing acute competition often in the form of fare wars. Consumers in general became much more price sensitive than ever before. In attempting to keep up with the competition, many carriers upgraded their service offerings, contributing to declining yields in a price-conscious market. Chronic excess capacity worldwide only exacerbated this situation.

Not surprisingly, there was a decline in passenger revenue yield in all geographic regions and the airlines were fighting an uphill battle to extract higher levels of efficiencies from their operating structures. (Exhibit 2 provides data on financial and operating statistics for the leading carriers by geographic region.) For example, passenger yield dropped by 1.9 percent and 2.5 percent in 1998 and 1999, respectively, in Europe and 0.8 percent

and 1.5 percent in North America during the same period. The drop was far more significant in the Asia-Pacific region where the yields fell by 3.9 percent and 4.1 percent in 1998 and 1999. A geographic region-wise summary of key trends in passenger traffic, growth potential, and major players follows.

North America

The North American region in general and the United States in particular is by far the most significant arena of competition in the international aviation industry. According to *Air Transport World*, a leading industry journal, U.S. traffic accounted for close to 40 percent of worldwide revenues and revenue passenger kilometers between 1997 and 1999 (see Exhibit 3). American Airlines, Delta Airlines, and United Airlines, who collectively accounted for roughly 58 percent of total U.S. airline revenues in 1999, dominated this market. Northwest Airlines, U.S. Airways, and Continental formed the second tier of the majors, accounting for approximately 29 percent of total revenues for U.S. carriers. Although

EXHIBIT 2

Key Financial and Operating Statistics for Global Air Passenger Carriers

	Cathay Pacific			Malaysia Airlines			Asia-Pacific Qantas			Singapore			Thai		
Inidicator	1997	1998	1999	1997	1998	1999	1997	1998	1999	1997	1998	1999	1997	1998	1999
Capacity															
Fleet Strength (Ns.)	62	72	65	-	99	103	97	98	98	80	86	96	74	77	79
Available ATK	10400	10857	11183	6149	6411	6649	10887	11151	11144	13501	14534	15652	6473	6838	7310
Passenger ASK	57104	60295	60295	40097	42294	45442	81440	81537	81765	73507	77219	83192	45353	48557	51907
Actual Traffic															
Overall RTK	7331	7213	7916	3707	3888	4031	7052	7055	7129	9512	10038	10766	4466	4585	5103
Passenger RPK	38962	40679	42713	27904	28698	30593	59199	58619	59863	54692	54441	60300	31288	32969	37585
Load Factors															
Overall (OLF)	70%	66%	71%	60%	61%	61%	64.8%	63.3%	64%	70%	69%	69%	69%	67%	70%
Passenger (PLF)	68%	67%	71%	70%	68%	67%	72.7%	71.9%	73.2%	74%	71%	72%	69%	68%	72%
Break-even Load	65%	66%	66%	59%	62%	64%	57.3%	55.5%	55.3%	66%	65%	67%	65%	59%	59%
Yield															
Overall (¢/RTK)	49.9	43.4	42.2	55.9	48.4	40.9	87	78.6	74.3	47.2	43.4	37.8	69.4	54.8	55.5
Passenger (¢/RPK)	7.18	5.83	5.74	6.5	5.6	4.5	7.9	7.2	6.7	6.4	6.1	5.1	7.0	5.5	5.3
Cargo (¢/FTK)	22.6	21.3	22.2	15.5	13.5	12.2	0	2.4	19.5	22.1	20.6	19.4	28.5	25.5	28.3
Operating Costs															
Staff (¢/ATK)	8.9	8.2	7.4	5.5	5.4	4.6	15.0	13.4	12.4	5.7	5.2	4.3	8.6	5.6	6.0
Fuel (¢/ATK)	5.5	4.0	4.1	5.6	4.9	3.8	6.4	5.4	4.3	5.3	4.7	3.6	7.6	6.0	6.0
M'ntnance (¢/ATK)	3.9	2.9	2.6	2.7	2.3	2.6	2.5			2.5	2.1	1.9	2.7	2.0	2.3
Tot. Oper. Costs/ATK	32.7	28.6	27.7	32.8	29.9	26.0	49.8	43.7	41.1	31.1	28.2	25.4	45.2	32.1	32.6
Financials															
Sales (local curr.—m)	30647	26695	28479	6564	7154	7536	7834	8132	8449	7222	7724	7795	84687	105493	108235
Oper. Income	4812	3144	5318	1573	1579	1406	820	955	1082	1795	1888	1767	18001	21234	21910
Oper. Margin %	15.7	11.8	18.7	23.9	22.0	19.1	10.5	11.7	12.8	24.8	24.4	22.6	21.2	20.1	20.2
Sales/empl. ($'000)	251	234	266	112.4	109.9	96.7	204	192	188	391	369	339	127	102	116

Definitions in Glossary of Terms.

SOURCE: Annual Reports and HSBC Research.

EXHIBIT 2 — Key Financial and Operating Statistics for Global Air Passenger Carriers (continued)

Europe

Indicator	British Airways			Lufthansa			KLM			Air France			Swissair		
	1999	2000	2001E	1998	1999	2000E	1997	1998	1999	1997	1998	1999	1997	1998	1999
Available ATK (bn)	25.11	25.84	25.58	20.13	21.84	23.21	12.33	12.83	13.12	94.75	101.1	102.3	5.68	6.21	6.90
Passenger ASK (bn)	167.27	168.36	166.68												
Passenger load factor	70.7%	69.8%	71.2%	70.4%	71.1%	71.3%	77.8%	75.1%	76.7%	75.5	75.2	76.1	71.9	71.0	71.8
Yield (¢/RTK)	49.28	47.01	49.21	1.40	1.34	1.39	105.3	103.3	103.8				0.65	0.80	0.22
Operating Costs															
Staff	2356	2481	2491	5608	6322	6764	3318	3544	3693				959	955	1107
Fuel	705	804	984	1690	1776	2437	1332	1170	1431				366	294	355
M'ntnance	660	661	640				463	1487	1533					537	541
Tot. Operating costs	8450	8856	9227	21027	23927	26139	11430	11477	12068				5355	5991	5905
Financials															
Sales (local curr.—m)	8932	8092	8556	25615	27789	30662	13364	13326	13875	58830	56692	67729	5619	5925	6414
Opr. Income (m)	1251	922	1087	4588	3862	4524	1934	1849	1807	2547	1755	2355	264	354	108
Opr. Margin %	14.0	11.3	12.7	17.9	13.9	14.8	14.5	13.9	13.0	4.3	2.9	3.5	4.6	6.0	1.7

USA

Indicator	American			United			Delta			Northwest			U.S. Airways		
	1999	1998	1997	1999	1998	1997	1999	1998	1997	1999	1998	1997	1999	1998	1997
Capacity															
Passenger ASM (bn)	161.21	155.29	153.91	176.8	174.0	169.1	144.0	140.14	136.8	99.44	91.31	96.96	59.25	56.86	58.5
Actual Traffic															
Passenger RSM (bn)	112.06	108.95	107.02	121.4	124.6	125.4	104.57	101.13	97.75	74.16	66.73	72.03	41.47	41.25	41.57
Passenger															
Load Factor	69.5%	70.2%	69.5%	71.8%	71.6%	71.0%	72.6%	72.2%	71.4%	74.6%	73.1%	74.3%	70.1%	72.7%	71.3%
Passenger yield (¢/RPM)	13.12	13.49	13.37	12.6	12.4	12.5	12.83	12.85	12.79	11.58	11.26	12.11	16.51	17.02	17.10
Operating Costs (m)															
Staff	6120	5793	5511	5018	5341	5670	4993	4850	4534	3393	3261	3024	3380	3101	3179
Fuel	1923	1604	1696	206	1788	1776	1360	1507	1722	1191	1097	1394	805	623	727
M'ntnance	1003	935	862	689	624	603	561	495	434	635	761	620	498	448	451
Tot. Operating costs	16574	15528	15362	16119	16083	16636	12841	12444	12063	9562	9236	9069	8459	7674	7930
Financials															
Sales (local curr.—m)	17730	17516	16957	17378	17561	18027	14711	14138	13594	10276	9045	10226	8595	8688	8514
Opr. Income (m)	1156	1968	1595	1259	1478	1391	1870	1694	1531	714	-191	1157	136	1014	584
Opr. Margin %	6.5	11.2	9.4	7.2	8.4	7.7	12.7	11.69	11.33	6.9	-2.1	11.3	1.5	11.6	6.85

SOURCE: Annual reports, S.G. Securities Research, ABN Amro.

EXHIBIT 3　Projected Airline Passenger Traffic Growth

Region	1987	1997	1998	1999	2000	2001
Africa	35.9	56.2	55.2	57.4	60.3	63.5
Asia/Pacific	253.5	639.5	630.1	657.2	696.0	744.0
Europe	494.2	655.2	691.5	721.9	763.1	808.9
Middle East	44.6	76.7	77.7	80.5	84.4	89.3
North America	684.6	1020.4	1042.1	1082.7	1123.9	1175.6
Latin America	76.7	125.1	133.8	139.3	147.2	156.8
World	1589.5	2573.1	2630.4	2739.1	2874.8	3038.0

Revenue Passenger Kilometers—billions.

SOURCE: International Civil Aviation Organization.

most of these large carriers had carved out significant regional markets in the United States where they continue to dominate, many are looking to alliances with overseas carriers to help meet growth targets. This was especially critical since U.S. airline companies witnessed a 16 percent decline in profitability in 1998 alone. A large part of the decline was blamed on operational inefficiencies and increases in input costs. For example, personnel costs had increased by three percent between 1997 and 1999. Increases in oil prices, it was feared, would further erode profit margins since all cost increases could not be passed along to consumers who were already price sensitive.

Europe

The European region was poised to grow between five percent and six percent annually between 2000 and 2001 according to ICAO (International Civil Aviation Organization) estimates. In 1999 this region accounted for 26 percent of total revenue passenger kilometers worldwide, placing it second to the North American market. Much of the region remained fragmented in terms of market dominance, although a small group of leaders had started establishing control over key routes. British Airways and Lufthansa comprised the top tier of this market and accounted for roughly 45 percent of total 1999 revenue passenger kilometers in the region while KLM, Iberia, Swissair, SAS, and Sabena formed the second tier with a little over 37 percent. With the enact-

ment of the EU (European Union) standards, all regulatory barriers had virtually evaporated between member countries. As a consequence, the market shares of national carriers in their own home markets fell by close to 15 percent on average between 1993 and 1998. The move to fare-based competition was still in its infancy. It was estimated that only two percent of Europe's travelers chose to fly on low-cost carriers as opposed to 18 percent in the United States. This may be an indication of the potential for low-cost competition in Europe.

Asia-Pacific Region

By 1999, traffic in the Asian region had become quite important to the overall success of the air transportation industry. Collectively, this region represented 24 percent of worldwide revenue passenger kilometers. The ICAO estimated that the Asia-Pacific region had grown annually by 9.7 percent over the last ten years. This upward trend was expected to continue albeit at slightly lower levels, moderating between six percent and seven percent until 2001. Trans-Pacific traffic was expected to grow at 6.6 percent and intra-Asia-Pacific traffic by five percent. Some analysts predicted that Asia would play a key role in over half of the top 20 international markets ranked in terms of revenue passenger miles by 2002 (see Exhibit 4).

The aviation market in Asia, while similar to Europe of the pre-EU era, did indeed have some dominant players. Japan Airlines and Singapore Air-

Rank	Region	1998–2002E	1998–2007E
1	Africa–South America	8.3%	8.2%
2	Northeast Asia–Southwest Asia	8.2%	8.2%
3	Africa–Southwest Asia	7.8%	7.8%
4	Central America–South America	7.7%	7.5%
5	CIS region–International	7.5%	7.3%
6	Europe–South America	7.4%	7.9%
7	Europe–Northeast Asia	7.3%	7.7%
8	Oceania–South America	7.2%	7.1%
9	China–Southwest Asia	7.1%	7.2%
10	Middle East–Northeast Asia	6.9%	7.6%
11	Europe–Southwest Asia	6.7%	6.8%
12	North America–South America	6.6%	6.7%
13	Africa–North America	6.6%	6.9%
14	North America–Southeast Asia	6.5%	6.9%
15	China–Europe	6.4%	6.8%
16	Africa–Middle East	6.2%	6.1%
17	China–Northeast Asia	6.0%	6.6%
18	Southeast Asia–Southwest Asia	5.9%	6.3%
19	Northeast Asia–Southeast Asia	5.7%	6.5%
20	North America–Northeast Asia	5.7%	6.2%

EXHIBIT 4 Top 20 International Markets Projected Growth in RPMs by Region

SOURCE: U.S. DOT Form 41, Boeing Corp.

lines were the clear leaders and together accounted for 40 percent of the market share. The second tier included Cathay Pacific, Thai, and Korean Air, which comprised 33 percent of the market.[1] Asian carriers in general had significantly lower operating costs compared to their American and European counterparts. For example, in 1998, according to Warburg, Dillon & Read, personnel costs for North American carriers accounted for approximately 32 percent of total revenues. For European carriers, it was 21 percent. However, for the Asia-Pacific carriers, it was only 17 percent. Most of the Asian carriers also had much higher labor productivity levels and lower unit labor costs than airlines in North America or Europe (see Exhibit 5). This location-specific advantage was a primary reason why carriers from other regions were setting up significant hub operations in the Asia-Pacific region. While the yields for many carriers such as China Airlines, Korean Air, Thai, and Malaysian, the second and third tier competitors, were much lower than international levels, the top tier carriers such as Japan Airlines, and Singapore Airlines had yields consistent with their North American and European counterparts. The avenues for differentiating airline services in this region were shrinking. The elite carriers who had built a reputation for superlative service such as Singapore Airlines were now facing stiff competition from carriers such as Thai Airways and Cathay Pacific, who had geared to deliver similar services. Thus, differentiation was becoming much more demanding and difficult to sustain.

EXHIBIT 5

Annual Staff Cost per Employee in the Global Airline Industry

Region/Airline	1999 U.S. $
Europe	
Swissair	47,000
KLM	56,000
Air France	58,000
Lufthansa	58,000
British Airways	59,000
SAS	60,000
North America	
Air Canada	46,000
American	50,000
Continental	58,000
United	60,000
Northwest	61,000
Delta	68,000
U.S. Airways	75,000
Asia-Pacific	
Malaysian Airlines	18,000
Thai Airways	24,000
Air New Zealand	36,000
Korean	38,000
Singapore Airlines	46,000
Qantas	50,000
Cathay	67,000
All Nippon Airways	96,000
JAL	104,000

NOTE: Data drawn from bar charts deemed approximate.

SOURCE: Warburg, Dillon & Read, *Airline Analyser,* Aug. 1999.

The Rise of Alliances

By the late 1990s alliances between air carriers in different parts of the world had become the norm rather than the exception. The initial drive to find alliance partners could be traced to the historic strategic moves by KLM and Northwest in 1992 to partner and begin offering code-share services. This arrangement gave KLM a foothold in the rapidly growing U.S. market and allowed Northwest to expand its horizons in Europe. Today, most of the leading carriers around the world were part of mega-alliances which had evolved to include several carriers under a single alliance brand. The Star Alliance, for example, included ten carriers representing Asia-Pacific, North America, Latin America, and Europe. Oneworld, a similar network of partnerships, encompasses eight carriers spanning a similar geographical territory to Star (see Exhibit 6). Alliances such as these were expected to redirect traffic, increase profitability, help leverage scale economies in operations, and differentiate services in the minds of consumers who wanted to buy travel services through a single carrier.

While they did seem like a wonderful strategic option even to established carriers, alliances brought their own set of thorny issues. There were invariably questions relating to level of service across carriers, safety records of the partners, and willingness to cede control to an alliance. The key issue seemed to be the difficulty in developing a consensus about how the partners would establish common safety, service, and performance standards. Further, in the European markets there was a potential for cross-shareholdings between carriers as privatization accelerated. It was feared that this could create a parallel network that might undercut alliances. Since individual airlines were typically allowed to negotiate side deals with other carriers on their own irrespective of their alliance membership, the likelihood of inter-network rivalry was also high.

Singapore International Airlines: Country and Company

History and Culture of Singapore

Singapore had witnessed bountiful growth and become the envy of many neighboring countries as it entered the new 21st century. Its per capita GNP increased by a phenomenal 75 percent between 1990 and 1999 and currently stood at S$39,724.[2] This meteoric rise could be directly traced to Mr. Lee Kuan Yew, the most powerful Prime Minister in Singapore's history. He was able to tap the patriotic

EXHIBIT 6   Major Partners in Global Airline Alliances (1999)

Star	Wings	Oneworld	Delta
Air Canada	KLM	American	Delta
Lufthansa	Northwest	British Airways	Austrian
SAS	Alitalia	Canadian	Sabena
Thai	Continental	Cathay Pacific	Swissair
United		Qantas	Air France
Varig		Finnair	
Air New Zealand		Iberia	
Ansett Australia		Lan Chile	
All Nippon Airways			

SOURCE: Merrill Lynch.

spirit of his people when he announced his intent to develop Singapore to rival Switzerland in terms of standard of living. His emphasis on superior education standards, a controlled labor environment, and significant outlays for training and development all helped to enhance the quality of human capital. At the end of 1999, Singapore boasted a literacy rate of 93 percent, among the highest in the region. Singapore's Confucian work ethic dovetailed very well with his ambitions. It emphasized responsibilities over rights and placed enormous value on attributes such as hospitality, caring and service. As a result of these efforts, Singapore today ranked among the best countries in terms of human capital and was often rated among the world's friendliest places to do business. Rising standards of living meant higher wages (see Exhibit 7). Coupled with the small size of the local population and a very low unemployment rate (3.2 percent in 1998), the availability of labor was seen as a potential stumbling block in the drive toward further growth. Many of the larger companies already depended on a sizable number of expatriates from neighboring countries as well as the West to staff positions.

A staunch believer in free trade and internally driven growth, Mr. Yew made it clear from the start that "the world does not owe Singapore a living." For example, in the air transportation sector,

Mr. Yew's government declared that SIA, although the national carrier, would not receive any subsidies, protection, financial assistance, or economic benefits from the government. It would have to sink or swim based on its own resources and ingenuity. Singapore literally adopted a free skies approach whereby foreign flag carriers from other countries were welcome to serve the city-state without any restrictions. This meant heightened competition for SIA right from the start. However, the free market philosophy also resulted in sharper rates of market growth. For example, roughly 35 percent of the equity base of Singapore was foreign in origin, and foreign investors owned 17 percent of all companies in the country, both testaments to the successful programs that attracted foreign capital and commerce to the island nation.

The tourism industry played a very significant role in the overall development of the country. Handicapped by the small size and the lack of natural resources, Singapore had to rely on service industries such as tourism and finance to generate growth. It had always enjoyed an enviable status as an important geographic hub dating back to the pre-British Colonization era. During its history as a British colony, Singapore provided an important stop-off point for travelers from Europe and Britain to the outlying colonies of Australia and New

Zealand. Building on this historical reputation, Singapore evolved into an important Asian tourist hub (see Exhibit 8).

Singapore International Airlines: The Company

SIA traced its roots to an organization called Malayan Airways that offered its first commercial passenger service in May 1947. The modern incarnation, SIA, was born in 1972 when the Malaysia Singapore Airlines was officially split into two new airline companies, SIA and Malaysian Airlines System (now called Malaysia Airways). The long association with the Malaysian counterpart had proved to be quite beneficial to the fledgling company. The crews garnered significant flight experience operating over rough geographical terrain in Southeast Asia. Their safety records were impeccable. This association also provided SIA personnel with crucial operating experience ranging from flight operations to matters of administrative importance. As part of the split, SIA got half the combined assets, most of the overseas offices, its headquarters building in Singapore, and a fairly new computer reservation system. SIA was ready to spread its wings in the international aviation industry while its erstwhile partner, Malaysian Airlines System, was intent on focusing on domestic flights within Malaysia. The

choice was actually pre-determined for SIA since Singapore was a very small city-state with a geographic area of only 240 square miles, smaller than New York City! In early 1999 SIA reached 95 destinations in 43 countries in Asia, Europe, North America, Middle East, Southwest Pacific, and Africa (see Exhibit 9). Its subsidiary Silk Air served feeder routes and reached 18 destinations in the Southeast Asian region.

SIA had established an enviable record both in terms of its operational performance and its profitability history. It was one of the few Asian airlines that had continuously posted profits even during lean years such as the 1990s economic downturns in Asia. Its return on equity (ROE) averaged roughly ten percent over the five-year period prior to 1999, while its return on sales was around 14 percent during the same period. These profitability metrics were far more superior to those posted by SIA's rivals, and in some cases as high as twice or thrice what the rivals were earning. SIA had positioned itself to execute a strategy of differentiation, predicated on offering its passengers a level of service that was seldom surpassed at the price levels that SIA offered.

On the Ground

SIA's legendary commitment to superior service began on the ground. It built a network of wholly

EXHIBIT 8   Tourist Arrivals and Outbound Departures to and from Singapore

	1993	1997	1998
Tourist Arrivals	6,425,800	7,198,000	6,241,000
Outbound departures	1,587,416	2,391,149	2,197,759
Tourists per capita		1.92	1.76
Departures per capita		0.64	0.61

SOURCE: Government of Singapore, Department of Statistics.

Primary Regions of Origin of Singapore Bound Tourists, 1998

Region/Country	Number
ASEAN	1,878,600
Japan	843,700
Australia	427,200
Taiwan	362,400
U.K.	357,900

SOURCE: Government of Singapore, Department of Statistics.

EXHIBIT 9   Route Structure for Singapore Airlines

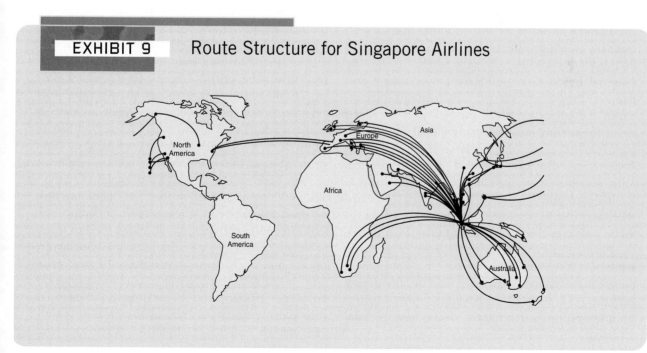

owned subsidiaries and joint ventures to provide operational support in areas such as catering, terminal management, and aircraft maintenance. These subsidiaries were largely managed as autonomous entities that had to bid for orders from the parent and were rated number one in many of their core areas. The Singapore Airlines Terminal Services (SATS) subsidiary was one of the largest in the group. It offered a variety of terminal management services including catering, passenger and baggage handling, and ramp operations. SATS operated one of the largest flight kitchens in the world at Changi International Airport, producing an average of 45,000 meals a day. It had an impressive client list that included British Airways, Qantas, Lufthansa, and Japan Airlines. It served more than 70 percent of all airlines flying into Singapore. SATS had also gone global through joint ventures in Beijing, Hong Kong, Ho Chi Minh City, Macau, Chennai, Male, Manila, Osaka, and Taipei.

The Changi International Airport was indeed a crown jewel for SIA. Given its status as a national flag carrier, it occupied pride of place at Changi, an airport that it also managed. The airport itself was rated among the best in the world by several global organizations. It often got top honors for its people-handling efficiency and cleanliness. For example, SIA made a promise to deliver a passenger's baggage within ten minutes upon arrival in Changi and consistently delivered on that promise. Such a high standard would be difficult but for the excellence of its subsidiary network, especially SATS. Changi was also the headquarters of SIA's Engineering Company, a subsidiary that provided aircraft maintenance and engine overhaul services. As a testament to its engineering prowess, many global carriers engaged SIA Engineering to service their fleets. SIA Engineering also had a global presence through joint ventures with reputable companies such as Rolls-Royce and Pratt & Whitney. It was expected that both SATS and SIA Engineering would be taken public in the near future to give them the independence and the incentive to grow faster internationally. It was unclear whether this move would dampen the control that SIA held in these subsidiaries and how it might impact the superior ground operations that these divisions have been instrumental in building.

The almost obsessive attention to detail began the moment the passenger decided to travel on SIA. The company was at the forefront of introducing electronic ticketing through its Web site. Online ticketing was being rolled out across all destinations in its network. To make it easy on the passengers, the company had introduced automated check-in systems on certain flights that tended to attract a large number of travelers. It embraced technology in a variety of forms, allowing check-in via e-mail, telephone, and fax. The Silver Kris Lounge that SIA offered its first and raffles class (business class) passengers could be best described as "oases of peace and quiet"[3] amidst the hustle and bustle of the airport. It featured an environment with plush armchairs, deep-pile carpeting, aquariums, tropical gardens, and a décor that included original paintings by Singapore artists. Top-of-the-line business equipment such as computers, fax services, and a stock ticker were standard amenities. It was one of the largest and most luxurious airport lounges in the world.

Fleet Acquisition and Management

Singapore Airlines came a very long way from its origins as a company that had a fleet of just ten aircraft serving a network of 22 cities. By late 1999 it operated a fleet of 96 aircraft, almost all of them capable of long-haul, large-capacity flights. It had 37 aircraft on firm order mostly with Boeing and another 36 on options to acquire should the need arise. It had planned its fleet acquisitions judiciously such that its fleet was only five years old on average.[4] It was the world's largest operator of the Boeing 747-400 Megatops, a roomy aircraft capable of long-distance flights. Among the largest air carriers in the world, Delta Airlines came closest to SIA in terms of fleet age with an average of roughly eight years. Most of the other carriers had large segments of their fleets in the 14-plus years range.[5] Continuously maintaining youth in its flight operations was no small achievement. It was a facet of competition that SIA took very seriously. It maintained an office in Seattle, Washington, just to liaise with Boeing designers and oversee the development of new additions to the SIA fleet. Newer aircraft were typically more fuel efficient and less maintenance intensive than older generations. SIA used a mix of leasing and outright purchase, primarily during economic lulls, to feed its appetite for new fleets, thus extracting maximum value for its investment.

SIA emphasized fleet selection because of its strong signaling value. It implicitly tells the potential customer that she/he can expect top-of-the-line technology, comfortable seating, and a safe trip, all of which are critical aspects around which differentiation can be built. Keeping up with the changes in technology allowed SIA to design aircraft interiors that encompassed the latest amenities. For example, SIA was among the first to offer a personal video screen in every seat, even in its economy class. Its in-flight entertainment system *Kris World* delivered 22 video channels, 12 audio stereo channels, and ten Nintendo game channels at every seat, with a Dolby surround sound system that was specially designed for SIA. Its first-class cabins became the gold standard in the industry. They were outfitted with armchair type seats that converted into comfortable beds at the push of a button. Clad in Connolly leather (the company that supplies leather products to Rolls Royce, Ferrari, and Jaguar) and trimmed in burl wood, the seats included built-in communication devices and an inflatable air mattress. The cabin crew provided a "turn-down" service where the bed linen was replaced on long trips. The famous French fashion house Givenchy designed all the serviceware. SIA tried to convey this air of exclusivity in its other cabins as well. Even in coach class, the seats were wider than average, with spacious legroom, leg rests, video screens, and ergonomic headrests. As part of its drive to be a top-notch air carrier, SIA had gathered several firsts along the way. In 1991, it was the first transcontinental carrier to introduce in-flight telephones using advanced communications technology. It was the first with the Dolby surround sound and personal video screens in coach. It was the first to offer fax services in the air. The list goes on. Plans were under way to upgrade the communications package to allow Internet access while in the air. It would shortly debut an on-demand entertainment system called *WISEMEN* in its first and raffles class cabins.

The Softer Side of SIA

The company firmly believed that its employees were the primary drivers of the success that it en-

joyed in the marketplace. Through a deft mixture of organizational culture, indoctrination, and ritual, SIA was able to meld the human assets into a formidable source of competitive advantage. A large number of its employees came from Singapore and Malaysia. As of 1999 it employed 27,400 people worldwide, of which roughly 11,000 worked in Singapore, making SIA the largest private sector employer in the country. The company established an expansive SIA Training Center in Singapore that served as the focal point for training programs targeted at cabin crew, commercial staff, flight crew, and flight operations personnel.

SIA executed a finely tuned recruitment and training strategy to keep its ranks stocked with exceptional talent. Most of the employees arrived at the company through either a cadetship (similar to an internship) program that attracted generalists or a specialist program geared to functional experts in areas such as computer services and finance. The cadetship was an intensive on-the-job training program that cycled employees through a variety of functions as they moved up the hierarchy. Its commitment to employee training and development was reflected in the fact that it spent roughly 14 times as much per employee as the average Singapore company. The company instituted a system of proven controls and mentoring guidelines that helped the employees develop their potential to contribute to the success of the organization. Over time, this built an enormous sense of camaraderie among the team, a very strong sense of identity and belonging where the employees truly took pride in their organization. For example, during the recent economic crisis that plagued Asia, SIA was able to manage without significantly trimming its workforce because many of its employees willingly turned down their annual wage increments while improving operational efficiency at the same time.

The pool of talent with respect to pilots was indeed global in complexion. At last count SIA had pilots from over 50 countries flying its fleet. Many of these pilots were expatriates drawn by the allure of flying the latest equipment under professional working conditions at very generous levels of compensation. The company operated its own flying college with campuses in Singapore and Jandakot, Australia, that focused on improving training efficiency and producing qualified pilots. The college served as an incubator for developing Singaporean pilots to meet SIA's growing demands. The company had a state-of-the-art flight training facility in Singapore which housed eight flight simulators where pilots were trained. All flight personnel were required to go through mandatory biennial proficiency checks. It was generally believed that the training programs in this regard were quite well administered as reflected in the very high levels of safety that the company was able to achieve. It was the long-term intent to induct more Singapore nationals into the cockpit, a daunting proposition especially since the number of local pilots available was quite low. This was augmented by graduates of the Singapore Armed Forces (SAF), which trained pilots for defense purposes. After completion of the mandatory employment with SAF, some of the trained personnel took up jobs with SIA. The company employed roughly 1,500 flight crew, of whom half were expatriates. Normally, the expatriates were more expensive since the company had to bear a variety of expenses such as housing, schooling for children, travel, etc., in addition to base pay.

The complement of cabin crew, numbering roughly 6,000, were chosen through a very rigorous selection process. SIA considered them to be the "brand ambassadors" who should reflect the high standards of service excellence that its passengers expected. Although they were drawn from many ethnicities within the South/Southeast Asian region (mainly Malaysia, India, Japan, Korea, Taiwan, and Indonesia), they were mostly Singaporean. Of late, this recruitment strategy had posed a stumbling block since the pool of available talent within Singapore was insufficient to draw from. Given the fact that SIA had some of the lowest labor costs among leading carriers, this home-based cost advantage had proven to be a critical ingredient in the success of the company. Any fall-off in the availability of local talent could adversely impact operating costs, especially if it necessitated the recruitment of expatriate personnel. Such a move would also raise questions about how globalizing its workforce would fit in with its historic branding approach, the *Singapore Girl*. When SIA was formed, it had to compete against other airlines that had much more sophisticated fleets and passenger options. In com-

bating this handicap and to distinguish itself in the marketplace, SIA launched the *Singapore Girl* as the embodiment of caring, comfortable, hospitable service. It also played well to the oriental mystique that was then prevalent in the Western world where the company sought to establish a footing.

The image of the *Singapore Girl* was carefully nurtured. It began with a rigorous selection process and extensive training soon thereafter. The training program emphasized aspects such as passenger handling, social etiquette, and grooming. While no different on the surface from other competitors, the SIA program was far more intense and demanding. For starters, it lasted much longer than competitors' training programs and embraced some nontraditional aspects. For example, many of its cabin crew spent extensive periods of their training program in homes for the aged to gain a better appreciation of the special needs of this fast-growing passenger segment. The company's approach to molding attitudes and service-oriented behaviors transcended mere internalization of a set of physical practices, and do's and don'ts by the cabin crew. The arduous training process was to be repeated periodically through preplanned refresher courses so that the crew could get acquainted with new cabin management technologies and service standards. Once in the fold of the organization, there was a marked effort on the part of management and staff to help each employee perform at his/her best potential. Various practices such as detailed performance reviews and feedback at all levels, career counseling, and performance-based reward systems were designed toward this end. SIA's in-cabin service became legendary, the standard that even other airlines aspired to reach. In a recent survey by *Condè Nast Traveler*, a well-respected travel magazine, SIA was ranked overall as the Best International Airline. This was the tenth time that SIA was chosen for the prestigious honor in eleven years that the award had been given. The respondents rated SIA's cabin service as the best in the world, a testament to the company's emphasis on excellence in this arena. Such awards were nothing new for SIA, which had garnered over 100 from august organizations such as Zagat, Condè Nast, Business Traveller, OAG Worldwide, ASEAN (Association of South East Asian Nations) Tourism Association, and Asia

Money. In January of 1999 alone, the company won an astounding 23 awards.

Competing in the New Millennium

By the late 1990s, competition in the airline business had become decidedly global, although very few carriers could legitimately claim to be global carriers. Carriers in the Asia-Pacific region had taken a page from the SIA playbook in offering premium services at consistently low fares. Those in Europe and North America had strengthened their positions through alliances. SIA had already taken some important steps to fortify its position globally. It had recently decided to join the Star Alliance, a powerful network of carriers that included Lufthansa, United, Ansett, Air New Zealand, All Nippon Airways, South Africa Airways, Air Canada, Thai, Varig, and SAS. It was believed that this would allow the members to offer code-sharing services, fine-tune traffic flows to increase revenues and efficiency, and combine their buying power to negotiate favorable terms for securing inputs. Translated from an SIA perspective, this could open up several destinations that SIA did not yet serve. It could take advantage of code sharing to carry a greater number of passengers to destinations within Europe and the United States. For example, as of 1999 it served only three major cities in the United States: Los Angeles, San Francisco, and New York. Hence, the relationship with United could extend that limited set of destinations to encompass a considerably larger number of primary and secondary cities. A similar argument could be made with respect to leveraging the new relationship with Varig to fly to more destinations in South America, a region that was not well represented in SIA's route structure. However, despite the obvious advantages, the alliance network did bring with it some concerns.

Thai Airlines, the nearest geographical neighbor for SIA in the alliance, announced its intent to step down from the Star Alliance since it believed that the relationship would not serve its best interests after SIA was allowed to join. This could indicate some simmering rivalry in the region, where Thai was taking active steps to upgrade its service levels and had reached a position where its service would be rated quite highly. From the perspective of loyal SIA passengers, it remained to be seen whether the other network carriers would be able to rise to the levels of SIA's hallmark service standards. Should there be shortfalls, it is quite likely that the brand image that SIA has so carefully nourished could be tarnished, especially among its loyal first and business class passengers. In essence, joining a network amounted to delegating some aspects of brand management to the collective group of companies such that the identity of the network would transcend the individual identities of the members. The loss of control over some key decisions such as scheduling and flight frequency could also pose challenges in the future. It also raised critical questions about the imitability of core competences. Would the partner firms be able to learn more about the critical aspects of SIA's recipe for sustainable competitive advantage? An alliance is usually not designed to last forever and hence should the partners learn firsthand about SIA's operations, it might be disadvantageous to SIA should the alliance be dissolved.

In balancing growth potential against the ability to control the alliance, SIA was considering equity investments. It acquired an 8.3 percent equity stake in Air New Zealand to cement a long partnership with the New Zealand carrier. Since Air New Zealand already owned 50 percent of Ansett Airways, SIA would have the benefit of the additional alliance with Ansett as well. It was expected that these moves would strengthen SIA's position in the Australasia market that was growing significantly.

Mr. Kong believed it was in SIA's best interest to pursue an equity investment in Virgin Airways as a further step toward achieving global status. His team discussed an investment proposal under which SIA would acquire 49 percent of Virgin Atlantic for roughly $975 million. This represented a valuation that was equivalent to four times prevailing market value for Virgin and about 1.2 times Virgin's sales revenues.[6] In return, SIA would gain access to the lucrative trans-Atlantic sector between the United States and the U.K., thus entering an arena that SIA could not enter previously given the roadblocks imposed by the British government. It would also obtain landing slots at Heathrow. The route structures of the two companies were quite complementary with very little overlap (see Exhibits 9 and 10). This would indicate greater potential for increasing revenues through code-sharing flights. While Sir Richard Branson was slated to continue managing Virgin, SIA had been promised three board memberships. Since both organizations adopted an almost obsessive attention to customer service and had similar operating philosophies, it was believed that they would function well as partners. However, Virgin appeared to be the more free-spirited company of the two and had a reputation as an iconoclast while SIA portrayed a buttoned-down, conservative image. The board was sure to raise issues of management compatibility, price to acquire, control of Virgin Atlantic, and how the new relationship could impact existing relationships that SIA had built with other carriers. For example, Virgin declared that it would soon launch a low-cost Virgin Australia division that would compete in the Australian market. This might place SIA in an awkward position since its ownership in Air New Zealand could technically make it a competitor to Virgin. Further, Virgin had repeatedly said that it would not join the Star Alliance. This could potentially pit SIA against Star Alliance members. For ex-

ample, SIA might want to funnel passengers to Virgin on its North Atlantic routes instead of United, a Star Alliance partner. Decisions such as this could muddy the alliance network that SIA currently belongs to. In essence, joining forces with Virgin might undo some of the benefits of belonging to the Star Alliance.

As Mr. Kong proceeded through Immigration at Changi, he was trying to assemble a mental map of how he wanted to position SIA in the near future. Besides the strategic issues relating to alliances and Virgin Atlantic, the mounting competitive intensity in the Asia-Pacific region also required immediate action. How should SIA continue to differentiate itself from the copycats who seemed to be doing a very creditable job at imitating SIA in terms of cabin service and amenities? What new signaling devices could SIA harness to set itself apart from the competition? Should SIA be wedded to the *Singapore Girl* concept that had historically helped distinguish their service offerings? Would SIA be able to achieve its global objectives while holding steady with its recruitment approach that focused primarily on Singaporeans and Malaysian personnel? Should SIA begin a full-blown strategy analysis based on Internet technologies that appear to be

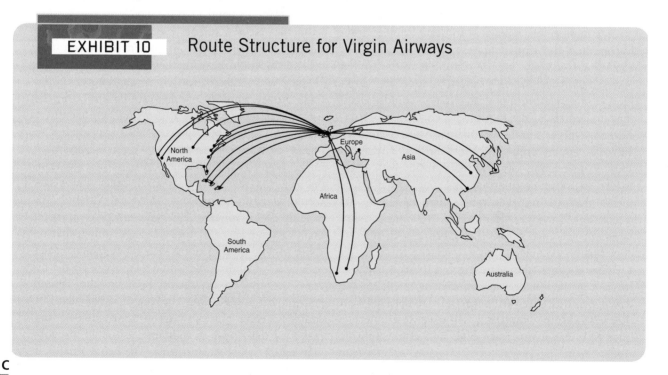

EXHIBIT 10 Route Structure for Virgin Airways

rewriting the rules of business? How could its potential be harnessed within SIA?

The chauffeur was holding the door open as Mr. Kong strode to the limousine. Mr. Kong wanted to get a few winks before the board meeting tomorrow. It was the best of times for SIA on some fronts, but there was uncertainty in the air. SIA was at a crossroads in its history. The next few strategic moves would determine whether it would rise from its status as a very good Asian airline to become a global player, commanding the respect of the world's largest carriers.

Notes

1. World Airlines in Review, *Interavia Business & Technology,* June 1999.
2. Government of Singapore, Department of Statistics, http://www.singstat.gov.
3. BBC program.
4. Fleet data and age obtained from http://www.singaporeair.com.
5. *Airline Analyzer,* Warburg, Dillon & Read, August 1999.
6. HSBC report, Feb. 7, 2000.

Glossary of Terms

Available Ton Kilometer (ATK)	A measure of capacity expressed in terms of aircraft payload multiplied by kilometers flown
Available Seat Kilometers (ASK)	A measure of seat capacity available defined by the number of seats multiplied by kilometers flown
Revenue Ton Kilometers (RTK)	The total traffic carriage measured by the revenue-generating weight (in tons) of load carried multiplied by kilometers flown
Revenue Passenger Kilometers (RPK)	A passenger traffic measure expressed as the total number of passengers carried multiplied by kilometers flown
Passenger Load Factor (PLF)	Passenger load factor in RPKs expressed as a percentage of ASKs, which indicates utilization of seat capacity (RPK/ASK)
Cargo Load Factor (CLF)	Cargo load in RTKs expressed as a percentage of ATKs, which indicates utilization of total capacity
Overall Load Factor (OLF)	Total passenger and cargo load expressed as a percentage of total passenger and cargo capacity (ATKs), which indicates utilization of total capacity
Break-Even Load Factor	Unit cost per ATK divided by overall yield—provides an indication of the load factor needed for the airline to break even at the operating profit level
Yield	Amount of revenue generated by each unit of load expressed in cents per RTK for cargo or cents per RPK for passengers
Unit Cost	Expenditure required to produce a unit of capacity expressed in cents per ATK for cargo or cents per ASK for passengers

United Airlines

Case 20A: United Airlines—"Rising"?

Derek Evers
Velislav Hristanov

Adam Kirst
Todd Robeson

Mathangi Shankar
M. Gail Christian

In December 2002 United Airlines, the nation's second largest airline carrier, filed for Chapter 11 bankruptcy protection. The airline had posted losses of nearly $3 billion in the prior 18 months and had been losing money from its operations at a rate of $7 million per day. At that time United's bankruptcy was the largest airline failure and the sixth largest bankruptcy in U.S. history.[1] United's downfall was caused by a combination of circumstances and events, including the terrorist attacks on September 11, 2001, that affected the entire airline industry. In this case, United, its competitors, and the airline industry are examined to determine if there is a light at the end of the tunnel for United Airlines.

UAL History

United Airlines, Inc. is the wholly owned, principal subsidiary of UAL Corporation, incorporated December 30, 1968, as UAL, Inc. In 2002 United Airlines carried, on average, more than 210,000 passengers per day. United flew more than 108 billion revenue passenger miles in 2001[2], carrying people, property, and mail to nearly 119 destinations in 26 countries and two territories.

United's history actually began much earlier than 1968. In 1925, an act of Congress made the carrying of mail by air a private operation under a system of competitive bidding.[3] United was formed a year later as an airmail service that carried mail between Pasco, Washington, and Elko, Nevada. This original venture evolved into a modern global airline.

Strong demand for air travel followed during the post World War II economic boom that swept the United States. In response, United expanded its workforce, acquired new routes, and purchased the company's first jet aircraft.[4] On June 1, 1961, United merged with Capital Airlines, then the fifth largest air transport company in the United States, and formed the world's largest commercial airline. In 1968, United's stockholders approved the formation of UAL, Inc., as a holding company, with United as a wholly owned subsidiary.

The next 20 years were turbulent times for the company and tested not only United, but the entire airline industry. The company had six different presidents between 1970 and 1989. Management

This case was written for purposes of class discussion only and is not intended to illustrate either effective or ineffective handling of an administrative situation. We would like to acknowledge the helpful comments of Robert E. Hoskisson on previous drafts of this case.

Reprinted by permission of Robert E. Hoskisson, Arizona State University, and team members Marilyn Gail Christian, Derek Evers, Velislav Hristanov, Adam Kirst, Todd Robeson, and Mathangi Shankar.

changes resulted in new directions and new images for United. The company acquired other non-airline businesses including rental car businesses and hotel properties, which were later sold. UAL, Inc., also changed its name to Allegis Corporation in 1986, and then changed it back to UAL, Inc., in 1988. On February 11, 1986, United purchased Pan American Airways' Pacific Division and began service to 13 Pacific cities, and in October 1990, it announced the purchase of Pan American's routes between the United States and London.

United sustained record losses in the early 1990s and worked to recoup them for several years. The company initiated a hiring freeze, grounded older aircraft, and sold its flight kitchens. However, the resulting $400 million reduction in operating expenses was not enough to enable United to avoid launching intensive labor costs negotiations with employee unions. The UAL board approved a proposal for 54,000 employees to exchange portions of their salaries and benefits for UAL stock, paving the way for the creation of the largest majority employee-owned company in the world on July 12, 1994.[5]

The newly created Employee Stock Option Plan (ESOP) environment conflicted with the company's prior culture because formerly control was centered in the top level executives. Subsequently, the chairman, president, CEO, and other key officials stepped down from their positions. One of the new management's first steps was to begin to transform the corporate culture from a "command-and-control" philosophy to one based on higher employee involvement, with an emphasis on better communication. Workplace innovations were quickly adopted, including telecommuting, elimination of the furlough policy, and the introduction of casual dress codes in non-public areas of the company.[6]

Perhaps the most substantial change resulting from the ESOP was the shift in the balance of power within UAL. Over the two-year period after its creation, the original 54,000 U.S. employees who launched the ESOP in mid-1994 were joined in ownership by many of their coworkers in Europe, South America, and Asia.[7] By 2002 a significant portion of the UAL workforce was represented by one of five different unions: the International Association of Machinists and Aerospace Workers (IAMAW), the Air Line Pilots Association (ALPA),

the Association of Flight Attendants (AFA), the Transport Workers Union (TWU), and the Professional Airline Flight Control Association (PAFCA).[8] With such a high level of union organization and enormous ownership stake in the company, UAL labor was able to create three employee representative positions on the 11-member board (see Exhibit 1). Over the next several years the labor force became very powerful in such decisions as the approval of mergers and the selection and removal of executive officers. Thus, the seats on the board gave employees significant control over major business decisions.

In response to the globalization of the airline industry in the early 1990s, United directed its strategy toward an international expansion through strategic alliances. In 1992, United entered into an alliance agreement with Air Canada, and in 1993 it announced a comprehensive marketing agreement with Lufthansa. With careful attention to antitrust regulations, United ensured that the company's alliances received antitrust immunity from the U.S. Department of Transportation. On May 14, 1997, United Airlines, Lufthansa, Air Canada, SAS, and Thai Airways International launched the Star Alliance network, which also included Austrian Airlines, Lauda Air, Varig Brazilian Airlines, Singapore Airlines, and others, bringing the total to 14 airline companies.

In 2002 Star Alliance, through its members, served customers at 729 airports in 124 countries with a fleet of 2,058 airplanes and a busy schedule of 10,728 departures per day. As a member of the Star Alliance, United received such benefits as the diversification of risks and the sharing of resources necessary for global competition. Increasing the number of destinations, creating a vast communication network, and enhancing marketing and sales activities were the key factors that favorably influenced the company's future growth and competitiveness. Its advertising slogan, "Rising," seemed well deserved.

Starting in 1995, United enjoyed three consecutive years of record-breaking profits. However, although United was named one of the ten best stocks for long-term investment in August 1999 by *Fortune* magazine, the company soon encountered turbulent times again. The pilots and machinists staged work slowdowns during the 2000 labor negotiations that resulted in canceled flights, angry customers, and a $700 million revenue shortfall. In an attempt to regain employee confidence, an agreement was made with the pilots' union that made United pilots the highest paid in the industry.[9] United then planned an all-cash acquisition of US Airways, hoping that its strong presence in the eastern United States would complement United's stronger nationwide and international network. Because it sought the acquisition without first obtaining union approval, employee confidence again waned. The deal was canceled in 2001 when the Justice Department indicated that it would block the merger because it would reduce competition.

Administrative expenses also increased substantially during this time, which, combined with 41 percent higher fuel expenses, resulted in fiscal year 2000 being one of United's poorest in the last decade. Financial information for UAL, Inc., is provided in Exhibit 2.

The Airline Industry

As an airline, United operates in a unique environment. Following the government deregulation of the airline industry in 1978, the industry began to evolve competitively into the model followed by most airlines today.

Regulation

The Airline Deregulation Act of 1978 phased out the federal government's control over airfares and services, allowing the airlines instead to rely on competitive market forces to determine the price, quantity, and quality of domestic air service. The two most important consequences of deregulation were lower fares and higher productivity. It was estimated that deregulated fares in 2002 were ten percent to 18 percent lower, on average, than they would have been when the airline industry was regulated. The savings to travelers were in the range of $5 billion to $10 billion per year.[10] Higher productivity was a result of increased flexibility in operations, introduction of the hub-and-spoke business model, and a more competitive industry environment.

Although deregulation allowed the airline companies to set their own prices and choose their own destinations, the industry was still regulated considerably in regard to taxation, air traffic control, and

EXHIBIT 2　UAL Financial Highlights

Income Statement ($ million)

Fiscal Year Ending	Dec. 01	Dec. 00	Dec. 99	Dec. 98	Dec. 97	Dec. 96	Dec. 95	Dec. 94
Net sales	16,138	19,352	18,027	17,561	17,378	16,362	14,943	13,950
Cost of goods	11,537	11,147	9,493	9,857	9,810	9,344	8,541	8,100
Gross profit	4,601	8,205	8,534	7,704	7,568	7,018	6,402	5,850
Sell gen. & admin. exp.	5,918	6,424	4,701	4,540	4,643	5,136	4,849	4,604
Depreciation & amort.	1,026	988	850	1,686	1,666	759	664	725
Net Income	−2,145	50	2,810	821	949	533	349	51

Balance Sheet ($ million)

Fiscal Year Ending	Dec. 01	Dec. 00	Dec. 99	Dec. 98	Dec. 97	Dec. 96	Dec. 95	Dec. 94
Annual Assets								
Cash	1,688	1,679	310	390	295	229	194	500
Mrktable securities	940	665	379	425	550	468	949	1,032
Receivables	1,047	1,216	1,284	1,138	1,051	962	951	889
Prop., plant, & equip.	21,996	22,566	20,717	18,827	15,890	14,206	12,677	11,956
Accumulated dep.	5,188	6,223	5,852	5,773	5,116	5,963	5,656	5,233
Net prop. & equip.	16,808	16,343	14,865	13,054	10,774	8,243	7,021	6,723
Total Assets	25,197	24,355	20,963	18,559	15,803	12,677	11,641	11,764
Annual Liabilities								
Accounts payable	1,268	1,188	967	1,151	1,030	994	696	651
Cur. long-term debt	1,217	170	92	98	235	165	90	384
Total current liab.	8,066	6,509	5,411	5,668	5,248	5,003	4,433	4,906
Total Liabilities	22,087	18,594	14,819	14,455	12,851	11,384	11,761	12,031
Shareholder Equity	3,110	5,761	6,044	4,004	2,438	1,262	−179	−316

SOURCE: Company annual reports obtained from Global Access (http://www.primark.com).

competitive behavior. The Airport Transportation Association claimed that the federal government taxed flying more heavily than cigarettes. Mergers, acquisitions, and alliances (global or domestic) were heavily scrutinized for monopolistic and anticompetitive behavior and were subject to approval by concerned regulatory organizations such as the Federal Aviation Administration (FAA). Many industry analysts in the United States believed that regulations, such as those limiting the domestic competition of foreign airlines, stood in the way of much needed changes in the industry.

Cost and Price Structure

The airline industry as a whole has been spectacularly unprofitable over the last two decades, with notable exceptions such as Southwest Airlines and JetBlue. The industry, even in the best of times, has been a low-margin, capital-intensive business, heavily burdened with high fixed costs and overcapacity. Between 1996 and 2001, larger carriers added three percent more capacity each year even when the market was mature.[11] Labor and fuel were the two major components of the cost structure, while unions played a significant role in driving up the labor costs.

Price competition also became fierce. Although business travelers were typically willing to pay much higher fares for unrestricted tickets when times were good, they were not willing to do the same during a downturn in the economy. Business travelers began to choose leisure fares with restrictions or to travel coach, and many turned to the Internet for discounted ticket prices.

Hub-and-Spoke versus Point-to-Point

Adopted first by American Airlines, the hub-and-spoke business model has been used by major airlines and alliances. Use of the hub-and-spoke model would enable an airline to serve a large number of destinations and provide frequent flights by channeling passengers through a hub airport on the way to their destinations using only a fraction of the aircraft that would be necessary if all flights were direct. One drawback of the hub-and-spoke model is the large upfront investment required to build the hub, which could result in increased fares to cover the investment and operation costs.

In contrast, the point-to-point system would provide customers with direct flights between two locations without making the additional stopover at a hub. Under this system, aircraft and crews typically worked harder and low-cost carriers such as Southwest and JetBlue relied on low fares to attract business. According to Aviation Economics, a London consultancy, "low cost carriers using the point-to-point system get 11 hours flying per day out of each aircraft, compared with only about nine hours for a network carrier using the hub-and-spoke system."[12] However, traditional carriers such as American and United continued to use the hub-and-spoke model because of its ability to service wider markets.

Competition

In 2002 the industry's top five players ranked in terms of sales were AMR (parent company of American Airlines), UAL (parent company of United Airlines), Delta, Lufthansa, and Japan Airlines. Most major airlines had formed global alliances to enable them to compete in international markets. Global alliances allowed airlines to circumvent national laws and other regulatory problems, as well as share resources to develop additional routes, global marketing strategies, and code-sharing agreements, all without incurring the high costs associated with expansion. The major alliances at that time were Star Alliance (14 member airlines, including United), Oneworld (eight member airlines, including American Airlines, British Airways, and Finnair), SkyTeam (six member airlines, including Delta Airlines, Air France, and Korean Air) and Wings (Continental, Northwest, and KLM Royal Dutch Airlines). Star Alliance was the 2001 industry leader in terms of number of passengers carried and market share for 2001. Throughout 2001 Star Alliance carried 112 million passengers and had 23 percent market share, based on passenger/kilometers traveled. Oneworld and SkyTeam were second and third with 17 percent and 13 percent market share respectively. (See Exhibit 3.)

While the major airlines used alliances to position themselves in the global market, they faced a slightly different set of rivals in their domestic market—low-cost, point-to-point carriers. Southwest Airlines, JetBlue, and Ryanair (Europe) emerged as new competitors who posed a significant threat to the larger carriers. They offered customers the convenience of point-to-point service combined with lower fares. In 2002 the market capitalization of Ryanair surpassed that of British Airways. In the United States, Southwest Airlines was the only profitable airline in 2001, and JetBlue, a growing U.S. airline, won rave reviews from American passengers.

Although the deregulation of the industry resulted in higher productivity, alarming trends developed to put the airline industry on a very bumpy course. United Airlines and the other members of the Star Alliance were not the only airlines facing critical strategic issues. The entire airline industry struggled, and underlying flaws in the dominant business model were exposed. Mergers and airline failures made the industry more concentrated at the national level than it was prior to deregulation. Poor profits, bankruptcies, predatory practices, extensive price discrimination, and terrorist activities tarnished the image of this once fascinating and glamorous industry.

Competitor Histories

Despite its competition, UAL managed to position itself as a frontline player in both the domestic and

EXHIBIT 3 — Alliances' Market Shares

Alliance	Passengers Carried (Mill)	Market Share* Percent
Star Alliance—Lufthansa, United	112.6	23
Oneworld—British Airways, American	85.6	17
SkyTeam—Delta, Air France	55.8	13
Wings—KLM, Northwest, Continental (may join SkyTeam)	67.8	11

*Based on passenger/kilometers traveled in 2001.
SOURCE: "How SkyTeam Measures Up," *Business Week*, September 9, 2002.

international markets. Although United competed regionally with low-cost carriers, the company's major competitors were hub-and-spoke airlines such as American, Delta, and Continental.

American Airlines

Aviation Corporation's directors created American Airlines in 1930,[13] and the company, held by AMR Corporation, had grown to be the world's largest airline carrier.[14] In April 2001, a merger with Trans World Airlines (TWA), orchestrated to compete against UAL's attempt to purchase US Airways, pushed American past United Airlines in overall size. The merger gave American access to more domestic cities and a few additional international destinations for a total of 177 destinations.[15] Although the merger resulted in the acquisition of more resources, American needed to improve its image with its customers and employees to capitalize on this advantage.

American also sought to compete through its Oneworld alliance with British Airways. This alliance was created in August 2001 after approval was received from U.S. Department of Transportation (DOT). Oneworld was a late entrant into the market because U.S. antitrust regulators blocked previous attempts at an alliance with British Airways. The Star Alliance had a firm position in world markets through its system of alliances, and Oneworld sought to play catch up (see Exhibit 4).[16] Financial information for AMR Corporation is provided in Exhibit 5.

Delta Air Lines

Delta Air Lines was founded in 1924 as the world's first aerial crop dusting organization. It started providing passenger flights in 1929 and in 2002 was the second largest airline in terms of passengers carried and third largest as measured by operating revenues

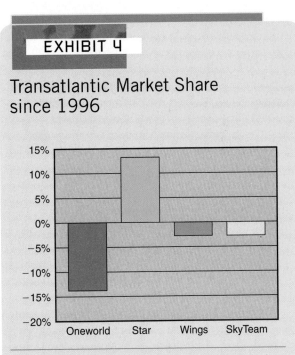

EXHIBIT 4

Transatlantic Market Share since 1996

SOURCE: http://www.american-britishairways.com/announcement.ppt.

EXHIBIT 5   AMR Financial Highlights

Income Statement ($ million)

Fiscal Year Ending	Dec. 01	Dec. 00	Dec. 99	Dec. 98	Dec. 97	Dec. 96	Dec. 95	Dec. 94
Net sales	17,484	18,117	16,338	16,309	15,866	15,136	14,503	13,910
Cost of goods	12,060	10,394	8,936	8,512	8,493	8,027	7,552	7,342
Gross profit	5,424	7,723	7,402	7,797	7,373	7,109	6,951	6,568
Sell gen. & admin. exp.	6,020	5,411	5,405	5,087	4,976	4,848	4,890	4,757
Depreciation & amort.	1,257	1,068	977	941	950	930	975	966
Net Income	−1,562	778	627	1,063	780	705	208	268

Balance Sheet ($ million)

Fiscal Year Ending	Dec. 01	Dec. 00	Dec. 99	Dec. 98	Dec. 97	Dec. 96	Dec. 95	Dec. 94
Annual Assets								
Cash	117	86	72	86	47	37	70	13
Mrktable securities	2,856	1,549	1,645	1,398	1,762	1,312	816	744
Receivables	1,371	1,242	1,124	1,153	1,057	1,087	1,013	877
Prop., plant, & equip.	26,760	25,469	22,661	19,720	17,419	17,501	17,787	17,829
Accumulated dep.	9,188	8,843	8,146	7,366	6,653	5,900	5,437	5,184
Net prop. & equip.	17,572	16,626	14,515	12,354	10,766	11,601	12,350	12,645
Total Assets	30,477	23,161	21,719	19,224	17,753	17,562	17,629	17,323
Annual Liabilities								
Accounts payable	1,717	1,178	991	940	855	914	742	831
Cur. long-term debt	421	108	61	23	21	22	49	49
Total current liab.	7,173	6,761	5,310	5,328	5,347	6,082	5,283	4,163
Total Liabilities	24,998	16,726	14,569	12,799	12,399	13,034	13,983	14,090
Shareholder Equity	5,479	6,435	7,150	6,425	5,354	4,528	3,646	3,233

SOURCE: Company annual reports obtained from Global Access (http://www.primark.com).

and revenue passenger miles flown.[17] In 2001, Delta operated 5,767 flights each day to over 425 cities in 76 countries. Through well-paced mergers, marketing agreements, and alliances, Delta managed to build a network that could offer passengers access to nearly 80 percent of the world's destinations.

In 2000, Delta's strategic action was to launch the SkyTeam global alliance, partnering with AeroMexico, Air France, and Korean Air (Alitalia and CSA Czech Airlines were also members of the alliance). The SkyTeam alliance believed that it had several key advantages that made it a strong global rival. First, the size of the alliance was efficient— large enough to cover the most important locations, but not so large that it was cumbersome to manage. Second, SkyTeam's strong network made the alliance a leader on the Transatlantic and in Europe, and provided a basis for growth in Asia and Latin America. Third, an important advantage was SkyTeam's regulatory freedom; it was the only alliance with anti-trust immunity among partners in the United States, Europe, and Asia. Finally, a key to success was the alliance's operational integration on all levels—technology, pricing, sales, connections to destinations, etc.[18] However, at the same time, Frederick Reid, president and chief operating officer of Delta, said "We want to grow some more—strategically—but we do not have aspirations to become a United Nations of the sky."[19]

Delta experienced four profitable years between 1997 and 2000 (see Exhibit 6). In 2001, however, the overall downturn in the economy brought net sales down by 17 percent. The company could not reduce its cost of goods sold accordingly and therefore recorded a loss of $1.2 billion. Delta also faced an increase of approximately $1.2 billion in its current liabilities, which the airline tried to meet by selling almost all of its marketable securities. Overall, the company's financial condition deteriorated in 2001, but with aggressive cost management efforts and an upward trend in passengers as the economy recovered, Delta strove to get its net income in the black again.

Delta posed a major threat to UAL with respect to global alliance competition. In order to match the marketing agreement between United and US Airways in July 2002, Delta announced a marketing agreement with Northwest and Continental Airlines, which included frequent flyer reciprocity. This move extended SkyTeam's service into Asia and Latin America and threatened to eliminate Star Alliance's dominance in these regions.

| EXHIBIT 6 | DAL Financial Highlights |

Income Statement ($ million)

Fiscal Year Ending	Dec. 01	Dec. 00	Dec. 99	Dec. 98	Dec. 97	Dec. 96	Dec. 95	Dec. 94
Net sales	13,879	16,741	14,883	14,597	14,057	13,594	12,455	12,194
Cost of goods	9,208	9,133	7,707	7,414	7,302	7,079	6,414	6,597
Gross profit	4,671	7,608	7,176	7,183	6,755	6,515	6,041	5,597
Sell gen. & admin. exp.	3,689	3,827	3,579	4,352	4,201	4,222	4,115	4,314
Depreciation & amort.	1,283	1,187	1,057	961	860	710	634	622
Net Income	−1,216	828	1,208	1,101	1,001	854	156	408

Balance Sheet ($ million)

Fiscal Year Ending	Dec. 01	Dec. 00	Dec. 99	Dec. 98	Dec. 97	Dec. 96	Dec. 95	Dec. 94
Annual Assets								
Cash	2,210	1,364	1,623	1,124	1,077	662	1,145	1,233
Mrktable securities	5	243	693	19	557	508	507	529
Receivables	368	406	492	602	938	943	968	755
Prop., plant, & equip.	24,444	22,616	19,495	17,972	14,980	13,486	11,414	12,598
Accumulated dep.	8,347	7,776	7,045	6,792	5,965	5,444	4,894	5,662
Net prop. & equip.	16,097	14,840	12,450	11,180	9,015	8,042	6,520	6,936
Total Assets	23,605	21,931	19,942	16,750	14,603	12,741	12,226	12,143
Annual Liabilities								
Accounts Payable	2,666	2,248	1,974	2,209	2,025	1,691	1,540	1,473
Cur. long-term debt	260	62	670	660	67	236	40	151
Total current liab.	6,403	5,245	5,514	5,392	4,577	4,083	3,638	3,441
Total Liabilities	19,836	16,588	14,815	12,107	10,405	9,254	9,765	10,196
Shareholder Equity	3,769	5,343	5,127	4,643	4,198	3,487	2,461	1,947

SOURCE: Company annual reports obtained from Global Access (http://www.primark.com).

Continental Airlines, Inc.

Walter T. Varney and his partner Louis Mueller founded Varney Speed Lines in 1934, which was renamed Continental Airlines in 1937. In addition to the flagship airline, by 2002 the company had two wholly owned airline subsidiaries, ExpressJet Airlines, Inc., (formerly Continental Express, Inc.) and Continental Micronesia, Inc. Continental operated flights to 123 domestic and 93 international destinations and offered additional connecting services through alliances with domestic and foreign carriers. In addition, ExpressJet Airlines, Inc., and Continental Micronesia, Inc., served 216 airports worldwide.[20]

Continental Airlines formed alliances with other airlines for a combined domestic and international route network reaching 500 cities around the globe. In 2002 it announced a broad code-sharing agreement that would fold the alliance of Northwest, KLM Royal Dutch Airlines, and Continental, the Wings alliance, into SkyTeam, the alliance of Delta, Air France, and others.[21] The agreement linked their schedules both domestically and internationally and also allowed their customers to use each other's frequent flyer programs and airport lounges. In addition to the well-known alliance with Northwest Airlines, KLM Royal Dutch Airlines, and Delta Airlines, Continental also maintained alliances with smaller domestic carriers, other international carriers, and joined with Amtrak in 2002 to begin the first air/rail code share in U.S. history.

Continental maintained its OnePass frequent flyer program to encourage repeat travel on its system. The OnePass program allowed passengers to earn mileage credits by flying on Continental and certain other carriers. Continental also sold mileage credits to credit card companies, phone companies, hotels, car rental agencies, and other companies who participated in the OnePass program. The number of frequent flyer awards used on Continental represented 7.3 percent of its total revenue passenger miles in 2001.[22] Financial information for Continental Airlines is provided in Exhibit 7.

US Airways

In 2002 US Airways was the largest air carrier east of the Mississippi River, a region the company had focused on since its beginnings as All American Aviation, an airmail carrier in western Pennsylvania.

Passenger service began in 1949, and the company was renamed Allegheny Airlines in 1953. Under this name, the company performed a number of mergers and acquisitions and became one of the largest airlines in the world during the 1970s, yet maintained its sole focus on the eastern United States. Upon expanding into the southern and western United States in 1979, Allegheny adopted the name US Airways. By 2002 US Airways served select destinations in Europe, the Caribbean, and eastern Canada, as well as 38 states. Its focus remained on the eastern United States, as evidenced by their hub locations in Pennsylvania and North Carolina.

USAir was one of the first airlines to use the marketing strategy of international alliances. In 1993, they joined British Airways in an attempt to enhance services. USAir broke this alliance in 1997, partly in an attempt to improve their rights at London's Heathrow Airport and to regain stock owned by British Airways. Even without the presence of alliances, code sharing remained a large part of the US Airways method of business—they considered themselves to be the innovator in this field. Financial information for US Airways is provided in Exhibit 8. Exhibit 9 highlights industry statistics for the individual airline companies and is provided for comparison purposes.

Changing Face of the Airline Industry

Each airline responded to the September 11 terrorist incident in different ways, but for all of them the safety and security of passengers and employees became an issue of major importance. United took immediate action to implement new security enhancements, which included reinforcing the cockpit doors, equipping and training pilots to use taser guns, providing security training for flight attendants, and implementing comprehensive passenger pre-screening programs. Interestingly, the security enhancements did not affect departure and arrival performance.

The September 11 tragedy also had an immediate effect on the airline industry's finances. Anticipating heavy financial losses, major U.S. carriers requested government assistance in hopes of staging a quick comeback. Two weeks after the tragedy, Congress passed the Air Transportation Safety and Sys-

EXHIBIT 7 CAL Financial Highlights

Income Statement ($ million)

Fiscal Year Ending	Dec. 01	Dec. 00	Dec. 99	Dec. 98	Dec. 97	Dec. 96	Dec. 95	Dec. 94
Net sales	8,969	9,899	8,639	7,927	7,194	6,360	5,825	5,670
Cost of goods	4,437	4,758	3,969	1,968	3,236	2,784	2,491	2,768
Gross profit	4,532	5,141	4,670	5,959	3,958	3,576	3,334	2,902
Sell gen. & admin. exp.	3,021	2,875	2,510	2,218	2,988	2,797	2,696	2,655
Depreciation & amort.	467	402	360	294	254	254	253	258
Net Income	−95	342	455	383	385	319	224	−613

Balance Sheet ($ million)

Fiscal Year Ending	Dec. 01	Dec. 00	Dec. 99	Dec. 98	Dec. 97	Dec. 96	Dec. 95	Dec. 94
Annual Assets								
Cash	1,132	1,371	1,198	1,399	1,025	1,061	747	396
Mrktable securities	N/A	24	392	N/A	N/A	N/A	N/A	N/A
Receivables	404	495	506	449	361	377	351	376
Prop., plant, & equip.	7,595	6,355	5,161	3,458	2,406	1,964	1,865	1,869
Accumulated dep.	1,442	1,192	988	803	618	522	404	276
Net prop. & equip.	6,153	5,163	4,173	2,655	1,788	1,442	1,461	1,593
Total Assets	9,791	9,201	8,223	7,086	5,830	5,206	4,821	4,601
Annual Liabilities								
Accounts payable	1,008	1,016	856	843	781	705	617	630
Cur. long-term debt	355	304	321	184	243	201	163	126
Total current liab.	3,191	2,980	2,775	2,442	2,285	2,104	1,984	2,408
Total Liabilities	8,387	7,349	6,630	5,782	4,672	4,322	4,206	4,419
Shareholder Equity	1,404	1,852	1,593	1,193	916	869	588	156

SOURCE: Company annual reports obtained from Global Access (http://www.primark.com).

tem Stabilization Act consisting of a $5 billion cash payment to the industry as an emergency aid and a potential $10 billion in guaranteed loans to air carriers. The event greatly depressed the air travel market and illuminated some serious problems in the industry—high costs, excess capacity, and poor management of resources. The hub-and-spoke business model used by traditional carriers was expensive to run (more gates to lease and idler crew on the ground).

Airlines responded to this situation by cutting costs. Numerous cost-cutting measures were imple-mented, to include reducing the number of flights, eliminating free services such as providing drinks and food, tightening refund requirements, and eliminating corporate discounts on cheap fares. The industry also pursued more marketing alliances to take advantage of economies of scale.

The results of these cost-cutting measures were still unclear in 2002. It was expected that airlines would be forced to get tough with unions and suppliers over the restrictive practices that raised costs in the past. It was also anticipated that the industry would be burdened with extra costs for fuel, security,

EXHIBIT 8   USAir Financial Highlights

Income Statement ($ million)

Fiscal Year Ending	Dec. 01	Dec. 00	Dec. 99	Dec. 98	Dec. 97	Dec. 96	Dec. 95	Dec. 94
Net sales	8,253	9,181	8,460	8,556	8,514	7,704	6,985	6,579
Cost of goods	1,553	1,659	1,086	932	4,862	4,614	4,091	3,731
Gross profit	6,700	7,522	7,374	7,624	3,652	3,091	2,894	2,847
Sell gen. & admin. exp.	4,955	4,951	4,714	5,794	2,667	2,421	2,322	2,977
Depreciation & amort.	362	329	292	290	401	301	337	387
Net Income	−1,989	−255	273	559	1,025	183	33	−716

Balance Sheet ($ million)

Fiscal Year Ending	Dec. 01	Dec. 00	Dec. 99	Dec. 98	Dec. 97	Dec. 96	Dec. 95	Dec. 94
Annual Assets								
Cash	537	496	228	612	1,092	950	880	429
Mrktable securities	485	773	624	598	870	636	20	22
Receivables	272	328	385	355	296	325	322	326
Prop., plant, & equip.	8,418	7,672	6,412	6,301	5,819	6,060	6,074	5,955
Accumulated dep.	3,924	2,983	2,786	2,641	2,429	2,382	2,223	2,006
Net prop. & equip.	4,494	4,689	3,626	3,660	3,390	3,678	3,851	3,949
Total Assets	7,941	8,986	7,497	7,870	8,266	7,393	6,824	6,676
Annual Liabilities								
Accounts payable	598	506	414	430	297	420	325	263
Cur. long-term debt	159	284	116	71	186	84	77	81
Total current liab.	2,932	2,823	2,366	2,269	2,451	2,983	2,576	2,318
Total Liabilities	10,571	9,475	7,683	7,277	7,164	7,478	7,135	6,949
Shareholder Equity	−2,630	−489	−186	593	1,102	−85	−311	−273

SOURCE: Company annual reports obtained from Global Access (http://www.primark.com).

and insurance. Realizing the urgent need for new and bold strategic initiatives, many airlines began to implement structural changes and cost-cutting measures. Individual airlines responded to these situations in different ways.

Competitor Reactions

American Airlines

Excess capacity resulting from the TWA acquisition became a problem as September 11 resulted in a major decrease in demand. American Airlines lost roughly $2.5 billion in the first year following the terrorist attacks.[23] In September 2002, the company's market capitalization had fallen by 87 percent from the previous year; its credit rating was also downgraded, further hindering its access to capital. A weak economy and struggling airline industry combined with declining financial strategies forced American to develop new strategies.

To adapt to the environment in 2002, American announced its new strategy, describing the change as "a combination of fundamental structural changes

EXHIBIT 9

AMR Statistical Highlights
(American Airlines—excludes TWA)

Year	MRQ (3rd)	2001	2000	1999	1998	1997
Revenue passenger miles (millions)	34	110	120	115	112	110
Available seat miles (millions)	47	160	167	167	160	158
Passenger revenue per available seat mile (cents)	8.18	9.22	10.18	9.13	9.46	9.3
Operating revenue per available seat mile (cents)	8.48	9.63	10.62	9.52	9.88	9.75
Operating expense per available seat mile (cents)	10.38	11.14	10.48	9.5	9.25	9.27
Operating aircraft at year end	826	988	978	965	857	840
Cost of aviation fuel/gallon (including taxes)		0.812	0.779	0.548		

Hubs: Dallas/Fort Worth, Chicago O'Hare, Miami, St. Louis, San Juan

UAL Statistical Highlights
(United Airlines)

Year	MRQ (2nd)	2001	2000	1999	1998	1997
Revenue passenger miles (millions)		117	127	125	125	121
Available seat miles (millions)		165	175	177	174	169
Operating revenue per available seat mile (cents)	9.89	9.8	11	10.2	10.1	10.3
Operating expense per available seat mile (cents)		12	10.6	9.4	9.2	9.5
Operating aircraft		543	604	594	577	575
Cost of aviation fuel/gallon (including taxes)		0.865	0.810	0.579	0.590	0.695

Hubs: Chicago O'Hare, Denver, Los Angeles, San Francisco, Washington Dulles

DAL Statistical Highlights
(Delta Air Lines)

Year	MRQ (2nd)	2001	2000	1999	1998	1997
Revenue passenger miles (millions)	26	102	113			
Available seat miles (millions)	36	148	155			
Operating revenue per available seat mile (cents)	9.69	9.39	10.8			
Operating expense per available seat mile (cents)	10.05	10.14	9.68			
Operating aircraft at year end	831	814	831			
Cost of aviation fuel/gallon (including taxes)		0.686	0.6738			

Hubs: Atlanta, Cincinnati, Dallas/Ft. Worth, Salt Lake City

EXHIBIT 9 *(continued)*

**USAir Statistical Highlights
(US Airways)**

Year	MRQ (2nd)	2001	2000	1999	1998	1997
Revenue passenger miles (millions)	11	46	47	42		
Available seat miles (millions)	15	67	67	60		
Operating revenue per available seat mile (cents)	10.96	10.92	12.51	13.02		
Operating expense per available seat mile (cents)	12.25	12.46	12.72	12.99		
Operating aircraft at year end	311	342	417	393		
Cost of aviation fuel/gallon (including taxes)		0.8628	0.9576	0.5861		

Hubs: Pittsburgh, Philadelphia, Charlotte

**CAL Statistical Highlights
(Continental Airlines)**

Year	MRQ (3rd)	2001	2000	1999	1998	1997
Revenue passenger miles (millions)	16	61	64	60	54	48
Available seat miles (millions)	21	84	86	82	75	68
Operating revenue per available seat mile (cents)	9.43	9.78	10.67	9.86	9.95	10.06
Operating expense per available seat mile (cents)	8.9	9.58	9.68	8.98	8.89	9.04
Operating aircraft at year end	366	352	371	363	363	337
Cost of aviation fuel/gallon (including taxes)		0.7832	0.8421	0.4656	0.4683	0.6291

Hubs: Newark, Houston, Cleveland

**LUV Statistical Highlights
(Southwest Airlines)**

Year	MRQ (2nd)	2001	2000	1999	1998	1997
Revenue passenger miles (millions)	12	44	42	36	31	28
Available seat miles (millions)	17	65	60	53	48	44
Operating revenue per available seat mile (cents)	8.37	8.51	9.43	8.96	8.76	8.58
Operating expense per available seat mile (cents)	7.48	7.54	7.73	7.48	7.32	7.4
Operating aircraft at year end	366	355	344	312	280	261
Cost of aviation fuel/gallon (including taxes)		0.7086	0.7869	0.5271	0.4567	0.6246

and tactical moves."[24] The plan set out to cut capacity by nine percent, eliminate 7,000 jobs, and retire inefficient planes by the end of 2005. First class seating would be eliminated, and cabins would have only two classes, business and coach.

American Airlines adopted the "rolling hub" system of holding fewer aircraft on the ground and squeezing more flight hours from each aircraft. It was anticipated that the future hub-and-spoke model would be more cost effective, but could result in lengthy layovers. "There will be less service, and it will be less convenient to travel," predicted Robert Crandall, the ex-chief of American Airlines.[25] However, by staggering the number of flights into a hub, reducing the time an airplane remained on the ground, and reducing the number of gates, the airline expected to achieve substantial savings, which was projected to be as much as $1.1 billion annually.

Delta Airlines

Delta Air Lines lost $1 billion in 2001 due to the recession, September 11, and the resulting significant decrease of business travel. The total costs for 2002 were high—resulting from insurance against war and terrorism, restrictions on airline transport of priority mail and cargo shipments, government-imposed passenger security fees, and government-mandated security changes (such as reinforced cockpit doors, additional ramp security, screening of caterers and training).[26] The company lost money for the first nine months of 2002. To counter the increased security costs, Delta reduced the number of its full-time workforce by 7,000 from the previous September.[27] In March 2002, Delta became the first airline to stop paying most commissions to travel agents, followed soon by the other airlines.

In August 2002, Delta announced the launch of a low-cost competition strategy built on the company's strengths to compete more aggressively with low-fare carriers such as AirTran Holdings Inc., Jet-Blue, and Southwest Airlines Co. Delta had good reason to explore this segment as approximately 30 percent of Delta's domestic revenue was derived from markets with low-fare competition.[28] Delta expected that its experience with its low-cost unit Delta Express, which was introduced in 1996 and offered low-price point-to-point flights from nine midwestern or northeastern markets to five Florida cities, would be an asset. Although Delta Express was not as successful as expected, Delta gained some expertise in that low-cost segment and thus had a chance to gain greater market share.

Continental Airlines

One of Continental's first reactions to September 11 was a reduction in its flight schedule. For the fourth quarter of 2001, the company reduced its system-wide available seat miles by approximately 14.9 percent, as compared with capacity for the same period in the prior year.[29] In August 2002, Continental announced that it would implement a series of revenue-generating and cost-saving initiatives that were designed to achieve improved pre-tax earnings potential.[30] The company then planned to remove an additional 11 MD-80 aircraft by the end of 2003. In addition, Continental implemented domestic capacity reductions that were among the largest in the industry. The airline would continue to monitor employment levels and hoped to avoid additional furloughs through a hiring freeze, retirements, voluntary leaves, and attrition.[31]

Continental experimented with ways to offer different levels of service to passengers paying different prices. Continental retained its full-service product for higher-revenue customers and adjusted services and fees to reflect customer demand for lower fares.[32] The company tried to match products and services to the amount passengers were willing to pay.[33] For example, those who bought the cheapest tickets might not get assigned seats or frequent flyer miles. Other measures the airline implemented included a $20 assessment fee for all domestic paper tickets, fees for services that low-fare customers selected, rigid enforcement of all fare rules, re-bidding of many supplier contracts, advanced technologies, and modification of select employee programs.

Regardless of its efforts, the *Wall Street Journal* reported that Continental Airlines, which had previously stated that it would soon return to profitability, did not expect its situation to improve before the end of 2002 or 2003.

US Airways

Due to its dependence upon the eastern United States, US Airways suffered the most following the terrorist attacks on September 11, 2001. One year later, the airline announced reorganization plans under Chapter 11. US Airways depended largely upon its negotiations with employees and vendors to achieve significant cost savings. The airline had a reputation for commendable service, in part due to the good relations maintained with employees. Chapter 11, for a large part, would aid US Airways in its arrangements with vendors. In addition, US Airways and United formed a marketing alliance in July 2002 to cut costs and improve services. Some of the highlights of this agreement included sharing frequent flyer programs and airport lounges. US Airways projected that the agreement would increase revenue by $200 million per year.

UAL's Reaction

United was losing money even before September 11,[34] and the terrorism attacks simply magnified United's failed acquisition of US Airways and its declining profits. The sudden combination of demand reduction, high debt, and management/labor difficulties left United facing possible bankruptcy with few obvious solutions. CEO Jim Goodwin wrote a letter to the board in October 2001 stating his concerns that the company was "literally hemorrhaging money" and that the airline might not have a future.[35] Only four days after the letter was received, Goodwin was replaced, primarily due to union pressures and lack of board confidence.[36] The recovery plan then formulated by the company is found in Exhibit 10.

Despite the spending cutbacks outlined in the plan, one of the most pressing concerns was cash flow. Because of uncertain future revenues, managing working capital became very unpredictable and difficult. Negative cash flows caused current liabilities to balloon, forcing UAL into a cash crisis near the end of 2002. In an attempt to avoid possible bankruptcy, management sought major concessions from all of the labor unions to secure $1.8 billion in loan guarantees from the federal government. Overall, the unions agreed to support $5.8 billion in concessions, usually in exchange for stock options.[37] Regardless of the concessions, the Air Transportation Stabilization Board rejected United's application for aid in early December. United Airlines declared bankruptcy on December 9, 2002.

Even while filing for the federal loan, United was having discussions with banks about bankruptcy financing. United knew that without the loan there would be no alternative to bankruptcy.[38] Four banks agreed to finance Chapter 11 for United, and they set up loan covenants with very stringent requirements. United was required to operate profitably within three months, stay in the black for the rest of 2003, and finish with $575 million in before-tax earnings.[39] Many suggested that the unions would be the ones to suffer. The Employee Stock Option Plan made them powerful stakeholders in the company and they used this power to become the most expensive workforce in the industry.[40] The company was not expected to liquidate,

| EXHIBIT 10 | Financial Recovery Plan[45] |

1. Non-essential capital spending projects as well as new aircraft purchases were delayed. UAL has delayed the delivery of most new aircrafts until 2004. These reductions were projected to reduce capital spending by an estimated 50 percent.

2. Relations with unions and other employees must be mended so that labor costs can be significantly reduced. As of October 2002, United Airlines employed roughly 84,000 laborers.[46] The labor now finds itself in a position where concessions must be made for the company to remain in service. During the second quarter of 2002, United's cost of labor was roughly 47 percent of revenues. As a point of comparison, JetBlue's labor costs only accounted for 25 percent.[47]

3. UAL is focused on maximizing revenues from every flight. Inventory studies, new product offerings, pricing of flights, and new flight schedules were examined thoroughly in an attempt to increasing revenues.

4. A financing plan to keep UAL alive while other aspects of the recovery plan are underway was formulated. This plan was heavily dependent upon government assistance as provided by the Air Transportation Safety and System Stabilization Act. Other plans included sale of assets and obtaining unsecured borrowings.

however, because its most valuable assets, the aircraft, were under financing by outside organizations that would rather have the planes flying than idle awaiting sale.[41] On another positive note, Lufthansa, United's main Star Alliance partner (who had remained profitable), was willing to help.[42]

Glenn F. Tilton became the CEO of United in 2002, following several others that same year. Tilton had recent experience trying to help the financially distressed company Dynegy.[43] Although his previous experience was within the oil industry, he remained confident that a recovery was possible, and referred to Chapter 11 as "Chapter One."[44] The challenges faced by Tilton and United were extreme, considering the difficulties of management/labor relations, a declining industry structure, and the strict loan requirements. The question was, would United be able to meet those challenges and remain in business, or would the company be liquidated?

Case 20B: United Airlines—Time to Fly

January 2005

Robert E. Hoskisson
M. Gail Christian

Attempts to Emerge from Bankruptcy and Continued Competition

With rising fuel costs, continuing disadvantages relative to the employment and pension costs associated with discount airlines, and increased competition in its global routes, legacy carriers such as United Airlines have a significant challenge ahead. Although United has won important concessions from its employees, it continued to struggle to emerge from bankruptcy for several years even though some progress has been made. Glenn F. Tilton, who took over the CEO position in 2002, has some difficult decisions to make. After slashing about one third of United's expenses, he may have to further reduce expenses by seeking debt relief through cutting one of labor's "sacred cows," its pension fund.[48] Major changes have been made, to include $7 billion in cost cuts, a decrease in its workforce of 6,200 people, lower pay for employees, more flight hours for pilots, and outsourcing. In addition, United has created its own low-cost airline, Ted. Ted is scheduled to fly out of Chicago's Midway and O'Hare airports. United has also added a new aircraft to its fleet, the Embraer 170, a regional jet that will have room for first class seats. However, they still have not emerged from bankruptcy, and other drastic actions may still occur. For instance, other U.S. legacy competitors have even closed significant hubs, as we indicate later.

Actions while under Bankruptcy Court Supervision and Continued Competition

United Airlines and its parent company, UAL, had applied for Air Transportation Stabilization Board (ATSB) loan guarantees worth $1.8 billion in December 2002. The rejection by the ATSB precipitated UAL's decision to enter Chapter 11 bankruptcy proceedings. Subsequently, on June 17 and June 28, 2003, the ATSB rejected two requests for loan guarantees worth $1.6 billion and $1.1 billion, respectively. To continue Chapter 11 proceedings without liquidation, United needed immediate assistance from its creditors as well as additional cost reductions.[49]

In order to avoid default, United negotiated an agreement with Debtors-in-Possession (DIP) for an additional $500 million. (DIP financing allows companies to continue operations while going through Chapter 11 proceedings and is considered attractive because it is done only under order from the Bankruptcy Court.[50]) Much of the $500 million comes from firms such as GE Capital, which has loaned airlines $7 billion since the 2001 terrorist attacks. GE is UAL Corp.'s largest creditor, having a $1.6 billion stake. GE continues to put money into airlines to avoid potential huge losses from airline collapse and liquidation. However, GE argues that it makes more money when airlines are in dire straits due to financial distress. If it has to take over the actual airplanes in default, it can lease them to other U.S. or foreign airlines.[51]

In July 2004, United Airlines took a different tact to avoid liquidation: it chose to avoid a $72 million payment owed to three of its unions' pension plans and indicated that it planned to skip more than $500 million in payments due in September and October. In essence, this may mean that the Pension Benefit Guaranty Corp. (PBGC), a government-subsidized corporation that helps to fund pension funds of bankrupt companies, would potentially have to continue funding the pension plans. The threat to PBGC would be that all the other airlines would follow suit. This would be a huge savings for airlines who have also suffered from high fuel prices, continued proliferation, and competition from low-cost discount carriers. The workers would get $1.9 billion less than expected, but the PBGC would have to cover $6.4 billion of the under funding that would result in ceased payments to United pensioners. Ultimately, this would cause the PBGC fund to go into default and require a multi-billion-dollar government bailout. Whether UAL would succeed in this ploy would depend on a ruling by the bankruptcy court judge.[52] The UAL default would be the largest corporate pension default ever, and, although PBGC could apply to obtain UAL's assets, their obligation would come after many other creditors who already have obligations filed with the bankruptcy court.[53]

Besides United, other airlines are in bankruptcy or have come close to it. USAir is in bankruptcy court for a second time. Delta Airlines, in December 2004, barely avoided bankruptcy with a last-hour concession by its labor unions to provide significant pay cuts. However, large "legacy" airlines such as United, Delta, and American Airlines have not been the only airlines to experience difficulties.

Although discount airlines have significant cost advantages over the legacy airlines, these airlines have also suffered from the competitive situation since the 2001 terrorist attacks. For instance, although AirTran made a profit in 2003, in 2004 it found itself being squeezed by even cheaper startup airlines such as Independence Air. Independence was offering a $59 fare between Atlanta and Washington, D.C. (a $20 reduction from its usual $79 fare), causing AirTran and others to follow suit. Furthermore, due to concessions made by Delta employees,

it was being squeezed from the larger legacy airlines such as Delta. AirTran and Delta both have hubs at the Atlanta airport. In fact, United Airways group has been able to slash pilot pay so low that its pilots make less than those at Southwest Airlines, the most successful discount carrier. In a similar squeeze, ATA Holdings Corp. filed for bankruptcy protection in October. JetBlue Airways, a very successful low-cost carrier, has recently seen its operating margins squeezed. For instance, it expects to post a rare fourth quarter loss in 2004.

However, the discount carriers have learned from the experiences of the larger airline alliances such as that among Delta, Continental, and Northwest. In an attempt to achieve similar advantages of economies of scale, ATA and Southwest Airlines have recently entered into a code-sharing alliance that coordinates ATA's and Southwest's reservation systems and flight schedules. Through the alliance, Southwest will now be able to offer service to such new markets as Boston Logan, New York La-Guardia, Newark, Washington National, San Francisco, and Honolulu, among others. The new code-sharing agreement combined with Southwest's expanded Chicago Midway operations and new Pittsburgh market (which it plans to enter in May 2005) will continue to put pressure on both its low-cost competitors and traditional airlines such as American and United.[54]

Although Delta still cannot match AirTran's prices for most round trip tickets, it has done other things to increase its competitiveness. It has dropped the requirement for a Saturday night stay for its cheapest fares, and it feels that it can justify higher prices because of its global network, well known frequent flyer program, and airport lounges.[55]

In an unusual yet creative attempt to use its frequent flyer program to lure customers away from the low-cost carriers, United recently announced a frequent flyer program for pets. Pet owners will receive 1,200 bonus miles on up to two round trip tickets when they fly with their pets before May 27, 2005. Jerry Dow, the managing director of Worldwide Advertising and Promotions for United said, "We recognize that pets are members of the extended family and an important part of our customers' lives."[56] In addition to appealing to pet owners, United made a much-needed effort to improve its image by publicly displaying a personal concern for its customers.

In another response to the discount threat, many U.S. carriers have been shifting more aircraft to fly on more profitable international routes. For instance, American indicated in 2004 that it would shift 12 percent of its capacity, and United suggested that it would shift 14 percent of its capacity to such international routes, including Shanghai and Vietnam. Cutting fares over routes in the north Atlantic is less risky than the competitive battles with discounters and other hardened and financially distressed carriers in the United States. However, European airlines are far more dependent on transatlantic travel, which accounts for 26 percent of their total traffic versus 13 percent for similar U.S. carriers. Thus European carriers are likely to fight this move by U.S. airlines because the north Atlantic routes are the largest profit contributors of members of the Association of European Airlines.[57]

Other discounters in other parts of the world are pursuing a discount strategy in these more profitable global routes. For instance, Emirates Group in Dubai, United Arab Emirates, has been growing passenger traffic at a 25 percent average annual rate over the last 20 years. It continues to fly and increased traffic even in its risky hub in Dubai in the Mideast. While others perceive flying into the Mideast as high risk, Emirates Group has continued to raise its passenger traffic significantly and force other airlines such as the combined Qantas New Zealand Air, a newly merged airline, to pursue more routes into the United States and Latin America versus competing with the low-cost approach of the Emirate Group in the Middle East and Pacific regions.[58]

Other legacy carriers have responded by pursuing other domestic cost-cutting approaches. For instance, Delta has closed down its hub in the Dallas-Ft. Worth airport. Others have restructured their fares to make them more simple as Delta did, and many airlines are following its lead.

Summary and Challenges

It appears that the government is not going to bail out the airlines through loan guarantees that are due to unsustainable profit structures compared to the discount airlines. Although creditors may continue to support airlines, this will depend on the bankruptcy judges such as in the United Airlines case. The regional hub systems have protected legacy airlines' positions relative to discounters, but the cost structures are still different enough to create problems for this continued strategy, and some hubs have been closed down. Many of the regional airlines have suffered bankruptcy in connection with this strategy. Global alliances have also supported legacy firms such as the Star Alliance in which United is tied. However, partner airlines cannot continue to subsidize a firm that is in bankruptcy proceedings. Although some legacy carriers are pursuing more profitable overseas routes, these routes are increasingly being squeezed by global discounters such as Emirates Group and Virgin Atlantic. A shift to transatlantic routes is likely to disrupt alliances with European airlines, which are also likely to fight back because they are more dependent on transatlantic routes.

Despite the tough decisions Glenn F. Tilton will be facing, he believes that the future looks bright for United. On Friday, January 21, 2005, the bankruptcy court gave United approval to extend its exclusivity period for another three months. Thus, United will have an additional three months to file its reorganization plan without interference from other parties. Its current extension was due to expire on January 31. In an interview with the Chicago *Tribune*, Tilton said that he expects United to emerge from bankruptcy in the fall of 2005 a different company. Although emergence from bankruptcy is no guarantee of success, Tilton optimistically believes that it will soon be "time to fly" for United.[59]

Notes

1. M. Amdt, How to keep United flying, *Business Week,* December 23, 2002, p. 34.
2. UAL Corporation (NYSE)—Business Description, *Yahoo,* October 16, 2002, http://yahoo.marketguide.com.
3. Era 2: 1926–1933, *United Airlines,* October 16, 2002, http://www.ual.com/page/middlepage/0,1454,2287,00.html.
4. Era 5: 1946–1958, *United Airlines,* October 16, 2002, http://www.ual.com/page/middlepage/0,1454,2290,00.html.
5. Era 8: 1990–1993, *United Airlines,* October 16, 2002, http://www.ual.com/page/middlepage/0,1454,2293,00.html.
6. Era 9: 1994–1999, *United Airlines,* October 16, 2002, http://www.ual.com/page/middlepage/0,1454,2294,00.html.
7. Ibid.

8   A. Abromitis, E-mail to Derek Evers, October 18, 2002.

9. C. Woodyard, M. Adams, & J. O'Donnell, United Airlines chief steps down, *USA Today,* October 29, 2001, http://www.informare.it/news/review/2001/usatodat0005.asp.

10. A. Kahn, Airline deregulation, *The Library of Economics and Liberty,* October 20, 2002, http://www.econlib.org/library/Enc/AirlineDeregulation.html.

11. Landing with a bump, *Economist,* August 15, 2002, http://www.economist.com

12. So many planes, so few passengers, *Economist,* September 19, 2002, http://www.economist.com.

13. American Airlines, Inc.—C.R. Smith, *Scripopholy,* September 29, 2002, http://www.scripophily.net/amairinc1.html.

14. Key facts for AMR Corp., *Wall Street Journal,* October 18, 2002, http://www.wsj.com.

15. L. Steffy & M. Schlangenstein, American's risky flight plan, *Bloomberg,* October 2, 2002, http://www.bloomberg.com/marketsmagazine/ft2_0106.html.

16. British Airways, American attempt new alliance, *USA Today,* August 3, 2001, http://www.usatoday.com/money/biztravel/2001-08-03-ba-american.htm.

17. Corporate information, *Delta Airlines,* October 15, 2002, http://www.delta.com/inside/investors/corp_info/index.jsp.

18. F. Reid, SkyTeam alliance strategy and hub network: Close up on Atlanta, *Delta Airlines,* September 18, 2002, http://www.delta.com/inside/investors/corp_info/speeches/index.jsp.

19. Ibid.

20. Continental Airlines, Inc (NYSE)—Business Description, *Yahoo,* September 29, 2002, http://yahoo.marketguide.com.

21. Continental Airlines, Delta Air Lines, Norwest Airlines in code-share pact, *The Wall Street Journal,* August 22, 2002. http://yahoo.marketguide.com.

22. Continental Airlines, Inc (NYSE)—Business Description, *Yahoo,* September 29, 2002, http://yahoo.marketguide.com.

23. American Airlines' losses continue to mount, *USA Today,* October 16, 2002, http://www.usatoday.com/money/companies/earnings/2002-10-16-american-airlines_x.htm.

24. S. Steinke, American changes strategy to survive, *Flug Revue,* October 1, 2002, http://www.flug-revue.rotor.com/FRheft/FRH0210?FR0210e.htm.

25. P. Coy and W. Zellner, Commentary: The airlines caught between a hub and a hard place, *Business Week Online,* August 5, 2002, http://www.businessweek.com/@@vKTPpoYQPOkivw0A/magazine/content/02_31/b3794112.htm.

26. L. Mullin, Boston Chamber of Commerce leading industries executive forum, *Delta Airlines,* July 29, 2002, http://www.delta.com/ docs/LFM_LeadingInd_72902.doc.

27. SEC filings, *Delta Airlines,* October 15, 2002, http://investor.delta.com.

28. M. Adams, Despite losses, Delta remains optimistic about future, *USA Today,* April 26, 2002, http://www.usatoday.com/money/covers/2002-04-26-delta.htm.

29. Continental Airlines, Inc (NYSE)—Business Description, *Yahoo,* September 29, 2002, http://yahoo.marketguide.com.

30. Continental Airlines, Responding to market changes, implements measures to increase revenue, reduce costs, *PR Newswire,* August 20, 2002, http://www.prnewswire.com.

31. Ibid.

32. Ibid.

33. It's showtime for the airlines, *Business Week Online,* September 2, 2002, http://www.businessweek.com.

34. Gone . . ., Economist.com, December 14, 2002.

35. C. Isidore, Union wants UAL CEO out, *CNN Money,* October 24, 2001, http://money.cnn.com.

36. UAL boss seeks sacrifices, *CNN Money,* October 29, 2001, http://money.cnn.com.

37. A. Bernstein, Stock options: Fuel of United's revival?, *Business Week,* November 8, 2002.

38. D. Bond, United's DIP loans require profit in 2003, *Aviation Week & Space Technology,* December 16, 2002.

39. Ibid.

40. S. Tully, Friendly skies aren't out of the picture, *Fortune,* December 30, 2002, p. 42; M. Amdt, How to keep United flying, *Business Week,* December 23, 2002, p. 34.

41. Cruel phoenix: United Airlines, *The Economist,* December 14, 2002, p. 56.

42. Ibid.

43. UAL Corp. announces appointment of Glenn F. Tilton as chairman, *United Airlines,* October 19, 2002, http://www.united.com.

44. The night of the killer zombies: Bankruptcy in America, *The Economist,* December 14, 2002, p. 55.

45. UAL Corporation, 2001, *Annual Report 2001.*

46. *Wall Street Journal* key facts for UAL Corp., *Wall Street Journal,* October 21, 2002, http://www.wsj.com.

47. S. Carrey, Can a big carrier book profit while battling a nimble rival?, *The Wall Street Journal,* September 9, 2002, http://www.wsj.com.

48. W. Zellner & M. Roman, 2004, Glenn Tilton: Flying on fumes, *Business Week,* July 12, 44.

49. S. Carey, H. Sender & A. Schatz, 2004, UAL again fails to get loan aids, hurting airline's Chapter 11 plan, *Wall Street Journal,* June 29, A3.

50. http://www.gacfo.com/products/debtor-in-possession.html.

51. S. McCartney, 2004, Middle seat: One reason airlines keep flying despite huge losses: GE, *Wall Street Journal,* December 15, D8.

52. A. Borrus, L. Woellert, N. Byrnes, J. W. Weber & B. Grow, 2004, Pensions on a precipice, *Business Week,* 52–53.

53. J. Helyar, 2004, Time to clear the air, *Fortune,* September 20, 39–42.

54. M. Sunnucks, 2005, Southwest/ATA deal puts more pressure on America West, *The Phoenix Business Journal,* January 21, 1, 58.

55. E. Perez and N. Harris, 2005, Despite early signs of victory, discount airlines get squeezed, *Wall Street Journal,* January 17, A1, A6.

56. J. Gardner, 2005, Friendly skies encouraging furry fliers, *Albany Democrat-Herald,* January 23, http://www.democratherald.com.

57. V. J. Racanelli, 2004, Coming: Not-so-friendly skies over the Atlantic, *Barron's,* November 8, MW10.

58. D. Michaels, 2005, From tiny Dubai, an airline with global ambition takes off, *Wall Street Journal,* January 11, A1, A15.

59. M. Skertic, 2005, Blue skies ahead, United chief says, *Chicago Tribune,* January 25, http://www.chicagotribune.com.

GLOSSARY

A

acquisition   a transaction in which a firm buys a controlling interest in another firm with the intention of either making it a subsidiary business or combining it with its current business or businesses

acquisition strategy   an action plan that the firm develops to successfully acquire other companies

administrative innovation   a new way of organizing and/or handling the organizational tasks firms use to complete their work

B

balanced scorecard   provides a framework for evaluating the simultaneous use of financial controls and strategic controls

benchmarking   the process of identifying the best practices of competitors and other high-performing firms, analyzing them, and comparing them with the organization's own practices

business-level strategy   an action plan the firm develops to describe how it will compete in its chosen industry or market segment

C

capabilities   result when the firm integrates several different resources to complete a task or a series of related tasks

competitive advantage   when the firm's core competencies allow it to create value for customers by performing a key activity *better* than competitors or when a distinctive competence allows it to perform an activity that creates value for customers that competitors can't perform

competitive M-form   an organizational structure in which there is complete independence between the firm's divisions

competitive rivalry   the set of actions and reactions between competitors as they compete for an advantageous market position

complementary resources   resources that each partner brings to the partnership that, when combined, allow for new resources or capabilities that neither firm could readily create alone

complementors   the network of companies that sell goods or services that are complementary to another firm's good or service

cooperative M-form   an organizational structure in which horizontal integration is used so that resources and activities can be shared between product divisions

cooperative strategy   an action plan the firm develops to form cooperative relationships with other firms

core competencies   capabilities the firm emphasizes and performs especially well while pursuing its vision

corporate entrepreneurship   an organization-wide reliance on entrepreneurship and innovation as the link to solid financial performance

corporate relatedness   achieved when core competencies are successfully transferred between some of the firm's businesses

cost leadership strategy   an action plan the firm develops to produce goods or services at the lowest cost

country specific or location advantages   advantages that concern the desirability of producing in the home country versus locating production and distribution assets in the host country

D

demographic trends   changes in population size, age structure, geographic distribution, ethnic mix, and income distribution

differentiation strategy   an action plan the firm develops to produce goods or services that customers perceive as being unique in ways that are important to them

distinctive competencies   core competencies that differ from those held by competitors

divestiture   a transaction in which businesses are sold to other firms or spun off as independent enterprises

due diligence   the rational process by which acquiring firms evaluate target firms

E

economic trends   the direction of the economy in which a firm competes or may choose to compete

economies of scale   the improvements in efficiency a firm experiences as it incrementally increases its size

economies of scope cost savings that the firm accrues when it successfully shares some of its resources and activities or some of its core competencies between its businesses

entrepreneurial culture encourages employees to identify and exploit new opportunities

entrepreneurial opportunities circumstances suggesting that new goods or services can be sold at a price exceeding the costs incurred to create, make, sell, and support them

entrepreneurs people who recognize entrepreneurial opportunities and then take risks to develop an innovation to pursue them

entrepreneurship a process of "creative destruction" through which existing products, methods of production, or ways of administering or managing the firm are destroyed and replaced with new ones

equity alliance an alliance in which each partner owns a percentage of the equity in a venture that the firms have jointly formed

exporting the process of sending goods and services from one country to another for distribution, sale, and service

external environment a set of conditions outside the firm that affect the firm's performance

F

financial controls focus on shorter-term financial outcomes

financial economies cost savings or higher returns generated when the firm effectively allocates its financial resources based on investments either inside or outside the firm

focus strategy an action plan the firm develops to produce goods or services to serve the needs of a specific market segment

focused cost leadership strategy an action plan the firm develops to produce goods or services for a narrow market segment at the lowest cost

focused differentiation strategy an action plan the firm develops to produce goods or services that a narrow group of customers perceive as being unique in ways that are important to them

foreign direct investment a process through which a firm directly invests (beyond exporting and licensing) in a market outside its home country

franchising the licensing of a good or service and business model to partners for specified fees (usually a signing fee and a percentage of the franchisee's revenues or profits)

functional structure an organizational structure consisting of a CEO and a small corporate staff

G

general environment the trends in the broader society that influence an industry and the firms in it

geographic-area divisional structure a decentralized organizational structure that enables each division to focus on a geographic area, region, or country

global matrix structure an organizational structure in which both functional and product expertise are integrated into teams so the teams will be able to quickly respond to requirements in the global marketplace

global strategy an action plan that the firm develops to produce and sell standardized products in different markets

global trends changes in relevant emerging and developed country global markets, important international political events, and critical changes in cultural and institutional characteristics of global markets

greenfield venture a venture in which a firm buys or leases land, constructs a new facility and hires or transfers managers and employees, and then independently launches a new operation (usually a wholly owned subsidiary) without involvement of a partner

H

horizontal acquisition the purchase of a competitor competing in the same market or markets as the acquiring firm

horizontal strategic alliance an alliance that involves cooperative partnerships in which firms at the same stage of the value chain share resources and capabilities

human capital includes the knowledge and skills of those working for the firm

I

industry a group of firms producing similar products

innovation the development of something new—a new good, a new type of service, or a new way of presenting a good or service

intangible resources assets that contribute to creating value for customers but are not physically identifiable

integrated cost leadership/differentiation strategy an action plan the firm develops to produce goods or services with a strong emphasis on both differentiation and low cost

internal environment the set of conditions (such as strengths, resources and capabilities, and so forth) inside the firm affecting the choice and use of strategies

internal-coordination or administrative advantages advantages that make it desirable for a firm to produce the good or service rather than contracting with another firm to produce or distribute it

J

joint venture a separate business that is created by an equity alliance

L

leveraged buyout (LBO) a restructuring strategy in which a party buys all or part of a firm's assets in order to take the firm or a part of the firm private

liability of foreignness the costs and risks of doing business outside a firm's domestic market

licensing the process of entering an international market by leasing the right to use the firm's intellectual property—technology, work methods, patents, copyrights, brand names, or trademarks—to a firm doing business in the desired international market

M

market power power that exists when the firm sells its products above competitive prices or when its costs are below those of its primary competitors

merger a transaction in which firms agree to combine their operations on a relatively equal basis

mission defines the firm's core intent and the business or businesses in which it intends to operate

multidivisional (M-form) structure an organizational structure in which the firm is organized to generate either economies of scope or financial economies

multidomestic strategy an action plan that the firm develops to produce and sell unique products in different markets

multiproduct strategy an action plan that the firm develops to compete in different product markets

N

nonequity alliance a contractual relationship between two or more firms in which each partner agrees to share some of its resources or capabilities

O

operational relatedness achieved when the firm's businesses successfully share resources and activities to produce and sell their products

opportunities conditions in the firm's external environment that may help the firm reach its vision

organizational culture the set of values and beliefs that are shared throughout the firm

organizational structure specifies the firm's formal reporting relationships, procedures, controls, and authority and decision-making processes

outsourcing acquiring a capability from an external supplier that contributes to creating value for the customer

P

political/legal trends the changes in organizations and interest groups that compete for a voice in developing and overseeing the body of laws and regulations that guide interactions among firms and nations

primary activities inbound logistics (such as sources of parts), operations (such as manufacturing, if dealing with a physical product), sales and distribution of products, and after-sales service

process innovations new means of producing, selling, and supporting goods and services

R

related-party transactions paying a person who has a relationship with the firm extra money for reasons other than his or her normal activities on the firm's behalf

resources the tangible and intangible assets held by the firm

S

simple structure an organizational structure in which the owner/manager makes all of the major decisions and oversees all of the staff's activities

social capital includes all internal and external relationships that help the firm provide value to customers and ultimately to its other stakeholders

sociocultural trends changes in a society's attitudes and cultural values

stakeholders individuals and groups who have an interest in a firm's performance and an ability to influence its actions

strategic alliance a relationsp between firms in which the partners agree to cooperate in ways that provide benefits to each firm

strategic business unit (SBU) a semiautonomous unit of a diversified firm with a collection of related businesses

strategic business unit (SBU) M-form an organizational structure in which the divisions within each SBU concentrate on transferring core competencies rather than on sharing resources and activities

strategic controls focus on the content of strategic actions rather than on their outcomes

strategic entrepreneurship the process of taking entrepreneurial actions using a strategic perspective by combining entrepreneurial and strategic management processes to enhance the firm's ability to innovate, enter new markets, and improve its performance

strategic intent the firm's motivation to leverage its resources and capabilities to reach its vision

strategic leaders the individuals practicing strategic leadership

strategic leadership developing a vision for the firm, designing strategic actions to achieve this vision, and empowering others to carry out those strategic actions

strategic management the ongoing process companies use to form a *vision, analyze* their external environment and their internal environment, and select one or more *strategies* to use to create value for customers and other stakeholders, especially shareholders

strategy an action plan designed to move an organization toward achievement of its vision

strategy implementation the set of actions firms take to use a strategy after it has been selected

strengths resources and capabilities that allow the firm to complete important tasks

substitute products goods or services that perform similar functions to an existing product

support activities provide support to the primary activities so that they can be completed effectively

switching costs the one-time costs customers incur when they decide to buy a product from a different supplier

T

takeover a specialized type of acquisition in which the target firm does not solicit the acquiring firm's offer

tangible resources valuable assets that can be seen or quantified, such as manufacturing equipment and financial capital

technological trends changes in the activities involved with creating new knowledge and translating that knowledge into new products, processes, and materials

threats conditions in the firm's external environment that may prevent the firm from reaching its vision

top management team the group of managers charged with the responsibility to develop and implement the firm's strategies

transnational strategy an action plan that the firm develops to produce and sell somewhat unique, yet somewhat standardized products in different markets

V

value chain consists of the structure of activities that firms use to implement their business-level strategy

value the satisfaction a firm's product creates for customers; can be measured by the price customers are willing to pay for the firm's product

vertical acquisition the purchase of a supplier or distributor of one or more of a firm's goods or services

vertical strategic alliance an alliance that involves cooperative partnerships across the value chain

vision contains at least two components—a mission that describes the firm's DNA and the "picture" of the firm as it hopes to exist in a future time period

W

weaknesses the firm's resource and capability deficiencies that make it difficult for the firm to complete important tasks

worldwide divisional structure a centralized organizational structure in which each product group is housed in a globally focused worldwide division or worldwide profit center

NAME INDEX

COMPANY INDEX

Risk (*continued*)
  in foreign direct
    investment, 204
  franchising and, 225, 226
  in innovating through
    acquisitions, 250
  internal innovation and,
    248
  international competition
    and, 191, 193, 203,
    204
  managerial motives and,
    149, 151
  multiproduct strategies
    and, 139, 149, 151
  outsourcing and, 94
  in resource/activity
    sharing, 144
  in strategic alliances,
    227–228
  strategic alliances to
    share, 220, 223, 226
  strategic entrepreneurship
    and, 251
Risk management
  acquisitions for, 172
  in strategic alliances,
    227–228
Risk taking
  entrepreneurship and, 37,
    243
  in strategic controls, 42
Rivalry, 8, 9–10
  with existing competitors,
    65–68, 116–117, 119
  international, 193, 195
Russia, 58, 97

S

Sales revenue
  at Best Buy, 6
  diversification and, 139,
    141
  due diligence and, 175
  multiproduct strategies
    and, 139
  outsourcing and, 235
  rapid increase in, 175
  same-store, 6
  at UPS, 139
Same-store sales, 6
Sarbanes-Oxley Act, 39, 40
Savings rates, 56
SBU. *See* Strategic business
    unit (SBU)
SBU M-form, 153–154
SEC. *See* Securities and
    Exchange Commission
    (SEC)

Secondary activities, 92
Securities and Exchange
  Commission (SEC), 40,
    85, 134
Sex discrimination, 48
Shared ownership, at TKG,
    26
Shareholder value, 32
  acquisitions and, 171
  business-level strategies
    and, 111
  of Disney, 41
Shareholders, 17
  acquisitions and, 172
  corporate governance
    and, 39
  employees as, 26
  outsourcing and, 221
  strategic alliances and,
    228
  strategic management
    and, 7
Simple structure, 124, 126
Singapore, 197
Single-business
  multiproduct strategy,
    139, 140–141, 143
  functional structure and,
    151
  at Wrigley, 140–141, 161,
    162
Skills
  innovation, 240, 250
  as intellectual property, 36
  internal innovation and,
    251
  in personal career, 254
  relational, 37
Small businesses
  Internet competition and,
    191
  organizational structure
    and, 124
  strategic leadership in, 18
Social capital, 6, 36, 37
  in career, 233
  customer service and, 89,
    90
  strategic alliances and,
    229
Social responsibility, 25–26,
    32
Society
  economic trends and,
    56–57
  exit barriers by, 67
  general environment and,
    55
  as stakeholder, 26
Sociocultural differences, 60

Sociocultural trends, 55, 58
South Africa, 25–26, 197
South Korea, 197
Soviet Union, former, 203
Spain, 162, 193
Spanish language, 53
Specialization
  information technology
    and, 225
  organizational structure
    and, 124, 125, 126,
    127
  outsourcing and, 94, 236
Specialized assets, 67, 68
Specialized know-how,
    greenfield venture and,
    202
Stakeholders, 11, 16–18
  controls and, 42
  economies of scope and,
    144
  ethics and, 19
  managerial motives and,
    149
  society as, 26
  strategic leadership and,
    19
  strategic management
    and, 7
Standardized products, 114,
    115, 125
  in global strategy, 197,
    199
  in transnational strategy,
    199
Standards, controls and, 41
Stock acquisition, 171,
    177
Storage costs, 67
Strategic alliances, 8, 10,
    216–236. *See also* Joint
    ventures
  acquisitions *vs.*, 224
  business-level, 221,
    222–224, 225, 227
  career and, 233
  in China, 217–218,
    219–221, 227
  for competitive
    advantage, 91–92
  as cooperative strategy,
    202, 218
  corporate-level, 224–226,
    227
  cross-border, 226, 227
  between Disney and
    Pixar, 223, 227, 228
  for diversification,
    224–225, 226
  by eBay, 189